The Big Book
of Beastly
Mispronunciations

Also by Charles Harrington Elster

THERE'S A WORD FOR IT!
A Grandiloquent Guide to Life

VERBAL ADVANTAGE®
(audiocassette program)

TOOTH AND NAIL
A Novel Approach to the New SAT

IS THERE A COW IN MOSCOW?
*More Beastly Mispronunciations
and Sound Advice*

THERE IS NO ZOO IN ZOOLOGY
and Other Beastly Mispronunciations

The Big Book of Beastly Mispronunciations

The Complete Opinionated Guide
for the Careful Speaker

Charles Harrington Elster

HOUGHTON MIFFLIN COMPANY

BOSTON · NEW YORK

For information about permission to reproduce selections from this book,
write to Permissions, Houghton Mifflin Company, 215 Park Avenue South,
New York, New York 10003.

Library of Congress Cataloging-in-Publication Data
Elster, Charles Harrington.
The big book of beastly mispronunciations : the complete opinionated
guide for the careful speaker / Charles Harrington Elster.
p.   cm.
Includes bibliographical references.
ISBN 0-395-89338-0
1. English language — Pronunciation — Dictionaries.
I. Title.
PE1137.E56   1999
423´.1 — dc21   98-47193   CIP

Printed in the United States of America

Book design by Robert Overholtzer

QUM   10 9 8 7 6 5 4 3 2

The author gratefully acknowledges permission to quote from the following:
Say It My Way by Willard R. Espy. Copyright © 1980 by Willard R. Espy. Used by
permission of Doubleday, a division of Bantam Doubleday Dell Publishing
Group, Inc. *Watching My Language: Adventures in the Word Trade* by William
Safire. Copyright © 1997 by The Cobbett Corporation. Reprinted by permission
of The New York Times Company. *The New Fowler's Modern English Usage,*
3rd ed., edited by R. W. Burchfield. Copyright © 1965, 1996 by Oxford University
Press. *A Dictionary of Modern English Usage* by H. W. Fowler. Copyright © 1926
by Oxford University Press. Reprinted by permission of Oxford University
Press. *The Harper Dictionary of Contemporary Usage,* 2nd ed., by William
and Mary Morris. Copyright © 1985 by William and Mary Morris. *Don't Say
It!* by John B. Opdycke. Copyright © 1939 by Funk & Wagnalls Company.
A Desk-Book of 25,000 Words Frequently Mispronounced, 4th ed., by Frank H.
Vizetelly. Copyright © 1917, 1919, and 1929 by Funk & Wagnalls Company.
You Don't Say! by Alfred H. Holt. Copyright © 1937 by Thomas Y. Crowell
Company. *We Who Speak English, and Our Ignorance of Our Mother Tongue*
by Charles Allen Lloyd. Copyright © 1938 by Thomas Y. Crowell Company.
Reprinted by permission of HarperCollins Publishers. By permission.
Webster's New International Dictionary of the English Language, 2nd ed.,
unabridged. Copyright © 1934 by Merriam-Webster, Inc. The December
1996 issue of *English Language Notes.* Reprinted by permission of
J. Wallace Donald of the University of Colorado, Boulder.

FOR JUDITH CHRISTINA

born September 23, 1997,
future cultivated speaker
of the 21st century

Acknowledgments

I am grateful to my editor, John "San Expédito" Radziewicz, for his long-time interest in my work and for the opportunity to transmute two good books into a new, better, and much bigger one. I am also indebted to Ralph H. Emerson for sharing his invaluable research and insight with me, to C. J. Bailey for sharing his erudition and opinions, and to Brian M. Sietsema for being a genial adversary in logomachy. Thanks to Deborah C. Schneider for being a great agent. Thanks to Nancy and Reinhardt Elster for being great parents. And special thanks to my wife, Myrna Zambrano, and my daughters, Carmen and Judith, for being a great family. I owe you girls a bunch of lazy weekends together.

Contents

Introduction

When it comes to pronunciation, there are two types of people: those who don't give the subject a second thought and those who do. This book is for those who do.

When I was growing up, one of the surest ways to raise the decibel* level of the already stentorian conversation at dinnertime was to raise the subject of pronunciation, or worse, to question how another family member pronounced a certain word. What would begin as an animated discussion often would degenerate into a shouting match and end with the contestants hunched and panting over an unabridged dictionary. If a clear victor emerged, the vanquished party was often sullen for weeks.

Were we fanatics, members of some fringe element of verbally obsessed freaks? Not at all. I have heard scores of testimonials about this sort of familial sparring from people all over the country. Were we nitpickers, smitten by the bug of phonetic correctness? You bet — and proud of it. In our home, words were nothing to trifle with. Language was the great, mysterious gift that distinguished the human being from the beast, and how you used words — and pronounced them — was a mark of character, intelligence, and refinement. It was an important lesson for a young person to learn, especially for one who would grow up to make pronouncements about pronunciation.

There are those, however, who would teach a much different lesson — that simply because we are human our speech can never be beastly:

Few people nowadays botch pronunciation. Americans are perfectly sensible in not caring a hoot about it. Inarticulateness, not mispronunciation, is what sends people to defeat in the Game. It used to be thought that a distinct and careful pronunciation was most desirable, but no one believes that anymore except a few speech teachers. . . . Most people are well advised not to worry

---

* See the Guide for the proper pronunciation of this word.

about a particular pronunciation. Say it the way you want and be proud of it. No party or parties decide the meaning of a word, and no one decides the pronunciation. . . . You needn't worry about pronunciation, since no one cares about that anymore.

— Robert C. Pinckert, *Pinckert's Practical Grammar* (1986)

It's hard to imagine any self-respecting person swallowing this nonsense. Telling us to pronounce words however we please and claiming that no one cares about how they are pronounced is an insult to our intelligence — and an invitation to disaster. Would you trust a driving instructor who told you not to worry about the rules of the road? Pinckert is like the writing teacher who, faced with a roomful of students eager to sharpen their skills, says, "Don't worry about grammar, spelling, punctuation, diction, syntax, and all that useless, boring stuff. There's no such thing as a mistake. Whatever you feel like writing is good." Those who take that counsel to heart no doubt will learn to write good and get a more better job.

The sad truth is that lots of people mispronounce words every day and plenty of other people notice. (Just listen to all the folks around you who say pro-*noun*-ciation instead of pro-*nun*-ciation!) And because we know that other people take note of how we speak, most of us *do* care about pronunciation, as this passage illustrates:

If you are like most of us, you are embarrassed when you mispronounce a word. You feel that mispronouncing common, or even uncommon, words marks you as not quite educated. And you are right. . . . Of course, you can still make a million, have friends, influence people, be admired for your good sense, be loved for your good heart, send your children to the best colleges, become President of the United States even if your pronunciation is not what it should be. But you will still be judged by the words you mispronounce. And you may not be judged kindly.

— Abraham and Betty Lass, *Dictionary of Pronunciation* (1976)

As the author of several books about language, I have had the opportunity to be a guest on several hundred radio shows throughout the United States and in Canada, and the experience has been ear-opening, to say the least. As I fielded questions, noted gripes, and listened to the lamentations of hundreds of listeners, one thing became persistently and incontestably clear: People do care about how the English language is spoken, and they care about it with a passion — sometimes a ferocious one.

The Big Book of Beastly Mispronunciations is the product of my lifelong interest in the spoken word. Specifically, it is the culmination of over a dozen years of observing the pronunciation of educated Americans, studying the pronunciations recorded in dictionaries from the 18th century to the present, and weighing the opinions of pronunciation experts on hundreds of disputed words (and various troublesome names as well). My focus naturally is on the present, but my analysis always takes in the past. What emerges from these pages is a snapshot of cultivated American speech at the end of the millennium with the entire 20th century in the background.

Although this volume incorporates my two earlier books on pronunciation, *There Is No Zoo in Zoology, and Other Beastly Mispronunciations* (1988) and *Is There a Cow in Moscow? More Beastly Mispronunciations and Sound Advice* (1990), it is by no means merely a reprint or rehash of their contents. Every entry in those books has been revised and updated and every ruling rigorously reexamined. I have expanded my list of Authorities Consulted and relied on the most recent editions of the leading dictionaries. I have also added a good deal of material; at least one-fifth of the entries in this book are new.

The Big Book of Beastly Mispronunciations is much more than a dry list of acceptable and unacceptable pronunciations. It provides historical background. It reports the opinions of numerous authorities. It offers pithy explanations and passionate opinion. It is replete with information you won't find in a dictionary or get from other pronunciation guides that simply present their preferences and do not bother to justify them. Only in these pages will you find a concise and accessible discussion of past and present usage, alternative pronunciations, levels of acceptability, analogies and tendencies, the vicissitudes of human nature, the terrible swift sword of phonetic justice — whatever variables may happen to bear upon a particular word.

Here you will get some straight talk on where the stress should fall in *harass(ment)*. You will find out why so many say *nucular* instead of *nuclear*, why you should think twice about sounding the *t* in *often*, and why the pronunciation for-TAY for *forte* (strong point) is a pretentious blunder. You will learn why we should articulate the middle *c* in *arctic* and pronounce *foliage* and *verbiage* in three syllables rather than two. You will get some sound advice on where to place the accent in *affluent, influence, mayoral,* and *electoral* and hear "the taint of preciosity"* in the hissing-*s* pronunciations of *controversial, negotiate,* and *species.* Words that unnerve or trip up many well-educated speakers — *deluge, heinous, milieu, flaccid, loath, niche, plethora, et cetera, clandestine, machination, philatelist, entrepreneur, unequivocally, paroxysm, xenophobia, assuage,* and *zoology* are but a few examples —you will pronounce hereafter with quiet confidence. In short, you will see how to *air* is human, to *ur* divine.

---

* The phrase is from *The King's English*, 3rd ed., by H. W. Fowler and F. G. Fowler; Oxford: Oxford University Press, 1985, p. 11.

Although *The Big Book of Beastly Mispronunciations* contains no shortage of my opinions, I have no particular ax to grind. I view sloppy speakers and ostentatious speakers with equal disdain. I frown upon affectation as well as carelessness. I take a few potshots at our neighbors across the pond (the British), but I am not interested in disparaging or promoting the speech of any group or region. I am sometimes accused of wanting to fix the language or erase all differences among speakers, but even the accusers know these are preposterous goals. "Sounds are too volatile and subtile for legal restraints," Dr. Johnson cautioned in the preface to his famous dictionary of 1755. "To enchain syllables, and to lash the wind, are equally the undertakings of pride, unwilling to measure its desires by its strength."

I am not opposed to change. Such a position would be untenable. I am skeptical of ignorant, pompous, and faddish change. I am annoyed when people invent pronunciations for unfamiliar words. I am exasperated when they can't be bothered to check the pronunciation of a word they look up in a dictionary. And I deplore our tendency to model our speech after those "whose abilities and character entitle [their] opinions to respect," as Noah Webster wrote, "but whose pronunciation may be altogether accidental or capricious." Change is inevitable, and only time can tell what will perish and what will prevail. In the meantime, however, pronunciations born of laziness and parrotry will feel the lash of my pen.

Over two hundred years ago, in 1791, the English elocutionist John Walker published *A Critical Pronouncing Dictionary and Expositor of the English Language,* a work of such extraordinary popularity that its influence could still be discerned in the 20th century. (See the footnote under *educate* for more on Walker's dictionary.) In many ways *The Big Book of Beastly Mispronunciations* is indebted to Walker, for he laid the ground rules for prescriptive commentary on pronunciation and set the tone for generations of authorities to come. "I do not pretend to be exempt from faults myself," he wrote in his preface;

> in a work like the present, it would be a miracle to escape them; nor have I the least idea of deciding as a judge, in a case of so much delicacy and importance, as the pronunciation of a whole people; I have only assumed the part of an advocate to plead the cause of consistency and analogy, and where custom is either silent or dubious, to tempt the lovers of their language to incline to the side of propriety; so that my design is principally to give a kind of history of pronunciation, and a register of its present state; and where the authorities of dictionaries or speakers are found to differ, to give such a display of the analogies of the language as may enable every inspector to decide for himself.

I have written this book for the same reasons Walker wrote his: to register the pronunciations of my time and give "a kind of history" of them; to plead for consistency and analogy; to tempt you to "incline to the side of propriety"; and, when authorities and speakers differ, to provide sufficient information to enable you to decide for yourself. Consider *The Big Book of Beastly Mispronunciations* an invitation to determine what constitutes acceptability or beastliness for you. Whether you are adamant or ambivalent about the spoken word, you will find a bold line here to guide you in drawing your own conclusions.

The late John Ciardi — poet, teacher, etymologist, and lover of the language — once asked,

> Are there any enduring standards of English usage? I think there are only preferences, "passionate preferences," as Robert Frost used to say, the level at which any English-speaking person chooses to engage the instrument — the orchestra — of the language. In the long run the usage of those who do not think about the language will prevail. Usages I resist will become acceptable. . . .
>
> It will not do to resist uncompromisingly. Yet those who care have a duty to resist. Changes that occur against such resistance are tested changes. The language is better for them — and for the resistance.*

Pronunciation, like life, is governed by repetition but rife with ambiguity, passion, and caprice; it is forever vulnerable to change and open to interpretation. This book is one man's informed opinion, based on a variety of reputable sources, about the pronunciation of a number of problematic words. I present it to you in the hope that it will assist, amuse, enlighten, and occasionally inflame you, and give you as much joy and distress in the reading as it did me in the writing.

Use *The Big Book of Beastly Mispronunciations* to settle arguments, start a colorful debate, or reevaluate your preferences. But more than anything, use it to "engage the instrument of the language" and have fun playing it.

> In words, as fashions, the same rule will hold,
> Alike fantastic, if too new or old;
> Be not the first by whom the new are tried,
> Nor yet the last to lay the old aside.
>
> — Alexander Pope

Charles Harrington Elster
San Diego, California
October 1998

---

* From the introduction to the *Harper Dictionary of Contemporary Usage*, 2nd ed., by William and Mary Morris; New York: Harper & Row, 1985, p. xxii.

The Key to Pronunciation

The following key was designed to indicate the majority of English speech sounds in a simple and comprehensible manner. I created it on the assumption that most readers do not enjoy trying to discern and decipher minute, arcane characters and symbols, and resent having to refer to the key for every word. Therefore, this key employs no signs, symbols, accent marks, or inverted letters; it is not phonetic or diacritical. It is what I call a *literal key* — it relies only upon lowercase and capital letters, combinations of letters, and underscored and boldfaced letters to indicate sound and stress.

No key is perfect, or even comprehensive. All must approximate in some fashion, and this one is no exception. In constructing it I have borrowed from various sources, but the key as a whole is my own, as is the responsibility for any weaknesses it may have. (Readers of *There Is No Zoo in Zoology* and *Is There a Cow in Moscow?* will notice that I have made a few refinements for this volume, but the bulk of the key remains the same.)

Vowel Sounds

A, a — flat, back, pass, exact
AH, ah — spa, father, hot, mop
AHR, ahr — car, jar, farm, alarm
AIR, air — hair, stare, bear, where
AY, ay — hay, wait, came, state
AW, aw — raw, all, walk, thought

E, e — let, yes, step, echo
EE, ee — see, beat, key, she
EER, eer — fear, pier, beer, mere
I, i — in, hit, sip, mix, pick
Y, y and EYE, eye — by, nice, pie, right, aisle
> *Note:* Y is used in combination with other letters to form a syllable: SLYT-lee (*slightly*). EYE is used when this sound by itself forms a syllable: EYE-l̲a̲nd (*island*).

OH, oh — go, sew, coat, approach
OO, oo — do, ooze, rule, true
OR, or — for, door, born, war
OOR, oor — poor, tour, allure, obscure
OW, ow — cow, out, tower, doubt
OY, oy — oil, loin, boy, annoy

UH, uh — up, dull, some, color; also, ago, allow, about
UR, ur — turn, stir, were, learn
UU, uu — pull, full, good, took, would

Obscure, Unstressed, Lightened, or Variable Vowel Sounds

a̱ — final, woman, elephant, balsam, librarian
e̱ — item, taken, moment, novel, difference
i̱ — edible, policy, charity, nation, imminent
o̱ — connect, polite, gallop, carrot, summon
u̱ — focus, lettuce, singular, column, raucous

Consonant Sounds

B, b — boy, cab, bubble
CH, ch — chip, catcher, peach
D, d — dog, add, sudden
F, f — fat, effort, staff
G, g — get, bigger, bogus, tag
H, h — hit, hope, behind
HW, hw — wheat, whither, whet
J, j — jug, juice, tragic, age
K, k — king, cup, take, actor, pack
L, l — leg, also, bell
'l — temple, ladle, cattle, turtle, apple, peddle*
M, m — my, humble, gem
'm — spasm, bosom, album, schism*
N, n — no, knee, end, winner
'n — hidden, cotton, open, satin, reason*
NG, ng — sing, anger, tank
P, p — pen, pepper, pop
R, r — red, arrive, car

---

* Apostrophe before L, M, or N ('l, 'm, 'n) indicates a "syllabic consonant," which *Webster's New World 3* (1997) defines as "a consonant pronounced in such a way as to form a complete syllable, or the main part of a syllable, entirely or almost entirely by itself, with little or no perceptible sound of a vowel in that syllable."

S, s — sit, ask, pass
SH, sh — she, rush, nation, conscious
T, t — top, sit, bitter, party
TH, th — thin, thirst, nothing, bath
<u>TH</u>, <u>th</u> — there, this, brother, bathe
V, v — very, even, live
W, w — will, wait, power
Y, y — yes, you, layer
(Y), (y) — indicates that some speakers employ the Y sound of *you* and
   others do not: N(Y)OO, *new;* D(Y)OO-tee, *duty;* uh-ST(Y)OOT, *astute.*
Z, z — zoo, daze, please
ZH, zh — vision, measure, azure, or French *je*

Foreign Sounds

<u>KH</u>, <u>kh</u> — German *ach,* Scottish *loch,* Hebrew *l'chaim*
   A guttural sound — called a voiceless velar fricative — like that of clear-
   ing the throat.
(N), (n) — French *vin, bon, blanc, garçon*
   A nasalized sound — the N is stopped in the nose.

Stress/Accent

- Syllables are separated by a hyphen [-].
- Syllables printed in CAPITAL letters are stressed.
- Syllables printed in lowercase (small) letters are not stressed.
- Words of one syllable are printed in CAPITALS.
- Words of two syllables in which each syllable receives roughly equal stress
  are also printed in CAPITALS: AY-MEN (*amen*), SHORT-LYVD (*short-
  lived*).
- Words of more than two syllables that have primary and secondary stress
  are transcribed in the following manner: the syllable with secondary
  stress is printed in CAPITALS, and the syllable with primary stress is
  printed in **BOLDFACED CAPITALS:** pruh-NUHN-see-**AY**-sh<u>i</u>n ED-<u>i</u>-
  fi-**KAY**-sh<u>i</u>n (*pronunciation edification*).

The Guide

A

a UH (as in *ago*); AY (as in *ate*) for emphasis only.

I am often asked if it is wrong to pronounce the indefinite article *a* like the letter *a* (AY). The answer is yes, except in special situations. Here are some expert opinions:

In *The Orthoepist* (1894), Alfred Ayres writes: "This vowel is pronounced [AY] as a letter, but [UH] as a word, except when emphatic. Then it has its full name sound. Thus: I said Cleveland is *a* [AY] large town, not *the* [THEE] large town of Ohio."

In *Comfortable Words* (1959), Bergen Evans states that "the pronunciation of the indefinite article depends on how emphatic we want to be. In normal, unemphatic speech ('There was a boy here looking for you'), it is always spoken *uh*. Anything else is an affectation. However, if we want to emphasize the idea of singleness ('I did not say *eight* boys; I said *a* boy!'), it is pronounced to rime with 'say.'"

In their *Pronouncing Dictionary of American English* (1949), Kenyon & Knott note that "the use of [AY], the stressed form of *a*, in places where the unstressed [UH] belongs, often gives an artificial effect to public address."

The precept is simple enough, and sensible to boot, yet few abide by it with any consistency, and charges of affectation and artificiality have done little to prevent the AY for UH substitution from becoming rampant. I have heard prominent public speakers, from President John F. Kennedy ("the torch has been passed to AY new generation") to erstwhile *Masterpiece Theatre* host Alistair Cooke use AY where unstressed UH belongs. Many speakers nowadays are fond of saying AY to give extra (imagined)

---

a = at / a̲ = final / ah = spa / ahr = car / air = fair / ay = hay / aw = saw
ch = chip / e = let / e̲ = item / ee = see / eer = deer / i = sit / i̲ = April
ng = sing / o̲ = carrot / oh = go / oo = soon / or = for / oor = poor
ow = cow / oy = toy / sh = she / th = thin / th̲ = this / u̲ = focus / uh = up
ur = turn / uu = pull, took / y, eye = by, I / zh = measure / (see full key, p. xiv)

weight to their words, many pop singers employ it, and if you listen carefully to TV and radio broadcasters you will catch nearly all of them using AY in unemphatic contexts frequently.

Try conducting your own informal survey of any radio or TV talk show and you may be surprised at what you hear. I once did this during a *Firing Line* conversation between William F. Buckley, Jr., and Barry Goldwater. In the course of a half-hour show (that's UH half-hour show, not AY), Goldwater used AY in unemphatic contexts four times; Buckley (who is sometimes accused of hyperenunciation) turned out to be a gold mine of overemphasis, using AY at least ten times in such phrases as *a major problem, a general rule, a balance of power,* and *a free man.*

I have a hunch why AY is so popular among broadcasters. No, it's not because they are trying to speak more clearly; AY actually is more difficult to say than UH, and overusing it makes one's speech less fluid, hence less clear. Nor have they been taught that it is proper, in formal speech, to overemphasize with AY. Instead, they have been taught — and for good reason — to avoid filling pauses in their speech with *uh* or *um.* Thus, if they happen to pause on the article *a* when pronouncing it UH, they will appear to have committed this cardinal sin.

This bit of overniceness unfortunately has led many to assume that it is *better* to say AY than UH — an understandable assumption, given how often today you hear educated speakers and broadcasters use unemphatic AY. But don't be fooled by all these AY-sayers. There is nothing preferable about AY; it has no noble pedigree. Nor is it any clearer or more natural than UH. In plain, unemphatic utterances, AY is neither wrong nor right; it's simply unnecessary. And, as Evans points out, it usually sounds affected. For clarity and simplicity's sake we should try to restrict AY to the name of the letter and to those rare situations that call for special emphasis.

abdomen AB-duh-men. Occasionally, ab-DOH-men.
Veteran radio commentator Paul Harvey says ab-DOH-men, with the accent on the middle syllable, and some speakers still insist that this is the proper pronunciation. Not so. Both ab-DOH-men and AB-duh-men have been used in cultivated speech for more than a hundred years, and both are acceptable. However, since the 1960s AB-duh-men has become so prevalent that it has nearly eclipsed ab-DOH-men.

The *Imperial Dictionary* (1884), Funk & Wagnalls *Standard* (1897), the *Century* (1889–1914), and *Webster 2* (1934) all countenanced AB-duh-men as an alternative pronunciation. Vizetelly (1929) noted that it was "gradually displacing the more formal" ab-DOH-men. Alfred H. Holt, in *You Don't Say!* (1937), remarks that "there is something too forthright and booming about 'ab-dó-men,' though it has long been standard. Five of the leading dictionaries now allow the first syllable accent, and one approves it." When Kenyon & Knott (1949) and *American College* (1952) gave AB-duh-men preference, it was clear old ab-DOH-men was taking it in the gut.

Today AB-duh-men is the norm, and though current dictionaries still list second-syllable stress in good standing, even Paul Harvey would probably tell you that it's only a matter of time before ab-DOH-men goes belly up.

aberrant a-BER-int, uh-BER-int, or a-BAIR-int, uh-BAIR-int.

The initial *a-* may be pronounced as in *hat* or as a schwa (an unstressed, obscure vowel): *uh-*. Be sure to stress the second syllable (*aberrant*). Easterners give this *e* a short sound, as in *bet*, while most other Americans blend the *e* into the *r* so that it sounds like *air*.

Aberrant is now often heard with first-syllable stress: AB-ur-int. This fairly recent (c. 1960–1970) aberration is listed second in *M-W 10* (1993) and *RHWC* (1997), and in *WNW 3* (1997) it is qualified by "also." *American Heritage 3* (1992) recognizes only the traditional a-BER-int. Stick with second-syllable stress.

abhor ab-HOR or uhb-HOR. Do not say uh-BOR.

Random House II (1987) and *American Heritage 3* (1992) give only ab-HOR, with the *a* clearly pronounced, as in *abject* or *absolute. WNW 3* (1997) and *M-W 10* (1993) also recognize uhb-HOR, in which the *a* is a schwa (obscure), as in *about.*

Be sure to pronounce the *h* in *abhor* and in the corresponding adjective *abhorrent:* ab-HOR-int (or, for eastern speakers, ab-HAHR-int). The beastly mispronunciation uh-BOR (which sounds like *a bore* or *a boar)* is not recognized by dictionaries.

abyss uh-BIS (rhymes with *amiss*), not AB-is (like *abbess*).

academia AK-uh-**DEE**-mee-uh.

This is the only pronunciation given in two recent American dictionaries, *American Heritage 3* (1992) and *M-W 10* (1993). *OED 2* (1989) sanctions only AK-uh-**DEEM**-yuh.

Avoid the beastly mispronunciations AK-uh-**DAY**-mee-uh and AK-uh-**DEM**-ee-uh, now popular among some academics and listed in a few dictionaries. There is no *day* or *dem* in *academia.* The word should rhyme with *anemia* and *Bohemia.*

Academia, the incestuous offspring of the professoriat, entered English in the 1950s. The word *academe* (sometimes capitalized, and pronounced AK-uh-**DEEM** or **AK**-uh-DEEM) is far older; it first appeared in 1588 (spelled *Achademe*) in Shakespeare's *Love's Labour's Lost.*

academician uh-KAD-uh-**MISH**-in (uh-KAD- as in *academy,* primary stress on -**MISH**-).

This is the only pronunciation in Funk & Wagnalls *Standard* (1897), the *Century* (1914), *Webster 2* (1934), and *OED 2* (1989), and it is the preference of Vizetelly (1929), Opdycke (1939), Lass & Lass (1976), and the *NBC Handbook* (1984).

The alternative AK-uh-di-**MISH**-in (with AK-uh pronounced as in *academic*) is the only pronunciation given by Worcester (1860) and *American Heritage,* new college edition (1969). Preferred by Phyfe (1926), it has been sanctioned by most dictionaries since the 1940s. Given this record of acceptance, one can hardly claim that AK-uh-di-**MISH**-in is wrong. The debate, however, is not yet academic. Careful speakers should note that throughout the 20th century the weight of authority clearly has been with uh-KAD-uh-**MISH**-in.

accelerate ak-SEL-uh-rayt. Do not say uh-SEL-uh-rayt. See **accept, acceptable**.

accent AK-sent (noun); ak-SENT (verb).

Properly, the AK-sent should fall on the second syllable of the verb to ak-SENT. Regrettably, most folks now ignore this nicety and pronounce both noun and verb with first-syllable stress. See **decrease** for an explanation of the rule for accenting (did you say ak-SEN-ting?) two-syllable words that function as nouns and verbs.

accept ak-SEPT; **acceptable** ak-SEP-tuh-buul.

First, take care to clearly pronounce the *t* in *accept.* Second, be sure to articulate the *ks* sound of the double *c* in these words. Don't change it to an *ss* sound and say uh-SEPT and uh-SEP-tuh-buul, as if they were spelled *assept* and *asseptable.* These are Un-ak-**SEP**-tuh-buul, certifiably beastly pronunciations.

In his delightful book *Say It My Way* (1980), Willard R. Espy, the dean of light verse on language, offers this advisory poem:

> In words with double C's, express
> C first as K, and then as S:
> A*k*-SEPT, a*k*-SEDE, a*k*-SESS-ory.
> (One time there was a silly lout
> Who always left the K sound out.
> He said a*ss*-EPT, he said su*ss*-INCT;
> He luckily became extinct
> Before he could propose that we
> Reverse the sounds of double C
> And say a*ss*-KEPT, a*ss*-KESS-ory.)

See the next two entries, and also **flaccid, succinct, vaccinate**.

accessible ak-SES-uh-buul. Do not say uh-SES-uh-buul.

Assess and *access* are different words, with distinct spellings and pronunciations. *Assess* (uh-SES) makes *assessable* (uh-SES-uh-buul); *access* (AK-ses for noun and verb) makes *accessible* (ak-SES-uh-buul). See previous entry, and also **flaccid** and **succinct**.

accessory ak-SES-uh-ree. Do not say uh-SES-uh-ree.

Despite what you may hear from the salesperson at your local department store, there is no such thing as an *assessory.* Pronounce the double *c* in *accessory* like *ks.* See the two previous entries, and also **flaccid** and **succinct**.

acclimate Traditionally, uh-KLY-mit. Now usually AK-luh-mayt.

This word came into the language in 1792, and for well over a hundred years was pronounced uh-KLY-mit (like *a climate)* in educated speech. This is the only pronunciation listed in Worcester (1860), Ayres (1894), *Century* (1914), *Webster's Collegiate* (1917), *New Century* (1927), and *OED 1* (1928).

AK-luh-mayt, with first-syllable stress, seems to have sprung up in the early part of the century, and by the 1920s and 1930s it was popular enough to attract the attention of various orthoepists. W. H. P. Phyfe (1926) called AK-luh-mayt "a very frequent error"; Vizetelly (1929) said, "The pronunciation of this word is sometimes confused with that of ACCLIMATION"; Lloyd (1938) complained that *acclimate* had "always been put down as [uh-KLY-mit], to the great distress of many who felt that [AK-luh-mayt] sounded better"; and Holt (1937), speaking of the adjective *acclimated,* says, "What seems to many Americans the more natural accentuation (on the first and third) is not yet the approved."

In 1934, *Webster 2* recognized AK-luh-mayt as an alternative pronunciation, and since then most dictionaries have followed suit, listing both pronunciations, usually with uh-KLY-mit first. In 1976, Lass & Lass duly reported that all four major dictionaries of the decade listed both pronunciations, and noted their preference for the traditional uh-KLY-mit. By the 1980s, the tide seemed to have turned in favor of the alternative AK-luh-mayt, which appeared as the preferred pronunciation in the fourth edition of *NBC Handbook* (1984).

Here's how the major current dictionaries weigh in on the matter: *RHWC* (1997) and *M-W 10* (1993) list AK-luh-mayt first; *WNW 3* (1997) and *American Heritage 3* (1992) list uh-KLY-mit first; and *OED 2* (1989) gives only uh-KLY-mit. Decide for yourself which pronunciation has the stronger tradition; I'm sticking with uh-KLY-mit. In the meantime, you may want to get accustomed to *acclimatize* (uh-KLY-muh-tyz). According to the *OED* lexicographer R. W. Burchfield in *The New Fowler's Modern English Usage* (1996), *acclimate* "has totally given way to *acclimatize* (1836) in the U.K. . . . and partially in the U.S. . . ." See **confiscate**.

accompanist uh-KUHM-puh-nist, not uh-KUHM-puh-nee-ist.

Accompanist has four syllables (ac-com-pa-nist), not five. Don't add an extra syllable and say *accompany-ist*. (*Accompanyist* once was a legitimate word — Dickens used it in *Oliver Twist* — but *accompanist* has long supplanted it.) Some dictionaries also sanction a three-syllable variant, uh-KUHMP-nist, which, because it is both less common and less articulate, is not recommended.

accouterment, accoutrement uh-KOO-tur-ṃint, not uh-KOO-truh-ṃint. The spelling *accoutrement,* which Burchfield (1996) and other sources note is chiefly British (it was originally French), has unhappily caused many speakers to think the word should be pronounced uh-KOO-truh-ṃint, with -truh- following -*tre*-. No matter which spelling you prefer, the overwhelming number of authorities prefer uh-KOO-tur-ṃint, and it is the only pronunciation countenanced for the -*ter*- spelling. We don't say THEE-uh-truh for *theatre* or SEN-truh for *centre,* so don't be a wiseacre. Say it in plain old American: uh-KOO-tur-ṃint.

An admonition for Francophiles: do not Gallicize the final syllable (-*ment*) by pronouncing it -maw(n). The Frenchified pronunciation a-KOO-truh-**MAW(N)** is an affectation unrecognized by English dictionaries (even really old ones).

accurate AK-yur-it; **accuracy** AK-yur-uh-see. Do not drop the Y sound in the second syllable and say AK-ur-it, AK-ur-uh-see, or worse, AK-rit, AK-ruh-see.

It grieves me to report that *Merriam-Webster's Collegiate Dictionary, Tenth Edition* (1993), the latest product of the storied house of lexicography in Springfield, Massachusetts, has, with unusually dogged permissiveness, recognized the ugsome pronunciations AK-ur-it and AK-rit for *accurate,* and AK-ur-uh-see and AK-ruh-see for *accuracy* — thus conferring upon these variants, at least within the pages of *M-W 10,* the lofty status of "standard."

Do not be fooled by this linguistic flimflammery. AK-ur-it and AK-rit are not standard, they have never been standard, and they have not suddenly become standard simply because the pronunciation editor of one dictionary has decided to list them, apparently in flagrant disregard of the fact that the vast majority of educated speakers consider these pronunciations, to put it mildly, slovenly and boorish.

If that seems too bold a generalization, then why is *M-W 10* alone in recognizing these abominations? Why do the three other major current American dictionaries — *WNW 3* (1997), *RHWC* (1997), and *American Heritage 3* (1992) — ignore AK-ur-it? Why do orthoepists — including Ayres (1894), Phyfe (1926), Vizetelly (1929), Gilmartin (1936), Holt (1937), Opdycke (1939), and Shaw (1972) — unanimously condemn AK-ur-it and its boorish brethren, often calling them "illiterate"? And why, under *accu-*

racy, does the notoriously permissive *Webster 3* (1961), the unabridged predecessor of *M-W 10,* bother to place an obelus [÷] before AK-uh-ruh-see and AK-ruh-see, indicating that many consider them unacceptable and "take strong exception" to them?

No, I'm afraid it just doesn't wash — or perhaps that should be *warsh*. That these beastly mispronunciations exist (and persist!) no one would dispute. That they are "the general practice of the nation" (Noah Webster's criterion for propriety), or even customary among educated speakers, is preposterous. Their appearance in a reputable dictionary, with no caveat or label whatsoever, is nothing less than an affront to all who aspire to speak well and who would sooner be dead wrong than AK-rit.

across uh-KRAWS. Don't add a T at the end and say uh-KRAWST.

In *Say It Right!* (1972), Harry Shaw issues this dictum: "Only *across* is acceptable in pronunciation and spelling. *Acrost* is substandard, either dialectal or illiterate."

Shaw is right in saying that *acrost* is substandard, but the mispronunciation is hardly confined to "dialectal or illiterate" speakers. I have heard many educated speakers say *acrost.* This is unfortunate, for as Shaw's words reveal, when an educated speaker makes an error that is considered illiterate, it can be very damaging.

We know that dialectal and illiterate speakers are at a disadvantage when it comes to using standard English, so when we hear them say *acrost* we tend to have more sympathy for their mistake, knowing that this is but one of many solecisms they will have to overcome. On the other hand, an educated speaker who says *acrost* lays himself open to disparagement or ridicule. *Substandard,* in dictionary lingo, means "unacceptable to educated speakers." The illiterate speaker who says *acrost* does not know his pronunciation is substandard and may not possess the means to find out. The educated speaker who says *acrost* has no such excuse. See **ask.**

actor AK-tur, not AK-tor. See **juror.**

acumen uh-KYOO-men, not AK-yuh-men. Stress the second syllable (the "Q").

The recessive-stress variant AK-yuh-men was first recognized by *Webster 3* (1961) but was ignored by most other dictionaries until the 1980s, by which time it had gained considerable ground on the traditional uh-KYOO-men.

Perhaps AK-yuh-men will ultimately prevail, like AB-duh-men for *abdomen* (see above); the spoken language is often partial to recessive stress. I cannot, however, shake off my suspicion in this case that AK-yuh-men was the innovation of younger (not-well-enough-) educated speakers who think nothing of shifting an accent here and there in an effort to sound more urbane or savvy. (The recessive-stressing Brits may be guilty, too; the *Oxford Guide* (1983) recommends "stress on 1st syllable.") Like most pseudosophisticated innovations, AK-yuh-men soon became a follow-the-herd pronunciation, and here we are today with two quite different ways of saying *acumen* countenanced by the dictionaries where one, in my opinion, would do just fine. (See **confiscate** for a discussion of recessive and progressive stress.)

address (noun, meaning "location, place where mail can be sent") uh-DRES or A-dres; (noun, meaning "speech") always uh-DRES; (verb) always uh-DRES.

Many have asked me: which is right, uh-DRES or A-dres? Do you ever wonder which is "more correct"? Read on.

Most of those doing the wondering believe (or have been taught to believe) that uh-DRES is proper for both verb and noun and that A-dres is wrong. Indeed, the first-syllable accent for the noun (I have never heard anyone say A-dres for the verb, though some say it is a frequent error) has been criticized by orthoepists in the past, and those infamous, heavy-handed English teachers of yore surely have contributed to the widespread notion that a careful speaker never says A-dres.

A-dres has been heard for over a hundred years, and has been attacked since its inception. Ayres (1894) prescribes uh-DRES for both noun and verb. Phyfe (1926) writes, "Although analogy may suggest the pronunciation [A-dres], it is not countenanced by any of the standard dictionaries." "Always stress the final syllable," advises Vizetelly (1929). And Lloyd (1938) says, "I very strongly favor 'adDRESS' over 'ADdress.'"

Webster 2 (1934) was the first to accept A-dres, noting that it was used especially for "the directions for the delivery of a letter, package, etc." This led Opdycke (1939) to predict that, although *address* "has stubbornly stood out for second-syllable accent as both noun and verb," it "will eventually fall in line" with the custom for two-syllable words that function as both nouns and verbs, where the former are accented on the first syllable and the latter on the second. (See **decrease** for more on this rule.) Opdycke then went so far as to recommend that we "help force this word into line — first-syllable accent as noun, second as verb."

Since *Webster 2*, A-dres has enjoyed good standing in the dictionaries. All current sources countenance first-syllable accent for the noun, though most give second-syllable accent precedence; several — including *American Heritage 3* (1992), *M-W 10* (1993), and *WNW 3* (1997) — qualify A-dres with the label *also*, indicating that it is less common in educated speech. I disagree. The judiciously prescriptive Morris & Morris (1985) prefer A-dres (in the place-mail-is-sent sense) and I have heard A-dres at least as often as uh-DRES from cultivated speakers in all parts of the country — more often in recent years since having an email address has become *de rigueur* (q.v.). What's more, I have frequently heard the same speaker use both pronunciations within a single conversation.

I usually say uh-DRES, but once in a while I say A-dres without the slightest twinge of self-consciousness. It all depends on the context — the flavor of the conversation and the syntax one chooses. For example, say aloud, "There were thirteen," and the accent falls on -teen; say, "There were thirteen men," and the accent shifts to the first syllable, *thir-*. Shifting accent in two-syllable words is "a tendency widely operative in present English speech," says *Webster 2* (1934). In some cases it is helpful to preserve a particular stress, especially when precision and clarity are at stake. But a shift in stress does not necessarily "harm" the language, and your accentuation, in this type of case, only reflects your personal preference — what you were taught or what you are accustomed to hearing from others.

If there is any distinction to be made, it should be this: for the verb, always say uh-DRES; for the noun, say uh-DRES or A-dres as you prefer, when you mean the place to which mail is sent or the place someone lives or works; however, when you use *address* to mean a speech, say uh-DRES (as in Gettysburg Address), the undisputed preferred pronunciation for that sense of the word.

adieu uh-DYOO, not uh-DOO.

Yes, you'll find the *y*-less uh-DOO in current dictionaries, and sometimes listed first; it's been acceptable since Kenyon & Knott (1949) and *American College* (1952) recognized it as an alternative. Bear in mind, however, that historically the weight of authority — including Worcester (1860), Funk & Wagnalls *Standard* (1897), Phyfe (1926), Vizetelly (1929), *Webster 2* (1934), Opdycke (1939), Lass & Lass (1976), *WNW Guide* (1984), the *NBC Handbook* (1984), and *OED 2* (1989) — favors uh-DYOO, with a *y* sound, probably for the same reasons I do: *adieu* comes from French, where it has the *y* sound; we always use the word to add a little French flavor to our speech (if we didn't we'd simply say "good-bye"); uh-DYOO is euphonious, uh-DOO is not; and finally, uh-DYOO avoids potential confusion with *ado*. The plural is uh-DYOOZ, preferably spelled *adieus*. See **dew**.

ad infinitum ad-IN-fi-NY-tum.

Note that the primary stress falls on -*ni*-, which should rhyme with *fly*, not *flee*.

adjective AJ-ik-tiv. Pronounce the *c* (like *k*). Do not say AJ-uh-tiv.

Some people drop the hard *c* (*k*) sound in *adjective* and say AJ-uh-tiv. What's worse, they often insist they're right in doing so. This AJ-itates me.

A voice talent I once worked with told me an English teacher had taught her that AJ-ik-tiv, with the hard *c* audible, was wrong. Sorry to be the teacher's pest, but if AJ-uh-tiv were preferable, or even acceptable, wouldn't most (if not all) authorities list it? Funny thing is, since *Webster 3* (1961) included the note "*rapid sometimes* [AJ-ud-iv]," only Merriam-Webster's dictionaries have recognized AJ-uh-tiv, and in *M-W 9* (1985) and *10* (1993) it is preceded by *also*, which in dictionary lingo means "appreciably less common." In my book, AJ-uh-tiv is appreciably less acceptable — in other words, beastly. Careful speakers vocalize the hard *c, even* in rapid dialogue.

admirable AD-mi-ruh-buul. Do not say ad-MY-ruh-buul.

Always stress the *ad* in *admirable.* Current authorities do not recognize the beastly ad-MY-ruh-buul (like *admire a bull*). "The pronunciation 'AD-mirable' is so well established," wrote Charles Allen Lloyd in *We Who Speak English* (1938), "that only children and uneducated people are likely to say 'adMIrable.'" See **formidable, comparable, irreparable, lamentable, preferable**.

adult (noun) uh-DUHLT or AD-uhlt; (adjective) uh-DUHLT.

Since the 1930s, when *Webster 2* (1934) recognized AD-uhlt, first-syllable stress has been acceptable in American speech, although, as Burchfield (1996) indicates, AD-uhlt is probably more common among educated British speakers than their American counterparts, who on the whole still show a preference for uh-DUHLT. (The *Oxford Guide* [1983], a British usage manual, recommends first-syllable stress for both the adjective and noun.)

Although you will occasionally hear Americans stress the adjective *adult* on the first syllable — for example, for *adult education* or *adult bookstore* some say AD-uhlt — careful speakers tend to preserve second-syllable stress. See **address, ally**.

adversary AD-vur-SER-ee. Do not say ad-VUR-sur-ee.

Dictionaries do not recognize ad-VUR-sur-ee, and it is not, as some may imagine, the customary British pronunciation; *OED 2* (1989) ignores it and the *Oxford Guide* (1983), a British source, says "stress on 1st syllable." Second-syllable stress is an example of what Follett (1966) calls an "eccentric pronunciation." See **controversy, faucet**.

advertisement AD-vur-TYZ-ment (American); ad-VUR-tiz-ment (chiefly British).

The pronunciation ad-VUR-tiz-ment, with the accent on the second syllable, has always been the standard in England, despite the preference of a number of English authorities — including Thomas Sheridan (1780), the celebrated elocutionist John Walker (1791), and James Knowles (1835) — for third-syllable stress. In the United States, the story is reversed. American authorities of the 1800s preferred or gave priority to ad-VUR-tiz-ment, but by the turn of the century AD-vur-**TYZ**-ment had caught on for good and was destined to prevail.

Funk & Wagnalls *Standard* (1897) was the first American authority to favor AD-vur-**TYZ**-ment. Though subsequent dictionaries, including the *Century* (1914) and *Webster 2* (1934), continued to give ad-VUR-tiz-ment precedence, the comments of contemporaneous orthoepists indicate a clear and widespread preference for AD-vur-**TYZ**-ment in early 20th-century America. Phyfe (1926) says: "[AD-vur-**TYZ**-m<u>e</u>nt] is more commonly heard in the United States of America." Vizetelly (1933) says: "[AD-vur-**TYZ**-m<u>e</u>nt] is a word the American pronunciation of which has jarred on the sensitive ears of our British friends." Holt (1937) says: "Ordinary Americans show a decided prejudice against the *ver* accent in *advertisement.*" Opdycke (1939) says: "*Advertisement* is preferably accented on the second syllable, as always in England. There is sound authority, however, for [AD-vur-**TYZ**-m<u>e</u>nt] and this is customary in the United States." And Lloyd (1938) says: "My own observation is that in America 'adver-TISE-ment' is heard more often, and this fact, combined with the fact that it is the one I have been familiar with from early childhood, makes it my personal choice."

I'm with Lloyd, all the way. For at least sixty years most Americans — ordinary and extraordinary alike — have preferred AD-vur-**TYZ**-m<u>e</u>nt, with the accent on the third syllable, and ad-VUR-tiz-m<u>e</u>nt, though still listed in good standing in current dictionaries, now sounds stilted coming from an American.

aegis EE-jis. Do not say AY-jis. See **algae, alumnae.**

aerie AIR-ee (like *airy*) or EER-ee (like *eerie*).

AIR-ee is the preference of most sources past and present, from the *Century* (1914) and *OED 1* (1928) to the *NBC Handbook* (1984), *Random House II* (1987), and *American Heritage 3* (1992). AIR-ee has prevailed probably because of its similarity to such words as *aerial, aerate, aerobic,* etc., in which *aer-* (a variant of *aero-,* air) is commonly pronounced AIR. This is fortuitous, however, for *aerie,* a nest in a high place, probably comes from a Latin word meaning "field" (later "nest") or another Latin word meaning "level spot" or "threshing floor."

EER-ee has been listed in most dictionaries since the early 1900s. It may be based on the alternative spellings *eyrie* and *eyry,* popular in the 18th and 19th centuries, or perhaps it came about from the notion that the *ae-* is the Latin diphthong (sometimes printed as a ligature: *æ*), which is pronounced like long *e* in such words as *Aeolian* (ee-OH-lee-<u>i</u>n) and *aegis* (EE-jis).

The variant AR-ee (A as in AT) appears in Kenyon & Knott (1949) listed as both a general and a Southern pronunciation. It has remained less frequent and probably is still regional, for of the major current dictionaries only *M-W 10* (1993) recognizes it.

Finally, there is the trisyllabic AY-ur-ee (AY- as in *day*), preferred by 19th- and early 20th-century authorities, including *Webster 2* (1934). It employs the older, hyperarticulate pronunciation of *aer-* in which *a* and *er* were pronounced separately: e.g., *aerial,* formerly ay-EER-ee-<u>u</u>l, now AIR-ee-<u>u</u>l; and *aeroplane,* first pronounced AY-ur-uh-playn, then AIR-uh-playn, then finally AIR-playn with the spelling *airplane.* (Vizetelly [1933] says: "[AY-ur-uh-playn], like *á er a ted* bread, is a mouthful, and airplane is much simpler.") *WNW 3* (1997) lists AY-ur-ee first, but other current dictionaries no longer recognize it, and I suspect it is fast on its way to its final nest.

Aesop EE-sup (usually listed first) or EE-sahp (my preference, usually listed second).

Some call this famed fabler AY-sahp (AY- as in *day*), a beastly variant for which there is no authority. See **algae**.

aesthetic es-THET-ik.

Be sure to pronounce the *th* in *aesthetic* and *anesthetic* (AN-es-**THET**-ik). The pronunciation slob drops the *h* and says es-TET-ik and AN-es-**TET**-ik. See **anesthetize**.

affluence AF-loo-ints; **affluent** AF-loo-int. Do not say uh-FLOO-ints, uh-FLOO-int.

The beastly vogue pronunciation uh-FLOO-ints for *affluence* and its uncouth cousin uh-FLOO-int for *affluent* have in the last twenty years grown steadily in popularity like a well-tended investment portfolio. Lass & Lass (1976) show that by the mid-1970s one dictionary had recognized them, and gradually the rest have followed suit, each time acknowledging greater currency and conferring greater status. In *WNW 3* (1988, 1997) they are preceded by the label "occasionally"; in *RHWC* (1991, 1997) by "sometimes"; in *M-W 9* (1985) and *10* (1993) by "also"; and in *American Heritage 3* (1992) they are full-fledged arrivistes, with no demeaning label at all.

Take my advice — especially all you Generation Xers: don't fall for these shallow, pseudosophisticated, upstart pronunciations, which I suspect have been foisted upon us by grasping Yuppies and egotistical boomers. Hold out for first-syllable stress in *affluence* and *affluent*. AF-loo-ints and AF-loo-int may not be earning as much interest right now, but they are solid performers with a lot longer record. See **influence**.

aficionado uh-FISH-ee-uh-**NAH**-doh or uh-FISH-yuh-**NAH**-doh; (chiefly British) uh-FIS-ee-uh-**NAH**-doh or uh-FIS-yuh-**NAH**-doh.

afternoon AF-tur-**NOON**.

Some speakers who never say NYOO for *new* or DYOO for *dew* will for some unfathomable reason insert a spurious, overrefined *y* into this word so that it comes out *after-nyoon*. What a NYOO-sins!

aged (adjective) AY-jid (rhymes with *say kid*); (participle) AYJD (rhymes with *raged*).

When *aged* is an adjective, meaning old or grown old, it is pronounced in two syllables: an *aged* (AY-jid) man. When it is a participle of the verb to *age*, to grow older or make ripe, it is pronounced in one syllable, AYJD: her troubles have *aged* (AYJD) her; this cheese has been *aged* (AYJD) for six months. See **learned**.

aggrandize uh-GRAN-dyz. Formerly, AG-ran-dyz.

Until the 1930s, when *Webster 2* (1934) recognized uh-GRAN-dyz, authorities preferred first-syllable stress. Since then second-syllable stress has predominated. "At some point between 1917 (when Daniel Jones's *English Pronouncing Dictionary* was first published) and 1963 (12th edn)," writes Burchfield (1996), "the main stress moved to the second syllable . . . from its traditional placing on the first." First-syllable stress is preferred by Lass & Lass (1976), the *Oxford Guide* (1983), the *NBC Handbook* (1984), and Daniel Jones (14th ed., 1991). The corresponding noun *aggrandizement* is properly pronounced uh-GRAN-diz-mint.

ague AY-gyoo (rhymes with *plague you*).

An ague is a chill or acute fever, often malarial, accompanied by fits of shivering. Though it looks as if it should be pronounced in one syllable — we don't say VAY-gyoo for *vague,* right? — looks can be misleading: the only recognized pronunciation is AY-gyoo, with two syllables. (Shakespeare buffs will recall from *Twelfth Night* the character Sir Andrew Aguecheek, pronounced AY-gyoo-cheek.) The adjective is *aguish* (AY-gyoo-ish).

albeit awl-BEE-it (like *all be it*), not al-BEE-it (like *Al be it*).

Albeit has nothing to do with a guy named *Al.* It is a Middle English contraction of *although it be.* The preposterous al-BEE-it first appeared in *Webster 3* (1961), where for some unfathomable reason it preceded the traditional awl-BEE-it. This undoubtedly led many speakers to believe that the *al-* pronunciation had greater authority. Not so. Post–*Webster 3* sources continue to favor awl-BEE-it: Lass & Lass (1976) and the *NBC Handbook* (1984) prefer it, and two of the four major current dictionaries — *WNW 3* (1997) and *RHWC* (1997) — recognize only this pronunciation.

Alcott (Louisa May and Bronson) AWL-kut.

This name is commonly mispronounced AL-kaht (like *Al cot*) or sometimes AWL-kaht (like *all cot*). Various current sources acknowledge these mispronunciations on account of their frequency, but more diligent examination of the historical evidence proves that, properly, *Alcott* should sound like *all cut* with the *cut* slightly swallowed. Jones (1991), the *NBC Handbook* (1984), the *Columbia Encyclopedia* (1963), *American College* (1952), Kenyon & Knott (1949), W. H. P. Phyfe (1926), *Webster's Collegiate* (1917), Funk & Wagnalls *Standard* (1897), and the *Century Cyclopedia of Names* (1897) all give only AWL-kut.

Ralph H. Emerson (1996), an authority on the pronunciation of English and American literary proper names and a consultant on that subject to *Merriam-Webster's Encyclopedia of Literature* (1995), informs me that "it's entirely safe to assume that [AL-kaht] is a spelling pronunciation through and through. In corroboration, I've noticed that bearers of other *-cott* names (like *Prescott*) tend to use [-kut] while those around them say

[-kaht] as we'd expect, since people tend to overpronounce unstressed vowels in words they know only (or mostly) by sight."

algae AL-jee. Do not say AL-jay, AL-jy, or (yuk) AL-gy.

The ligature (LIG-uh-chur) æ, Æ (now usually printed *ae, Ae*) occurs in words from Latin and Greek. It is properly pronounced with a long *e* (as in *be* or *need*). See **aegis, Aesop, alumnae, antennae, formulae, larvae, minutiae, papilla(e), vertebrae,** in which *ae* should have the long *e* sound.

alleged uh-LEJD.

Both the past tense verb (*She alleged that . . .*) and the adjective (*the alleged criminal*) are properly pronounced in *two* syllables. The three-syllable variant uh-LEJ-id, undoubtedly modeled on the pronunciation of the adverb *allegedly* (uh-LEJ-id-lee), was first recognized by *Webster 3* (1961), which labeled it "appreciably less frequent." Today it is appreciably *more* frequent, but still listed after the traditional two-syllable pronunciation, uh-LEJD. See **supposed.**

all right See **already.**

ally (noun) AL-eye (my preference) or uh-LY; (verb) uh-LY.

Vizetelly (1929), one of the last authorities to object strenuously to AL-eye for the noun, claims that the first-syllable stress "is based on false analogy" with the rule for bisyllabic words that function both as nouns and verbs, where the noun is stressed on the first syllable and the verb on the second. (See **decrease** for more on this rule.) He then quotes the influential *Critical Pronouncing Dictionary* (1806 ed.) of the English orthoepist John Walker:

> A few years ago [*circa* 1785] there was an affectation of pronouncing this word, when a noun, with the accent on the first syllable; and this had an appearance of precision from the general custom of accenting nouns in this manner, when the same word, as a verb, has the accent on the last; but a closer inspection into the analogies of the language shewed this pronunciation to be improper, as it interfered with an universal rule, which was, to pronounce the *y* like *e* in a final unaccented syllable. But, whatever was the reason of this novelty, it now seems to have subsided; and this word is now generally pronounced with the accent on the second syllable, as it is uniformly marked by all the Orthoepists in our language.

"When the Entente Cordiale of 1914 became, in English, the Allies," writes Holt (1937), "and the latter word, usually accented on the first syllable, entered our everyday speech, it was the *coup de grâce* in the losing fight dictionary-makers have been waging for years to keep *allies* rhyming with *advise*. The first syllable accent is now permitted. Not in the verb, however."

Sixty years later, AL-eye for the noun is entrenched. Burchfield's *New Fowler's MEU* (1996) says, "Originally stressed, both as noun and verb, on the second syllable. As a verb it still is, but as a noun is now normally stressed on the first. The adjective *allied* is stressed on the first syllable when it precedes a noun (*the Allied forces*), otherwise on the second."

When the *a* in *ally* is unstressed, some speakers — William F. Buckley, Jr., is a prominent example — do not pronounce it as a schwa, or obscure vowel (uh), but instead take pains to give it a clear short sound, as in *album* or *alto:* al-EYE. To my ear this overmeticulous pronunciation, which most dictionaries do not recognize, only draws unnecessary attention to itself. Say it naturally, with a schwa: uh-LY.

almond Preferably, AH-mund, but AM-und is also standard, and AHL-mund, AL-mund, and AWL-mund are now often listed (though not recommended).

I won't say I like it, but it looks as if I'll have to live with it: the *l* sound in *almond* is here to stay.

In my first book on pronunciation, *There Is No Zoo in Zoology*, I took speakers to task for sounding the *l* in *calm, palm, balm, qualm, psalm*, and *alms*. Several readers wrote me to protest this ruling, which they found arbitrary and regionally biased.

Columnist James J. Kilpatrick complains that I insist "on a New England Yankee pronunciation of the *-alm* words, so that *calm* comes out KOM, *balm* as BOMB, and *palm* as POM. We Southerners are bound to object. . . . There's no way to reproduce phonetically the Southern pronunciation of these things, but those of us who speak the puah speech tend to say pahl-um, bahl-um, cahl-um, psahl-um, and the like. My New England friends tend to drop the *l* altogether: pahm, bahm, psahm, and so on." (It may surprise Kilpatrick to learn that, back in the 1940s, Kenyon & Knott noted that the variant AL-mund was "frequent" in New England.)

Julie Glenn of Birmingham, Alabama, agrees with Kilpatrick. "Although I acquiesce to the demise of the 'l' sound in 'psalm,' 'salmon,' and perhaps 'almond,'" she writes, "I must tell you that you've been talking to entirely too many Yankees if you think that sound has gone also from 'walk,' 'talk,' and 'balk.' It hasn't, here in the South. . . . Among educated, well-spoken Southerners, 'talk' does *not* sound like half the vocabulary of a clock; 'walk' *cannot* be confused with a Chinese cooking pot; and 'balk' is *not* a revered German composer!"*

Well, as William Safire says in these situations, I stand corrected. The *l* in *almond* is a tough nut to crack, so I won't risk breaking my teeth on it.

---

* Of course, TAHK, WAHK, and BAHK (all rhyming with *sock*) for *talk, walk,* and *balk* are also regional pronunciations, which I have heard used by various New Englanders, Pennsylvanians, and Midwesterners. The "dictionary standard" pronunciation for these words has an AW (as in *paw*), not an AH (as in *pot*), sound, with the *l* silent: TAWK, WAWK, BAWK. For the revered German composer the preferred pronunciation is BAHKH, with a German guttural CH. See **Bach.**

With so many accepted pronunciations of the word, common sense dictates that the prudent orthoepist, like the circumspect politician, refrain from issuing a dictum and instead defer to regional and personal preference — in common parlance, go with the flow. If you are accustomed to pronouncing the *l* in *almond*, then more power to you. Besides, it's not as if the *l* sound is new on the scene. Funk & Wagnalls *Standard* (1897) recognizes AL-mund as an alternative, and both Vizetelly (1929) and Worcester (1860) list AHL-mund, citing William Perry's *Royal Standard English Dictionary* (1775) as their original source.

In an amusing (and, in retrospect, revealing) comment on the sounding of *l* in *almond, alms, balm, calm, palm, psalm, qualm,* and *salmon,* Bergen Evans, in *Comfortable Words* (1959), says,

> All dictionaries agree that the *l* is not pronounced in any of these words in standard speech. . . . Against this may be set the evidence of our ears. The *l* is now heard more often than not in *almond* and *salmon* and frequently in *palm.* In fact many educated people, even, are astonished to hear any questioning of it. I have never heard the *l* pronounced in *psalm* or *calm.* . . . It is correct at present not to pronounce the *l*, but like many a correctness it may soon be the mark of an old fogy and in time a downright error. [pp. 23–24]

Perhaps, as Evans suggests, the *l*-sounders are both the truth of the past and the wave of the future, and I, at forty, am already the old fogy.

In defense of all you AH-mund sayers, however, I can't let the *l*-sounders get off scot-free. All my current sources still list AH-mund first (with AM-und usually next); Lass & Lass (1976), the *NBC Handbook* (1984), and Morris & Morris (1985) prefer AH-mund; *Random House II* (1987) and *RHWC* (1997) call AL-mund a spelling pronunciation; and *American Heritage 3* (1992) does not recognize any variants with an *l* sound. Though the *l*-influenced pronunciations may be widespread, AH-mund still prevails, not only in the dictionaries but also on the airwaves and on Main Street, U.S.A. (some households excepted). No matter how many variants exist for *almond,* or how loudly some may insist on the primacy of an *l*-influenced pronunciation, the traditional pronunciation, with silent *l*, continues to be the undisputed leader of the pack. At the close of the 20th century AH-mund is still the most widely heard and widely accepted way of saying this word, and — Evans's dire prognostications notwithstanding — it shows no signs of relinquishing its preeminent status.

alms AHMZ. Do not say AMZ (rhymes with *hams*), which is beastly, or AHLMZ, which is dialectal; in general American speech the *l* is silent. Of the four major current dictionaries, three — *RHWC* (1997), *WNW 3* (1997), and *American Heritage 3* (1992) — give only AHMZ, and only *M-W 10* (1993) recognizes AHLMZ. Of *almoner,* the recipient of alms, Burchfield

(1996) says, "The *OED* (1884) and Daniel Jones (1917) gave preference to the pronunciation [AL-muh-nuh, American: -nur], but [AHM-] is now customary, doubtless after the analogy of *alms* [AHMZ]." See **balm, calm, palm, psalm, qualm,** and, for general commentary on *-alm* words, **almond.**

already   awl-RED-ee. Also, AWL-red-ee.

Try not to drop the *l* and say aw-RED-ee or AW-red-ee.

How often have you heard people, even the most careful speakers, say *awright, awready* for *all right, already?* In casual, rapid speech, we often drop the *l* in these words — so often, in fact, that one would suppose the dictionaries would have recorded the dropped-*l* pronunciations. Not so. Only *Webster 3* (1961) does; its most recent abridgments, *M-W 9* (1985) and *10* (1993), revert to the standard awl-RED-ee and also list the alternative AWL-red-ee. The other major current dictionaries — *WNW 3* (1997), *RHWC* (1997), and *American Heritage 3* (1992) — sanction only awl-RED-ee.

I do not hesitate to confess that I, too, am sometimes guilty of dropping the *l* in *already* and *all right* in informal conversation, but in situations that call for more precise speech (when I go on the radio, for example) I am careful to say these words in the standard manner, as the dictionaries mark them.

aluminum   uh-LOO-mi-num (four syllables).

The British spell it *aluminium* and pronounce it in five syllables: AL-yoo-**MIN**-ee-um.

alumnae   uh-LUHM-nee. Do not say uh-LUHM-ny.

Alumnae is the Latin feminine plural of *alumna* (uh-LUHM-nuh), a female graduate. The word is often mispronounced uh-LUHM-ny (-ny as in *night*), which is the proper pronunciation for *alumni,* the Latin masculine plural of *alumnus* (uh-LUHM-nus), a male graduate. *Alumni* can mean male graduates, or male and female graduates. *Alumnae* (uh-LUHM-nee) refers only to female graduates, as the *alumnae* of Smith and Wellesley. See **algae, antennae, larvae, minutiae, papilla(e), vertebrae.**

alveolar   al-VEE-uh-lur. Do not say AL-vee-OH-lur.

An *alveolus* (al-VEE-uh-lus) is a little pit or cavity, as in a honeycomb; an air cell or sac, as in the lungs; or the socket of a tooth. The plural is *alveoli* (al-VEE-uh-ly, with *-li* pronounced like *lie,* not *lee*). The adjective is *alveolar* (al-VEE-uh-lur). All three words have their stress on *-ve-*. Dictionaries do not recognize an alternative pronunciation.

Alzheimer's   (disease) AHLTS-hy-murz (AHL- as in *Oliver* or rhyming with *doll*).

No one has any trouble with *-heimer's* (hy-murz); it's the *Alz-* that's at issue. What's the proper way to pronounce the first syllable?

AHLTS-, recommended here, has the clear weight of authority behind it. Preferred by the *NBC Handbook* (1984), AHLTS-hy-murz is the only pronunciation in *WNW 3* (1997) and the first listed by other major current dictionaries. The runner-up is ALTS- (ALT- as in *shalt*), listed in three current sources, and third place goes to AWLTS- (rhyming with *halts* or *waltz*), listed by two sources.

I have heard some speakers (including a gerontologist) pronounce the first syllable AWLZ- (rhymes with *calls* and *falls*), or ALZ- (rhymes with *pals* and *gals*), in which the German *ts* sound for the *z* has been anglicized. At present only one source, *American Heritage 3* (1992), recognizes AWLZ-, and there is no authority for ALZ-. Careful speakers pronounce the *z* like *ts*, as in *Mozart* (MOH-tsahrt).

amateur AM-uh-tur.

The pronunciation of *amateur* has been a subject of controversy for many years, and, as Shaw (1972) remarks, how one said the word was "often considered a test of one's degree of culture and education." Problem was, there was little agreement among the educated what precisely *was* the cultured way to pronounce the word. Should it be AM-uh-chur, AM-uh-toor, AM-uh-tyoor, AM-uh-tur, or [your pronunciation here]?

The -toor and -tyoor variants are best avoided, partly because they are much less common today and partly because, as Holt (1937) advises, "Vain attempts at the French *-eur* should cease." (See **connoisseur, de rigueur, entrepreneur, liqueur, restaurateur** for more on the pronunciation of *-eur*.)

AM-uh-chur and AM-uh-tur, which authorities have sanctioned since the 1930s, are the variants now most often heard in educated speech. Be aware, however, that AM-uh-chur, though sanctioned, was still often maligned by some, and it still seems to be the pronunciation most disdained by those who choose not to use it. Though preferred by the *NBC Handbook* (1984), AM-uh-chur retains a vaguely lowbrow aroma, perhaps because of its popularity among those paragons of pronunciation, sportscasters. For that reason I recommend AM-uh-tur — preferred by, among others, Holt (1937), Opdycke (1939), Lass & Lass (1976), and Burchfield (1996) — in the belief that it is least likely to raise eyebrows, cause dyspepsia, or induce sneers.

ambassador am-BAS-uh-dur, not am-BAS-uh-dor.

There is no *door* in *ambassador*. The regrettable frequency of the self-conscious overpronunciation am-BAS-uh-dor has prompted current dictionaries to list it after the traditional am-BAS-uh-dur. See **juror**.

ambidextrous AM-bi-**DEK**-strus.

This word has four syllables. Do not add a syllable and say AM-bi-**DEK**-stur-us (like *ambidexterous*), which is archaic, says Opdycke (1939), or AM-bi-**DEK**-stree-us (like *ambidextrious*), which is beastly, sez me. Also, pronouncing *ambi-* as AM-by or AM-bee is uncultivated. Keep the *i* short, as in *bid* and *bit.* See **disastrous.**

ambience (or **ambiance**) AM-bee-ints, not AHM-bee-ahnts.

I prefer the spelling *ambience,* though it is less commonly used, because it better reflects the anglicized pronunciation recommended above.

Ambience (from the French *ambiance*) has been an English word for a little over a hundred years. As late as *Webster 3* (1961), American dictionaries recorded only the two-syllable French pronunciation, with the *m* and *n* nasalized: aw(n)-BYAW(N)S. Today, however, the French pronunciation is on the brink of extinction, kept alive only by some dictionaries' deferential recognition of the dwindling group of older speakers who grew up treating the word as a foreignism. Now we often hear the half-anglicized (and, to borrow one of H. W. Fowler's favorite put-downs, half-educated) AHM-bee-ahnts (or sometimes ahm-bee-AHNTS). This trendy, pseudo-French variant, which appears only in *M-W 10* (1993), is favored by those who wish to affect a familiarity with the word's Gallic origin. Little do they know that, as Lass & Lass (1976) and Morris & Morris (1985) show, *ambience* has been fully anglicized since the late 1960s, when it became a vogue synonym for *atmosphere* and *environment.* If you're still too young to collect Social Security, you should say this word in plain English: AM-bee-ints. See **penchant.**

amen AY-MEN. In singing, AH-MEN.

Amen comes from a Hebrew word meaning truly, certainly. The traditional pronunciation, AY-MEN (AY- rhyming with *say*), is often considered rural or uneducated. Nothing could be further from the truth. From John Walker's landmark *Critical Pronouncing Dictionary* (1791) to the dictionaries of today, British and American authorities alike have bestowed their blessing upon AY-MEN, sometimes noting that in verse and especially in hymns the word is commonly pronounced AH-MEN, with the more resonant open *a* we are asked to make at the dentist's.

Though both pronunciations have coexisted, like rival sects, for many years, AY-MEN without question has enjoyed widespread currency both in and out of church, while AH-MEN, until recently, has largely been confined to the choir loft. AH-MEN's rise in currency in the past fifty years has led most current dictionaries to list it without qualifying comment. I suspect, however, that the spread of AH-MEN is the work of votaries and proselytizers who believe the open *a* is more refined. There is no authority whatsoever to support that claim.

In *The American Language* (1937), H. L. Mencken relates this anecdote about the pseudosophistication of AH-MEN: "E. W. Howe tells a story of a little girl in Kansas whose mother, on acquiring social aspirations, entered the Protestant Episcopal Church from the Methodist Church. The father remaining behind, the little girl had to learn to say *amen* with the *a* of *rake*

when she went to church with her father and *amen* with the *a* of *car* when
she went to church with her mother" (pp. 337–38).

AH-MEN for singing, AY-MEN for speaking, says the *NBC Handbook*
(1984). I recommend following that sage advice, for no matter how stri-
dently the AH-MEN sayers sing the praises of their open *a*, AY-MEN still
sits on high, and it probably will take an act of God to change that.

A final note to this little homily: several current sources mark *amen* as
receiving equal stress on each syllable, as I have marked it here. Only in
singing, however, is the stress usually even; in speech it may vary, as in the
amen (AY-men) *corner* and *I'll say amen* (ay-MEN) *to that, sister!* Such
variation, authorities agree, is perfectly acceptable.

amenable uh-MEE-nuh-buul.
The alternative pronunciation uh-MEN-uh-buul, which perhaps arose
because of its similarity to *amend,* has existed for over a hundred years. In
its early days it was rejected by Ayres (1894), Phyfe (1926), and Vizetelly
(1929); *Webster 2* (1934) is the first of my sources to recognize it. Current
dictionaries all list it second after uh-MEE-nuh-buul, which Shaw (1972)
says "is generally considered preferable." Lass & Lass (1976) and *NBC
Handbook* (1984) concur. Pronounce the second syllable like *me*, not *men*.

amenity uh-MEN-i-tee (rhymes with *serenity*); **amenities** (plural) uh-
MEN-i-teez.
ABC news correspondent Jeff Greenfield pronounces *amenities* as uh-
MEE-ni-teez, with a long instead of a short *e* in the second syllable. Is he
correct? Let's see.

Worcester (1860) gives only the -MEN- pronunciation, citing Walker
(1791) and Smart (1836) among his authorities. Funk & Wagnalls *Standard*
(1897), the *Century* (1889–1914), *Webster's Collegiate* (1917), and *OED 1*
(1928) also list only uh-MEN-i-tee(z). The -MEE- variant, however, has
been heard (and castigated) since at least the late 1800s, for Ayres (1894),
Phyfe (1926), and Vizetelly (1929) all proscribe it.

Webster 2 (1934) is the first of my sources to recognize uh-MEE-ni-
tee(z). Subsequent authorities are divided: Holt (1937), Opdycke (1939),
Lass & Lass (1976), and the *NBC Handbook* (1984) prefer uh-MEN-i-tee(z),
and this is the only pronunciation listed in *New Century* (1927), Kenyon &
Knott (1949), Funk & Wagnalls *New Practical Standard* (1962), and *Webster's New Twentieth Century* (1983). Witherspoon (1943), *American College*
(1952), and *Webster 3* (1961) list uh-MEE-ni-tee(z) as an alternative. Since
the 1960s the -MEE- variant has been sanctioned by most dictionaries,
though -MEN- continues to be listed first.

The upshot is this: uh-MEE-ni-tee(z) has become an acceptable alternative pronunciation, but I must stress the word *alternative.* Most American speakers say uh-MEN-i-tee(z) — so many, in fact, that Mr. Green-

field's -MEE- pronunciation, though acceptable, still smacks of eccentricity — or nouveau Englishness. Although *OED 1* (1928), as noted above, does not recognize the -MEE- variant, *OED 2* (1989) lists it first, and *OED 2*'s editor, R. W. Burchfield, in his *New Fowler's MEU* (1996) notes that today "the dominant pronunciation" among educated English speakers is uh-MEE-ni-tee, while uh-MEN-i-tee prevails "in regional and overseas varieties of English."

Stick with uh-MEE-ni-tee(z) if that's what you are accustomed to, but if you're straddling the fence or trying to settle a debate, remember this: in American speech, both tradition and "the general practice of the nation" (Noah Webster's standard of acceptability) favor uh-MEN-i-tee(z).

American(s) uh-MER-i-kin(z) or uh-MAIR-i-kin(z).

Do not pronounce *American(s)* in three syllables, uh-MAIR-kin(z), or, as Lyndon Johnson did, uh-MUR-kin(z). Make sure to say it in four syllables: *A-mer-i-can(s)*.

Amish AH-mish (AH- as in *spa*).

Most older authorities preferred AM-ish (AM- as in *ham*), with AH-mish as the alternative. Since the 1940s, however, AH-mish has gradually become dominant. *Webster 3* (1961), which lists AH-mish first and labels AM-ish less frequent, also gives a third variant, AY-mish, labeled "sometimes." This pronunciation, if memory serves, is popular in New York City (where I grew up in the 1960s) and environs. It appears, listed last, in *WNW 3* (1997) and *M-W 10* (1993), and is not recommended. The generally American pronunciation, preferred by the *Winston Dictionary* (1951) and the *NBC Handbook* (1984), is AH-mish.

anachronism uh-NAK-ruh-niz'm (stress -*nach*-, which rhymes with *back*).

Anachronistic is pronounced uh-NAK-ruh-**NIS**-tik.

Anaïs (Nin) See **Nin, Anaïs**.

anal AY-nal (AY- rhyming with *say*).

I include this word in the hope of preventing impressionable speakers from following (and overzealous lexicographers from recording) the poor example of former congressman William Dannemyer of California.

In an April 10, 1989, interview on NPR's *Morning Edition*, Dannemyer pronounced *anal* to rhyme with *channel*. This bit of beastliness does not appear in any of my sources (thank goodness), and I have never heard anyone else say it that way. Perhaps Dannemyer thought his pronunciation more delicate. Unfortunately, that's no excuse for being wrong.

If dictionaries sanction more than one pronunciation for a word, in most cases that means you can use the one you prefer. But please, don't invent pronunciations. Chances are you will only make an ass of yourself.

analogous uh-NAL-uh-gus.

Don't say uh-NAL-uh-j<u>u</u>s (it's beastly). The *g* is hard, as in *gum* or *gusto*.

ancillary AN-s<u>i</u>-ler-ee (rhymes with *cancel merry*). Stress the first syllable.

The variant an-SIL-uh-ree, with the accent on the second syllable, has been around since at least the 1930s — when Opdycke (1939) counseled, "Don't accent *sil* or *la*" — but it did not appear in a dictionary until the 1980s. *American Heritage 3* (1992) does not recognize it, and *RHWC* (1997) and *M-W 10* (1993) label it "especially British." I would call it "definitely not American and only recently British." *OED 1* (1928) does not recognize an-SIL-uh-ree, *OED 2* (1989) lists it second, and Jones (1991) prefers it.

anesthetize uh-NES-th<u>i</u>-tyz.

Anesthetize is a mouthful of a word that causes many speakers pain. For example, I have heard Senator Joseph Biden (on NPR's *Morning Edition,* August 17, 1989) mispronounce it uh-NES-th<u>i</u>-syz. Biden slipped up on the last syllable, -*tize*, which he pronounced like *size* instead of like *ties*. That is how many speakers — including many educated ones — mispronounce the word. Another common blunder to watch out for is uh-NEST-uh-thyz (like *a nest o' thighs*). There is only one acceptable pronunciation: uh-NES-th<u>i</u>-tyz.

angst AHNGKST.

The rise in respectability of the science of psychology during the 1940s and 1950s helped make *angst,* a borrowing from German, a naturalized English word. It first appeared in *Webster 3* (1961) with two pronunciations: AHNGKST (rhymes with *honks* + *t*) and ANGKST (rhymes with *thanks* + *t*). A survey of current sources reveals that the former pronunciation has dominated, at least in American English. Although the British *OED 2* (1989) countenances only ANGKST, with the flat *a* of *bank,* and *M-W 10* (1993) recognizes it as an alternative, AHNGST, with the broad *a* of *father,* is the preference of the *NBC Handbook* (1984) and the only pronunciation listed in Lass & Lass (1976), *American Heritage 3*·(1992), *RHWC* (1997*)*, and *WNW 3* (1997).

anise AN-is (rhymes with *Janice*).

Occasionally I hear educated speakers pronounce this word like *a niece.* That is a bogus, Anglo-French affectation. AN-is is the only recognized pronunciation.

anomie AN-uh-mee.

antarctic ant-AHRK-tik. Do not say ant-AHR-tik, or worse, an-AHR-dik.

Antarctica is pronounced ant-AHRK-tik-uh, with all the *c*'s and *t*'s articulated. A rebus I saw recently in the children's magazine *Highlights* proves that the cultivated pronunciation is still alive and well. The puzzle showed an ant + an ark + a tea bag + the letters *ca.* See **arctic.**

antennae an-TEN-ee. Do not say an-TEN-eye.

There is no *eye* in *antennae.* It should be an *e.* Words from Latin that form their plurals in -*ae* properly have a long *e* sound at the end. If you don't like that rule, say *antennas*. See **algae, alumnae, formulae, larvae, minutiae, papilla(e), vertebrae.**

antepenult AN-tee-**PEE**-nuhlt or AN-tee-pi-**NUHLT**.

This is a toss-up. Historically, there is sound authority for both pronunciations. Current American sources tend to favor the former while British sources favor the latter, but many educated Americans place the primary stress on -*nult*, perhaps because of the adjective *antepenultimate*, which is pronounced AN-tee-pi-**NUHL**-ti-mit. See **penult.**

anti- AN-tee.

For all words beginning with this combining form, Holt (1937) offers this sensible advice, which I wholeheartedly endorse: "Don't bother with a long *i*. Just rhyme *anti* with *panty*. Similarly with *semi*; think of *seminary*." Opdycke (1939) allows the long *i* "only when contrast or other emphasis is desired," but that exception, I would argue, throws the door wide open for abuse, which is why so many speakers overpronounce these *anti-* words today. See **semi-.**

anticlimactic AN-tee-kly-**MAK**-tik.

The pronunciation slob drops the second *c* and says *anticlimatic*. There is no *mat* in this word. The last two syllables rhyme with *tactic*.

Antigua (West Indies) an-TEE-wuh; (Guatemala) an-TEE-gwuh.

apartheid uh-PAHRT-hayt (like *apart hate*).

Apartheid is "correctly pronounced [uh-PAHRT-hayt] in standard English," writes R. W. Burchfield (1996), editor of *OED 2* (1989), which sanctions only this pronunciation. The *Oxford Guide* (1983) says, "3rd syllable like *hate*. Not *apart-ite* or *apart-hide*." The *NBC Handbook* (1984) and Jones (1991) concur, the latter noting that uh-PAHRT-hayt is the pronunciation in Afrikaans.

Although I strongly recommend uh-PAHRT-hayt, I differ with the *Oxford Guide* regarding the variant *apart-ite* (uh-PAHR-tyt). Lass & Lass (1976) prefer it and several American dictionaries list it first, so I'm persuaded to accept it as an alternative.

Never say uh-PAHR-thyd (-thyd like *thigh* + *d*). There is no *thigh* in *apartheid*. This ugly spelling pronunciation is not recognized by any authority I have consulted.

aphrodisiac AF-ruh-**DIZ**-ee-ak (**DIZ**-ee like *dizzy*).

Many speakers pronounce this word AF-ruh-**DEE**-zee-ak, and I have also heard some say AF-ruh-**DEE**-zhee-ak (with *s* pronounced as in *vision*). The latter variant has no authority; the former did not appear in a dictionary until the mid-1980s. Lass & Lass (1976), who record the variants listed in the four leading desk dictionaries of the early 1970s, give only AF-ruh-**DIZ**-ee-ak. Today, three of those four dictionaries recognize AF-ruh-**DEE**-

zee-ak: *RHWC* (1997) and *M-W 10* (1993) list it first; *American Heritage 3* (1992) lists it second. *WNW 3* (1997) and *OED 2* (1989), the British authority, sanction only AF-ruh-**DIZ**-ee-ak.

Whenever a new pronunciation suddenly rises to prominence, I become suspicious. Why did people start pronouncing *aphrodisiac* differently? It's doubtful that many consciously changed their pronunciation from -DIZ- to -DEE-; they probably never knew the proper pronunciation to begin with. Upon first coming across the word, it's likely they didn't bother to look it up in a dictionary and simply adopted the pronunciation of a friend or coworker or teacher — someone, as Noah Webster wrote in his *Dissertations* (1789), "whose abilities and character entitle his opinions to respect, but whose pronunciation may be altogether accidental or capricious." (See **capricious,** which is properly pronounced kuh-PRISH-u̲s.) "With respect to many words, I have been in the same uncertainty," Webster continues, "and used formerly to change my pronunciation, in conformity to the practice of the last man of superior learning whom I heard speak."

When we mimic someone else's pronunciation — assuming, without evidence, that it is correct — we only make monkeys of ourselves. The popularity of AF-ruh-**DEE**-zee-ak, attained in a mere decade, smacks of this sort of monkey-say-monkey-doism. For careful speakers who want to get dizzy with desire, Dr. Elster recommends taking an aphro-*dizzy*-ac.

aplomb uh-PLAHM (recommended) or uh-PLUHM.

The second syllable of this word, -*plomb,* traditionally rhymes with *Tom* or *bomb.* Until relatively recently, that was the only recognized pronunciation of the word. Current sources, however, now also recognize the variant uh-PLUHM (second syllable like *plum*). Burchfield (1996), who recommends uh-PLAHM, says "the pronunciation [uh-PLUHM] is not wrong but is now a minority one," but Morris & Morris (1985) claim uh-PLUHM "is at least as widely used" and grant it equal status. The original, French-influenced pronunciation uh-PLAW(N), often listed in older sources, is now obsolete. The word has been anglicized for so long (it entered English in the 1820s) that uh-PLAW(N) now sounds stilted, if not downright unintelligible.

apotheosis uh-PAH-thee-**OH**-sis. Less often, AP-uh-**THEE**-uh-sis.

The word means deification, glorification, "supreme exaltation of any person, principle, etc., as if to divine honor; as, the *apotheosis* of womanhood," says Funk & Wagnalls *Standard* (1897).

> Take heart, take heart, O Bulkington! Bear thee grimly, demigod! Up from the spray of thy ocean-perishing — straight up, leaps thy apotheosis!
> — Herman Melville, *Moby-Dick*

Vizetelly (1929) traces the penultimate stress (accent on the second-to-last syllable, the *o* of *-osis*) all the way back to the early dictionaries of John Entick (1764) and James Barclay (1774), and then quotes T. R. Lounsbery's *Standard of Pronunciation* (1904): "The accentuation of the penult of *apotheosis* has made great headway of late years. It is authorized by several modern dictionaries. It is not unlikely that it may come to prevail generally."

An edifying aside here: did you notice Lounsbery's litotes? Are you wondering what litotes is (or maybe are)? *Litotes,* pronounced LY-tuh-teez, denotes a rhetorical device where one uses a negative to subtly express an affirmative; "thus, 'a citizen of no mean city'" says the *Century* (1914) "means one 'of an illustrious city.'" In the quotation above, Lounsbery combines two no's to make a yes. By predicting that "it is *not unlikely*" uh-PAH-thee-**OH**-sis will prevail, he asserts his belief — with appropriately genteel reluctance — that it will, as indeed it has.

In 1934, *Webster 2* gave precedence to penultimate stress. Since then only Witherspoon (1943), the *Winston Dictionary* (1951), Lass & Lass (1976), and Frierson (1988) prefer the accent on the antepenult (the third-to-last syllable, pronounced AN-tee-**PEE**-nult). All my other authorities, from Opdycke (1939) to the *NBC Handbook* (1984), prefer uh-PAH-thee-**OH**-sis, which all current dictionaries list first.

Appalachia AP-uh-**LAY**-chee-uh, AP-uh-**LACH**-ee-uh, -**LAY**-chuh,
   -**LACH**-uh.
Appalachian AP-uh-**LAY**-chee-in, AP-uh-**LACH**-ee-in, -**LAY**-chin,
   -**LACH**-in.
Should the third syllable of *Appalachia* and *Appalachian* be pronounced *lay* or *latch?* There is equal authority for both pronunciations. There also is good authority for pronouncing these words either in four or five syllables, although the five-syllable variants seem to have the edge among both older and newer sources. The variants with long *a* (like *lay*) appear first in most sources since the 1960s; before that authorities generally favored short *a* (like *latch*).

Webster 3 (1961) notes that the short *a* is preferred in the southeastern United States. From what I can glean, that appears to be true. Reflecting the southern preference, Dr. David Frierson (1988), a South Carolinian orthoepist and emeritus professor at the University of the South (Sewanee, Tennessee), says AP-uh-**LACH**-ee-in, and I have heard Charles Frazier, author of the best-selling novel *Cold Mountain* (1997), speak of AP-uh-**LACH**-in folktales and his childhood in the southern AP-uh-**LACH**-inz (*The Newshour with Jim Lehrer,* November 20, 1997). Reflecting the predilection in network broadcasting for so-called Northern and Midland speech, the dominant American dialects, W. Cabell Greet, who was a professor of English at Barnard College and speech consultant to CBS for many years, lists AP-uh-**LAY**-chin first in *World Words* (1948), and AP-uh-**LAY**-chee-in is the preference of the *NBC Handbook* (1984), edited by Eugene Ehrlich, professor emeritus at Columbia University.

"Somewhere in mid-Virginia people start to pronounce it *latch*," an employee of the Appalachian Trail Project of the National Park Service in Harpers Ferry, West Virginia, opined when I called there to see if they had any insight to offer on the question. "North of there it's *lay*," she said. To be sure, the woman was no dialectician, and she was from California to boot, but I'll wager there's more than a grain of truth in the theory. Since then several other folks from various parts of the region have echoed this north-south bifurcation hypothesis, and one — an eminent phonetician who grew up in "a town in the southern Kentucky Appalachians" — told me that around his parts it was "considered hugely vulgar" to pronounce *Appalachian* with a long *a*.

You may hear some speakers who use the long *a* change the CH to an SH sound: AP-uh-**LAY**-shuh or AP-uh-**LAY**-shee-uh. These variants are not countenanced by dictionaries and are not recommended.

apparatus AP-uh-**RAY**-tus or AP-uh-**RAT**-us.

Avoid, at all costs, the beastly, affected, Latin-English hybrid AP-uh-**RAH**-tus. You may put a *ray* or a *rat* in your *apparatus,* as you please, but not a *rah.* The plural is *apparatus,* or sometimes *apparatuses.* See **data, erratum, gratis, status**.

applicable AP-li-kuh-bul, not uh-PLIK-uh-bul.

As in *applicant* and *applicator,* the stress in *applicable* should be on the first syllable.

The variant uh-PLIK-uh-bul, with second-syllable stress, has been around for much of the century (Kenyon & Knott recognized it in the 1940s), and although it is sanctioned by current dictionaries (*OED 2* excepted), not one lists it first, and no orthoepist with a reputation to lose prefers it. Why? I suspect because uh-PLIK-uh-bul has always been the darling of the half-educated, who, in my experience at least, take delight in displaying it like a Boy Scout badge of urbanity. Little do they know that every pronunciation authority of the last two hundred years — including Walker (1791), Worcester (1860), Phyfe (1926), Vizetelly (1929), Gilmartin (1936), Holt (1937), Opdycke (1939), Lass & Lass (1976), the *Oxford Guide* (1983), *WNW Guide* (1984), *NBC Handbook* (1984), Jones (1991), and Burchfield (1996) — favors AP-li-kuh-bul. In this book that's called "the weight of authority," and in this case it's clearly something to be reckoned with.

apricot AY-pri-kaht or AP-ri-kaht.

American authorities preferred long *a* (as in *April* and *apron*) until the

1970s, when dictionaries began to reflect a gradual shift over to the short *a* (as in *apt* and *apropos*). The *NBC Handbook* (1984) opted for short *a,* and in 1987 *Random House II* took the liberty of altering the way the word had always been divided, changing it from *a-pri-cot* to *ap-ri-cot,* probably to reflect the new preference in pronunciation. Burchfield (1996) says the word is pronounced AY-pri-kaht in British English, but "mostly" AP-ri-kaht in American English. I'm not so sure; the evidence of my ears, to use Bergen Evans's phrase, says otherwise.

Although I grew up hearing and saying AP-ri-kaht, I was surprised to find that hardly anyone I encountered outside my region (New York City and New England) pronounced it that way. In California, where I have lived since 1981, I hear people say AY- far more often than AP-, not only natives of the state but also transplants from the Northwest and Midwest. Either way you choose to pronounce it, you will not be wrong. However, on account of its longer tradition in the dictionaries (and because I love to protract a controversy about words), I'm going with AY-pri-kaht.

aqua, aqua-   AK-wuh.

Aqua comes directly from Latin and means water. The prefix *aqua-,* sometimes spelled *aqui-,* which denotes water, appears in a number of English words including *aquaculture* (or *aquiculture*), *aquacade, aquifer,* the trademark *Aqua-Lung, aquamarine, aquanaut, aquaplane,* and *aquatint.* All of these have their primary accent on the first syllable, which is preferably pronounced AK- (rhyming with *sack*).

Older dictionaries favored the pronunciation AY-kwuh for *aqua,* and marked *aquamarine* and *aquatint* (the other words hadn't yet made it into the dictionaries) as having a long *a.* By the 1930s, however, the long *a* was fading into obscurity, and *Webster 2* (1934) gave precedence to the short *a* of AK-. But even then a new variant, AHK-wuh (AHK- rhyming with *sock*), was already on the rise. In 1937, Alfred H. Holt made this comment on *aqua:* "Most of the dictionaries prefer that we begin with a long *a,* Webster's preference is for 'ack,' and everyone who has had even a smattering of twentieth century Latin says 'ah.'" That little learning soon proved a dangerous thing. When *Webster 3* appeared in 1961, AHK-wuh had taken up residence alongside AK-wuh, and it has appeared in dictionaries since.

I recommend the short *a* of AK-wuh for the group of words noted above for two reasons: (1) because the weight of authority in this century favors it; and (2) because it is pure English rather than a Latin-English hybrid. My gripe with AHK-wuh is that, as Holt suggests, it appears to have been foisted upon us by those who felt compelled to show off their smattering of classical Latin, and since the 1960s, when Latin began falling out of the curriculum, I suspect it has been embraced by those who know no Latin but who felt the broad *a* was somehow more refined. In this case, however, the more refined and natural pronunciation is the anglicized one, with a short *a:* AK-wuh.

aquatic uh-KWAT-ik (rhymes with *an attic*).

This word may also be pronounced uh-KWAHT-ik, with the second syllable rhyming with *lot.* I recommend uh-KWAT-ik, however, because it has a considerably longer tradition in the dictionaries: I traced uh-KWAT-ik as far back as John Walker (1791); the earliest citation I could find for uh-KWAHT-ik was in *Webster 2* (1934), where it is listed as an alternative. Orthoepists since then have been divided. Opdycke (1939) and the *NBC Handbook* (1984) prefer uh-KWAHT-ik; Witherspoon (1943), Lass & Lass (1976), and Frierson (1988) prefer uh-KWAT-ik, as I do for the reasons noted in the last paragraph of the previous entry.

aqueduct AK-wi-duhkt.

This is the only recognized pronunciation. Do not say AH-kwuh-duhkt. (In case you're wondering, *aqueduct* begins with *aque-* instead of *aqua-* because it comes from the Latin *aquae,* the genitive of *aqua,* water.)

aqueous AY-kwee-us

"Rimes with *they see us,*" says Opdycke (1939). "There is also authority for *ak' we us.* The former, however, is preferred." That statement remains true today. Current dictionaries all list AY-kwee-us first, and Lass & Lass (1976) and the *NBC Handbook* (1984) prefer it.

aquiline AK-wi-lin or AK-wi-lyn. (The first syllable rhymes with *pack,* not *sock.*)

"Usage is pretty evenly divided between these two forms," says Phyfe (1926). Vizetelly (1929) shows that orthoepists and lexicographers have also been fairly evenly divided since as far back as Thomas Sheridan (1780), who favored AK-wi-lyn, and John Walker (1791), who favored AK-wi-lin. It's still a toss-up today. Take your pick.

archaeology AHR-kee-**AHL**-uh-jee, not AHR-kay-**AHL**-uh-jee.

Pronounce the second syllable like *key,* not *kay* (which is beastly).

archangel AHRK-ayn-juul (like *ark angel).*

archetype AHRK-uh-typ (like *ark a type).*

The adjective is *archetypal,* which may be stressed either on the third or first syllable: AHR-kuh-**TYP**-al or **AHRK**-uh-TYP-al.

archive, archival, archivist AHR-kyv, ahr-KY-vul, AHRK-uh-vist.

arctic AHRK-tik. Do not say AHR-tik.

Burchfield (1996) — the latest in a long line of authorities that includes Walker (1791), Ayres (1894), Phyfe (1926), Larsen & Walker (1930), Opdycke (1939), Witherspoon (1943), Lass & Lass (1976), the *Oxford Guide* (1983), and the *NBC Handbook* (1984) — duly admonishes us to pronounce the word "with the first *c* fully in place."

"This [word] was formerly spelt without the front *c,* but now that it's there it should be used," advises Holt (1937). Want to know what I say? If you value your reputation as a speaker, don't even *think* about dropping that medial *c.* Without coming right out and saying so, Burchfield and Holt are politely trying to inform you that if you drop the medial *c,* many educated speakers will think you're a boor.

But who pays attention to us orthoepists? Despite all our admonitions, *arctic* is frequently mispronounced, and since the 1950s most dictionaries have sanctioned AHR-tik, especially for the winter boots called *arctics.*

Webster 3 (1961) tells us that "the pronunciation without the first *k* is the original one in English . . . and has centuries of oral tradition behind it." Well, I suppose that settles that, right? With "centuries of oral tradition" and the redoubtable Merriam-Webster imprimatur behind AHR-tik, who could possibly challenge its acceptability? Let's try Frank H. Vizetelly, general editor of Funk & Wagnalls *New Standard Dictionary* (1913).

In his *Desk-Book of 25,000 Words Often Mispronounced* (1929), Vizetelly casts his vote for AHRK-tik and refers us to the entry for *antarctic.* There he acknowledges that "this word was formerly pronounced as spelled — without the medial *c,*" and then goes on to say this: "The medial *c* has been indicated as pronounced by every lexicographer since 1721, when [Nathan] Bailey's dictionary was published." A check of *OED 2* (1989) — which, by the way, sanctions only AHRK-tik — reveals that the *arc-* spelling of *arctic* dates from 1556 and that by about 1700 the medial *c* had become the norm. In light of this, how could *Webster 3* throw its weight behind a vestigial variant based on an obsolete spelling and simply ignore the fact that for nearly 250 years AHRK-tik had been the only acceptable pronunciation in cultivated speech?

In *Comfortable Words* (1959), the distinguished (but in this case wrong-headed) professor and linguist Bergen Evans offers this artful defense of AHR-tik:

> How much parental energy has gone into the seemingly hopeless task of trying to get children to pronounce the first *k* sound in *arctic!* What moves the slovenly little devils to leave it out, especially after Papa (who is a mod'l of pr'cise 'nunciation) has pointed it out to them?
>
> It's the nature of the language, Papa, and you might as well give up. Had you consulted a dictionary before the lesson in articulation, you would have noticed that either pronunciation is correct and had you consulted a linguist you might have learned that the concession, in allowing either pronunciation, is not to the slovenly omission but to the meticulous inclusion.

A concession — if I may interject — that has been *the norm for more than two centuries* and *the preference of all authorities.* Even if you accept the implication here that today's standard pronunciation AHRK-tik, which dates from 1700, is only a corruption of the original AHR-tik, which dates from Chaucer's time, you can't help noticing Evans's revealing choice of words. Which would *you* rather be guilty of, a "slovenly omission" or a "meticulous inclusion"?

Let's let Evans finish his argument:

> The difficulty is that some scholar inserted the first *c* of the Latin *arcturus* into the established English *artic,* ignoring the fact that the occurrence of two *k* sounds so close together in one word runs counter to ease in speaking. By a process known as dissimilation, we usually eliminate the first of two such bothersome sounds or change it to another.

He concludes by wryly declaring that

> anyone who puts the first *k* sound into *antarctic* practically has to withdraw from the conversation while he arranges his mouth. A good, clean enunciation of all the consonants in *antarctic* is an impressive performance.

Evans's irony notwithstanding, it *is* impressive when you enunciate a difficult word properly, which is why I say dissimilation be damned! Is it really "the nature of the language" we're talking about here, or human nature?

Sometimes it seems that linguists exist simply to identify a "process" or invent a polysyllabic label that will mask or mollify some bit of laziness or ignorance. So it's too tough to put an *ark* in *arctic* and *antarctic,* is it? Well, tough boogies. If it was so arbitrary and unnatural to insert that medial *c* into "the established English *artic,*" then why didn't we just chuck it after a decade or two of fruitless experimentation? Why instead, against all odds and in defiance of "linguistic process," have cultivated speakers of the last three centuries embraced this awkward medial *c?*

It's hard to fathom how Evans could suggest that any pronunciation that "runs counter to ease in speaking" is "bothersome" and not worth attempting to master. That is tantamount to saying that trying to speak carefully and clearly is a waste of time. Would you excuse schoolchildren from learning how to multiply because memorizing times tables is bothersome? Would you refrain from correcting errors of grammar and syntax in their compositions because it might run counter to ease in their writing? Would you tell them it doesn't really matter if they misspell words? (For surely, if you scrutinize the *OED,* you can find some writer from centuries ago who used that very "misspelling.") When survey after survey reveals that what millions of Americans dread most is speaking in public, and when business executives continually report that verbal competence is the first thing they look for when interviewing a job candidate, it is at the very least disingenuous for anyone to suggest that speaking precisely is a negligible skill.

The thing that Evans, his fellow linguists, and today's dictionaries will never tell you — and it's a crying shame they won't — is that for generations good speakers have considered an *ark*-less *arctic* beastly, and despite AHR-tik's renewed popularity today, a heck of a lot of educated people still think that if you can't pronounce the medial *c* in *arctic* and *antarctic* you might as well wear a sign around your neck proclaiming, "I'm a pronunciation slob and proud of it." See **February, library, nuclear.**

areola Traditionally, uh-REE-uh-luh. Now often AIR-ee-**OH**-luh.

I would guess that most educated people know this biological term in its anatomical sense, which *RHWC* (1991) defines as "a ring of color, as around the human nipple." I would also guess that most educated people have no idea that uh-REE-uh-luh is the *only* recognized pronunciation of the word.

Does that surprise you? It did me. I have always said AIR-ee-**OH**-luh and I have always heard AIR-ee-**OH**-luh (even from medical personnel). Until someone asked me recently whether the first syllable should be pronounced AIR- (as in *hair*) or AR- (as in *arid*), I had no idea there was any other way of saying the word, let alone that uh-REE-uh-luh, with second-syllable stress, was the only pronunciation countenanced by dictionaries.

This made me wonder: how could our intrepid pronunciation editors, who are always on the *qui vivre* for any variant occurring among educated speakers, manage to turn a deaf ear on AIR-ee-**OH**-luh, which (according to the evidence of my woefully amateurish ears) has all but supplanted uh-REE-uh-luh in educated speech? I'm afraid I can't answer that question, but I can at least offer an explanation of how AIR-ee-**OH**-luh became so prevalent.

OED 2 (1989) shows that *areola* entered English from Latin in 1664; the variant *areole,* pronounced AIR-ee-ohl or AR-ee-ohl, came along from French in 1856. Although *areole* never outdid *areola* in print, in pronunciation the variant undoubtedly exerted pressure on the traditional form. Add to that *areola*'s similarity and etymological relation to the word *area* (in Latin, *areola* is the diminutive of *area*) and you have the makings of a hypothesis.

Theories, however, do not alter the fact that AIR-ee-**OH**-luh is nowhere to be found in a dictionary, which, *ipso facto,* must lead any reasonable person to conclude that the traditional uh-REE-uh-luh is still the better (and safer) bet.

argot AHR-goh (rhymes with *cargo*) or, less often, AHR-gut (almost rhymes with *target*).

The word means jargon, specialized vocabulary, the phraseology peculiar to a certain group, as *adolescent argot.*

Argot came into the language about 1860 from French. The pronunciation AHR-goh is closer to the French, and AHR-gut is anglicized (more English). Since about 1900, most dictionaries have given both, with AHR-goh first. Holt (1937), Opdycke (1939), Lass & Lass (1976), and the *NBC Handbook* (1984) prefer AHR-goh.

Arkansas (the state) AHRK'n-saw. For the river, also ahr-KAN-zis (like *are Kansas*).

According to Paul Dickson's *Labels for Locals* (1997), residents of Arkansas call themselves *Arkansawyers* (**AHRK**'n-SAW-yurz), which has a nice buzz to it, or *Arkansans* (ahr-KAN-zinz). In *Leaves of Grass* Walt Whitman used *Arkansian,* says Dickson, but this variant "is exceedingly rare today."

For Arkansas City, Kansas, the local pronunciation is ahr-KAN-zus. For Arkansas City, Arkansas, however, it's like the state: AHRK'n-saw.

Don't add a *z* sound to the end of *Arkansas.* AHRK'n-sawz (-sawz like *saws*) is beastly and not listed in dictionaries. (Exception: the possessive *Arkansas's.*) See **Illinois, Missouri, Oregon**.

arthritis ahr-THRY-tis.

Arthritis has three syllables. Don't add a syllable and pronounce the word like *arthuritis* (an aversion to men named Arthur).

asbestos as-BES-tus or az-BES-tus.

Watch out for the last syllable here. Some speakers mispronounce this word as-BES-tohs (or az-). Dictionaries do not recognize this pronunciation. The -tus in *asbestos* should rhyme with *us* or *kiss,* not with *dose*.

ask pronounced as spelled, to rhyme with *task.*

Many speakers in New England and the South pronounce the *a* in *ask* with a sound halfway between the flat *a* of *cat* and the broad *a* of *arm* or *dark*. In England, *ask* is pronounced *ahsk,* with a broad *a;* this pronunciation is an affectation coming from an American speaker.

I am often asked about the pronunciation AKS (like *ax* or *axe*). Is it truly an illiteracy? Bergen Evans offers these comments in *Comfortable Words* (1959):

"My little boy persists in saying *axe* for *ask,*" laments a mother. "What should I do about it?"

Nothing whatever — unless he's deaf.

If you nag him enough, he may take to stammering and then you'll both have a real problem. If you let him alone, he will in time perceive that nowadays more people put the *s* sound before the *k* sound in this word, not after it. And so he will change his pronunciation. At least most people do, for almost all children say *axe* for *ask* but very few adults do.

They used to, though. It's interesting that children make this particular change, because *axe* is the old form — the "correct" form, if you want to call it that. The Anglo-Saxon verb was *acsian.* The modern pronunciation is the result of metathesis — which is a learned way of saying that the *s* slipped out of place. For some reason children feel an urge to put it back. It hasn't been out of place very long, either. Wyclif has: "Axe and it shall be gyven unto you." Caxton (1490) spelled the past tense *axyd*. And as late as 1806 Noah Webster said he preferred *axe*.*

There are many words in the language in which a similar sound change has occurred. *Lisp* was formerly *lips*, *tax* was *task*, and *wasp* was *wops*.

In *The American Language* (1937), H. L. Mencken says "the old form *ax* for *ask* is now confined to a few dialects; in the current vulgate *ast* is substituted for it." AST, which still persists in the vulgate, is uncultivated; the admonition of Opdycke (1939) still holds true today: "*Ast* for *ask, assd* for *asked, assing* for *asking* are vulgarisms." Though AKS is no longer acceptable in standard English, it is still common in the dialects of Black English and the so-called mountain speech of certain isolated rural areas — both of which are known for their tendency to preserve archaic forms.

I do not believe, as some assert, that the language is threatened by this dialecticism. As Evans points out, most people who say AKS (or AST) but who otherwise speak reasonably good, standard English will eventually realize that this is not the way the word is pronounced by the overwhelming majority of speakers in the country, and they will correct the error. If they don't, it's much more their problem than the language's. See **across**.

aspartame   Originally, uh-SPAHR-taym or as-PAHR-taym. Now also AS-pur-taym.

Both the word *aspartame* and the sweetener it denotes come from *aspartic* (uh-SPAHR-tik) *acid*, an amino acid found in molasses. *OED 2* (1989) traces the word's origin in print to 1973. At first it was pronounced with second-syllable stress, uh-SPAHR-taym, but within a decade, perhaps through association with *aspirin*, an alternative pronunciation with first-syllable stress, AS-pur-taym, had become popular enough to achieve recognition in *Random House II* (1987).

Since then it's been a toss-up. *WNW 3* (1988) recognizes only as-PAHR-taym (with a fully enunciated initial *a*), but its latest revision, *WNW 3* (1997), recognizes only AS-pur-taym. *American Heritage 3* (1992) and *M-W 10* (1993) list AS-pur-taym first, *RHWC* (1997) lists uh-SPAHR-taym first, and *OED 2* (1989) sanctions only uh-SPAHR-taym. Now that's *ex*-AS-pur-*ating!*

---

* Webster also argued for the form *you was*, favored the flat *a* of *hat* for *quality, quantity,* and *quash,* advocated the broad *a* of *arm* in *ant, pass, staff, half, path, after, clasp, grant, slander,* and various other words in which the flat *a* is entrenched, and even recommended the broad *a* in *chamber, gape,* and *bracelet.* Thank goodness the language somehow works itself out, despite what anyone says. (See **aunt** and **rather** for more on flat vs. broad *a*.)

My ruling? There's no sweet way out of this mess. I'm sticking with the original uh-SPAHR-taym, but AS-pur-taym is also fully accepted and nobody can snub you for saying it that way.

assembly uh-SEM-blee. Don't add a syllable and say uh-SEM-buh-lee.

assuage uh-SWAYJ.

Do not say uh-SWAYZH (beastly), uh-SWAHZH (beastlier), or uh-SWAHJ (beastliest). Here's a mnemonic:

> All the world's a stage,
> And that's how you rhyme *assuage*.

Assuage has been in the language for seven hundred years, and since dictionaries began indicating pronunciation in the mid-1700s there has been only one acceptable way to say the word: uh-SWAYJ. This has been the proper pronunciation from Walker (1791) to *Webster 3* (1961). Recently, however, two upstart variants — uh-SWAYZH (rhymes with *beige*) and uh-SWAHZH (rhymes with *mirage*) — have achieved enough currency to gain recognition in certain dictionaries. *Random House II* (1987) and its abridgment, *RHWC* (1991, 1997), countenance uh-SWAYZH. *M-W 9* (1985) and *10* (1993) list both uh-SWAYZH and uh-SWAHZH, preceded by the label *also* to show they are "appreciably less common."

After centuries of calm agreement, who is rocking the boat, and why? The misguided speakers who have adopted these eccentric variants very likely have read widely and command a large vocabulary, for *assuage* is not the sort of word you encounter every day in the newspaper or on TV. Apparently, though, they have never heard it pronounced correctly (or pronounced by anyone else at all). Chances are they simply guessed how to say it, and I doubt they ever bothered to check if their conjecture was sanctioned by a dictionary (or two).

To their credit, *OED 2* (1989), *American Heritage 3* (1992), and *WNW 3* (1997) do not recognize these beastly new variants. They, along with the *NBC Handbook* (1984), *WNW Guide* (1984), and *Everyday Reader's* (1985), are content with good, old-fashioned uh-SWAYJ.

asterisk AS-tuh-risk. The plural *asterisks* is pronounced AS-tuh-risks.

"The little typographical flower that sends you down to the footnote," writes William Safire in *I Stand Corrected* (1984), "is not, as some say, an 'asterick.' People who say that also say 'ek cetera,' as they bunk into each other."

As you can see, mispronouncing this word is regarded, on the ladder of literacy, as but one weak rung above beastliness. Even the diversity-embracing *M-W 10* (1993) throws out its warning sign — the symbol ÷ (called an obelus, pronounced AHB-uh-lus) — before "asterick(s)" to indicate that it "is considered by some to be unacceptable." It's not hard to say it right: combine *aster* and *risk* quickly and you have *asterisk*.

atelier at'l-YAY or AT'l-yay (rhymes with *tattle day*).

You may stress either the first or the last syllable. Worcester (1860), *Webster 2* (1934), Kenyon & Knott (1949), *American College* (1952), and *OED 2* (1989) prefer first-syllable stress; the *Century* (1914), Phyfe (1926), Vizetelly (1929), the *Winston Dictionary* (1951), Lass & Lass (1976), and the *NBC Handbook* (1984) prefer second-syllable stress. *M-W 10* (1993) and *American Heritage 3* (1992) list only at'l-YAY, while *RHWC* (1997) and *WNW 3* (1997) countenance both pronunciations. *Webster 3* (1961), Jones (1991), and Burchfield (1996) recognize a variant with second-syllable stress, uh-TEL-yay, which is uncommon in the U.S. and best avoided.

athlete ATH-leet; **athletics** ath-LET-iks.

Do not say ATH-uh-leet, with three syllables instead of two, or ATH-uh-LET-iks, with four syllables instead of three. These errors are regrettably common, especially among athletes themselves, as well as among sportscasters, who should know better. Don't pick up their bad habit. "Learn to leap from *th* to *l* without benefit of bridges," writes Holt (1937). There is no vowel between the *h* and the *l* in *athlete* and *athletics*, and no justification for adding a syllable to these words.

atmospheric at-mus-FER-ik. Regionally, at-mus-FAIR-ik.

Do not say at-mus-FEER-ik (like *atmosphere* + ik). The *pher-* in *atmospheric* should be pronounced like *fer-* in *ferry*, not like the word *fear*.

In 1961, *Webster 3* recognized at-mus-FEER-ik and listed it first. Since then this variant has taken the word by storm, and defenders of the traditional pronunciation are beginning to dwindle. Nevertheless, the weight of authority still rests with at-mus-FER-ik. Lass & Lass (1976) and the *NBC Handbook* (1984) prefer it, it is the first pronunciation listed in *American Heritage 3* (1992), *RHWC* (1997), and *WNW 3* (1997), and it is the only pronunciation countenanced by *OED 2* (1989). See **hemispheric, spherical**.

atoll AT-awl (like *at all*, with stress on *at*).

There is also sound authority for uh-TAHL (rhymes with *a doll*). However, AT-awl (or sometimes AT-ahl) is the preference of most American authorities, and therefore recommended.

Attila AT'l-uh (like *battle-uh* without the *b*). This is the traditional pronunciation.

Are you surprised that the stress is properly on the first instead of the second syllable? Would it surprise you even more if I told you that AT'l-uh, with first-syllable stress, was the only recognized pronunciation until the 1960s? The many who now favor the upstart (and etymologically illogical) variant with second-syllable stress, uh-TIL-uh (rhymes with *gorilla*), perhaps will hasten to point out that the *NBC Handbook* (1984) and *WNW Guide* (1984) prefer uh-TIL-uh, the latter noting that "[AT'l-uh], the older pronunciation, is still sometimes heard."

My response to that is a belligerent grimace (which I pronounce gri-MAYS — see the entry), for it comes down to this: those who say AT'l-uh know what they are talking about, and those who say uh-TIL-uh don't. History and the weight of lexical authority are soundly behind first-syllable stress. It is also supported by etymology: *WNW 3* (1997) notes that *Attila* combines the Gothic *atta*, baby talk for "father," and the diminutive suffix *-ila;* hence, *atta-la* or *att-ila*, not *a-til-a*. And if that's not enough, AT'l-uh is still the first pronunciation listed by all four major current dictionaries: *WNW 3* (1997), *American Heritage 3* (1992), *M-W 10* (1993), and *RHWC* (1997).

aunt ANT (like *ant*). Regionally, AHNT (rhymes with *want*).

"Some people insist that *ahnt* is necessary to distinguish their kinswoman from an insect," writes Bergen Evans in *Comfortable Words* (1959). "One can only wonder from what crawling kind they come that they think the confusion is possible."

"The usual vowel of AUNT in the United States is the (a) of *rant*," says *Random House II* (1987), "except in New England and eastern Virginia," where AHNT prevails. "Elsewhere, the 'broader' *a* is chiefly an educated pronunciation, fostered by the schools with only partial success ('Your relative isn't an insect, is she?'), and is sometimes regarded as an affectation." *Random House II* also notes that the flat *a* pronunciation of *aunt* (ANT) was established in America well before the broad *a* (AHNT) became the standard in British English.

In *The American Language* (1937), H. L. Mencken theorizes that the peculiar New England Yankee predilection for the broad *a* in *aunt* and *tomato,* and the half-broad *a* in *ask, dance, laugh, rather,* and various other words, is largely due to the single-handed efforts of Noah Webster, whose "immense authority was sufficient to implant the broad *a* firmly in the speech of the Boston area."

That seems rather a tall order for one "severe, correct, humorless, religious, temperate man who was not easy to like, even by other severe, religious, temperate, humorless people," as Bill Bryson describes Webster in *The Mother Tongue* (1990). Nevertheless, although his readership often ignored his preferences, Webster was nothing if not dogged and his influence was great; few today recall that his *American Spelling Book* (1788), "with the possible exception of the Bible," writes Bryson, "is probably the best-selling book in American history," going through at least 300 editions and selling more than 60 million copies. Webster, says Bryson, "appears to have left us with our pronunciation of *schedule* rather than the English 'shedjulle,' and with our standard pronunciation of *lieutenant* which was then widely pronounced 'lefftenant' in America, as it still is in England today" (see pp. 154–57).

On several occasions I have been asked why many African-American speakers prefer the broad *a* in *aunt*, regardless of what part of the country they live in or hail from. Having noticed this myself, I thought the question worthy of investigation. I dug around the public library but came up empty-handed. Then, to my surprise, I found the very question posted on the Internet at a Web site called Ask a Linguist. Unfortunately, the linguists who responded could only speculate.

Aunt with a broad *a* "is very widespread among African-American communities both within and outside of the South," wrote Benji Wald of UCLA. "In those areas of the South where blacks but not whites commonly use [AHNT], some whites who are aware of it ascribe it to the influence of New England education extended to Southern blacks during emancipation." Elaborating on this notion, Frank Anshen of SUNY at Stony Brook offered this explanation, admittedly with "no substantiating evidence":

> After the Civil War, a number of "Freedmen's Schools" were set up in the south for the education of slaves. Among the staff were a number of maiden ladies from New England with strong abolitionist ideals. Such women would have been of an age and position to be addressed as "Aunt" or "Auntie" and would, like my own aunts, have insisted that they were "onts," "ants" being small insects. As I said, no way to prove it, but it does seem plausible.

John R. Rickford, professor of linguistics at Stanford and an expert on (among other things) African-American vernacular English, dismisses this theory as improbable. "That puts a heavy burden of responsibility on teaching," he told me in a telephone interview, pointing out (as the above quotation from *Random House II* suggests) that education is not known to have a profound influence on speech compared with the powerful influence of home and community. "Having some small quantity of teachers down there wouldn't have that great an effect," he said.

So why do a significant number of African-American speakers in various parts of the country say AHNT for *aunt* and AHN-tee for the diminutive *auntie?** The answer remains elusive. Neither Rickford nor several other linguists I queried could offer anything definitive, although Charles-James N. Bailey, an expert on southern U.S. phonetics, did adduce the

---

* One salient example comes from the TV sitcom *Fresh Prince of Bel Air*. At one point in the show's theme song we hear AHN-tee, with a broad *a,* in the line, "You're movin' with your auntie and your uncle in Bel Air." In the show's dialogue, the star, Will Smith, uses both the broad and the flat *a* (mostly the latter), and his Uncle Phil, a prominent judge, says AHNT with a broad *a.*

beginnings of a credible theory: "I can hazard two possibilities," Bailey writes:

> Less likely, (1) they might have copied the broad-**a** of eastern Virginia or the Caribbean-Tidewater semibroad-**a** of Charleston — prestige areas of the South two or three generations ago — in order to elevate the title's prestige; more likely, (2) the broad-**a** grew up in (Cajun- and Gumbo-speaking) parts of Louisiana and Mississippi where Haitian Creole French and Acadian French prevailed — and where most of the African-American population in the Midwest States came from; these speakers may have had an effect on African Americans from elsewhere in the South — who would in turn have easily influenced their back-home relatives.*

automaton aw-TAHM-uh-tahn or aw-TAHM-uh-t<u>u</u>n.

These pronunciations have equal authority. Worcester (1860), the *Century* (1914), Phyfe (1926), Opdycke (1939), the *Winston Dictionary* (1951), and Lass & Lass (1976) prefer -tahn for the final syllable, as I do. *Webster 2* (1934), the *NBC Handbook* (1984), and *OED 2* (1989) prefer -t<u>u</u>n. Kenyon & Knott (1949), *American College* (1952), and all four major current American dictionaries list both pronunciations.

autopsy AW-tahp-see. Pronounce the second syllable like *top*.

American dictionaries usually also list the variant AW-t<u>u</u>p-see, a pronunciation I have never heard uttered by an American speaker. In *Moscow* I wrote that it was chiefly British, but on reinspection I can find no solid evidence of that. Instead, Holt (1937) and others note the British often accent the *top*. *OED 2* (1989) does list aw-TAHP-see, but after AW-tahp-see, which I recommend to all speakers, particularly Americans.

auxiliary awg-ZIL-yuh-ree.

Be sure to articulate the *y* sound in the third syllable. Don't say awg-ZIL-uh-ree. Dictionaries now countenance this *y*-less pronunciation, but careful speakers do not.

avant-garde AH-vahnt-**GAHRD** or AV-ahnt-**GAHRD**. Also, uh-vahnt-**GAHRD**.

Burchfield (1996), the *OED* lexicographer, remarks that this word, which first appeared in English in the 15th century, "continues to be used with great frequency, but still retains its quasi-French pronunciation." I beg to differ. In America the quasi-French, *t*-less variants AH-vahn-**GAHRD** and A-vahn-**GAHRD** (with the *n* sometimes nasalized) were once preferred by many authorities — even as recently as Lass & Lass (1976) and the *NBC Handbook* (1984). The evidence of my ears, however, tells me they are now heard infrequently. *American Heritage 3* (1992) sensibly recognizes only

---

* Personal correspondence, March 1998.

two variants, AH-vahnt-**GAHRD** (with the AH of *father*) and AV-ahnt-**GAHRD** (with the AV of *have*), and I would agree that these are the most common pronunciations among educated American speakers today, with uh-vahnt-GAHRD running a rather distant third.

awry uh-RY (like *a rye*).

This is the only recognized pronunciation. Anything else is beastly.

"A friend of mine who possesses a Ph.D. conferred by Harvard told me he pronounced it [AW-ree] for many years," writes Lloyd (1938), "until it dawned on him that it is simply the word 'wry' with 'a' before it. . . ." (How embarrassing.)

Azores AY-zorz or uh-ZORZ.

It's hardly worth making *a zore* point about a few dots on the map. Older sources preferred or listed only uh-ZORZ; many current sources give AY-zorz precedence, and the *NBC Handbook* (1984) prefers it. Take your pick.

B

Babel BAY-bul (rhymes with *fable*), not BAB-ul (rhymes with *rabble*).
Properly, the *a* in *Babel* is long, not short: BAY-bul. This is the only
pronunciation countenanced by older authorities. The current popularity
of the alternative BAB-ul, with a short *a* as in *lab,* probably is due to the
influence of *Babylon* and the verb *babble.* These are convenient but misguided associations. Among current sources, the traditional long *a* still
prevails: *RHWC* (1997) and *M-W 9* (1985) and *10* (1993) list BAY-bul first,
Lass & Lass (1976) and the *NBC Handbook* (1984) prefer it, and it is the
only pronunciation in *WNW 3* (1997) and *OED 2* (1989).

bacchanal BAK-uh-**NAL**.
This is the preference of Lass & Lass (1976) and the *NBC Handbook* (1984)
and the only pronunciation sanctioned by *WNW 3* (1997).

Older authorities preferred BAK-uh-nul, and although current sources
usually list this pronunciation, it now appears to be chiefly British: *OED 2*
(1989) and Jones (1991) prefer it. The variant BAH-kuh-**NAHL**, with the
broad *a* of *father* in the first and last syllables, first appeared in *Webster 3*
(1961) and is now countenanced by several dictionaries. It probably arose
from a broad-*a* mispronunciation of *Bacchus* (see next entry).

Bacchus BAK-us, not BAHK-us.
The name of this Greek god of wine and drunken revelry is properly
pronounced with the short *a* of *back,* not, as one increasingly hears, with
the broad *a* of *father.*

Bach BAHKH.
KH is the German guttural *ch* — or, as linguists put it, voiceless velar

---

a = at / a̱ = final / ah = spa / ahr = car / air = fair / ay = hay / aw = saw
ch = chip / e = let / e̱ = item / ee = see / eer = deer / i = sit / i̱ = April
ng = sing / o̱ = carrot / oh = go / oo = soon / or = for / oor = poor
ow = cow / oy = toy / sh = she / th = thin / tẖ = this / u̱ = focus / uh = up
ur = turn / uu = pull, took / y, eye = by, I / zh = measure / (see full key, p. xiv)

fricative — which is "produced like the sound of clearing the throat," says *WNW Guide* (1984).

We do not anglicize Beethoven, Mozart, and Wagner; we say BAY-toh-vin (not BEE-thoh-vin), MOHT-sahrt (not MOH-zahrt), and VAHG-nur (not WAG-nur). Why do certain speakers (and some authorities) make an exception for Bach, anglicizing it to BAHK (rhymes with *flock*)?

BAHK apparently has been heard for most of the 20th century. Though Phyfe (1926), Vizetelly (1929), *Webster 2* (1934), *American College* (1952), and the *Columbia Encyclopedia* (1963) do not recognize the anglicized pronunciation, Opdycke (1939) says *Bach* should rhyme with *lock* and Kenyon & Knott (1949) list BAHK first. Most current authorities continue to favor the German *ch;* BAH<u>KH</u> appears first in *American Heritage 3* (1992) and *M-W 10* (1993), and it is the only pronunciation in *Random House II* (1987) and *RHWC* (1997). Only the *NBC Handbook* (1984) and McConkey (1986) prefer BAHK.

So we must conclude, albeit reluctantly, that BAHK is now an approved alternative; however, it is far less common than its dictionary recognition makes it appear. *WNW 3* (1997), which prefers BAH<u>KH</u>, no doubt is right in labeling BAHK occasional and eastern. Among musicians, music buffs, and classical music disc jockeys BAH<u>KH</u> is *de rigueur,* and that's what the all-American *Reader's Digest* (1972) recommends: "Bach (the composer) retains its German pronunciation: the *a* as in *father,* the *ch* a guttural sound." *WNW Guide* (1984) says "most Americans try to reproduce the German *ach* sound" — and most Americans, I would add, have no trouble doing so.

Do not say BAK (like *back*), or worse, BAYCH. Both are beastly.

bade (past tense of *bid*) BAD, not BAYD.

American Heritage 3 (1992) and *M-W 10* (1993) have sanctioned the spelling pronunciation BAYD, but *RHWC* (1997) and *WNW 3* (1997) countenance only BAD, and Lass & Lass (1976), *WNW Guide* (1984), the *NBC Handbook* (1984), and Burchfield (1996) agree that this (gradually disappearing, it seems) past tense of *bid* should rhyme with *sad,* not with *made.* Compare **forbade**.

badminton BAD-min-tin.

Badminton comes from the name of the countryseat of the Duke of Beaufort in England, where the game was first played.

Take care to make the middle *n* in *badminton* audible. The word is often mispronounced BAD-mit'n (like *bad mitten*). This is sloppy. All sources, past and current, indicate the pronunciation with *n.* If you are not accustomed to saying it that way, try this exercise: pronounce the city of Edmonton (Alberta, Canada) — ED-min-tin — then substitute BAD- for ED- in the first syllable. After a few times switching back and forth you should have no trouble saying BAD-min-tin.

Bahamian buh-HAY-mee-in.

balk BAWK. Do not say BAWLK.

The *l* is silent, as in *talk, walk, stalk, caulk,* and *chalk.* See **almond**.

balm BAHM (like *bomb*). See **almond, calm**.

Balmoral (Castle, cap, and boot) bal-MOR-ul or bal-MAHR-ul.

The second, stressed syllable may sound like *more* or *mar.* Note: the castle is always capital *B;* the cap is sometimes capital *B;* the boot is lowercase *b.*

balsamic bawl-SAM-ik. Don't say bawl-SAHM-ik.

Despite what you may hear from some slippery-tongued chefs on those gourmet cooking TV shows, the stressed second syllable of *balsamic* rhymes with *ham,* not *calm.*

banal BAY-nul or buh-NAL. Formerly, BAN-ul. British also buh-NAHL.

Banal is a word of many pronunciations, each of which has its outspoken and often intractable proponents. Though it may pain some to hear it, let the record show that BAY-nul is the variant preferred by most authorities (including me). Here's how dictionaries and orthoepists of the last hundred-odd years weigh in on the word:

Worcester (1860) gives BAY-nul. The *Century* (1914) gives BAN-ul. Funk & Wagnalls *Standard* (1897) lists only BAN-ul but the *New Standard* (1913) switches to BAY-nul. *Webster's Collegiate* (1917) and Phyfe (1926) countenance BAN-ul and BAY-nul, while *OED 1* (1928) reverses that order. Vizetelly (1929) and Witherspoon (1943) prefer BAY-nul. *Webster 2* (1934), Kenyon & Knott (1949), and *American College* (1952) sanction, in this order, BAY-nul, buh-NAL, buh-NAHL, and BAN-ul.

Opdycke (1939) says *banal* "may be pronounced [BAY-nul] or [buh-NAL] (riming with *a pal*), or [buh-NAHL] (riming with *a doll*), or [BAN-ul] (riming with *flannel*). It is therefore one of the few words in English that would appear to be impossible of mispronunciation. . . . The order above given is the order of preference."

Holt (1937) says, "I favor following an analogy which gives a good approximation of the French pronunciation of *banal:* rhyme it with *canal.*"

Lass & Lass (1976) prefer BAY-nul. The *Oxford Guide* (1983), a British source, says "2nd syllable like that of *canal* or *morale* (Amer. rhymes with *anal*)." *WNW Guide* (1984) says BAY-nul, buh-NAL, or buh-NAHL.

Curiously, the *NBC Handbook* (1984) prefers the chiefly British buh-NAHL, which, also curiously, *OED 2* (1989) lists *after* BAY-nul. In his *New Fowler's MEU* (1996), *OED 2* lexicographer R. W. Burchfield calls buh-NAHL the British standard and notes that in American English *banal, banality,* and *banally* are commonly pronounced BAY-nul, bay-NAL-i-tee, and BAY-nuh-lee, "but there is much variation," he adds. Although BAY-nul is the dominant pronunciation in American speech, buh-NAL is a close runner-up and may eventually lead the pack. Three of the four major current American dictionaries now list buh-NAL first.

Bangor (Maine) BANG-gor (like *bang gore*).

Often mispronounced *banger* (BANG-ur), like the English sausage. Although BANG-gor is preferred by all sources, BANG-gur is also sanctioned by many authorities.

bankruptcy BANGK-ruhpt-see.

Don't say BANGK-rup-see. Careful speakers preserve the *t* sound in this word.

banquet BANG-kwit (like *bang* + *quit*).

Baptist BAP-tist. Don't say BAB-tist.

This word has been "mispronounced by millions of people, particularly in the South," says Frierson (1988), a southern orthoepist. "They say *Bab-tist*, with a *b* instead of a *p*."

baptize bap-TYZ or BAP-tyz.

The traditional pronunciation, preferred by many clerics (and by me), stresses the second syllable. Outside of church, however, first-syllable stress is now common. See **blasphemous, trespass.**

Barabbas buh-RAB-us. There is no authority for first-syllable stress.

barbiturate bar-BICH-ur-it.

Many speakers fail to articulate the second *r* in *barbiturate*. Don't say bar-BICH-oo-it or bar-BICH-uh-wit. Take care to put the *r* in there: *barbi*-chur-*ate*.

When *barbiturate* came into the language in the late 1920s, it had two acceptable pronunciations, bar-buh-TYOOR-it and bar-BICH-uh-rayt. Both appear in current dictionaries but are rarely heard.

basal BAY-sul, not BAY-zul (*s* as in *case*, not as in *rose*).

American Heritage 3 (1992), *M-W 10* (1993), and *RHWC* (1997) list BAY-sul first, and *WNW Guide* (1984), the *NBC Handbook* (1984), *Everyday Reader's* (1985), Jones (1991), Burchfield (1996), and *WNW 3* (1997) prefer it. Only one modern source, Lass & Lass (1976), prefers BAY-zul.

basalt buh-SAWLT.

This is the first pronunciation listed in all four major current American dictionaries and the preference of the *NBC Handbook* (1984) and *Everyday Reader's* (1985). An acceptable alternative is BAY-sawlt, which is preferred by Lass & Lass (1976).

bases (plural of *basis*) BAY-seez; (plural of *base*) BAY-siz.

I have often heard well-educated speakers — professionals and academics — carelessly use the plural *bases* (BAY-seez) when their sentence requires the singular *basis* (BAY-sis). For example, a lawyer may say, "There is no BAY-seez for this charge," meaning *There is no basis for this charge.* Of course, no educated person would ever write "There is no bases for this charge," but unfortunately, to many the error is less obvious in speech.

The problem is chiefly one of overpronunciation, which *Random House II* (1987) defines as speaking "in an exaggerated, affected, or excessively careful manner." In this case, the exaggerated attempt at correctness (called *hypercorrection*) causes the speaker to flip-flop into solecism. Like the grammatical errors "for him and I" and "between you and I," in which *I* should be *me*, saying BAY-seez for *basis* is a sign that an insecure speaker is trying too hard to be precise. See **crisis, diagnosis, thesis.**

basil Traditionally, BAZ-il (BAZ- rhyming with *has*). Now usually BAY-zil.

In *There Is No Zoo in Zoology* (1988), after noting that *Webster 3* (1961) was the first of my sources to recognize the variant BAY-zil, I complained that "thirty years of saying BAY-zil hardly seems enough to justify granting it . . . precedence over BAZ-il, which was the only recognized pronunciation until the middle of the century." Today, however, despite the fact that all four major current American dictionaries — *American Heritage 3* (1992), *RHWC* (1997), *M-W 10* (1993), and *WNW 3* (1997) — list BAZ-il first, and the *NBC Handbook* (1984) prefers it, there is no denying the evidence of my ears. Without doubt, the upstart BAY-zil — the preference of Lass & Lass (1976) — is now the dominant pronunciation at all levels of American speech. Rarely do I hear someone use the traditional BAZ-il, and when I do it's usually someone from another English-speaking country. Nevertheless, I cling to my obsolescent preference, ignoring the strange glances of my misguided fellow Americans, secure in the knowledge that, if challenged, I have plenty of authority to back me up. See **cumin.**

basilisk BAZ-i-lisk or BAS-i-lisk.

For the first syllable, American authorities favor BAS-, while British authorities prefer BAZ-. On this one, along with the *NBC Handbook* (1984), I'm with the Brits. The *z-s* combination sounds better than the hissing *s-s*, don't you agree? Of course, one could argue that such sibilance befits a word denoting a weird tropical lizard or a fabled serpent with a deadly look and killer breath. Your call.

bas relief BAH ri-LEEF.

Properly, the *s* is silent.

bathos BAY-thaws. See **pathos.**

Baton Rouge (Louisiana) See **rouge.**

beaucoup boh-KOO or BOH-koo (as in the informal expression *beaucoup bucks*).

Certain dictionaries say *beaucoup* is sometimes spelled *bookoo* or *boocoo* and pronounced BOO-koo. Here's what I say: those spellings are facetious at best, illiterate at worst, and BOO- for *beau* is either simpleminded or simply in *geste*. (I wonder how long it will be before some prickmedainty* decides to say boh-KYOO!) See **bouquet, boutique, coupon.**

---

* *Prickmedainty,* which *OED 2* (1989) traces to 1529, means a man or woman who is compulsively fastidious about dress, appearance, and manners.

because bee-KAWZ or, in rapid speech, bi-KAWZ.

The word *cause* rhymes with *gauze,* but you will hear some careless speakers rhyme *cause* with *loss.* This mispronunciation is far more frequent when *be-* precedes *cause.* Many educated speakers, who would never rhyme *cause* with *loss,* say bee-KAWS, with a "pure" or "sharp" *s,* instead of bee-KAWZ, with a "soft" *s.* Take care to make the *s* in *because* sound like *z.*

The pronunciation bi-KUHZ (famously rendered in the lyric from the 1939 film *The Wizard of Oz:* "bi-KUHZ of the wonderful things he does") is not, as some claim, beastly. Kenyon and Knott (1949) sanction it, and current sources list it as an alternative.

behemoth bi-HEE-muth (also -mawth). Formerly, BEE-uh-mawth (or -muth).

"Modern usage," says Vizetelly (1929), "as reflected by [Funk & Wagnalls *New Standard* (1913), the *Century* (1914), and *OED 1* (1928)], accents the penult" — the next-to-last syllable, pronounced PEE-nuhlt (like *peanut* with an *l: peanult*).

Beijing bay-JING, or, with roughly equal stress, BAY-JING.

Do not say bay-ZHING or bay-SHING.

In 1989, as Americans listened to reports of the struggle of the Chinese student protesters in Tiananmen Square, they heard two things: the story of a heroic plea for freedom and a persistent mispronunciation of *Beijing.* Over and over, newscasters on all the networks were saying bay-ZHING, with the *zh* sound of *azure* for the *j.* (I call this the "French *j.*") Local announcers picked up the error, and soon it seemed most of America was saying it wrong.

It never ceases to amaze me how our proclivity for mimicry and affectation can turn tradition and convention on their heads and introduce a new "standard" almost overnight. I could indict the media, who have as much responsibility to render the news with proper grammar and pronunciation as they do to report it accurately, but that would be the easy way out and not altogether fair, for some newscasters do take pains to pronounce things properly (especially proper nouns). In truth, the gravamen* rests with *vox populi* (VAHKS PAHP-yoo-ly) — the voice of the people — which habitually separates the wheat from the chaff and regurgitates the chaff. What I fail to understand is why we are so impressionable. When we hear a questionable pronunciation on radio or television, why don't more of us take the sixty seconds it requires to check it in a dictionary?

For example, before about 1980 you rarely heard American broadcasters (or anyone else, for that matter) pronounce the first *t* in *negotiate* and

---

* *Gravamen,* pronounced gruh-VAY-min, is a legal term meaning the most serious part of a charge or accusation.

negotiation with a pure *s* instead of an *sh* sound. Then suddenly the spurious sibilance of nego-*see*-ate and nego-*see*-ation was hissing all over the airwaves, and before long it seemed that every other speaker you met was saying it that way. In no time at all this epidemic of affectation became so widespread that the dictionaries, which had always given only one pronunciation for these words — nego-*shee*-ate and nego-*shee*-ation — began to record the "see" sound as an acceptable alternative.

"The 'see-for-she' substitution is rampant on television," writes William Safire of *The New York Times,* in *I Stand Corrected* (1984, p. 387). "Phil Donahue . . . pronounces *controversial* as 'contro-ver-seeul,' rather than 'controvershul.' . . . In the same way, elitist newscasters knock the 'she' out of *negotiate* in their chichi pronunciation, 'nego-see-ations.' 'She' is right; 'see' is incorrect and an affectation." (For more on these "chichi" words, see **consortium, controversial, negotiate, oceanic, Social Security,** and **species.**)

All of which is to say that in the matter of *Beijing* there is no room for nego-*see*-ation. The proper pronunciation, says Safire, is "bay-JING — with the *j* as in *Joe* or *jingle* — rather than bay-SHING" (*The New York Times Magazine,* "On Language," July 2, 1989). In the old days we spelled it *Peking* and pronounced it pee-KING. In even older days we spelled it *Peiping* and pronounced it pay-PING (or bay-PING). Today the standard pinyin spelling is *Beijing,* for which, at the time of the crisis in Tiananmen Square, there was only one recognized pronunciation: bay-JING. (The *NBC Handbook* transcribes the second syllable as "-jeeng," which perhaps shows more of the authentic Chinese inflection.) In *Is There a Cow in Moscow?* I wrote that "no authority I have consulted lists either bay-SHING or bay-ZHING." Now, eight years later, one dictionary — *WNW 3* (1997) — has capitulated. All other current sources, however, still sanction only bay-JING (or the evenly stressed BAY-JING).

beneficent buh-NEF-uh-sint.

Don't say buh-NIF-uh-sint; there is no *-nif-* in *beneficent.* Be careful with the second syllable, which should rhyme with *chef.* See **maleficent.**

beneficiary BEN-i-FISH-ee-er-ee, not BEN-i-FISH-ur-ee.

Beneficiary has six syllables, not five. Say *bene-fishy-ary,* not *bene-fishery.* See **judiciary, subsidiary.**

benignant buh-NIG-nint.

Benign (buh-NYN) and *benignant* follow the pronunciation of *malign* (muh-LYN) and *malignant* (muh-LIG-nint).

bequeath bi-KWEETH.

Properly, the *th* is voiced, meaning it should sound like the *th* in *this* and *bathe,* not like the *th* in *thin* and *path.*

Bernstein (Leonard) BURN-styn (rhymes with *turn sign*).

Commonly, but erroneously, pronounced BURN-steen, even among musicians and music buffs. This composer-conductor's name "even gets abused by disk jockeys on classical music stations — normally a most fastidious group," says McConkey (1986). See **bolivar**.

besiege bi-SEEJ. See **siege**.

bestial BES-chuul or BEST-yuul. British, BES-tee-ul or BEST-yuul.

Don't say BEES-chuul. Also, be careful not to mush the *bes-* into *besh-*.

Since the 1960s dictionaries have listed BEES-chuul as an alternative because many misguided speakers had erroneously begun to model their pronunciation of *bestial* after the word *beast*. Unfortunately, our dictionary-makers are too self-importantly egalitarian to inform you that many educated speakers consider this variant thoroughly beastly. Why? Because it distinguishes those who pay attention to propriety and tradition in speech from those who do not, and who simply make uninformed guesses or follow the herd. It separates the cultivated speakers from the crude, the more evolved beings from the vulgar boors. That may seem arbitrary, and perhaps even ridiculous, but all custom is arbitrary and ridiculous in a way. The proper pronunciation of this word, more so than many others in this book, is a matter of etiquette and a mark of refinement, like handling your silverware properly or covering your mouth when you cough. If that sort of thing matters to you when it comes to speech, then you should know that BES-chuul is the *best* pronunciation and BEES-chuul is *beastly*.

The corresponding noun *bestiality* is pronounced BES-chee-**AL**-i-tee.

bête noire bayt NWAHR or bet NWAHR.

"Literally, a black beast," says *Webster 2* (1934); hence, "a person or object of fear, detestation, or aversion." As I always say, the prescriptive orthoepist is the descriptive linguist's *bête noire*.

Biloxi (Mississippi) bi-LUHK-see, not bi-LAHK-see.

There are no *lox* in *Biloxi*. It's Bi-*luck*-see.

bipedal by-PED'l or BY-ped'l.

Not long ago I heard some anthropologist on NPR's *Talk of the Nation* say by-PEED'l, with the long *e* of *impede*. Since I had never in my life heard that pronunciation, I did what all good language mavens do — run to the dictionaries! After a rigorous hunt through sources past and present, I found four and a half citations. The half is John Walker (1791), who gives the peculiar BIP-pee-dal (in later dictionaries rendered BIP-i-dul, now an obsolescent variant). It popped up next in Vizetelly (1929), who found it in John Ogilvie's *Imperial Dictionary* (1882). Then came *Webster 3* (1961), where it was preceded by the label "also." This odd bird appeared again, as the *preferred* pronunciation, in Jones (1991), a British source, and finally in the thoroughly American *WNW 3* (1997) — where, to my astonishment, it was listed first, followed by by-PED'l.

My conclusion? I think by-PEED'l doesn't have much of a leg to stand on. The spoor is too spotty, and smells vaguely British (or Anglophilic). I say stick with by-PED'l, which is the only pronunciation in *American Heritage 3* (1992), *M-W 10* (1993), and *RHWC* (1997). First-syllable stress, preferred by the *Century* (1914), *Webster 2* (1934), and *OED 2* (1989), is also acceptable.

blasphemous BLAS-fuh-mus. Do not say blas-FEE-mus.

Always stress the *blas-* in *blasphemous*. Stressing the second syllable, *-phe-*, is beastly. The noun *blasphemy* is pronounced BLAS-fuh-mee, with the accent again on the second syllable. The verb *blaspheme* is traditionally (and usually among the clergy) pronounced blas-FEEM, with the accent on the second syllable, but first-syllable stress is now also acceptable. See **baptize, posthumous, trespass.**

blithe BLYTH (rhymes with *writhe*).

When a monosyllabic word ends in *-the*, the *th* is usually sounded or "voiced," as in *clothe, breathe, lathe, seethe,* and *soothe.* When the *th* is final, it is usually "voiceless," as in *cloth, broth, breath, death,* and *forsooth. Blithe* follows this rule, and so is pronounced with the *th* of *then* and *there,* not with the *th* of *path.*

Since *Webster 3* (1961), Merriam-Webster's dictionaries have listed the voiceless *th* pronunciation BLYTH (TH as in *thin*) first. If a Merriam-Webster is the only dictionary you own, you should know that their previous unabridged dictionary, *Webster 2* (1934), gives only BLYTH (TH as in *then*), all three other major current American dictionaries list BLYTH first, and the voiced *th* is preferred by (among many others) Kenyon & Knott (1949), Lass & Lass (1976) and the *NBC Handbook* (1984).

Boca Raton BOH-kuh ruh-TOHN.

The name of this Florida city comes from Spanish and means literally "mouse mouth." *Boca* is rarely if ever mispronounced, but some speakers mispronounce *Raton* as ruh-TAHN, with the short *o* of *top.* The *o* is properly long, as in *tone.*

Bodleian (Library) bahd-LEE-in or BAHD-lee-in.

Bodleian as an adjective means "of or pertaining to the famous library at Oxford University in England, opened in 1602, or to its founder, Sir Thomas Bodley."

The weight of authority is for second-syllable stress. The *Century* (1914), Phyfe (1926), *OED 1* (1928), *Webster 2* (1934), *Random House II* (1987), and *OED 2* (1989) all list bahd-LEE-in first, and Vizetelly (1929) and the *NBC Handbook* (1984) prefer it. Worcester (1860) and the *Columbia Encyclopedia* (1963) list BAHD-lee-in first, and Jones (1991) prefers it.

Boeotian bee-OH-shin (like *be ocean*).

Boeotia (bee-OH-shuh), one of the divisions of ancient Greece, was a region "known for its thick atmosphere," says the *Century* (1914). According to the Athenians, this torpid climate was "supposed to communicate its dullness to the intellect of the inhabitants." Although three of Greece's greatest men of letters — Hesiod (HEE-see-u̱d), Pindar (PIN-dur), and Plutarch (PLOO-tahrk) — were native Boeotians, Athenian city slickers reveled in reviling these simple country folk.

Today a *Boeotian* is a dull, stupid, ignorant person, and the adjective *Boeotian* means stupid, boring, obtuse. *Boeotian ears,* says *Brewer's Dictionary of Phrase and Fable,* are "ears unable to appreciate music or rhetoric."

Boise (Idaho) BOY-see (local and recommended) or BOY-zee.

The *NBC Handbook* (1984) prefers BOY-zee, but other authorities show that this is not the authentic pronunciation. Kenyon & Knott (1949) and W. Cabell Greet's *World Words* (1948) give only BOY-see, and *Random House II* (1987) says -see is the local pronunciation. Mary Reed, director of the Latah County (Idaho) Historical Society and a Boise native, confirms this ruling.

Boleyn, Anne BUUL-in (like *bull in*) or buu-LIN.

Surprised, are you, by the first pronunciation given? So was I when I read this passage in *We Who Speak English* by Charles Allen Lloyd (1938):

> It probably makes no difference to Anne Boleyn, and possibly not a great deal to anybody else, but some of my readers may be interested to know that reference books usually give the pronunciation of her surname as "BULLin," not "BoLIN," as we frequently hear it.

Lloyd is right. All my references up to the *Columbia Encyclopedia* (1963) give BUUL-in for the last name of this second wife of Henry VIII of England and mother of Elizabeth I. Vizetelly (1929), who sanctions buh-LIN as an alternative, is the only exception. Kenyon & Knott (1949) note that Shakespeare spelled the name *Bullen.* Since the 1960s, however, authorities have sanctioned second-syllable stress, with the first syllable pronounced variously buu-, buh-, or boh-. *American Heritage 3* (1992), *RHWC* (1997), and *WNW 3* (1997) list BUUL-in first, but the *NBC Handbook* (1984) prefers buu-LIN and *M-W 10* (1993) lists it first. *M-W 10* also records buu-LEEN, an eccentric variant for which I can find no other authority.

bolivar boh-LEE-vahr.

I recommend this one pronunciation for both the monetary unit of Venezuela and the name of the 19th-century South American liberator (Simón Bolívar). It is a personal preference, based on the following assumptions:

1. There seems to be a tendency among educated speakers and the broadcast media to pronounce foreign personal names as they are pronounced in the language they come from. In cases where the native pro-

nunciation would cause spasms in the English-speaking tongue, we try to come as close as possible without mangling the name or the organ of speech. We also must be mindful not to sound *too* foreign, lest we sound affected, or simply goofy.

2. It is your inalienable right to demand that your name be pronounced the way you want it to be pronounced. Unfortunately, this right is not very often respected, especially with celebrities and historical figures (see **Bernstein, Carnegie, Chavez, Dreiser, Marquez, Nin, Rand**). Mr. Bolívar is no longer here to plead his case, so I will have to do it for him. In Spanish as well as in English orthography there is an accent mark over the *i* in *Bolívar*. It is not there for embellishment; that is where the stress falls. There is also an accent in the man's first name. The entire Spanish-speaking world calls him Simón (see-MOHN) Bolívar (boh-LEE-vahr). As that is quite pronounceable by English speakers I see no reason why we shouldn't do the same.

3. Finally, the name of the unit of currency comes from the name of the historical figure. Therefore, using the same pronunciation for both is sensible and consistent. For the plural of the monetary unit, I recommend the spelling *bolivars* and the pronunciation boh-LEE-vahrz.

bona fide BOH-nuh-FYD or **BAH**-nuh-FYD. Avoid BOH-nuh FY-dee.

Reader's Digest (1972) offers this sound advice: "Join the common people and say [**BOH**-nuh-FYD]; the Latin scholars who add the extra syllable [BOH-nuh FY-dee] sound pedantic." The four-syllable pronunciation, says Burchfield (1996), is usual "in English contexts"; it is most decidedly not so in the U.S.

The *o* in *bona* may be long, as in *bone,* or short, as in *bonnet.* Current dictionaries list the long *o* pronunciation first (which usually indicates greater currency) and some authorities — e.g., *Everyday Reader's* (1985) and the *NBC Handbook* (1984) — give only long *o;* however, the short *o* — sanctioned in good usage at least since *American College* (1952) and preferred by Lass & Lass (1976) — is fully standard.

N.B. The noun *bona fides,* meaning "credentials," if it must be used at all, is best pronounced BOH-nuh FY-deez, and not, as it often is colloquially, **BOH**-nuh-FYDZ (-FYDZ rhyming with *sides*), which *M-W 10* (1993) labels as "unacceptable" to many.

Bonaparte BOH-nuh-pahrt, not BAHN-uh-pahrt.

The *o* is long, as in *bone,* not short, as in *bonnet.*

bon mot bawn MOH or, with a French nasalized *n,* baw(n) MOH.

Bon mot, literally "a good word," means a clever remark or witty saying. For *bon,* some authorities prefer bohn- (like *bone*) or bahn- (rhymes with *on*). For the plural *bon mots,* add a *z* sound at the end: bawn MOHZ. The *t* should never be pronounced.

boudoir BOO-dwahr.

Boudoir should rhyme with *food bar,* not *good bar.* Most authorities prefer first-syllable stress, but stressing the second (boo-DWAHR) is now also acceptable.

bougainvillea BOO-gin-**VIL**-yuh or -**VIL**-ee-uh. Sometimes, -**VEE**-yuh.

The first syllable is properly BOO-, as in *boot,* not BOH-, as in *boat.*

bouillabase BOO-yuh-**BAYS** or BOOL-yuh-**BAYS**.

Older authorities — including Opdycke (1939), Kenyon & Knott (1949), and, more recently, Lass & Lass (1976) — prefer the anglicized BOOL-yuh-**BAYS,** with an audible *l.* Current authorities show a preference for the de-anglicized (or re-Frenchified) BOO-yuh-**BAYS,** with the *l* silent. The *NBC Handbook* (1984) prefers BOO-, all four major current American dictionaries list BOO- first, and one of them, *M-W 10* (1993), does not even recognize BOOL-.

Primary stress on the first syllable is now also acceptable; you may say **BOO**-yuh-BAYS or **BOOL**-yuh-BAYS. However, pronouncing the final syllable BAYZ (rhymes with *raise*) or BEZ (rhymes with *fez*) is incorrect. According to Morris & Morris (1985),

> the correct pronunciation of the name of this French seafood dish is boo-yuh-BASE. Some fairly appalling pronunciations have been heard on broadcasts, even from cooks who should know better. One such was bull-yuh-BEZ from the lips of one of the highest-priced "talents" on the air. Ah, well.

bouquet boo-KAY (boo- as in *boot*) or boh-KAY (boh- as in *boat*).

Holt (1937) says, "Though Webster [2] lists 'bo-kay'' as a possibility, most of the authorities plainly look on it as a ridiculous half breed. The French is, of course, 'boo-kay.' Yet most of us, for reasons unknown, were brought up on 'bo-kay'." These remarks are revealing, for since *Webster 2* (1934) recognized boh-KAY as an alternative it has gained greatly in popularity and appears to have outpaced boo-KAY, except when the word is used to mean an aroma, as in "the bouquet of this wine," for which the pronunciation boo-KAY is still favored.

Why such a distinction is necessary — boh-KAY for a bunch of flowers, boo-KAY for an aroma — is beyond me. Maybe it came about because the connoisseurs all stuck to boo- after hoi polloi had cast their ballots for boh-. Now I suppose we'll have to say, "The boo-KAY of your boh-KAY is mighty fine, ma'am." Frankly, that smells a bit fishy to me, but *de gustibus non est disputandum.* Take your pick — but remember, the accent must be on the second syllable. I'm sticking with the perennial boo-KAY. See **beaucoup, boutique, coupon**.

bourgeois (adjective and noun) boor-ZHWAH or BOOR-zhwah. Pronounce the *r.*

Two reminders regarding this word: you may place the stress on either the second or the first syllable, depending on your syntax; and for the first syllable, eschew (es-CHOO) the beastly variants boo- and buuzh-, with no *r* sound, and also buush- (like *bush*), with an *sh* instead of a *zh* sound.

Bourgeois is one of the few words in the language that is easier to speak than to spell. In *Say It My Way* (1980), Willard Espy relates an anecdote about a college professor who asked his students to write about the *bourgeoisie* (BOOR-zhwah-**ZEE**). Not only did the professor find out that three-fourths of the class could not spell the word, but also that they spelled it in no fewer than 84 different ways.

The plural noun is *bourgeois,* spelled and pronounced the same. The feminine form, not often used, is *bourgeoise* (boor-ZHWAHZ), plural *bourgeoises* (boor-ZHWAHZ; the three-syllable alternative boor-ZHWAH-ziz, listed in some dictionaries, is not recommended.)

bourgeoisie See **bourgeois.**

boutique boo-TEEK.

The beastly mispronunciation boh-TEEK — created, I imagine, on analogy with the pronunciation boh-KAY for *bouquet* — "is now widespread," says *WNW Guide* (1984), which prefers boo-TEEK. Regrettably, that assessment is true. Nevertheless, you should know that all current authorities prefer boo-TEEK, and only one dictionary, *WNW 3* (1997), recognizes boh-TEEK, which appears with the vaguely incriminating label "often." Such collective disregard among modern lexicographers is rare, and may reasonably be taken as a sign that there is probably something less than savory about boh-TEEK. See **beaucoup, bouquet, coupon.**

bowdlerize BOWD-luh-ryz (BOWD- rhyming with *loud*).

Bowdlerize is the gift to the language of one Thomas Bowdler, an uptight English physician now infamous for publishing an expurgated edition of Shakespeare's works in 1818. It means to delete from a text anything considered indecent or objectionable. "Bowdler so thoroughly purged both Shakespeare and Gibbon," writes Robert Hendrickson in his *Dictionary of Eponyms* (1972), "that they would have screamed in pain from the bloodletting had they been alive."

Why, you may be wondering, do I recommend BOWD-luh-ryz and not BOHD-luh-ryz? After all, Funk & Wagnalls *Standard* (1897), the *Century* (1914), the *Quintessential Dictionary* (1978), the *NBC Handbook* (1984), and *Everyday Reader's* (1985) all prefer BOHD-luh-ryz, with the long *o* of *low* and *tow,* and three of the four major current American dictionaries list this pronunciation first. Nevertheless, historically the weight of authority falls clearly on the side of BOWD- (rhymes with *loud*) for the first syllable. BOWD-luh-ryz is the preference of *Webster 2* (1934), Holt (1937), Opdycke (1939), Kenyon & Knott (1949), the *Winston Dictionary* (1951), *American College* (1952), Lass & Lass (1976), Barnhart (1988), *OED 2* (1989), and Jones

(1991), and the first pronunciation listed in the *Columbia Encyclopedia* (1963) and *WNW 3* (1997).

Finally, H. W. Fowler (1926) says, "pronounce bow-" to rhyme with *cow*. If that highbrow dictum from the legendary logogogue* doesn't make you kowtow to BOWD-luh-ryz, perhaps nothing will.

braggadocio BRAG-uh-**DOH**-shee-oh.

Take note of the -shee- in the penultimate syllable.

Astonishing: a variant I have never heard, BRAG-uh-**DOH**-see-oh, is listed *first* in *American Heritage 3* (1992) and *M-W 10* (1993). Surely this is yet another piece of prissiness adopted by the painfully overrefined, for there is no authority — zero, zip, zilch — for substituting -see- for -shee- in this word. If your restless tongue must find an alternative to BRAG-uh-**DOH**-shee-oh — the preference of only about a gazillion sources from Walker (1791) and Worcester (1860) to *Webster 2* (1934) and *OED 2* (1989) — then how about BRAG-uh-**DOH**-chee-oh, a variant preferred by Jones (1991), a British source, but no longer recorded in American dictionaries. At least it follows the Italian custom of pronouncing *c* before *i* like *ch* in *church,* whereas this prissy -**DOH**-see-oh is pure poppycock.

brassiere bruh-ZEER.

Brassiere entered English about 1910 directly from the French *brassière,* bodice. At first it had a Frenchified pronunciation, brah-SYAIR or bras-ee-AIR (like *brassy air*), but within two decades the anglicized bruh-ZEER and the clipped form *bra* had asserted themselves for good. (Another clipped form, *brass,* also had a brief lifespan, but it died presumably for want of a *brassy air* to support it.)

Of bruh-ZEER, Holt (1937) complained that "a pronunciation so totally unjustified by the spelling seems to me unfortunate." Gilmartin (1936) and *Webster 2* (1934) had already countenanced it, however, and they were soon followed by Kenyon and Knott (1949), who put bruh-ZEER first, and the influential *American College* (1952), which sanctioned only bruh-ZEER. By the 1970s the Frenchified pronunciation had disappeared from the dictionaries, and today even the grave accent (*brassière*) is rare. See **lingerie**.

Brobdingnagian BRAHB-ding-**NAG**-ee-<u>in</u>.

Be sure to pronounce the second syllable like the word *ding*. It is often mispronounced like *dig*, probably because the word is prone to the misspelling *Brobdignagian*. Also, the first syllable, *Brob-*, rhymes with *blob* and *sob*, not with *robe*.

Brobdingnagian (did you hear a *ding?*) refers to the gigantic inhabitants

---

* *logogogue* (LAHG-uh-gahg, like *log agog*), a language dictator, pontificator on words.

of the imaginary land of Brobdingnag (BRAHB-ding-nag) in Swift's *Gulliver's Travels,* or to anyone or anything like them. It should be capitalized.

Brontë (sisters Charlotte, Emily, and Anne) BRAHN-tee (rhymes with *Monty*).

This surname is commonly mispronounced BRAHN-tay (-tay rhyming with *day*), and sometimes (*mon dieu!*) brahn-TAY.

"The name is not French," explains Ralph H. Emerson (1996), an authority on the pronunciation of literary names, in his article on that subject for *English Language Notes* (December 1996).

> Far from indicating foreignness, the dots on the *e* are simply a quaint device for showing that the letter is to be said in a separate syllable, much as in *reëlect* and *coöperate.* (Serving in this capacity, the dots are called a dieresis rather than an umlaut.) They alert the reader that *Brontë* ends in *tea* instead of being plain *Bront* — a mispronunciation one might be tempted into if the *e* were unadorned, for most extra *e*'s at the ends of English names are mere silent decorations which can be safely ignored, as in *Browne, Wilde, Crabbe, Trollope,* and many others. . . .

BRAHN-tee, Emerson adds in a note to me, "is furthermore the pronunciation still used in Haworth, Yorkshire, where the family lived."

brooch BROHCH.

Brooch and *broach* are, historically, the same word. Over time these spellings came to designate separate words, with *brooch* denoting an ornamental clasp and *broach* meaning to introduce a subject, bring something up. Both words are properly pronounced with a long *o* (as in *broke*).

The long *o* pronunciation for *brooch,* notes Vizetelly (1929), was first recorded in William Perry's dictionary of 1775; the spelling pronunciation BROOCH (rhyming with *smooch*) is just as old, dating back to Thomas Sheridan (1780) and John Walker (1791). Although it enjoyed currency through the mid–20th century — when Holt (1937) predicted, "Eventually, the approved rhyme for *brooch* will be *hootch,*" and Clement Wood, in his *Rhyming Dictionary* (1936), did indeed rhyme *brooch* with *hooch, mooch,* and *pooch* — and although dictionaries today still list BROOCH as an alternative, it has steadily fallen out of use and favor. *WNW Guide* (1984) calls it less common, and modern authorities — including Lass & Lass (1976), the *NBC Handbook* (1984), Barnhart (1988), and Jones (1991) — prefer BROHCH.

brothel BRAHTH-ul (*o* as in *hot, th* as in *thin*).

Of the four variants for this word — the others being BRAWTH-ul (like *broth* + *el*), which is often listed, and BRAHTH-ul (*th* as in *then*) and BRAWTH-ul, which are now rarely listed — the one recommended above is by far most often preferred or given first by authorities past and present.

Broun (Heywood) BROON (rhymes with *moon*).

bruit BROOT (like *brute*). Don't say BROO-it.

Buckingham (palace and duke) BUHK-ing-<u>um</u>.

There is no *ham* in *Buckingham*.

Buenos Aires BWAY-nohs EYE-rays (like *I race*).

The anglicized pronunciation BWAY-nuhs AIR-eez is undoubtedly more common, but I recommend the one above, along with Greet (1948), as both easy to pronounce and more faithful to the Spanish (which is BWE-naws EYE-res, with a rolled *r*). Opdycke (1939) says, "*bway' nos* riming with *say gross*, and *eye' race* riming with *my face*, are insisted upon by those who are meticulous in regard to native pronunciation of place names."

buffet (sideboard or self-service meal) buh-FAY, buu-FAY, or boo-FAY.

According to Burchfield (1996), the British pronunciation is BUHF-it (rhymes with *rough it*) for the sideboard and BUU-fay or BUHF-ay for the self-service meal.

In American speech, the *u* in *buffet* may have the sound of the *u* in *but*, or *oo* in *book*, or *oo* in *boot*. Regardless of which sound you prefer for the *u* (and many educated speakers will vary from one to another, which is no crime), the accent should be on the second syllable. *Random House II* (1987) notes that first-syllable stress is common when the word is used as an adjective, as in *buffet dinner*, *buffet service*, and *buffet car*. This distinction, which is relatively recent, seems a natural and inoffensive extension of the process of shifting stress (e.g., *the* un*known man* and *a man un-known to us*). For the noun, however, second-syllable stress is the norm and first-syllable stress should be resisted. See **address** for more on shifting stress.

bulimia byoo-LIM-ee-uh; **bulimic** byoo-LIM-ik.

The variants byoo-LEE-mee-uh, boo-LEE-mee-uh, and buh-LEE-mee-uh — and, for the adjective, byoo-LEE-mik, boo-LEE-mik, and buh-LEE-mik — are recent and regrettably common mispronunciations. There is no *lee* in *bulimia* and *bulimic*. The second, stressed syllable should properly sound like *limb*.

OED 2 (1989) traces the history of the noun *bulimia*, which means literally "ox hunger" — the earlier term in medicine was *bulimy* (BYOO-li-mee) — all the way back to 1398, but the word remained obscure to most until the late 1970s, when the medical condition known as *bulimia nervosa*, colloquially called the "binge-purge syndrome," burst upon the mass cultural scene and was subsequently shoved down our collective throats. Until then the only recognized pronunciation of *bulimia* was byoo-LIM-ee-uh. Once the word leapt from the medical manuals into the vernacular, however, there was widespread confusion over its pronunciation, and in response *Random House II* (1987) dutifully recorded the following variants: byoo-LEE-mee-uh, boo-LIM-ee-uh, boo-LEE-mee-uh, buh-LIM-ee-uh, and buh-LEE-mee-uh. (The last is now undoubtedly, and unfortunately, the most common).

The imbroglio (im-BROHL-yoh, a confused or embarrasing state of affairs) over *bulimia* and *bulimic* proves yet again that human stupidity is rampant at *all* levels of speech, from the most ignorant, beastly mispronouncer to the most erudite, self-important egghead. What is wrong with everybody, anyway? Is the word really so hard to pronounce properly? Why didn't the newscasters and TV "Movie of the Week" directors take five seconds to check the *NBC Handbook* (1984), which gives byoo-LIM-ee-uh? In the rush to be trendy, didn't anyone bother to look it up?

I try to be fair-minded, so I'll accept boo- instead of byoo- for the first syllable (there's an obsolescent alternative spelling *boulimia* that would require boo-); if you push me I'll even grant you buh-. But LEE-mee-uh instead of LIM-mee-uh for the rest is outrageous. It's like saying LEE-muh-rik for *limerick* or uh-LEE-muh-nayt for *eliminate*. There's got to be a LEE-mit to this sort of thing.

It may be a bit disconcerting at first to be the only one in the neighborhood who says byoo-LIM-ee-uh, but I guarantee you'll get used to it. You will also be *right*. And if some wiseacre tries to call you on it, show him this entry and direct him to *Webster 3* (1961), which gives only byoo-LIM-ee-uh, and *American Heritage 3* (1992) and *RHWC* (1997), which list it first.

buoy BOO-ee (recommended) or BOY. British, BOY.
Both BOO-ee and BOY are acceptable. American authorities formerly preferred BOY, but BOO-ee is now more frequently heard in the U.S. at all levels of speech. (For the compound word *life buoy*, however, BOY is the more usual pronunciation, no doubt due in part to the extensive advertising for the soap called "Lifeboy.")

BOY remains afloat for the verb (to *buoy* up), but BOO-ee is winning the regatta for the noun: *NBC Handbook* (1984) and *WNW Guide* (1984) prefer BOO-ee, and three of the four major current American dictionaries list it first. (A third variant, BWOY, which Opdycke declared obsolescent in 1939, no longer appears in current sources.) Conversely, for *buoyant* and *buoyancy* the pronunciations BOY-int and BOY-in-see now prevail over BOO-yint and BOO-yin-see, which, though still listed in good standing, are beginning to sound weatherbeaten and are therefore not recommended.

bursar BUR-sur (rhymes with *cursor*), not BUR-sahr.
"Americans, even in their traditional haste," writes Holt (1937), explaining his predilection for BUR-sahr, "find time to pay a certain amount of respect to that last syllable — a tendency which should not be discouraged."

I disagree. To my ear, BUR-sahr (-sahr rhyming with *car*) is an overpronunciation, a phonetic peccadillo of pompous proportions that somehow has crept into various current dictionaries. English has a pile of disyllabic nouns that end in *-ar* and have their accent on the first syllable, and in nearly every one the final *-ar* is pronounced -ur. We don't say -ahr (like *are*) for the second, unstressed syllable in *sugar, burglar, liar, altar, polar, lunar, hangar, cougar, molar, velar, pedlar, pillar, friar, cellar, stellar, collar,* and *dollar.* To do so would be mighty peculi-*ahr*, wouldn't it?

The only common exceptions to this ingrained convention are *jaguar, feldspar, lodestar* (which, as a compound of *star*, doesn't really count), *quasar* (an abbreviation of *quasi-stellar*), and the acronyms *radar*, which stands for "radio detecting and ranging," and *sonar*, which stands for "sound navigation and ranging." Longer words ending in *-ar* follow this custom as well, including *regular, popular, similar, circular, vinegar, jocular, molecular, particular, triangular, spectacular, vehicular, vernacular, lumbar* (traditionally like *lumber* but now often LUHM-bahr), and *scimitar*, which is properly SIM-i-tur — the only recognized pronunciation from Walker (1791) to *Webster 3* (1961) — but which is now sometimes overpronounced SIM-i-tahr. The small handful of exceptions (not counting foreign names like *Zanzibar* or trade names like *Mylar* and *Vivitar*) includes a few exotic loanwords — *caviar, avatar, jemadar* (an officer in the Indian army) — the mineral and color *cinnabar*, and *registrar*, which is pronounced **REJ**-i-STRAHR probably because of the unusual presence of two *r* sounds in the final syllable and to distinguish the word from *register.*

Holt, by the way, has no allies in his defense of BUR-sahr. BUR-sur is the preference of Phyfe (1926), Vizetelly (1929), Opdycke (1939), Kenyon & Knott (1949), Lass & Lass (1976), the *NBC Handbook* (1984), and *WNW Guide* (1984), and it is the only pronunciation given in the *Century* (1914), *Webster 2* (1934), *American College* (1952), *OED 2* (1989), and *RHWC* (1997).

business BIZ-nis.
  M-W 10 (1993) recognizes the variant BID-nis, labeling it Southern. Other current sources do not countenance this pronunciation, and most careful speakers in other parts of the U.S. consider it substandard (i.e., beastly).
Butte (Montana) BYOOT (like *beaut-* in *beautiful*).
Byzantine BIZ-in-teen (most common) or bi-ZAN-tin (my preference).
  Current dictionaries sanction other variants, most often BIZ-in-tyn, which *OED 2* (1989) lists second after bi-ZAN-tyn, the dominant pronunciation in Great Britain, according to Burchfield (1996) and Jones (1991). Evidence indicates that BIZ-in-teen now prevails in America, so go with it if you like safety in numbers. I'm sticking with bi-ZAN-tin, the preference of the *Century* (1914), *Webster 2* (1934), and other older American authorities. Though it's a bit musty now, all four major current American dictionaries still list it in good standing. Moreover, it retains the accent of the place it refers to, *Byzantium*, which in American speech is traditionally pronounced bi-ZAN-shee-um, with the *ti* like *sh*. (The British prefer bi-ZAN-tee-um.) See **consortium.**

C

cache KASH (like *cash*).

cachet ka-SHAY (like *cash hay* said quickly).

cacophony kuh-KAHF-uh-nee.

Stress the second syllable, -*coph*-, which should rhyme with -*soph*- in *philosophical*.

NPR reporter Brooke Gladstone (as heard on *All Things Considered*, November 20, 1997) mispronounces this word kuh-KAF-uh-nee, as if it were spelled *cacaphony*, and unfortunately she has much company among educated speakers. There is no *calf* in *cacophony*. Note that the word begins with the combining form *caco*-, bad. Also, don't say kuh-KAWF-uh-nee; for neither is there a *cough* in *cacophony*. At all costs avoid **KAK**-uh-FOH-nee (rhymes with *back a pony*), which is half-literate and beastly. *American Heritage 3* (1992), *RHWC* (1997), and *WNW 3* (1997) sanction only one pronunciation: kuh-KAHF-uh-nee.

cadre KAD-ree (recommended); now usually KAH-dray. British, KAH-dur or KAH-druh.

The word comes through French and the Italian *quadro*, frame, from the Latin *quadrum*, a square. *OED 2* (1989) cites examples of its use in print dating from 1830.

In the first half of the century dictionaries gave the pronunciation KAH-dur, after the French, or sometimes KAD-ur. Then they began recording another pronunciation, KAD-ree, common among the military. *Webster 3* (1961) gave precedence to KAD-ree, and since then most authori-

---

a = at / a̱ = final / ah = spa / ahr = car / air = fair / ay = hay / aw = saw
ch = chip / e = let / e̱ = item / ee = see / eer = deer / i = sit / i̱ = April
ng = sing / o̱ = carrot / oh = go / oo = soon / or = for / oor = poor
ow = cow / oy = toy / sh = she / th = thin / t̲h̲ = this / u̱ = focus / uh = up
ur = turn / uu = pull, took / y, eye = by, I / zh = measure / (see full key, p. xiv)

ties have continued to prefer it; however, another variant, KAH-dray, which has also been recorded since the 1960s, has overtaken KAD-ree and is now the dominant American pronunciation.

To my ear, KAH-dray sounds affected. It is what I call a de-anglicized pronunciation, an attempt to return to what speakers imagine is the original, or foreign, pronunciation of the word. In this case, KAH-dray makes the word sound as if it came from Italian or Spanish rather than French. If a word has already been fully anglicized, there is little purpose in returning halfway; invariably, this sort of half-baked etymological regression winds up creating some peculiar phonetic hybrid. To say, as the British do, KAH-dur, which is closest to the French (and about as close to the French as the Brits like to get), strikes me as more sensible than saying KAH-dray, which is neither French nor English. To say KAD-ree may not sound pretty, but it is definitely English.

KAD-ree is preferred by Lass & Lass (1976), the *NBC Handbook* (1984), and *WNW Guide* (1984), and it is the first pronunciation listed in *American Heritage 3* (1992), *WNW 3* (1997), and *RHWC* (1997). See **forte**.

caduceus kuh-D(Y)OO-see-<u>us</u>.

The *caduceus* is that "snakie wand," as Edmund Spenser put it, that serves as the emblem of the medical profession and the insignia of the U.S. Army Medical Corps: a rod or staff entwined by two snakes, with a pair of spread wings at the top.

caisson KAY-sahn (like *case on*) or KAYS'n (rhymes with *Jason*).

calliope kuh-LY-uh-pee.

In San Diego there's a Greek restaurant named *Calliope's* that its employees and patrons call KAL-ee-**OH**-payz, a lame affectation of the modern Greek pronunciation of *Calliope,* which is kahl-YOH-pee. Of course they may call the restaurant whatever they like, but in English the traditional and proper pronunciation of *calliope,* the whistling musical instrument, and *Calliope,* the Greek muse of eloquence and epic poetry, is kuh-LY-uh-pee, with the accent on the second syllable, like *Penelope.*

Current dictionaries note that the instrument is sometimes called a KAL-ee-ohp (rhymes with *galley rope*), and *American Heritage 3* (1992) sanctions this as an alternative pronunciation without comment. My evidence shows that although KAL-ee-ohp dates back at least a hundred years it was ignored by older dictionaries and unanimously disliked by orthoepists. Ayres (1894) calls it "unauthorized," Phyfe (1926) proscribes it, Opdycke (1939) calls it incorrect, and Vizetelly (1933), Kenyon & Knott (1949), Lass & Lass (1976), the *NBC Handbook* (1984), and Jones (1991) all prefer second-syllable stress.

calm KAHM. The *l* is properly silent. Do not say KAHLM or KAWLM.

In general American speech, *calm* rhymes with *bomb*. Among many New

England speakers who use what is sometimes called the intermediate *a* (a sound between the broad *a* of *father* and the short *a* of *hat*), *calm* rhymes with *clam*.

M-W 10 (1993) recognizes the variants with *l* audible, but *RHWC* (1997) labels KAHLM a spelling pronunciation — a pronunciation based on how a word is spelled, which differs from the traditional, established pronunciation. KAHM, with silent *l*, is the only pronunciation in *American Heritage 3* (1992) and *WNW 3* (1997). See **almond**.

candida KAN-di̱-duh. Stress the first syllable.

Candida albicans is pronounced KAN-di̱-duh AL-bi̱-kanz.

candidate KAN-di̱-dayt, not KAN-di̱-dit.

"Do not omit the first *d*," cautions Shaw (1972). Pronouncing this word like *can a date* or *can a dit* is beastly. See **delegate**.

cantaloupe KAN-tuh-lohp (like *can't elope* said quickly).

This has been the dominant American pronunciation since *Webster 2* (1934). The British prefer KAN-tuh-loop and often spell it without the final *e*.

capricious kuh-PRISH-u̱s, not, as is commonly heard, kuh-PREE-shu̱s.

The second syllable should rhyme with *wish*, not *we*.

No one, as far as I know, gives the sound of long *e* (ee) to the *i* in the second, accented syllable in *delicious, suspicious, judicious, avaricious, officious,* and *malicious.* Why, then, do so many speakers today say kuh-PREE-shu̱s instead of kuh-PRISH-u̱s? The answer most likely is that kuh-PREE-shu̱s, which was first recognized by dictionaries in the 1960s, is a spelling pronunciation based on the corresponding noun *caprice* (kuh-PREES). The traditional pronunciation, kuh-PRISH-u̱s, is listed first in all four major current American dictionaries, it is the only pronunciation sanctioned by *OED 2* (1989), and it is the preference of Lass & Lass (1976), *WNW Guide* (1984), the *NBC Handbook* (1984), and *Everyday Reader's* (1985). See **prestigious**.

caramel Traditionally, KAR-uh-mu̱l or KAR-uh-mel. Now also KAHR-mu̱l.

"*Caramel* has a second syllable that careful speakers pronounce, however lightly," says Shaw (1976). For the final syllable, past and present authorities are about evenly divided between -mu̱l (which sounds like -*mel* in *camel*) and -mel (as in *smell*); both the lexicographic evidence and the evidence of my ears indicate the former is now more common.

In the 1940s and 1950s dictionaries began listing the two-syllable variant KAHR-mu̱l but seemed insecure about its standing. Kenyon & Knott (1949) add the vague comment, "In many places [KAHR-mu̱l] is often heard." *American College* (1952) says, "Midwest often KAHR-mu̱l." *Webster 3* (1961) labeled it unacceptable to many. Since then, however, KAHR-mu̱l has risen from the gutter of descriptive lexicography into widespread acceptance, a sweet-toothed success story in which the influence of TV's candy bar commercials cannot be overlooked. Today all four major current American dictionaries recognize KAHR-m<u>u</u>l, and two of them list it first.

Caribbean KAR-<u>i</u>-**BEE**-<u>i</u>n (preferred and recommended).

Although kuh-RIB-ee-<u>i</u>n, with second-syllable stress, has been listed as an alternative pronunciation since *Webster 2* (1934), most authorities of the last century — from Ayres (1894) and Phyfe (1926) to the *NBC Handbook* (1984) and Morris & Morris (1985) — prefer the accent on the third syllable, KAR-<u>i</u>-**BEE**-<u>i</u>n, and the evidence of my ears tells me this is still the prevailing pronunciation in the U.S. today, at least among the non–jet set. John R. Rickford, a professor of linguistics at Stanford and a native of Guyana, also prefers KAR-<u>i</u>-**BEE**-<u>i</u>n and tells me it is probably the dominant pronunciation in the Caribbean itself. Burchfield (1996) notes that "in Britain the standard pronunciation has the main stress on the third syllable."

Third-syllable stress is also the preference of W. Cabell Greet, a professor of English at Columbia who for many years was a speech consultant to CBS. In his geographical pronunciation guide *World Words* (1948), Greet writes that "the pronunciation [kuh-RIB-ee-<u>i</u>n] is a variation mysterious in origin. It has a 'British' quality to American ears, and to the British it sounds like an American invention." He then quotes these intriguing comments from an article in *American Speech* (vol. 17, p. 284) by the phonetician John S. Kenyon (of Kenyon & Knott):

> A competent phonetically trained observer in the Caribbean region tells me that repeated inquiries elicit the information that Caribbe'an is almost universally recognized as the old established pronunciation but that many informants "have recently heard Carib'bean and supposed it must be right." I find no evidence that the neophony issues from England but some evidence that it may have spread from New York City.

The moral of the story? When in doubt, blame it on those snooty New Yorkers. The fact is, despite more than sixty years of use in educated speech, kuh-RIB-ee-<u>i</u>n, wherever it came from, still retains a mysterious aroma of oily pseudosophistication. By contrast, KAR-<u>i</u>-**BEE**-<u>i</u>n exudes nothing more than the pleasantly musty odor of tradition and unimpeachable authority.

Carnegie (Andrew) kahr-NEG-ee, not KAHR-nuh-gee.

No pronunciation maven with a reputation to lose sanctions first-syllable stress in this name — and why would anyone when, as Phyfe (1926) notes, the man himself informs us, "The accent is on the second syllable."

Webster 2 (1934) says, "The pronunciation with ā [kahr-NAY-gee] was that of Mr. Carnegie himself, but as the Scotch ā is 'stopped,' that is, pronounced with no terminal glide, it sounds like ĕ [kahr-NEG-ee] to many."

For the famous concert hall in New York City, general practice has followed local custom in placing the accent on the first syllable, although some speakers (even in New York) still stress the second. For the renowned friend maker and people influencer Dale Carnegie, first-syllable stress is most commonly heard. See **bolivar.**

caryatid KAR-ee-**AT**-id (KAR-ee like *carry,* -**AT**-id rhyming with *batted*).

In architecture, a *caryatid* is a female figure, dressed in long robes, serving as a supporting column.

KAR-ee-**AT**-id was the only recognized pronunciation until 1961, when *Webster 3* (1961) listed the variants KAR-ee-uh-tid and kuh-RY-uh-tid. Don't be misled by this apparent approbation. KAR-ee-**AT**-id is still the established and proper pronunciation; it is preferred by Lass & Lass (1976), the *NBC Handbook* (1984), *WNW Guide* (1984), and *Everyday Reader's* (1985), and it is the only one countenanced by *OED 2* (1989) and *American Heritage 3* (1992).

catarrh kuh-TAHR (rhymes with *guitar*).

The adjective *catarrhal* is pronounced kuh-TAHR-u̱l.

Cather (Willa) KA̱TH-ur (rhymes with *gather*).

In *Klee as in Clay* (1986), Wilfred J. McConkey gives KAWTH-ur, which is wrong. Ralph H. Emerson (1996), a more scholarly and reliable authority on literary names, says *Cather* "rhymes with *gather;* it is not said as in *Catherine.*" His opinion is corroborated by a number of my other sources, including *Webster 2* (1934), the *NBC Handbook* (1984), and *American Heritage 3* (1992).

catsup See **ketchup.**

caveat KAY-vee-at or KAV-ee-at.

Until the 1960s, dictionaries listed only one pronunciation for this word: KAY-vee-at (KAY- as in *cave,* -at like *at*).* *Webster 3* (1961) is the first of my sources to record an alternative: KAH-vee-aht. Later authorities sanctioned numerous other variants: KAV-ee-at, preferred by Lass & Lass (1976) and the *NBC Handbook* (1984); KAV-ee-aht, listed first in *M-W 10* (1993) and *RHWC* (1997) and preferred by Barnhart (1988); the pseudo-Latin KAH-vay-aht; as well as variations on these variants in which the *a* in the final syllable is a schwa (pronounced obscurely like the *a* in *ago* or *final*).

In this mad market of possibilities, I say *caveat emptor* (which I pronounce EMP-tor but some pronounce EMP-tur), let the buyer beware.

---

* I can find only one exception among my sources: Funk & Wagnalls *Standard* (1897) sanctions KAV-ee-a̱t as an alternative after KAY-vee-at.

The pronunciation with the best warranty is KAY-vee-at. Its satisfied customers go back at least two centuries to Walker (1791), and it is still the trusted choice of many today: *Everyday Reader's* (1985) and *OED 2* (1989) prefer it, and it is listed first in *American Heritage 3* (1992) and *WNW 3* (1997). Second place goes to KAV-ee-at, which Ayres (1894) and Phyfe (1926) proscribed but which has since gained widespread acceptance. According to Burchfield (1996), *caveat*, "which until the mid–20th century was regularly pronounced [KAY-vee-at], is now just as regularly pronounced with a short *a* in the first syllable."

cavil KAV'l (rhymes with *gravel*).

celebratory SEL-uh-bruh-tor-ee. Also, but now fading, suh-LEB-ruh-tor-ee.

Since this word entered the language in 1926 there have been two acceptable pronunciations in American speech — one with primary stress on the first syllable, the other with primary stress on the second — and educated usage has gradually settled on first-syllable stress as the preferred form.

Webster 2 (1934) sanctions only second-syllable stress, but *Webster 3* (1961) reverses that ruling and gives only SEL-uh-bruh-tor-ee. Likewise with *WNW 2* (1984), which prefers suh-LEB-ruh-tor-ee, and *WNW 3* (1988 & 1997), which prefers SEL-uh-bruh-tor-ee. *Random House II* (1987) lists both, with SEL-uh-bruh-tor-ee first, but its most recent abridgment, *RHWC* (1997), countenances only first-syllable stress. *American Heritage 3* (1992) also lists both, with SEL-uh-bruh-tor-ee first, but *M-W 9* (1985) and *10* (1993) do not recognize suh-LEB-ruh-tor-ee.

The variants SEL-uh-bray-tur-ee and sel-uh-BRAY-tur-ee are British and — notwithstanding *M-W 10*'s curious inclusion of the latter as an unlabeled alternative — would sound peculiar or stilted coming from an American speaker.

cellulite SEL-yuh-lyt (like *sell ya light*), not SEL-yuh-leet.

Since it made its rapid entrance into English from French in the late 1960s, *cellulite* has had two competing pronunciations. Some speakers say SEL-yuh-leet (-leet rhyming with *meat*), after the French pronunciation of the suffix *-ite*, but most use the anglicized pronunciation SEL-yuh-lyt (-lyt like *light*). Should we retain the French flavor or follow the anglicizing majority? Is one way more "authentic" than the other?

Cellulite was anglicized almost immediately upon its adoption into English. This happened for three reasons: terminal *-ite* is pronounced with a long *i* (as in *bite*) in dozens of English words (e.g., *impolite, satellite, appetite, dynamite, parasite, underwrite, reunite, sulfite, Brooklynite*); in the related word *cellulitis*, the suffix *-itis* has a long *i*; and *cellulite* became a trendy word.

Analogy with related English words exerts a strong pull toward anglicization, but perhaps the most significant influence is how often the word occurs in print, on the airwaves, and in everyday conversation. When a word makes a mad dash from another language into our mass-cultural vocabulary, when it is cut from the wilderness of words and run through the English-language lumber mill, it is inevitable that it will emerge with an English sound, and often an English look.

That is why the anglicized form, SEL-yuh-lyt, is more "authentic" than SEL-yuh-leet, which has no aural sibling in English (unless you want to stretch it and count *elite*, the only common English word, also from French, in which *-ite* is pronounced -eet). From the outset most educated speakers anglicized *-lite* to -lyt, and dictionaries have recorded their preference. SEL-yuh-lyt is the first pronunciation listed in *The Second Barnhart Dictionary of New English* (1980), the earliest source in which I found the word, as well as in *OED 2* (1989), *M-W 10* (1993), *WNW 3* (1997), and *RHWC* (1997). It is the only pronunciation sanctioned by *American Heritage 3* (1992).

Celtic SEL-tik.

My way of dealing with the words *Celtic* and *Keltic* is to pronounce the former SEL-tik and the latter KEL-tik — and, since the latter spelling is on the wane, I almost never have to say KEL-tik and I can promote my preference, SEL-tik. Sound simple enough to you? Not so fast, Mr. Pronunciation Man.

For *Celtic*, the *NBC Handbook* (1984) prefers KEL-tik and three of the four major current American dictionaries list this pronunciation first; only *WNW 3* (1997) puts SEL-tik first. That strikes me as odd — first, because these sources give *Celtic* as the preferred spelling, and second, because the *s* for *C* and *k* for *K* division has been established for a long time and makes perfect sense to the eye and ear. Besides, have you ever heard anyone call the Boston basketball team the KEL-tiks? They're the SEL-tiks. Are they now going to be the only exception?

Let's take a brief look at the *Celtic/Keltic* situation diachronically (across time). Worcester (1860) gives SEL-tik for *Celtic*, noting that this is also the marking of the English lexicographers John Craig (1849) and Benjamin Humphrey Smart (1836), as well as the American lexicographer Noah Webster (1828). Funk & Wagnalls *Standard* (1897), the *Century* (1914), Phyfe (1926), Vizetelly (1929), *Webster 2* (1934), Kenyon & Knott (1949), and *American College* (1952) all mark *Celtic* SEL-tik and *Keltic* KEL-tik, with *Webster 2* and *American College* noting that KEL-tik for *Celtic* is especially British.

Opdycke (1939) agrees: "*Celtic* may also be spelt *Keltic*, and the two forms are accordingly pronounced — *sell'tik* and *kell'tik*. . . . In England the *k* spelling and pronunciation of these words is preferred, in the United States the *c* spelling and pronunciation."

Contemporaneous British sources, however, differ with that assessment.

[64]

OED 1 (1928) sanctions only SELT for *Celt* and SEL-tik for *Celtic,* and in *Modern English Usage* (1926) H. W. Fowler writes, "The spelling *C-,* & the pronunciation s-, are the established ones, & no useful purpose seems to be served by the substitution of k-." But that was then and this is now: *c-* is out and *k-* is in. *OED 2* (1989) recognizes the *k-* pronunciation, listing it after the *s-,* and Burchfield (1996), my most current commentator on British ways, declares the *K-* spelling dead and says "except for the football club *Celtic* (in Glasgow), which is pronounced [SEL-tik], both *Celt* and *Celtic* are pronounced with initial /k/ in standard English." So the Brits have embraced the illogical KEL-tik for *Celtic* after all, but must we Americans sell out to KEL-tik too?

Hard-line *k*-sayers on either side of the Atlantic who believe their pronunciation is authentically *Celtic* or *Keltic* should know that the *k*-pronunciation and spelling are not derived from the Indo-European sub-family of languages of that name. *Celt* and *Celtic* go back through the French *Celte* and *Celtique,* where they apparently got their *s-* sound, to the Latin *Celta* (for *Celt*) and *Celticus* (for *Celtic*), in which the *c* was pronounced like *k,* and the Greek *Keltoi,* the Gauls. Thus, those who insist on the *k-* sound are perpetuating a pedanticism by following Latin and Greek rather than modern English.

I know some speakers will be annoyed with me for trying to kill their KELT, so just to show there are no hard feelings, here's a compromise: try going to a Boston Celtics game and yelling, "Go, KEL-tiks!" If you get out of there without being slam-dunked, you can say it however you want.

centenary SEN-ti-NER-ee (recommended). Now often sen-TEN-ur-ee. *Centennial* always has its accent on the *ten,* but what about *centenary?*

Traditionally, in American speech, the stress has been on the first syllable, although stress on the second has been heard since the early 20th century and has been approved since *Webster 2* (1934) sanctioned it as an alternative. Phyfe (1926), Vizetelly (1929), and Opdycke (1939), however, all prefer the accent on *cent-,* and Holt (1937) argues vehemently for it:

> While Webster [2] has decided that we may now accent the *ten* if we want to, there is such a good reason for distinguishing between this word and *centennial* in accentuation — namely, the double *n* — that I favor accenting the *cent.* If the two are to be pronounced so nearly alike, one or the other will die, and writers who would avoid repetitions will have one more headache-producer.

Holt's dire prediction has not come true probably because, as Burchfield (1996) indicates, *centenary* has become "the more usual term in Britain," while elsewhere *centennial* prevails. In British English, the preferred pronunciation places the accent on the second syllable, which sounds like *tea.* This may have influenced the spread of second-syllable stress in American speech. Modern American authorities who prefer stress on *cent-* include Lass & Lass (1976), the *NBC Handbook* (1984), and *Everyday Reader's* (1985).

centimeter SEN-ti-MEE-tur.

Some speakers insist on pronouncing this word **SAHN**-ti-MEE-tur, with the first syllable rhyming with *don*. This eccentric French-English hybrid is based on the French pronunciation of *centimetre,* the source of the word; it appears as an alternative in *Webster 2* (1934), *Webster 3* (1961), *M-W 9* (1985) and *10* (1993), and *WNW 3* (1997).

The problem is that *centimeter* — along with *centigrade, centigram,* and *centiliter* — entered English way back in 1801 and has been fully anglicized for over a hundred years. Today, unless you're French, or lamely attempting to speak French, there's no excuse for affecting a French pronunciation of these established English words. The weight of authority overwhelmingly favors **SEN**-ti-MEE-tur: Phyfe (1926), Vizetelly (1929), Opdycke (1939), Kenyon & Knott (1949), Lass & Lass (1976), the *NBC Handbook* (1984), *WNW Guide* (1984), *Everyday Reader's* (1985), and Jones (1991) prefer it, and it is the only pronunciation given in Funk & Wagnalls *Standard* (1897), the *Century* (1914), *Webster's Collegiate* (1917), *American College* (1952), the *Winston Dictionary* (1951), *American Heritage 3* (1992), and *RHWC* (1997).

cerebral SER-uh-brul. Now very often suh-REE-brul.

Avoid SEER-uh-brul and SEER-brul, which are beastly.

The traditional pronunciation, SER-uh-brul, places the stress on the first syllable. This is the only pronunciation countenanced by Funk & Wagnalls *Standard* (1897), the *Century* (1914), *Webster 2* (1934), and *OED 2* (1989), and it is the preference of Kenyon & Knott (1949), Lass & Lass (1976), and the *NBC Handbook* (1984). The variant suh-REE-bral, with second-syllable stress, has been around for over seventy-five years. Phyfe (1926) and Opdycke (1939) frowned upon it, and dictionaries did not recognize it until the late 1940s. *American College* (1952) is the first of my sources to record it. In 1961 *Webster 3* listed it first, and since then it has gained greatly in popularity. Today all four major current American dictionaries sanction it, and Morris & Morris (1985) claim it is "rather more commonly heard." Though the weight of authority still favors SER-uh-brul, which I recommend, at this point one cannot legitimately find fault with those who prefer suh-REE-brul.

cervical (American) SUR-vi-kuul; (chiefly British and Canadian) sur-VY-kuul.

Any American speaker who stresses the second syllable in *cervical* is putting on the dog.

The *Oxford Guide* (1983), a British source, says "stress either on 1st syllable (with last two syllables as in *vertical*) or on 2nd (rhyming with *cycle*); both pronunciations have been common for at least a century and a half (Amer. only the first pronunciation)." Although Jones (1991), another British source, prefers second-syllable stress, Burchfield (1996), my most recent British source, notes that the emergence of the word from the laboratory, "where it was normally pronounced with the main stress on the second syllable," into widespread use has caused a general shift in pronunciation. "A counting of heads," he says, "would probably show that the dominant pronunciation now is [SUR-vi-kuul]."

chaise longue shayz-LAWNG.

Chaise longue comes directly from French and means literally "long chair." Note that the *ch* in *chaise* is pronounced like *sh* in *shade,* and the word rhymes with *raise.* Do not say, as many do incorrectly, CHAYS (like *chase*), or sometimes SHAYS.

What about the pronunciation shayz-LOWNJ (or chays-LOWNJ) and the spelling *chaise lounge?* Is *lounge* incorrect? The short answer is no, it's just more plebeian,* but let us inquire a bit further into the matter.

"One of the most remarkable misunderstandings in the history of languages," writes Charles Allen Lloyd rather hyperbolically in *We Who Speak English, and Our Ignorance of Our Mother Tongue* (1938), "is concerned with the name of the article of furniture known as a 'chaise longue.'

> Please note the spelling of the last word. It is not l-o-u-n-g-e, but l-o-n-g-u-e, being the French word for "long" in its feminine form. . . . The spelling of the word "lounge" is so near to that of this French word "longue," that probably the majority of people — and of furniture dealers — confuse the two and call it a "chaise lounge," the confusion being aided by the fact, of course, that the chaise longue is intended for lounging.

In American English today, says Burchfield (1996), "the word sometimes turns up, esp. in trade advertisements, as *chaise lounge.*" I can attest that it turns up in numerous other places too — for example, I found it in *The 27-Ingredient Chili Con Carne Murders* by Nancy Pickard. In *Comfortable Words* (1959), Bergen Evans asks,

> Shouldn't it be *chaise longue,* the French for "elongated chair"? Not if the American people decide they prefer a "corrupt" English word to a correct French word. And a glance at the furniture ads in any newspaper ought to convince the most obdurate that the people have so decided. The dictionaries haven't recorded the change yet, but they will. . . .

Actually, at the time Evans made that prediction, one old dictionary had in fact recorded *chaise lounge* and a new one was about to. *OED 2* (1989),

---

* *plebeian* (pli-BEE-in), of the common folk; also, coarse or unrefined [from Latin *plebs,* the common people].

which does not recognize the *lounge* variant, notes that in the Scottish lexicographer John Ogilvie's *Imperial Dictionary* (either the 1850 edition or the 1882 revision, it does not say) it is "called *chaise-lounge*." The variant next appeared in *Webster 3* (1961), and since then most American authorities have listed it as standard. Many educated Americans, however, still find the *lounge* variant objectionable: Morris & Morris (1985) report that 91 percent of their usage panel would not use it in writing and 88 percent would avoid it in speech.

If you consult a current dictionary you will see that the corrupted form, *chaise lounge,* has evolved from the original form, *chaise longue,* by what lexicographers call "folk etymology," a term that *American Heritage 3* (1992) — which, by the way, sanctions only *chaise longue* — defines as "a change in the form of a word or phrase resulting from a mistaken assumption about its composition or meaning, as in *shamefaced* for earlier *shamfast,* 'bound by shame,' or *cutlet* from French *côtelette,* 'little rib.'"

So if some say it's now okay to spell it *chaise lounge,* at least in furniture ads and mystery novels, what about the pronunciation? Aha, now there's the rub — or the flub, as the *chaise* may be. Current authorities agree that when it is spelled *chaise longue* you must always say shayz-LAWNG; when it is spelled *chaise lounge* you may say -LOWNJ but you should still say shayz- for *chaise.* The way I see it, you might as well spell it *chaise longue,* pronounce it shayz-LAWNG, and relax. (For more on how pronunciation influences spelling, see **minuscule**.)

chamois SHAM-ee.

Unless you are referring to the goat antelope *Rupicapra rupicapra,* any pronunciation other than SHAM-ee is beastly.

chamomile KAM-uh-myl.

Properly, there is no *meal* in *chamomile,* which may also be spelled *camomile.* Make it a *mile.* Although the *NBC Handbook* (1984) prefers KAM-uh-meel, this alternative did not appear in a dictionary until *Webster 3* (1961), which labeled it "appreciably less frequent." Other current authorities favor the traditional *mile* pronunciation, which all four major current American dictionaries list first.

chary CHAIR-ee (rhymes with *scary* and *wary*).

chassis CHAS-ee or SHAS-ee.

CHAS-ee, listed first by three of the four major current American dictionaries, is probably now the dominant pronunciation in the U.S. Only one current source, *M-W 10* (1993), recognizes the variant CHAS-is, labeling it "appreciably less frequent."

chastise chas-TYZ (recommended) or CHAS-tyz.

Chastise, like *baptize* (which see), is traditionally stressed on the second syllable, but first-syllable stress is also standard. Although Shakespeare favored CHAS-tyz (but switched to chas-TYZ when it suited him), since Samuel Johnson's landmark dictionary (1755) chas-TYZ has been preferred. In the mid–20th century, CHAS-tyz made a strong comeback and is now fully acceptable. Most current authorities, however, still favor chas-TYZ. See **chastisement**.

chastisement CHAS-tiz-ment (recommended) or chas-TYZ-ment.
Ayres (1894), Phyfe (1926), Gilmartin (1936), Holt (1937), and Opdycke (1939) all proscribe second-syllable stress in this word, and *Webster 2* (1934) ignores it; however, Vizetelly (1929), who sanctions chas-TYZ-ment as an alternative, notes that the dictionaries of Nathan Bailey (1732), Samuel Johnson (1755), and William Perry (1775) indicate chas-TYZ-ment, but that Thomas Sheridan (1780) and John Walker (1791) preferred CHAS-tiz-ment "and have been supported by all the other lexicographers." The revival of chas-TYZ-ment, which has been standard since Kenyon & Knott (1949) and *American College* (1952), is no doubt largely due to the dominance, in American speech, of third-syllable stress in *advertisement*. If one is to believe *Webster 3* (1961) and *M-W 8* (1975) through *10* (1993), which label CHAS-tiz-ment "appreciably less common," the traditional pronunciation may be on its way out. If so, then I, for one, will at least do it the courtesy of escorting it to the door. See **chastise**.

chauvinism SHOH-vi-niz'm (SHOH- like *show*, rhyming with *slow*).
It is beastly to pronounce the first syllable SHAW- (rhymes with *jaw*), and even beastlier to pronounce it SHOW- (rhymes with *cow*).

Chavez (César) CHAH-vez (*ch* as in *chop*).
The *ch* in *Chavez* should sound like the *ch* in *chop*, not like *sh* in *shop*. Don't be misled if you happen to consult *American Heritage 3* (1992), which recognizes the variant SHAH-vez. There is no authority whatsoever for this beastly mispronunciation, or for the even beastlier shuh-VEZ. Pronounce *Chavez* as the *NBC Handbook* (1984) marks it: CHAH-vez. For the man's first name, you may say SAY-sahr, like the Spanish, or anglicize it to SEE-zur (as in Julius Caesar).

chemise shuh-MEEZ.
M-W 10 (1993) lists shuh-MEES as a less-frequent alternative; other current sources do not recognize it. It is best avoided.

chic SHEEK. Formerly also SHIK. Do not say CHIK.
This smart little word, which made its sophisticated way into English from French in the 1850s, was in times past often pronounced SHIK (rhyming with *stick*). Although disapproved of by Phyfe (1926), Vizetelly (1929), and Lloyd (1938), SHIK had some formidable authority behind it; Funk & Wagnalls *Standard* (1897) and *Webster 2* (1934) sanctioned it as an alternative, and the *Century* (1914) and *Webster's Collegiate* (1917) preferred it. Since the 1960s it has fallen steadily out of use, and today all four major

American dictionaries — *American Heritage 3* (1992), *M-W 10* (1993), *WNW 3* (1997), and *RHWC* (1997) — countenance only SHEEK (rhymes with *sleek*).

A word to the wise: *Random House II* (1987) cautions that "the spelling pronunciation (chik) is considered nonstandard except when used facetiously."

chicanery shi-KAY-nur-ee, not chi-KAY-nur-ee.

Older dictionaries do not recognize chi- for the first syllable, and the current ones that do list it as an alternative after shi-KAY-nur-ee, which is preferred by Lass & Lass (1976), the *Quintessential Dictionary* (1978), the *NBC Handbook* (1984), *WNW Guide* (1984), *Everyday Reader's* (1985), Barnhart (1988), *OED 2* (1989), and *WNW 3* (1997).

Chicano chi-KAH-noh.

This is the preference of the *NBC Handbook* (1984) and Burchfield (1996), and the only pronunciation in *WNW 3* (1997). Barnhart (1988) gives chee-KAH-noh, the Spanish pronunciation.

Despite their appearance as alternative pronunciations in three current American dictionaries, shi-KAH-noh and chi-KAN-oh (KAN like *can*) are flat-out wrong. *OED 2* (1989) also lists chi-KAY-noh and shi-KAY-noh, which are downright bizarre. There is no authority for any of these beastly variants. They got into the dictionary probably because a few hapless Anglos, either unfamiliar or uncomfortable with this ethnic word, stumbled over it while a pronunciation editor was busy listening. In the case of shi-KAH-noh, among Americans the most common of the beastly variants, people somehow got the bright idea to Frenchify a word that comes from Spanish, conveniently forgetting that we don't say *nosho* for *nacho*, *shilly* for *chili*, *sheeno* for *chino*, or *shocolate* for *chocolate*. Properly, there is no *sh* in *Chicano*. And don't put a *can* (or worse, a *cane*) in there, either. The second syllable should sound like *con*. See **Chavez, Chilean**.

chiefs CHEEFS (rhymes with *briefs*). Do not say CHEEVZ (rhymes with *leaves*).

Thief becomes *thieves* and *leaf* becomes *leaves*, but *chief* does not become *chieves* or *cheaves*.

Chile See **Chilean**.

Chilean CHIL-ee-in (like *chilly in*, or rhymes with *Lillian*).

Do not say chi-LAY-in and do not pronounce the *Ch-* like *sh*. Of all my sources, *M-W 9* (1985) and *10* (1993) are the only ones that recognize the spurious, faddish, and beastly chi-LAY-in.

The panic in the news of March 1989 concerning a putatively poisonous pile of *Chilean* fruit rotting on American docks stirred up the usual accompanying epidemic of mispronunciation. Why is it that whenever something gets beaten to death in the media the language always takes a beating too? It would seem that we are guided by a foreign policy — and by "foreign" I mean *strange:* "If the word's in the news," we say, "then it's ours to abuse."

A fear of chi-LAY-in fruit is unfounded for the simple reason that there is no such thing as chi-LAY-in fruit, just as there is no such thing as a *nucular* weapon and no such thing as *pronounciation.* No matter how many times careless speakers utter these slovenly pronunciations, they do not become standard; like the nonword *irregardless,* popular among the half-educated, they remain illegitimate because most of us refuse to accept them while some of us (like me) denounce them vociferously. In the case of *Chilean* it is as plain as a rotten peach that speakers who stress the second syllable have no idea their pronunciation is beastly and no doubt think it's more "faithful" to the Spanish. (The Spanish adjective is *chileno;* there is no *chileano* en Español.) The simple, incontestable fact is that the only proper, acceptable pronunciation for the English adjective that means "of or pertaining to Chile" is CHIL-ee-in, with the accent on the first, not the second syllable.

For *Chile,* the nation, the English pronunciation is CHIL-ee (like *chilly*), which I strongly recommend for all English-language contexts. The Spanish pronunciation is CHEE-le, which a native English speaker usually turns into CHEE-lay. (Warning: slipping in a Spanish CHEE-lay when speaking English may be perceived as pompous or pedantic.) Sometimes we hear English speakers say CHIL-ay; this is a false hybrid, neither English nor Spanish, and should be scrupulously avoided. It is no doubt from the erroneous CHIL-ay that the bogus and affected chi-LAY-in comes.

Here's a moral for you: don't buy poisoned chi-LAY-in fruit, insist on unspoiled CHIL-ee-in fruit, and ban all *nucular* weapons.

chimera ky-MEER-uh (recommended) or ki-MEER-uh.
"I had been pronouncing 'chimera' as 'shimmera' for years," confesses William Safire, language columnist for *The New York Times Magazine,* "until some wiseguy little kid insisted rightly it was 'ky-MEER-a.'" There's no shortage of beastly mispronunciations for this fabulous beast or wild fancy, the most common employing shuh-, shy-, chuh-, and chy- for *chi-*. Like Safire's "shimmera," all are wild and fabulous inventions with no sound authority. (See next entry.)

chimerical ki-MER-i-kul (ki- as in *Kim*) or ky-MER-i-kul (ky- as in *kite*).
Don't say ki- or ky-MEER-i-kul; properly, there is no *miracle* in *chimerical.* "The accent and the last three syllables are the same as in *numerical,*" counsels Holt (1937), who prefers the short *i* (ki-) in the first syllable, as do I. See **chimera**.

chiropodist ki-RAHP-uh-dist or ky-RAHP-uh-dist. Do not say shi-RAHP-uh-dist.

Once derided as "a high-flying term for a 'corn-cutter,'" says Burchfield (1996), this word "is now in ordinary use for one who treats the feet and their ailments."

The *ch* in *chiropodist* is properly pronounced like *k*, and not, as comedian Woody Allen pronounced it in an appearance early in his career on *The Jack Paar Show*, like *sh*. The variant shi-RAHP-uh-dist, which is listed as an alternative in most current dictionaries, is a pseudosophisticated blunder that bamboozled its way into educated speech. It first appeared in *Webster 3* (1961) labeled with an obelus [÷] to show that many speakers took "strong exception" to it. Why did they take such strong exception? Because it was an awkward and ignorant attempt at cultivated speech that took a combining form from Greek (*chiro-*, hand) and mercilessly Frenchified it. The same *chiro-* appears in *chiropractor*, which no one but an ignoramus would pronounce *shiropractor*. What does saying *shiropodist* prove, other than that one is content to follow the herd and make a silly word sillier?

Until about 1960, authorities preferred a long *i* in the first syllable (ky-RAHP-uh-dist), and this is my preference too, if only because it preserves a nice companionship in sound between *chiropodist* and *chiropractor*. Since then the preference has clearly shifted to a short or obscure *i* (ki- or ki-RAHP-uh-dist), and the long *i* variant is now sometimes labeled infrequent or old-fashioned.

chivalrous SHIV-ul-rus. Stress the first syllable.

This is the only recognized pronunciation in the four major current American dictionaries. Do not say shi-VAL-rus, which is beastly. For the adjective *chivalric*, however, modern authorities prefer second-syllable stress: shi-VAL-rik. See **heraldic**.

chocolate CHAWK-lit or CHAWK-uh-lit; CHAHK-lit or CHAHK-uh-lit.

The *choc-* may be pronounced either like *chalk* or like *chock*.

The two-syllable pronunciation of *chocolate* was once criticized, but is now entirely acceptable. *Chocolate* has been altered by a linguistic process called syncope (SING-kuh-pee), the loss or dropping of a letter, sound, or syllable from the middle of a word, as in AWF-lee for *awfully*, DIF-rints for *difference*, FAM-lee for *family*, KUHMF-tur-buul for **comfortable**, DY-pur for *diaper* (formerly DY-uh-pur), GROHS-ree for **grocery**, PRIV-lij for *privilege*, PREF-rins for *preference*, SEV-rul for *several*, VAK-yoom (or VAK-yum) for *vacuum* (formerly VAK-yoo-um), VEJ-tuh-buul for **vegetable**, and WAR-yur for *warrior*.

The old-school elocutionists and rulebook-thumping schoolteachers may disagree with me, but I maintain that losing a weakly stressed syllable here and there is nothing to get bent out of shape about (along with putting prepositions at the ends of sentences when they are idiomatic).

Syncope is chipping away at English words all the time, and has been for hundreds of years. Without syncope, poetry would *never* have *ne'er,* the third day of the week would not be WENZ-day, and our work would be tedious *busy-ness* instead of *business.* It's difficult to see anything but intransigence and paranoia in the claim that these elisions constitute a threat to the language.

Syncope is acceptable most of the time because it improves the fluidity of speech without garbling the word. In certain cases, however, when the syncopated form is resisted by most educated speakers and criticized as slurred, slovenly, or illiterate, pains should be taken to preserve the unstressed syllable. See, along with the boldfaced words above, **foliage, maintenance, mayonnaise, usual, verbiage.** For more on syncope, see **temperature.**

cholesterol kuh-LES-tur-awl.

Should the final syllable of *cholesterol* sound like *all* or *roll?* Both pronunciations have been recognized since the word entered English in the 1890s. Numerous modern authorities — including Lass & Lass (1976), the *NBC Handbook* (1984), *Everyday Reader's* (1985), and Barnhart (1988) — prefer *roll,* but there is plenty of good authority for *all,* which is the only pronunciation in *OED 2* (1989) and my three medical dictionaries — *Taber's* (1970), *Stedman's* (1972), and *Mosby's* (1990).

Since the 1970s, when *cholesterol* became a household word, the *all* pronunciation — no doubt reinforced by other *all* words such as *parasol, alcohol, menthol, protocol, vitriol,* and *folderol* — has spread ineluctably, like a middle-aged waistline. Today, the evidence of my ears says the *roll* pronunciation is far less common than its unlabeled presence in current dictionaries would indicate; in fact, I would argue that it is now rare enough to sound peculiar and raise eyebrows, and I wouldn't be surprised if it disappears from the dictionaries by 2025. When faced with a choice between two rival pronunciations with equally legitimate credentials, it is often prudent to go with the flow if a flow can be discerned. In this case the current is rapid and powerful, and the choice is clear: when it comes to *cholesterol,* it's *all* or nothing.

Some unfortunate speakers pronounce the word kluh-RES-tur-awl, as if it were spelled *chloresterol.* This hopelessly garbled bit of beastliness probably is the result of confusion with words beginning with *chlor-.*

civilization SIV-i-li-ZAY-shin.

Although *OED 2* (1989) lists this pronunciation first, British and Canadian speakers often say SIV-i-ly-ZAY-shin (and sometimes spell it *civilisation*).

"These are the voyages of the Starship *Enterprise,*" says Canadian actor William Shatner (aka Captain James Kirk) in his voice-over introduction to the classic TV series *Star Trek.* "Its five-year mission," he continues,

". . . to seek out new life and new civilizations. . . ." Wait, stop the tape. Did you hear anything unusual there? I don't think you have to be a "Trekkie" to notice that Shatner pronounces the third *i* in *civilizations* like the word *eye*. This long *i*, says Opdycke (1939), "is used in England to a great extent but is not preferred in the United States." That has been the case for well over a hundred years: SIV-i-li-**ZAY**-shin is the only pronunciation in Worcester (1860), Funk & Wagnalls *Standard* (1897), and the *Century* (1914), and it is the only pronunciation listed in all four major American dictionaries today.

In American speech, the verbal suffix *-ize* is pronounced like *eyes* and the noun suffix *-ization* is pronounced with a lightened or obscure *i* (as in *edible* or *sanity*). Say the following pairs of words aloud and you will hear the change from *eyes* (*-ize*) to *is* (*-zation*): capitalize, capitalization; characterize, characterization; dramatize, dramatization; institutionalize, institutionalization; organize, organization; pasteurize, pasteurization; realize, realization; sterilize, sterilization; visualize, visualization.

clandestine klan-DES-tin (klan- like *clan,* -DES-tin like *destin-* in *destiny*). This is the only acceptable pronunciation. There is no legitimate authority (other than ignorant, bullheaded frequency of error) for the beastly variants klan-DES-tyn, klan-DES-teen, KLAN-di-styn, KLAN-di-steen, and KLAN-di-stin.

Clandestine is so often mispronounced by educated speakers (John F. Kennedy was one prominent example) that you have to wonder whether the correct pronunciation is a well-guarded secret. But you don't need to invoke the Freedom of Information Act to find out how to say it right. Just check any dictionary or pronunciation guide, American or British, from the past or present, and you'll find that nearly all record only one pronunciation, klan-DES-tin, and the handful that recognize one or more alternatives still list klan-DES-tin first. A survey of current sources shows that klan-DES-tin is the only pronunciation in *OED 2* (1989), *American Heritage 3* (1992), *RHWC* (1997), and *WNW 3* (1997), and it is the preference of Lass & Lass (1976), the *Quintessential Dictionary* (1978), *WNW Guide* (1984), the *NBC Handbook* (1984), *Everyday Reader's* (1985), Barnhart (1988), and Burchfield (1996).

clangor KLANG-ur. Now infrequently KLANG-gur.
Older authorities preferred KLANG-gur, and although current dictionaries still list this pronunciation, only *M-W 10* (1993) correctly labels it with *also* to indicate it is "appreciably less common." In the U.S., KLANG-gur survives chiefly among older speakers and it is doubtful that many young speakers have ever heard it. Lass & Lass (1976) and the British *Oxford Guide* (1983) hold out for KLANG-gur, but the *NBC Handbook* (1984), *WNW Guide* (1984), and *Everyday Reader's* (1985), along with another British authority, Jones (1991), prefer the now-dominant KLANG-ur.

clapboard KLAB-urd (as if spelled *clabberd*).

Most older authorities preferred the spelling pronunciation KLAP-bord and often called KLAB-urd colloquial. For example, *Webster 2* (1934), which lists KLAP-bord first, notes in its front matter that the *p* is silent in *cupboard* and *clapboard,* and Vizetelly (1929), who also sanctions KLAB-urd as an alternative, calls *clapboard* "a word that is analogous to *cupboard,* and which, in some regions, is pronounced with the p silent. This colloquial pronunciation may, perhaps, be traced to the spelling *clabords,*" which dates back to 1641. As with *cupboard,* which every native speaker of English pronounces *cubberd,* the linguistic process of assimilation (making neighboring sounds similar) has done its work in *clapboard,* making it sound like *clabberd.* Today, the colloquial pronunciation prevails in the U.S., and the spelling pronunciation now sounds awkward and stilted; despite its appearance in current dictionaries, it is fast fading away. Lass & Lass (1976), the *NBC Handbook* (1984), and *WNW Guide* (1984) all prefer KLAB-urd, the last noting that KLAP-bord is heard only occasionally.

cliché klee-SHAY, not kli-SHAY.

Careful speakers always stress the second syllable and rhyme the first with *see,* which is probably why klee-SHAY is the first pronunciation in *M-W 10* (1993) and *RHWC* (1997), the only pronunciation in *American Heritage 3* (1992) and *WNW 3* (1997), and the preference of Lass & Lass (1976), *WNW Guide* (1984), and the *NBC Handbook* (1984). See **clique**.

clientele kly-un-TEL.

This word has been used in English to mean "a body of clients or customers" since the mid-1800s.

The usual pronunciation in the U.S. today, kly-un-TEL, has been standard for over a hundred years: *Webster's New International* (1909) and Phyfe (1926) were two of the earliest authorities to prefer it. A number of older American authorities — including Worcester (1860), Funk & Wagnalls *Standard* (1897), the *Century* (1914), and Vizetelly (1933) — preferred kly-un-TEEL or KLY-un-teel. These have passed out of use in American speech, but kly-un-TEEL is apparently still heard in England, for *OED 2* (1989) lists it first. Some older American speakers (my mother, for example) prefer a Frenchified variant, klee-ahn-TEL, which *OED 2* lists second and three other British authorities, *Oxford Guide* (1983), Jones (1991), and Burchfield (1996), prefer. (Jones marks it klee-un-TEL.) American authorities have never much cared for it, and although all four current American dictionaries recognize it, two label it *also,* indicating it is far less frequent. The evidence of my ears says it is well on the road to retirement.

clique KLEEK, not KLIK.

This word should rhyme with *sleek,* not *slick.*

"The late Frank Colby in his *American Pronouncing Dictionary* claimed that most Americans prefer KLIK," write Morris & Morris (1985), "but we suspect that his ear was attuned to Western American speech, rather than to the speech patterns of the country as a whole. Those who are aware of the French origin of the word are more likely to pronounce it KLEEK." See **cliché**.

clitoris KLIT-ur-is. (British often KLY-tur-is.)

Do not say kli̱-TOR-is. Stress the first syllable.

This is the story of how beastly mispronunciation can cause inestimable trouble, especially when perpetrated on national TV. Specifically, in the case of one Jerold Mackenzie, it meant loss of livelihood, a tarnished reputation, and a long legal ordeal.

Mackenzie, a former executive with the Miller Brewing Company, "was fired from his $95,000-a-year job in 1993," said an Associated Press report appearing in my local paper, "after he discussed a racy episode of 'Seinfeld' with a female co-worker." When Mackenzie sued for damages, the pronunciation of *clitoris* had its day in court.

"In the episode of the NBC sitcom cited at trial," said the report,

> Jerry Seinfeld's character can't remember the name of his girlfriend, only that it rhymes with a female body part. Jerry and his friends try a few guesses, including "Mulva" and "Gipple." Only after the woman realizes that Jerry doesn't know her name and runs off does he remember and scream out, "Dolores!" . . . Mackenzie testified that he never said the word of the body part, and instead showed [the female co-worker] a photocopied page from the dictionary with the word "clitoris" on it.*

Don't you love that phrase, "the dictionary"? It's never "a" dictionary, always "the" dictionary — as if there were only one such book in existence, which we can turn to in times of need for The Last Word in matters of language.

But let us return to our story. It does indeed say something about the prevalence of the pronunciation kli̱-TOR-is that Seinfeld and his writers would hang the episode's climactic punchline on it. Clearly they assumed their audience would naturally rhyme *clitoris* with *Dolores*. But would they? And what about that dictionary?

Had Mackenzie taken a closer look, and had the patience to decipher those often inscrutable diacritical marks, no doubt he would have been surprised to discover that the first pronunciation listed did not rhyme with *Dolores*. Moreover, if the dictionary he consulted happened to be *WNW 3* (1988, 1997) or *American Heritage 3* (1992), he would have been even more surprised that the variant with second-syllable stress was nowhere to be found. Likewise with any desk dictionary printed before 1980.

---

* *The San Diego Union-Tribune*, Wednesday, July 16, 1997, p. A-6.

Although Mr. Mackenzie won his lawsuit and was awarded a whopping $26 million by a jury, in my opinion he is guilty on three counts: for not reading the dictionary entry carefully, for assuming that his coworker would say kli-TOR-is and get the joke, and for harassing someone with a beastly mispronunciation.

Despite the recent voguish embrace of second-syllable stress, KLIT-ur-is remains the established American pronunciation, listed first in all four major current American dictionaries and preferred by Lass & Lass (1976), *Oxford American* (1980), the *NBC Handbook* (1984), *WNW Guide* (1984), Barnhart (1988), and all three of my medical dictionaries — *Taber's* (1970), *Stedman's* (1972), and *Mosby's* (1990).

The adjective *clitoral* is pronounced KLIT-ur-ul to rhyme with *literal*. Don't say kli-TOR-ul. See **electoral, mayoral, pastoral.**

coeval koh-EE-vul.

cognoscenti KAHN-yuh-**SHEN**-tee (or, for the first syllable, KOHN-
    or KAWN-).

The more anglicized variant KAHG-nuh-**SHEN**-tee (KAHG- like *cog*) is now also standard, but most current sources still favor the *gn* rolled as in *lasagna* (luh-ZAHN-yuh). The first syllable may be KAHN- (as in *confident*), KOHN- (like *cone*), or the more Italian KAWN- (rhymes with *dawn*); choose the one you are most comfortable with. Be sure to put the primary stress on the third syllable (-*scen*-) and give the *sc* the sound of *sh*.

Cognoscenti, which comes from Italian, is a plural noun meaning experts or connoisseurs, especially in the fine arts, literature, or *haute couture* (OHT koo-TUUR), high fashion. The singular is *cognoscente*, in which the first three syllables are pronounced the same but the last changes to -tay: KAHN- (or KOHN- or KAWN-) -yuh-**SHEN**-tay. See **connoisseur, Modigliani, seraglio.**

coherent koh-HEER-int, not koh-HAIR-int or (Eastern and Northern)
    koh-HER-int.

Properly, there is no *hair* in *coherent*. In *adhere* and *adherent, inhere* and *inherent, cohere* and *coherent,* the stressed syllable should sound like *here*. The co-*hair*-ent (or short *e* of *herald*) variant is a vogue pronunciation — a mistake that somehow becomes a fad — that first gained recognition in *Webster 3* (1961). It has since become widespread, but no authorities prefer it, and all four major current American dictionaries give priority to koh-HEER-int. See **inherent.**

coitus KOH-i-tus.

This word is often mispronounced. The problem comes from not knowing where to put the stress, and those who shift it to the second syllable are then unsure how to pronounce the *i*. This insecurity can produce some astonishing results — I have heard koh-EYE-tus, koh-AY-tus, and KOYt_us, all of which may be in the Kamasutra but which are decidedly un-ko-sher in cultivated speech. (The first two variants do not appear in any dictionary I have consulted; *M-W 10* (1993) is the only source that, regret-tably, recognizes the last.) Several current dictionaries countenance one alternative pronunciation with second-syllable stress, koh-EE-t_us, which Lass & Lass (1976) prefer. However, an overwhelming number of sources — including the *Century* (1914), *Webster 2* (1934), *American College* (1952), *Webster 3* (1961), the *NBC Handbook* (1984), *Random House II* (1987), *OED 2* (1989), and *RHWC* (1997) — say there's only one way to do it, and that's KOH-i-t_us.

colander KUHL-an-dur or, now more often, KAHL-an-dur.

Traditionally, the first syllable rhymes with *dull,* not *doll,* but read on.

Colander was first recorded about 1450. Like many old English words, it was spelled in a variety of strange ways over the years. By the end of the 19th century the field had narrowed to two standard spellings: *colander* and *cullender.* After another half-century of duking it out, *colander* won the preferred spelling title and *cullender* won the more tenuous second prize — pronunciation. In a winner-takes-all society, however, the runner-up rarely gets any respect. As it became clear that *colander* had the edge in spelling (c. 1920–1930), many people started pronouncing it as it was spelled. Although Phyfe (1926) and Vizetelly (1929) proscribed the KAHL-pronunciation, *Webster 2* (1934) and Kenyon & Knott (1949) accepted it as an alternative; Opdycke (1939) dubbed it "preferable," as did Lass & Lass (1976) almost forty years later. Today, although three of the four major current American dictionaries list KUHL-an-dur first and the *NBC Handbook* (1984) and Burchfield (1996) prefer it, there is no question that, at least in American speech, KAHL-an-dur has taken the lead and seems destined to eclipse its rival.

Coleridge (Samuel Taylor) KOHL-rij.

This name is perennially mispronounced — even by English teachers — in three syllables, either KOH-luh-rij (like *cola ridge*) or KAH-luh-rij (like *collar ridge*). Properly, it is pronounced in two syllables, KOHL-rij (like *coal ridge*).

I can hear some English teachers saying, "Oh, really? If KOH-luh-rij is wrong, then why do my colleagues say it that way and and why is that pronunciation listed in all four major current American dictionaries?" The answer is simple: it is listed precisely because so many teachers have been content to perpetuate a misnomer in the guise of educated speech, instill-ing the error in generations of unsuspecting students. If you think it's correct to pronounce *Coleridge* in three syllables, then answer me this: why is the two-syllable KOHL-rij listed first in all four of those dictionaries? Why is it the only pronunciation countenanced by *Webster 2* (1934), the *Columbia Encyclopedia* (1963), and *Random House II* (1987), and the preference of orthoepists from Phyfe (1926) to the *NBC Handbook* (1984)? Moreover, why would Ralph H. Emerson (1996), an expert on the pronunciation of literary names, assert that KOHL-rij is in accord with the poet's own usage and call the three-syllable variants wrong? English teachers of America, perhaps it's time to brush up on your KOHL-rij.

colloquial kuh-LOH-kwee-ul. Do not say kuh-LOH-kee-ul.

Take care to preserve the -kwee- sound of the -*qui*- in *colloquial* ("of everyday speech, conversational") and *colloquialism* ("an informal expression"). I have heard may speakers (including those masters of colloquial lingo, radio talk show hosts) mangle them by changing -kwee- to -kee- and rhyming *colloquial* with *parochial* and pronouncing *colloquialism* like *collokialism*. These are not kuh-LOH-kwee-ul pronunciations; they are macaws in the menagerie of beastly speech.

column KAHL-um.

Do not say KAHL-yum or KAHL-yoom. There is no *yum* or *yoom* in *column*. "It is altogether wrong," says Holt (1937), "to put a *y* sound into the ordinary *column*." Likewise, *columnist* is pronounced KAHL-um-nist. Anything else is beastly.

comity KAHM-i-tee (like the nonsense phrase *comma tea*).

Some speakers (e.g., Assistant Treasury Secretary Lawrence Summers) pronounce this word with a long *o*, KOH-mi-tee. This variant does not appear in any of my sources before the 1970s and is recognized by only one current source, *M-W 10* (1993).

commingle kuh-MING-gul, not koh-MING-gul.

Commingle is often mispronounced as if it were spelled *co-mingle*, and no doubt because of the mispronunciation the spelling *co-mingle* occasionally appears in print.* An examination of *OED 2* (1989), which sanctions only kuh-MING-gul, reveals that the spelling *co-mingle* dates back to Shakespeare, who used it in *Hamlet*, but for over a hundred years it has been considered obsolete and therefore nonstandard (which may be taken to mean "unacceptable in educated usage"). *Commingle*, on the other hand, has enjoyed good standing at least since Sir Francis Bacon used it in 1626. Like *commit, commend, commence, commemorate, commiserate, commission, commodity, community, commuter, commercial,* and various other words in which *com-* is followed by a stressed syllable beginning with *m*,

---

* Two examples: (1) In a sidebar appearing in *The New York Times* (September 28, 1997, National section, p. 16) that profiled the members of the advisory board for President Clinton's Initiative on Race and Reconciliation, Thomas H. Kean, former governor of New Jersey and president of Drew University, was quoted as saying that "we see clubs and we see even churches where we don't have a chance to *co-mingle* with people who are not like us." (2) "'Somehow, if you're on the left you can *co-mingle* (funds) and no one seems to notice,' The Associated Press quoted Gingrich as saying" (Lionel Van Deerlin, *The San Diego Union-Tribune*, January 29, 1997, p. B-5).

the first syllable of *commingle* has an obscure *o* and the word sounds like *come mingle* spoken rapidly. Dictionaries do not recognize the *co-mingle* spelling and pronunciation, but if prominent people keep saying it that way and *The New York Times* and The Associated Press keep spelling it as people mispronounce it, then, as surely as the sun rises and sets, future dictionaries will bestow their blessing upon the bastardly *co-mingle*. (For more on words where mispronunciation has influenced spelling, see **Brobdingnagian, chaise longue, conservatism, daiquiri, doctoral, entrepreneur, loath,** and **minuscule.**)

communal kuh-MYOO-nul. British, KAHM-yuh-nul.

comparable KAHM-pur-uh-buul. Do not say kum-PAIR-uh-buul.

The beastly mispronunciation kum-PAIR-uh-buul, with second-syllable stress, is "considered by some to be unacceptable," according to *M-W 10* (1993). I would change that "some" to "many" or "most." Burchfield (1996), echoing the preference of generations of careful speakers, says, "The main stress falls on the first syllable. . . . Nonstandard speakers frequently place it on the second syllable." One further caveat: do not say KAHM-pruh-buul, in three syllables. *Comparable* should have four clearly articulated syllables. See **admirable, formidable, incomparable, irreparable, reparable.**

compensatory kum-PEN-suh-TOR-ee.

Occasionally one hears an eccentric speaker say KAHM-pen-SAY-tur-ee. The *Oxford Guide* (1983), a British source, says "the older (and Amer.) pronunciation has stress on 2nd syllable, but stress on 3rd is now common." Common, presumably, in England. In standard American English, however, there is no authority for this beastly variant.

comptroller kun-TROH-lur (just like *controller*). Do not pronounce the *p*.

"*Comptroller* is an erroneous spelling of *controller*," explains Bergen Evans in *Comfortable Words* (1959),

> introduced about the year 1500 by some zealous pedant who had found out that the French word for *account* was *compte*. This absurd spelling became established in the titles of certain positions and in these titles it remains. Thus it is the Comptroller General of the United States, so fixed by law. But it is still pronounced *controller* — though one hears *comp-troller* every now and then from some earnest soul who just can't believe that *mp* is ever pronounced *n*.

conch KAHNGK (like *conk*).

"Though Sir William Golding consistently pronounced the word as [KAHNCH] in a lecture that he gave on *The Lord of the Flies* and other matters at the University of Oxford in February 1990," says Burchfield (1996), "the more usual standard pronunciation is [KAHNGK]."

Sir William's preference, a so-called spelling pronunciation, is not without precedent; in fact, *OED 2* (1989), which lists KAHNCH second, suggests that it may be the original pronunciation, based on the earlier English spelling *conche,* from French. *Webster's New International* (1909), as quoted in Phyfe (1926), says "formerly, and still by some, pronounced konch or konsh," Lass & Lass (1976) prefer KAHNCH, Barnhart (1988) calls it "more common," and current dictionaries all sanction it. KAHNGK's lineage in cultivated speech, however, goes back more than two hundred years, and a survey of numerous sources from Walker (1791) to the present shows that the weight of authority is clearly in its favor.

The plural is preferably spelled *conchs* and pronounced KAHNGKS (like *conks).*

concierge KAHN-see-**AIRZH** or KAWN-see-**AIRZH**. French, kaw(n)-SYAIRZH.

Concord (New Hampshire and Massachusetts) KAHNGK-urd.

When referring to the capital of New Hampshire, the town in Massachusetts, the wine, and the grape, *Concord* should sound like *conquered* (or rhyme with the imaginary word *bonkered*). However, for various other U.S. cities of this name, for the noun *concord* (harmony, agreement), and for *Concorde,* the trademark of the supersonic transport, the pronunciation is KAHN-kord or KAHNG-kord (-kord like *cord*).

concupiscence kun-KYOO-pi-sins.

Stress the second syllable (*-cu-*), not the third (*-pis-*). Once used in philosophy to denote a soulful longing for that which gives delight, *concupiscence* has become a twenty-dollar word for strong sexual desire. The adjective *concupiscent* is pronounced kun-KYOO-pi-sint.

confiscate KAHN-fi-skayt. Formerly, kun-FIS-kayt.

Don't get sloppy with the first syllable of this word, changing *con-* to *com-*. Saying *com*fiscate is a Bozo no-no; dictionaries do not recognize it. Be sure to say *con*fiscate.

OED 2 (1989) says, "As in other words of the same form, *compensate, concentrate, contemplate,* etc., the stress is now usually on the first syllable, but till c[*irca*] 1864 the dictionaries had only [kun-FIS-kayt]." In the 19th century, *demonstrate* and *expurgate* also had their accent on the second syllable. Say aloud the nursery rhyme, "Mary, Mary, quite contrary," and you will hear the former pronunciation of *contrary.* Around the turn of century (give or take a decade or so, depending on the word) dictionaries began to recognize, and orthoepists began to sanction, a shift in stress to the first syllable in these words, which had become predominant in educated speech. Today, second-syllable stress in any of them would sound, as William Safire puts it, "like something a visiting Martian would say."

The trend at work in these words has been called "recessive accent" or "recessive stress." Certain other three-syllable words, however, yielded their second-syllable stress less willingly. Though many (and in some cases most) speakers today stress the first syllable in *precedence, infiltrate, acclimate, minuscule, inculcate, vagaries,* and *obfuscate,* not a few speakers (some young as well as old) retain the accent on the second syllable, and their traditional pronunciation is still listed in good standing in current dictionaries. *Confiscate* no longer belongs to this class of holdouts against recessive stress. If you are one of the few speakers who still accent the second syllable in this word, surely you must know you are part of a vanishing breed.

The English language is a restless, unwieldy creature, and the accent in many English words has shifted back and forth (or forth and back) over time. While recessive stress pushes back the accent in certain words, a companion trend called "progressive stress" pushes the accent forward. Progressive stress is now at work on various three-syllable words that traditionally have been stressed on the first syllable. For example, we often hear speakers stress the second syllable in *affluent, clitoris, congruent, disparate, exquisite, influence, integral, mayoral, pastoral,* and *pectoral.* At present, progressive stress in all these words is frowned upon by careful speakers and I exhort you to resist it. See the individual discussions of these words, and also **acclimate, acumen, despicable, formidable, hospitable, inculcate, infiltrate, lamentable, minuscule, obfuscate, precedence, preferable, promulgate, sonorous, vagaries.** For more on recessive and progressive stress, see H. W. Fowler's *Modern English Usage,* pp. 486–87, and R. W. Burchfield's *New Fowler's Modern English Usage,* pp. 657–58.

congratulations kun-GRACH-uh-**LAY**-shinz, not kun-GRAJ-uh-**LAY**-shinz.

The issue here is the sound of the *t* in the second syllable. Whenever I'm a guest language maven fielding questions on a radio show, invariably someone calls in to complain about speakers who pronounce this word as if it were spelled *congradulations* and had something to do with *graduation.* This informal and rather sloppy pronunciation has become so frequent among educated speakers that some current dictionaries now recognize it. Cultivated speakers, however, take care to pronounce the *t* like *ch* in *congratulate, congratulatory,* and *congratulations.*

congruent KAHNG-groo-wint. Stress the first syllable.

Congruent, congruence, congruous, and *congruency* all properly have their accent on the first syllable, not the second. (The noun *congruity,* however, is pronounced kahng-GROO-i-tee.) Progressive (forward-moving) stress has besieged these words and also *incongruent* since about the 1930s, thanks to a growing contingent of semiliterate speakers who apparently feel that stressing the second syllable is somehow more sophisticated. Most decidedly, it is not. For *congruent*, Lass & Lass (1976), the *NBC Handbook* (1984), *Everyday Reader's* (1985), Barnhart (1988), and *OED 2* (1989) all prefer the established pronunciation with first-syllable stress. KAHNG-groo-wint also appears first in two of the four major current American dictionaries, and a third, *WNW 3* (1997), does not recognize the voguish and beastly kang-GROO-wint and IN-kahng-**GROO**-wint.

N.B. When you stress the first syllable in *congruent* and its brethren noted above, take care to preserve the -groo- sound. Don't omit the *u*, drop a syllable, and pronounce them as if they were spelled *congrent, congrence, congress,* and *congrency.* These two-syllable variants are utterly beastly. See **incongruent, incongruous,** and, for a discussion of progressive and recessive stress, **confiscate.**

connoisseur KAHN-uh-**SUR**. Do not say KAHN-uh-**SOOR** or KAHN-uh-**SOO**-ur.

The final syllable, which receives the primary stress, should sound like *sir,* not *sewer.* Holt (1937) rhymes the word with *on a spur.* The old vaudevillian line illustrates the vulgarity of the *sewer* pronunciation: "I'm a common-sewer of fine wines." Although some dictionaries now recognize this mispronunciation (because of its unfortunate frequency), properly there is no *sewer* in *connoisseur.* See **amateur, de rigueur, entrepreneur, liqueur, restaurateur.**

conservatism kun-SUR-vuh-tiz'm. Do not say kun-SUR-vuh-tiv-iz'm.

There is no *conservative* in *conservatism.* The word has five syllables, not six. The spelling *conservativism,* modeled after the mispronunciation, is also nonstandard.

consortium Traditionally, kun-SOR-shee-um, not kun-SOR-tee-um.

The variant kun-SOR-shum, although recognized by some dictionaries, is also not recommended. The word properly should have four clearly enunciated syllables.

This just in from the Bureau of Beastly Mispronunciation: your vigilant pronunciation maven recently heard — from the lips of a Ph.D., no less, who is a top-level administrator at a prestigious California university — a horrifying and outrageously affected new mispronunciation of *consortium:* kun-SOR-see-um. It's common knowledge that the ivory tower is surfeited with consortia (kun-SOR-shee-uh), so I'm concerned that I may have detected the first sign of an epidemic about to emanate from the groves of academe. This ob-nock-see-us new breed of beastly mispronunciation is not in any dictionary yet (thank goodness), and let's make sure it never gets there. Let's avoid this prissy consor-see-um like the proverbial plague.

Now on to other matters. The paramount issue with *consortium* is whether the *ti* should be pronounced like *sh* or like the word *tea.* To do the latter, I am convinced, is to be guilty not only of spelling pronunciation, which is venial, but also of vogue pronunciation, which is far more grievous (pronounced in two syllables, please, as GREE-v<u>us</u>, not the beastly GREE-vee-<u>us</u>). Vogue pronunciations — to borrow a phrase or two from the legendary prescriptivist H. W. Fowler — are "taken up merely as novel variants on their predecessors," often only for "the joy of showing that one has acquired them." One unfortunate characteristic of vogue pronunciations is that they have a certain snob appeal (and of course that irresistible novelty) which seduces many educated speakers into thinking they must be more refined or proper or intellectual; then, what were once mere eccentricities or risible affectations suddenly acquire cachet and become mass-media-marketed commodities. Before you know it every shlub in Lower Slobbovia has to have 'em, they become the aural equivalent of kitsch, and they go straight into the dictionaries, where the shlubs can point and smugly say "You see? I'm right!" It's enough to drive a pronunciation maven mad!

Let us trace the vogue displacement of *she* in favor of *tea* in *consortium*. As far as I can tell, it probably took root in the 1950s. Before *Webster 3* (1961) — which gives k<u>un</u>-SORSH-ee-<u>um</u>, k<u>un</u>-SORSH-<u>um</u>, and k<u>un</u>-SOR-dee-<u>um</u> — authorities sanctioned only k<u>un</u>-SOR-shee-<u>um</u>. Lass & Lass (1976), who prefer k<u>un</u>-SOR-shee-<u>um</u>, show that only one of the four major American dictionaries of the 1970s — *M-W 8* (1975), which was based on *Webster 3* — recognized k<u>un</u>-SOR-tee-<u>um</u>. In the 1980s we see that the *NBC Handbook* (1984), *WNW 2* (1984), and *Everyday Reader's* (1985) stick by k<u>un</u>-SOR-shee-<u>um</u>, but *WNW Guide* (1984) accepts all three variants and the redoubtable *OED 2* (1989) recognizes k<u>un</u>-SOR-tee-<u>um</u> as a standard alternative. Finally, in the 1990s the latest editions of those same four major American dictionaries all countenance k<u>un</u>-SOR-tee-<u>um</u>, with two listing it first. (Only two list k<u>un</u>-SOR-sh<u>um</u>.)

In *There Is No Zoo in Zoology* (1988) I argued that "tradition favors k<u>un</u>-SOR-shee-<u>um</u>, analogy with similar words in which *ti* is pronounced like *sh* (e.g., *nasturtium, Byzantium, nation, partial, patient, tertiary*) justifies it, and general practice still prefers it." Ten years later I still vigorously agree with the first two assertions but must confess I have lost confidence in the last. Undoubtedly there are many careful speakers out there who preserve the *she* in *consortium*, but just as undoubtedly there are many more who don't. And now, with at least two generations of computer-savvy speakers coming of age in the age of the Pentium® Processor (yup, that's PEN-tee-<u>um</u>), I have to wonder if the traditional pronunciation will survive. The vogue, once perceived as elevated, has become vulgar and hence victorious. See **Beijing, controversial, negotiate, oceanic, Social Security,** and **species**.

consul KAHN-s<u>u</u>l; **consulate** KAHN-suh-lit.

Don't say KOWN-s<u>u</u>l and KOWN-suh-lit, as if the words were spelled *council* and *councilate*. These are regrettably common beastly mispronunciations, which I have heard from numerous educated speakers. *Council* and *counsel* are pronounced KOWN-s<u>u</u>l, but there is no *cow* in *consul* (KAHN-s<u>u</u>l), *consular* (KAHN-suh-lur), and *consulate* (KAHN-suh-lit).

consummate (adjective) k<u>u</u>n-SUHM-it; (verb) KAHN-suh-mayt.

Stress the adjective on the second syllable and the verb on the first. This is the traditional distinction, preferred by Ayres (1894), Phyfe (1926), Vizetelly (1929), Gilmartin (1936), Holt (1937), Opdycke (1939), Kenyon & Knott (1949), Lass & Lass (1976), the *NBC Handbook* (1984), *WNW Guide* (1984), *Everyday Reader's* (1985), and Morris & Morris (1985). The adjective is now often stressed on the first syllable, but *American Heritage 3* (1992), *WNW 3* (1997), and *RHWC* (1997) list k<u>u</u>n-SUHM-it first.

contemplative k<u>u</u>n-TEM-pluh-tiv, not **KAHN**-t<u>u</u>m-PLAY-tiv.

Second-syllable stress (k<u>u</u>n-TEM-pluh-tiv) has a venerable history. It is preferred by (among others) Walker (1791), Worcester (1860), Funk & Wagnalls *Standard* (1897), the *Century* (1914), Phyfe (1926), Vizetelly (1929), Opdycke (1939), the *Winston Dictionary* (1951), Lass & Lass (1976), *Oxford Guide* (1983), *WNW Guide* (1984), the *NBC Handbook* (1984), and *OED 2* (1989). Authorities advocating primary stress on the first syllable (**KAHN**-t<u>u</u>m-PLAY-tiv) are few and far between.

contiguous k<u>u</u>n-TIG-yoo-<u>u</u>s.

Be sure to articulate the -yoo- in the third syllable. Of the four major current American dictionaries, *M-W 10* (1993) is the only one that marks the word k<u>u</u>n-TI-gyuh-w<u>u</u>s, with a schwa (obscure vowel sound) in the third syllable. The other three mark it -yoo-, which is also the preference of Lass & Lass (1976), the *NBC Handbook* (1984), and *WNW Guide* (1984).

controversial KAHN-truh-**VUR**-sh<u>u</u>l, not KAHN-truh-**VUR**-see-<u>u</u>l.

The *-sial* in *controversial* is properly pronounced as one syllable.

Today we often hear the five-syllable pronunciation KAHN-truh-**VUR**-see-<u>u</u>l (or, much less frequently, KAHN-truh-**VUR**-shee-<u>u</u>l). This variant is not, as some believe, a British import; the opposite is more likely the case, with the BBC announcers picking it up from their American counterparts and passing it along to the average Brit. *OED 2* (1989) and Jones's *English Pronouncing Dictionary* (1991), both authorities on standard British pronunciation, give only the four-syllable KAHN-truh-**VUR**-sh<u>u</u>l.

The five-syllable KAHN-truh-**VUR**-see-<u>u</u>l has existed in American speech for much of the 20th century; until recently, however, it was not commonly heard and received scant attention in the dictionaries. (I don't recall ever hearing it myself until the early 1980s, when I was in my mid-twenties.) Lass & Lass (1976) — who prefer the traditional KAHN-truh-**VUR**-sh<u>ul</u> — note the appearance of KAHN-truh-**VUR**-see-<u>ul</u> in one dictionary of the 1970s, *Webster 3* (1961) sanctions it, Kenyon & Knott (1949) list it as an alternative, and Opdycke (1939), attesting to its ugsome existence sixty years ago, offers this advice: "Don't say *con tro ver'si al;* this is a four-syllable word."

Beginning in the late 1970s and early 1980s, the hitherto unpopular five-syllable variant suddenly became a vogue pronunciation. One after another — perhaps first in an effort to appear more articulate, then later in an effort to sound like the other guy — newsreaders and program hosts on radio and television (Phil Donahue was a prominent example) adopted the pseudosophisticated KAHN-truh-**VUR**-see-<u>ul</u>, and soon much of the public copied their poor example. By 1991 all four major American desk dictionaries listed KAHN-truh-**VUR**-see-<u>ul</u> second. Today so many Americans prefer the five-syllable upstart that it seems poised to become the dominant pronunciation, which it already appears to be for speakers under twenty-five or thirty, who have grown up during its rapid rise from obscurity to prominence.

If you currently pronounce *controversial* in five syllables, ask yourself this: have you always done so? Are you sure that — maybe eight, or ten, or twelve years ago — you didn't just slip into pronouncing it with an extra syllable because some of your coworkers or peers were saying it that way, or that's how you often heard it on radio and TV? Do you recall, when you were growing up, how your family members and friends pronounced it? Did your teachers and professors say it in four syllables or five? If you're over thirty and you answer these questions honestly, I'll bet you'll wind up admitting that somewhere along the way you adopted the five-syllable KAHN-truh-**VUR**-see-<u>ul</u> and that the traditional, unaffected, four-syllable KAHN-truh-**VUR**-sh<u>ul</u> was in fact your original pronunciation. If not, all I can say is, you're weird.

(By the way, it's interesting to note that while the language has numerous words ending in *-tial* and *-cial* that are pronounced -sh<u>ul</u> — e.g., *partial, initial, spatial, nuptial, commercial, official, crucial, financial,* etc. — the only common English word ending in *-sial* is *controversial.* Perhaps this spelling peculiarity tempted speakers to treat it differently in pronunciation.) See **Beijing, negotiate, oceanic, Social Security, species.**

controversy KAHN-truh-VUR-see.

Primary stress on the first syllable, secondary stress on the third — that is the only acceptable pronunciation of the word in American speech.

A pronunciation with second-syllable stress, k<u>u</u>n-TRAHV-ur-see, is heard in British speech (and is noted as British by some current American dictionaries); however, contrary to popular belief, it is not the traditional British pronunciation. *OED 2* (1989) and Jones (1991) prefer first-syllable stress. "The pronunciation with stress on 2nd syllable seems to be increasingly common, but it is strongly disapproved by many users of RP [Received Pronunciation]," says the *Oxford Guide* (1983). The British novelist Kingsley Amis (1998) puts that sentiment more bluntly: "Only a berk stresses the second syllable." According to Burchfield (1996), "the mood of the moment is to challenge orthodoxy by placing the main stress on the second syllable. . . . My verdict is that the traditional pronunciation with initial stressing is at risk, but is still, just, dominant among RP speakers in the UK." See **adversary, controversial.**

conversant kun-VUR-sint.

Second-syllable stress has completely won out in this word. Walker (1791) gave both first- and second-syllable stress as acceptable in cultivated speech and advocated the former; authorities of the first half of the 20th century preferred first-syllable stress. Current dictionaries still list first-syllable stress as an alternative and Lass & Lass (1976) prefer it, but I have never heard an American speaker use this pronunciation. Burchfield (1996), who notes that the accent was originally on the third syllable, recommends second-syllable stress, which the *NBC Handbook* (1984), *WNW Guide* (1984), and *Everyday Reader's* (1985) prefer.

Copenhagen KOH-pin-HAY-gin (also KOH-pin-**HAY**-gin), not **KOH**-pin-HAH-gin.

"*Copenhagen* is the English variant of the Danish *Köbenhavn*," explains W. Cabell Greet, professor of English at Columbia and speech consultant to CBS, in *World Words* (1948). "It should be pronounced as English with long *a* as in *Haig and Haig*. A broad 'ah', as in *Harvard*, does not give the native pronunciation. . . ."

KOH-pin-HAH-gin first appeared in *Webster 3* (1961). No doubt its currency has received a boost from the popular ice cream that goes by the (meaninglesss and pseudo-Scandinavian) trade name *Häagen Dazs*. Although current sources — including *Webster's Geographical Dictionary,* third edition (1997) — sanction the broad *a*, it remains an affectation. The *Columbia Encyclopedia* (1963) and the *NBC Handbook* (1984) prefer **KOH**-pin-HAY-gin.

corpuscle KOR-puh-sul or **KOR**-PUHS'l.

The difference between these two pronunciations amounts to only a slightly lighter or heavier articulation of the second syllable, resulting either in an obscure *u* as in *focus* (KOR-puh-sul) or a short *u* as in *must* (**KOR**-PUHS'l). Authorities in the first half of the 20th century favored the short *u;* authorities in the second half generally have shifted in favor of the obscure *u*. Second-syllable accent in *corpuscle* is now obsolescent, and the affected variant kor-PUHS-kyool (as if the word were spelled *corpuscule*) is ludicrous.

cosmos KAHZ-m<u>u</u>s (-m<u>u</u>s as in *Amos*).

KAHZ-m<u>u</u>s has been the prevailing American pronunciation since Kenyon & Knott (1949). It is the first pronunciation listed in all four major current American dictionaries and the preference of Lass & Lass (1976), the *NBC Handbook* (1984), *Everyday Reader's* (1985), and Barnhart (1988). KAHZ-mahs (-mahs with the broad *a* of *father*), favored by various older American authorities, is now chiefly British. KAHZ-mohs (-mohs as in *most*) has appeared in most dictionaries since the 1960s; *M-W 10* (1993) and *WNW 3* (1997) label it less common, but the evidence of my ears says it is very common and is now challenging KAHZ-m<u>u</u>s for the lead. See **ethos, pathos.**

costume KAHS-tyoom (recommended) or KAHS-toom.

"If you are one of those who can say [KAHS-tyoom] without making it [KAHS-choom], and without sounding affected, you have the privilege," says Holt (1937). "The rest of us will probably say 'cos-toom.'" Good advice, I say. If KAHS-tyoom, with the long *u*, comes naturally to you, fine; if not, say -toom. No one can legitimately find fault with you for using either pronunciation.

coupon KOO-pahn.

"Why do Americans have such a time with the French *ou?*" asks Alfred H. Holt in *You Don't Say!* (1937). "When we are not putting a long *o* into *bouquet* and *cantaloup* [*sic*], we are putting an initial 'Q' into *coupon*. It's simply 'coo'pon,' rhyming with 'Do, Don.'"

The pronunciation KYOO-pahn, with the spurious Q, is widespread and used by many otherwise conscientious speakers — Vincent Price, for example. Neither analogy nor spelling justifies it, however. We do not say SYOOP for *soup*, byoo-TEEK for *boutique*, or TYOOR-n<u>i</u>-kit for *tourniquet,* or insert a Y before the OO in *nouveau riche, coup d'état,* and *haute couture*. Why stick *cue* into *coupon?*

Although dictionaries have listed KYOO-pahn as an alternative pronunciation since the late 1940s, not a single one lists it first (not an insignificant coincidence), and I can find only two orthoepists who sanction it: Kenyon & Knott (1949) and Shaw (1972). By contrast, Vizetelly (1933), Gilmartin (1936), and Opdycke (1939) proscribe KYOO-, and *Webster 2* (1934) labels it incorrect. Phyfe (1926), Witherspoon (1943), Lass & Lass (1976), the *NBC Handbook* (1984), and *WNW Guide* (1984) all prefer KOO-pahn, the last noting that "KYOO pahn is common but is generally disapproved by those who say KOO pahn." See **beaucoup, bouquet, boutique, cantaloupe, percolator.**

courtesan KOR-t<u>i</u>-zin.

On the radio I once heard *New York Times* book reviewer John Leonard say KOOR-t<u>i</u>-zin. Dictionaries do not recognize this pronunciation. Formerly, say *Webster 2* (1934) and *WNW 3* (1997), the word was pronounced KURT-uh-zin. Some current dictionaries still list this pronunciation without comment; it is not recommended. The British stress the last syllable and rhyme it with *man:* KOR-ti-**ZAN**.

couturier koo-TUUR-ee-ur (recommended) or koo-**TUUR**-ee-AY.

This French word meaning "dressmaker, seamstress," entered English about 1900; it now refers to a designer of high-fashion clothing for women or an establishment that sells such expensive clothing. We native speakers of English are by nature cool toward French and wary of using it in everyday conversation. When it comes to the Francophilic world of high fashion, however, we become positively starry-eyed and silver-tongued. Lass & Lass (1976), the *NBC Handbook* (1984), and *WNW Guide* (1984) prefer the Frenchified koo-**TUUR**-ee-AY. *WNW 3* (1997) and *OED 2* (1989) mark the word as foreign (meaning it should be printed in italics) and prefer the even more Frenchified koo-tuur-YAY. I say there's already enough froufrou and foofaraw in high fashion and the word's been English for a hundred years. Three current dictionaries — *American Heritage 3* (1992), *M-W 10* (1993), and *RHWC* (1997) — list the anglicized koo-TUUR-ee-ur first, and I predict that if this is not already the dominant pronunciation, it surely will be soon. For the feminine form, *couturière,* if it must be used at all, I recommend the same pronunciation.

covert Traditionally, KUH-vurt (like *cover* + *t*). Now usually KOH-vurt.

In his *New Fowler's MEU,* Burchfield (1996) sums up the KUH-vurt vs. KOH-vurt situation nicely: "The traditional pronunciation [KUH-vu(r)t] is still favoured by most people in Britain, but the current pronunciation [KOH-vurt] is gaining ground outside the U.S. all the time. The American pronunciation is perhaps derived from the spelling . . . but, more likely, is influenced by its antonym *overt.*"

KOH-vurt didn't see the light of dictionary until *Webster 3* (1961). As far as I can determine it has been heard in American speech since the 1930s, when Opdycke (1939) disapproved of it: "It is pronounced *kuv′ ert,* not *kove ′rt,* not *kahv′ ert.*" My guess is that it probably got a big boost during the McCarthy era, when certain folks were worried about spies in the pumpkin patch and under the streets and needed a particularly ugly and alarming way to pronounce that. After its debut in *Webster 3,* KOH-vurt kept a low profile for a while, hanging out in the back rooms of shadowy hotbeds of subterfuge like the Pentagon, State Department, and the CIA. Then came Watergate, and people had something really ugly to be alarmed about — they saw that even the president of the United States can be unscrupulous and underhanded! With Watergate, KOH-vurt came out of the closet, paraded itself on radio and TV, and made it clear that from now on it would be calling the shots. Since then I don't believe I have heard a single American broadcaster say KUH-vurt (no, make that one — *me*), and even Lass & Lass (1976) and the *NBC Handbook* (1984) prefer KOH-vurt. That is indeed alarming.

I know that by championing KUH-vurt over KOH-vurt (and the even beastlier koh-VURT, which has come into vogue in the past ten or fifteen years and which no authority with a reputation to lose prefers) I am on the losing side of the war. But current dictionaries still list KUH-vurt in good standing, and there are still enough of us, I remain convinced, to fight the good fight for at least another generation. After that, who knows? In the meantime I shall continue to give aid and sympathy to the underdog. That's the American way, isn't it?

Cowper (William) KOO-pur.

coyote ky-YOH-tee (recommended). Now less often, KY-oht.

Both the disyllabic KY-oht and trisyllabic ky-YOH-tee have been heard in educated speech since the word first appeared in dictionaries in the late 1800s. Until the 1960s most authorities gave priority to KY-oht. Since then the weight of authority has shifted in favor of ky-YOH-tee. Although Merriam-Webster's dictionaries have listed KY-oht first since *Webster 2* (1934), there is no question that the dominant pronunciation today is ky-YOH-tee, and KY-oht now is heard chiefly in the western U.S.

credo KREE-doh or KRAY-doh.

Both pronunciations are equally acceptable in cultivated speech. The word is Latin for "I believe"; KREE-doh shows the so-called English, or anglicized, pronunciation, KRAY-doh the "Roman" or "classical" pronunciation. The evidence of my ears tells me that KRAY-doh probably is now more common, but if you like to pick nits, which I do, then you could argue (or take it on faith) that KREE-doh is preferred by more authorities (including me), especially those in the first half of the century. Just don't expect to win the debate.

crème de cacao See **crème de menthe**.

crème de la crème See next entry.

crème de menthe KREM duh MAHNT (KREM rhyming with *Clem*, MAHNT rhyming with *want*).

The variants KREEM (like *cream*) for *crème* and MENTH (as in *menthol*) or MINT (like *mint*) for *menthe* first appeared in *Webster 3* (1961) and now enjoy the blessing of most current dictionaries. They are not recommended here, however, for the same reason I would advise against pronouncing *crème de la crème* as KREEM duh lah KREEM instead of KREM duh lah KREM: they're clunky anglicizations that fall flat upon the ear like a failed soufflé. The way I see it, if you're going to stuff an ostentatious chunk of French into your conversation, you might as well try to give it some flair.

The quasi-French (see **quasi-**) KREM duh MAHNT (without the slightly guttural *r* and just a smidgen of nasalized *n*) is listed first in *American Heritage 3* (1992) and *WNW 3* (1997) and is the preference of the *NBC Handbook* (1984). It is the pronunciation I would use if I ever had to, but frankly I try to stay away from the stuff. Likewise with *crème de cacao,* which is pronounced KREM duh kuh-KOW.

crisis (singular) KRY-sis; **crises** (plural) KRY-seez (like *cry seize*).

Do not say KRY-seez (*crises*) when you are referring to a single KRY-sis (*crisis*), as I have all too often heard well-educated speakers do. And at all costs avoid the beastly misspelling *crisises* and its accompanying beastly mispronunciation KRY-si-seez. As Burchfield explains in his *New Fowler's MEU* (1996), "Some common words regularly retain the Latin pl[ural], e.g., *bases, crises, oases, theses* (not *basises, crisises, oasises, thesises*)." See **basis, diagnosis, thesis.**

croissant kruh-SAHNT.

French bugs me. When French words enter English, it always raises the difficult question of how to walk that fine line between sounding like a pompous toad or sounding like an ignorant toad. The question becomes even more irritating when you ponder how, in this world of all-important first impressions, the act of pronouncing the name of a falciform blob of flaky dough can make you sound like a gump.*

If you say kwah-SAH(N) or kwah-SAW(N), with a Frenchified *r* and *n,* they'll think you're a supercilious snob. If you say kwah-SAHNT, with a Frenchified *r* and anglicized *n,* they'll think you're a supercilious slob. And if you say kruh-SAHNT, with an anglicized *r* and *n,* they'll probably think that nothing but junk food has ever passed your lips and that your brains are as adipose as your diet. Current dictionaries, which sanction both the French and anglicized variants, are of little help. So what can you do? Allow me to feed you some simple advice.

For me, the answer is plain. To borrow a fine phrase from Alfred H. Holt (1937), vain attempts at the French should cease. Unless you are French, or fluent in French, this is one tough word to pronounce in French, so for most of us there's no point in trying. And unless you prefer the sort of company in which ostentatious displays of Continentalism (perhaps over a continental breakfast featuring the flaky, falciform blob of dough in question) are the expected method of establishing one's social and intellectual credentials, the pseudo-French kwah-SAH(N) and half-anglicized kwah-SAHNT seem equally pointless and pompous. *Croissants* have been part of English for a hundred years now — the first citation in *OED 2* (1989) is from 1899 — and speakers of English who like to eat them de-

---

* *Gump,* a complete nitwit, "a silly, stupid fellow," says *Webster 2.*

serve some lingual relief. It's time to stop torturing and contorting our organs of speech over this word and say it in a manner comfortable to the English tongue (and nose). To some the pronunciation kruh-SAHNT, with a normal English *r* and *n*, may seem lowbrow now, but it is sensible and comprehensible, and it will undoubtedly prevail.

culinary Properly, **KYOO**-li-NER-ee. Now usually **KUHL**-i-NER-ee.

"This word, which means 'pertaining to the kitchen,' is often mispronounced *cullinary* as though the *u* were short," says Gilmartin (1936). "Make it long, sounding the first syllable exactly like the letter *q*," he admonishes, echoing the advice of his fellow orthoepists Phyfe (1926), Vizetelly (1929), Holt (1937), Lloyd (1938), and Opdycke (1939).

It is a matter of no small irony that the pronunciation **KUHL**-i-NER-ee — which of course has thriven despite these caveats — may have been imported from Britain, which is hardly renowned for its culinary art. According to *OED* lexicographer Burchfield (1996), the first syllable is pronounced kuhl- in British English, and although *OED 2* (1989) lists kyoo- first, another respected British authority, Jones (1991), gives kuhl- and calls kyoo- "old-fashioned."

The kuhl- variant did not appear in an American dictionary until the 1960s; since then it has proliferated in American speech. Nevertheless, only the Merriam-Webster dictionaries have listed it first, and of all my American sources published since 1960, only Barnhart (1988) prefers it. The traditional **KYOO**-li-NER-ee is the first pronunciation given in *American Heritage 3* (1992), *RHWC* (1997), and *WNW 3* (1997); it is the only pronunciation in Funk & Wagnalls *New Practical Standard* (1962), *Scribner-Bantam* (1979), *Oxford American* (1980), and *Everyday Reader's* (1985); and it is preferred by Lass & Lass (1976) and the *NBC Handbook* (1984).

Note: I have heard some speakers, including a reporter on NPR, say KOO-li-NER-ee (KOO- as in *cool*). Current dictionaries do not recognize this variant. Be sure to make the *u* long, as in *cute*.

cumin KUHM-in, not KYOO-min or KOO-min.

Cumin (which formerly was also spelled *cummin*) should rhyme with *summon*, not with *human*. Think of "I'm comin'" and you'll remember how to say it.

For several years I had the audacity to believe, without any evidence, that KYOO-min was correct. Can you imagine my chagrin when someone politely asked if that was the proper pronunciation and I finally took the time to take my own advice and look it up? At that time (the late 1980s) only one solitary source, *Random House II* (1987), recognized K(Y)OO-min, undoubtedly because enough fools like me had somehow gotten it into their head that the *yoo* or *oo* sound was more "elegant." Of course that's balderdash, but dictionaries will record any sort of nonsense if enough people decide to swallow and regurgitate it. In the ensuing decade two more dictionaries — *M-W 10* (1993) and *American Heritage 3* (1992) — have countenanced K(Y)OO-min as an alternative pronunciation (with KUHM-in still listed first). *OED 2* (1989) and *WNW 3* (1997), however, sanction only the traditional KUHM-in, which I recommend as the only unaffected and unimpeachable pronunciation. See **basil**.

cumulative KYOOM-yuh-luh-tiv (recommended) or **KYOOM**-yuh-LAY-tiv.

Both pronunciations are acceptable in educated speech; the one recommended is, by the evidence of my ears, more commonly heard. A historical examination reveals that although current dictionaries accord the two pronunciations equal authority, most sources since the mid-1800s favor KYOOM-yuh-luh-tiv. Phyfe (1926), Kenyon & Knott (1949), and *American College* (1952) prefer **KYOOM**-yuh-LAY-tiv, and the formidable *Webster 2* (1934) lists it first; however, Worcester (1860), Funk & Wagnalls *Standard* (1897), the *Century* (1914), Vizetelly (1929), the *Winston Dictionary* (1951), Lass & Lass (1976), *Oxford American* (1980), the *NBC Handbook* (1984), and *OED 2* (1989) prefer KYOOM-yuh-luh-tiv.

cupola KYOO-puh-luh.

This is the only standard pronunciation, as a lexicographer might say, or, as I would put it, the only acceptable pronunciation in educated speech.

For some reason *cupola* has proved to be a tongue twister for many speakers. There are two beastly mispronunciations to avoid: KYOO-puh-loh, which makes the word sound as if it were spelled *cupalo,* and KOO-pyoo-luh, which makes it sound as if it were spelled *coopula.* Both variants appear in *Webster 3* (1961) labeled with an obelus [÷], meaning that many consider them unacceptable. *Webster 3*'s latest abridgment, *M-W 10* (1993), does not list KOO-pyoo-luh and also labels KYOO-puh-luh substandard. All other current sources sanction only KYOO-puh-luh. For more on beastly mispronunciations involving sound flip-flops, see **dimunition, irrelevant, jewelry, jubilant, nuclear.**

curator Traditionally, kyuu-RAY-tur. Now usually KYUUR-ay-tur or KYOOR-ay-tur or, less often (but customarily in law), KYUUR-uh-tur. Lass & Lass (1976), the *NBC Handbook* (1984), and Barnhart (1988) prefer second-syllable stress, and three of the four major current American dictionaries put it first, but the variants with first-syllable stress now predominate in American speech.

cyclic SY-klik or SIK-lik; **cyclical** SY-kli-kul or SIK-li-kul.

Both SY-klik (like *sigh click*) and SIK- (like *sick lick*) are correct. Current authorities generally prefer the former, which is more common today. I prefer the latter; the rhyme created by the two short *i* sounds seems more mellifluous to my ears. It is not true that SY-klik is American and

[93]

SIK-lik British. The British *OED 1* (1928) gives only SIK-lik and the 1924 edition of Daniel Jones's *English Pronouncing Dictionary* lists it first, but *OED 2* (1989) and the 14th edition of Jones (1991) put SY-klik first. Meanwhile, older American authorities — including Worcester (1860), Funk & Wagnalls *Standard* (1897) and *New Standard* (1913), *Webster's New International* (1909), the *Century* (1914), and Phyfe (1926) — prefer SIK-lik, and Vizetelly (1929) says the "best modern usage gives the *y* the sound of *i* as in 'pin.'" The difference is not national or cultural, but one of a general shift in custom over time. "Modern usage" now clearly favors SY-klik, but SIK-lik is still listed in good standing.

cynosure SYN-uh-SHOOR (or -SHUUR).

First syllable like *sign* is the traditional American pronunciation. The British prefer *sin* for the first syllable and sometimes -ZHOOR or -SYUUR for the last.

D

Daedalus DED'l-l<u>u</u>s.

Veteran radio broadcaster Paul Harvey says DAYD'l-<u>us</u>, which is flat-out wrong. There is no authority for this eccentric mispronunciation. *Daed-* should sound like *dead,* making *Daedulus* rhyme approximately with *peddle us.* The British make it *deed* and rhyme it with *needle us.* The adjective is *Daedalian* (d<u>i</u>-DAY-lee-<u>i</u>n).

daguerreotype duh-GAIR-uh-typ, not duh-GAIR-ee-uh-typ.

Properly, the word is pronounced in four syllables, not five. This early photographic process was developed in 1839 by Louis Daguerre (duh-GAIR). The word has three elements, *Daguerre, -o-,* and *-type,* in which the *-o-,* being unstressed, has an intermediate or obscure sound. "Rhyme the whole business with 'a *pair* o' snipe,'" says Holt (1937).

The five-syllable variant duh-GAIR-ee-uh-typ, which arose possibly by association with *stereotype,* has been listed in good standing by most dictionaries since the 1930s. That acceptance is not by any means universal, however. Among current sources, *OED 2* (1989) and *American Heritage 3* (1992) countenance only duh-GAIR-uh-typ, and Lass & Lass (1976), the *NBC Handbook* (1984), and Barnhart (1988) all prefer the four-syllable pronunciation. Moreover, *WNW 3* (1997), *RHWC* (1997), and *M-W 10* (1993) all list duh-GAIR-uh-typ first, with the last labeling the five-syllable variant "appreciably less common."

I recommend duh-GAIR-uh-typ for the following reasons: you cannot divide the word into five syllables in print — it would be incorrect to

---

a = at / <u>a</u> = final / ah = spa / ahr = car / air = fair / ay = hay / aw = saw
ch = chip / e = let / <u>e</u> = item / ee = see / eer = deer / i = sit / <u>i</u> = April
ng = sing / <u>o</u> = carrot / oh = go / oo = soon / or = for / oor = poor
ow = cow / oy = toy / sh = she / th = thin / <u>th</u> = this / <u>u</u> = focus / uh = up
ur = turn / uu = pull, took / y, eye = by, I / zh = measure / (see full key, p. xiv)

hyphenate it *daguerr-eotype;* the proper pronunciation of this eponymous word is more than a nicety — it is an act of historical preservation; and the weight of authority, as noted above, favors four syllables, and careful speakers continue to say it that way. See **bolivar, decibel.**

daiquiri DY-kuh-ree (recommended). Often DAK-uh-ree.

At a '50s-retro restaurant in San Diego, a sign over the bar advertises a concoction called a "tunafish daiquiri." (Possible sales pitch: "Perfect for designated drivers. One sniff and you've had enough.") The form *tunafish* is irregular, but that's of no concern here. What I was taken by was the *i*-less spelling *daquiri,* which I had never seen before. Was it, as I suspected, a misguided attempt to spell the word like the oft-heard variant pronunciation DAK-uh-ree?

First, this news: the species of rum cocktail under discussion was named after Daiquirí, Cuba (Spanish pronunciation: dy-kee-REE), the town where it is said to have originated. The word entered English about 1920, when F. Scott Fitzgerald used it in *This Side of Paradise:* "If you ask me, I want a double Daiquiri." (Just go easy on the tuna, Fitz.) *Daiquiri* didn't appear in a dictionary until the late 1940s *(American College),* and by then the variant DAK-uh-ree had caught on and was listed after DY-kuh-ree.

OED 2 (1989) lists *daquiri* as a variant spelling, for which it provides two obscure citations from 1929 and 1935, the latter from a cookbook that in giving the recipe for the drink manages to commit two solecisms in a single sentence: "Fill your tumbler with dry crusted ice, and pour over Baccardi rum." (It's Bacardi rum, of course, and it makes a lot more sense to pour the rum over the ice instead of the other way around.) A few "tunafish daquiris" with "Baccardi" rum do not an alternative spelling make, I'm afraid, which is probably why American dictionaries have never sanctioned *daquiri.* (The word is an American invention.) It remains to be seen, however, whether the growing popularity of DAK-ur-ee will eventually establish the *i*-less spelling.

If you follow my advice, it won't, because I say DY-kuh-ree has the pedigree here and DAK-uh-ree is illegitimate. Anyone who has had even the slightest exposure to Spanish knows that DY- preserves the proper Spanish diphthong and the flavor of the drink's Cuban birthplace, whereas DAK- bears no resemblance to Spanish and comes straight out of nowhere. My guess is that DAK- was a product of the Anglophone's characteristic sloppy-lipped handling of foreign names, which familiar repetition over time has dignified. That's why you'd never catch Ricky Ricardo drinking DAK-uh-reez, but when he's off rehearsing at the club, Lucy might share a pitcher of them with Ethel and Fred.

Here's how current authorities weigh in on the matter. *WNW Guide* (1984) prefers DAK- and *WNW 3* (1988, 1997) labels DY- less frequent.

Although it pains me to admit it, that may now be true, which is probably why *M-W 10* (1993) lists DAK- first, reversing the order of previous Merriam-Webster dictionaries. Holding the line for DY- are Lass & Lass (1976), *Oxford American* (1980), and the *NBC Handbook* (1984), and *American Heritage 3* (1992) and *RHWC* (1997) list DY- first. For more on pronunciation influencing spelling, see **commingle, entrepreneur, minuscule**.

dais DAY-is, not DY-is.

Burchfield (1996) points out that *dais* was pronounced in one syllable (rhyming with *lace*) until the beginning of the 20th century but in two syllables since then. What he neglects to comment on is the question we are concerned with here — whether the first of those two syllables should be pronounced like *day* or like *die*.

The answer is, never say *die*. Those who do, though blatantly wrong, are sufficient enough in number to have won recognition in the dictionaries. Those who say *day*, however, can point to every 20th-century authority to support their claim of propriety. All the orthoepists — from Phyfe (1926), Opdycke (1939), and Kenyon & Knott (1949) to Lass & Lass (1976), the *NBC Handbook* (1986), and Barnhart (1988) — prefer DAY-is. From *Webster 2* (1934) to *OED 2* (1989), dictionaries list DAY-is first; some (including the two just cited) do not recognize DY-is, and even the chronically charitable *M-W 10* (1993) sternly labels it "considered by some to be unacceptable."

Nevertheless, as Morris & Morris (1985) note, "an astonishing number of otherwise educated people say [DY-is], which is incorrect." Those who pronounce the first syllable *die* are wrong not simply because most educated speakers pronounce it *day*. (Tyranny of the majority, by itself, rarely constitutes a compelling case for me, and I often find it repugnant.) They are wrong because they treat the *a* and *i* not as separate vowels to be sounded distinctly, but as a diphthong with a single, gliding sound; then, in the second syllable they again pronounce the vowel (the *i*) that they have already incorporated in the first. Thus, to justify the pronunciation DY-is, *dais* would have to be spelled with two *i*'s — *daiis*. For more on this type of mistake, see **zoology**.

data DAY-tuh.

DAY-tuh is the first pronunciation listed in all four major current American dictionaries — *American Heritage 3* (1992), *M-W 10* (1993), *RHWC* (1997), and *WNW 3* (1997) — and it is preferred by Lass & Lass (1976), the *NBC Handbook* (1984), *OED 2* (1989), and Burchfield (1996). The alternative pronunciation DAT-uh has been recorded since the 1940s, but has always been listed after DAY-tuh. Another variant, DAH-tuh (with the broad *a* of *father*), is sometimes listed third; it dates to the 19th century, or perhaps earlier, and is infrequently heard today.

Data is pronounced DAY-tuh, with a long *a,* because it comes from Latin and follows the rules for the so-called English pronunciation of Latin. According to this method, says *Webster 2* (1934), "Vowels, when ending accented syllables, have always their long English sounds, as *pater* [PAY-tur], *homo* [HOH-moh]." The first syllable of *data* is accented and ends in the vowel *a;* therefore, the *a* is long, as in *day.* See **apparatus, erratum, gratis, status.**

-day In days of the week, -day or -dee; elsewhere, now usually -day.

For the days of the week and *yesterday,* I prefer the so-called spelling pronunciation -day (SUHN-day, etc., YES-tur-day) rather than the long *e* sound of *me* that some speakers prefer (SUHN-dee, etc., YES-tur-dee). For many years I thought (naturally) that my -day was correct and refined and their -dee was beastly and Boeotian. (See **Boeotian.**) Not so at all, I have since learned. Here's the difference a *-day* makes:

"When *ay* comes immediately after the accent in a final syllable, like *ai,* it drops the [long *a* sound], in the colloquial pronunciation of the days of the week," wrote the esteemed early English elocutionist John Walker (1791). "Thus as we pronounce *captain, curtain,* &c. as if written *captin, curtin,* &c. so we hear *Sunday, Monday,* &c. as if written *Sundy, Mondy,* &c. A more distinct pronunciation of *day,* in these words, is a mark of the northern dialect."

Nearly a century and a half later, *Webster 2* (1934) sanctioned -dee for *-day* for all the days of the week except Saturday, for which it gives both -dee and -day. "**Saturday** and **yesterday,** when they have a light rhythmic accent on **-day,** are occasionally pronounced [SAT-ur-day, YES-tur-day], but ordinarily are [-di]," *Webster 2* explains. "But when **-day** has a secondary accent, it is [-day]," as in *weekday, workaday, payday, heyday, everyday, doomsday, mayday,* and *holiday.*

From this you might conclude that the pronunciation -day, with the long *a* sound, is a mid-20th-century development that spread from *Saturday* and *yesterday* to all the days of the week. Not so, again. Vizetelly (1929), in his discussion of *Monday,* says the -di (short *i*) or more common -dee (long *e*) pronunciation for *-day* "should be discouraged in favor of one that is more distinct. This should approximate to the sound of *a* in 'chaste,' and was formerly so heard in Scotland, the north of England, and in Ireland. Fenning (1760), Perry (1777), and Sheridan (1780) so indicated it, but Walker (1791) gave to the *a* the sound of *e* in 'me.'"

Today, although current American dictionaries all list the -dee pronunciation in good standing, the evidence of my ears agrees with *WNW 3* (1997), which marks -dee for all the days of the week and *yesterday* as either less frequent or occasional.

debacle di-BAH-kul. Do not say DEB-uh-kul.

The accent should be on the second syllable, which is preferably pro-nounced -BAH-, as in *box,* but which may also be pronounced -BAK-, like *back.* The first syllable may be pronounced with a lightened *e,* like *de-* in *defeat* or *depend,* or with a long *a* sound, as in *décor* (day-KOR) and *détente* (day-TAHNT). The former is recommended, but the latter is counte-nanced by many authorities.

With several acceptable variants, you'd think it would be nearly impos-sible to mispronounce *debacle.* In recent years, however, speakers who are fond of innovation or who are unfamiliar with the word (or both) have begun saying DEB-uh-kul, with the stress on the first syllable. This mis-pronunciation appears in *M-W 9* (1985), but *M-W 10* (1993), in an abrupt turnabout, labels DEB-uh-kul unacceptable to some, and *WNW 3* (1997) and *RHWC* (1997) do not recognize it.

debridement di-BREED-mint; **debride** di-BREED.
There's always one in the bunch who likes to play Stump the Teacher. One night about ten years ago I was speaking at a San Diego bookstore known for its cultured clientele, and when it came time to field questions from the audience, sure enough, a savvy person (who works with doctors) asked me about *debridement.*

Gulp! I take pride in my vocabulary, and I have spent much time developing it, the way some folks build their muscles. But goshdarnit if I wasn't stumped on this one. *Debridement?* It looked like a legal term for defloration or the breaking off of an engagement.

When I shared that impression I got a laugh, thank goodness, which mitigated some of the stigma of "ignorance" I felt not knowing the word. This stigma, however, is more imagined than real; it is usually self-imposed and, in the long run, always detrimental. I have learned that it is best to admit right away that I do not know a word, for experience has taught me an important lesson about vocabulary and intelligence: no matter how large your vocabulary, there will always be words you don't know. To come across a new one, therefore, is always a blessing, an opportunity to expand your knowledge of the world; it is never a verdict on your intelligence. As you grow older there are many things you cannot do as well as you once did. But you can always improve your vocabulary, and each word learned yields great rewards. There is no attendant embarrassment in that activity, only a sense of wonder and accomplishment. And so that night I tossed aside my self-consciousness and learned a fascinating word, which I now can share in this book.

Debridement (sometimes spelled with an accent, *débridement*) is a surgi-cal term used chiefly by doctors and dentists. *WNW 3* (1997) defines it as "the cutting away of dead or contaminated tissue or foreign material from a wound to prevent infection." The woman who asked me about it had heard it pronounced several ways, and she wondered if doctors said it one way and dentists another. I have found no evidence indicating a professional distinction.

Debridement came into English from French about 1840 and for over a hundred years the only recognized pronunciation was the French, day-breed-MAW(N). *Webster 3* (1961) is the first of my sources to countenance the anglicized alternative di-BREED-mint, which has since become the dominant pronunciation. A poll of current sources shows that *M-W 9* (1985) and *10* (1993), *WNW 3* (1988, 1997), *Random House II* (1987), and *RHWC* (1997) all list di-BREED-mint first, and the *Quintessential Dictionary* (1978) and *Everyday Reader's* (1985) give only this pronunciation. (Some authorities also note day- for the first syllable.)

The French pronunciation, day-breed-MAW(N), is still acceptable: *American Heritage 3* (1992) lists it first and *OED 2* (1989) and my three medical dictionaries — *Taber's* (1970), *Stedman's* (1972), and *Mosby's* (1990) — prefer it. However, considering how long the word has been in the language and how often it must be used today by medical professionals, the French pronunciation seems stilted. Since I learned the word I have heard a few surgeons use it, and I have asked a few doctors and dentists their preference, and they all said di-BREED-mint. That's not a scientific survey, of course, just some anecdotal evidence offered to bolster my contention that the anglicized pronunciation is more natural for American speakers and in time will undoubtedly eclipse the French.

The woman who *debrided* (di-BREE-did) my brain with this word also asked me if the spelling pronunciation di-BRYD-mint (-BRYD- like *bride*), which she had sometimes heard from her fellow health professionals, was kosher. When she posed the question ten years ago no dictionary had recognized it, and the same is true today; it is safe to say, then, that di-BRYD-mint is nonstandard and should be avoided.

debris (American) duh-BREE; (British) DEB-ree or DAY-bree.

Debussy (Claude) DEB-yuu-**SEE**.

A survey of current sources shows that there are two acceptable English pronunciations for this French impressionist composer's surname: DEB-yuu-**SEE** and duh-BYOO-see. In the former, a long *a* sound is also acceptable: DAYB-yuu-**SEE**. *RHWC* (1997) lists an adjective, *Debussyan*, pronounced duh-BYOO-see-in.

I recommend DEB-yuu-**SEE** here for two reasons: my upbringing as the son of two conservatory-trained, professional musicians and the evidence of my adult ears suggest that it is more common in educated speech; and it does little or no offense to the original French.

debut (verb) day-BYOO; (noun) day-BYOO or DAY-byoo.

decathlon di-KATH-lahn or di-KATH-lun.

Decathlon and *pentathlon* (pen-TATH-lahn or -l<u>u</u>n) have three syllables. Don't add a fourth and pronounce the words *decath-a-lon* and *pentath-a-lon*. Dictionaries do not recognize these four-syllable pronunciations, and *WNW Guide* (1984) calls them "not standard." I call them beastly.

decibel DES-i-bel, not DES-i-buul.

Don't slur the last syllable. Properly, there is no *bull* in *decibel*. Make sure to pronounce the *e* as clear as a *bell*.

The *bel* in this word comes from Alexander Graham Bell. An *ohm* (named after George Simon Ohm) is never called an *um*, nor is a *watt* (named after James Watt) ever called a *what*. The legacy of an important man is at stake here.

The slurred pronunciation of -*bel* probably arose out of false analogy with *decimal*. Although two current dictionaries list DES-i-buul first and the *NBC Handbook* (1984) prefers it, the weight of authority is resoundingly on the side of DES-i-bel: it is the preference of *Webster 2* (1934), Kenyon & Knott (1949), *American College* (1952), Lass & Lass (1976), *Everyday Reader's* (1985), and *OED 2* (1989). See **bolivar, daguerreotype**.

décolletage DAY-kawl-**TAHZH** (recommended).

The primary stress should fall on the final syllable. The second syllable may be pronounced like *call*, like *col-* in *college*, or like *coal*. Standard variants, all of which are fashionable in educated speech, include DAY-kahl-**TAHZH,** DAY-kohl-**TAHZH,** DAY-**kahl-uh-TAHZH,** DAY-kawl-uh-**TAHZH,** and DAY-kohl-uh-**TAHZH.** Less often listed, and not recommended, are DEK-uh-luh-**TAHZH** and DEK-luh-**TAZH.**

Décolletage entered English in the 1890s. The earliest sources in which I found it are *Webster's Collegiate* (1917) and Phyfe (1926), which give DAY-kawl-**TAHZH,** the pronunciation recommended above. This is also the preference of *Webster 2* (1934), *American College* (1952), Jones (1991), and *American Heritage 3* (1992); the *NBC Handbook* (1984) prefers the almost identical DAY-kahl-**TAHZH.** The four-syllable variants are all at least fifty years old, and were first catalogued by *Webster 3* (1961). The most popular today appears to be DAY-kah-luh-**TAHZH,** which *RHWC* (1997), *WNW 3* (1997), and *M-W 10* (1993) list first. Only Lass & Lass (1976) prefer the more anglicized variant DEK-uh-luh-**TAHZH,** which appears in *RHWC;* a three-syllable version of this, DEK-luh-**TAZH,** appears in *M-W 10*.

décor day-KOR.

decrease (noun) DEE-krees; (verb) di-KREES.

Throughout this book I refer to something I call "Phyfe's rule," which is this:

In words of two syllables . . . that do double duty as nouns or adjectives on the one hand and as verbs on the other, it is the custom, with a few exceptions, to accent the nouns and adjectives upon the *first* syllable and the verbs upon the *last*.

— W. H. P. Phyfe, *18,000 Words Often Mispronounced* (1926)

In his *New Fowler's Modern English Usage* (1996), R. W. Burchfield echoes Phyfe:

When, for historical reasons, a word is made to do double duty as a noun and a verb, the language from almost the earliest times has shown a strong tendency to differentiate the two by pronunciation. . . . A large number of disyllabic nouns and verbs are also distinguished by the placing of the stress, the normal pattern being shown in e.g. *áccent* (noun), *accént* (verb); *cómpound* (noun), *compóund* (verb).

This custom, or general tendency, from which Phyfe's rule springs applies to many words today. Following is a partial list (in which the bold-faced examples appear as separate entries in this book):

Disyllabic (DY-si-**LAB**-ik) words that function as both nouns, with the accent on the *first* syllable, and verbs, with the accent on the *second* syllable, include *abstract,* **accent** (now often AK-sent for both noun and verb), *addict, affect, affix,* **ally** (a few speakers still say uh-LY for both noun and verb), *annex* (many speakers now also stress the first syllable for the verb), *combat, combine, commune, compact, compound, compress, conduct, confine, conflict, conscript, console, consort, contest, contract* (often KAHN-trakt for the verb in business contexts), *contrast, converse, convert, convict,* **defect** (though often di-FEKT for the noun as well), *descant, desert,* **digest,** *discharge, discord, discount, discourse, escort, essay, excerpt, exploit, export, extract,* **ferment,** *import, imprint, incense, incline,* **increase,** *inlay, insert, insult, intrigue, object,* **perfume, permit,** *pervert, prefix,* **presage,** *present,* **produce, progress, project, protest** (in America often PROH-test for the verb as well), *rebel, record,* **refund,** *refuse, reject, relapse, relay, reprint, subject, survey, suspect, torment,* **transfer,** and *transport.**

In a far smaller category we have the disyllabic words that function as both adjectives, with *first*-syllable stress, and verbs, with *second*-syllable stress. These include *absent,* **frequent,** *perfect, present,* and *suspect.*

Exceptions to Phyfe's rule — and of course, as with all rules, there are plenty — include *access* (the verb, which comes from the jargon of computer science and dates back to 1966, is pronounced AK-ses, like the noun); **address** (formerly always uh-DRES for noun and verb but now often A-dres for the noun); *bias; burden; butcher; cement; comment; compact* (the

---

* Although I loathe the word *impact* used as a voguish substitute for *influence,* I must note, reluctantly, that it also belongs in this list.

adjective is often stressed on the second syllable); *consent; contact; critique; decline; defeat; delay;* **deluge;** **detail** (some authorities prefer second-syllable stress for the noun); *dictate* (the British generally preserve the noun-verb distinction, but Americans no longer do); *dirty; disdain; disgust; dispute; distance;* **divine;** *doctor; effect; elbow; empty; finance* (some speakers say fi-NANS for noun and verb while others prefer FY-nans for both); *format* (the verb, a 1964 creation from computer science, is pronounced FOR-mat, like the noun); **grimace** (traditionally, gri-MAYS for both noun and verb); *handle; harangue; lower; lumber; master; mistake; neglect; notice; outrage; parade; parent; people; preface;* **process;** *profile;* **program; research** (properly, ri-SURCH for both noun and verb); *raffle; ruffle; salute; select; service; silence; spirit; total; tutor;* and *weather.*

Larsen and Walker (1930) point out that most disyllabic words beginning with *re-* have their stress on the second syllable, "whether used as verbs, nouns, or adjectives" — for example, *refrain, relate, release, remove, reply, repeal, report, request, respect, result, retreat, return, revenge, revolt,* and *reward.* (See **recess, recourse, redress, repeat,** and **research,** which traditionally have their accent on the second syllable but which in varying degrees have been bucking the trend.)

Newscasters are some of the worst offenders of Phyfe's rule, especially with the words *decrease* and *increase.* Sometimes they shift the accent of the noun to the second syllable (which sounds extremely strange), and very often they shift the accent of the verb to the first syllable. In the first case I suspect it is mere affectation. In the second case I suspect they are prompted by the misguided notion that emphasizing the contrasting prefixes *in-* and *de-* will make them sound more articulate and ensure our comprehension. Not only is this unnecessary, it is condescending; anyone is capable of understanding these and analogous words when they are pronounced properly. The newscasters who say "crime has *de*creased in the past year" or "a chance of showers *in*creasing overnight" do not serve clarity; they merely display their ignorance of Phyfe's rule — the distinction that educated speakers customarily make between the nouns *decrease* (DEE-krees) and *increase* (IN-krees) and the verbs to *decrease* (di-KREES) and *increase* (in-KREES).

defect (noun) DEE-fekt (recommended) or di-FEKT; (verb) di-FEKT.
Many older authorities prefer second-syllable stress for both noun and verb, and this is still acceptable. However, in the past sixty years or so there has been a strong trend, which I support, to make the word conform with Phyfe's rule (discussed under *decrease* above) by stressing the noun on the first syllable and the verb on the second. Reflecting this trend, the four major current American dictionaries list DEE-fekt first for the noun. Many Americans stress the second syllable in the phrase *birth defect(s),* but elsewhere di-FEKT is becoming rare.

defendant di-FEN-dint or dee-FEN-dint. Do not say di-FEN-dant or dee-FEN-dant.

Despite what you may hear from certain pompous lawyers, judges, and jurists, there is no *ant* in *defendant.* In cultivated, nonlegal English the *-ant* is pronounced with a schwa (a lightened or obscure vowel sound), as in *pendant, mordant,* and *discordant.* See **juror.**

defense di-FENS. In sports, often DEE-fens.

In the beer-guzzling, chip-munching, peanut-cracking, hotdog-scarfing, statistic-spewing world of American sports fandom, *defense* is DEE-fens and *offense* is AH-fens (or AW-fens), and *at this point in time* (a favorite redundancy of our sportscasters) there ain't nuthin' gonna change that.

Making an exception for sports usage is fine with me, as long as we do not change the pronunciation of *defense* and *offense* in their other, traditional senses. One's justification for a position is always one's di-FENS. Lawyers do not prepare a DEE-fens for a client, psychiatrists do not speak of DEE-fens mechanisms, nor is America's di-FENS managed by the Department of DEE-fens. The same is true for *offense:* an insult, infraction, assault, or breach of moral conduct is always an uh-FENS, and one always gives or takes uh-FENS, never AH-fens (or AW-fens).

Some dictionaries note that first-syllable stress is often heard when *offense* is used to mean the act of attacking or the person, army, or side that attacks. I am skeptical of that judgment. For example, under the definition "the act of attacking; attack or assault," *Random House II* (1987) gives the sample phrase *weapons of offense.* I think most speakers would pronounce that *weapons of* uh-FENS, not *weapons of* AH-fens; moreover, they would wonder why the phrase is not *offensive weapons,* which is far more common.

It's a question of idiom: an assault on nature is an uh-FENS (not AH-fens) against nature; we stage an *offensive* (uh-FEN-siv), not an *offense;* and only in sport do we *go on offense* (AH-fens); everywhere else we *go on the offensive.* However, unlike in football, we rarely refer to a person, army, or nation as the *offense* in an encounter or war; the person is usually the *attacker* or *offender* and the army or nation the *aggressor.*

Before things get out of hand, why not keep it simple — and idiomatic? When sportscasters and fans speak of DEE-fens and AH-fens, just relax and enjoy the game. In all other contexts, however, hold the line for second-syllable stress. See **error.**

deity DEE-i-tee, not DAY-i-tee.

Rhyme the noun *deity* with *see a tree* and the verb *deify* with *see a fly.*

A little Latin can be a dangerous thing. I suspect that the vogue variant DAY-i-tee got started because certain speakers, possessed of the awesome erudition that a smattering of Latin picked up in school or church confers, could not resist displaying their classical know-how by modeling their pronunciation of the English *deity* after the Latin *deus,* god, pronounced DAY-uus. One example should suffice to illustrate the point: when William Safire of *The New York Times* appealed to his readers, "For God's sake, don't say DAY-ity when you refer to the Deity (say DEE-ity)," one such Latin-deluded reader self-righteously responded, "I don't agree with you at all about *deity.* Think for a moment; it comes from *deus* and you know how to pronounce that, don't you."*

The beastly hybrid DAY-i-tee first gained recognition in *Webster 3* (1961), where it was labeled *sometimes,* meaning it was "infrequent." Today, unfortunately, it is quite frequent — so frequent, in fact, that Burchfield (1996) laments that "the traditional pronunciation [DEE-i-tee] is now regrettably yielding to [DAY-i-tee]." Under such circumstances one would imagine that all our current dictionaries, whose editors typically are always on the qui vivre for any new variant that infiltrates educated speech, would recognize DAY-i-tee. Yet it is remarkable that of the four major American dictionaries only *M-W 10* (1993) lists DAY-i-tee while the others — *American Heritage 3* (1992), *RHWC* (1997), and *WNW 3* (1997) — sanction only the traditional DEE-i-tee. Are these editors going deaf, or, for God's sake, could they perhaps be trying to tell us something? See **homogeneity, spontaneity.**

déjà vu DAY-zhah-**VOO.** Don't say DAY-zhah-**VYOO** (-VYOO like *view*).
Vain (and inane) attempts at the French should cease. Follow the example of *American Heritage 3* (1992) and *WNW 3* (1997), which give only DAY-zhah-**VOO.**

delegate (noun) DEL-uh-git or, less often, DEL-uh-gayt; (verb) DEL-uh-gayt.
It is not true that DEL-uh-gayt (final syllable like *gate*) was once the only proper pronunciation for both noun and verb. DEL-uh-git for the noun can be found in American dictionaries as far back as Funk & Wagnalls *Standard* (1897) and Worcester (1860). Gilmartin (1936) says, "The sound of the *a* is as in *senate* and not as in *plate.* For the verb, the *a* is long as in *fate.*" Lass & Lass (1976) prefer -gayt for both noun and verb, but *WNW Guide* (1984) and the *NBC Handbook* (1984) agree with Gilmartin and three of the four major current American dictionaries list DEL-uh-git (or -git) first for the noun.

This pattern of -it (or -it as in *charity* or *senate*) for the noun or adjective and -ayt (rhymes with *late*) for the verb can be heard in the analogous words *advocate, aggregate, alternate, animate, appropriate, approximate, associate, certificate, conglomerate, degenerate, desolate, duplicate, elaborate, estimate, graduate, incarnate, initiate, laminate, moderate, postulate, precipitate, separate, sophisticate, subordinate,* and *syndicate.*

---

* See *Coming to Terms* (1991), pp. 301–2.

[105]

Candidate remains an exception to the pattern, probably because the word functions almost exclusively as a noun and the rare verb to *candidate* shows little promise of gaining currency. *Random House II* (1987) lists it, but its most recent abridgment, *RHWC* (1997), and the three other major current American dictionaries do not.

deluge (noun and verb) DEL-yooj (like *dell* plus *huge* without the *h*).

Deluge is an exception to Phyfe's rule, discussed above under **decrease**. Both the noun and the verb are pronounced the same, with the accent on the first syllable.

Deluge takes a little practice to pronounce correctly. Difficulty with it has resulted in a DEL-yooj of variants. *RHWC* (1997) gives DEL-yooj first and then lists a ridiculous number of variants: DEL-yoozh, DEL-ooj, DEL-oozh, di-LOOJ, and di-LOOZH — all testimony to the fact that this word causes uncertainty and confusion for a heck of a lot of educated speakers. *M-W 10* (1993) countenances DEL-yooj and DEL-yoozh and then labels di-LOOJ and DAY-looj with an obelus [÷], meaning these variants are "considered by some to be unacceptable." *American Heritage 3* (1992) and *WNW 3* (1997) sensibly give only DEL-yooj, which is also the preference of Lass & Lass (1976), the *NBC Handbook* (1984), *WNW Guide* (1984), and Jones (1991).

deluxe di-LUHKS (second syllable like *lucks*) is recommended.

Less often, di-LUUKS (second syllable rhyming with *books*). Now rarely, di-LOOKS (second syllable rhyming with *dukes*). For the first syllable, dee- (rhyming with *me*) is an overpronunciation.

Deluxe comes from the French *de luxe* (literally, of luxury) and first appeared in English in 1819. The British *OED 2* (1989) gives only the bifurcated French spelling, but most current American authorities prefer the unified *deluxe*.

There are three ways to pronounce the word: di-LUHKS (most anglicized); di-LUUKS (half-anglicized); and di-LOOKS (closest to the French). The first, di-LUHKS, prevails in American speech today. It has been standard for over 70 years; *Webster 2* (1934) listed it in good standing and Opdycke (1939) gave it his blessing. The second, di-LUUKS, once was dominant but is now, in dictionary lingo, "appreciably less common." The third, di-LOOKS, is obsolescent both in the U.S. and Britain.

The transition from di-LUUKS to di-LUHKS as the prevailing pronunciation in American speech has occurred in about the last 30 years. Lass & Lass (1976) prefer di-LUUKS, and Shaw (1972) says it is "more often used by careful, educated speakers." *WNW Guide* (1984) says that di-LUUKS and di-LOOKS "are becoming less and less frequent." All four major current American dictionaries list di-LUHKS first, and only two still record di-LOOKS.

Demeter di-MEE-tur.

All pronunciation mavens have an Achilles heel (or two), and I must confess that until recently the weak spot of mythological magnitude in my spoken vocabulary was *Demeter.* I had always pronounced the name of this Greek goddess of agriculture and fertility with the accent on the first syllable, DEM-i-tur. Then, a few years ago, when the actress Demi Moore was getting a lot of attention for a film or something, I was puzzled when broadcasters would stress the second syllable of her first name, saying di-MEE Moore instead of DEM-ee Moore, which seemed more logical to me. Wondering if *Demi* was perhaps short for *Demeter,* this hapless maven went to a dictionary, and then another dictionary, and then another, and so on, until Zeus finally took pity on me and turned me into a parking meter in midtown Manhattan, where for the rest of time I could listen to New Yorkers saying, "Hey, did ya feed *Demeter?*"

demonstrable di-MAHN-struh-buul.

demonstrative di-MAHN-struh-tiv.

Occasionally one hears some misguided soul stress the first syllable, **DEM**-un-STRAY-tiv. Dictionaries do not recognize this beastly mispronunciation.

demur di-MUR. Do not say di-MYOOR.

Pronounce -*mur* as in *murder,* not as in *mural.*

Demur (di-MUR) and *demure* (di-MYOOR) are frequently confused. The verb to *demur* means to object, take exception to, as in "He accepts and you *demur.*" The adjective *demure* means shy, reserved, or affectedly modest, coy. Many educated speakers slip up by saying *demure* when they mean *demur.* This is an error of overrefinement, like saying AF-tur-**NYOON** for *afternoon.* Take care not to insert a *y* sound between the *m* and *u* in *demur:* di-MUR. In *demure,* however, there is a *y* sound: di-MYOOR. Always stress both *demur* and *demure* on the second syllable.

demure See **demur**.

denouement DAY-noo-**MAH(N)**.

This is the only pronunciation given by *American Heritage 3* (1992), *WNW 3* (1997), and *RHWC* (1997), and the preference of other current American authorities including the *NBC Handbook* (1984) and *Everyday Reader's* (1985). The pronunciation day-NOO-mah(n), with second-syllable stress, is British. *Webster 3* (1961) painstakingly records the anglicized variants duh-NOO-mint and duh-NOO-mahnt, labeled *sometimes,* which I am thankful for. These should be studiously avoided.

Denouement comes directly from French and means literally "an untying"; in English it refers to the final unraveling and resolution of the plot in a drama or novel. Perhaps because *denouement* is a highbrow literary word, confined chiefly to college classes, book reviews, and stuffy cocktail parties, it retains its French flavor in pronunciation. The accent is on the final syllable, -*ment,* in which the *t* is silent, the *n* is nasalized (as in the French *vin* or *mon*), and the whole element has a sound somewhere between the *ma-* in *mama* and the *maw-* in *mawkish.*

depot DEE-poh.

Many authorities mark the alternative pronunciation DEP-oh as chiefly military and British. American usage has always favored DEE-poh, and it seems reasonable to use it for all the word's senses.

deprivation DEP-ri-**VAY**-shin, not DEE-pry-**VAY**-shin.

The small number of speakers who prefer the eccentric pronunciation DEE-pry-**VAY**-shin may pedantically point out that *deprive* is part of the word, or that it is formed from the prefix *de-,* which in this case serves as an intensifier, and *privation,* pronounced pry-VAY-shin; hence, the long vowel sounds. If you follow this sort of specious etymological reasoning, then you ought to say dee-FY-nyt for *definite,* dee-FEER-ints for *deference,* DEE-pree-**DAY**-shin for *depredation,* and so on — which, I dare say, would be REE-pree-*hensible.*

Here are the bare facts about *deprivation:* DEE-pry-**VAY**-shin appears to be an early 20th-century British innovation that has since caught on among those British and American speakers who have a proclivity for hyperarticulate pronunciations. The venerable H. W. Fowler sanctions it, although it does not appear in *OED 1* (1928). My current authorities on British English — *Oxford Guide* (1983), *OED 2* (1989), and Burchfield (1996) — prefer DEP-ri-**VAY**-shin, with Jones (1991) listing DEE-pry- as a less-common alternative. The American elocutionists Vizetelly (1929) and Opdycke (1939) disapproved of DEE-pry-, which first appears as an alternative in *Webster 3* (1961) labeled "appreciably less frequent." Only two of the four major current American dictionaries recognize DEE-pry-, and both label it infrequent.

M-W 9 (1985) is anomalous in dividing the word *de•pri•va•tion.* However, its successor, *M-W 10* (1993), rejoins the rest of the pack, who divide it *dep•ri•va•tion,* which clearly suggests the pronunciation DEP-ri-**VAY**-shin.

depths DEPTHS (with the *p* immediately followed by a *th* as in *tooth*).

Don't say DEPS, with no *th* sound.

Phyfe (1926) says that "the three consonant sounds, occurring in immediate succession, render this word difficult of articulation." No kidding — but no excuse nonetheless. Be sure to lightly smack your lips then slip your tongue between your teeth as you say *depths,* exactly as it is spelled.

de rigueur du-ree-GUR or du-ri-GUR.

In a broadcast of a Cubs vs. Pirates baseball game some years ago, Vin Scully, who is generally a very respectable speaker, stepped just a bit too far out of his ken to reach for the gusto with this line: "Shinguards [for batters] are now day-ri-GAIR." Tom Seaver, his partner in the pronunciation penalty box, gently corrected him in his response, pronouncing this French phrase day-ri-GUR. You could almost hear the umpire shouting, "Vin — you're outta here!" and "Tom — almost, but no SEE-gahr."

I had to sympathize with both gentlemen, for though I knew how to pronounce *rigueur* properly, I too had been mispronouncing *de* as *day*. This French *de*, says *Webster 2* (1934), has the so-called mute *e*, which is like English *e* in *maker*. Its sound is in between UH as in *up* and UU as in *pull* and *look*. Try saying UR as in *purr*, and then again, dropping the double *r*. The vowel sound you are left with is the quality of the *e* in *de*. For lack of an appropriate literal symbol I have transcribed this unusual sound simply as a schwa, du-, as most dictionaries do (they use an upside-down and backwards *e*).

Rigueur may be pronounced ree-GUR, rhyming with *see her* (stress on *her*), or ri-GUR, like *rigor* with the stress on *-gor*. Don't say ri-GAIR, rhyming with *fair*, as Scully did, or ri-GYOOR, rhyming with *pure*. Both are nonstandard (i.e., beastly). For more on the pronunciation of *-eur*, see **amateur, connoisseur, entrepreneur, liqueur, restaurateur**.

Desdemona DEZ-duh-**MOH**-nuh.
Des Moines (Iowa) duh-MOYN.
despicable Traditionally, DES-pik-uh-buul. Now usually di-SPIK-uh-buul. In *There Is No Zoo in Zoology* (1988), I fell in line with my fellow pronunciation mavens, past and present, and fought the good fight for first-syllable stress in *despicable*. A little more than ten years later, I'm ready to give up and go home. It is clear that the devotees of Daffy Duck, the slobbering cartoon character with the penchant for expectorating the second syllable in *despicable*, have won this battle. Occasionally I'll hear an actor in a historical drama, usually a British one, say DES-pik-uh-buul, but among educated Americans of all ages today first-syllable stress has just about gone the way of the dodo. The same is true on the other side of the Atlantic. "In *The Spoken Word* (1981) I recommended [DES-pik-uh-buul], with the stress on the first syllable, i.e. the traditional pronunciation," writes Burchfield (1996), echoing my lament, "but the tide seems now to have turned in favour of [di-SPIK-uh-buul]."

If you are a lifelong di-SPIK-uh-buul speaker, I have no illusions that you will jump ship to join the dwindling band of DES-pik-uh-buul do-does. For the record, however, and for anyone who may care to know, other modern authorities who have registered a preference for first-syllable stress include Shaw (1972), Lass & Lass (1976), *Oxford American* (1980), the *NBC Handbook* (1984), and *OED 2* (1989), and three current dictionaries — *American Heritage 3* (1992), *RHWC* (1997), and *WNW 3* (1997) — still bravely list it first.

desuetude DES-wi-T(Y)OOD.

This twenty-dollar word meaning "a state of disuse" should be pronounced in three syllables, with primary stress on the first syllable. (A long *u* as in *mute* in the final syllable is recommended but optional.) Speakers familiar with the word from literature but unsure how to pronounce it will often hazard a guess and say di-SOO-i-tood, shifting the stress to the second syllable and adding an extra syllable to the word. Apparently, enough educated speakers have used this conjectural pronunciation to attract the attention of the editors at Merriam-Webster, who have recognized it as an alternative in their dictionaries since *Webster 3* (1961). Other current dictionaries do not countenance it, however, and authorities from Walker (1791) to the present favor the three-syllable pronunciation.

desultory DES-ul-TOR-ee (rhymes with *wrestle story*).

Place the primary stress on the first syllable, secondary stress on the third. Avoid saying DEZ- for *des-* and do not accent the second syllable: di-SUHL-tur-ee is wrong.

deteriorate di-TEER-ee-uh-rayt.

Be sure to pronounce all five syllables in *deteriorate*, and all six in *deteriorating* (di-**TEER**-ee-uh-RAY-ting). Do not drop a syllable, as Ross Perot does, and say di-**TEER**-ee-AYT-ing. Perot may be all ears, but his tongue falls apart on this word. Lass & Lass (1976) include *deteriate* for *deteriorate* in a list of slovenly pronunciations "that make their perpetrators sound at least a trifle uneducated," some of the others being *heighth* for *height*, *mischeevious* for *mischievous*, *athalete* for *athlete*, *irrevelant* for *irrelevant*, and *jewlery* for *jewelry*.

detritus di-TRYT-us (rhymes with *arthritis*). Stress the second syllable.

Detritus is debris, disintegrated material; specifically, rock fragments that have worn away from a mass.

Over the years I have heard a number of well-educated people mispronounce this word DE-tri-tus, with the accent on the first syllable instead of on the second. The mispronunciation evidently has been around for quite some time, for Vizetelly (1929) warns not to stress the first syllable. One might suspect the British, with their penchant for recessive accent, are the culprits, but both *OED 2* (1989) and Jones (1991) countenance only second-syllable stress. I suspect it is simply the age-old mistake of the literate mispronouncer who discovers the word in reading, looks up the definition but fails to check the pronunciation, and then simply guesses how to pronounce it based on what "sounds right." And what may sound right is probably a false analogy with *detriment*. Though *detritus* is related etymologically to *detriment*, it differs in accentuation. *Detriment* is stressed on the first syllable, *detritus* on the second. There is no authority for first-syllable stress in *detritus*. All my sources, past and present, sanction only second-syllable stress.

de trop du̱-TROH. (For a discussion of du̱-, see **de rigueur**.)

deus ex machina DAY-uus EKS MAH-ki-nah (Latin); DEE-u̱s EKS MAK-i-nuh (English).

Pronouncing *machina* muh-SHEE-nuh, like *machine* + *uh*, is beyond beastly.

Both pronunciations given above are acceptable, but the evidence of my ears says the Latin has the upper hand in American English today. Current authority also favors it. Although *WNW 3* (1997) gives only the anglicized version, the *Quintessential Dictionary* (1978), *American Heritage 3* (1992), *M-W 10* (1993), and *RHWC* (1997) list the Latin first, and the *NBC Handbook* (1984) and *Everyday Reader's* (1985) prefer it.

dew Preferably, DYOO. Commonly, DOO.

Did you know that not everyone pronounces *dew* like *do?* The truly fascinating people in the world say DYOO, with a YOO or long *u* sound, because that is the way what were once called "the best speakers" have pronounced it for centuries. But the times they've been a'changing, and the traditional long *u* has almost evaporated from *dew*.

There is a long-standing tendency in American speech to change the YOO or long *u* sound in many words (as in *music* and *beauty*) to an OO sound (as in *soon* and *true*). Some words seem invulnerable to the process, particularly those in which YOO/long *u* occurs after the letters *f, m*, and *p* — e.g., *few, feud, fuel, refuse, refute, music, amuse, ammunition, remunerate, pewter, putrid, dispute, ampule*, etc. Many others, however, are variously affected. Since the 19th century we have been steadily engaged in dropping YOO/long *u* from such words as *assume, aptitude, attitude, astute, constitute, enthusiasm, hirsute, institute, minute, neutral, numerical, numerous, nutrition, opportune, platitude, presume, student, stupor, tune*, and *tutor*. After *d*, especially initial *d*, the YOO/long *u* has long been under fire, and most speakers now unquestionably prefer OO in *adduce, deuce, Deuteronomy, dual, duel, duet, duke, during, duty, dutiful, endure, endurance, induce, produce, reduce, traduce*, etc. Following initial or medial *st*, all but the most punctilious American speakers (like me) now say STOO-pid for *stupid* and DES-ti̱-toot for *destitute*. Following initial *s*, YOO/long *u* is almost never heard from Americans. We say SOOT for *suit*, SOO-pur for *super*; and soo-PREEM for *supreme*. And following *l* — in such words as *absolutely, allude, alluring, flute, illusion, illuminate*, and *lute* — the YOO/long *u* has disappeared from cultivated speech in the U.S. and is obsolescent in Britain.

The YOO/long *u* sound occurs in about half of the handful of English words ending in or incorporating -*ew*. It is intact (for now) in *askew, few, hew, mew, nephew, pew(ter), phew, sinew, spew*, and *view* (along with *re-*

[111]

view, interview, and *purview*). It is giving way to OO in *curlew, gewgaw, knew, mildew, stew(ard)*, and *dew*. It would be nice if those who consider themselves careful speakers took pains to preserve the YOO/long *u* in these words — with the single exception of *lewd*, which, because *-ew* follows *l*, makes the long *u* sound appropriate only when coming from the mouths of Elizabethan actors.

Many authorities now prefer DOO, and most dictionaries now list it first, but no matter how many people say it that way I just can't bring myself to accept it. To me, *the DYOO is on the grass* is crisp, clean English, while *the DOO is on the grass* never fails to invoke the image of a pet owner who has neglected to pick up after his pooch. Although I don't lose sleep over the loss of YOO/long *u* in many words, I most emphatically do mourn its disappearance in *dew*. If your concern for propriety in speech extends to beauty and harmony, I urge you to join me in preserving the cultivated and euphonious DYOO. And with that appeal, I bid you adieu.* See **dual/duel, due, duty, new**.

diabetes DY-uh-**BEE**-teez (recommended) or DY-uh-**BEE**-tis.

In DY-uh-**BEE**-teez, the last syllable sounds like *tease*. In DY-uh-**BEE**-tis, the last syllable rhymes with *kiss*.

DY-uh-**BEE**-tis was labeled "colloquial" by Phyfe (1926) and *Webster 2* (1934) and "popular" by Funk & Wagnalls *New Practical Standard* (1962). Its popularity can be traced back, and perhaps in no small degree attributed, to the influential English elocutionist John Walker, who, in his *Critical Pronouncing Dictionary* of 1791, marks the final *e* as short, so that *-tes* rhymes with *less*. It is an easy and natural step from *-tes* to *-tis* in this unstressed syllable, so that DY-uh-**BEE**-tis is what we often hear today.

Kenyon & Knott (1949) and *American College* (1952) are the earliest sources in which I found DY-uh-**BEE**-tis listed first, and current sources listing it first include *WNW Guide* (1984), *American Heritage 3* (1992), and *RHWC* (1997). None of my sources prefer it, however, and the weight of 20th-century authority is clearly on the side of DY-uh-**BEE**-teez, the only pronunciation sanctioned by *OED 2* (1989) and my three medical dictionaries — *Taber's* (1970), *Stedman's* (1972), and *Mosby's* (1990) — and the preference of orthoepists from Vizetelly (1929) and Opdycke (1939) to Lass & Lass (1976) and the *NBC Handbook* (1984).

I recommend DY-uh-**BEE**-teez both for that reason and because it follows the custom of pronouncing terminal *-es* as *-eez* in the host of loanwords and names from Greek and Latin: e.g., *appendices, diagnoses,*

---

* Preferably pronounced uh-DYOO, of course. For more on YOO/long *u* vs. OO, and some interesting historical perspective, see the entries for LU and U in H. W. Fowler's *Modern English Usage* (1926); Larsen & Walker's *Pronunciation: A Practical Guide to American Standards* (1930), § 129; and Alfred H. Holt's *You Don't Say!* (1937), § II of the preface, pp. xi–xv.

theses, crises, axes (plural of *axis*), *feces, antipodes, isosceles, indices* (plural of *index*), *amanuenses* (plural of *amanuensis*), *cacoethes* (KAK-oh-**EE**-theez, a mania, compulsion, irresistible urge), *meninges* (muh-NIN-jeez, what meningitis affects), *Socrates, Aristophanes, Euripides, Hermes, Hades, Pleiades, Pisces,* etc.

For *diabetes mellitus,* the proper pronunciation of *mellitus* is muh-LY-tis, rhyming with *arthritis.* I must register my strenuous objection to the variant MEL-i-tus, with first-syllable stress, which is of quite recent and erroneous vintage. It appears as an alternative to muh-LY-tis in *AHSC* (1985) and *Random House II* (1987), and (either by mistake or with egregious disregard for tradition) as the *only* pronunciation in *M-W 7* (1972). Since then, if you judge by the four major current American dictionaries, the upstart pronunciation has taken the traditional one by storm: muh-LY-tis is the only pronunciation in *WNW 3* (1988, 1997), but *American Heritage 3* (1992) lists MEL-i-tus second and *M-W 10* (1993) and *RHWC* (1991, 1997) recognize only MEL-i-tus.

Mellitus is a Latin loanword that means "sweetened with honey." If you were speaking Latin you would pronounce it me-LEE-tuus, and apparently some speakers think they can get away with that in English, for *Webster 3* (1961) recognizes the pseudo-Latin variant muh-LEE-tis (which, like a serious disease that begins with *p,* should be rigorously avoided). According to the customary method of anglicizing loanwords from Latin and Greek, when the stress in the original language falls on a syllable ending in a vowel, the vowel in English has its alphabetic or long sound. That's why there's a *date* in *data,* a *cry* in *crisis,* a *no* in *diagnosis,* a *ray* in *foramen,* a *rye* in *arthritis,* a *bee* in *diabetes,* and a *lie* in *mellitus.* Perhaps the recent graduates of our medical schools, unaware of the oral tradition of their clinical vocabulary, are responsible for encouraging this shift to first-syllable stress.* Whatever the reason, I deplore it — and a pox on Random House and Merriam-Webster for ignoring the traditional muh-LY-tis and for making it appear that cultivated speakers have abandoned it.

diagnosis DY-ig-**NOH**-sis (also -sis).

The plural *diagnoses* is pronounced DY-ig-**NOH**-seez (-seez like *seize*).

---

* A friend of mine, a former chief resident at a major hospital who is now in private practice, tells me that MEL-i-tus is *de rigueur* among American physicians and medical school professors and he has heard muh-LY-tis only from British and Canadian clinicians. The reason for the mass shift, he suggests, may be a conscious effort to avoid confusion by distinguishing *mellitus* from the host of medical terms ending in the suffix *-itis,* which means "inflammation." If that theory is true, which it may well be, then the American medical establishment is guilty of misdiagnosis and overmedicating a nonexistent problem. Shifting the stress was unnecessary because *mellitus* is never used without the common *diabetes* in front of it, and no doctor — at least no doctor I would trust — could possibly confuse *diabetes mellitus* with an inflammatory condition.

Take care not to confuse the singular and plural pronunciations. Many speakers incorrectly say diagno-*seez* when they mean diagno-*sis*. See **basis, crisis, thesis.**

diaspora dy-AS-puh-ruh (dy- rhyming with *dry,* -AS- rhyming with *pass*).
Do not de-anglicize the first syllable, *di-*, as if you were attempting to utter the word in the original Greek, and say dee-AS-puh-ruh. *M-W 10* (1993) recognizes this erroneous bit of pretentiousness, but other current sources sanction only dy-AS-pur-uh.

dictator DIK-tay-tur.
This is now unquestionably the dominant American pronunciation. In England, dik-TAY-tur still prevails. Americans also stress the verb *dictate* on the first syllable, while the English stress the second. For *dictatorship,* both dik-**TAY**-tur-SHIP and **DIK**-tay-tur-SHIP are standard in America, with the former still more common in news broadcasts and formal speech.

didactic dy-DAK-tik.
This pronunciation, in which the first syllable sounds like *die,* has been dominant in American speech for at least sixty years. It is preferred by American authorities from Opdycke (1939) and Kenyon & Knott (1949) to the *NBC Handbook* (1984) and Barnhart (1988), and it is the only pronunciation sanctioned by *American College* (1952), *American Heritage 3* (1992), and *RHWC* (1997). The alternative pronunciation di-DAK-tik (or di), preferred by Lass & Lass (1976), Vizetelly (1929), the *Century* (1914), and various other older authorities, is obsolescent in America. It survives in Britain, however, for Jones (1991) prefers it and it is the only pronunciation in *OED 2* (1989).

diesel DEE-zul, not DEE-sul. The word should rhyme with *easel.*
Diesel comes from Rudolf Diesel (DEE-zul), a German automotive engineer who in 1892 patented an internal-combustion engine that now bears his name. In German, explains *Webster 2* (1934), the letter *s* is pronounced "like English **s** in **rose** . . . before a vowel." We should follow this rule when we say *diesel* for it breaks no rule of English nor does it pose any difficulty to the tongue. Modern authorities preferring DEE-zul, with the *z* sound, include Lass & Lass (1976), Funk & Wagnalls *Standard* (1980), *Oxford American* (1980), *WNW Guide* (1984), the *NBC Handbook* (1984), and *OED 2* (1989). See **Dreiser.**

digest (verb) di-JEST (recommended) or dy-JEST; (noun) DY-jest.
Digestion is preferably di-JES-chin, *digestive* di-JES-tiv. The noun *digest* is always DY-jest.

In the first syllable of *digest,* both the short or obscure *i* (di- or di-) and the long *i* (dy-) are standard, and only the smallest of minds would impugn one or the other. One cannot say it both ways, however, so a choice must be made. And because it is the business of this book to make distinctions and defend preferences, I am casting my vote with Alfred H. Holt (1937), who recommends the short or obscure *i,* as in the first syllable of *divide,* for the following words and their derivatives: *digest, digress, dilute, direct, diverge, diverse, divert, divest,* and *divulge.*

Of course the long *i* sound in these words is also standard and particularly common today in *digest, digress, dilute,* and *diverse.* Nevertheless, I advocate the short or obscure *i* on these grounds: because it has the longer tradition and is still the customary pronunciation in American speech; because American authorities generally favor it; because the consistency of sound is sensible and pleasing;* and because, as Jones (1991) indicates, in all these words (with the exception of *digest*) the long *i* is now the British preference, and it goes without saying that any self-respecting American speaker should avoid the appearance of Anglophilia at all costs. See **direct, dissect, divine**.

digress di-GRES (or di-) is recommended over dy-GRES. See **digest**.

dilapidated di-**LAP**-i-DAY-tid.

In my town — San Diego — we once had an elected official who pronounced *dilapidated* as though it were spelled *dilapitated,* with two *t*'s instead of two *d*'s. In her bid for reelection she was defeated by a political novice. Does pronunciation affect credibility? I suppose it depends which issues you are mispronouncing about, but I have seen campaigns won or lost — and reputations spared or ruined — over a few key words. So don't let your pronunciation of *dilapidated* fall apart. Make sure it's -*dated,* not mis-*tated,* at the end.

dilatory DIL-uh-TOR-ee.

dilemma di-LEM-uh (or di-), not dy-LEM-uh.

"The short *i* is preferred," says Holt (1937), and Worcester (1860), Ayres (1894), Lass & Lass (1976), the *NBC Handbook* (1984), *Oxford Guide* (1983), and *WNW Guide* (1984) agree. Vizetelly (1929) acknowledges that the variant dy-LEM-uh is recognized "as alternative" by Funk & Wagnalls *Standard* (1897), *Webster's New International* (1909), the *Century* (1914), and *OED 1* (1928), but pronounces it "distinctly provincial." Although Burchfield (1996) warns that "the traditional pronunciation [di-LEM-uh], with short *i* answering to the short iota in Gk δίλημμα, is now being threatened by initial [dy-]," one wouldn't necessarily conclude that from a survey of current American dictionaries. *American Heritage 3* (1992) and *RHWC* (1997) sanction only di-LEM-uh, and *M-W 10* (1993) and *WNW 3* (1997) say *also* dy-, meaning, as the former puts it, that dy-LEM-uh is "appreciably less common."

---

* It's weird to hear someone mix the short and long *i* sounds and say something like this: *I won't* dy-*gress. I'll be* di-*rect. This is no time for the company to* dy-*vest. We must continue to* di-*versify.*

dilute di-LOOT (or dį-) is recommended over dy-LOOT. See **digest**.

diminution DIM-į-**N(Y)OO**-shįn.

Beware the beastly and regrettably common flip-flop mispronunciation DIM-yoo-**NISH**-įn, which makes the word sound as if it were spelled *dimunition*. This word should rhyme with *elocution* or *institution*, not with *ammunition*.

dinghy (American) DING-ee; (British) DING-gee or DING-ee.

American authorities of the first half of the 20th century countenanced only DING-gee, but this pronunciation has since become rare. (I, for one, have never heard it.) Except for the *NBC Handbook* (1984), current American authorities prefer DING-ee, the only pronunciation given by *American Heritage 3* (1992) and *RHWC* (1997).

diocese **DY**-uh-SEES or **DY**-uh-SIS; **diocesan** dy-AHS-į-sįn.

"The different spellings of this word have influenced its pronunciation," notes Vizetelly (1929). *OED 2* (1989) traces the word back, through some twenty-odd variant spellings, to the 14th century. Today's standard spelling, *diocese,* was in use by the 16th century, but at that time the forms *diocesse* and *dioces* were already established. In his dictionary of 1755, Samuel Johnson preferred *diocess,* and many later authorities, including Walker (1791), followed suit, indicating the pronunciation as **DY**-uh-SES. *Diocess* was in use through much of the 19th century, and **DY**-uh-SES appears as an alternative in some early 20th-century sources. From this *diocess*/**DY**-uh-SES apparently has come the modern pronunciation **DY**-uh-SIS.

In the first half of the 20th century, British and American pronunciation was sharply divided. H. W. Fowler (1926) says, "The right spelling is -*ese,* but the pronunciation is usually weakened to -es or -is," and his British contemporaries Jones (1924), Wyld (1932), and *OED 1* (1928) agree. *Webster 2* (1934), on the other hand, labels **DY**-uh-SIS "especially British," and Funk & Wagnalls *Standard* (1897) and *New Standard* (1913), the *Century* (1914), and Kenyon & Knott (1949) give only **DY**-uh-sees. "The long 'ee' is more American than British," says Holt (1937).

Today, however, the British DY-uh-sis is probably more often heard in America, and many American authorities — including Lass & Lass (1976) and the *NBC Handbook* (1984) — prefer it. Several current dictionaries also record **DY**-uh-SEEZ (-seez like *seize*), but this variant, which first appeared in *Webster 3* (1961), has little authority. I recommend **DY**-uh-SEES on the grounds that it is both a historically regular form and the traditional American pronunciation.

diphtheria dif-THEER-ee-uh, not dip-THEER-ee-uh.

The *ph* should be pronounced like *f,* as in *telephone, phonetics,* and *ophiolatry* (AHF-ee-**AHL**-uh-tree), worship of snakes. "However, with the exception of doctors and nurses," note Morris & Morris (1985), who prefer dif-THEER-ee-uh, "it is doubtful that one in ten Americans pronounces this word any way other than [with dip- in the first syllable]." It is equally doubtful that one in a hundred orthoepists would recommend the dip-pronunciation, despite its popularity. *Taber's Medical* (1970) and *Stedman's Medical* (1972) countenance only dif-, but *Mosby's Medical* (1990), bowing to popular usage, sanctions both pronunciations. Although current American dictionaries list dip-THEER-ee-uh, *WNW 3* (1997) precedes it with the subtly pejorative qualifier *widely* and *M-W 10* (1993) labels it with an obelus [÷] to indicate that some speakers find it objectionable. Among those objecting are Lass & Lass (1976), the *NBC Handbook* (1984), *Everyday Reader's* (1985), and Burchfield (1996). For more on -*phth*-, see **diphthong, ophthalmology.**

diphthong DIF-thawng or DIF-thahng.

As all good speakers know, there is no *dip* in *diphthong* — at least not anymore.

If you were taught, as I was, to put a *dif*- in *diphthong,* it will probably come as a surprise to you that the pronunciation *dip-thong* was formerly, and for many years, not only acceptable but preferred by many authorities.

The early English elocutionist John Walker (1791), whose *Critical Pronouncing Dictionary* was as popular in 19th-century America as the works of Noah Webster,* decreed that "*ph* is generally pronounced like *f,* as in *philosophy, phantom,* &c.," but "in *diphthong* the sound of *p* only is heard." Vizetelly (1929), who prefers DIF-, shows that during much of the 19th century, through the influential dictionaries of Worcester (1860) and Stormonth (1871), the weight of authority was on Walker's side.

After that the *f* sound seizes the day. The *Century* (1889–1914) lists dif- first, and Funk & Wagnalls *Standard* (1897), Webster's *International* (1909), Phyfe (1926), *OED 1* (1928), and *Webster 2* (1934) all prefer it. In *Modern English Usage* (1926), H. W. Fowler probably hoped he was sounding the death knell for DIP- when he wrote, "[DIFTH-] is the right sound, & [DIPTH-] a vulgarism."

Nevertheless, this modern-day vulgarism, like a powerful virus, has persisted and flourished despite strong resistance. Today DIP- appears as an alternative in general dictionaries — with a few exceptions, most notably *OED 2* (1989). Contemporary authorities, however, unanimously prefer DIF-, and Burchfield (1996) calls the DIP- pronunciation "highly irregular." See **diphtheria, ophthalmology.**

direct di̱-REKT; **directly** di̱-REKT-lee (avoid DREK-lee, which is chiefly British).

---

* For more on Walker's popularity, see the footnote under **educate.**

Be sure to make the *t* audible in *direct* and *directly*. Don't say dị-REK, dị-REK-lee. It is also beastly to put the stress on the first syllable.

For *direct* and *directly*, the preferred pronunciation in American speech, which dictionaries consistently list first, has a short or obscure *i* and the accent on the second syllable: dị-REKT, dị-REKT-lee. The variant with a long *i*, dy-REKT and dy-REKT-lee, is often heard in British and Canadian speech but is considerably less common in the U.S. The early British authority John Walker, in his influential *Critical Pronouncing Dictionary* (1791), approved of the long *i* variant for *directly* in "emphatical or colloquial use" when "we wish to be very distinct and forceful. . . ." American dictionaries of the 19th and early 20th century did not record the long *i* variant, but evidence shows it was afoot in the U.S. over a hundred years ago, for Ayres (1894) proscribed it, as did Phyfe (1926). Vizetelly (1929), however, sanctioned the long *i* and remarked that it "has an increasing vogue in the United States and in Great Britain." Larsen & Walker (1930) give a different assessment:

> In England generally there is a tendency to the use of the [long *i* like *eye*] sound (ī) in such words as *direction, civilization,* and *organization,* and in words ending in *-ile,* such as *agile* and *docile.* New England and Southern speech do not seem to approximate to that of England in this respect; in General American the (ĭ) sound [short *i* as in *pit*] is almost universal.

The British *OED 1* (1928) was the first dictionary to record dy-REKT and dy-REKT-lee as alternative pronunciations, and the American *Webster 2* (1934) soon followed suit. Since then both American and British authorities have listed the long *i* in good standing, but always after the established pronunciation with short or obscure *i*, which Lass & Lass (1976), *WNW Guide* (1984), and the *NBC Handbook* (1984) prefer.

In American speech, the short or obscure *i* in *di-* is also customary in these related words and phrases: *direction, director, directory, directive, direct current, direct mail, direct deposit, direct dial, direct examination, indirect,* and *redirect*. See **digest, dissect, divine.**

dirigible DIR-ị-jị-buul. Stress the first syllable, not the second.

"This word must not be accented on the *rig*," says Gilmartin (1936). "The second syllable, which is *i*, is unstressed, the accent going clearly on the first, *dir.*"

The variant dị-RIJ-ị-buul, with second-syllable stress, has been listed as an alternative in American dictionaries since the 1960s. Kenyon & Knott (1949), in their *Pronouncing Dictionary of American English,* call it British, but I suspect it is merely an affectation. The British *OED 2* (1989) sanctions only first-syllable stress, and another important British authority, Jones (1991), prefers it, as do the American authorities Lass & Lass (1976) and the *NBC Handbook* (1984).

disastrous di-ZAS-tr<u>u</u>s.

Disastrous, like *disaster*, has three syllables. Do not add an extra syllable and say di-ZAS-tur-<u>us</u>, as though the word were spelled *disasterous*. This is a di-ZAS-tr<u>u</u>s-lee careless pronunciation. See **ambidextrous**.

discern di-SURN. Formerly, and still occasionally, di-ZURN.

From Walker (1791) through the *Century* (1914), authorities sanctioned only one pronunciation: di-ZURN, with a so-called soft *s* sound, as in *rose*. But in the early 20th century di-SURN, with a hard or pure *s* as in *sir*, began to catch on. Phyfe (1926) and Vizetelly (1929) disapproved of di-SURN, but *Webster 2* (1934) saw fit to recognize it as an alternative in good standing, and since then it has enjoyed widespread currency in cultivated speech. Current dictionaries list di-ZURN without qualification, but there is no doubt that di-SURN is the dominant pronunciation today and di-ZURN is becoming rare. Although Lass & Lass (1976) hold out for di-ZURN, *WNW Guide* (1984), *NBC Handbook* (1984), and *Everyday Reader's* (1985) prefer di-SURN, and *OED 2* (1989) says it is now the usual pronunciation.

disenfranchisement DIS-<u>i</u>n-**FRAN**-chiz-m<u>i</u>nt or DIS-<u>i</u>n-**FRAN**-chyz-m<u>i</u>nt.

There is no authority for placing the accent on *-chise-* in *disenfranchisement*. Both *disenfranchise* (DIS-<u>i</u>n-**FRAN**-chyz) and *disenfranchisement* are properly accented on *-fran-*.

Older authorities and one current dictionary, *WNW 3* (1997), give only the first pronunciation listed above, which I prefer and recommend. However, the alternative, a spelling pronunciation, is listed first in three current dictionaries and is probably more common.

dishabille dis-uh-BEEL.

Opdycke (1939), who rhymes *dishabille* with *hiss a deal*, defines the word as "a loose dress or negligée, or the condition of being loosely and carelessly dressed." The pronunciation dis-uh-BEEL is also the preference of Phyfe (1926), *Webster 2* (1934), Holt (1937), Lass & Lass (1976), the *NBC Handbook* (1984), *WNW Guide* (1984), and *WNW 3* (1997). The word is occasionally spelled *deshabille*, in which case it is appropriate to say dez-uh-BEEL. The *Quintessential Dictionary* (1978) stresses the first syllable, DIS-uh-beel, which is eccentric, unattested elsewhere, and not recommended.

disparate DIS-puh-rit, not di-SPAR-it (or -SPAIR-it).

Stress the first syllable, not the second. Also, avoid compressing the word to two syllables: DIS-prit. *Disparate* should have three distinct syllables.

OED 2 (1989) traces *disparate* back to a 1608 sermon ("two disperate species and sorts of men"). The oldest dictionary in which I found the word is Worcester (1860), who gives DIS-puh-rit. The beastly mispronunciation di-SPAR-it is the product of progressive stress — pressure to move the accent forward in a word — reinforced by false analogy with *disparity* and *disparage*. It appears to have crawled out of the woodwork in the 1920s or 1930s. Opdycke (1939) is the earliest of my sources to report that *disparate* "is frequently misaccented on the second syllable." No one else paid any attention to the problem until suddenly, and most mysteriously, di-SPAR-it appeared in *Webster 3* (1961) listed *first*, with — here's the real shocker — the traditional pronunciation, DIS-puh-rit, labeled "appreciably less frequent."

Lexicographers tend to play down the influence their editorial decisions have on the populace (probably less out of professional modesty, nowadays, than from fear of liability); nevertheless, there can be no doubt that the preeminence of di-SPAR-it in a major — and controversial — dictionary abetted its spread immeasurably. As a result, current American dictionaries all list di-SPAR-it, but not one — including *Webster 3*'s latest abridgment, *M-W 10* (1993) — lists it first, and *WNW 3* (1997) labels di-SPAR-it less common. Lass & Lass (1976), *WNW Guide* (1984), the *NBC Handbook* (1986), Barnhart (1988), and *OED 2* (1989) all prefer the traditional DIS-puh-rit. For more on progressive (and regressive) stress, see **confiscate**.

dissect di-SEKT (or di̱-). Stress the second syllable, *not* the first.
Properly, there is no *die* in *dissect*. The *i* should be short or obscure, as in *dissent, dissolve,* and *dissuade*. That is the traditional pronunciation, but it is now under attack, as Morris & Morris (1985) explain:

> Used by the general public mainly to mean "to examine' or "to analyze," *dissect* has been subjected by radio and TV announcers to several pronunciations other than the traditional dis-SECT. The most frequent variation is DIE-sect, probably because of a mistaken idea that *dissect* is analogous to "bisect." The trouble with that theory is that the prefix in "bisect" is "bi-," meaning "two," and hence "bisect" means to cut into two equal parts. The prefix in *dissect* is "dis-," which means "apart," and hence *dissect* means to cut apart.* While the newer dictionaries enter DIE-sect as a third pronunciation (after dis-SECT and die-SECT), the preferred pronunciation remains dis-SECT.

The variants dy-SEKT and DY-sekt first appeared in *Webster 3* (1961), which labels them with an obelus [÷] to indicate they are unacceptable to many. *Webster 3*'s most recent abridgment, *M-W 10* (1993), slaps the same warning label on these variants, and none of my sources prefer them. *OED 2* (1989) sanctions only di-SEKT, and all four leading current American dictionaries list the short or obscure *i* first. See **digest, direct**.

---

* I suspect this false analogy in pronunciation between *dissect* and *bisect* was exacerbated by the fact that in some words the prefix *dis-*, apart, away, becomes *di-* (e.g., *digress*, to go apart, *dilapidated*, falling apart, *dilute*, to wash away, *diverge*, to turn away), and also by a confusion of *dis-* with the prefix *di-*, meaning "two, twice, double."

divan di-VAN.

This is the only pronunciation in *American Heritage 3* (1992), the first listed in *OED 2* (1989), *M-W 10* (1993), and *RHWC* (1997), and the preference of the *NBC Handbook* (1984) and Burchfield (1996). The variant DY-van, preferred by Lass & Lass (1976) and most older authorities, is now much less common. Dictionaries sometimes record the pretentious di-VAHN, which should be avoided.

diverge di-VURJ (or di̱-) is recommended over dy-VURJ. See **digest**.

diverse di-VURS (or di̱-) is recommended over dy-VURS.

Stress the second syllable, not the first. The short or obscure *i*, as in *divide*, is also recommended in *diversity.* See **digest**.

divert di-VURT (or di̱-) is recommended over dy-VURT. See **digest**.

divest di-VEST (or di̱-) is recommended over dy-VEST. See **digest**.

divine di̱-VYN. Don't say dee-VYN.

"A common mistake is to make the first syllable 'dee,'" says Holt (1937). The *i* in the first syllable should be short or obscure, as in *divide.* See **direct**.

divisive di-VY-siv. Don't say di-VIS-iv.

If you asked people what they can recall from former President George Bush's speeches, they would probably regurgitate the phrases "a kinder, gentler nation" and "a thousand points of light." Aside from Bush's infamous "here I stand, warts and all" misquotation,* what I remember most is his mispronunciation, in his inaugural address, of the word *divisive.* Instead of saying di-VY-siv (-VY- rhyming with *tie*) — the pronunciation 99 percent of us have heard and used all our lives — Bush said di-VIS-iv (-VIS- as in *vista*). Was this just a venial bit of Ivy League snobbery, or was the president letting fly with a beastly mispronunciation?

Bush's di-VIS-iv does not appear in any of my sources, either American or British, before *Webster 3* (1961), which labels it "appreciably less frequent." A poll of sources published since then reveals a smattering of recognition for di-VIS-iv and a humongous heap of authority for di-VY-siv. *OED 2* (1989) sanctions only di-VY-siv. The *American Heritage* dictionaries — *AHNC* (1969), *AHSC* (1985), and *American Heritage 3* (1992) — sanction only di-VY-siv. And the Random House dictionaries — *Random House II* (1987) and *RHWC* (1991, 1997) — sanction only di-VY-siv. It is the only pronunciation in *Scribner-Bantam* (1979), *Oxford American* (1980), and Funk & Wagnalls *Standard* (1980), and Lass & Lass (1976) and *Everyday Reader's* (1985) prefer it. The *NBC Handbook* (1984) doesn't even

---

* Bush, with the misguided aide of his speechwriter, Peggy Noonan, attributed these words to Abraham Lincoln. In his essay "Public Eloquence," David Reid writes, "Of course it was Martin Luther who said, 'Here I stand,' and Oliver Cromwell who had the warts, but according to the London *Times* the garbled quotations worked magic. 'With [Noonan's] help, Bush has certainly found his voice, warts and all.'" (From pp. 270–71 of *The State of the Language*, edited by Christopher Ricks and Leonard Michaels.)

have an entry for *divisive,* presumably because there is no question how the word should be pronounced.

WNW 2 (1984) and *WNW Guide* (1984) record di-VY-siv and di-VIS-iv as equally common and acceptable, but *WNW 3* (1988, 1997) revises that judgment and applies the label *also* to di-VIS-iv, indicating that the variant is less common and, presumably, less than equally acceptable.* *M-W 9* (1985), which also slaps the *also* label on di-VIS-iv, goes on to record the variants di-VIZ-iv and di-VY-ziv, with a *z* sound for the *s.* I have heard some Southern speakers say di-VY-ziv, and since the medial *i* is long (as in *devise*), I can accept it as a reasonable alternative. All other variants, however, are outré.

Frankly, I'm surprised that di-VIS-iv got into dictionaries at all, because the evidence of my ears tells me it is far less frequent in educated speech — and far less acceptable to most educated speakers — than the *also* label makes it appear. As you can imagine, I am a careful observer of speech, and in the last ten years I have heard exactly two people say di-VIS-iv: President Bush and the host of a popular talk radio show in Denver, on which I was a guest. Can somebody tell me where all these purported di-VIS-iv sayers are hiding?

"Any pronunciation that is too conspicuous is ineffective," declares *Reader's Digest* (1972). Although I wouldn't agree with that assertion in every case — sometimes it *is* effective to be conspicuous, particularly when

---

* In its front matter, *WNW 2* (1984) has this to say about the order in which pronunciations are listed: "In most cases, the order indicates that on the basis of available information, the form given first is the one most frequent in general cultivated use. Where usage is about evenly divided, since one form must be given first, the editors' preference generally prevails. Unless a variant is qualified, as by *now rarely* or *occasionally* or some such note, it is understood that any pronunciation here entered represents a standard use."

I could write a treatise on this passage and what it reveals, explicitly and implicitly, about how so-called descriptive dictionaries record pronunciation, but as this is merely a footnote to another discussion I shall limit myself to two pertinent points: first, that any careful reader of that passage will have cause to wonder, upon seeing two or more pronunciations listed for a word, whether the first one given is "most frequent in general cultivated use" or the preference of the editors, or both; and second, that the clear implication of the last sentence is that "any pronunciation here entered" is standard *unless the variant is qualified.*

WNW 3 (1988, 1997) puts things a bit differently, and more tersely: "Two or more pronunciations are often given for the same word. One or more of the additional pronunciations may have a qualifying note (such as *also, often, occas., chiefly Brit,* or the like). If no such note is given, each pronunciation shown is equally acceptable in American English, regardless of the order in which the pronunciations appear." The careful reader will discern from this explanation the same implication as in the earlier one — that pronunciations are "equally acceptable" only when no qualifying note is given.

The Merriam-Webster dictionaries from *Webster 3* (1961) on define their *also* label as "appreciably less frequent" or "appreciably less common," and their *sometimes* label as "infrequent" or "even less common."

you are *right* — in this instance it certainly applies. To say di-VIS-iv is like pronouncing **controversy** or **adversary** with the accent on the second syllable, or pronouncing **isolate** the British way, to rhyme with *dissipate*. It sounds foreign and eccentric and, yes, even precious. One cannot help dwelling on the irony of Bush's calling for "a kinder, gentler nation" and then saying *divisive* in a pseudosophisticated way that is alien to the overwhelming majority of speakers in the country.

For more on beastly mispronunciation of political words, see **electoral, inaugural, mayoral**. For more on beastly mispronunciations by politicians, see **American, anal, anesthetize, clandestine, nuclear, preferable**.

divulge di-VUHLJ (or di̱-).

This is the only pronunciation in *American Heritage 3* (1992) and *WNW 3* (1997) and the first in *M-W 10* (1993) and *RHWC* (1997). The variant dy-VUHLJ is more common in Britain than in America. See **digest**.

doctoral DAHK-tur-u̱l. Do not say dahk-TOR-ee-u̱l.

Doctoral properly has three syllables, stress on *doc-*.

The eccentric dahk-TOR-ee-u̱l, with the accent on the second syllable, is sometimes heard from educated speakers who should know better. Beware, all ye budding doctors, of any "institution of higher learning" offering a *doctorial* degree. As Prof. Laurence McNamee and Kent Biffle note in *A Few Words* (1988), "Despite the ring of authenticity that deans give to 'doctorial' as they consistently mispronounce it, dictionaries continue to spell it 'doctoral' with the accent on the 'doc.'"

True, but not quite the whole story. First-syllable stress in *doctoral* has been preferred for at least 250 years, as evidenced by the dictionaries of Samuel Johnson (1755) and John Walker (1791). However, as *OED 2* (1989) shows, the variant *doctorial*, pronounced in four syllables, was relatively common for most of the 18th century and much of the 19th. Although the last citation in *OED 2* dates from 1858, *doctorial* appears in nearly all the other major unabridged dictionaries of the past hundred years: Funk & Wagnalls *Standard* (1897), the *Century* (1914), *Webster 2* (1934), *Webster 3* (1961), and *Random House II* (1987). Despite this long lexicographic trail, however, there is nothing to suggest that *doctorial* has had any currency in the 20th century. Other, less voluminous dictionaries ignore it, commentators on usage have nothing to say about it, and I for one have never seen it in edited writing — have you? Thus it is doubtful that the variant spelling has fueled the modern mispronunciation; more likely it is the persistence of the mispronunciation that has kept the vestigial spelling on life support. *Doctorial*'s anomalous presence in one current dictionary — *RHWC* (1991, 1997) — should not be construed as evidence of a revival, and all authorities continue to agree that *doctoral* is the preferred spelling and DAHK-tur-u̱l the proper pronunciation. For more on how pronunciation influences spelling, see **minuscule**.

Dodgson (Charles Lutwidge) DAHD-sun, not, as commonly heard,
DAHJ-sun.

Dodgson (1832–1898) is perhaps better known by his pen name, Lewis
Carroll. His middle name is pronounced LUHT-wij.

Nearly all sources countenance only the spelling pronunciation DAHJ-
sun, which most speakers assume is authentic, but only *M-W 10* (1993),
which lists DAHD-sun first, has it right. According to Ralph H. Emerson,
an expert on the pronunciation of literary names, Dodgson and his family
preferred a silent *g*, as if the name were spelled *Dodson*. "His niece wrote to
the BBC to say so a long time ago, after hearing it mispronounced on one
of their radio shows," Emerson informs me.* He also notes that Dodgson's
model for Alice was Alice Liddell, pronounced "LIDDLE, like *fiddle*," the
daughter of the renowned classical scholar Henry Liddell, co-editor of *Liddell and Scott's Greek-English Lexicon*.

domicile DAHM-uh-syl, not DOH-muh-syl.

Pronounce the *dom-* as in *dominate*, not like *dome*. The *-cile* rhymes with
tile.

Formerly, the prevailing pronunciations for *domicile* were DAHM-uh-
sil (-sil with a short *i*, rhyming with *pill*) and DAHM-uh-sil (-sil with an
obscure *i*, as in *evil* and *pupil*). Current dictionaries still list the latter,
but *WNW Guide* (1984) correctly notes that it is "no longer common."

"Many, especially in England, pronounce [*domicile*] to rime with
comma style, but the long *i* in the last syllable has no authority in this
country," says Opdycke (1939), apparently unaware that Vizetelly (1929)
had sanctioned DAHM-uh-syl as an alternative and Phyfe (1926), citing its
appearance in *OED 1* (1928), had given it his tentative blessing. Although
Webster 2 (1934) and Kenyon & Knott (1949) do not recognize DAHM-uh-
syl, it resurfaces in *American College* (1952) and since then it has become
the dominant American pronunciation, with DOH-muh-syl (long *o* as in
dome), which first appeared in *Webster 3* (1961), as its only serious con-
tender.

The long *o*, however, has a limited following — of all my sources only
Lass & Lass (1976) prefer it. *Oxford American* (1980), *WNW Guide* (1984),
and the *NBC Handbook* (1984) prefer DAHM-uh-syl, and all four major
current American dictionaries list it first, with *WNW 3* (1997) labeling
DOH-muh-syl less common.

Don Quixote See **quixotic**.

doppelgänger DAHP-ul-**GANG**-ur (rhymes with *topple hanger*).

Some authorities still prefer a German pronunciation, but I say this word
is pompous enough without subjecting it to a throat-and-noseful of that.
English has employed *doppelgänger* for almost 150 years, and there's no

---

* Personal correspondence of July 2, 1997, and January 20, 1998.

excuse not to anglicize it. Current orthography favors lowercase *d* but retains the umlaut or dieresis (dy-ER-i-sis) over *ä*.

double entendre DUHB'l (like *double*) ahn-TAHN-druh.

The *NBC Handbook* (1984) and Barnhart (1988) prefer the Frenchified DOO-blah(n)-**TAH(N)**-druh, and *WNW Guide* (1984) and *M-W 10* (1993) list it first. Given that, I can't say it's wrong. However, *double entendre* has been used in English since the 1670s, more than time enough for *double* to take on its normal English sound. Moreover, the phrase is obsolete in French, which makes the Frenchified pronunciation an ostentatious waste of time.

dour DOOR (rhymes with *poor, tour,* and *lure*) or DUUR (UU as in *book* and *took,* so that the word almost rhymes with *stir* or *fur*). Commonly, but erroneously, DOW-ur, a spelling pronunciation based on false analogy with *our, hour, flour, sour, scour,* and *devour.*

"*Dour* meaning stubborn, gloomy, sullen, is first recorded in English about 1470," says *The Barnhart Dictionary of Etymology* (1988). It is related to the verb *endure* and may have come from the same source, the Latin *durus,* hard, also stern, severe. The pronunciation DOOR (rhyming with *poor*) and the spelling *dour* come from Scottish.

"Pronounce door, not dowr," advises the venerable H. W. Fowler in his classic *Modern English Usage* (1926). "The only standard pronunciation in Britain is [DOOR], rhyming with *tour* not *sour;* but [DOW-ur] is common in AmE and Australia," says Fowler's successor, R. W. Burchfield, in his *New Fowler's Modern English Usage* (1996).

A survey of American sources of the last hundred years reveals that DOOR was the only recognized pronunciation until the 1940s, probably because until then it was uncommon in American speech and writing. Funk & Wagnalls *Standard* (1897) and the *Century* (1914) marked it Scottish, and *Webster 2* (1934) labeled it "chiefly Scottish." By the next decade, however, it was clear that Americans had finally sunk their teeth into *dour* and were hard at work flossing away its quaint Scottish flavor.

"It is pronounced to rime with *boor,* not with *door* or *flour,*" complained Opdycke (1939), but did anyone listen? Ten years later, in their *Pronouncing Dictionary of American English* (1949), Kenyon & Knott recognized three pronunciations of the word: DOOR, DUUR, and DOW-ur. Then the influential *American College Dictionary* (1952) sanctioned DUUR and DOW-ur. Then the controversial *Webster 3* (1961) put the upstart spelling pronunciation DOW-ur first, followed by DUUR, and finally DOOR, labeled "Scottish." Three decades later, however, *M-W 10* (1993), the latest abridgment of *Webster 3,* reversed that verdict and put DUUR first and DOW-ur second (with DOOR apparently having moved quietly back to Scotland).

Clearly the door has been flung open for DOW-ur, but no current authority prefers it and the traditional DOOR and its cousin DUUR* still wear the plaid in the family. Lass & Lass (1976), the *NBC Handbook* (1984), and *OED 2* (1989) prefer DOOR. *Everyday Reader's* (1985) prefers DUUR, which *American Heritage 3* (1992), *RHWC* (1997), and *WNW 3* (1997) list first.

dramaturge DRAM-uh-turj; **dramaturgy** DRAM-uh-TUR-jee.

For the first syllable in these words, DRAH- is also acceptable. Be sure to pronounce the *g* like *j*, as in *surge* and *dirge*. Do not say DRAM-uh-turg.

Dramaturgy is the art of theatrical composition and representation. Originally, *dramaturge* was a fancy synonym for a playwright; the word now usually refers to a literary consultant for a theater who assists playwrights and directors, helps select and edit scripts for production, researches historical matters, and advises on the techniques of theatrical representation.

Some of my friends who work in theater have taken to pronouncing *dramaturge* and *dramaturgy* with a hard *g* (as in *gurgle* and *burger*) rather than a soft *g* (as in *urge, purge,* and *merge*), and I have heard a number of actors and prominent theater professionals say it this way. I am not sure where this peculiar innovation came from or what the motivation for it is (Stanislavsky?), but I can assure you of one thing: it is without question an illogical, erroneous, and beastly mispronunciation. And don't be misled by the *e*-less — and illogical, erroneous, and ugly — variant spelling *dramaturg,* which two current dictionaries, *M-W 10* (1993) and *RHWC* (1997), now recognize. *All* my sources, past and present, countenance only a soft *g,* as in *urge,* in *dramaturge* and *dramaturgy.* See **zounds.**

Dreiser (Theodore) DRY-zur, not DRY-sur. The *s* is properly soft, as in *rose* and *raise.*

The immensely influential *Webster 2* (1934), the earliest source in which I found *Dreiser* listed, gives DRY-sur, with the hard *s.* Does that mean it's correct? Let's see.

In the world of reference it is commonplace for new works to borrow from earlier works, and when the earlier work is of the stature of *Webster 2,* several generations of reference books often will rely heavily on its authority. Such was the case with *Dreiser,* apparently, for every source since *Webster 2* that I have checked sanctions DRY-sur; the *Columbia Encyclopedia* (1963), the *NBC Handbook* (1984), *WNW Guide* (1984), and McConkey (1986) prefer it, and all four major current American dictionaries list it first, with DRY-zur second. The problem is, even great dictionaries make mistakes, and when they do the error can, by fiat, become the norm.

---

* The origin of DUUR is mysterious. It may have been a regional variant, like RUUM for *room,* BRUUM for *broom,* and RUUF for *roof,* in which the customary full OO sound (as in *doom*) in these words is cut to a UU sound (as in *look*).

Webster 2 and its copycats are wrong, says Ralph H. Emerson, an authority on the pronunciation of literary names who served as a consultant on that subject to *Merriam-Webster's Encyclopedia of Literature* (1995). In an article published in *English Language Notes* (December 1996), he writes that *Dreiser* is properly pronounced "DRIZER, like *early riser*," with the same German *z* sound for the *s* that one hears in the last name of Paul Reiser, co-star of the TV sitcom *Mad About You*, or Theodor Geisel (GY-zul), the real name of Dr. Seuss.

On what does Emerson base his claim? I asked him in a telephone interview.* Two pieces of evidence, he said. First, in a book called *What's the Name, Please?* (1938) by the respected lexicographer Charles Earle Funk, which reports (on the basis of information obtained from mailed questionnaires) how more than 1,500 celebrities of the time pronounced their own names, *Dreiser* is said to rhyme with *geyser* or *riser*. Although that would appear to dictate a *z* sound for the *s*, Emerson pointed out that it was still faintly ambiguous because in the 1930s *geyser* was occasionally pronounced with the hard *s* of *gas* rather than the soft *s* of *rise*. "So I tracked down one of Dreiser's nieces," he told me, who confirmed it was DRY-zur. "She said it was a German name and they pronounced it the German way." See **diesel**.

drowned DROWND.

Drowned has one syllable. The pronunciation DROWN-děd is beastly.

dual, duel DOO-ul or DYOO-ul (my preference).

Dual and *duel* have two syllables, not one. Don't rhyme these words with *fool*. The sloppy speaker says DOOL personalities, DOOL purposes, and DOOL-ing banjos. The careful speaker says D(Y)OO-ul and D(Y)OO-uh-ling.

Du Bois (W. E. B.) doo-BOYS (rhymes with *you voice*).

ducat DUHK-it (like *duck + it*, rhyming with *bucket*).

A *ducat* is a type of coin, usually made of gold, formerly used by various European countries. *Ducats* figure prominently in tales and movies about marauders on the bounding main. Don't be misled by Errol Flynn or any other Hollywood swashbucklers who mispronounce this word DOOK-it or DYOOK-it. The only recognized pronunciation is DUHK-it.

due Traditionally, DYOO. Commonly, DOO. See **dew, dual/duel, duty**.

duodenum D(Y)OO-uh-**DEE**-num (recommended). Also, doo-AHD'n-um.

The adjective *duodenal* is pronounced D(Y)OO-uh-**DEE**-nul. WNW 3 (1997) marks the *o* in the second, unstressed syllable of *duodenum* and *duodenal* as long (as in *go*), but all other current sources mark it as a schwa (as in *carrot* or *summon*).

---

* January 13, 1998.

The *duodenum* is the first section of the small intestine, which extends from the stomach to the jejunum (ji-JOO-num), the middle section. Traditionally the word receives secondary stress on the first syllable and primary stress on the third. The alternative pronunciation doo-AHD'n-um, with second-syllable stress, apparently caught on in the 1930s and was instantly attacked as spurious. "The 'odd' accent is a myth," asserted Holt (1937). "Accent the 'dee,'" Opdycke (1939) said. "The affected pronunciation *dew odd' e num* has no sanction." As is often the case, despite the criticism of these and other authorities, doo-AHD'n-um was taken up both by physicians and regular folk. In 1961 *Webster 3* recognized it, and since then it has been listed in good standing.

A poll of 16 sources published since then, however, reveals that the weight of authority still heavily favors the traditional D(Y)OO-uh-**DEE**-num. It is listed first by all four major current American dictionaries and by *Stedman's Medical* (1972), *WNW Guide* (1984), *Random House II* (1987), and *Mosby's Medical* (1990). It is preferred by *Taber's Medical* (1970), Funk & Wagnalls *Standard* (1980), *Oxford American* (1980), the *NBC Handbook* (1984), *Everyday Reader's* (1985), *OED 2* (1989), and Jones (1991). Only Lass & Lass (1976) prefer doo-AHD'n-um.

Some speakers (including me) prefer to pronounce the first syllable with a long *u* sound: DYOO-.

Durrell (Lawrence George) DUR-ul (rhymes with *squirrel*).

duty Traditionally, DYOO-tee. Commonly, DOO-tee.

It is beastly to say DOO-dee (like *doody,* a variant of *doo-doo*). Pronounce the *t.*

If we counted heads in America today, I doubt if one in a hundred speakers would pronounce *duty* in the traditional manner, with the long *u* [dūty] to rhyme with *beauty*. Although orthoepists from Walker (1791) to Phyfe (1926) to Lass & Lass (1976) have favored the long *u* and frowned upon DOO-tee, by Phyfe's time the -oo- for *u* sound had gained widespread acceptance. "In America, at least, the [oo] sound is widely used by the educated," says *Webster 2* (1934). "Though Lowell nearly a century ago satirized this pronunciation as 'dooty,' Grandgent and other competent observers have ascertained that it is in cultivated use very generally."

All this is still true today, of course. Nevertheless, duty compels me to side with the pronunciation mavens of the past and advocate for the long-suffering DYOO-, even as it lies dying like a dog amid a vociferous chorus of DOO-. Like W. H. Auden's "Ironic points of light" that "Flash out wherever the Just / Exchange their messages,"* we who still do our duty with a long *u* shall know in a flash, when we meet, that the messengers of justly cultivated speech have not yet fled America. See **dew, due, new.**

---

* See the magnificent final stanza of "September 1, 1939."

E

ebullient i-BUHL-yint or i-BUUL-yint.

Ebullient should be pronounced in three syllables. In the second, accented syllable the *u* may have the sound of the *u* in *bulk* or *bull.*

ebullition EB-uh-**LISH**-in, not EB-yoo-**LISH**-in.

Ebullition should rhyme with *abolition,* not *ammunition.* Say *ebb-olition.*

ecology i-KAHL-i-jee.

This is the preference of all current authorities, with the exception of *WNW Guide* (1984) and *WNW 3* (1997), which prefer ee-KAHL-i-jee. Only *M-W 9* (1985) and *10* (1993) recognize a short *e* (as in *bet*) in the first syllable; this variant is best avoided.

economic(al) For the first syllable, both long *e* (as in *seek*) and short *e* (as in *peck*) are acceptable.

Economy and *economist* should have a lightened long *e:* i-KAHN-i-mee, i-KAHN-uh-mist.

ecstatic ek-STAT-ik.

Some sloppy speakers drop the first *c* and say i-STAT-ik. This is beastly.

eczema EK-suh-muh or EG-zuh-muh. Stress the first syllable, not the second.

Edinburgh (Scotland) ED'n-bur-uh or ED'n-buh-ruh.

These (relatively indistinguishable) pronunciations are authentic and recommended. Various American sources, including Kenyon & Knott (1949) and the *NBC Handbook* (1984), give an Americanized pronunciation with a long *o* sound at the end: ED'n-bur-oh or ED'n-buh-roh. This is also

---

a = at / a̱ = final / ah = spa / ahr = car / air = fair / ay = hay / aw = saw
ch = chip / e = let / e̱ = item / ee = see / eer = deer / i = sit / i̱ = April
ng = sing / o̱ = carrot / oh = go / oo = soon / or = for / oor = poor
ow = cow / oy = toy / sh = she / th = thin / th = this / u̱ = focus / uh = up
ur = turn / uu = pull, took / y, eye = by, I / zh = measure / (see full key, p. xiv)

acceptable. Some sources recognize a clipped variant, ED'n-bruh, as chiefly British. Never, never say ED'n-burg. There's an ED'n-burg in Texas, but to a Scot (and probably to a Brit as well), this variant is beastly.

educate EJ-i-kayt; **educable** EJ-i-kuh-buul; **education** EJ-i-**KAY**-shin (EJ- like *edge*).

Some speakers, in an effort to avoid what they deem the vulgar sound of *j* in these words — the *edge* sound — take pains to say ED-yoo-kayt, ED-yuu-kuh-buul, and ED-yoo-**KAY**-shin. (For *educate* and *education*, the *u* is also pronounced -yuh-). Are these variants acceptable or affected? Here's the story in a nutshell:

Way back in 1791, the English elocutionist John Walker called the *edge* pronunciation "the most polite" and "the most agreeable to rule." Despite Walker's formidable influence,* many British and American authorities of the 19th century, and some in the early 20th century, including Phyfe (1926) and Vizetelly (1929), disdained the *edge* sound and preferred a *y* (or long *u*) sound in the second syllable. However, four major American dictionaries — the *Century* (1889–1914), Funk & Wagnalls *Standard* (1897), *Webster's New International* (1909), and *Webster 2* (1934) — sided with Walker (and, presumably, "the best usage" of their time), and by 1940 the *y* sound was fast on its way out. Of *educate, educator, education(al), educable,* and *educative*, Opdycke (1939) says, "In all of them *du* is preferably *ju* but it may be cleared — *ed' eu kate.*" Kenyon & Knott (1949) and *American College* (1952) countenance only the *edge* sound, and Lass & Lass (1976), who prefer *edge,* show that by the 1970s only one of the four leading American dictionaries recorded the *y* sound. Although the *y* sound survives today in ed-*yoo*-cated British speech, in America it is as rare and unappealing as steak tartare.

Avoid, at all costs, the peculiar variants ED-oo-kayt (*educate*) and ED-oo-**KAY**-shin (*education*), for which there is no modern authority.

e'er AIR (like *air*). See **ere**.

egregious i-GREE-jus (three syllables).

Eiffel (Tower) EYE-ful; (A. G. Eiffel) e-FEL, like the letters *f-l,* with stress on *l.*

A. G. Eiffel, the engineer who designed the famous tower, was French (*naturellement*), and according to Phyfe (1926) "his countrymen pronounce the word as if spelled Effel, with the accent on the *final* syllable."

---

* In *Dictionaries: The Art and Craft of Lexicography* (1984), Sidney I. Landau calls Walker's *Critical Pronouncing Dictionary* "one of the most popular and influential dictionaries ever published. It went through countless editions and remained in widespread use well into the nineteenth century. The work had an incalculably great effect on the treatment of pronunciation in other dictionaries as well as on schoolbooks, and many pronunciations still taught as correct in our schools can be traced to Walker's dictionary" (p. 57).

either EE-<u>thur</u>.

Though both EE-<u>thur</u> and NEE-<u>thur</u> (EE- and NEE- rhyming with *see*) and EYE-<u>thur</u> and NY-<u>thur</u> (EYE- and NY- rhyming with *high*) occur in educated American and British speech, authorities agree that EE-<u>thur</u> and NEE-<u>thur</u> have been and still are the customary American pronunciations, while EYE-<u>thur</u> and NY-<u>thur</u> prevail in England.

We could dispense with the issue right there, but a brief examination of the historical record on *either* and *neither* is enlightening.

Webster 2 (1934) notes that EYE-<u>thur</u> "is more prevalent in England (esp. in southern England) than in America. In the 17th century, the word was pronounced [AY-<u>thur</u>]. . . . Both [EE-<u>thur</u>] and [EYE-<u>thur</u>] were in general use by 1790."

In his influential *Critical Pronouncing Dictionary* (1791), the celebrated English elocutionist John Walker writes,

> *Either* and *neither* are so often pronounced *eye-ther* and *nigh-ther* that it is hard to say to which class they belong. Analogy, however, without hesitation, gives the diphthong the sound of long open *e*, rather than that of *i*, and rhymes them with *breather,* one who breathes. . . . We sometimes, indeed, hear the diphthongs in these words sounded like slender *a*, as if written *ay-ther* and *nay-ther;* but this pronunciation must be carefully avoided.

"Between [EE-<u>thur</u>] and [EYE-<u>thur</u>] there is little, in point of good usage, to choose," rules another oft-quoted English elocutionist, Benjamin Humphrey Smart, in his 1836 revision of Walker's dictionary, "but usage, as well as regularity, favors the sound of *e* in these two words."

By the end of the 19th century, the long *i* in *either* and *neither* "came to predominate in standard British speech," says *Random House II* (1987), but American authorities — from Ayres (1894) and Vizetelly (1929) to Lass & Lass (1976) and the *NBC Handbook* (1984) — have resolutely preferred the long *e* and tolerated the long *i* as a relatively harmless Anglophilic aberration. For example, Phyfe (1926), noting that three of the five major dictionaries of his time list long *e* first and the other two give only long *e,* concludes that "the consensus . . . is decidedly in favor of [EE-<u>thur</u>]; although [EYE-<u>thur</u>] is the pronunciation of a very respectable minority in the United States."

Random House II has more to tell us about this "very respectable minority" as it manifests itself today. "In American English," says the dictionary's pronunciation note, EYE-<u>thur</u> and NY-<u>thur</u> "reflect a recent borrowing from British speech rather than a survival from the time of early settlement, influenced as well by the *ei* spelling, which is pronounced (ī) in such words as *height* and *stein*." EYE-<u>thur</u> and NY-<u>thur</u> now "occur occasionally," claims *Random House II,* "chiefly in the speech of the educated and in the network standard English of radio and television."

Although it is true, as Morris and Morris (1985) note, that the long *i* is chiefly heard in New England and along the eastern seaboard, it is also true, as *Random House II* reports, that it is "a recent borrowing from British speech" used by many educated speakers throughout the U.S. and in the broadcast media. This raises an interesting question: why is it that *educated* Americans have adopted the long *i* pronunciation of *either* and *neither?* Could it be to call attention to their education, urbanity, or class?

Speech, like dress, is often a form of social statement. Among certain educated Americans, EYE-thur and NY-thur are but two examples of a predilection for "sophisticated" pronunciations, which these speakers apparently imagine will make them seem more polished and respectable and distinguish them from hoi polloi. Students of common sense, however, know that careful pronunciation in an American speaker is not necessarily a sign of intelligence, and poor pronunciation in an American speaker is not necessarily a sign of ignorance, but British pronunciation in an American speaker is almost always a sign that someone is putting on the dog.

Well aware of this canine tendency, Opdycke (1939) tactfully says it's okay to use a long *e* or long *i,* "but please adopt one or the other and stick to it. Don't say *eether* during your working hours, and *eyether* during your social hours." The American journalist and critic Richard Grant White (1821–1885) puts things more bluntly: "For the pronunciation [EYE-thur] and [NY-thur], with the *i* long, which is sometimes heard, there is no authority, either of analogy or of the best speakers. It is an affectation, and, in this country, a copy of second-rate British affectation. Persons of the best education and the highest social position in England generally say *eether* and *neether.*"

It is interesting to compare White's dictum with what the eminent *OED* lexicographer R. W. Burchfield (1996) has to say over a century later: "Both [EYE-thur] and [EE-thur] are used [in England] with approximately equal frequency. In 1984 a correspondent informed the Oxford dictionaries that the Queen's private secretary had told him . . . that the Queen pronounces the word herself as [EYE-thur]. Doubtless the Queen, like the rest of us who use the same pronunciation, regards the alternative one with a degree of amiable tolerance." The celebrated British novelist Kingsley Amis, in his posthumously published usage manual *The King's English* (1998), agrees. "Personally speaking," he writes, "I find [EE-thur] a trifle underbred."

Clearly, the sword cuts both ways, and American pronunciation in a British speaker won't do either. (Now, how did you pronounce that last word?)

electoral i-LEK-tur-ul. The accent is properly on the second syllable.

Don't say EE-lek-**TOR**-ul, with the primary accent on the third syllable, and don't add a syllable to the word and say EE-lek-**TOR**-ee-ul, as if it were spelled *electorial*. The former is beastly, the latter illiterate.

The trendy EE-lek-**TOR**-ul, with the primary accent on the third syllable, is regrettably rampant among radio and TV newsreaders and "analysts," who may have invented it and who have passed it on to the rest of us like the common cold. This variant, which apparently sprang up sometime after World War II, appears in *Webster 3* (1961) labeled with an obelus [÷] to indicate that many speakers found it objectionable. It did not appear in another dictionary for more than twenty-five years. In the 1980s it spread across the airwaves and infected the population, and today it is especially common among younger (under forty) speakers, some of whom may never have heard the proper pronunciation. As a result of this newfound popularity, EE-lek-**TOR**-ul reappears in *WNW 3* (1988) preceded by the label *often* (which only the cognoscenti would interpret as subtly pejorative),* and *M-W 10* (1993) lists it as an acceptable alternative. However, *American Heritage 3* (1992) and *RHWC* (1991, 1997) sanction only i-LEK-tur-ul, and no pronunciation maven with a reputation to lose would recommend anything else.

In *Watching My Language* (1997), William Safire relates a remarkable moment in broadcasting history. On election night in November 1992, when Bill Clinton defeated George Bush for the presidency, "at NBC, an assistant producer of *Today*, Chris Brown, reminded those on the air that *electoral* was pronounced 'e-LEC-tur-ul,' not the voguish 'e-lec-TOR-al.'" Chris Brown, you deserve my coveted Courageous Corrector Award! (I only hope you didn't lose your job.) See **mayoral, pastoral, pectoral**.

eleemosynary EL-uh-**MAHS**-i-ner-ee.

Eleemosynary means pertaining to or supported by charity. The pronunciation recommended above, with six syllables, is the first one listed in the four major current American dictionaries — *American Heritage 3* (1992), *M-W 10* (1993), *WNW 3* (1997), and *RHWC* (1997) — and the preference of an overwhelming number of authorities in the last hundred years, from the *Century* (1914) and Opdycke (1939) to Lass & Lass (1976) and the *NBC Handbook* (1984). Many American authorities also sanction the seven-syllable variant EL-ee-uh-**MAHS**-i-ner-ee, but *Webster 3* (1961) labels it "appreciably less frequent." My three current British authorities — *OED 2* (1989), Jones (1991), and Burchfield (1996) — prefer another seven-syllable variant, EL-i-ee-**MAHS**-i-nur-ee, which hasn't appeared in an American dictionary since *Webster 2* (1934), which lists the six-syllable EL-uh-

---

* See note 2 under *divisive* for more on the coded implications of pronunciation labels in modern dictionaries.

MAHS-i-ner-ee first. Although there is good authority for pronouncing the *s* like *z*, I doubt many say it that way anymore (except perhaps in Britain). Avoid the eccentric variant EL-uh-**MOH**-si-ner-ee, which appears only in *M-W 9* (1985) and *10* (1993).

elegiac EL-i-**JY**-ik.

This word is sometimes mispronounced EL-i-**JAY**-ik, as if the *i* and *a* were switched and the word were spelled *elegaic*.

EL-i-**JY**-ik (or sometimes the overenunciated EL-i-**JY**-ak), with the main stress on the third syllable, has been the preference of most American and British authorities from *OED 1* (1928) and *Webster 2* (1934) to Lass & Lass (1976) and the *NBC Handbook* (1984). Before 1930, most American authorities preferred i-**LEE**-jee-ak, with the stress on the second syllable. Although i-**LEE**-jee-ak still appears in current American dictionaries, *WNW Guide* (1984) says it is "heard occasionally" and *M-W 10* (1993) labels it "appreciably less common."

elephantine EL-uh-**FAN**-teen or EL-uh-**FAN**-tin or EL-uh-**FAN**-tyn.

However you choose to say it, be sure to stress the third syllable.

EL-uh-**FAN**-teen is listed first in all four major current American dictionaries and preferred by *WNW Guide* (1984) and the *NBC Handbook* (1984). EL-uh-**FAN**-tin is my favorite; it is the preference of most older American authorities and one recent one, *Everyday Reader's* (1985), but it is infrequent nowadays and some current dictionaries do not list it. EL-uh-**FAN**-tyn is originally and still chiefly British, although current American dictionaries recognize it and Lass & Lass (1976) prefer it.

The variants EL-uh-fun-teen and EL-uh-fun-tyn, with the accent on the first syllable rather than the third, are best avoided. They first appeared in the assiduously admissive *Webster 3* (1961), and the evidence of my ears tells me they are popular today mostly among younger speakers who no doubt modeled their pronunciation after *elephant* and never bothered to check a dictionary. No authority prefers these variants, however, and no current dictionary lists them first.

Elysian i-**LIZH**-in; **Elysium** i-**LIZH**-ee-um or i-**LIZ**-ee-um.

These are the pronunciations given priority in current dictionaries and preferred by most modern authorities. If you prefer the pseudoclassic sound of -**LEE**- in the second syllable, or any other oddball variant, then that's between you, your dictionary, and the Guard of the Glittering Fields of the Next World. See **Parisian**.

emeritus i-**MER**-i-tus.

"More than one radio announcer has come a cropper on this," says Holt (1937). "Just take *demerit*, knock the *d* off, and add *us*."

enclave EN-klayv, not AHN-klayv.

Burchfield (1996) notes that *enclave*, which entered English from French in the 1860s, was pronounced in a French manner — roughly aw(n)-KLAV — through the 1920s but is "now routinely" pronounced EN-klayv. Routinely in Britain, perhaps, but in America AHN-klayv is often heard. Historical evidence indicates that this hybrid was not a result of anglicization, providing a transition from the French pronunciation to the fully anglicized EN-klayv. Instead it arose after EN-klayv already was established, and therefore must be considered a de-anglicized pronunciation — a misguided and often affected attempt to reinstate some of the foreign flavor of an anglicized loanword. "Some of the worst offenders are newscasters," write Morris & Morris (1985), "who seem to think it adds a touch of elegance to their pear-shaped tones to say ON-clave and ON-voy."

The anglicized EN-klayv has been the preferred pronunciation since *Webster 2* (1934). AHN-klayv, which first received recognition in *Webster 3* (1961), has not one champion among my authorities. All four major current American dictionaries list EN-klayv first, and *M-W 10* (1993) labels AHN-klayv as objectionable to some speakers. See **envelope, envoy.**

endive EN-dyv (like *end dive* said quickly). British, EN-div.

You know what I think of the variant ahn-DEEV (or AHN-deev)? I think *phooey!* It's beyond high time to drop the pseudo-French and pronounce this venerable word in English. After all, it's been English since the 14th century. Is that long enough for you? Current American dictionaries recognize ahn-DEEV and AHN-deev but all of them list EN-dyv first. *WNW Guide* (1984) and the *NBC Handbook* (1984) prefer EN-dyv.

enigmatic EN-ig-**MAT**-ik. Occasionally, and formerly, EE-nig-**MAT**-ik.

Should the *e* in *enigmatic* be short, as in *pen,* or long, as in *seen?* Both pronunciations have a long history in cultivated speech — more than two hundred years. Sheridan (1780), for example, preferred the long *e* while Walker (1791) preferred the short *e*. Most 19th-century authorities sided with Sheridan, but early in the 20th century the short *e* began a strong comeback, gaining the acceptance of numerous American and British authorities. Today the short *e* is so widespread that it has almost run the long *e* out of town. *OED 2* (1989) prefers long *e* but concedes that short *e* is now usual. Three of the four leading current American dictionaries label long *e* less frequent, and *American Heritage 3* (1992) countenances only short *e*.

en masse en-MAS (recommended) or ahn-MAS.

This phrase has been in the language for about 200 years, and it has been anglicized for at least 75 years — *Webster 2* (1934), Kenyon & Knott (1949), and *American College* (1952) all prefer en-MAS and do not recognize ahn-MAS, which first appears in *Webster 3* (1961). To say ahn- (like *on*) for *en,* especially when *masse* is anglicized to sound like *mass,* strikes me as pseudo-French. In my book it makes little sense to cling to a foreign pronunciation or to affect a half-foreign, half-English pronunciation of a word when a fully anglicized pronunciation has been listed in good standing and been used by careful speakers for the better part of a century. I will admit, however, that my distaste for ahn-MAS is a crotchet and does not reflect the reigning mood, for many educated speakers use the hybrid pronunciation and various authorities — including Lass & Lass (1976), the *NBC Handbook* (1984), and *Everyday Reader's* (1985) — prefer it. See **en rapport, en route,** and, for more on *en-* and pseudo-French, **enclave, envelope,** and **envoy.**

en rapport AW(N) ra-POR (or ruh-POR).

Unlike *en masse,* this phrase has *not* been fully anglicized and may never be, probably because the *t* has always been silent in *rapport* (and shows no signs of asserting itself). A half-anglicized AHN (like *on*) for *en* is now acceptable, but the French AW(N), with a nasalized *n,* is still generally preferred. See **en masse, en route.**

en route en-ROOT (recommended) or ahn-ROOT.

Although they are often heard, en-ROWT and especially ahn-ROWT are not listed or labeled infrequent by some current dictionaries — reason enough, as far as I'm concerned, to avoid them. The French-flavored ahn-ROOT is probably more common today than the anglicized en-ROOT; it is the preference of numerous authorities, past and present, and the fact that ahn- sounds like *on* (as in *on the way*) no doubt has added to its popularity among educated speakers. The anglicized version is recommended here, however, for consistency's sake, to bring *en route* in line with the many other common words and phrases in which *en-* has been anglicized. See **en masse, en rapport, envelope,** and **route.**

enthusiast en-THOO-zee-AST, not en-**THOO**-zee-IST.

The final syllable, *-ast,* is properly pronounced to rhyme with *fast,* not with *fist.*

   Webster 3 (1961) was the first dictionary to countenance -IST for the last syllable of this word, which entered English in 1609. Despite its popularity, current authority still favors the traditional pronunciation, en-**THOO**-zee-AST. *M-W 10* (1993), *RHWC* (1997), and *WNW 3* (1997) list it first, the *NBC Handbook* (1984) prefers it, and it is the only pronunciation sanctioned by *Oxford American* (1980), *American Heritage 3* (1992), and *OED 2* (1989). See **gymnast.**

entirety en-TY-ur-tee (or en-TYR-tee), not en-TY-ruh-tee.

You wouldn't say en-TY-ruh-lee for *entirely,* would you? Of course not. Everyone says en-TY-ur-lee (or en-TYR-lee). So why do so many speakers today say en-TY-ruh-tee for *entirety?* Two reasons, I think. Most do so because it's easier to say than the proper pronunciation, and some do so because they want to show they can spell.

Unfortunately, all the current dictionaries now sanction the preposterous en-TY-ruh-tee, so any boob can point to them and assert his right to mispronounce the word. Yet the curious thing is that all of them also divide the word *en · tire · ty*. Not a one gives *en · ti · re · ty*. That is cause enough, in my opinion, to view en-TY-ruh-tee with suspicion. Add to that the fact that no orthoepist I have consulted countenances en-TY-ruh-tee and you have the makings of a beastly mispronunciation. Careful speakers are hereby advised to preserve the *tire* in *entirety*.

entrepreneur AHN-truh-pruh-**NUR** (last syllable rhymes with *sir* and *fir*). English speakers have such a devil of a time with this French loanword that the best thing we could do would be to chuck it and use *enterpriser* or *business venturer* or some such thing instead. But *entrepreneur* has been with us for over a century now, and in recent years it has become so widely used that even the uneducated now happily mispronounce it. Clearly there's a need for this word, so we had better put some effort into saying — and spelling — it properly.

Entrepreneur is one of a class of words that many people misspell according to their pronunciation — which in most cases is a beastly mispronunciation. As any good English teacher will tell you, fools spell as fools speak, and here are some regrettably common examples: *miniscule* for *minuscule,* the verb *loathe* used where the adjective *loath* is meant, *momento* for *memento, expresso* for *espresso, unequivocably* for *unequivocally, doctorial* for *doctoral, Brobdignagian* for *Brobdingnagian, conservativism* for *conservatism, daquiri* for *daiquiri, crisises* as the plural of *crisis,* and, last but not least, *pronounciation* for *pronunciation.* (See the entries for all these words — under their correct spellings, of course.)

In the case of *entrepreneur,* careless speakers often omit the *r* in the next-to-last syllable, pronouncing it -puh- instead of -pruh-, and this beastly mispronunciation now sometimes appears in print as *entrepeneur,* even in so-called "edited writing." One example should suffice: "Our code of entrepeneurial [*sic*] individualism . . ." wrote Michiko Kakutani of *The New York Times Magazine* (December 7, 1997, p. 38). When a mispronunciation weasels its way into that level of print, it's bound to weasel its way into the dictionaries, and sure enough the aurally unslumbering editors at Merriam-Webster — in *Webster 3* (1961) through *M-W 10* (1993) — recognize the slovenly -puh- for the penultimate syllable. No other current dictionary does, but I'm not placing any bets that Merriam-Webster will be alone for long.

The other perennial problem people have with *entrepreneur* is mispronouncing the final syllable, -*neur,* as -**NOOR**, or worse, -**NYOOR** (both rhyming with *tour* and *boor*). As in *connoisseur, voyeur, chauffeur, liqueur, colporteur* (KAHL-por-tur), *raconteur* (RAK-ahn-**TUR** or RAK-<u>un</u>-**TUR**), and *restaurateur* (RES-tuh-ruh-**TUR** — do not pronounce and spell it with the *n* of *restaurant*), the -*eur* in *entrepreneur* properly should rhyme with *sir*. The unfortunate prevalence of the pseudosophisticated -**NOOR** and -**NYOOR** variants has led dictionaries to recognize them, but all four current American dictionaries give priority to -**NUR** for the final syllable, and I am aware of only one modern authority — *WNW Guide* (1984) — that prefers -**NOOR**. See **amateur, connoisseur, de rigueur, liqueur, restaurateur**. For more on how mispronunciation influences spelling, see **loath, minuscule, memento**.

envelope (noun) EN-vuh-lohp, not AHN-vuh-lohp.

Of *envelope, enclave,* and *envoy,* Morris & Morris (1985) have this to say:

> All three are borrowings from French and all three are victims of people using what they take to be an approximation of the French accent by pronouncing the first syllable as ON. The results are ON-vel-ope, ON-voy, and ON-clave, fair examples of what someone once called "bargain basement French."
>
> In the case of the first, EN-velope is unquestionably the more logical pronunciation. . . . [T]here is no sense to the pseudo-French pronunciation of ON-velope, but so many well-educated people use it that all American dictionaries enter it as an . . . acceptable pronunciation.

Kenyon and Knott (1949) also call AHN-vuh-lohp "pseudo-French." Holt (1937) asks, "Why keep the French 'on' when the French spelling *(enveloppe)* has long been discarded?" *M-W 10* (1993), which labels AHN-vuh-lohp unacceptable to some speakers, offers this explanatory note:

> The \'en\ and \'än\ pronunciations are used with about equal frequency, and both are fully acceptable, though the \'än\ version is sometimes decried as "pseudo-French." Actually \'än\ is exactly what one would expect to hear when a French word like *entrepreneur* is becoming anglicized. *Envelope,* however, has been in English for nearly 300 years, plenty of time for it to become completely anglicized and for both of its pronunciations to win respectability.

That AHN-vuh-lohp is acceptable, I will grudgingly admit. That it is respectable is open to debate. Whenever I hear someone say AHN-vuh-lohp I think of the hackneyed phrase uttered ad nauseam every year during the Academy Awards — that interminable, tawdry tribute to the narcissism of Hollywood: *the ON-velope, please.* Do you think all those grinning, glib celebrities pronounced it that way before they joined the glitterati? I doubt it, *dahling.* Certainly Hollywood's annual self-love fest, established in 1927, has played no small part in making AHN-vuh-lohp "respectable," but somehow its phony aroma never managed to go away.

Three of the four major current American dictionaries and *OED 2* (1989) list EN-vuh-lohp first, and it is preferred by Lass & Lass (1976), the *NBC Handbook* (1984), and Burchfield (1996), who says it "is now dominant." See **enclave, envoy**.

environment en-VY-urn-m̲e̲nt or en-VY-r̲u̲n-m̲e̲nt.

Be sure to pronounce the middle *n*. Don't say en-VY-ur-m̲e̲nt, as if the word were spelled *envirement*. This beastly mispronunciation is now so common that *M-W 9* (1985) and *10* (1993) recognize it. But many careful speakers frown upon it, including *New York Times* language maven William Safire, who is tolerant and sometimes downright liberal when it comes to pronunciation. Safire says he will never accept en-VY-ur-m̲e̲nt, sans the middle *n*, in his *liberry* — and I'm with him all the way. We've lost the *n* in *government*. Please help hold the line on our poor *environment*.

envoy EN-voy, not AHN-voy.

AHN-voy is pseudo-French. "No authority for the fake-French 'on,'" says Holt (1937). "The *en* is just 'en.'" See **enclave, envelope**.

ephemeral i̲-FEM-uh-r̲u̲l.

Although some current sources recognize the three-syllable variant i̲-FEM-ruul, *ephemeral* is traditionally and preferably pronounced in four syllables. Lass & Lass (1976), the *Quintessential Dictionary* (1978), *WNW Guide* (1984), the *NBC Handbook* (1984), *Everyday Reader's* (1985), and Barnhart (1988) all prefer i̲-FEM-uh-r̲u̲l, which is the only pronunciation sanctioned by *American Heritage 3* (1992) and *RHWC* (1997).

Listening to NPR one day, I heard a British psychiatrist say i̲-FEE-muh-r̲u̲l, rhyming the second, accented syllable with *seem* rather than *hem*. How peculiar, I thought — and therefore worthy of investigation. First I went to my chief British source, *OED 2* (1989), and found only i̲-FEM-uh-r̲u̲l. After digging around for a while I found i̲-FEE-muh-r̲u̲l in only three sources: *Webster 3* (1961) calls it "chiefly British"; Jones (1991), another leading British authority, labels it "somewhat less common" than i̲-FEM-uh-r̲u̲l; and I was amazed to discover that *M-W 10* (1993), America's best-selling dictionary, lists i̲-FEE-muh-r̲u̲l with no qualifying label at all.

Conclusion: say i̲-FEM-uh-r̲u̲l.

epitome i̲-PIT-uh-mee.

Stress the *pit* and pronounce *epitome* in four syllables. "It rhymes with 'She *hit* a bee,'" says Holt (1937). There is no *tome* in *epitome*. The three-syllable EP-i̲-tohm is beastly.

E-PIT-o-mē is kind and fair.
Of evil EP-i̲-tōm beware.

> Of mispronunciation he
> Is clearly the e-PIT-ome.
> — Willard R. Espy, *Say It My Way* (1980)

epoch EP-u̲k.

EP-u̲k, the dominant American pronunciation of *epoch*, sounds almost the same as *epic* (EP-ik), but there is a slight difference: the *o* in *epoch* is obscure — like the *o* in *hillock* or *cassock*, or the *a* in *stomach* — whereas the *i* in *epic* is short, as in *pick*. The variant EP-ahk (-ahk rhyming with *clock*) is also recognized by dictionaries but thankfully less often heard. (It sounds painfully overpronounced to me.) Another variant, EE-pahk, is the usual British and Canadian pronunciation, notes *WNW 3* (1997).

Stress the adjective *epochal*, like *typical*, on the first syllable: EP-uh-ku̲l.

equable EK-wuh-buul.

American usage and the weight of authority have favored this pronunciation, with a short *e* sound, since *Webster 2* (1934). The long *e* sound, EE-kwuh-buul, although duly recorded in current dictionaries, is far less often heard. Among current authorities only Lass & Lass (1976) prefer it. See **equi-**.

equanimity EE-kwuh-**NIM**-i̲-tee.

From Phyfe (1926) to Kenyon & Knott (1949) to the *NBC Handbook* (1984), the weight of orthoepic authority favors a long *e* (ē) sound, as in *me*, for the first syllable. Although EK-wuh-**NIM**-i̲-tee, with a short *e* (ĕ) sound, as in *wreck*, for the first syllable, has been an acceptable alternative since *Webster 2* (1934), only *WNW Guide* (1984) gives it priority and among current dictionaries only *WNW 3* (1997) lists it first.

equatorial EE-kwuh-**TOR**-ee-u̲l.

The short *e* of *peck* has been standard since the 1940s, but the long *e* of *equal* — preferred by *Webster 2* (1934), Opdycke (1939), Lass & Lass (1976), and the *NBC Handbook* (1984) — is recommended as having greater authority.

equi- 1. Authority favors EE-kwi̲- or EE-kwuh, with the long *e* sound of *meet*, in most words where the first syllable is stressed: *equidistant, equilateral, equilibrium, equine,* and *equinox*. Authority favors the short *e* of *met*, however, in *equity, equitable,* and *equipage* (which see), and is about evenly divided between long and short *e* in *equipoise* (I prefer the latter). See also **equable**. 2. When the first syllable is unstressed, as in *equipment, equivalent, equivocal, equivocate,* and *equilibrist*, the *e* is lightened and sounds like the short *i* of *sit* or the *i* in *sanity*. 3. The same lightened *e* is heard in *equality, equator,* and *equestrian*.

equilibrate i-KWIL-i̲-brayt (ee- for the first syllable is also acceptable but less frequent).

This has been the dominant pronunciation in America for at least 50 years, rapidly replacing EE-kwi-**LY**-brayt, which authorities generally preferred until the 1950s. *American Heritage 3* (1992) and *M-W 10* (1993) list only i-KWIL-i-brayt, and *WNW 3* (1997) labels EE-kwi-**LY**-brayt infrequent. See **equi-**.

equilibrium EE-kwi-**LIB**-ree-um. See **equi-**.

equinox EE-kwi-nahks. See **equi-**.

equipage EK-wi-pij (rhymes with *sacrilege* and *get a bridge*).

This is the only acceptable pronunciation. Stressing *-quip-* is beastly, and Frenchifying *-page* to -pahzh is affected. Only *Webster 3* (1961) lists these variants, labeling them either objectionable or infrequent. Other authorities, including all four major current American dictionaries and *OED 2* (1989), sanction only EK-wi-pij. See **equi-**.

era EER-uh (like *ear* + *uh*).

Authorities formerly preferred EE-ruh, with the long *e* of *be,* but since the 1930s this hyperarticulate pronunciation has given way to the more fluent EER-uh, in which the long *e* blends into the *r* as in *hero* and *zero.* The variant with short *e*, pronounced ER-uh (or, by many, AIR-uh) so that the word sounds like *error* pronounced by a terminal *r*-dropper, first appeared in *Webster 3* (1961). This homegrown American vogue pronunciation has little to recommend it other than its popularity. Lass & Lass (1976), Funk & Wagnalls *Standard* (1980), the *NBC Handbook* (1984), and *OED 2* (1989) prefer EER-uh, and all four major current American dictionaries list it first.

ere AIR (like *air*). See **e'er**.

err UR, not ER or AIR.

Traditionally, *err* rhymes with *her* and *sir,* not with *hair* and *fair.* Also, *erred* rhymes with *bird* and *erring* with *stirring.*

"Though [ER/AIR] is now common," says *WNWG* (1984), which prudently prefers UR, "it is still objected to by some." What an understatement! In my book, ER/AIR for *err* is right up there in the competition for the Great Beastly Mispronunciation of All Time. While those who don't know how it should be pronounced are blissfully AIRing and being YOO-man, the beleaguered legions of those who will not forgive fight a divine battle to preserve what has abided for generations. (All right, it's not really a holy war, just a beastly mispronunciation.) Here's the situation:

The trouble perhaps may have begun with the English elocutionist John Walker (1791), who, in his immensely influential *Critical Pronouncing Dictionary,* ambiguously indicates the short *e* sound of *met* not only for *err* but also for *-er* in *deter, prefer, refer, inter, aver,* and *transfer,* as well as in *herd, heard, hermit,* and *ferry, merry, berry,* and *bury.* No doubt that confused some of the many Americans who relied on Walker, but American authorities of the 19th century were in no way ambiguous about the correct pronunciation. For example, in Worcester (1860), Webster (1867 "academic edition"), and Funk & Wagnalls *Standard* (1897), *err* rhymes with *her* and *term* or has the sound of *-er* in *over*. An 1898 handbook called *Ten Thousand Words: How to Pronounce Them* ("Indispensable for Cultured People," boasts the title page), in its key to pronunciation, gives *err* to illustrate the diacritic ė, apparently content that readers would discern from this one example that the vowel sound being indicated was the same as in *fur* and *sir*.

Authorities of the first half of the 20th century were no less definite in their preference for UR, but because ER/AIR had by now begun to spread, they were no longer nonchalant. Gilmartin (1936) says, "This little verb is often confounded with the noun *error*. It has but one syllable and should rhyme with *purr*." Opdycke (1939) insists that *err* "must be pronounced to rime with *were*, not with *ware*; . . . *erred* rimes with *herd*, and . . . *erring* rimes with *purring*." And Holt (1937) writes, "In spite of *error* and *errant*, don't say, 'We have *aired* and strayed from thy ways like lost sheep.' Let the thought of *deterring* deter you from a mispronunciation of *erring*."

Some argue that *err* is the etymological cousin (through Latin *errare*, to wander, stray) of *error* and *errant*, and so should be pronounced similarly. Considering that for at least 150 years UR was the only acceptable pronunciation in educated speech, this argument strikes me as a feeble attempt to find a legitimate reason for a mistake — which of course is how ER/AIR started out: a pronunciation mistakenly arrived at (a) through ignorance of the established pronunciation, and (b) by false analogy with *error*. If *err* means to commit an *error*, people reasoned, surely two words so close in meaning and spelling must have the same sound. The problem with this line of thinking was that it ignored the fact that UR for *err* was a longstanding idiosyncrasy of English pronunciation, like *herd* and *heard* having the same pronunciation, or *cough* and *rough* having dissimilar sounds. Clearly the speakers who first adopted ER/AIR did so without so much as a peek into a dictionary, and the speakers who copied them simply took it on faith that what they had embraced was right.

ER/AIR did not appear in a dictionary until the 1960s, but since then it has rapidly been displacing the traditional pronunciation. Modern authorities, however, such as *WNW Guide* (1984) cited above, have given the variant a cool reception. Only the *NBC Handbook* (1984) prefers it, and of the four major current American dictionaries only *M-W 10* (1993) lists it first. *OED 2* (1989) does not recognize ER/AIR, and *WNW 3* (1997) gives UR followed by the subtly deprecating "*widely* er." Nevertheless, as you may have surmised, if we do not conscientiously continue to UR today, our children will surely ER/AIR tomorrow, for as William Safire has said, "In pronunciation and ultimately in usage, when enough of us are wrong, we're right." I'm not sure I agree with that, but I'll admit it's hard to dispute.

erratum i-RAY-t<u>u</u>m; **errata** i-RAY-tuh.

The de-anglicized (or re-Latinized) pronunciations i-RAH-t<u>u</u>m and i-RAH-tuh have been recognized by dictionaries since the 1940s and are preferred by some current sources, including the *NBC Handbook* (1984). The weight of modern authority, however, favors the anglicized *ray* for the second syllable. Don't put a *rat* in these words: avoid i-RAT-<u>u</u>m and i-RAT-uh. See **data**.

error ER-ur or AIR-ur. Do not say AIR.

Sportcasters, particularly those who cover baseball, are notoriously careless pronouncers of this word. Many say it in one syllable instead of two, compressing *error* into *air*. Affected speakers, on the other hand, overpronounce the terminal *-or* by giving it a full OR sound, like *oar*. Both of these pronunciations are, in dictionary lingo, "nonstandard," which in this book means beastly. A third variant, ER-uh, with the final *r* silent, is not listed in dictionaries but is acceptable from speakers who normally drop their *r*'s (e.g., some New Englanders, New Yorkers, and Southerners) and pronounce, for example, *carrier* as KAR-ee-uh and *father* as FAH-<u>th</u>uh. The pronunciation ER-ur, with *e* as in *pet*, is chiefly Eastern and Southern; the pronunciation AIR-ur (AIR- as in *pair*), chiefly Midwestern and Western. Use the one you are comfortable with. Just remember to pronounce the word in two syllables. See **furor, mirror,** and, for more on the overpronunciation of *-or*, **juror.**

erudite Traditionally, **ER**-uh-DYT (or **AIR**-). Now usually **ER**-yuh-DYT (or **AIR**-).

Before we get into the matter of whether 'tis nobler to pronounce the *u* in *erudite* with or without a *y* sound, let me point out that this *u*, with or without the *y* sound, may acceptably have any of three different pronunciations: -oo- as in *rude*, -uu- as in *wood*, or -uh- as in *mud*. Variation from one of these sounds to another is also common and acceptable in cultivated speech. The four major current American dictionaries reflect this variation: *WNW 3* (1997) gives -oo- and -uh-; *RHWC* (1997) gives only -uu-; and *American Heritage 3* (1992) and *M-W 10* (1993) give only -uh-. I am using -uh- here only because it is probably the most common of the three, but all three are permissible.

Now let us consider the *y* sound in the second syllable: should we say **ER**-uh-DYT or **ER**-yuh-DYT? Doesn't it sound rather more erudite to insert the *y* (creating a quasi-long *u*)? If your answer to that rhetorical question was yes, then you can take comfort in the fact that you are in the majority, for nearly everyone nowadays says **ER**-yuh-DYT. If your answer was no, then chances are you know something more about this word than simply its definition and how most everyone else pronounces it.

Okay, now let's get pedantic. *Erudite* comes from the Latin *eruditus*, educated, the past participle of *erudire*, to instruct, polish, which is formed in turn from *e-* (*ex-*), without, and *rudis*, rude, unschooled. By derivation it means "free from rudeness." The traditional pronunciation of *erudite*, with -uu- or -uh- in the second syllable, is a subtle and refined reminder of the word's origin — *e-* (without) -*rudite* (rudeness). The popular pronunciation, **ER**-yuh-DYT, with the *y* inserted, ignores the *rude* dwelling within *erudite* and illogically transforms the short Latin vowel into a long English one.

ER-yuh-DYT was a vogue pronunciation that gained popularity in the early 20th century. Although *Webster 2* (1934) recognized it as an acceptable alternative, contemporaneous authorities disapproved of it. "Preferably, not 'air-yoo' but 'air-oo'," said Holt (1937). Opdycke (1939) advised, "Don't pronounce *u* long — it is not *ewe*." Since the 1960s, when dictionaries began giving priority to **ER**-yuh-DYT, it has been the dominant pronunciation in American speech.

So why do I choose to fight the lonely fight for the pure, *y*-less **ER**-uh-DYT? Because of my nagging suspicion that it has always been those members of society who would fashion themselves as fashionable who thought it better to pronounce this learned word in a superficially more learned way, though you will never hear these same people taking pains to pronounce the long *u* in *duty* or *assume* or say the DYOO (*dew*) has fallen rather than the DOO has fallen. Though **ER**-yuh-DYT may now prevail, it is still, in my estimation, pseudocultivated.

By the way, my preferred pronunciation of *erudite* is not as disused as it may seem. Most British speakers — who typically pronounce the long *u* in words like *opportunity, presume, minute, tutor, endure, deuce, neutral,* and *astute* and who always say *nyew* and *dyew*— do not put a *you* in *erudite*. Jones (1991) gives priority to **ER**-oo-DYT, and *OED 2* (1989) sanctions only **ER**-uh-DYT. Now isn't that interesting? See **garrulous, querulous, virulent.**

escape ẹ-SKAYP.

Be careful not to say ek-SKAYP, as if the word were spelled *excape*. Some say this beastly mispronunciation is an offense confined to the uneducated, but that is not the case, as one example should illustrate. Some years ago on TV's *Saturday Night Live* I heard the comedian Dennis Miller say ek-SKAYP during his "Weekend Update" segment, and, I can assure you, he wasn't joking.

"Possibly because so many English words begin with *ex, escape* is often mispronounced," writes Harry Shaw in *Say It Right!* (1972), which is why so many educated adults are also guilty of the beastly mispronunciations *expresso* for *espresso* and *ek cetera* for *et cetera*. In most cases *excape* for *escape* is a vestigial error from childhood, a time when we all struggle to master the many challenging and often confusing consonant clusters in the language — sometimes with ludicrous results like *puh-sketty* for *spaghetti* and *pacific* for *specific*. Most of us eventually hear these errors and correct them, but for others a solecism like *excape* may slip by, become a habit, and then a liability. Parents and teachers faced with children who say *excape* are hereby advised to give gentle guidance, good example, and be patient. See **ask, especially, espresso, et cetera, library**.

eschew   es-CHOO. Do not say e-SHOO or e-SKYOO.

Traditionally and properly, there is no *shoe* in *eschew,* and no *skew* either. It's *chew.*

From time to time I correspond with Brian M. Sietsema (SEET-suh-muh), Ph.D., pronunciation editor of Merriam-Webster, Inc., and the man behind the pronunciations in their latest opus, *Merriam-Webster's Collegiate Dictionary, Tenth Edition,* referred to in this book as *M-W 10* (1993). We have a healthy professional respect for each other, but we both know we stand on opposite sides of a linguistic Mason-Dixon line. Sietsema's job is to describe; mine is to prescribe. He records; I remonstrate. He defends what I decry. He deals with what is, while I deal with what is versus what should be.

As you can imagine, we frequently agree to disagree, and such was the case when I wrote him in December 1996 regarding his treatment of the pronunciation of *eschew.*

"Can it be true," I asked, "that, in the *Tenth,* you give 'e-shü [e-SHOO] . . . *also* e-skyü [e-SKYOO]' for *eschew?* Heaven forfend, sir! Say it ain't so, Sietsema. There is no *shoe* in *eschew,* and only the vocally imbalanced would pronounce the word *askew.* What in the name of Orthoëpicus possessed you to countenance these cockamamie mispronunciations? I respectfully request — no, make that demand — an explanation."

Sietsema is a busy lexicographer who I imagine must spend a lot of his time collecting variant pronunciations — like a lepidopterist in search of new species of moths and butterflies, or the Starship *Enterprise* in search of "new civil-*eye*-zations." The following July he sent a lengthy reply:

The short answer to your questions about the first and last pronunciations listed in the entry in *Merriam-Webster's Collegiate Dictionary, Tenth Edition,* is the same answer that I would give to a question about almost any pronunciation in the book: we include it because we have collected citations for it over a span of years from educated native speakers of English. It is possible that the last variant in the *Tenth Collegiate* [e-SKYOO] and the pronunciation which you favor [es-CHOO] both qualify as spelling pronunciations in their own way — the latter because it has perhaps always been so, and the former because it appears to have died out and been resurrected later on by those attentive to spelling (or etymology), somewhat like the pronunciation of *schism* with a velar consonant.

There is an interesting comparison of these two pronunciations in John Walker's *A Critical Pronouncing Dictionary and Expositor of the English Language*. (I have the fifth printing of 1810 in my office.) No slouch as a prescriptive orthoepist, Walker seems to have favored the sentiments of a certain Mr. Elphinston, who wrote in defense of the spelling *eskew* and the pronunciation appropriate thereto, over and against the spelling *eschew* and its common pronunciation (the one you prefer).

> "No wonder *eskew,* (he says,) often falsely articulated because falsely exhibited *eschew,* was ocularly traced from the old *scheoir* (afterwards *echoir*) to devolve or escheat, rather than from *esquiver,* to parry, avoid, or *eskew;* by those to whom the body of the child and the soul of the parent were equally unknown." The etymological abilities of this gentleman in the French and English languages are unquestionable; . . .

Walker, however, ends up recommending your variant, but admits that he does so only in order to go with the flow of majority usage:

> . . . but the pronunciation of this word seems fixed to its orthography; and beyond the reach of etymology to alter. Words, like land, have a limitation to their rights. When an orthography and pronunciation have obtained for a long time, though by false title, it is perhaps better to leave them in quiet possession, than to disturb the language by an ancient, though perhaps better claim.

Rather sound advice, don't you think? Perhaps Messrs. Elphinston and Walker would have rejoiced to see our day, when the pronunciation to which they grant etymological bragging rights is again countenanced by a reputable dictionary. In any case, if your preferred *chew* pronunciation gains its place "by false title," certainly the *shoe* pronunciation which so many use nowadays has no falser a title. It is clear from the list of alternate early spellings in the *Oxford English Dictionary, Second Edition* that the *shoe* pronunciation is pretty old as well, and it is clear from our citation files that the *shoe* variant is used at least as much as if not more than the *chew* variant. And so we include all those variants in the *Tenth Collegiate* for the same reasons that motivated Walker to include your preferred variant: in the words of Noah Webster, "The general practice of a nation is the rule of propriety."

This is such an excellent argument that I hate to pick it apart, but I'm afraid I must. After all, as a careful speaker you deserve to know how and why this distinguished pronunciation editor's defense of e-SHOO and e-SKYOO is wrongheaded and flawed.

To begin with, I must contest that "the *shoe* variant is used at least as much as if not more than the *chew* variant." If the *shoe* variant were as common as Sietsema claims, wouldn't it be reasonable to expect to find it in at least one other dictionary? Well, you won't find it anywhere, not even in another Merriam-Webster dictionary and not in the two leading American dictionaries — *RHWC* (1997) and *WNW 3* (1997) — published after Sietsema's *M-W 10* (1993). In fact, not a single dictionary or authority, past or present, countenances the *shoe* variant, and no source I am aware of even mentions its existence. (Nobody — other than the obscure Elphinston, whose *Principles of the English Language Digested* was published in 1765 — gives the time of day to e-SKYOO either.) Given such conspicuous lack of recognition, it's hard to believe Sietsema's assertion of currency. Yet he says it's all strictly scientific, based on citations collected "over a span of years from educated native speakers of English." How can you argue with that?

I'll tell you how. While prescriptive language mavens like me are always on the lookout for verbal blunders, descriptive lexicographers like Sietsema are always on the qui vivre for linguistic variation. It's a matter of perspective. When I hear a pronunciation that deviates from established usage, I make a note of it and put it in a file labeled "Beastly Mispronunciations." When he hears the same thing, he fills out a citation slip and puts it in a file labeled "For Possible Inclusion in the Next Merriam-Webster Dictionary." It's no wonder, then, that Sietsema's citation files are stuffed with examples of the *shoe* variant. It's what he listens for, what catches his ear; it represents variation, change, perhaps a new order for the ages. The traditional *chew* pronunciation, like your parents when you were a teenager, is *boring*.

Sietsema's *M-W 10* recognizes not one but two variants for a word that has' had only one acceptable pronunciation since the 18th century, when dictionaries first began recording pronunciation. How is it that lexicographers at other houses, who were presumably engaged in the same activity of noting the occurrence of variant pronunciations, managed to overlook the frequency of e-SHOO, the first pronunciation in *M-W 10*, and the "appreciably less common" e-SKYOO in educated speech? Could it be that they determined, based on their own evidence, that these variants were not prevalent or respectable enough to warrant inclusion in their dictionaries? With all due respect for Merriam-Webster's diligence, I am not prepared to accept on their good word the propriety of two new pronunciations that other contemporary American dictionaries — and *OED 2* (1989) as well — have failed to note or chosen to ignore. I would like, at the very least, a second opinion.

"If your preferred *chew* pronunciation gains its place 'by false title,'" writes Sietsema, "certainly the *shoe* pronunciation which so many use nowadays has no falser a title." That is a clever way of dismissing my objections by saying that if two pronunciations are equally illegitimate, one cannot be deemed more acceptable than the other. The point is irrelevant, of course. Most words, especially older ones, deviate from their origins, and the origin of *eschew*, as Walker indicated, is so ancient and buried that even in his day it was already "fixed to its orthography; and beyond the reach of etymology to alter." This is a word that came into English in the 14th century, that until the 17th century was spelled in well over a dozen ways, that Dr. Johnson, in his famous dictionary of 1755, called "almost obsolete," and that stubbornly refused to die. When the dust had finally settled and it was clear the word was here to stay, the spelling and pronunciation of record were *eschew* and es-CHOO. That is not gaining a place by false title. That is earning your keep by usage. And more and more usage. And consistent recognition by dictionaries and orthoepists from Walker to the present day. The *shoe* variant, on the other hand, has only one dictionary, an indeterminate number of late 20th-century followers, and a couple of obsolete spellings from the 14th and 15th centuries to recommend it. Those are pretty flimsy credentials, I'm afraid.

Walker's advice to leave well enough alone in cases of long-standing usage is indeed sound, which is why I'm surprised Mr. Sietsema didn't follow it himself. In sanctioning es-CHOO, Walker was only bestowing his blessing upon a pronunciation that had already "obtained for a long time." In listing e-SHOO and e-SKYOO, however, Sietsema and *M-W 10* have not recognized "the general practice of a nation," only the obstinate malpractice of some of its citizens.

As for my own citation files, I can attest to hearing the *shoe* variant occasionally, the *skew* variant never. The former is undoubtedly a vogue pronunciation and the latter is probably a pedanticism, as Sietsema himself suggests. The eccentric Elphinston might have been delighted to see e-SKYOO countenanced by a reputable dictionary, but Walker and Webster, I'll wager, would have questioned the propriety of both variants and wondered aloud, as I have done, why on earth *M-W 10* is disturbing the language with them. For more on Brian M. Sietsema, see **flaccid, paroxysm.**

esoteric ES-uh-**TER**-ik (-**TER**- as in *terrace*).

There is no authority for ES-uh-**TEER**-ik (-**TEER**- rhyming with *fear*).

especially e-SPESH-uh-lee (or i̲- for the first, unstressed syllable).

Speakers who say eks-SPESH-uh-lee (like *x-specially*) are *especially* beastly. See **ask, escape, espresso, et cetera.**

espresso es-PRES-oh.

Watch out for the beastly mispronunciation ek-SPRES-oh. There is no *ex-* in *espresso*. The word is properly pronounced *s · press · oh*.

Occasionally you will see this word misspelled *expresso* after the mispronunciation, especially in the names of or ads for the gourmet coffee shops that have proliferated in recent years. Although current dictionaries, including *OED 2* (1989), now record *expresso* as a variant spelling — for which they give the pronunciation ek-SPRES-oh — anyone who wishes to be considered a careful speaker is wise to steer clear of it. The prevailing standard form is *espresso* (from the Italian *caffè espresso*, literally "pressed-out coffee"), and many speakers deride the spurious *expresso*, which Burchfield (1996) says "was presumably invented under the impression that It[alian] *espresso* meant 'fast, express.'" See **ask, escape, especially, et cetera**.

et cetera et-SET-uh-ruh.

Also sanctioned, but not recommended, is the two-syllable et-SE-truh. Careful speakers clearly pronounce the *t* in *et* and make sure that *cetera* has three syllables.

The variant ek-SET-ur-uh (or EK SE-truh), "heard increasingly nowadays, is not considered standard," says *WNW Guide* (1984). In other words, it's beastly. Burchfield (1996), also noting that *et cetera* is "quite frequently, but wrongly" pronounced ek-SET-ur-uh, says "this comes about because no other common word in English begins with /ets-/, whereas words beginning with /eks-/ abound. . . ." See **ask, escape, especially, espresso**.

ethos EE-thahs.

This is the only pronunciation in three of the four major current American dictionaries, and the preference of Lass & Lass (1976), *WNW Guide* (1984), the *NBC Handbook* (1984), *Everyday Reader's* (1985), Barnhart (1988), *OED 2* (1989), and Jones (1991). The variants EE-thohs and ETH-ahs, which appear in *RHWC* (1997), are not sanctioned by any other authorities and should be avoided. See **pathos**.

evil EE-vuul. Do not say EE-vil.

The second syllable, -*vil*, rhymes with *full*, not *hill*.

"Some persons, desiring to seem exact in pronunciation, pronounce this word ē-vĭl," says Phyfe (1926). "It displays as much ignorance to introduce a sound that is superfluous as to neglect one that is requisite."

evolution EV-uh-**LOO**-shin.

The pronunciation EE-vuh-**LOO**-shin is British.

execrable EK-si-kruh-bul. Stress the first syllable.

exemplar eg-ZEM-plur.

This is the pronunciation preferred by most authorities from Phyfe (1926) and Kenyon & Knott (1949) to the *NBC Handbook* (1984) and *OED 2* (1989). However, *Webster 2* (1934) sanctions eg-ZEM-plahr, with the broad *a* of *far*, as an alternative, *M-W 10* (1993) lists it first, and Lass & Lass (1976) and *American Heritage 3* (1992) prefer it. The first syllable may also be pronounced ig-. The adjective *exemplary* should have second-syllable stress: eg-ZEM-pluh-ree. See **bursar, Templar**.

experiment ek-SPER-uh-mint or ek-SPAIR-uh-mint. The first syllable is often, and acceptably, lightened to ik-.

Do not say ek-SPEER-uh-mint. Properly, there is no *spear* in *experiment*.

expertise EK-spur-**TEEZ**. Do not say EK-spur-**TEES**.

The last syllable, *-tise,* should sound like *tease.* Do not pronounce it to rhyme with *piece* or *fleece.* The diligently permissive *M-W 10* (1993) lists EK-spur-**TEES** as an alternative and *WNW 3* (1997) labels it less frequent, but *American Heritage 3* (1992) and *RHWC* (1997) do not recognize it and Lass & Lass (1976), *WNW Guide* (1984), and *Everyday Reader's* (1985) prefer EK-spur-**TEEZ**. Occasionally one hears speakers place the accent on the first syllable, but authorities recognize only third-syllable stress.

explicable EK-spli-kuh-buul. Now often ek-SPLIK-uh-buul.

EK-spli-kuh-buul, with the accent on the first syllable, was the only pronunciation listed in dictionaries until 1961, when ek-SPLIK-uh-buul, with the accent on the second syllable, appeared in *Webster 3,* listed first. Among current authorities, however, only *M-W 10* (1993) lists ek-SPLIK-uh-buul first. Lass & Lass (1976) and the *NBC Handbook* (1984) prefer first-syllable stress, and EK-spli-kuh-buul is the only pronunciation in *Oxford American* (1980), *OED 2* (1989), and *American Heritage 3* (1992).

I have always suspected that some pronunciations are preferred simply because they are challenging and because there is a certain satisfaction in mastering them. (See **arctic,** for example.) It takes a cultivated speaker to say *explicable* right, and by that I don't mean a pompous or pretentious speaker, but a careful, conscientious, practiced one. If you are unaccustomed to saying EK-spli-kuh-buul, give it a try right now. Hit the EKextra hard and let the rest roll off your tongue. You may have some trouble at first, but don't give up. With a little practice it will become easy and natural, and you will leave the sialoquent* sayers of ek-SPLIKuh-buul in the dust. See **despicable, hospitable, inexplicable, lamentable, summarily**.

exquisite Traditionally, EK-skwi-zit. Now usually ek-SKWIZ-it.

The accent is properly on the *first* syllable.

Before I share my thoughts on this word, consider these comments from various other pronunciation mavens:

Gilmartin (1936): "If you are inclined to say that a thing is *exquis'ite* rather than *ex'quisite,* don't. The latter is the correct pronunciation."

Holt (1937): "Though the 'quiz' accent is common, there is no authority for it. The only excuse for it is (according to Webster) 'occasionally, especially for emphasis.'" (The actual wording in *Webster 2* is "*occas., esp. by way of emphasis.*")

---

* *Sialoquent,* pronounced sy-AL-uh-kwint, means spraying saliva when speaking.

Opydycke (1939): "**ex'qui site** has been called the most frequently mis-pronounced word in the language. But it has a good alibi. Authorities agree that it should be accented on the first syllable. But they follow up by saying 'occasionally, especially by way of emphasis, it may be accented on the second syllable.' Inasmuch as this is one of the socalled [*sic*] 'feminine adjectives,' that is, adjectives used principally by the fair sex, it follows that this word is usually pronounced with emphasis; thus, *ex qui' site.* But the correct pronunciation is *eks' kwi zit.* . . ." ("Feminine adjectives"? It's amazing what foolishness men thought they could get away with in those days.)

RHWC (1991, 1997): "The pronunciation of EXQUISITE has undergone a rapid change from (ek'skwi zit) to (ik skwiz'it). While the newer pronunciation is criticized by some, it is now more common in both the U.S. and England, and many younger educated speakers are not even aware of the older one."

Burchfield (1996): "The placing of the main stress in this word has steadily changed in standard speech in the last two centuries from the first to the second syllable. . . . By 1963 Daniel Jones gave preference to first-syllable stressing but commented that the alternative pronunciation was 'becoming very common'. J. C. Wells [*Longman Pronunciation Dictionary*] (1990) reported that 69% of the members of his poll panel opted for . . . second-syllable stressing. My personal preference is to stay with the other 31%."

The variant ek-SKWIZ-it first appears as an alternative, without qualification, in *American College* (1952), and *Webster 3* (1961), *WNW Guide* (1984), and *M-W 9* (1985) and *10* (1993) list it first. The traditional pronunciation, EK-skwi-zit, appears first in *OED 2* (1989), *American Heritage 3* (1992), *WNW 3* (1997), and *RHWC* (1997), and is preferred by Lass & Lass (1976), *Oxford Guide* (1983), the *NBC Handbook* (1984), and Barnhart (1988).

There you have it. Now it's time to take sides, and I'm with Burchfield and what remains of the EK-skwi-zit bunch, for better or for worse. (Since 1963 that 31 percent has probably dwindled to 20 percent or even less, at least in America.) I am convinced that ek-SKWIZ-it, like most vogue pronunciations, was picked up first by those who thought they knew better (or who wanted others to think so) and then by those who didn't know any better than to imitate this *soi-disant* smart set. The pseudosophisticated appeal of accenting the second syllable for emphasis has long since worn off, however, and ek-SKWIZ-it is now banal. Maybe in a generation or so the smart set, in search of new pleasures, will revive EK-skwi-zit — believing, of course, that it's a charming innovation. A pronunciation maven can only hope.

extant EK-stint (rhymes with *sextant*).

This is the pronunciation listed first by the *Century* (1914), *Webster 2* (1934), and all current dictionaries, and the one preferred by most 20th-century authorities, from Holt (1937) and Opdycke (1939) to Lass & Lass (1976) and the *NBC Handbook* (1984). The variant ek-STANT, which puts the accent on the second syllable, is listed first by Kenyon & Knott (1949) and preferred by Barnhart (1988), but it has been gradually passing out of use and by 2025 it may no longer be extant.

extempore ek-STEM-puh-ree.

Do not say ek-STEM-puh-ray, EK-stem-**POR**-ay, EK-stem-**POR**-ee, or ek-STEM-por. All these beastly variants have no authority.

extraordinary ek-STROR-di-ner-ee, not EK-struh-**OR**-di-ner-ee.

Yes, the word is spelled *extra-ordinary*, and the spelling pronunciation EKS-truh-**OR**-di-ner-ee has appeared as an alternative in dictionaries for a long time, but you shouldn't say it that way. Why not? Two compelling reasons: because pronouncing the word in six syllables proves only that you can spell and that you probably think the rest of us can't; and because custom, good usage, and the preponderance of authority since John Walker (1791) have favored the five-syllable ek-STROR-di-ner-ee. Burchfield (1996) affirms it is "the dominant pronunciation in standard English" — as if anyone needed to be told.

When *extraordinary* is used in the sense of "beyond the official duties of" or "sent upon an unusual or special mission," as, an ambassador or minister *extraordinary,* some sources say it is permissible to pronounce the word in six syllables. *Extraordinary* is rarely used in this sense, however, which is yet another reason the five-syllable ek-STROR-di-ner-ee prevails. I recommend it for all senses of the word.

extricable EK-stri-kuh-buul.

Stress the first syllable. See **inextricable.**

F

facet FAS-it (rhymes with *pass it*). Don't say FAW-sit or FAHS-it (like *faucet*).

Some time ago I phoned an old friend who is now a professor of physics at a distinguished university. During our conversation I was surprised to hear him say what clearly sounded like *faucet* when I knew he meant *facet*. Apparently the mispronunciation has been around for a while, for Phyfe (1926) and Opdycke (1939) warn speakers not to confuse *facet* and *faucet* in spelling and pronunciation.

This type of mistake is what Wilson Follett calls eccentric pronunciation. "It is likely that every person retains from early days one or two homemade deviations from usage," he writes in *Modern American Usage* (1966). "Thus, cultivated speakers have been heard to say *laxadaisical* for *lack-* and *laythal* for *lethal; cut-and-dry* for *cut-and-dried*. The only advice here is 'Look and listen.'"

Everyone, surely, has a story about someone's use of an eccentric pronunciation, and many of us have stories about overcoming our own goofy deviations from good speech. Some of them are quite eccentric, indeed, to our ears today. A fellow writer once told me how she never had trouble spelling *psychology* in grade school because her father always pronounced the *p*.* Another off-the-wall tale comes from a former news director at my

---

* Later I was surprised to discover that in the early part of the 20th century some authorities in fact preferred sounding the *p* in most words beginning with *ps-*. Although the *Century* (1914) countenances only silent *p*, *Webster 2* (1934) lists the voiced *p* as alternative and Opdycke (1939)

a = at / a̱ = final / ah = spa / ahr = car / air = fair / ay = hay / aw = saw
ch = chip / e = let / e̱ = item / ee = see / eer = deer / i = sit / i̱ = April
ng = sing / o̱ = carrot / oh = go / oo = soon / or = for / oor = poor
ow = cow / oy = toy / sh = she / th = thin / t̲h̲ = this / u̱ = focus / uh = up
ur = turn / uu = pull, took / y, eye = by, I / zh = measure / (see full key, p. xiv)

local public radio station. His high school chemistry teacher, he told me, preferred to pronounce the name of his subject with a *ch* instead of a *k* sound: CHEM- instead of KEM-is-tree. If a student demurred (see **de-mur**), he would go to the blackboard and write down a few words beginning with *ch-* (*church, chair,* and so on), then announce to everyone, "In my classroom, it's CHEM-is-tree." He also foisted other outlandish pronunciations on them, such as ahk-SEE-jin for *oxygen.* Was the man just a quack, or was he a misanthrope (MIS-un-throhp) indulging in a cruel joke?

Mispronunciation enforced by authority should be a punishable offense. It is, literally, a form of verbal abuse. But mispronunciation that is the result of mistraining or oversight deserves only the gentlest admonishment, for everyone makes mistakes, and it is another form of cruelty to put every petty offense on trial. (For one example of my own "homemade deviations from usage," see **Demeter.**)

faience fy-AHNS or fay-AHNS.

faineant FAY-nee-int (recommended).

The adjective *faineant* means lazy, idle, indolent; as a noun, a *faineant* is a lazy, good-for-nothing person. The corresponding noun is *faineance,* pronounced FAY-nee-ins.

If you look up *faineant* in a current dictionary you will find it spelled with an accent, *fainéant,* and you will usually find the French pronunciation, fay-nay-A(N), listed first or sometimes listed alone. Frankly, I find that perplexing, because two of the 20th century's most respected arbiters on American pronunciation, *Webster 2* (1934) and Kenyon & Knott (1949), both prefer the anglicized pronunciation FAY-nee-int, and the latter spells the word without the accent. *Webster 3* (1961) also renders the word sans accent and gives only the anglicized pronunciation, but its two latest abridgments, *M-W 9* (1985) and *10* (1993), curiously reverse that ruling and give precedence to the Frenchified spelling and pronunciation. Likewise, *AHNC* (1969) prefers the anglicized FAY-nee-int and lists the French as alternative, but its successors, *AHSC* (1985) and *American Heritage 3* (1992), countenance only the French fay-nay-A(N). The same strange deanglicization occurs yet again between *Random House II* (1987), which puts FAY-nee-int first, and its latest abridgment, *RHWC* (1991, 1997), which

---

says, "It is permissible to sound the initial *p* if you care to try . . . [and] if you can do it gracefully." *OED 1* (1909 ed.) called the silent *p* "an unscholarly practice often leading to ambiguity," and H. W. Fowler (1926) predicted that "with the advance of literacy the pronunciation of the *p* in words beginning thus is likely to be restored except in *psalm* & its family, e.g. in the compounds of *pseud(o)-* & such important words as *psychical* and *psychology.*" Burchfield (1996) remarks that "nothing of the kind has happened and all English words beginning with *ps* . . . are now pronounced with initial /s/, not /ps/." See **psychiatry.**

prefers the French spelling and pronunciation and labels the anglicized versions less common.

From this evidence one cannot help wondering if there's a conspiracy afoot to prevent this unusual and lovely word from becoming fully English. The noun *faineant* entered the language in the early 1600s and the adjective came along in the mid-1800s. After so much time, anglicization is entirely reasonable, and often inevitable. And when an anglicized pronunciation has existed in educated speech for fifty years or more (in this case at least seventy), clinging to the foreign pronunciation makes little sense and probably is futile. In the case of *faineant*, which cries out for anglicization, retaining the accent and reviving the French pronunciation seems foolish and pretentious. I say it's high time to bring this word in line: spell it *faineant* and say FAY-nee-int.

In addition to the sources noted above, *American College* (1952), *Everyday Reader's* (1985), and *WNW 3* (1997) also prefer the anglicized pronunciation.

fait accompli FAY-tuh-KAHM-**PLEE** (also, "more French," FET-uh-KAHM-**PLEE**).

The plural, *faits accomplis,* may be pronounced the same.

Most recent authorities — for some strange reason — still prefer the French pronunciation, which is approximately FET-ah-KAW(N)-**PLEE**. If you can say it in French without drawing undue attention to yourself, fine. More *pouvoir* to you. Keep in mind, however, that most educated American speakers today would not even care to try, preferring instead to use regular English sounds in this French phrase, which has been used in English since 1845. I'm with those folks all the way, as are *Oxford American* (1980), the *NBC Handbook* (1984), and *M-W 10* (1993). The British go one step further and say FAYT-uh-**KAHM**-plee. Americans may eventually embrace this logical anglicization, but for now the primary stress remains on the final syllable.

familial fuh-MIL-yul or fuh-MIL-ee-ul.

There is no *me* in *familial.* Don't say fuh-MEE-lee-ul. See **filial, memorabilia, -philia.**

farrago fuh-RAY-goh or fuh-RAH-goh.

A *farrago* is a confused mixture, jumble, hodgepodge.

There is equal authority for both pronunciations. Most older authorities, from Walker (1791) to *Webster 2* (1934), prefer fuh-RAY-goh, but fuh-RAH-goh has been heard in educated speech at least since it appeared in Funk & Wagnalls *Standard* (1897), and various authorities of the past twenty-five years prefer it. I say fuh-RAY-goh because a broad *a* in a stressed syllable of an established English word strikes me as anomalous, more like Latin (the source of *farrago*) than English. Traditionally, in words taken directly from Latin, a vowel has its long English sound when it ends a stressed syllable — e.g., *magi* (MAY-jy), **data** (DAY-tuh), **status** (STAY-tu̱s), *afflatus* (uh-FLAY-tu̱s), **erratum** (i̱-RAY-tu̱m), *desideratum* (di̱-SID-uh-**RAY**-tu̱m).

The plural is *farragoes* in American English, *farragos* in British English. The adjective is *farraginous*, pronounced fuh-RAJ-i̱-nu̱s.

February FEB-roo-ER-ee.

"Don't forget the first *r*," says Opdycke (1939). "*Feb you ary* is an illiterate pronunciation."

In recent years, certain dictionaries and guides have taken great pains in their pronunciation notes on this word to tell you that a fancy linguistic process called dissimilation is at work here, in which similar sounds that follow closely in a word tend to become dissimilar, the result being that most educated speakers now replace the first *r* in *February* with a *y* and say FEB-yoo-ER-ee.

That is a very convenient explanation, which makes a mispronunciation look right because so many people use it and makes the correct pronunciation look wrong because only a few people take the trouble to say the word properly. For some reason current dictionaries love to make elaborate excuses for errors of this nature, perhaps because it makes people feel better and sells more dictionaries. This book, however, was written on the assumption that you are an educated speaker who has consulted these pages not for encouragement to adopt the next person's whims, copy your neighbor's mistakes, or follow one authority blindly, but to obtain information on the opinions of various authorities and find advice on what pronunciation is best and why, especially in situations where there is a controversy over how or how not to say a word. Therefore, I will not dissemble about dissimilation (to paraphrase that well-known crude expression, "It happens"), nor will I feed you some malarkey about how FEB-yoo-ER-ee is legitimately based on analogy with *January*. The fact is that *February* is a different word and a different month, with a peculiar spelling, a peculiar pronunciation, and a very peculiar number of days, all of which adds up to the fact that we must treat the creature with particular respect.

The traditional and proper pronunciation, FEB-roo-ER-ee, is hard to say, and so most people say FEB-yoo-ER-ee because it is easier and because so many others do, not because it is right. As far as current dictionaries are concerned, that's enough to make it standard. As far as this book is concerned, however, the -yoo- variant may now be standard, but it is still beastly. Perhaps the lingering aroma of slovenliness surrounding -yoo- is why Shaw (1972), Lass & Lass (1976), the *NBC Handbook* (1984), Morris & Morris (1985), and Burchfield (1996) stand by the traditional FEB-roo-ER-ee, and why three of the four major current American dictionaries

— *American Heritage 3* (1992), *WNW 3* (1997), and *RHWC* (1997) — list
FEB-roo-ER-ee first. The fourth, *M-W 10* (1993), puts the -yoo- variant
first but labels it with an obelus [÷] (AHB-uh-l<u>u</u>s) to show that it "occurs
in educated speech" but "is considered by some to be unacceptable." The
way I see it, as long as those cultivated "some" still exist, **FEB**-roo-ER-ee
will be the preferred pronunciation in careful speech. (With a month like
February, you can make that kind of leap of faith.) See **arctic, library,
nuclear**.

fecal FEE-k<u>u</u>l.
I have heard writers and professors pronounce this word with an *s* instead
of a *k* sound for the *c:* FEE-s<u>u</u>l. This eccentric pronunciation is not recognized by dictionaries. *Fecal* has a hard *c* (like *k*), FEE-k<u>u</u>l, while the corresponding noun *feces* has a soft *c* (like *s*), FEE-seez.

fecund FEK-<u>u</u>nd (rhymes with *beckoned*) or FEE-k<u>u</u>nd.
Authority is about evenly divided between these two pronunciations. Both
have been standard for at least two hundred years: John Walker, in his
Critical Pronouncing Dictionary (1791), preferred the short *e* of FEK-; William Enfield, in his *General Pronouncing Dictionary* (1807), preferred the
long *e* of FEE-. Burchfield (1996), referring to England, calls the short *e*
"the more usual pronunciation," and that is probably now true in America
as well.

fellatio fuh-LAY-shee-oh, not fuh-LAH-tee-oh.
Fellatio should rhyme with *Horatio*.
   Although *OED 2* (1989) traces the origin of *fellatio* in print to 1887, it
apparently did not have much currency outside of the clinical arena until
the 1960s, when novelists Saul Bellow *(Herzog)* and John Updike *(Couples)*
and various critics helped make it a respectable verbal member of society.
As far as I can tell, *Webster 3* (1961) is the first dictionary to record it, indicating these pronunciations: fuh-LAY-shee-oh (or fe- for the first syllable) and fuh-LAH-dee-oh.* With both pronunciations recognized at the
outset, you could argue that it's a standoff, a "you say tuh-MAY-toh, I say

---

* From the layperson's perspective, one of the quirks in *Webster 3*'s linguistically meticulous but
often inscrutable treatment of pronunciation is the use of *d* instead of *t* for any word that in
educated American speech has anything less than "a strongly articulated, aspirated, distinctly
heard \t\." For example, *Webster 3* transcribes *party, editor,* and *attitude* as PAHR-dee, ED-uh-
dur, and AD-uh-tood, whereas in other dictionaries and in this book they appear as PAHR-tee,
ED-<u>i</u>-tur, and AT-<u>i</u>-t(y)ood — the use of *t* here being understood to encompass the various
subtle gradations American English speakers naturally give to *t* in these words, making it more
distinct in *editor*, less so in *attitude*, and least so in *party*, where it often does sound almost —
but not quite — like pure *d*. And that *not quite*, I suspect, is why other dictionaries — even
subsequent Merriam-Webster dictionaries — do not follow *Webster 3*'s practice, and why you
will see *t* used in all such instances here.
   Why don't other authorities follow the practice? Because it is frequently perplexing and even

tuh-MAH-toh" debate, except there's one big difference: tuh-MAH-toh is a regional English pronunciation, while fuh-LAH-tee-oh (or fe-) is classical Latin. Anyone who says fuh-LAH-tee-oh is speaking another language (and a dead one, too), treating the word as a foreignism when it is not. That strikes me as ostentatious.

Not surprisingly, the weight of authority since *Webster 3* heavily favors the anglicized fuh-LAY-shee-oh. Lass & Lass (1976), the *Quintessential Dictionary* (1978), Funk & Wagnalls *Standard* (1980), and the *NBC Handbook* (1984) prefer it, and *OED 2* (1989), *American Heritage 3* (1992), and *RHWC* (1997) list it first. *M-W 9* (1985) lists the Latin fuh-LAH-tee-oh second, but it is conspicuously absent from *M-W 10* (1993), which sanctions only fuh-LAY-shee-oh (or fe-). Only *WNW Guide* (1984) and *WNW 2* (1984) — which had the same pronunciation editor — put fuh-LAH-tee-oh first. The latter also lists another variant best avoided, the half-anglicized fuh-LAT-ee-oh. *WNW 3* (1988, 1997), however, jettisons the Latin and half-Latin and countenances only the anglicized fuh-LAY-shee-oh and the three-syllable fuh-LAY-shoh.

feral FEER-ul.

FEER-ul (or, in some older sources, FEE-rul) is the traditional pronunciation, and the only one recognized by my sources until *Webster 3* (1961). Since then FER-ul — or FAIR-ul in much of the Midwest and Western U.S. — has been listed as an alternative. Burchfield (1996) claims it is now the dominant pronunciation in England, but *OED 2* (1989) and Jones (1991), two other British authorities, give precedence to FEER-ul, which is listed first by all four major current American dictionaries and preferred by Lass & Lass (1976), the *NBC Handbook* (1984), and Barnhart (1988).

ferment (noun) FUR-ment; (verb) fur-MENT. See **decrease**.

fetid FET-id (FET- rhyming with *pet*).

This is, and has been for some time, the preferred American pronunciation. The alternative FEE-tid still appears in current dictionaries, but *WNW 3* (1997) marks it less common and *M-W 10* (1993) labels it espe-

---

misleading to a nonlinguist who is unfamiliar with the "voiced flap consonant" and "leveling" and who consults the dictionary for general edification and guidance. I wonder, for example, how a speaker is better informed by *Webster 3*'s two pronunciations of *better* — BED-ur and BET-ur — than by the one pronunciation in *Webster 2* (1934) or *Random House II* (1987) or *American Heritage 3* (1992): BET-ur. Of course, neither BET-ur nor BED-ur is the actual pronunciation used by most educated Americans; the *t* sound is neither so sharp (BET-) nor so dull (BED-), but falls somewhere between those two extremes. But since the precise sound cannot be simply rendered (only described in dense front-matter notes that most people ignore), the question is, Which method of transcription better serves the average user of the dictionary? I think you will agree that if presented only with the sharp pronunciation, American speakers will naturally and unconsciously soften the *t* sound slightly. If presented with both sharp and dull options, they will wonder whether they should pronounce *better* like a gruff New Yorker or like a *t*-loving Brit.

cially British. However, Jones (1991) lists FET-id as the dominant English pronunciation, and *Oxford Guide* (1983) and Burchfield (1996) agree. The variant spelling *foetid* is obsolescent.

fetish FET-ish. Formerly, FEE-tish.

Pronounce the *e* as in *fetter,* says the *Oxford Guide* (1983).

I have never seen *fetish* spelled *fetich,* but *OED 2* (1989) has citations from the 18th and 19th centuries and current dictionaries still list *fetich* as an alternative spelling. (The word comes from the French *fétiche.*) Dictionaries also still record the pronunciation FEE-tish (like *feet* + *-ish*), but the evidence of my ears tells me it is moribund. *WNW Guide* (1984) and *M-W 10* (1993) label FEE-tish less frequent, and Burchfield (1996) pronounces it dead.

fief FEEF (rhymes with *beef*); **fiefdom** FEEF-dum.

There is no authority for rhyming *fief* with *wife.* The word that does rhyme with *wife* is *fife,* a small, high-pitched, transverse flute.

fifth FIFTH or FITH.

If you can pronounce the second *f,* good for you. But there's nothing slovenly or improper about dropping it and rhyming *fifth* with *pith* and *myth.* It is beastly, however, to drop the *h* and say FIFT or drop the *th* and say FIF.

figure FIG-yur. Don't say FIG-ur.

In proper British speech, *figure* rhymes with *bigger,* but never so in educated American speech. "The British pronunciation is sometimes heard in AmE," says Burchfield (1996), "but is usually condemned as substandard." You're damn tootin', buster! See **inaugural**.

filet fi-LAY; **fillet** (slice) fi-LAY; **fillet** (band) FIL-it.

filial FIL-ee-ul or FIL-yul.

There is no *feel* in *filial.* The beastly overpronunciation FEEL-ee-ul, which dictionaries do not recognize, is pseudo-Latin. See **familial, memorabilia, -philia.**

finis FIN-is. Occasionally, FY-nis. The popular variant fee-NEE is wrong.

Finis is not French for "finished," as many apparently imagine. It comes through Middle English from the Latin *finis* and means "the end, conclusion." In the so-called classical system of Latin pronunciation, *finis* is pronounced FEE-nis; this variant appears only in *Webster 3* (1961) and is not recommended. In the so-called English system of Latin pronunciation, *finis* is pronounced FY-nis. Authorities of the 19th and first half of the 20th century preferred FY-nis and some — Opdycke (1939), for example — proscribed FIN-is. However, since FIN-is was recorded as an acceptable alternative in Kenyon & Knott (1949), it has been the preference of most authorities — including Lass & Lass (1976), the *NBC Handbook* (1984), *WNW Guide* (1984), and Barnhart (1988) — and the first pronunciation listed in most dictionaries.

FIN-is is now under siege (that's SEEJ, not SEEZH) by the ridiculous, but ridiculously popular, fee-NEE. This pseudo-French variant appeared, unlabeled, in *RH College* (1968) but did not surface elsewhere until the 1980s, when *WNW 2* (1984) noted that *finis* was "*often taken as Fr.* [fee-NEE]." The current editions of all four leading American dictionaries recognize this beastly variant, but it is worth noting the differences in their treatment of it. As in previous Random House dictionaries, *RHWC* (1997) lists fee-NEE second, between FIN-is and FY-nis, with no comment. *American Heritage 3* (1992) and *M-W 10* (1993) list fee-NEE third, after FIN-is and FY-nis, except that *M-W 10* doesn't quite get it right and gives fuh- for the first syllable, making it sound like *funny* with the accent on *-ny* (a phonological Freudian slip, perhaps?). *WNW 3* (1997) also lists it third, but with a curious label: *jocosely.* This would seem to imply that the people who say fee-NEE are just joking around and know full well the word isn't French and shouldn't be pronounced that way. I doubt it. I'm convinced they think it's French and are using it in the same playful way that people usually use *voilà.* I can only hope that someday they will say, "Voilà! It is FIN-is for fee-NEE!"

flaccid FLAK-sid, not FLAS-id.

As far back as I can remember, my omnierudite mother impressed upon me the importance of pronunciation. She taught me that the well-spoken person will be well received, while the poor speaker will be scorned like a dinner guest who mishandles the silverware and wipes his mouth on his sleeve. My mother was always right about pronunciation, and if anyone in the family mispronounced a word she would not fail to point it out — during dinner, during an argument, even while we were on the phone. On a side table in the living room lay the family dictionary — *Webster 2* (1934) — to which she would send us for confirmation if we tried to put up a fight. This hefty tome was the ultimate authority in our disputes, which of course she always won. We figured she had that great book memorized.

As I got older it became more difficult to accept her admonishment. Once, when I was home from college on vacation, I used the word *flaccid,* pronouncing it FLAS-id. She stopped me right away.

"You mean FLAK-sid, dear," she said.

"Oh, come on, Mom, you're kidding. Nobody says it that way."

"Well, *I* say it that way, and that's the proper way to pronounce it."

"But my English professor doesn't pronounce it that way."

She smiled serenely. "Then your English professor is wrong."

My professor, wrong? Such hubris must be punished, I thought. I marched off to the dictionary, fully expecting to return triumphant and rub her nose in the page. Instead I found that my professor and I and scores of other supposedly smart folks I knew were indeed wrong. The pronunciation FLAK-sid stared limply back at me; FLAS-id was nowhere to be found. Could my mother ever have imagined that in such mortifying moments pronunciation mavens are born?

Apparently, the flabby FLAS-id has been limping around in educated circles for most of the 20th century, for both Phyfe (1926) and Opdycke (1939) frown upon it. *Webster 3* (1961) was the first dictionary to recognize FLAS-id, labeling it with its esoteric symbol of disrepute, the obelus [÷] (pronounced AHB-uh-l<u>us</u>), meaning that it occurred in educated speech but that many took "strong exception" to it. For the next two decades only the Merriam-Webster line of *Collegiate* dictionaries, based on *Webster 3*, countenanced FLAS-id. *M-W 7* (1972) and *8* (1975) both list it as an alternative with no warning label, and *M-W 9* (1985) lists FLAK-sid second and FLAS-id first.

Then, in a stunning reassessment of reality, truth, and the American Way, Merriam-Webster's most recent dictionary, *M-W 10* (1993), gives FLAS-id — but lo! once again labeled with the Obelus of Opprobrium — and then FLAK-sid preceded by *also* to indicate it is "appreciably less common" than FLAS-id. Translate this dictionary shorthand into plain English and you have this message (rhetorically retouched by your friendly pronunciation maven): FLAS-id is now more common in educated speech than FLAK-sid. However, the majority who say FLAS-id probably have no idea that their pronunciation is an upstart, that FLAK-sid is the traditional pronunciation, and that the minority who say FLAK-sid consider FLAS-id spurious and ridiculous.

Although the FLAK-sid-sayers are now in the minority, there's no denying it's one heck of a respectable minority. A survey of sources published since the 1960s reveals that an overwhelming number of authorities prefer FLAK-sid. These include *RH College* (1968), *AHNC* (1969), Lass & Lass (1976), *Quintessential Dictionary* (1978), *Scribner-Bantam* (1979), *Oxford American* (1980), *WNW Guide* (1984), the *NBC Handbook* (1984), *Everyday Reader's* (1985), Jones (1991), *OED 2* (1989), and Burchfield (1996). Only *one* — Barnhart (1988) — prefers the spineless FLAS-id. Even Merriam-Webster's own pronunciation editor, Brian M. Sietsema, Ph.D. (the man responsible for the illuminating revision in *M-W 10* noted above), eschews FLAS-id. Like me, Sietsema is a postcollegiate, Johnny-come-lately convert to the truth. "I used to pronounce flaccid as FLASS-id," he confessed to a reporter from *The New York Times*.* "And now? It's FLAK-sid. . . ."

Flaccid is a book-learned word, more often read than uttered, which may in part explain why so many educated speakers in the past thirty years have swallowed the beastly FLAS-id without giving a second thought

---

* July 22, 1993, p. C8.

to how more common analogous words are pronounced. No educated speaker free of speech impediments says *assident* for *accident, susseed* for *succeed,* or *essentric* for *eccentric.* In these and similar words — where *cc* precedes an *i* or *e* — the double *c* should be pronounced like *x* or *k-s,* as in *accept, vaccinate, accentuate, accede, occidental, occipital,* and *succedaneum* (SUHK-si-**DAY**-nee-u̲m, a substitute). See **accessible, accessory, succinct.**

flutist FLOO-tist.

The word *flutist* was first recorded in 1603, and FLOO-tist has been and still is the only acceptable pronunciation for it. The variant *flautist* was adapted from the Italian *flautista* in 1860. The preferred pronunciation for *flautist* is FLAW-tist (FLAW- like *flaw*). The variant FLOW-tist (FLOW-rhyming with *cow*), which mimics the Italian pronunciation of *-au-,* appears in current dictionaries but only the *NBC Handbook* (1984) prefers it. Unless you have some special reason for preferring Italian spellings and pronunciations, stick with the English *flutist* (FLOO-tist), which is both traditional and unaffected. See **pianist, viola.**

foliage FOH-lee-ij.

In Woody Allen's 1989 movie *Crimes and Misdemeanors,* there is a scene in which Allen tries to dissuade Mia Farrow from accepting an assignation with a sleazy producer (played by Alan Alda), insisting that the man has no interest in her career and wants only to seduce her. They have a witty exchange that reveals the extent to which pronunciation can affect our impressions of others.

"Don't worry," Farrow assures him. "I've never been seduced by a guy who wears loafers and no socks, much less one who says *nucular.*"

"Yeah," declares Allen, "and he says *foilage,* too!"

Foliage (don't misspell it *foil-*) is properly pronounced in three syllables. Do not say FOH-lij, which is erroneous, or FOY-lij, which is erroneous and illiterate. I could leave it at that, except that one current dictionary, Merriam-Webster's *Tenth Collegiate* (1993), has decided to stick up for these beastly two-syllable variants. After labeling FOH-lij and FOY-lij with an obelus [÷] to show they are "considered by some to be unacceptable," *M-W 10* offers this analysis in a usage note:

> The disyllabic pronunciation[FOH-lij] is very common. Some commentators insist that *foliage* requires a trisyllabic pronunciation because of its spelling, but words of a similar pattern such as *carriage* and *marriage* do not fall under their prescription. The pronunciation [FOY-lij] is disapproved because it suggests the transposition of the *l* and *i* in the spelling. It is not as common as [FOH-lij] and may be associated with the nonstandard spelling *foilage.*

It is sad, in my estimation, that the leading desk dictionary in the U.S. would devote space to such rubbish. On the surface (and couched in a reputable dictionary) these remarks appear impartial, but in fact they are subtly misleading — and you, as an educated speaker and dictionary user, deserve to know why.

First, the claim is made that FOH-lij "is very common" — as if this alone justifies it. If it were *as* common, and certainly if it were *more* common, a tenable argument could be advanced for its acceptability. But lots of usages that are "very common" are also very objectionable, not just to "some commentators" but to many and often most educated people. For example, as the exchange between Farrow and Allen indicates, although it is "very common" to hear people pronounce *nuclear* as if it were spelled *nucular,* this pronunciation is frowned on mightily and can make you the butt of jokes. Although the evidence of my ears tells me *he could have ran* and *I should have went* are "very common" today — regrettably so among younger college-educated Americans — there isn't an editor or English teacher in the land who would consider these phrases correct. And even though it is "very common" to see, in a supermarket, a sign over the express lane that says *10 Items or Less,* that does not alter the fact that in proper English this directive should be *10 Items or Fewer.* Just because something is common doesn't make it acceptable or right — in life, I might add, as well as in language. And although no language maven with half a brain would dispute that usage is an essential component of acceptability, it is equally absurd to assume that propriety is determined solely by usage. (That's like arguing that there must be something wholesome in tobacco because so many people smoke.)

"Some commentators insist that *foliage* requires a trisyllabic pronunciation because of its spelling," says *M-W 10,* "but words of a similar pattern such as *carriage* and *marriage* do not fall under their prescription." This is a not-so-veiled dig at pronunciation mavens like me, an insinuation that our pronouncements are arbitrary and preposterous. To begin with, I have not insisted, nor would I ever insist, on a three-syllable pronunciation for *foliage* simply because of its spelling. That would indeed be arbitrary and preposterous, like demanding that *cupboard* be pronounced like *cup* + *board* instead of *cubberd.* I insist on FOH-lee-ij not because I idiosyncratically think it ought to be the proper pronunciation but because the historical record shows that it is. That's the way educated people have pronounced it for a long, long time and that's the only pronunciation to be found in dictionaries — until quite recently. If insisting, on preponderant authority, that we ought to continue saying FOH-lee-ij is somehow arbitrary or preposterous, then to imply that FOH-lij is equally acceptable because it is now "very common" is at best ludicrous.

M-W 10's suggestion that pronunciation mavens single out *foliage* for special treatment compared with similarly formed words such as *carriage* and *marriage* is particularly disingenuous. The comment makes it appear that there is a sizable family of words ending in -*iage* when in fact there are very few. In addition to *foliage* there are *marriage* (and its variants *remarriage* and *intermarriage*), *carriage* and *miscarriage, verbiage,* and the uncommon *ferriage,* which means transportation by ferry or the fare paid for passage on one. Eliminate the variants and you have just five words: *marriage, carriage, foliage, verbiage,* and *ferriage. Marriage* and *carriage* do not fall under my prescription because, as no one will dispute, educated speakers have pronounced them in two syllables for over two hundred years. *Foliage* and *verbiage* do fall under my prescription because, as authorities from Walker (1791) and Worcester (1860) to *Webster 2* (1934) and *WNW 3* (1997) show, educated speakers have pronounced them in three syllables for over two hundred years. As for *ferriage,* even *M-W 10* agrees that the only acceptable pronunciation has three syllables: FER-ee-ij. Thus the disyllabic *marriage* and *carriage* are the exceptions here and do not constitute a majority or indicate a prevailing tendency, as *M-W 10* would have us believe.

M-W 10 has a more difficult time mustering enthusiasm for FOY-lij, choosing instead simply to report, with clinical detachment, that this variant "is disapproved because it suggests the transposition of the *l* and *i* in the spelling. It is not as common as [FOH-lij] and may be associated with the nonstandard spelling *foilage.*" This glosses over the truth. FOY-lij doesn't simply *suggest* the transposition of the *l* and *i,* it *accomplishes* it, as the existence of the abominable spelling *foilage* plainly attests. Moreover, as the conversation between Farrow and Allen demonstrates, FOY-lij is "disapproved" because the transposition from *foliage* to *foilage* is not only careless but also laughably ignorant.

M-W 10 and its brethren M-W 7 (1972), 8 (1975), and 9 (1985) also practice subtle deception by dividing *foliage* into two syllables: fo · liage. Other dictionaries — including the unabridged mother of *M-W 7–10, Webster 3* (1961) — divide the word into three syllables: fo · li · age.

Finally, *M-W 10*'s disparaging use of the phrase "some commentators" suggests there are certain other current commentators who embrace FOH-lij and who are willing to don armor and defend it. Alas, poor *M-W 10* stands alone in the lists. "FOH-lij is heard occasionally, but is considered careless speech," says *WNW Guide* (1984), and I say this: show me an authority on pronunciation who prefers FOH-lij and I'll show you the proverbial philosopher's stone, said to transmute base metal into gold. All my (non-Merriam-Webster) sources prefer FOH-lee-ij, and only one, *American Heritage 3* (1992), recognizes FOH-lij as an alternative. Outside of *M-W 10,* the preposterous FOY-lij is nowhere to be found.

for When stressed, FOR, rhyming with *door;* when unstressed, FUR, rhyming with *her* (or FUH among *r*-droppers).

I have been on many radio talk shows where someone calls in to complain about the pronunciation of *for* as *fur* or *fuh.*

"My teachers always taught me to say FOR, not FUR," the person says, "and I just can't stand how people slur the pronunciation of that word. Isn't it awful?"

"No, I'm sorry, it's not," I respond. "In fact, their pronunciation is the natural and proper one, and yours is overnice. Unfortunately, your teachers gave you the wrong advice. Consult any dictionary or pronunciation guide and you will see that the pronunciation of *for* is different in stressed and unstressed contexts."

Right about here the host usually cuts in. "You mean when Johnny says, 'What FUR, Mom?' that it's okay?"

"No," say I, "because in that sentence *for* is stressed, so Johnny should properly give the word its full sound. Compare these sentences and you'll see what I mean: if you say, 'What is it for?' the stress is on *for,* so it is pronounced FOR. But in the sentence 'He came for the book,' *for* is in a weak position and the natural pronunciation is FUR. Likewise in these sentences: 'What is she waiting for?' (stressed FOR); 'She is waiting for her friend' (unstressed FUR). In more cases than not *for* is unstressed, so it is more often pronounced FUR. As many authorities have noted, this distinction is perfectly natural English, and to impose FOR in all instances is at best stagy and at worst affected."

Next caller, please. See **forget**.

forbade fur-BAD.

The spelling pronunciation fur-BAYD has flourished since *Webster 3* (1961), in opposition to all previous authority, arbitrarily indicated that *forbade* should be pronounced fur-BAYD and the *e*-less *forbad* should be pronounced fur-BAD. Given that the spelling *forbad* was already obsolescent, that pretty much put the kibosh on fur-BAD. Burchfield (1996), in a peculiar burst of unsubstantiated permissiveness, claims that fur-BAYD "cannot be said to be wrong"; nevertheless, other recent authorities prefer the traditional fur-BAD and current dictionaries list it first. The controversy may soon be academic: the evidence of my ears says that *forbid* is fast replacing *forbade* as the past tense of *forbid.* Compare **bade**.

forehead FOR-id, FAHR-id, FOR-hed, or, occasionally, FAHR-hed.

All four variants are acceptable, and all have been heard for over two hundred years. FOR-hed and FAHR-hed have often been criticized as spelling pronunciations, but from the mid-1700s to the mid-1800s they were preferred by many authorites and heard in cultivated speech on both sides of the Atlantic. From the late 1800s to the 1940s, authorities almost universally preferred FAHR-id. Since then FOR-hed has reasserted itself with a vengeance, FOR-id has gained currency and respectability, FAHR-id is trailing far behind, and FAHR-hed is passing out of use.

I'll tell you, the whole thing is enough to give a pronunciation maven a sore throat and a headache "this big." However, for all you armchair lexicographers and for anyone slapping his forehead (or someone else's) over this word, here is a more thorough historical overview.

Worcester (1860) gives both FAHR-id and FOR-hed, then polls the leading authorities since the 1770s and shares these results: FAHR-id is the preference of Barclay (1775) and Sheridan (1780); FAHR-hed is the preference of Jones (1798), Fulton & Knight (1802), and Knowles (1835); and FOR-hed is the preference of Perry (1777), Walker (1791), Enfield (1807), Jameson (1827), Craig (1849), and Smart (1836), who labels FAHR-id colloquial.

In the late 1800s, the *Century* (1889–1914) sanctions FAHR-id and FOR-hed while Ogilvie, in his *New Imperial Dictionary* (1884), prefers FOR-hed. However, Ayres (1894), who prefers FAHR-id, remarks that FOR-hed "nowadays is hardly permissible," even though "there is a long list of orthoëpists that favor this pronunciation."

Now we enter the heyday of FAHR-id, which is preferred by numerous American and British authorities, including Funk & Wagnalls *Standard* (1897), Phyfe (1926), Fowler (1926), the *New Century* (1927), *OED 1* (1928), Vizetelly (1929), *Webster 2* (1934), Gilmartin (1936), Opdycke (1939), and Witherspoon (1943).

At this point things shift again. Kenyon & Knott (1949) and *American College* (1952) list FOR-id, FAHR-id, and FOR-hed, and these are the first three pronunciations in *Webster 3* (1961). Lass & Lass (1976) prefer FAHR-id but note that three of the four leading American dictionaries of the 1970s list FOR-id and FOR-hed appears in all four.

Sources in the 1980s and 1990s show the scars of so many years of confusion. There seems to be a preference for FOR-id and some reluctance to acknowledge the frequency (and growing dominance) of FOR-hed, but you may draw your own conclusion from the following evidence: the *NBC Handbook* (1984) prefers FOR-id. *Random House II* (1987), *American Heritage 3* (1992), and *WNW 3* (1997) list FOR-id first, but all of them also sanction the popular FOR-hed and the less common FAHR-id, which is my preference and the first pronunciation in *M-W 9* (1985) and *10* (1993). Only *WNW Guide* (1984) prefers FOR-hed, asserting — no doubt accurately — that FOR-id and FAHR-id "are fast losing ground."

Here's a postscript to the discussion offering a view from the other side of the pond, as they say. In *The King's English* (1998), the late British novelist Kingsley Amis writes, "I unconsciously said *forrid* until the sincere incomprehension of a lecture-class in the 1950s brought me round to *fawhed* and to hell with Longfellow's little girl. . . .

> There was a little girl and she had a little curl
> Right in the middle of her forehead,
> And when she was good she was very very good,
> But when she was bad she was horrid."

foreword FOR-wurd (like *four* + *word*). For *r*-droppers, FAW-wuud.
Don't say FOH-wurd (FOH- rhyming with *go*). See **forward**.

forget fur-GET. Don't say fur-GIT.
The slurring of -GET to -GIT in *forget* has become a very common mis-
pronunciation. Note that *for-*, because it is unstressed, is lightened to fur-.
To say for-GET, with a fully articulated *for-*, is an overpronunciation.
See **for**.

formidable FOR-mi-duh-buul, not fur-MID-uh-buul.
The accent is properly on the *first* syllable. The beastly mispronunciation
fur-MID-uh-buul, which shifts the accent to the second syllable, is a FOR-
mi-duh-buul one. Numerous language mavens have attacked, stigmatized,
and scorned it for decades — Kingsley Amis (1998), for example, says
"only a berk [an unpleasant fool] stresses the second syllable" — yet it
continues to spread insidiously like a virus. Nevertheless, it has gained little
attention in the dictionaries and authorities are still firmly opposed to it.
Lass & Lass (1976), *WNW Guide* (1984), the *NBC Handbook* (1984), *Everyday Reader's* (1985), Morris & Morris (1985), and Burchfield (1996) all favor
the traditional FOR-mi-duh-buul, and it is the only pronunciation sanctioned by *OED 2* (1989), *American Heritage 3* (1992), and *WNW 3* (1997).

formulae FORM-yuh-LEE, not -LY.
The last syllable should rhyme with *flee*, not *fly*.
 So you learned a little Latin back in high school or college, and you've
been wondering ever since what you can do with it. Well, why not proudly
display your classical erudition when pronouncing those pesky Latin plurals ending in -*ae*? As every science-savvy person knows, *antennae, larvae,
papillae,* and so on have a long *i* sound at the end, right? Wrong. Words
borrowed from Latin that form their plurals in -*ae* properly have a long *e*
sound at the end. That's why, for example, we say AL-jee for *algae*. The
long *i* sound may be good classical Latin, but it's lousy English. If you must
use the pompous *formulae* (the anglicized *formulas* is much more user-
friendly, in my opinion), at least pronounce it in the same language as the
rest of your sentence. See **algae, alumnae, antennae, larvae, minutiae,
papilla(e), vertebrae**.

forte (strong point) properly FORT, now usually FOR-tay; (musical direction) FOR-tay.
Do not stress the second syllable. For either sense of the word, for-TAY is
wrong.

In a television promo for Disney's *Beauty and the Beast: The Enchanted Christmas* video, the male voice-over says that the actor Tim Curry plays an "evil pipe organ" called *Forte,* which he pronounces for-TAY, with second-syllable stress. For all I know, Disney's video may be a beauty, but the pronunciation for-TAY is a real beast. I'll explain why in a moment. First, a little history.

Forte comes from the French *fort,* strong. It entered English in 1648 as a fencing term meaning "the strongest part of a sword blade"; by 1682 it had acquired the figurative sense of "a strong point or area of expertise." *Forte* acquired its final *-e* in the 1700s; "as in other adoptions of French," says *OED 2* (1989), "the feminine form [was] ignorantly substituted for the masculine." In the 20th century a confusion of *forte,* strong point, with the Italian musical direction *forte,* meaning "play loudly or forcefully," gave rise to the variant pronunciation FOR-tay, first recorded in *Webster 3* (1961). FOR-tay was readily adopted by hoi polloi no doubt because of its Continental cachet and because it served the handy purpose of distinguishing *forte,* an elegant word, from the pedestrian *fort.* By the late 1980s FOR-tay had won recognition in all the leading dictionaries and current evidence (which I will not dispute) indicates it is the dominant pronunciation on both sides of the Atlantic.

The variant for-TAY, which shifts the stress to the second syllable, was first recorded in *M-W 9* (1985), and *M-W 10* (1993) is the only current dictionary that recognizes it. (It also lists the peculiar FOR-tee, pronounced like *forty,* which I have never heard — and hope I never do.) The ugsome for-TAY is doubly beastly because it's not only erroneous but also illogical, a preposterous hybrid of Italian and French. The pretentiousness of for-TAY would be laughable if the variant were not so damnably common today. Morris & Morris (1985) have this to say about it:

> *Forte* (derived from the French word "fort"), meaning "one's strong point," is sometimes pronounced for-TAY. This is wrong. The final "e" is a false feminine ending, acquired by analogy to words such as "morale" and "locale."
>
> Those who say for-TAY do so on the false assumption that all French words ending in "e" have the final syllable pronounced AY. This is true only of words ending in "é" with an acute accent. Actually the final feminine "e" in French is always silent.

In English we say AY at the end of *émigré, papier mâché, protégé, habitué,* and *naiveté,* but for-TAY is outré — for the time being, at least. Recently I discovered this sentence in my local newspaper: "Sailing isn't the only forté of . . . Olympic bronze medalist J. J. Isler."* The columnist who wrote that

---

* *The San Diego Union-Tribune,* January 21, 1998, p. B-1.

is a professional acquaintance who occasionally consults me on matters of language. I immediately faxed her a "Language Alert" in which I explained, as gently as possible, that there is no authority for *forte* with an accent and that the pronunciation for-TAY was pseudosophisticated. "Here's hoping you'll hold the *forté*," I concluded. A pronunciation maven can never be too vigilant.

So, now that we've subjected the heretical for-TAY to an auto-da-fé (AW-toh-duh-**FAY**), what do we do about the now-dominant FOR-tay? We live with it, because it's here to stay. I hope you will join me in pronouncing *forte* in one syllable, like *fort,* but if that seems too old-fashioned or downright bizarre to you, then go ahead and pronounce it like the Italian musical direction, FOR-tay. Just be sure to stress the *first* syllable for both senses of the word, never the second.

forward   FOR-wurd (like *four + word*).

What has happened to the *for* in *forward?* In recent years I have heard more and more speakers, on the street and on the air, changing it to foh- (rhymes with *toe*) so that *forward* comes out like *foe word* or *faux word.* This is not a simple matter of *r*-dropping, because these same speakers retain the second *r,* in *-ward,* and most of them are not native *r*-droppers who *pahk the cah* and eat with a *fawk* and say *fah-wood (or faw-wood) mahch.* Native *r*-droppers pronounce *-or-* roughly as -aw- or -ah-, but these folks are pronouncing it -oh-, with a long *o* as in *go.* I have to conclude that it is simply an eccentricity, an instance of what might be called *r*-slopping. C'mon, everybody, there is no *foe* in *forward.* You either pronounce both *r*'s, or, if you're an *r*-dropping Southerner or New Englander or New Yorker, swallow them both.

Also, don't confuse *forward* with *froward,* which means stubborn, willful, refractory, and is pronounced FROH-wurd. See **foreword**.

foyer   FOY-ur.

This word came into English from French in 1859. The French pronunciation, still listed by some authorities, is fwah-YAY, and FWAH-yay, with first-syllable stress, is occasionally heard in Britain, says Burchfield (1996). In American speech these Frenchified pronunciations are extremely rare. The half-anglicized pronunciation FOY-ay (rhymes with *joy way*) still has many adherents, some of whom mistakenly believe that the fully anglicized pronunciation FOY-ur (rhymes with *lawyer*) is wrong.

FOY-ur has been heard in educated American speech for at least a hundred years. Although Phyfe (1926) objected to it, Vizetelly (1929) sanctioned it, Opdycke (1939) recommended it, and Holt (1937) said it "is certainly better than the half-French, half-English form that some dictionaries allow." *Webster 2* (1934) listed FOY-ur as a standard alternative, and the *New Century* (1927) and Kenyon & Knott (1949) gave it priority. Since then it has been the dominant American pronunciation. Lass & Lass (1976) and the *NBC Handbook* (1984) prefer FOY-ur, and all four major current American dictionaries list it first.

Anglicization — the process by which words taken from other languages gradually conform to English standards of spelling, usage, and pronunciation — is natural and necessary. Moreover, it is inevitable if the word is to remain in the language. FWAH-yay and fwah-YAY, the Frenchified pronunciations of *foyer,* are no longer intelligible to American speakers. The half-anglicized FOY-ay is intelligible, but many cultivated speakers now find it affected or old-fashioned. Although dictionaries still list it as standard, for several decades it has been superseded, as it should be, by the fully anglicized FOY-ur. See **cadre, junta, lingerie, penchant.**

fracas FRAY-k<u>i</u>s, not FRAK-<u>i</u>s.

The first *a* is properly long. When you enter the *fray* (rhymes with *day*), you enter a FRAY-k<u>a</u>s. "Unduly influenced by La Belle France," writes Holt (1937), "the British struggle with 'frack'ah.' . . . We sensibly rhyme it with '*Make* us!'"

Fracas entered English in 1727. FRAY-k<u>i</u>s was the only sanctioned pronunciation until *Webster 3* (1961), which listed FRAK-<u>i</u>s as an "appreciably less frequent" alternative. Since then dictionaries have continued to list FRAY-k<u>i</u>s first, and all my recent authorities prefer it.

fragile (American) FRAJ-<u>i</u>l; (British) FRA-jyl.

For a discussion of American vs. British pronunciation of *-ile,* see **textile.**

frequent (adjective) FREE-kwent; (verb) free-KWENT.

Properly, the adjective is stressed on the first syllable and the verb on the second. You are a *fre*quent customer at a restaurant but you fre*quent* the restaurant. Until the mid–20th century, most educated speakers observed this distinction. Although most current dictionaries continue to list free-KWENT first for the verb, the evidence of my ears tells me that first-syllable stress is now predominant. Nevertheless, the careful speaker is advised not to follow the herd. See **decrease.**

Freudian FROY-dee-in (FROY- rhymes with *boy*).

Have you ever heard anyone mispronounce this word FRAWD-ee-in (FRAWD- like *fraud*)? Watch out for this FROY-dee-in slip.

Friday see -**day.**

frustrated FRUH-stray-tid.

There is no *l* in this word. Don't get flustered and say FLUH-stray-tid.

fundamental FUN-duh-**MEN**-t<u>u</u>l.

This word is frequently mispronounced without the *d* and *t* sounds, as if it were spelled *funnamennel.* Athletes (ATH-leets, not ATH-uh-leets) and sportscasters, who never seem to tire of talking about fundamentals, are perhaps most guilty of the mispronunciation. See **gentle, kindergarten, mental, rental, ventilate.**

fungi (plural of *fungus*) FUN-jy (soft *g* as in *age,* long *i* as in *sigh*).

"Never [FUNG-gy]," admonished Vizetelly (1929), but current dictionaries now list this variant as an alternative. FUNG-gy may be a British import, for Jones (1991) and Burchfield (1996) prefer it, although *OED 2* (1989) sanctions only FUN-jy. However, 20th-century American authority — from *Webster 2* (1934) and Kenyon & Knott (1949) to Lass & Lass (1976) and the *NBC Handbook* (1984) — overwhelmingly favors the traditional pronunciation, FUN-jy.

Fungicide, something that kills a fungus, is pronounced FUN-ji̱-syd.

furor FYUUR-or, not FYUUR-ur.

Most English nouns ending in -*or* are pronounced like those ending in -*er*. Thus *actor, factor, governor, juror, sector, vendor, visitor,* and so on, all have the same -ur sound at the end as *maker, officer, seller, thinker,* and the like.

Furor, however, is an exception, for we pronounce the -*or* to rhyme with *more,* not *her.* Exceptions are sometimes impossible to explain, and the best explanation I can offer in this case is that FYUUR-or has been the cultivated pronunciation since dictionaries began recording pronunciation in the 18th century. *Webster 3* (1961) was the first dictionary to recognize the -ur variant. It does not appear again in any of my dictionaries until *M-W 9* (1985), and current dictionaries all list FYUUR-or first. The *NBC Handbook* (1984), playing the maverick, is the only authority that prefers -ur.

FYUUR-ur may be the result of increasing pressure to make the word conform with all the others ending in -*or* that are pronounced -ur. But I suspect another influence — the vicissitudes of history. FYUUR-ur is the anglicized pronunciation of *führer* (or *fuehrer*), the German word for leader and the title assumed by Adolf Hitler. After the terror and destruction of World War II, it is conceivable that in the public mind a *furor* (rage, frenzy, uproar) became linked with *der Führer,* the symbol of unfathomable rage and the perpetrator of world uproar.

Whatever the reason, we now have two pronunciations where one has always sufficed. Let's try to keep the German separate from the English: FYUUR-ur for *führer* and FYUUR-or for *furor.* See **juror** for more on the pronunciation of -*or.*

futile (American) FYOO-ti̱l; (British) FYOO-tyl.

For a discussion of American vs. British pronunciation of -*ile,* see **textile**.

G

gala GAY-luh.

"Over the radio recently," writes Frank H. Vizetelly in *How to Speak English Effectively* (1933), "a glamorous new movie star said '*gahla*' (gala), and on another program the same evening a popular master of ceremonies said '*galla*.' How many admirers of each will say the same thing, regardless of the fact that the only correct pronunciation of the word is '*gayla*.'"

Indeed, since the 1930s these two variants have gained ground, but current American sources still prefer GAY-luh. GAL-uh is usually listed second, and GAH-luh, which often appears third, is British, says *Random House II* (1987) and *RHWC* (1997). In his *New Fowler's Modern English Usage* (1996), the *OED* lexicographer Robert Burchfield recommends GAH-luh but confirms that GAY-luh is the traditional pronunciation and the dominant one in American English.

Galápagos (Islands) guh-LAH-puh-gu̱s or -gohs.

Stress the second syllable (that's why there's an accent mark over the second *a*). Third-syllable stress is beastly. You may pronounce the final syllable either like -*gus* in *Angus* or like *ghos*- in *ghost*. Also acceptable, but less often listed, is the fully anglicized guh-LAP-uh-gu̱s (second syllable like *lap*).

Galileo GAL-i̱-**LEE**-oh.

GAL-i̱-**LEE**-oh is the anglicized pronunciation, preferred by numerous authorities from Worcester (1860) to *Webster 2* (1934) to the *NBC Handbook* (1984) and the first pronunciation listed in three of the four major

---

a = at / a̱ = final / ah = spa / ahr = car / air = fair / ay = hay / aw = saw
ch = chip / e = let / e̱ = item / ee = see / eer = deer / i = sit / i̱ = April
ng = sing / o̱ = carrot / oh = go / oo = soon / or = for / oor = poor
ow = cow / oy = toy / sh = she / th = thin / t̲h̲ = this / u̱ = focus / uh = up
ur = turn / uu = pull, took / y, eye = by, I / zh = measure / (see full key, p. xiv)

current American dictionaries. GAH-lee-**LAY**-oh is the Italian pronunciation, duly noted alternatively by older sources but almost never heard today. The half-anglicized GAL-i-**LAY**-oh, which combines a flat English *a* with an Italian *e,* has been recorded since the 1960s and is now very popular. It's a half-baked variant, used by the let's-sound-Continental-and-sophisticated crowd. It took 400 years for the Roman Catholic Church to vindicate this unfairly persecuted scientist. Why are we now making linguistic mincemeat of his name?

gamut GAM-it (rhyming, approximately, with *slam it*).

A radio talk show host once told me he had heard *gamut* pronounced guh-MOOT. This is a good example of what Wilson Follett (1966) calls eccentric pronunciation, a "homemade deviation" from standard usage. The eccentric guh-MOOT sounds like a failed attempt to pronounce the unusual word *gemot* (guh-MOHT), an Anglo-Saxon historical term meaning a conference, assembly. For *gamut,* the only recognized pronunciation is GAM-it. For more on eccentric pronunciation, see **facet**.

garage guh-RAHZH (recommended) or guh-RAHJ.

Regionally (chiefly New England and Canadian), guh-RAZH or guh-RAJ.)

In 1934, *Webster 2* ruled that this word was "generally pronounced" guh-RAHZH, with the second *g* as in *rouge,* but that it was sometimes "loosely" (meaning less acceptably) pronounced guh-RAHJ, rhyming with *lodge.* Since then the "loose" pronunciation has gained both currency and respectability and is now listed in good standing in current dictionaries alongside guh-RAHZH. Shaw (1972) says, "The preferred pronunciation is guh-RAHZH, but guh-RAHJ is also acceptable. The British are more likely to say GAR-ahzh or GAR-ij." Kenyon & Knott (1949) say that "the fully Anglicized [GAR-ij] is not general in American cultivated use."

garrote (noun and verb) guh-RAHT or guh-ROHT.

Garrote has several senses, all of them suffocating. The *garrote* was a method of execution used in Spain in which an iron collar was fastened around the neck and tightened slowly until the victim strangled. A *garrote* may also be an implement (especially something thin, such as a cord or wire) used to strangle someone, or the act of strangulation itself. To *garrote,* the verb, means to strangle.

I almost strangled myself when I found out I had been mispronouncing this word GAR-it (like *garret*). In vain I interrogated my dictionaries for corroboration of my preference, nearly throttling them when I did not find what I wanted. Finally I had to admit defeat. Only *Webster 3* (1961) and its latest abridgments, *M-W 9* (1985) and *10* (1993), list GAR-it — last, of course.

There is no question about it: *garrote* is properly stressed on the second syllable, which may sound like *rot* or *rote.* Older authorities tend to favor guh-ROHT, current ones guh-RAHT; *WNW Guide* (1984), for example, prefers the latter and says the former is heard "occasionally." I've decided to use the *rot* pronunciation both to stay in line with current preferences and because it makes *garroted* (guh-RAH-tid) rhyme with *carotid* (kuh-RAH-tid), the major artery in the neck. How's that for a nice bit of poetic mnemonics?

garrulous GAR-uh-l<u>u</u>s (recommended). Less often, GAR-yuh-l<u>u</u>s.

Nearly all authorities since Worcester (1860) have preferred GAR-uh-l<u>u</u>s, with the *u* in the second syllable pronounced as in *focus* or *pull.* However, two alternative pronunciations date back at least to Worcester's time: GAR-yuh-l<u>u</u>s and GAR-yoo-l<u>u</u>s, with a *y* sound inserting itself before the *u.* Ayres (1894) disapproved of these variants, and Funk & Wagnalls *Standard* (1897), the *Century* (1889–1914), and *Webster's Collegiate* (1917) did not recognize them. In 1934, however, *Webster 2* gave priority to the *y* sound, marking the *u* as lightened or variable, as in *unite.* Kenyon & Knott (1949) and *American College* (1952) listed GAR-yuh-l<u>u</u>s as an alternative, and most sources since have countenanced the *y*-influenced pronunciation.

If you have always said GAR-yuh-l<u>u</u>s you have ample authority to support your preference. However, if you are just learning the word or trying to decide which pronunciation you feel more comfortable with, it may be helpful for you to know that all four major current American dictionaries give priority to the *y*-less GAR-uh-l<u>u</u>s, which is the only pronunciation in *OED 2* (1989) and the preference of Lass & Lass (1976), *WNW Guide* (1984), the *NBC Handbook* (1984), *Everyday Reader's* (1985), and Barnhart (1988). That is strong evidence that GAR-uh-l<u>u</u>s is still the dominant pronunciation in educated speech today.

The corresponding noun *garrulity* is pronounced guh-ROO-l<u>i</u>-tee. See **erudite, querulous, virulent**.

gaseous GAS-ee-<u>u</u>s (recommended) or GASH-<u>u</u>s.

All four major current American dictionaries list GAS-ee-<u>u</u>s first, as does *OED 2* (1989). The *NBC Handbook* (1984) prefers GAS-ee-<u>u</u>s and Burchfield (1996) says it is "the dominant pronunciation now in standard English." Opdycke (1939) frowned upon the two-syllable GASH-<u>u</u>s, but Kenyon & Knott (1949) recognized it, Lass & Lass (1976) prefer it, and many good speakers use it today.

Gawain (Sir) GAH-win, GAH-wayn, or guh-WAYN.

There are almost as many ways to say the name of this famous knight and nephew of King Arthur as there were seats at the Round Table. In *How I Grew,* the first volume of her autobiography, Mary McCarthy insists that the proper pronunciation is GOW-wayn (GOW- rhyming with *cow,* -wayn like *Wayne*). I would be interested to know on what authority she based her preference, for GOW-wayn is the one variant that does not appear in any of my sources. GOW-win, which comes close, is listed third in two current dictionaries. Other recognized variants include GAW-win and GAW-wayn.

The pronunciation most often preferred by older authorities is GAH-win, with GAH-wayn and GAW-win the runners-up. Three of the four major current American dictionaries, however, list the recently minted (c. 1960s) variant guh-WAYN first, and three list GAH-wayn second. GAH-wayn seems overpronounced to me (like saying KAP-tayn for *captain*), and guh-WAYN has little other than its popularity to recommend it, which leaves me with the unobjectionable GAH-win. Take your pick.

gazebo guh-ZEE-boh, not guh-ZAY-boh.

Have you ever heard anyone say guh-ZAY-boh for *gazebo?* Until recently I never had, and I was shocked when I did. I was shocked again when I ran a quick check on the word. What I thought was just another harmless beastly mispronunciation turned out to be the *first* pronunciation listed in three of the four leading current American dictionaries.

What is wrong with these dictionaries? I wondered. Are the editors tippling in their guh-ZEE-bohz? In my whole life I have heard only one person say guh-ZAY-boh and suddenly I'm supposed to believe that it's the usual pronunciation? Give me a break. This goofy guh-ZAY-boh shouldn't even be listed at all, and I'll tell you why.

Apparently there has been a long-standing confusion both in spelling and pronunciation between the words *gazabo* (guh-ZAY-boh) and *gazebo* (guh-ZEE-boh). *Gazabo* is an old slang term for a fellow, guy, especially an eccentric or gawky guy, says *Webster 2* (1934). Wentworth and Flexner's *Dictionary of American Slang* (1975) says the word dates back to about 1805. It is believed to have evolved from the Spanish *gazapo,* literally a young rabbit, and figuratively a shrewd fellow, sly customer, or sharpie, or a lie, blunder, or howler. (From "sly guy" to "gawky guy" is a curious transition, but that's just the beginning of this twisted tale.)

The familiar *gazebo,* the turret-shaped open pavilion or small summerhouse that usually commands a nice view, dates back to about 1750 and its origin is uncertain. The *Century* (1914) says it is apparently formed from the verb to *gaze,* "simulating the form of a Latin verb of the 2nd conjugation, in the future indicative 1st person singular (like *videbo,* 'I shall see'), as if meaning 'I shall gaze.'" That's some weird word making, but you ain't seen nuthin' yet.

In classical Latin, *videbo* would be pronounced wi-DAY-boh, but in the English system for Latin pronunciation it would be vy-DEE-boh or vi-DEE-boh. Thus it is conceivable that *gazebo,* a pseudo-Latin coinage, could be pronounced guh-ZEE-boh in anglicized Latin and guh-ZAY-boh in pseudoclassical Latin. Add to this the fact that *gazabo* was occasionally misspelled *gazebo* and *gazebo* was occasionally misspelled *gazabo* and you start to have a serious problem. Does the *gazabo* enjoy the view from the *gazebo* or the other way around?

It took a while for the confusion to infiltrate the dictionaries. Worcester (1860), who doesn't list the slang *gazabo*, records *gazebo*, with the alternative spelling *gazeebo*, and one pronunciation: guh-ZEE-boh. Funk & Wagnalls *Standard* (1897) and the *Century* (1914) do the same, and *Webster's Collegiate* (1917), which drops the alternative *gazeebo*, also gives only guh-ZEE-boh. The slang *gazabo* first appears in *Webster 2* (1934), and it is here that things start getting out of hand. *Webster 2* says *gazabo* is pronounced guh-ZAY-boh, and *gazebo* guh-ZEE-boh, but it lists *gazebo* as an alternative spelling for *gazabo* and vice versa.

Webster 3 (1961) moved *gazabo* into the *gazebo* permanently by listing guh-ZAY-boh first for the spelling *gazebo*, meaning the pavilion. Since then the dictionaries seem to have given up on making a clear distinction, so it looks as if it's up to us. Most of us, thankfully, don't have trouble keeping the two words straight, since most of us, I think, have never even heard the slang *gazabo*. But to all you *gazabos* out there who are mispronouncing *gazebo*, I issue this heartfelt plea: you're making a mess of the dictionaries, and lots of people like me are going nuts trying to figure out why you're saying it that way. And while I'm at it, if any lexicographers are listening, I have three words for them: *get with it.*

geisha GAY-shuh.

Geisha entered English in 1891 and, despite the fact that the dictionaries all recorded its pronunciation as GAY-shuh, the word was soon badly mispronounced. "Don't say *guy'sha* or *gesh'a,*" admonishes Opdycke (1939). Those beastly utterances have disappeared (thank goodness), but another upstart variant, GEE-shuh, was first recorded in *Webster 3* (1961) and now appears in all four of the leading American dictionaries (two label it less common). I have yet to find an authority who prefers it, and I certainly don't.

genealogy Properly, JEE-nee-**AL**-uh-jee, not JEE-nee-**AHL**-uh-jee.

The question with *genealogy* is, should the *a* affect the pronunciation? In other words, since the tail end of the word is spelled *-alogy* instead of *-ology,* should the pronunciation reflect that? Purists would say yes, and in this case I cast my whole vote (every ounce of it) with them. In my book, the antepenultimate, accented syllable should be pronounced like the name *Al,* and to pronounce it like the *Ol-* in *Oliver* is beastly.

Authorities of the 18th and 19th centuries all agreed there was no AHL in *-alogy;* it was an unequivocal AL. Instead, the divisive issue was the first syllable: should it be pronounced JEN- or JEE-? Walker (1791), Smart (1836), and other orthoepists preferred JEE-, which Vizetelly (1929) says is "a Scottish pronunciation" (I can find no corroboration of that claim), while Sheridan (1780), Worcester (1860), Webster-Mahn (1864), and others favored JEN-. By the early 20th century, JEN- was faltering, and by mid-century JEE- was ascendant and JEN- was on the wane. Although JEN-ee-**AL**-uh-jee is rarely heard today, most current dictionaries still list it in good standing.

But back to who put the AHL in -*alogy*. As JEN- gave way to JEE- in the first syllable, so did AL begin to give way to AHL in the third. Though orthoepists such as Phyfe (1926), Holt (1937), and Opdycke (1939) wagged bony fingers at the beastly substitution of -*ology* for -*alogy*, the false analogy was too compelling and the mispronunciation became entrenched. Kenyon & Knott (1949) noted that the AH sound for -*alogy* "is found in all parts of the US and Canada. The -*ology* words have influenced it." *American College* (1952) records -**AHL**-uh-jee for -*alogy*, and dictionaries since have followed suit.* Of the four leading current American dictionaries, only one — *WNW 3* (1997) — lists -**AL**-uh-jee first, and *M-W 10* (1993) is quite correct in preceding it (and the obsolescent JEN-) with the label *also*, meaning it is now "appreciably less common." Even some modern authorities have caved in to the -*ology* trap. *WNW Guide* (1984) gives -**AHL**-uh-jee priority, and Lass & Lass (1976) prefer it. (The Lasses are strangely inconsistent, however, in their preference for the traditional pronunciation of -*alogy* in *mineralogy* rather than the erroneous but now acceptable -*ology* variant.)

One almost has to laugh at this replacement of JEE-nee-**AL**-uh-jee by JEE-nee-**AHL**-uh-jee. In a society so committed to momentary pleasure and so oblivious of even the recent past, the careless changing of -*alogy* to -*ology* in a word that means the study of family descent is an exquisite irony. Already the word is frequently misspelled informally, and no doubt someday some enterprising writers and editors will decide it is time to change the spelling to reflect the pronunciation, the world will embrace its *geneology*, and the debate will be forgotten. Perhaps even the meaning of the word will change to "the study of genes" and we will pronounce it *gene-ology*. Yet if, as they say, history repeats itself, then maybe those speakers who know this word's pedigree (Greek *genea*, race, descent, and -*logy*, science or theory of, from Greek *logos*, word), and who are careful to distinguish between -*ologies* and -*alogies*, will once again prevail. As one who believes that the ways of the past did not exist simply to be ignored or overthrown, I am committed to that end. In the Elster clan, at least, we will study JEE-nee-**AL**-uh-jee, never JEE-nee-**AHL**-uh-jee. See **mineralogy**.

---

* Although the painstakingly permissive *Webster 3* (1961) lists the -**AHL**-uh-jee variant first, it commendably labels it with an obelus [÷], meaning that many consider the pronunciation objectionable.

genre ZHAN-ruh, not JAHN-ruh.

This loanword from French (ultimately from the Latin *genus,* kind, sort, class) retains much of its French flavor in pronunciation. Thus the *g* is pronounced as in *rouge, massage,* and *mirage.* (Linguists call this a voiced sibilant.)

gentle JENT'l, not JEN'l; **gentleman (-men)** JENT'l-mun, not JEN'l-mun.

Be sure to pronounce the *t* in these words. Don't say *gennel* and *gennelman.* See **fundamental, kindergarten, mental, rental.**

genuine JEN-yoo-in.

There is no *wine* in *genuine.* Do not say JEN-yoo-wyn; this pronunciation has always been stigmatized. Holt (1937) says that circus barkers popularized it. Those who use it are looked upon by many as careless or uneducated speakers, or as caricaturing them.

gerrymander Properly, **GER**-ee-MAN-dur. Now usually **JER**-ee-MAN-dur.

Gerrymander means to slice up voting districts in such a way as to give one party an advantage. The word, which was coined in 1812, is a combination of *salamander* and the last name of Elbridge Gerry (GER-ee), governor of Massachusetts from 1810 to 1811 and vice president under James Madison from 1813 to 1814. (Gerry died in office at the age of 70.) When Gerry's party *gerrymandered* Essex County, Massachusetts, his opponents noticed that the new map resembled a salamander, and they did the only politic thing under the circumstances: they invented a disparaging word with his name in it to express their contempt for the underhand maneuver.

Although **JER**-ee-MAN-dur, with a soft *g* (which sounds like *j*), is more commonly heard today and is listed first in all four major current American dictionaries, two of those dictionaries — *American Heritage 3* (1992), which includes an interesting note on the birth of the word, and *M-W 10* (1993) — acknowledge that the original and proper pronunciation is **GER**-ee-MAN-dur, with a hard *g* as in *get.* Though I have yet to find proof of it, I suspect that the pronunciation with *j* may have been influenced by the connotative relation of the words *jury-rig* (c. 1780) and *jerry-built* (c. 1865). *Webster 2* (1934) was the first major American authority to sanction it (as an alternative).

One reason for saying *gerrymander* with a hard *g* is to show that you know the eponymous history of the word and the proper pronunciation of the source's name. But if you prefer to eschew that sort of pedantry and would rather follow a respectable role model, you can take your cue from the Great Communicator: during his presidency, Ronald Reagan said **GER**-ee-MAN-dur. He may not have heard very well, but when it came to speaking, the man was no slouch.

gewgaw Properly, GYOO-gaw. Now often GOO-gaw. See **dew.**

gibberish JIB-ur-ish.

This is the prevailing pronunciation on both sides of the Atlantic, and GIB-ur-ish (with the *g* of *go*) is obsolete in the U.S. and obsolescent in Britain.

giblet JIB-lit, not GIB-lit.

Gibran, Kahlil ji-BRAHN (-BRAHN as in *bronze*), kah-LEEL.

In her fine novel *Breathing Lessons*, Anne Tyler writes, "At the wedding, she had pronounced Gibran with a hard *g*. Today the *g* was soft. Maggie had no idea which was correct."

Poor Maggie. How I longed to tell her she is not alone. Confusion and mortification over one's pronunciation can strike at any moment, and if you believe in Murphy's Law, as I do, that moment is invariably the most inopportune one, when you are nowhere near a dictionary (or this book) and you know whoever is listening is doing so with a discriminating ear.

In this case, one does not need to consult a prophet for the proper pronunciation. *Go* and *get* have a hard *g*. A soft *g* occurs in *giant* and *ginger*. There is another type of soft *g* that sounds like *zh*; it occurs chiefly in words from French, such as *mirage* and *genre* (which see). *Gibran* is often mispronounced with this French soft *g*, zhi-BRAHN, or sometimes with a hard *g*, gi-BRAHN. Both are incorrect. Use the soft *g* that sounds like *j*, ji-BRAHN. (Some authorities mark the *i* as a schwa, ji-BRAHN or juh-BRAHN.) The author's first name is often pronounced KAH-leel or KAH-lil, with the accent on the first syllable. These also are incorrect. The *NBC Handbook* (1984), *RHWC* (1997), and *WNW 3* (1997) place the accent on the second syllable, which rhymes with *feel:* kah-LEEL.

Gila (monster) HEE-luh.

Dictionaries do not recognize the spelling pronunciation GEE-luh.

Above my desk I have posted a cartoon by the wonderfully gifted Leo Cullum that appeared in *The New Yorker*. The drawing shows a lab-coated physician advising a distraught man with a very large Gila monster hanging from his nose. "It's pronounced 'hee-la' monster," the doctor tells the patient. "The 'g' sounds like an 'h.'"

glaucoma glaw-COH-muh (glaw- rhyming with *law*).

Glaucoma entered English in the 1880s. The variant pronunciation glow-COH-muh (glow- rhyming with *how*) was first recorded in *Webster 3* (1961). *Taber's Medical* (1970) and *Stedman's Medical* (1972) do not countenance it, but *Mosby's Medical* (1990), bowing to its popularity even within the medical profession, recognizes it as an alternative. Current authorities are split: *American Heritage 3* (1992) and *M-W 10* (1993) list glow-COH-muh first; *RHWC* (1997) and *WNW 3* (1997) list glaw-COH-muh first. Lass & Lass (1976) and the *NBC Handbook* (1984) embrace the newfangled glow-; *WNW Guide* (1984), *Everyday Reader's* (1985), and Barnhart (1988) favor the traditional glaw-. Despite the widespread acceptance of the glow-

pronunciation, I cannot recommend it because it is based on an erroneous notion of how to pronounce the vowel combination *au*.

In English, *au* is occasionally pronounced as a diphthong (DIF-thawng or -thahng), which *Webster 2* (1934) defines as "a continuous glide from one sound to another," but in nearly all of the words in which it appears it is pronounced as a digraph (DY-graf), which *RHWC* (1997) calls "a pair of letters representing a single speech sound," as *th* in *path*, *ea* in *beat*, *eo* in *people*, *ou* in *group*, and *au* in *laud*. *Au* is a diphthong, with the gliding sound of OW as in *out*, in *umlaut* and *sauerkraut*. It is a digraph, with the sound of AW as in *saw*, in *sauce, taut, caught, applaud, flaunt, maudlin*, etc., and in practically every word it initiates: *author, audience, automobile, auspicious,* and so on.

There are a great many more English words in which *au* is treated as a digraph, and properly *glaucoma* is among them. The pronunciation with glow- for the first syllable is popular but eccentric and unjustifiable — unless you want to argue that it's the Latin pronunciation, in which case you will have to explain why you are speaking Latin and not English. The traditional glaw-COH-muh, on the other hand, is perfectly English, and perfectly consistent with analogous English words. See **flutist, trauma**.

golf GAHLF or GAWLF. Do not say GAHF, GAWF, or (ugh) GUHLF.

M-W 10 (1993) wins this pronunciation guru's uncoveted "Ear to the Ground Award" for recording more variants for *golf* than any other source: GAHLF, GAWLF, GAHF, GAWF, and "sometimes" (excuse me while I gag) GUHLF. By contrast, the other three leading current American dictionaries are more chary in their assessment of which pronunciations are acceptable in educated speech. *American Heritage 3* (1992) lists GAHLF and GAWLF; *WNW 3* (1997) lists GAWLF and GAHLF; and *RHWC* (1997) gives GAHLF and GAWLF followed by "British also" GAHF.

That GAHF (like *goff*) is common in British speech is contraindicated by British authorities. The *Oxford Guide* (1983) says "the pronunciation goff is old-fashioned" and labels it a form "especially to be avoided." Jones (1991) gives priority to GAHLF and adds "sometimes by players" GAHF. And Burchfield (1996) says "the standard pronunciation is [GAHLF]," noting that GAHF, which is imitative of the Scottish pronunciation GOHF, "is now seldom heard."

On this side of the Atlantic there is no question that GAHLF and GAWLF, with an audible *l*, are the prevailing pronunciations, and some authorities label GAHF and GAWF old-fashioned or infrequent in educated speech. American speakers are advised to use either GAHLF or GAWLF and avoid all other variants (especially the odious GUHLF).

gondola GAHN-duh-luh. Do not say gahn-DOH-luh.

The stress is properly on the *first* syllable.

In the 1986 movie *Heartburn,* based on Nora Ephron's book, a woman says, "Arthur's idea of romance is Venice, *gon*dolas," stressing the first syllable. "Gon*do*las," her husband interrupts, stressing the second syllable in an irritated tone of voice that implies he has corrected her often. "Yes, of course," she says, and changes the subject.

That is precisely the sort of unfortunate situation I had in mind when I decided to write this book, and I hope you will use what is written here as ammunition in your defense should you become the victim of what I like to call "erroneous correction." Correcting someone's pronunciation (or grammar or diction or anything else) can be one of the most obnoxious things a person can do, but it doesn't have to be. When I find myself impelled to do it, I try to follow these three rules:

1. Don't ever interrupt the speaker.
2. Whenever possible, make your comments in private.
3. Make damn sure you're right!

In this case the woman was right to put the accent on the *gon-* in *gondola,* and her partner, who apparently had never checked the pronunciation in a dictionary, broke all three rules and made an ass of himself.

Second-syllable stress in *gondola* has been heard since the early 20th century; it was denounced by a passel of authorities, including Phyfe (1926), Vizetelly (1929), Gilmartin (1936), Holt (1937), and Opdycke (1939), and did not gain enough respectability to get into a dictionary until the 1960s. Since then, as gahn-DOH-luh grew more popular, a debate arose whether *gondola* should have first-syllable stress for certain meanings and second-syllable stress for others. *Random House II* (1987) and its abridgment, *RHWC* (1991, 1997), sanction GAHN-duh-luh but add that gahn-DOH-luh is used especially for the Venetian boat. *WNW Guide* (1984), on the other hand, asserts that GAHN-duh-luh "is usual for the boat" and gahn-DOH-luh "is more common for other meanings." *M-W 9* (1985) and *10* (1993) also cite GAHN-duh-luh as the customary pronunciation for the boat.

The debate seems rather ridiculous, for ultimately the point is this: whether you say gahn-DOH-luh for the boat, the cable car, or any other sense of the word, you've missed the boat. Past and present authorities prefer GAHN-duh-luh, with the accent on the first syllable, and all current dictionaries list this pronunciation first.

government GUHV-urn-mint.

Pronounce the *r* and preserve the first *n,* pronouncing the second syllable -urn- rather than -ur- or -uh-.

Government is one of a number of words that careful speakers are particularly diligent about pronouncing precisely. In other words, how you say it is an indication of whether you are an average educated speaker or a cultivated one.

The variant GUH-vur-mịnt, in which the *n* is not articulated, and the variants GUH-vuh-mịnt and GUHV-mịnt, in which both the *n* and the *r* are inaudible, have been heard in educated American speech for most of the 20th century. Although Phyfe (1926) and Opdycke (1939) sternly disapproved of GUH-vur-mịnt and *Webster 2* (1934) sanctioned only GUHV-urn-mịnt, Kenyon & Knott (1949) recognized GUH-vur-mịnt, GUH-vuh-mịnt, and GUHV-mịnt, noting that "no competent observer can doubt [their] prevalence . . . among the leading statesmen of US and England, even in formal public address."

That is true; however, a great many speakers today still make an effort to say GUHV-urn-mịnt, and nearly all current authorities still consider this pronunciation preferable. Shaw (1972), Lass & Lass (1976), the *NBC Handbook* (1984), and Morris & Morris (1985) prefer it, *RHWC* (1997) and *WNW 3* (1997) list it first, and it is the only pronunciation sanctioned by *American Heritage 3* (1992). In his *New Fowler's MEU* (1996), R. W. Burchfield remarks that "while preparing my booklet *The Spoken Word* (1981) for the BBC, I found that [*government*] belonged to a small group of words that gave a maximum of offence to listeners if pronounced in a garbled manner, with the first *n* silent, i.e. as [GUHV-uh-mịnt] or even [GUHV-mịnt]."

gramercy gruh-MUR-see.

Gramercy is an archaic interjection used to express surprise or thanks. It is a contraction of the phrase *grand mercy,* which is why the accent falls on the second syllable, the *mer-* of *mercy.* For Gramercy Park in New York City, however, the customary local pronunciation is GRAM-ur-see (like *grammar + see*).

granary Properly, GRAN-uh-ree. Popularly, GRAY-nuh-ree.

Look up this word in several current dictionaries and you will see something curious. Some divide it *gran • a • ry,* the first syllable being *gran-;* others divide it *gra • na • ry,* with the first syllable *gra-.* Now, if you look closely you will see that those that mark the first syllable *gran-* give priority to the pronunciation GRAN-uh-ree — *American Heritage 3* (1992) and *WNW 3* (1997) — while those that mark it *gra-* give priority to the pronunciation GRAY-nuh-ree — *M-W 10* (1993) and *RHWC* (1997). Of course there are a few dictionaries that divide the word *gra • na • ry* and list GRAN-uh-ree first, or divide it *gran • a • ry* and list GRAY-nuh-ree first, but that's goofy. Perhaps at the root of the problem are the obsolete spelling variants *grainary* and *grainery.* The former was obsolete by the 19th century, but the latter appears in *Webster 2* (1934) and *Webster 3* (1961) with the pronunciation GRAY-nuh-ree. Although *granary* has been the dominant spelling of the word in educated usage since the 18th century, over the years these *grain*-influenced spellings have steadily influenced the pronunciation of the word.

And so the controversy rages in the dictionaries, and there is no way to resolve it but to take sides. If you think pronunciation should reflect meaning, and that word division should reflect pronunciation, imagine that *granary* comes from English *grain*, divide it *gra • na • ry*, and say GRAY-nuh-ree. If you favor traditional pronunciations and respect the influence of etymology, as I do, remember that the word comes from Latin *granarium* (from *granum*, grain, seed), divide it *gran • a • ry*, and say GRAN-uh-ree. With the former you won't be wrong, but with the latter you'll have a few more authorities to back you up.

grandiloquent gran-DIL-uh-kwint. Don't say gran-DEL-uh-kwint (like *grand eloquent*).

When I was publicizing my 1996 book *There's a Word for It!* on the radio, not a few silver-tongued talk show hosts had a tough time spitting out the subtitle, *A Grandiloquent Guide to Life.* They'd say *grand-**el**-oquent* instead of *grand-**ill**-oquent.*

gratis GRAT-is or, chiefly British, GRAY-tis. Don't say GRAH-tis.

GRAT-is (first syllable rhyming with *cat*) appears first in three of the four leading current American dictionaries and is preferred by Lass & Lass (1976) and the *NBC Handbook* (1984). *WNW 3* (1997) gives priority to GRAY-tis (first syllable like *gray*), which the other three American dictionaries also recognize. Older American authorities preferred this pronunciation, but it is now infrequent in American speech; however, as Jones (1991) and Burchfield (1996) attest, it prevails in Britain. A third variant, GRAH-tis (with broad *a,* as in *father* and *harp*), is now often heard in America. The evidence from "across the pond," as it were, strongly indicates that it is a British import. It is also a pretentious de-anglicization, an unnecessary and unjustifiable revival of the classical Latin pronunciation of this 15th-century loanword. Only one American dictionary, *American Heritage 3* (1992), recognizes GRAH-tis. I can only hope it stays that way.

greasy GREE-see (*s* as in *crease*) or GREE-zee (*s* as in *easy*).

Both pronunciations are acceptable, although the first, GREE-see, probably is used by the majority of educated American speakers.

How you pronounce the *s* in *greasy* depends mostly on where you're from. The pronunciation note in *Random House II* (1987) explains that

GREASY is almost always pronounced as [GREE-zee], with a medial (z), in the South Midland and Southern U.S. and as [GREE-see], with a medial (s), in New England, New York State, and the Great Lakes Basin. Speakers of New Jersey and eastern Pennsylvania are divided, with some using (s) and some using (z). . . . Both pronunciations were brought to the colonies, where the present U.S. pattern emerged.

Many British speakers use both pronunciations, depending on the meaning intended. According to Jones (1991) and Burchfield (1996), GREE-see is usual for the literal sense "covered with grease," while GREE-zee is usual for the figurative sense "slippery, slimy," used either of slippery things or slimy people.

grievous GREE-vus. Don't say GREE-vee-us.

Be sure to say this word in *two*, not three, syllables, rhyming it with *leave us*. The three-syllable GREE-vee-us is an old and stubbornly persistent beastly mispronunciation — perhaps in part because, as Holt (1937) observes, it is "a common mistake among ministers." See **mischievous, heinous, intravenous**.

grimace Traditionally, gri-MAYS (-MAYS rhyming with *place*). Now usually GRIM-is.

Here is the story of how a gri-MAYS became a GRIM-is. The noun *grimace* came into the language from French in the mid-1600s, the verb came along in the mid-1700s, and for nearly two hundred years after that cultivated speakers stressed both on the second syllable, and authorities sanctioned only that pronunciation. The variant GRIM-is, with first-syllable stress, appears to have taken root sometime in the late 1800s, for Ayres (1894) counsels us to avoid it. By the 1930s it had begun to spread, leading Opdycke (1939) to write, "Don't say *gri'maze* or *grim'ass*." In 1947 *American College* recognized GRIM-is as an alternative, and in 1961 *Webster 3* listed it first. Then came the inane McDonald's restaurant advertising campaign with Ronald McDonald the clown and his puppet sidekick GRIM-is, and poor old gri-MAYS swiftly became as strange as a square hamburger. Lass & Lass (1976) are the only modern American authorities I can find who prefer gri-MAYS, and *WNW 2* (1984) and *3* (1988, 1997) are the only American dictionaries that list it first. *OED 2* (1989) and Jones (1991), both British authorities, prefer gri-MAYS, but Burchfield (1996) notes that first-syllable stress has been gaining ground in England. (Could the worldwide proliferation of McDonald's restaurants be partly to blame?)

One of the tragic aspects of capriciously changing the pronunciation of an old, established word is the loss of its conventional rhythm and rhyme. The traditional pronunciation, gri-MAYS, rhymes easily with many words, and its pleasing iambic meter — with a short syllable followed by a long one — is the most common foot in English poetry. The newfangled GRIM-is, with its obscure second syllable and heavier trochaic meter — a long syllable followed by a short one — is virtually impossible to rhyme, as the following verse makes clear:

The Painful Case of Poor Grimace

Gri*mace* is dead! Long live gri*mace!*
*Grim*ace has usurped its place.
Defiant of three hundred years,
An upstart strain has seized our ears,
And twisted English to its limits,
Declaring: "There's no rhyme for *grim*ace!"

This offspring of recessive stress
Transfixed us with its ugliness;
It warped its rhythm, shed its rhyme,
Became a fixture on prime time.
Though what we saw and what we heard
Was not the real or proper word,
Still all rushed headlong to embrace
This modish *grim*ace — goodbye gri*mace!*

Gri*mace* is dead! Long live gri*mace!*
*Grim*ace has usurped its place.
The arriviste has put a curse
Upon all English prose and verse,
And left our writers but the dimmest,
Slimmest hope of rhyming *grim*aced.

But such is life in the language game,
Where nothing seems to stay the same.
Tomorrow will today erase:
*Grim*ace is in, gone is gri*mace.*
Yet, friend — in secret, unobserved —
I vow to see tradition served;
When I put on a nasty face,
I'll still call it a gri*mace.*

grocery GROH-suh-ree or GROHS-ree.
The word is acceptably pronounced either in three or two syllables. Avoid, please, with all your might, the ugsome GROH-shuh-ree and GROHSH-ree. Only one dictionary, *M-W 10* (1993), recognizes the slovenly GROHSH-ree, which is straight out of Lower Slobbovia.

grovel GRAH-vul or GRUH-vul.
Older dictionaries countenanced only GRAH-vul, and some authorities — Phyfe (1926), for example — disapproved of GRUH-vul. However, *Webster 2* (1934) recognized GRUH-vul as an acceptable alternative and Kenyon and Knott (1949) noted that it "shows the original vowel" and GRAH-vul is a spelling pronunciation. Recent authorities are divided. Lass

& Lass (1976) and the *NBC Handbook* (1984) favor GRUH-vul, but *OED 2* (1989) gives only GRAH-vul and three of the four major current American dictionaries list it first. I say GRAH-vul. Take your pick.

guacamole GWAH-kuh-**MOH**-lee or GWAH-kuh-**MOH**-lay.

The first pronunciation is standard throughout the U.S. The second is common in California and the Southwest.

guillotine GIL-uh-TEEN, not **GEE**-yuh-TEEN. Pronounce the *l*'s.

This word entered English in 1793 and quickly became anglicized. Throughout the 19th century the accent wavered, with some authorities favoring it on the third syllable and others favoring it on the first. All agreed, however, that the double *l* was pronounced as in English *quill* and *willow*. By the early 20th century the accent had generally settled on the first syllable, where it has since firmly remained for the noun, although the verb is sometimes stressed on the final syllable. Lass & Lass (1976), the *NBC Handbook* (1984), and Barnhart (1988) prefer **GIL**-uh-TEEN, and all four major current American dictionaries list this pronunciation first. (Two medical dictionaries — *Taber's* (1970) and *Stedman's* (1972) — also prefer **GIL**-uh-TEEN for the surgical instrument called a *guillotine* that is used in excising a tonsil and growths in the larynx.)

The popular variant **GEE**-yuh-TEEN, with the *l*'s silent, is a de-anglicization first recorded in *Webster 3* (1961). Originally a pseudo-French affectation, it is now threatening to overtake the traditional anglicized pronunciation. Careful speakers are expected to help hold the line on this one — on pain of beheading!

Guyana gy-AH-nuh (gy- rhyming with *fry*).

gymnast JIM-nast, not JIM-nist.

Gymnast is properly pronounced to rhyme with *swim fast*, not *slim fist*.

Webster 3 (1961) was the first to record the slurred JIM-nist for this word, which entered English in 1594. Of the four major current American dictionaries, three give priority to the traditional JIM-nast, and *WNW 3* (1997) sanctions only JIM-nast. JIM-nast is also the only pronunciation in Funk & Wagnalls *Standard* (1980) and *OED 2* (1989), and it is the preference of the *NBC Handbook* (1984), Frierson (1988), and Jones (1991). Only *Oxford American* (1980) prefers JIM-nist.

You should clearly pronounce the *-ast* in *bombast* and *bombastic, iconoclast* and *iconoclastic, encomiast* and *encomiastic, dynast* and *dynastic, sarcast* (a sarcastic person) and *sarcastic, epiblast* and *epiblastic, fantast* (a dreamer, visionary) and *fantastic, enthusiast* and *enthusiastic, gymnast* and *gymnastic.* See **enthusiast.**

gynecology GY-nuh-**KAHL**-uh-jee. Less often, and usually among older speakers, JIN-uh-**KAHL**-uh-jee, or occasionally JY-nuh-**KAHL**-uh-jee. The attempt to ascertain a proper or preferred pronunciation for *gynecology* has exasperated pronunciation gurus almost since the word entered the language in the 1840s. How should the *gy-* be pronounced? JI- as in *gin*, JY- as in *gyre*, or GY- like *guy*?

Phyfe (1926), taking his cue from dictionaries of the early part of the century, which preferred the *j* (or soft *g*) pronunciations, gives JIN- and JY-nuh-**KAHL**-uh-jee. Vizetelly (1929) also prefers the *j* pronunciations, but notes one 19th-century source that sanctions GY-, with a hard *g* as in *go*. The comments of Gilmartin (1936) reflect the rising influence of the hard *g* and the mounting confusion of so many variants: "The first *g*," he writes, "may have the sound of *j*, or may be hard as in *girl*. The first syllable may be *jin* to rhyme with *sin*, or *ji* to rhyme with *cry*, or *gi* to rhyme with *try*." Opdycke (1939) throws his hands up and says, "It is impossible to say which is preferred by the dictionaries; all are given, sometimes one standing first, sometimes another. The medical profession probably prefers [GY-]."

The confusion continued, of course. Kenyon & Knott (1949) give JY- and GY- but not JIN-, noting that "one form is as 'correct' as the other. The first is more Englished." *American College* (1952) lists GY-, JY-, and JIN-, in that order. And *Webster 3* (1961) covers all the bases, as usual, by recording every variant imaginable.*

In recent years, as the GY- (*guy*) pronunciation began to predominate among speakers of all ages and in the medical profession, authoritative preference for it has jelled. *Taber's Medical* (1970) bravely countenances only GY-, and *Stedman's Medical* (1972) sanctions GY- first and JIN- as alternative. Lass & Lass (1976) — who report the variants recorded by the four leading dictionaries of their time, then note their own preference — favor GY-. And Morris & Morris (1985) say, "Even those who specialize in the field do not all agree as to the pronunciation of this [word] but the one preferred is gy-nuh-KOL-uh-jee (with a hard 'g' and long 'i' sound for 'y'). Jy-nuh-KOL-uh-jee and jin-uh-KOL-uh-jee are considered acceptable also."

Today GY-nuh-**KAHL**-uh-jee is without doubt the dominant pronunciation on both sides of the Atlantic. The four major current American dictionaries and the British *OED 2* (1989) all give priority to GY-, and it is preferred by Jones (1991), a British authority, the *NBC Handbook* (1984), and *WNW Guide* (1984), which notes, somewhat elegiacally, that the JY- and JIN- pronunciations "are still sometimes heard, especially among older speakers."

That should settle it, right? GY- has prevailed, and the variants with *j*

---

* In the *Harper Dictionary of Contemporary Usage* (1985), 2nd ed., Morris & Morris write, "The editors of the Merriam-Webster dictionaries, beginning with the Third International (1961) [called *Webster 3* in this book], have been at some pains to record every conceivable variant pronunciation on the theory that whatever is is acceptable. . . . Obviously no effort has been made to discriminate between what the educated speaker would consider proper and improper pronunciations" (p. 493).

have become old-fashioned. But one question remains. Should those who still prefer the soft *g* (JIN- or JY-) now conform? If you feel awkward using an outmoded pronunciation, yes; otherwise, absolutely not. If you were taught to say JIN- or JY-nuh-**KAHL**-uh-jee, if that's the way you've always said it, if that's what you are convinced is correct, or if the GY- pronunciation makes you uncomfortable, then by all means go ahead and keep saying it your way. You have every right to pronounce *gynecology* as you prefer. The only right time has taken from you is to declare the GY-pronunciation wrong.

H

Halley's (comet) HAL-eez, not HAY-leez.

The comet comes around once in a lifetime, but its name comes up far more often than that, so be smart and say it right. Here's the skinny: *Halley's comet*, which appears about every 76 years, was named after the English astronomer Edmund Halley (1656–1742). *Random House II* (1987) suggests that the variants HAY-leez and the less frequent (and anachronistic) HAW-leez may have come from the various spellings of the astronomer's name (*Hailey, Haley, Hawley*), which were used interchangeably during his time. By the 19th century, the spelling *Halley* and the pronunciation HAL-ee had become fixed. Today, notes *Random House II*, HAL-ee for the astronomer and HAL-eez for the comet are the prevailing pronunciations, and these are the pronunciations modern astronomers usually recommend. Moreover, the preponderance of modern authority — from *Webster 2* (1934) to the *Columbia Encylopedia* (1963) to the *NBC Handbook* (1984) — favors HAL-eez, and even the infamously permissive *Webster 3* (1961) acknowledges that HAY-leez is objectionable to many.

Hammett, Dashiell HAM-it, duh-SHEEL (rhymes with *reveal*).

That's right: duh-SHEEL for the writer's first name, not DASH-ul, as it's so often mispronounced. You don't believe me? *Random House II* (1987) lists duh-SHEEL first, and it is the only pronunciation in the *Columbia Encyclopedia* (1963). Ralph H. Emerson, an authority on the pronunciation of literary names who also prescribes duh-SHEEL, explains that "the name was originally French; generations earlier it had been spelled 'de Chiel.'"

---

a = at / a̲ = final / ah = spa / ahr = car / air = fair / ay = hay / aw = saw
ch = chip / e = let / e̲ = item / ee = see / eer = deer / i = sit / i̲ = April
ng = sing / o̲ = carrot / oh = go / oo = soon / or = for / oor = poor
ow = cow / oy = toy / sh = she / th = thin / th̲ = this / u̲ = focus / uh = up
ur = turn / uu = pull, took / y, eye = by, I / zh = measure / (see full key, p. xiv)

---

handkerchief HANG-kur-chif. Don't say HANG-kur-cheef.

There is no *chief* in *handkerchief*— at least not in its pronunciation. You don't say KUR-cheef for *kerchief* or MIS-cheef for *mischief,* do you? Authorities from John Walker (1791) to the present overwhelmingly favor -chif in the final syllable.

harass Answer below.

Harass, hands down, wins the Most Hotly Debated Pronunciation in the Language award. Whenever I happen to mention to someone that I'm a pronunciation maven, the person is certain to ask me about this word. And whenever I'm on the radio discussing language, invariably someone calls to ask whether 'tis nobler to say HAR-is (like the name *Harris*) or huh-RAS (rhymes with *alas*), or suffer the slings and arrows of outrageous lawsuits. I'm not qualified to give legal advice, but I do dispense advice on language, and this word to the wise is free: the pronunciation of *harass* is not worth the breath expended arguing about it, because it's a non-issue, a done deal, a fait accompli. Both pronunciations are legit.

HAR-is is the original and traditional pronunciation, dating from the 17th century when the word entered English from French, but huh-RAS has been heard in both cultivated and uncultivated speech for over 150 years, judging by the note in Joseph Emerson Worcester's dictionary of 1860: "This word is sometimes heard pronounced, erroneously, with the accent on the second syllable, [huh-RAS]; but this pronunciation is not countenanced by any of the orthoepists." *Webster's New International* (1909) echoed that sentiment, but *Webster 2* (1934), its illustrious successor, recognized huh-RAS, and from that day forth second-syllable stress was kosher. Kenyon & Knott (1949) observed that "[huh-RAS] instead of the older [HAR-is] appears to be on the increase," and *Webster 3* (1961) — known for taking bold (and occasionally cockamamie) stands in the pronunciation department — listed huh-RAS first. According to *Random House II* (1987), huh-RAS is now more common in the U.S. "especially among younger educated speakers, some of whom have only minimal familiarity with the older form." (Update on *RH II*'s statement: in the harassment-happy 1990s — from the Anita Hill hearings to the various charges against President Bill Clinton — during which the words *harass* and *harassment* saturated the broadcast media, lots of "younger educated speakers" were exposed, and sometimes indecently exposed, to both pronunciations. That many, if not most, of them still say huh-RAS is now more likely the result of conscious choice rather than "minimal familiarity with the older form.")

Before I tell you my own history with *harass,* let me share with you the opinions of three respected arbiters of language, the first two American, the last British.

Harass and *harassment* should be pronounced "with the stress on the first syllable," say Morris & Morris (1985). "However, many respected announcers and commentators, to say nothing of average literate users of the language, have been paying little attention to the 'authorities.' As a result, huh-RASS and huh-RASS-ment are widely heard in the speech of educated people and both pronunciations must now be deemed acceptable."

William Safire is one of those "respected commentators" who favor, and ardently defend, huh-RAS. Here is what he has to say in *Watching My Language* (1997):

I ran into Justice Antonin Scalia at a dinner party and asked him about the question most often put to me: how to say *harassment*. For days, my own answer to the frantic inquiries from broadcasters on this controversy was "I prefer to accent the second syllable, which I will not pronounce for fear of giving offense." (Somebody has to stand up for prudery.) Justice Scalia pronounced it the other way: "HAR-ass-ment." I promptly cross-examined him on *lamentable, despicable, hospitable* — he was consistent and principled, stressing the first syllable in all cases, as we were once taught to do.

He's not incorrect, but he is no longer in the mainstream of pronunciation preference. The increased preference for "ha-RASS-ment" is unmistakable, and has been reflected in the change in most leading dictionaries. Professor Anita Hill repeatedly changed her pronunciation, using both "HAR-ass-ment" and "ha-RASS-ment"; Dan Rather of CBS and Peter Jennings of ABC went with the more modern "ha-RASS," but Tom Brokaw tossed the *NBC Handbook of Pronunciation* [1984, which prefers huh-RAS] into the ashcan and went with the traditional "HAR-ass."

Finally, let's view the situation from the other side of the Atlantic and consider the comments of the editor of *OED 2* (1989), R. W. Burchfield, in his *New Fowler's Modern English Usage* (1996):

Nothing is more likely to displease traditional RP [Received Pronunciation] speakers in Britain than to hear *harass* pronounced with the main stress on the second syllable. . . . John Walker (1806), the *OED* (1899), Daniel Jones (1917), *COD* [*Concise Oxford Dictionary*] (7th edn, 1982) gave only first-syllable stressing, and that is the pronunciation I recommend. But second-syllable stressing (also in *harassment*) is dominant in AmE [American English] and, since about the 1970s, seems to be becoming the pattern favoured by the younger generation in Britain. It is hard to tell how long the traditional line can withstand the assault being made on it.

And now for my tale of *harassment*. As a "younger educated speaker" growing up in New York City in the 1960s, I had always heard huh-RAS (and believe me, living in that city I heard it a great deal). One evening I turned on the news and for the first time heard the word pronounced HAR-<u>i</u>s. Apparently someone in the newsroom had gotten hold of a dictionary (or received an irate letter from a language watchdog) and realized that HAR-<u>i</u>s was the traditional pronunciation — the white-collar way to say it, if you will, versus the blue-collar huh-RAS. And that's what I found out too when I hastened to the family dictionary, *Webster 2* (1934), to check it myself. For some time after that, broadcasters around the U.S. seemed to favor HAR-<u>i</u>s, but now its occurrence on the air has fallen way off, and huh-RAS is once again commonly heard. As the comments quoted above indicate, before too long this hardy huh-RAS may hound the senescent HAR-<u>i</u>s out of existence — but not while Tom Brokaw is still on the air and Justice Scalia is still on the Supreme Court.

Until time — or the Supreme Court — decides the issue, then, it's high time to bury the hatchet and stop *harassing* each other. With this word, I say do as you will and live and let live. Want to know what I do? In the early 1980s I abandoned the gruff huh-RAS of my inner-city youth in favor of the more genteel HAR-<u>i</u>s. Why? Partly to be consistent in my preference for traditional pronunciations (and to help preserve this one), partly to avoid the indelicate sound of the stress on -*ass,* and partly to nettle anyone (my mother, for example) who importunately insists that the word should be pronounced huh-RAS.

Hawaii huh-WY-ee or huh-WAH-ee.
Most speakers say either huh-WY-ee (sometimes transcribed huh-WAH-yee) or huh-WAH-ee, and these are the pronunciations most often countenanced by current authorities. *Random House II* (1987) also lists hah-VAH-ee; I am told by various reliable sources that this pronunciation is preferred by many Hawaiians, but it is not in general use throughout the continental U.S. A fourth variant, huh-WAH-yuh (which sounds like *how are you* spoken by an *r*-dropper), appeared often in older dictionaries but is now rarely heard.

heartrending HAHRT-REN-ding (three syllables).
There is no *render* in *heartrending.* Don't add a syllable and say *heart-rendering.*

hegemony hi-JEM-uh-nee. Less often, **HEJ**-uh-MOH-nee.
Hegemony comes from the Greek *hegemon,* leader, and means leadership or dominance. Since the late 19th century, at least eight pronunciations have been recognized in various dictionaries: hi-JEM-uh-nee, **HEJ**-uh-MOH-nee, hee-JEM-uh-nee, **HEE**-juh-MOH-nee, hi-GEM-uh-nee, hee-GEM-uh-nee (H. W. Fowler's preference), **HEG**-uh-MOH-nee, and most eccentric of all, hee-GEE-muh-nee (tee-hee to that hee-GEE-).

William Safire has stated that today the preferred pronunciation is hi-JEM-uh-nee, and he's right. From *Webster 2* (1934) to *WNW 3* (1997),

American dictionaries have consistently listed hi-JEM-uh-nee first, and authorities from Opdycke (1939) to Lass & Lass (1976), the *NBC Handbook* (1984), and Barnhart (1988) prefer it. **HEJ**-uh-MOH-nee is the most commonly listed alternative, **HEE**-juh-MOH-nee is occasionally listed but rarely heard, and hi-GEM-uh-nee, with a hard *g* (as in the original Greek), is now chiefly British. The rest of the variants noted above are either obsolescent or obsolete.

hegira (also **hejira**) Properly, HEJ-i̱-ruh. Commonly, hi-JY-ruh.

All four major current American dictionaries list hi-JY-ruh first, and numerous authorities — including Lass & Lass (1976), the *NBC Handbook* (1984), *Everyday Reader's* (1985), and Barnhart (1988) — prefer it. I, however, favor the second pronunciation the dictionaries sanction: HEJ-i̱-ruh. Why buck the trend? Because HEJ-i̱-ruh is the historically accurate pronunciation, and I can be a stickler about such things — even to the point of obnoxious pedantry. Here's my evidence: *OED 1* (1928) and *2* (1989) both label hi-JY-ruh "erroneous." *Webster's New International* (1909) says that "[HEJ-i̱-ruh] is etymologically the correct pronunciation, but [hi-JY-ruh] is much more widely used both popularly and among scholars." Vizetelly (1929) explains that HEJ-i̱-ruh,

> the correct pronunciation of the word as indicated by all modern authorities, was noted first by Bailey (1732), then Johnson (1755), Barclay (1774), Rees (1826), and Smart (1840). An erroneous pronunciation, noted by Ash (1775), Perry (1777), Sheridan (1780), Walker (1791), Scott (1797), Jones (1798), Fulton & Knight (1802), Jameson (1827), and Knowles (1835), is still noted as alternative by *Standard, Stormonth, & Webster,* but as preferred by *Worcester* — [hi-JY-ruh].

Don't count your chickens, those of you who say hi-JY-ruh. Lately I've heard HEJ-i̱-ruh here and there on the airwaves, and given the predilection these days for "authentic" pronunciations of "foreign" words (most people have no idea that *hegira* has been English for over four hundred years), I think the etymologically correct pronunciation may make a comeback. Stay tuned.

height HYT (rhymes with *night*).

It is incorrect to pronounce *height* with a *th* sound at the end. Don't say HYT-th (like *high + t + th*) and don't say HYTH (like *high + th*). These are vestigial pronunciations from the 17th and 18th centuries, when several variants were in common use — including one that rhymed with *weight* — and the word's spelling was unstable. For example, Shakespeare, whose spelling was inconsistent, used *height* and *hight,* Ben Jonson and Edmund Burke used *heighth,* and Milton preferred *highth.* In his influential *Critical Pronouncing Dictionary* of 1791, John Walker called the HYTH variant "vulgar," and since then his preference, HYT, has prevailed. "Current usage is a compromise," says *OED 2* (1989), "retaining the spelling *height* (which has been by far the most frequent written form since 1500), with the pronunciation of *hight*."

To all who still say HYT-th or HYTH, I make this appeal: modern authorities and cultivated speakers do not countenance these pronunciations. Your day is long past; stop being perverse and go with the flow. Besides, what can you rhyme the word with when you pronounce it that way?

heinous HAY-n<u>i</u>s.

This word is so frequently mispronounced by well-educated speakers (who ought to know better) that you'd think the dictionaries would have caved in by now and countenanced the blunder. To their credit, they have not. HAY-n<u>i</u>s is the only acceptable pronunciation of this word. Do not say HEE-n<u>i</u>s or HEE-nee-<u>i</u>s (HEE- as in *heat*), both of which are HAY-n<u>i</u>s and long-standing members of the Most Unwanted Beastly Mispronunciations Hit List. *Heinous* has two syllables, not three, and the first syllable is pronounced like the word *hay*, never like *he*. See **mischievous, grievous, intravenous**.

Helena (Montana) HEL-uh-nuh. Stress the first syllable.

helicopter HEL-<u>i</u>-KAHP-tur, not **HEE**-l<u>i</u>-KAHP-tur.

Here the proper pronunciation is a matter of etymology and analogy. Words hailing from the Greek *helix*, a spiral, employing the combining form *helic(o)-*, "spiral-shaped," are pronounced with a short *e* (as in *pet*) in the first syllable: *helical, helicoid, heliport, helicopter. Helix* (HEE-liks) itself is the only exception. The more numerous family of words hailing from the Greek *helios*, sun, employing the combining form *heli(o)-*, are pronounced with a long *e* (as in *me*) in the first syllable: *helium, heliotrope, heliocentric, heliotherapy*, etc.

Helsinki (Finland) HEL-sing-kee. Stress the first syllable, not the second.

hemispheric HEM-is-FER-ik, not HEM-is-**FEER**-ik.

Properly, there is no *fear* or *sphere* in *hemispheric*. Don't say hemis-*fear*-ic. The *e* in the stressed penultimate syllable should be short (as in *ferry*), as it is in the analogous words *generic, cleric(al), hysteric(al), numeric(al)*, and *esoteric*. See **atmospheric, spherical**.

heraldic huh-RAL-dik (-RAL- as in *rally* and *corral*).

Rampant and couchant mispronouncers have devised two beastly ways of misspeaking this noble word: the erroneous huh-RAWL-dik (-RAWL-rhyming with *all*) and the preposterous HER-<u>u</u>l-dik, with the accent on the first syllable. Valiant and chivalrous (SHIV-<u>u</u>l-r<u>u</u>s) speakers, however, know three things: (1) *heraldic* has nothing to do with TV's Geraldo Rivera or a guy named Harold Dick; (2) the accent falls on the second syllable; and (3) the *a* is short, as in *pal*.

herb URB. Do not pronounce the *h,* unless you happen to be British.
Your pronunciation of this word may indicate how Anglophilic you are.
Here is some historical perspective:

"The initial *h,*" says the *Century* (1914), "as regular in words coming
from Latin through Old French, was silent in Middle English and is properly silent in Modern English, but is now sometimes pronounced, in conformity to *herbaceous, herbarium,* and other forms in which the *h* is properly pronounced, as being recently taken from the Latin."

"The *h* was mute until the 19th century," say *OED 1* (1928) and *2* (1989),
"and is still so treated by many."

"The historical pronunciation is [URB]," says *Webster 2* (1934), "which
still prevails in the best usage in the United States, although [HURB] is also
used. In England [HURB] has increased in use since about 1800, and now
apparently prevails in the best usage."

"The English are so sensitive about their difficulties with *H* that they are
now sticklers for 'hurb,'" writes Holt (1937), "while Americans carry on
quite blissfully with the historic [*sic*] 'urb.'" Echoing that theme, Opdycke
(1939) says, "Uncle Sam more frequently uses [URB] than [HURB], perhaps just to show John Bull that he can take an *h* or leave it alone."

The initial *h* should be pronounced in *herbicide, herbaceous* (hur-BAY-
sh<u>u</u>s), *herbivore, herbivorous* (hur-BIV-ur-<u>u</u>s), and *herbarium* — all Modern English words derived directly from Latin. It is properly silent only in
the older, Middle English words *herb* and *herbage.* In *herbal* and *herbalist*
it's optional; the evidence of my ears tells me most Americans don't bother
with it.

herculean hur-KYOO-lee-<u>i</u>n (recommended) or HUR-kyoo-**LEE**-<u>i</u>n.
Until the 1930s it was considered incorrect to say HUR-kyoo-**LEE**-<u>i</u>n, with
the primary accent on the penultimate syllable. Worcester (1860) cites nine
authorities who prefer hur-KYOO-lee-<u>i</u>n and only one who prefers HUR-
kyoo-**LEE**-<u>i</u>n. Ayres (1894), the *Century* (1914), *Webster's Collegiate* (1917),
and Vizetelly (1929) all give only hur-KYOO-lee-<u>i</u>n, and Phyfe (1926) dis-
approves of penultimate accentuation. H. W. Fowler (1926) devotes an
entire article to a defense of hur-KYOO-lee-<u>i</u>n, noting that the second-syllable accent "is not a modern blunder to be avoided, but is established by
long use. In the only three verse quotations given by the *OED,* [HUR-
kyoo-**LEE**-<u>i</u>n] is twice impossible, and once unlikely."

Nevertheless, *Webster 2* (1934) recognized HUR-kyoo-**LEE**-<u>i</u>n without
comment; since then censure has ceased and dictionaries have listed the
pronunciation in good standing. Today, in fact, three of the four major current American dictionaries list HUR-kyoo-**LEE**-<u>i</u>n first, the *NBC
Handbook* (1984) prefers it, and Burchfield (1996) says it is now the dominant pronunciation. However, Lass & Lass (1976) prefer hur-KYOO-lee-<u>i</u>n,
and *OED 2* (1989) sanctions *only* this traditional pronunciation. In appre-

ciation of that tradition, I say and recommend hur-KYOO-lee-in, but I cannot criticize HUR-kyoo-**LEE**-in, which is now equally acceptable.

Say the word as you please — just please don't say HUR-kyoo-**LAY**-in.

Herzegovina HAIRT-si-goh-**VEE**-nuh. Also HURT- for the first syllable.

In Serbo-Croatian the primary stress falls on -*go*-, but in English — where we have our own established spellings and pronunciations for foreign places, called *exonyms** — we stress the penultimate syllable, -*vi*-. HAIRT-si-goh-**VEE**-nuh is the preference of the *NBC Handbook* (1984) and the only pronunciation in W. Cabell Greet's *World Words* (1948), the *Columbia Encyclopedia* (1963), *RHWC* (1997), and *WNW 3* (1997). *Webster's Geographical* (1949) prefers HURT-si-goh-**VEE**-nuh, but the third edition (1997) of that work gives priority to HAIRT-si-**GOH**-vee-nuh, perhaps because of the prevalence of this de-anglicized pronunciation among broadcasters today.

Himalaya(s) Usually, HIM-uh-**LAY**-uh(z), the anglicized pronunciation, which is recommended. "More native" but less frequently, hi-MAH-la-yuh(z).

I had never heard anyone pronounce this word with the accent on the second syllable until the late 1980s, when I heard hi-MAHL-uh-yuhz from an editor who loves to travel and who had done some climbing in those mountains. Now, this fellow was a competent professional and a decent guy, but like millions of other decent, competent people he wasn't always as sharp as he could be in his speech. So when I heard him say hi-MAHL-uh-yuhz I was startled and thought it was an affectation. However, upon investigation (a mad dash to the dictionaries the moment I arrived home) I discovered not only that the man had some authority to back him up, but that sometimes an editor actually can teach a writer a thing or two.

Webster 2 (1934) notes that what are commonly called the Himalayas are more correctly called the Himalaya, for which *Webster* gives the four-syllable pronunciation hi-MAH-luh-yuh, adding "often, less correctly, [HIM-uh-**LAY**-uh]." Kenyon & Knott (1949) list hi-MAHL-yuh(z), hi-MAH-la-yuhz, HIM-uh-**LAY**-uh(z), noting that "in England the traditional anglicized pronunciation still prevails (Jones says [hi-MAH-la-yuh(z)] is rare), as it once did in America, but the pronunciation more like the native one has recently become more frequent here." For *Himalayan, OED 1* (1928) prefers hi-MAH-luh-yin and says that HIM-uh-**LAY**-in, "though incorrect, is still frequent." *OED 2* (1989), however, revises that ruling, saying that hi-MAH-luh-yin, "though etymologically correct, is now infrequent." So who's right?

---

* In *Crazy English* (1989), Richard Lederer defines this useful new term — yet to be recorded in a dictionary — as "a place name that foreigners use instead of the name that natives use: *Cologne* for Köln, *Florence* for Firenze, *Morocco* for Maroc."

As anyone who studies pronunciation, even cursorily, knows well, the orthoepist's labels "wrong" and "right" and "more correct" and "less correct" quite often have little or no bearing on what prevails. Today, the "less correct," anglicized HIM-uh-**LAY**-uh(z) is without doubt the dominant pronunciation, which explains why the *NBC Handbook* (1984) and *WNW Guide* (1984) prefer it (the latter calls second-syllable stress rare) and why all four major current American dictionaries list it first. Even the equable R. W. Burchfield (1996) is down on second-syllable stress: "There seems no good reason to abandon the traditional English pronunciation [HIM-uh-**LAY**-uhz], stressed on the third syllable, or the traditional form (pl. in -*s*), in favour of the cultish form *Himalaya,* pronounced [hi-MAH-l<u>a</u>-yuh]. . . ."

Cultish? I knew there was something peculiar about that editor. Frankly, I'm relieved that current authority supports the "less correct" pronunciation, because I just wouldn't feel comfortable putting the accent on the second syllable. You may say what you like, but I'm going with the HIM-uh-**LAY**-in flow.

Hiroshima More English, HEER-uh-**SHEE**-muh or HIR-uh-**SHEE**-muh. Long *o* as in *hero* is also acceptable. More Japanese, and less often, hee-ROH-shee-muh or h<u>i</u>-ROH-shuh-muh.

Authorities countenance both the "more English" and "more Japanese" pronunciations, but it is worth noting that all four major current American dictionaries and *Webster's Geographical* (1997) give priority to the "more English" HEER-uh-**SHEE**-muh, which is also preferred by *WNW Guide* (1984) and the *NBC Handbook* (1984).

Holocaust HAHL-uh-KAWST. Don't say **HOH**-luh-KAWST or **HAWL**-uh-KAWST.

There is no *hole* in *holocaust.* There is also no *haul* in *holocaust.* The first syllable, *hol-*, is properly pronounced as in *hollow* and *Holland.* The last syllable, -*caust*, is pronounced like *cost.*

John Walker, in his *Critical Pronouncing Dictionary* of 1791, defines *holocaust* in its original sense of "a burnt sacrifice" and marks the word /hol′o kawst/, accent on the first syllable, first *o* as in *not* and the *a* in the last syllable as in *fall.* In this book that translates to **HAHL**-uh-KAWST, and this was the only pronunciation countenanced by authorities from Walker's day until 1961, when *Webster 3* (1961) recorded both *hole-ocaust* and *haul-ocaust* as alternative pronunciations. Since then both pronunciations have become widespread; the *hole-* variant, which is the more common of the two, probably was encouraged by the word's association with the phrase *wholesale destruction (of life).*

Do not be misled by *Webster 3*'s latest abridgment, *M-W 10* (1993), which gives priority to the *hole-* variant. It is an anomaly. The weight of modern authority still heavily favors Walker's pronunciation. The three other major current American dictionaries — *American Heritage 3* (1992), *RHWC* (1997), and *WNW 3* (1997) — give priority to **HAHL**-uh-KAWST, which is the preference of Lass & Lass (1976), *WNW Guide* (1984), the *NBC Handbook* (1984), and Jones (1991).

homage HAHM-ij. Pronounce the *h*.

Homage is one of the oldest words in the language, dating back to the 13th century. Until the 18th century the *h* was silent, but since then pronouncing it has been *de rigueur*. (See **de rigueur.**) Walker (1791), Worcester (1860), Funk & Wagnalls *Standard* (1897), *Webster's Collegiate* (1917), and *OED 1* (1928) sanction only the pronunciation with *h*, and Ayres (1894), Phyfe (1926), and Holt (1937) proscribe AHM-ij. But old ways die hard, and rarely are such questions cut-and-dried. The *Century* (1914) and *Webster 2* (1934) countenance AHM-ij as an alternative, and Opdycke (1939) says "the *h* may be silent." Three of the four major current American dictionaries list HAHM-ij first, however, and Lass & Lass (1976), the *NBC Handbook* (1984), *OED 2* (1989), and Jones (1984) prefer it. Only Barnhart (1988) favors the *h*-less AHM-ij.

homicide HAHM-i-SYD, not **HOHM**-i-SYD.

Properly, there is no *home* in *homicide*. The *hom-* should rhyme with *Tom*, not with *comb*.

This word entered English in 1375. John Walker (1791), my oldest source, indicates the short *o* of *not* in the first syllable, and this is the only pronunciation given by subsequent authorities, including Worcester (1860), the *Century* (1889–1914), *OED 1* (1928), and *Webster 2* (1934). In 1961, *Webster 3* recognized the variant **HOHM**-i-SYD, which dictionaries since then have listed as an alternative. All four major current American dictionaries give priority to the traditional **HAHM**-i-SYD.

Of all the authorities I checked (perhaps two dozen or so), I found only one — Opdycke (1939) — who favors the long *o* pronunciation. "Authorities disagree in regard to the *o*," Opdycke writes, perhaps meaning that *he* disagrees with all the other authorities, who prefer a short *o*. "It is preferably long, as in the original Latin, in contradistinction to the Greek prefix *homo* in which the first *o* is preferably short. The preferred pronunciation is *home'i side* but there is authoritative sanction (many police departments in particular) for the short *o* — *hahm'i side*." Careful speakers would be wise to smile politely at those misguided remarks and follow the advice of Morris & Morris (1985), who say, "While this word is sometimes given the pronunciation of HOME-ih-side, the preferred pronunciation is HOM-ih-side, with the first syllable rhyming with 'Tom.'" Modern dictionaries — with the peculiar exception of *M-W 7* (1972) through *M-W 10* (1993), which list **HAHM**-i-SYD first — divide the word *hom·i·cide*, which reflects the proper pronunciation.

homogeneity HOH-moh-ji-**NEE**-i-tee, not HOH-moh-ji-**NAY**-i-tee.

There is no *nay* in *homogeneity;* it's a *knee.* The accented antepenultimate syllable should be pronounced with a long *e,* as in *see.*

Webster 3 (1961) was the first to record the *-nay-ity* variant, labeling it "infrequent." It is now frequent enough that three of the four major current American dictionaries list it as an alternative. *RHWC* (1997), however, sanctions only *-knee-ity.* Burchfield (1996) says, "Pronounce the stem of the word [*-neity*] . . . with the stressed syllable having the sound of *bee* not of *bay,*" and Lass & Lass (1976), the *NBC Handbook* (1984), *Everyday Reader's* (1985), and Jones (1991) agree. See **deity, spontaneity**.

hospitable Traditionally, HAHS-pit-uh-buul. Now usually hah-SPIT-uh-buul.

Second-syllable stress in *hospitable* was once a beastly mispronunciation that stubbornly refused to go away. Ayres (1894) admonished against it, Phyfe (1926) and Vizetelly (1929) called it a frequent mispronunciation, and Opdycke (1939) said *hospitable* " — don't ever forget — is accented on the first syllable. . . . But the Britisher says *hos pit' a ble.*" *Webster 2* (1934) also calls second-syllable stress British, but H. W. Fowler (1926) says, "The stress should be on *hos-,* not on *-pit-,*" adding that "the stress on *hos-* is as old as Shakspere & Drayton."

In their *Pronouncing Dictionary of American English* (1949), Kenyon & Knott call hah-SPIT-uh-buul "much less frequent," but it was much more frequent in the estimation of *Webster 3* (1961), which listed it first. Most modern authorities, British as well as American, continue to prefer first-syllable stress, and three of the four major current American dictionaries list it first; however, Burchfield (1996) acknowledges that "second-syllable stressing is very common and may prevail as time goes on." I must sadly agree. Jones (1991) gives second-syllable stress as the dominant pronunciation in England, and that is no doubt true now in the U.S. as well.

That said, I will still make my case for HAHS-pit-uh-buul. To begin with, pronouncing this word in the traditional manner, in my opinion, is still one of the hallmarks of a cultivated speaker. And certainly one attractive advantage in saying HAHS-pit-uh-buul is that you avoid stressing the *spit,* which, considering the word's meaning, sounds rather *in*HOS*pitable.* As Holt (1937) puts it, "This is a pleasant sounding word if properly accentuated on the first syllable and not on the *spit.*" See **despicable, (in)explicable, lamentable, summarily**.

hostile (American) HAHS-til; (British) HAHS-tyl.

For a discussion of American vs. British pronunciation of *-ile,* see **textile**.

houses HOW-ziz, not HOW-siz or HOW-sis.

Houses is pronounced like *how's* + *is.* In the singular *house* the *s* is pronounced like the *s* in *mouse,* but in the plural *houses* the middle *s* changes to a *z* sound, as in *busy* and *rouse,* and the final, pluralizing *s* also is pronounced like *z*, as in *boxes, churches, sentences.* This change from an *s* to a *z* sound likewise occurs in the verb to *house* (HOWZ).

Houston (Texas) HYOO-stun; (Street in New York City) HOWS-tun (like *house ton*).

Be sure to pronounce the *h* for the city in Texas. Careless speakers say YOO-stun.

hovel HUHV-ul. Also, HAHV-ul. Do not say HOH-vul.

Older authorities preferred HAHV-ul, in which the *o* is pronounced as in *hot,* but by the 1940s HUHV-ul was the dominant American pronunciation. Kenyon & Knott give it priority in their *Pronouncing Dictionary of American English* (1949) and say "much less frequently" HAHV-ul. All four major current American dictionaries list HAHV-ul, but all give priority to HUHV-ul and *WNW 3* (1997) labels HAHV-ul less common. Modern authorities are neatly divided, with the British favoring HAHV-ul and the Americans favoring HUHV-ul. See **hover, grovel**.

hover HUH-vur. Infrequently, HAH-vur.

Do not say HOO-vur or HOH-vur, which are eccentric and beastly.

Both HUH-vur, rhyming with *cover* and *lover,* and HAH-vur, with the *o* as in *hot,* date back to the 18th century. Perry (1775) and Sheridan (1780) favored the latter, but Walker (1791), Smart (1836), Worcester (1860), and various other authorities preferred the former, which has prevailed in the U.S. since the 19th century. Although 20th-century American sources continue to list HAHV-ur, Kenyon & Knott (1949) and *WNW 3* (1997) label it infrequent. I have heard it only occasionally, most notably from Ted Koppel of ABC, who I have been told was educated in England, where — as the *Oxford Guide* (1983), Jones (1991), and Burchfield (1996) indicate — HAHV-ur is preferred. See **hovel**.

huge HYOOJ. Pronounce the *h*.

human HYOO-min. Pronounce the *h*.

humble HUHM-b'l. Pronounce the *h*.

Over the years I've been a guest on numerous radio talk shows, and sometimes the host, in a burst of hyperbole, will tout me as being a pronunciation doctor, or a Doctor of Pronunciation. Here is an excerpt from one of those programs:

Caller: "I'm wondering about the word *humble.* I've heard certain clergy drop the *h* and say UHM-b'l. Is that correct?"

Dr. P.: "Sounds like the David Copperfield Syndrome to me, or perhaps a symptom of Eliza Doolittle Distemper."

Host: "I've heard UHM-b'l too — from Pentecostal ministers, actually. Maybe when the evangelicals get all worked up it just comes out that way. Or maybe they think it sounds more HUHM-b'l to say UHM-b'l. Whaddayou think, Doc?"

Dr. P.: "Well, whoever says it that way, I say it's time to eat humble pie. UHM-b'l is an obsolescent pronunciation — it's passing out of use. Some British speakers, Cockneys in particular, still drop the *h*, but in America and the rest of the English-speaking world the *h* is usually pronounced."

That's the way it's been for over a hundred years. Ayres (1894) says "there is a growing tendency to aspirate the *h* of this word," *OED 1* (1928) lists only HUM-b'l, and *Webster 2* (1934) says UHM-b'l is the former pronunciation. Most current dictionaries recognize UHM-b'l but none give it priority and no authorities prefer it.

hundred HUHN-drid.

Don't transpose the *r* and *e* in *hundred* and say *hunderd*. Also avoid the even more beastly HUH-nurd, where the *r* and *e* are switched and there is no medial *d* sound at all. These pronunciations are slovenly and uneducated.

hygienic hy-JEN-ik (my preference) or hy-JEE-nik; **hygienist** hy-JEN-ist (probably the preference in the dental profession) or hy-JEE-nist or HY-jee-nist (my preference).

Modern dictionaries are a maze of variants and there is no consensus among authorities regarding these words. Therefore I must rely on the evidence of my ears, which tells me that the pronunciations given above are the most common and acceptable ones in educated American speech. Use whichever ones feel most comfortable to you. I have indicated my preferences only to satisfy your curiosity, not to sway you in my direction.

hyperbole hy-PUR-buh-lee.

I always thought that anyone who knew the meaning of this word did not mispronounce it. Then, to my surprise, a friend told me she heard a fancy-pants Los Angeles lawyer say HY-pur-bohl. It was an important hearing involving a settlement of millions of dollars, the media were out in full force, and in front of everyone this poor fellow said HY-pur-bohl. How embarrassing! I'm surprised the judge didn't throw the book at him — or at least a dictionary. Apparently the law schools need to spend more time teaching their students how to talk like the rest of us. Any Joe Blow sports fan will tell you that there's a Super Bowl, a Sugar Bowl, a Cotton Bowl, and a Rose Bowl, but there is no *Hyper Bowl*. It's an open-and-shut case. The only recognized pronunciation is hy-PUR-buh-lee. See **epitome**.

hysteria Properly, hi-STEER-ee-uh. Now usually hi-STER-ee-uh.

The traditional pronunciation, given by Worcester (1860), Funk & Wagnalls *Standard* (1897), the *Century* (1914), and *Webster 2* (1934), has a long *e* that naturally blends into the following *r* to make the second, accented syllable sound like *steer*. The variant pronunciation hi-STER-ee-uh, no doubt based on analogy with the more common word *hysterical,* was frowned upon by Opdycke (1939) but was recorded in Kenyon & Knott (1949), who labeled it "less frequent." It next appeared as an alternative in *American College* (1952), then *Webster 3* (1961) listed it first, and today all four major American dictionaries give it priority.

That hi-STER-ee-uh is the dominant pronunciation I will not contest. That it is the correct pronunciation, the better pronunciation, the more cultivated pronunciation, I most certainly will contest. For the record, the analogy with *hysterical* is false. The words are divided differently — *hys·te·ri·a* and *hys·ter·i·cal* — which indicates their distinction in pronunciation. The proper analogy is with *cafeteria, bacteria, criteria, wisteria,* and *diphtheria* (dif-THEER-ee-uh), in which *-eria* is pronounced -EER-ee-uh. See **diphtheria, wisteria.**

I

idea eye-DEE-uh. Do not say eye-DEER.

Vizetelly (1933) remarks that "many a delightful and cultured voice and utterance is marred by the introduction of an 'r' in words that end in 'a,' of which the most horrible example is 'idear.'" *Idea* has three syllables (*i-de-a*) and does *not* have an *r* at the end.

ideology EYE-dee-**AHL**-uh-jee (recommended) or ID-ee-**AHL**-uh-jee.

Both pronunciations are acceptable, but the recommended one, EYE-dee-**AHL**-uh-jee, has the weight of 20th-century authority behind it and is more common in contemporary American speech. *Webster 2* (1934) gives priority to the short *i* (as in *idiot*), but Funk & Wagnalls *Standard* (1897) and the *Century* (1914) countenance only the long *i* (like *eye*), and *American College* (1952), *Webster 3* (1961), and *Random House II* (1987) list the long *i* first. All four major current American dictionaries give priority to the *eye-* pronunciation, and Lass & Lass (1976) and the *NBC Handbook* (1984) prefer it. In case you're wondering if the short *i* might be British, *OED 2* (1989) countenances only EYE-dee-**AHL**-uh-jee and Jones (1991) indicates that it is the dominant pronunciation in England.

ignominy IG-nuh-MIN-ee.

There is no *nominee* in *ignominy*. Don't say ig-NAHM-i-nee. Stress the first syllable, *ig-*, not the second. The mispronunciation with second-syllable stress appears in the dictionaries of Merriam-Webster, from *Webster 3* (1961) on, and Random House, from *Random House II* (1987) on. The other major current American dictionaries — *American Heritage 3* (1992)

---

a = at / a̱ = final / ah = spa / ahr = car / air = fair / ay = hay / aw = saw
ch = chip / e = let / e̱ = item / ee = see / eer = deer / i = sit / i̱ = April
ng = sing / o̱ = carrot / oh = go / oo = soon / or = for / oor = poor
ow = cow / oy = toy / sh = she / th = thin / th = this / u̱ = focus / uh = up
ur = turn / uu = pull, took / y, eye = by, I / zh = measure / (see full key, p. xiv)

and *WNW 3* (1997) — as well as *OED 2* (1989), do not recognize it, and no authority I know of prefers it.

ignoramus IG-nuh-**RAY**-m<u>u</u>s, not IG-nuh-**RAM**-<u>u</u>s.

This word entered English in its current sense of "a foolish, ignorant person" in 1615, when George Ruggle used it as the title of a play in which he exposed "the ignorance and arrogance of the common lawyers." Walker (1791) gives *ray* for the stressed penultimate syllable, as do subsequent authorities until *Webster 3* (1961), which records the *ram* variant labeled "infrequent." Today it is listed after the proper pronunciation in three of the four major American dictionaries, a testament to the fact that there are plenty of fools out there who depend on ignoramuses to defend them from beastly mispronunciations. No authority I am aware of prefers *ram*.

-ile, words ending in, American vs. British pronunciation of: see **textile**.

Illinois IL-uh-**NOY**.

There is no *noise* in *Illinois*. *Random House II* (1987) says, "The pronunciation of ILLINOIS with a final (z), which occurs chiefly among less educated speakers, is least common in Illinois itself, increasing in frequency as distance from the state increases." Even as far away from Illinois as New York and California, careful speakers consider IL-uh-**NOYZ** a lowbrow pronunciation.

illustrative <u>i</u>-**LUHS**-truh-tiv, not **IL**-uh-STRAY-tiv.

Stress the second syllable, not the first. *American Heritage 3* (1992), *M-W 10* (1993), and *WNW 3* (1997) give priority to <u>i</u>-LUHS-truh-tiv, which is the only pronunciation in *OED 2* (1989) and *RHWC* (1997) and the preference of Lass & Lass (1976) and the *NBC Handbook* (1984).

imbroglio im-**BROHL**-yoh. See **seraglio**.

immature See **mature**.

impetus **IM**-pi-t<u>u</u>s.

Always stress the *im-*. Don't shift the accent to the second syllable and say im-PEE-t<u>u</u>s or im-PET-<u>u</u>s. These are beastly mispronunciations.

impious **IM**-pee-<u>u</u>s, not im-**PY**-<u>u</u>s.

There is no *pie* in *impious*. The stress is properly on the *imp*.

Don't be misled by the fact that *pious* is hidden in *impious,* or by the fact that you may find the mispronunciation im-PY-<u>u</u>s listed as an alternative in a dictionary. Dictionaries of the first half of the 20th century countenanced only first-syllable stress, it is the only pronunciation in *OED 2* (1989) and *WNW 3* (1997), and no modern authority with a reputation to lose sanctions anything other than IM-pee-<u>u</u>s.

imprimatur **IM**-pri-**MAH**-tur or **IM**-pri-**MAY**-tur.

The *a* may be broad, as in *spa,* or long as in *mate.* Older authorities gave their imprimatur to the long *a,* the anglicized pronunciation. Most, but by no means all, current American authorities favor the broad *a,* which is more Latin. (The British prefer the long *a*). Because the word comes directly from Latin and is rather esoteric, the Latin pronunciation is appropriate and cannot reasonably be called an affectation. *Webster 3* (1961) indicates that the anglicized -**MAY**- is "appreciably less frequent" than the Latinate -**MAH**-, and that is no doubt even more true in American speech today, for all four major current American dictionaries give priority to -**MAH**-.

"Don't accent the second syllable," says Opdycke (1939). Avoid the beastly variants im-PRIM-uh-t(y)oor and im-PRY-muh-tur. Also, don't make the *a* short, as in *mat*. Other unacceptable or obsolete variants include IM-pry-**MAY**-tur and IM-pry-**MAH**-tur (there is no *pry* in *imprimatur*), and the thoroughly eccentric IM-prim-uh-**TOOR**, a pronunciation that only a pretentious twiddlepoop would use.

inaugural i-NAW-gyur-ul, not i-NAW-gur-ul, and *especially* not the beastly i-NAW-grul.

Properly, there is no *augur* (AW-gur) in *inaugural, inaugurate,* and *inauguration*. Careful speakers have always pronounced the third syllable in these words -gyur-, never -gur-. However, to paraphrase William Safire, when enough folks get it wrong, they eventually get it right. Since Kenyon & Knott (1949) and *American College* (1952) recognized the -gur- variants, they have gradually achieved the status of acceptable alternative pronunciations — but with the emphasis on *alternative*. No authority prefers them and no dictionary lists them first. Funk & Wagnalls *Standard* (1980), *Oxford American* (1980), *OED 2* (1989), and *American Heritage 3* (1992) do not bother to recognize them, and even the painstakingly permissive *Webster 3* (1961) labels them "unacceptable to many."

Whatever you do, don't say i-NAW-grul. This three-syllable variant, though occasionally found in dictionaries, is illiterate. In educated speech *inaugural* always has four syllables. See **figure**.

incarnadine in-**KAHR**-nuh-DYN.

For the final syllable, -DIN (like *din*) and -DEEN (like *dean*) are also acceptable; however, -DYN (like *dine*) is the first pronunciation listed in all four major current American dictionaries and the preference of Lass & Lass (1976) and Jones (1991).

incendiary in-**SEN**-dee-ER-ee.

Opdycke (1939) rhymes *incendiary* with *in Wendy airy*. Don't slur the pronunciation to in-SEN-dree, he counsels, "as the Britisher is likely to do." The noun *incendiarism* is pronounced in-SEN-dee-uh-riz'm.

incidents IN-suh-dints (three syllables).

Take care not to add a syllable and say **IN**-suh-DIN-siz, like the nonword "incidences." This is a confusion of *incidents* with *instances,* and a beastly mispronunciation.

inclement in-KLEM-int. Stress the second syllable, not the first.

Clement and *inclement* are both properly stressed on *clem.*

The egregiously permissive *Webster 3* (1961) records the beastly mispronunciation IN-kluh-ment, labeling it "infrequent," and subsequent Merriam-Webster dictionaries slavishly list it as an acceptable alternative. It is not. Other dictionaries and authorities countenance only in-KLEM-int.

According to Morris & Morris (1985), "The consistent inconsistency of the English language is reflected in the pronunciation of *inclement:* in-CLEM-n't. This is so despite the fact that both 'increment' and 'implement' are pronounced with the accent on the first syllable." Actually, this is so because *clement* resides within *inclement,* whereas there is no *crement* or *plement* residing within *increment* and *implement.* The analogy is properly with words like *indecent, inconstant, insolvent, incredible, incapable, incompetent, indefinite, inelegant,* and so on. Do you see any inconsistency in that? I don't.

incognito Traditionally, in-KAHG-ni-toh. Now usually IN-kahg-**NEE**-toh. Today most speakers stress the *knee* in *incognito,* but the point is still worth making that properly the stress should fall on *cog,* as in these lines from the English poet and diplomat Matthew Prior (1664–1721):

> 'Twas long ago
> Since gods came down incognito.

Incognito comes through the Italian *incognito,* stress on *cog,* which in turn comes from the Latin *incognitus,* stress also on *cog.* The word entered English in the mid-1600s, and from the dictionaries of Samuel Johnson (1755) and John Walker (1791) to *Webster 2* (1934) and *American College* (1952), the only acceptable pronunciation was in-KAHG-ni-toh. The first dictionary to recognize IN-kahg-**NEE**-toh was *Webster 3* (1961), which listed it first but labeled it unacceptable to many; the traditional in-KAHG-ni-toh appears as an "appreciably less frequent" but otherwise unobjectionable alternative.

Since the 1960s penultimate stress (on *knee*) has become acceptable to many and antepenultimate stress (on *cog*) has gone undercover. Three of the four major current American dictionaries list penultimate stress first, and most authorities — including the *NBC Handbook* (1984), *Everyday Reader's* (1985), Barnhart (1988), and Burchfield (1996) — prefer it. Only *OED 2* (1989) and *WNW 3* (1997) give priority to antepenultimate stress, and only Lass & Lass (1976) prefer it.

incomparable in-KAHM-pur-uh-buul. Five syllables, not four.

There is no *pair* in *incomparable.* Stress the second syllable, *-com-.* See **comparable.**

incongruent in-KAHNG-groo-wint. Do not say IN-kahn-**GROO**-wint.

Stress the *-cong-*, not the *-gru-*. The variant with third-syllable stress is so often heard today that current dictionaries now recognize it. Be advised, however, that it is a vogue pronunciation that anyone aspiring to cultivated speech should scrupulously avoid. See **congruent, incongruous.**

incongruous in-KAHNG-groo-wus. Do not say IN-kahn-**GROO**-wus.

Put the accent on *-cong-*, not on *-gru-*. Stressing the third syllable is a beastly mispronunciation that (hallelujah) no current dictionary countenances. In the four-syllable noun *incongruity,* however, the accent shifts to *-gru-*. See **congruent, incongruent.**

increase (noun) IN-krees; (verb) in-KREES. See **decrease.**

inculcate in-KUHL-kayt or **IN**-kul-KAYT.

The pronunciation with first-syllable stress is originally British. It has been used by cultivated American speakers and countenanced by American authorities since the early 20th century. Modern American authorities still favor second-syllable stress, however. All four major current American dictionaries list it first, and the *NBC Handbook* (1984), *Everyday Reader's* (1985), and Barnhart (1988) prefer it. Only Lass & Lass (1976) prefer first-syllable stress. See **infiltrate** and, for a discussion of recessive (backward-moving) and progressive (forward-moving) stress, see **confiscate.**

indefatigable IN-di-**FAT**-i-guh-buul.

This word is often mispronounced IN-di-fuh-**TEEG**-uh-buul by the unwary, apparently through association with the word *fatigue* (fuh-TEEG). The only pronunciation recognized by dictionaries and sanctioned by authorities, however, is IN-di-**FAT**-i-guh-buul, with the primary stress on the third syllable, *-fat-*.

indict in-DYT (rhymes with *in sight*).

indigestion IN-di-**JES**-chin, not IN-dy-**JES**-chin.

The *i* in the second syllable is short, not long. See **digest.**

industrial in-DUHS-tree-ul.

Don't say in-DUHS-trul. *Industrial* has four syllables, not three.

inexplicable in-EK-spli-kuh-buul.

Stress the *-ex-* in *inexplicable,* if you can, rather than the *-plic-*. It's a sure sign of a cultivated speaker. See **explicable.**

inextricable in-EK-stri-kuh-buul.

Inextricable is now often pronounced IN-ek-**STRIK**-uh-buul, but cultivated speakers generally have resisted progressive (forward-moving) stress in this word and the weight of modern authority supports the traditional accent on the second syllable. Three of the four major current American dictionaries list in-EK-stri-kuh-buul first, as do *WNW Guide* (1984) and *Everyday Reader's* (1985). Lass & Lass (1976), the *NBC Handbook* (1984), and *OED 2* (1989) prefer it.

If you are accustomed to placing the accent on *-tric-* instead of on *-ex-*, you probably think it's easier to articulate all the syllables by stressing it that way. But who said pronunciation had to be easy? Try reading this sentence aloud: "*Inexorable, inexpiable,* and *inextricable* all have their stress on *-ex-.*" Chances are you pronounced *inexorable* (in-EKS-ur-uh-buul) and *inexpiable* (in-EK-spee-uh-buul) correctly with no trouble, so why not *inextricable*? It's not *that* hard, and you're already two-thirds of the way there. See **arctic, explicable, extricable.**

infiltrate in-FIL-trayt or IN-fil-TRAYT.

The pronunciation with the primary accent on the first syllable is a British import that first appeared in *Webster 3* (1961) labeled "appreciably less frequent." A scant four decades hence it is probably more common than the traditional pronunciation with the accent on the second syllable, but the weight of authority still favors second-syllable stress — for the time being. I wouldn't be at all surprised if in the next four decades **IN**-fil-TRAYT subverts in-FIL-trayt. See **inculcate** and, for a discussion of recessive (backward-moving) and progressive (forward-moving) stress, **confiscate.**

infinitesimal IN-fi-ni-**TES**-i-mul.

The *s* is properly hard and hissing, as in *test,* not soft and buzzing, as in *tease.*

influence IN-floo-ints, not in-FLOO-ints.

"A common mispronunciation is an accented 'floo,'" says Holt (1937). "There is no authority for this." Stress the *in,* not the *flu.*

Although no modern authority would touch the beastly in-FLOO-ints with a ten-foot tongue, I was not surprised to find it in the dogmatically descriptive *Webster 3* (1961), which labels it "infrequent." Today two of the four major American dictionaries list it, with one — *M-W 10* (1993) — labeling it "especially Southern." Do not be duped by this creeping recognition. Educated speakers nationwide have long favored first-syllable stress in *influence,* and second-syllable stress is either a regional aberration or, among non-Southerners, an affectation.

inherent in-HEER-int (-HEER- like *here* and *hear*).

Do not say in-HAIR-int or (Eastern and Northern) in-HER-int (-HER- as in *herald*).

Properly, there is no *hair* in *inherent.* We don't say in-*hair* for *inhere,* we don't say co-*hair* for *cohere,* and we don't say ad-*hair* for *adhere* or ad-*hair*-ent for *adherent.* Why do so many people put a *hair* in *coherent* and *inherent*?

There's no rhyme or reason to it. These *hair* pronunciations are simply goofy deviations from normal, accepted usage that somehow managed to become trendy. In other words, they are vogue pronunciations — mistakes that gain a smarmy veneer of respectability when they are snapped up by people who imagine that these signs of mediocrity and tastelessness are emblems of intelligence and refinement. The vogue pronunciation in-HAIR-int first gained recognition in *Webster 3* (1961); by the 1970s it was so popular that all four major American dictionaries recognized it. The current editions of those same four dictionaries, however, as well as *WNW Guide* (1984) and *Everyday Reader's* (1985), all give priority to in-HEER-int, which Lass & Lass (1976) and the *NBC Handbook* (1989) prefer.

A postscript: the craze for the *hair* variant in American speech may have been fueled by the flowering popularity of in-HER-int in British speech. (The British employ a short *e* as in *hem* and *herald,* not the *hair* sound.) Although *OED 2* (1989) sanctions only the traditional in-HEER-int and Jones (1991) lists in-HER-int as less common, Burchfield (1996) says that "in standard English either [in-HER-int] or [in-HEER-int] is acceptable. J. C. Wells (1990) reports that his poll panel of R[eceived]P[ronunciation] speakers showed a 66% preference for the first of these." That's scary. See **coherent**.

inhospitable Traditionally, in-HAHS-pit-uh-buul. Now usually IN-hah-SPIT-uh-buul. See **hospitable**.

inquiry in-KWYR-ee. Also, IN-kwi-ree.

Contrary to what some may think, the pronunciation IN-kwi-ree, with first-syllable stress, is not British. As Burchfield (1996) and Jones (1991) indicate, it has no currency in Britain today, and if it ever had any at all, it wasn't much. Vizetelly (1929) claims that it appears in William Perry's dictionary of 1775, but John Walker (1791) and subsequent authorities countenance only second-syllable stress. A quotation in Worcester (1860), who sanctions only in-KWYR-ee, suggests that IN-kwi-ree may be Scottish in origin, and thus perhaps brought to the U.S. by Scottish immigrants. That sounds more likely to me.

However it got going in America, there is no doubt that IN-kwi-ree has carved out its niche in educated speech. But I hasten to point out that it is only a niche, while in-KWYR-ee, the dominant pronunciation of the 19th and 20th centuries, shows no sign of relinquishing its preeminence. In 1909, *Webster's New International* noted that IN-kwi-ree (which it did not sanction), "though not recognized by orthoëpists, is sometimes used by good speakers," and the situation hasn't changed much since then. IN-kwi-ree, first listed by *Webster 2* (1934), remains the less common alternative; in-KWYR-ee is preferred.

insouciant in-SOO-see-int.

Insouciant and *insouciance* (in-SOO-see-ints) came lightheartedly skipping into English from French, the latter about 1800 and the former in 1829. Current dictionaries sometimes give the French pronunciation for them, which I do not recommend. These words have been anglicized for at least a hundred years. The *Century* (1889–1914) and *Webster's Collegiate* (1917) record the anglicized pronunciations, which the vast majority of educated speakers today prefer.

instrumental See **mental**.

insurance in-SHUUR-ints.

In cultivated speech the accent always falls on the second syllable.

The dictionaries of Merriam-Webster from *Webster 3* (1961) to *M-W 9* (1985) label the variant IN-shuur-ints, with first-syllable stress, as "chiefly Southern." The latest Merriam-Webster, *M-W 10* (1993), labels it "appreciably less common." The careful speaker would be wise to disregard these comments and follow the other three major current American dictionaries, which countenance only second-syllable stress.

integral IN-tuh-grul.

Webster 3 (1961) was the first dictionary to recognize the variant in-TEG-rul, with second-syllable stress, labeling it less common. Although current dictionaries now countenance it as an alternative, no authority I am aware of prefers it and I have heard numerous educated speakers express their disdain for it. First-syllable stress is *de rigueur* in mathematics.

By all means avoid the beastly mispronunciation IN-truh-gul, which makes the word sound as if it were spelled *intregal*.

intelligentsia in-TEL-i-JENT-see-uh.

Some intellectuals — William F. Buckley, Jr., for example — pronounce this word with a hard *g*, as in *get*, and Lass & Lass (1976) prefer this pronunciation. However, a soft *g*, as in *gentleman* and *intelligent*, has been more commonly heard in educated speech for most of the 20th century. (The word entered English from Russian in 1907.) *Webster 2* (1934) and Kenyon & Knott (1949) list the soft *g* first, and Holt (1937), Opdycke (1939), the *NBC Handbook* (1984), *Everyday Reader's* (1985), Barnhart (1988), and Jones (1991) prefer it. Morris & Morris (1985) explain that *intelligentsia*

> was coined in Russia as "intelligentsiya" to mean intellectuals as a class, and the Russian "g" is hard as in "go" or "get." When it was first introduced in this country (without the "y"), purists insisted that it be pronounced with a hard "g." However, words like "intelligent" and "intelligence" came into English from Latin by way of French at the time of the Norman Conquest and thus acquired the French soft "g." With these pronunciations well established before *intelligentsia* entered English . . . the Russian word has become completely Americanized and the soft "g" prevails.

inter- IN-tur-.

In casual speech, *inter-* often loses its *t* and becomes *inner-*. This can result in ear-splitting solipsistic solecisms such as *inner-connected* for *interconnected*, *inner-change* for *interchange*, and *inner-mission* for *intermission*, as well as the ubiquitous, blubber-lipped, in-your-face blunder of sportscasters, *innerference* for *interference*. The careful speaker, it goes without saying, is especially careful to preserve the *t* in *inter-*. See **interesting**.

interdict IN-tur-**DIKT**.

interesting IN-tris-ting or IN-tur-uh-sting or **IN**-tur-ES-ting.

All three pronunciations are acceptable, though not so long ago only the second was considered cultivated while the first was considered British and the third was frowned upon by some authorities. One reason there are so many accepted pronunciations is that most educated speakers do not say *interesting* in exactly the same way every time. Slight, unconscious variation is natural in rapid and informal speech, and when a certain variation recurs often enough in educated speech, it usually becomes the norm.

The three-syllable IN-tris-ting is a victim of syncope (SING-kuh-pee), the loss or omission of a sound or syllable from the middle of a word, as in FAM-lee for *family* and KUHMF-tur-buul for *comfortable* (which see). It is now probably the most commonly heard pronunciation in American speech. The noun and verb *interest* is also a victim of syncope and is usually pronounced in two syllables, IN-trist, although the older IN-tur-ist is still heard. The verbal adjective *interested* is often pronounced in four syllables, **IN**-tur-ES-tid, but the evidence of my ears says the three-syllable IN-tris-tid is more common.

The four-syllable variant IN-tur-uh-sting, once the preferred pronunciation, is now much less common than the syncopated IN-tris-ting. The somewhat overpronounced **IN**-tur-ES-ting never had great currency. Speakers who normally say IN-tris-ting will sometimes use it for emphasis or ironically, drawing out the syllables, as in the stock phrase *very interesting*.

Avoid pronouncing *interesting* as if it were spelled *inneresting*. The *t* of *inter-* must be preserved at all costs! Also don't say IN-tur-sting, as if the word were spelled *intersting*. These are both beastly mispronunciations.

For more on syncope, see **chocolate, temperature**.

interpret in-TUR-prit; **interpretation** in-TUR-pri-**TAY**-shin.

There is no *pit* in *interpret* and *interpretation*. Be sure to pronounce the *r* in the third syllable (*pre*) of each word. The *r*-less in-TUR-pit and in-TUR-pi-**TAY**-shin are beastly.

intravenous IN-truh-**VEE**-nus. Don't say IN-truh-**VEE**-nee-us.

This word has four syllables, not five, with the last two, -*venous*, pronounced like the planet *Venus*. See **grievous, heinous, mischievous**.

introduction IN-truh-**DUHK**-shin.

Don't pronounce *intro-* like *inner-*. See **inter-**.

Iran i-RAHN or i-RAN.

Karl V. Teeter, emeritus professor of linguistics at Harvard, offers this sensible advice for the pronunciation of foreign names: "My general rule is to do it the way the natives would if I know that, but not if that pronunciation is so exotic as to attract attention."*

I recommend i-RAHN for the following reasons: 1. It is the pronunciation closest to the native one (which is ee-RAHN, with a slightly rolled *r*). 2. It is not exotic nor likely to attract unfavorable attention. 3. It is not difficult to pronounce. 4. It was in common use even before the country's name was officially changed (from Persia) in 1935, and many educated speakers say it that way today. 5. It is preferred by many older authorities and listed first by several current ones, including *WNW Guide* (1984), the *NBC Handbook* (1984), and *M-W 10* (1993).

If you are uncomfortable saying i-RAHN, then use the anglicized alternative i-RAN, which appears first in many current sources and is used widely in the broadcast media. I strongly urge you, however, not to use the fully anglicized variant eye-RAN. Although current American dictionaries recognize this pronunciation, the evidence of my ears tells me that eye-RAN is heard chiefly from louts and jingoists. I admit that is a subjective and rather snobbish judgment, but we all have pet peeves, certain uncouth pronunciations that grate on the nerves, and for me eye-RAN is one. Whenever I hear it I want to ask, "You ran where?"

For *Iranian,* I recommend i-RAHN-ee-in; an acceptable alternative is i-RAY-nee-in. Most authorities do not recognize i-RAN-ee-in, and I'm sure you can guess how I feel about eye-RAY-nee-in. Compare **Iraq**.

Iraq i-RAHK or i-RAK; **Iraqi** i-RAHK-ee or i-RAK-ee.

There is no *eye* in *Iraq*. Pronounce the *I-* as in *irritate* and the *-raq* like *rock* or *rack*. The comments regarding **Iran** (above) apply equally to *Iraq(i)*.

irascible i-RAS-i-buul or eye-RAS-i-buul.

The *c* is silent, and the second syllable, *-ras-*, receives the stress. The initial *i* may be short as in *irritate* or long as in *irate*.

irony EYE-ruh-nee (like the name *Ira + knee*). Don't say EYE-ur-nee.

The *r* in *irony* is properly pronounced like the *r* in *ironic*, not like the *r* in *iron*.

irrefutable IR-i-**FYOO**-tuh-buul (also EER-) or i-REF-yoo-tuh-buul.

Where should we place the stress in *irrefutable* — on the second syllable or the third? Most modern authorities prefer second-syllable stress, and three of the four major current American dictionaries give it priority, but historically there is greater authority for third-syllable stress.

In his influential *Critical Pronouncing Dictionary* (1791), John Walker says, "All our Dictionaries place the accent on the third syllable of this word." Indeed, Samuel Johnson (1755), William Perry (1775), Thomas

---

* Personal correspondence of October 14, 1989.

Sheridan (1780), Noah Webster (1828), Benjamin Humphrey Smart (1840), Joseph Emerson Worcester (1860), the *Century* (1889–1914), and Funk & Wagnalls *Standard* (1897) and *New Standard* (1913, 1931) all prefer the accent on the third syllable, and *Webster's New International* (1909), *Webster's Collegiate* (1917), Phyfe (1926), and *OED 1* (1928) give it priority. In 1934, *Webster 2* listed i-REF-yoo-tuh-buul first, and most sources since have followed this example.

Analogy with words such as *incomparable, irreparable, irrevocable,* and *disreputable* has reinforced second-syllable stress. There is one prominent exception to this pattern, however: *indisputable.* This synonym of *irrefutable* used to have its accent on the second syllable, but in American and British speech alike *indisputable* is now almost always pronounced with the primary stress on the third syllable. It can be argued, both on historical and denotative grounds, that *irrefutable* belongs in a separate class with *indisputable,* and that second-syllable stress is only a modern imposition of a more "elegant" pronunciation. Such is my case for preferring IR-i-**FYOO**-tuh-buul, but I can't say it's irrefutable. The call is yours.

irrelevant i-REL-uh-vint (near rhymes with *an elephant*).

Be careful not to transpose the *l* and *v* sounds in this word and say i-REV-uh-lint, as though the word were spelled *irrevelant.* This is called metathesis, the transposition of a word's letters, syllables, or sounds. It occurs also in the beastly mispronunciations NOO-kyuh-lur for *nuclear,* JOO-luh-ree for *jewelry,* and AKS for *ask.* Simply put, *metathesis* is a big word that means you are making a big mistake. See **ask, cupola, diminution, February, jewelry, nuclear, Realtor.**

irreparable i-REP-uh-ruh-buul, not EER-uh-**PAIR**-uh-buul.

Irreparable does not incorporate the word *repair,* and should not be pronounced as if it does. The word is divided *ir · rep · a · ra · ble* (not *ir · re · par · a · ble*) and the accent should be on the second syllable (*-rep-*). See **irrevocable, reparable.**

irrevocable i-REV-uh-kuh-buul, not EER-uh-**VOH**-kuh-buul.

Analogy with *revoke* tempts some speakers to stress the third syllable, but custom and authority place the accent squarely on the second. The misplaced accent is heard often enough for the phonetically catholic *M-W 10* (1993) to list it with the label *sometimes.* The other three major current American dictionaries — *American Heritage 3* (1992), *WNW 3* (1997), and *RHWC* (1997) — sanction only second-syllable stress. See **irreparable.**

isolate EYE-suh-layt.

This is the preferred American *and* British pronunciation. Some 19th-century American and British authorities favored IZ-uh-layt, which has disappeared; others favored IS-uh-layt (IS- as in *miss*), which is never heard in America and survives, barely, in Britain. Although I have heard IS-uh-layt

[213]

from BBC reporters and here and there from other Brits on radio and TV, *OED 2* (1989) gives priority to EYE-suh-layt and Jones (1991) recognizes only this long *i* pronunciation.

Israel IZ-ree'l or IZ-ray'l.

Do not slur your pronunciation into IZ-ru̲l. *Israel* should have three syllables, though in the final one, *-el,* the vowel is obscure, as in *kernel* and *people.*

In liturgical contexts and in ecclesiastical singing the word is often intentionally overpronounced **IZ**-ray-EL or **IZ**-ry-EL, or with a pure *s* as in *soft,* **IS**-ray-EL or **IS**-ry-EL (sometimes with a slightly rolled *r*). These "ritualistic" pronunciations are not appropriate in everyday speech. See **Judaism, yarmulke, Yom Kippur.**

issue (American) ISH-oo; (British) ISH-(y)oo, also IS-yoo (rhymes with *miss you*).

Contrary to popular belief, IS-yoo is not the prevailing pronunciation in Britain. Jones (1991) gives ISH-oo as the dominant pronunciation in educated British speech, *OED 2* (1989) lists it first, and the *Oxford Guide* (1983) and Burchfield (1996) prefer it. "It is ISHoo," declares the late British novelist Kingsley Amis (1998), "and to say ISSyoo is a piece of pressi-OSSity."

With *issue* and *tissue,* I'm a bit of a maverick. I pronounce them with a long *u* sound: ISH-yoo and TISH-yoo. Walker (1791) stipulated this pronunciation, Funk & Wagnalls *Standard* (1897), Phyfe (1926), and Vizetelly (1929) prefer it, and *Webster 2* (1934) lists it first. Right around there, whatever popularity the long *u* sound had swiftly hit the skids. The four leading current American dictionaries list only ISH-oo, but *OED 2* gives ISH-(y)oo, meaning that some speakers insert a *y* or long *u* sound. American speakers always use a long *u* in *value, continue, rescue, curlicue, barbecue, imbue,* and *venue,* and many also use it in *revenue* and *avenue.* Few still use it in *due* and words employing it: *residue, overdue,* and *subdue.* I preserve the long *u* sound in all these words. I may be a maverick, but at least no one can accuse me of being inconsistent.

Italian i-TAL-yi̲n.

Only a dork puts an *eye* in *Italian* — and risks getting a black eye for using this ignorant and disparaging pronunciation. *Random House II* (1987) puts that sentiment more politely, noting that *eye-talian* "is heard primarily from uneducated speakers" and "is usually considered offensive."

J

jaguar JAG-wahr.

WNW Guide (1984), which gives JAG-wahr, adds that "JAG-yoo-ahr is occasionally heard." Not in standard American speech it isn't — nor, for that matter, in standard British speech, where the pronunciation is JAG-yoo-ur (swallow the *r*). I have heard JAG-yoo-ahr in commercials for the British luxury car of that name, where it struck me as yet another example of the vocal affectation common in ads for upscale products. Apparently Madison Avenue thinks the average American consumer associates affluence and prestige with fake British accents or an affected Continental intonation. American speakers should heed the advice of Opdycke (1939): "The *u* is pronounced *w*. Don't say *jag' you are*, but *jag' wahr*. There are two syllables, not three." And for goodness' sake don't say JAG-wyr (-wyr like *wire*), which my wife reported hearing from a wildlife conservationist interviewed on NPR recently. That's a truly beastly mispronunciation.

jalousie JAL-uh-see (rhymes with *fallacy*).

Formerly, dictionaries marked this word zhal-oo-ZEE. The British moved the accent to the first syllable: ZHAL-oo-zee. In modern American speech the word has been completely anglicized to JAL-uh-see, which is preferred by all current sources. Do not say juh-LOW-see.

Japanese JAP-uh-**NEEZ**.

The last syllable preferably should sound like *knees*, not like *niece*.

"The pronunciation of the termination of Proper Names in *ese*, as *Chinese, Genevese, Genoese, Japanese, Javanese, Portuguese*, etc., is not set-

---

a = at / a̱ = final / ah = spa / ahr = car / air = fair / ay = hay / aw = saw
ch = chip / e = let / e̱ = item / ee = see / eer = deer / i = sit / i̱ = April
ng = sing / o̱ = carrot / oh = go / oo = soon / or = for / oor = poor
ow = cow / oy = toy / sh = she / th = thin / t̲h̲ = this / u̱ = focus / uh = up
ur = turn / uu = pull, took / y, eye = by, I / zh = measure / (see full key, p. xiv)

tled," says Phyfe (1926). "As between $\bar{e}z$ and $\bar{e}s$, most orthoëpists favor the first." Most authorities since have continued to favor the -EEZ pronunciation for the termination -*ese*. For *Japanese*, the four leading current American dictionaries list -EEZ first, and the *NBC Handbook* (1984), *OED 2* (1989), and Jones (1991) prefer it.

jargon JAHR-g<u>un</u> (rhymes with *bargain*).

This is the only pronunciation given in *American Heritage 3* (1992) and *WNW 3* (1997) and the preference of Lass & Lass (1976), *WNW Guide* (1984), the *NBC Handbook* (1984), and Jones (1991). JAHR-gahn, preferred until the 1940s, is now an overpronunciation.

Jekyll (Dr.) JEK'l (rhymes with *freckle*).

This is now the dominant pronunciation in America, although JEEK'l (rhymes with *fecal* and *treacle*) is the original and proper pronunciation.

I was quite shocked to discover that this seemingly normal name — which comes, of course, from Robert Louis Stevenson's story *The Strange Case of Dr. Jekyll and Mr. Hyde* — has developed (before my very ears, as it were) a split personality, or perhaps I should say a split "pronunciality."*

Yes, rigorous scientific examination reveals that JEK'l — the pronunciation I grew up with and have heard from plebeians and professors alike — is a pernicious imposter that has warped the minds and mouths of millions of speakers everywhere. Phyfe (1926) provides irrefutable evidence of this truth. JEEK'l, not JEK'l, he says, and then quotes an unimpeachable corroborating source: R. L. Stevenson himself. "The family in England so pronounce it," says the author.

As if that were not enough to commit even a mildly deviant pronunciation, we also have the testimony of a battery of expert witnesses: *Webster 2* (1934) and Witherspoon (1943) give only JEEK'l, and Vizetelly (1929), Kenyon & Knott (1949), and *American College* (1952) list JEEK'l first. Are these authorities too old for you? The *NBC Handbook* (1984) gives JEEK'l, period.

But wait. Before you start muttering "I've always relied on the kindness of strangers" and prepare to surrender yourself to Nurse Ratched for *de-*JEK'l-*ization* treatment (say, was that a *Hollywood* mixed metaphor?), consider this: who cares how the English family pronounces *its* Jekyll? *This* Jekyll is part of classic literature and popular culture now, the phrase *Jekyll and Hyde* is in the public domain, and that means the name is ours to mangle as we please.

---

* This nonce word may be defined as the innate aural identity of a word, that is, the sum of its phonological, cosmological, and zoological characteristics. Experts in psychobabble have classified various types of "pronunciality" based on a complex theory called "the hearing-is-believing syndrome."

That, for better or for worse, is precisely what American speakers have done. Just as the poor doctor was compelled to drink his hateful potion time and again until his dreaded alter ego destroyed him, so we have slipped into saying JEK'l until the vulgar mispronunciation has become our norm. Can you imagine any American today saying that someone has a JEEK'l and Hyde personality? Three of the four leading current American dictionaries list JEK'l first, and it is the only pronunciation in *Oxford American* (1980). Apparently, even the British are beginning to abandon JEEK'l, for Jones's *English Pronouncing Dictionary* (1991) lists the vying variants as equally common and notes that JEK'l is frequently heard in the phrase *Jekyll and Hyde*.

At this point any reasonable pronouncer must conclude that the split has gone too far to stop, and to try to force Dr. Jekyll's "pronunciality" into line now may prove damaging beyond repair. So here is Dr. Elster's diagnosis: if you meet an English person named Jekyll who happens to be a doctor, go ahead and say, "Dr. JEEK'l, I presume." Otherwise, say JEK'l in all contexts, for I'm afraid if you attempt to pronounce it "properly" they may take you away.

Jerusalem juh-ROO-suh-l<u>e</u>m.
Don't slur the word and say juh-ROOS-l<u>e</u>m. *Jerusalem* should have four syllables.

Traditionally, the *s* in *Jerusalem* is pronounced like *s* in *salad* or *c* in *place*. Since the 1970s dictionaries have recorded an alternative pronunciation, juh-ROO-zuh-l<u>e</u>m, with *s* pronounced like *z*. The traditional pronunciation, which is recommended, is preferred by the *NBC Handbook* (1984) and *OED 2* (1989) and listed first in three of the four major current American dictionaries. See **Judaism**.

Jesuit JEZH-oo-it or JEZ-oo-it. British, JEZ-yoo-it.
Avoid the noncanonical variants JES-oo-it and JEZ-wit.

jewel(s) JOO-wuul(z). Don't say JOOL(Z).
There is no *Jules* in *jewels*. *Jewel(s)* is a two-syllable word. See **jewelry**.

jewelry JOO-wuul-ree. Don't say JOO-luh-ree.
Transposing the adjacent *e* and *l* in *jewelry* and pronouncing it as if it were spelled *jewelry* is a major-league beastly mispronunciation. Lass & Lass (1976) put *jewlery* for *jewelry* at the top of a list of slovenly pronunciations "that make their perpetrators sound at least a trifle uneducated," some of the others being *heighth* for *height, mischeevious* for *mischievous, athalete* for *athlete, irrevelant* for *irrelevant,* and *deteriate* for *deteriorate.* The *jewlery* booboo may have been aggravated by the alternative spelling *jewellery,* preferred by the British. To pronounce *jewelry* properly, first say *jewel* and then add *-ry.* See **cupola, diminution, irrelevant, nuclear, Realtor**.

jocose joh-KOHS (rhymes with *no dose*). Stress the second syllable.

jocund JAHK-und. The first syllable rhymes with *sock*.

joist JOYST (rhymes with *moist*).

Don't drop the *t* and pronounce this word like the name *Joyce*. The variant JYST (rhymes with *iced*) is also nonstandard. Also take care with the plural *joists:* the proper pronunciation is JOYSTS (rhymes with *hoists*), not JOY-siz.

joust JOWST. Formerly, JOOST or JUST.

OED 2 (1989) says, "The historical English spelling from the 13th century is *just*. . . . Under later French influence *joust* was used sometimes by Gower, Caxton, Spenser, and Milton, was preferred by Johnson, and used by Scott." It is now the only standard spelling. "When written as *just*," explains Burchfield's *New Fowler's MEU* (1996), "the word seems to have been pronounced [JUST] in the 19c. For the form *joust* the standard pronunciation (as given by Daniel Jones) in 1917 was [JOOST]. By 1932 A. Lloyd James (*Broadcast English*) recommended [JOWST], and this pronunciation has now entirely supplanted the older [JOOST] in Br[itish]E[nglish]."

JOWST has entirely supplanted the earlier pronunciations in American English as well. Since the 1960s most dictionaries have listed JOWST first and sometimes marked the older pronunciations as occasional or rare. The *NBC Handbook* (1984) is the only modern authority I know of that prefers JUST. In *You Don't Say!* (1937), Alfred H. Holt, writing around the beginning of the transition to JOWST, says this: "If you favor the pronunciation 'just,' spell it that way. The rhyme with *roost* is not much liked here. Americans who use the *ou* of *jounce* cannot be greatly censured, as this is the Hollywood version of it. I feel that the rough-and-tumble association with *roust* gives this pronunciation the edge over the ambiguous 'just.'"

jubilant JOO-bi-lint.

Be careful to avoid the beastly JOO-byoo-lint, as if the word were spelled *jubulant*. See **similar**.

Judaism JOO-dee-iz'm or JOO-day-iz'm or JOO-duh-iz'm.

Judaism should have four syllables. Do not say JOO-diz-um — which *M-W 10* (1993) labels British although Jones (1991) and *OED 2* (1989) give only JOO-day-iz'm.

If you examine the three standard pronunciations of *Judaism* listed above, you will see that they vary only in the sounding of the second syllable, *-da-*, which you may pronounce like the word *day*, like the letter *d*, or with an obscure *a*, as in *Judah* (JOO-duh). There is sound authority for each pronunciation; JOO-dee-iz'm, preferred by Lass & Lass (1976), the *NBC Handbook* (1984), and *American Heritage 3* (1992), is probably most commonly heard in American speech.

There is less variation allowed for the following related words, for which the preferred pronunciations are given:

Judea (also *Judaea*): joo-DEE-uh, not joo-DAY-uh.

Judean (also *Judaean*): joo-DEE-in, not joo-DAY-in.

Judaic: joo-DAY-ik.

Judaica: joo-DAY-i-kuh.

Judeo- (as in *Judeo-Christian*): joo-DEE-oh. This combining form is a simplified spelling of *Judaeo-*, in which the *ae* is a ligature traditionally pronounced like long *e*, as in *me* or *idea* (eye-DEE-uh). Thus the correct pronunciation, and the only one sanctioned by older sources such as *Webster 2* (1934), is joo-DEE-oh; the pseudoclassical joo-DAY-oh, however, is now so common that it is listed first in some current dictionaries. Note that the accent is on the second syllable of *Judeo-*. Do not stress the first: JOO-dee-oh and JOO-day-oh, though recorded by some current dictionaries, are incorrect. See **Israel, Jerusalem, yarmulke, Yom Kippur**.

judiciary joo-**DISH**-ee-ER-ee, not joo-DISH-ur-ee.

Judiciary properly has five syllables, not four. Say *ju-dishy-ary*, not *ju-dish-ary*. See **auxiliary, beneficiary, penitentiary, plenipotentiary, subsidiary**.

junta HUUN-tuh. Formerly, JUHN-tuh.

Junta has gone through a process I call de-anglicization. This is when a foreign word that has been fully anglicized once again takes on foreign characteristics, though not always ones it had formerly and sometimes not even those of the language of origin.

"When the word JUNTA was borrowed into English from Spanish in the early 17th century, its pronunciation was thoroughly Anglicized to [JUHN-tuh]," explain *Random House II* (1987) and *RHWC* (1997). "The 20th century has seen the emergence and, esp[ecially] in North America, the gradual predominance of the pronunciation [HUUN-tuh], derived from Spanish [HOON-tah] through reassociation with the word's Spanish origins. A hybrid form [HUHN-tuh] is also heard."

Normally I am skeptical of de-anglicized pronunciations and reluctant to accept them until they prove themselves more than just an affectation or a fad. In my estimation, the de-anglicized HUUN-tuh has passed the test. Since gaining dictionary recognition in the 1960s, HUUN-tuh has done what juntas so often do — take over completely. It is preferred by most recent authorities, including Lass & Lass (1976) and the *NBC Handbook* (1984), it is now the dominant pronunciation among radio and TV newscasters, and it is the first pronunciation listed in all four major current American dictionaries. The traditional, anglicized JUHN-tuh is usually listed next; it is standard in the U.K. but now almost obsolete in the U.S. The hybrid HUHN-tuh is not often listed and not recommended.

juror JOOR-ur, not JOOR-or.

The -*or* in *juror* should rhyme with *her*, not *for*.

"Every time I have served on jury duty in New York County (Manhattan)," writes the lexicographer Sidney I. Landau in his excellent and informative survey *Dictionaries: The Art and Craft of Lexicography* (1984),

> I have been struck by the unusual and emphatic pronunciation of the second syllable of *juror* when uttered by lawyers or judges. It received equal stress with the first, as though equal stress on every syllable were somehow suitable for dignified and solemn occasions as befit a court of law. The same measured kind of Gilbert and Sullivan pronunciation was heard for the last syllable of *defendant*, which left no doubt as to the -*ant* spelling. Perhaps these pronunciations have long traditions in the legal profession, but I wonder whether they are not uttered, by way of many intermediaries, in obedience to [John] Walker's admonitions in 1791 against the "slurring" of unaccented syllables. [pp. 58–59]

"Don't get hysterical about the quality of an unaccented vowel," advises Holt (1937). In Walker's day it may have been fashionable to give unstressed sounds their due, but in contemporary English speech anyone who hyperarticulates an unstressed syllable sounds like a popinjay — "a strutting supercilious person," as *M-W 10* (1993) defines it — which perhaps explains why so many in the legal profession favor the overpronounced JOOR-or and dee-FEN-dant.

The terminal -*or* in *juror* comes from Latin and corresponds to the English -*er*. Both are noun (or agent) endings, and in educated American speech both are traditionally and properly pronounced -ur. Thus the -*or* in *donor, perpetrator, oppressor, protector, inventor,* and *prosecutor* (to cite only a few of many such words) should sound the same as -*er* in *doer* or *maker*.

Some speakers, however, insist on saying AK-tor for *actor* instead of AK-tur, VEN-dor for *vendor* instead of VEN-dur, RAP-tor for *raptor* instead of RAP-tur, PRED-uh-tor for *predator* instead of PRED-uh-tur, and so on. These are overpronunciations, a form of hyperarticulate speech. They are exceptions to the norm imposed by speakers trying too hard to sound exceptional. In *color, odor, honor, harbor, valor, mayor, pastor, governor, conqueror, spectator, conductor, orator,* and dozens more words, -*or* is properly pronounced like -*er*, and there is no good reason not to be consistent about it.

The inclination to exaggerate the sounds of certain words may come in part from a phenomenon of mass culture that I call "sci-fi pronunciation" or "Hollywood Hyperspeak." American science-fiction movies and TV shows commonly employ an alien standard of speech to heighten the illusion of otherworldliness. Unstressed vowels in the names of characters, fictitious places, and imaginary planets are never lightened or elided as they are in natural, conversational English, and the many androids, robots, and extraterrestrials we encounter tend either to affect a peculiar and inconsistent form of British accent or overpronounce each syllable in the monotonous manner of early synthesized speech. Because these creatures appear to be free of the linguistic idiosyncrasies (and often the intellectual imperfections) of human beings, they can be intimidating as well as strange.

For example, in TV's original *Star Trek,* Mr. Spock, the hyperarticulate character played by Leonard Nimoy, overpronounces *sensor, sector, factor,* and *record,* saying SEN-sor, SEK-tor, FAK-tor, and (the British) REK-ord instead of SEN-sur, SEK-tur, FAK-tur, and (the American) REK-urd. Spock, being Vulcan (and fictional to boot), can say whatever he likes, but we earthlings have our own standards to uphold. However, since it is the nature of Hollywood to sell, and because the overprecise speaker always touches a self-conscious nerve in us, Mr. Spock's and numerous other pseudoprecise sci-fi pronunciations have permeated American popular culture and been adopted by many otherwise unaffected speakers. Today their influence is particularly noticeable in the jargon (sometimes overpronounced JAHR-gahn) of hi-tech, where the cognoscenti confer in acronyms and a word process-*ur* becomes a word process-*or.* See **defendant, mentor, predator, vendor.**

juvenile JOO-vuh-nil (recommended) or JOO-vuh-nyl.

JOO-vuh-nil (-nil like -*nal* in *annal*) is the traditional American pronunciation. JOO-vuh-nyl (-nyl rhyming with *pile*) is originally British; it is increasingly heard today in the U.S., particularly for the noun a *juvenile* (and especially in the criminal justice system). Three of the four major current American dictionaries now list JOO-vuh-nyl first, but pronunciation mavens from Holt (1937) and Opdycke (1939) to Lass & Lass (1976), the *NBC Handbook* (1984), and Barnhart (1988) prefer the traditional JOO-vuh-nil. See **textile.**

K

karaoke KAR-ee-**OH**-kee.

Only two current American dictionaries list this word, which the supplement to *OED 2* (1989) shows was first recorded in English in 1979. *M-W 10* (1993) gives three variants: KAR-ee-**OH**-kee, a reasonable anglicization and the most commonly heard pronunciation; kuh-ROH-kee, a clumsy, loutish pronunciation and an abomination in both English and Japanese; and KAH-rah-**OH**-kay, an approximation of the Japanese. *RHWC* (1997) gives one pronunciation: KAR-ee-**OH**-kee. Go with the one.

karate kuh-RAH-tee. Do not say kuh-RAH-tay or kuh-RAT-ee.

Every so often I hear someone claim that kuh-RAH-tay (-tay rhyming with *day*) is the proper pronunciation, but there is no authority to support that notion. *Karate* came into English from Japanese about 1955. *Webster 3* (1961), the first of my sources to record the word, gives one pronunciation: kuh-RAH-tee. Out of twenty dictionaries published since then that I consulted, only three — one hardcover, *AHNC* (1969), and two paperbacks, Funk & Wagnalls *Standard* (1980) and *Webster's II New Riverside* (1984) — list kuh-RAH-tay, and not one recognizes the eccentric variant kuh-RAT-ee, which is occasionally heard. *OED 2* (1989) and all four leading current American dictionaries — *American Heritage 3* (1992), *M-W 10* (1993), *RHWC* (1997), and *WNW 3* (1997) — sanction only kuh-RAH-tee. Given the one-sidedness of this evidence, I must conclude that -tay for the last syllable is at best pseudo-Japanese and at worst an affectation.

---

a = at / a̱ = final / ah = spa / ahr = car / air = fair / ay = hay / aw = saw
ch = chip / e = let / e̱ = item / ee = see / eer = deer / i = sit / i̱ = April
ng = sing / o̱ = carrot / oh = go / oo = soon / or = for / oor = poor
ow = cow / oy = toy / sh = she / th = thin / th = this / u̱ = focus / uh = up
ur = turn / uu = pull, took / y, eye = by, I / zh = measure / (see full key, p. xiv)

Keltic See **Celtic**.

Kenya KEN-yuh.

Sometimes a politician can have a powerful effect upon the language. In the case of *Kenya*, for instance, the predominance of KEN-yuh over KEEN-yuh in American and British speech today can be attributed to the great British statesman and orator Winston Churchill — or at least so says W. Cabell Greet, who was a professor of English at Columbia University and speech consultant to the Columbia Broadcasting System (CBS) for many years. "The more correct (and the BBC) pronunciation is [KEEN-yuh]," Greet writes in *World Words* (1948). "Our efforts to inculcate this pronunciation at WCBS were enfeebled when Prime Minister Churchill repeatedly said [KEN-yuh]."

KEEN-yuh has survived on the BBC, but Jones (1991), a current British authority, gives KEN-yuh as the prevailing pronunciation in England, adding that in Kenya itself both pronunciations are heard. In American speech today one rarely hears KEEN-yuh; the *NBC Handbook* (1984) prefers KEN-yuh and all four leading current American dictionaries list it first. It is also worth noting that the first president of independent Kenya was Jomo Kenyatta, whose last name is pronounced with a short *e*, ken-YAH-tuh.

ketchup KECH-up.

"The word, however spelled," writes Evans (1959), "is an attempt to present in English the Malayan word *kechap* (sauce), which, in turn, seems to have been an attempt to present a Chinese phrase in Malayan." The Chinese is *ke-tsiap* or *ketsiap*, which Shaw (1972) translates as "pickled-fish brine" and *Random House II* (1987) says is akin to Chinese words for *eggplant* and *juice*. *Ketchup* is without question the dominant spelling today. Current dictionaries list *catsup* and *catchup* as alternative spellings but fail to note that while the former is still fairly common the latter is rarely used by anyone over the age of ten.

Regardless of how you prefer to spell the word, or what the label on your favorite brand says, the pronunciation most commonly heard is KECH-up. The alternative KACH-up, based on the spelling *catchup*, is less common but acceptable. The variant KAT-sup, based on the spelling *catsup*, is sometimes heard, and dictionaries politely list it in good standing. To my ear, though, KAT-sup has a look-at-me quality that makes me wonder if the speaker expects to be congratulated for demonstrating a preference for the alternative spelling.

Keynes (John Maynard) KAYNZ (like *canes*).

khaki KAK-ee (rhymes with *tacky*). Now less often, KAH-kee (like *cocky*).

Khaki comes from Urdu, Hindi, and Persian words meaning dusty or dust-colored. KAH-kee was once the only correct way to pronounce the word; Holt (1937), for example, states flatly that "the flat 'ack' is not acceptable." However, in the years since Kenyon & Knott (1949) sanctioned KAK-ee and *American College* (1952) listed it first, usage and good authority have firmly established KAK-ee as the dominant pronunciation in the U.S. All four leading current American dictionaries list KAK-ee first, and Lass & Lass (1976), the *NBC Handbook* (1984), and Barnhart (1988) prefer it. KAH-kee remains the standard in Britain, and *WNW Guide* (1984) and *M-W 10* (1993) note that in Canada one often hears KAHR-kee, like *car key* (the word was formerly sometimes spelled *karkee*).

kibosh KY-bahsh (recommended). Now less often, ki-BAHSH.

The expression *to put the kibosh on* (something), meaning to put an end to, squelch, quash, has been used informally in American English for over 150 years. The origin is unknown. The first citation in *OED 2* (1989) is from an English writer: in *Sketches by Boz* (1836), Charles Dickens wrote, "'Hoo-roar', ejaculates a pie-boy in parenthesis, 'put the kye-bosk [*sic*] on her, Mary.'" *The Barnhart Dictionary of Etymology* (1988) explains that "*kye-bosk* is Dickens' representation of a Cockney variant of *kibosh*," and that the spelling *kibosh* "is first recorded in *The Slang Dictionary* (1869), defined as nonsense, stuff, humbug, a meaning influenced by *bosh* (1850)."

The oldest sources in which I found *kibosh* were Funk & Wagnalls *Standard* (1897), which gives ki-BAHSH, and the *Century* (1889–1914), which says ki-BAHSH or ky-BAHSH. *Webster's Collegiate* (1917, 1923), however, lists KY-bahsh first followed by ki-BAHSH, and that is what you'll find in every dictionary published since then (I checked a baker's dozen or so), including the four leading current American dictionaries and *OED 2* (1989). The *NBC Handbook* (1984), Morris & Morris (1985), and Barnhart (1988) prefer KY-bahsh, and only Lass & Lass (1976) favor ki-BAHSH.

Kierkegaard (Søren) **KEER**-kuh-GAHRD.

The Danish pronunciation (very approximately) is **KEER**-kuh-GOR (first name, SUUR-u̱n). *Webster 2* (1934), *American College* (1952), and the *Columbia Encyclopedia* (1963) prefer this pronunciation, but the anglicized pronunciation given above, which the *NBC Handbook* (1984) prefers, is the one listed first in current dictionaries and the one used by most educated American speakers today. Avoid the hybrid -GAHR for the last syllable.

kiln Traditionally, KIL (with silent *n*). Now usually KILN.

"'Kill' sounds illiterate to many who are not aware that it is preferred to 'kiln' by almost all the authorities," says Holt (1937). "There is no convincing reason for dropping the *n*, however, as there is in the case of *damn* or *limn*. The *n* of *kiln* was inherited from [Latin] *culina*, the ancestor of *culinary*."

In *Comfortable Words* (1959), Bergan Evans explains why there is "no convincing reason" to drop the *n:*

Most people who work professionally with kilns call them "kills." That is, they omit the final -*n* in their pronunciation. This is startling to the layman, however accustomed he may be to the vagaries of English spelling and pronunciation. But that's probably because few laymen ever have an occasion to say *kiln*. We omit some other final *n*'s, but since we have left them silent so long that we don't include them in the spelling any more, we're not aware that they're no longer there. *Ell*, in "Give him an inch and he'll take an ell," was formerly *elln*. And our common word *mill* (from the Latin *molina* . . .) had a final *n* up until a few centuries ago. Caxton spelled the plural *myllenes*.

KILN, the spelling pronunciation, has been acceptable in educated speech since *OED 1* (1928) and *Webster 2* (1934) countenanced it as an alternative to the traditional KIL. The four leading current American dictionaries give both pronunciations; two list KIL first and two list KILN first. Lass & Lass (1976) and the *NBC Handbook* (1984) prefer KIL, but Burchfield (1996) says the word is "now normally pronounced" KILN and Jones (1991) notes that KIL "appears to be used only by those concerned with the working of kilns." Based on this evidence, here's my advice: if you want to show you know something more about this word than how to spell it, say KIL. If you think saying KIL will make you sound pedantic or weird, or both, pronounce the *n*.

kilometer By analogy, **KIL-uh-MEE-tur**, but pronounced ki-LAHM-i-tur by many.

The metric system prefixes *centi-*, *deci-*, *deca-* (or *deka-*), *milli-*, and *hecto-* are accented on the first syllable. We do not say cen*tim*eter, de*cil*iter, mil*lim*eter, etc., nor do we stress the second syllable in *kilocycle* or *kiloliter*. Why say ki-*lom*-eter?

The pronunciation note in *Random House II* (1987) suggests that when *kilometer* came into English about 1800–1810, it was pronounced **KIL-uh-MEE-tur**. But almost right away an alternative pronunciation, with the stress on the second syllable, was recorded. "From 1828 to 1841," says the usage note in *M-W 9* (1985) and *10* (1993), "Noah Webster indicated only second syllable stress, and his successor added a first syllable stress variant in the first Merriam-Webster dictionary of 1847."

Later authorities did not share Webster's preference. Worcester (1860), Funk & Wagnalls *Standard* (1897), the *Century* (1889–1914), and Phyfe (1926) do not recognize ki-LAHM-i-tur, and *Webster's Collegiate* (1917) — which is based on *Webster's New International* (1909), the first unabridged Merriam-Webster dictionary of the 20th century — gives only **KIL-uh-MEE-tur**. "Analogy with various 'meters' has led to a faulty accent here," writes Holt (1937). "Emphasize the 'kill' and, secondarily, the 'mee.'" Nevertheless, since Webster's time ki-LAHM-i-tur has persisted alongside **KIL-**

uh-MEE-tur — reinforced, says *Random House II*, "by words for instruments (rather than units) of measurement ending in -*meter*, as *thermometer*, *barometer*, and *speedometer*" — and no amount of orthoepic disfavor has had the slightest effect upon its popularity.

By the 1930s, lexicographic resistance to ki-LAHM-i-tur began to break down. "Sometimes [ki-LAHM-i-tur] by false analogy with barometer, etc.," says *Webster 2* (1934); "much less frequent," note Kenyon & Knott (1949); used "occasionally," claims *American College* (1952). In 1961, *Webster 3* listed ki-LAHM-i-tur first but labeled it unacceptable to many. Since then the many have become few. Today "both pronunciations are venerable," rule *M-W 9* (1985) and *10* (1993), and *Random House II* (1987) concludes that both "are used by educated speakers, including members of the scientific community."*

I won't presume to tell members of the scientific community how to pronounce *kilometer* (they have their own arcane rules), but I will say this to you, the educated speaker, who may be waffling or consulting this entry to settle a debate: when two pronunciations have coexisted for well over 150 years, when they are used by relatively equal numbers of speakers at all levels of society, and when they are recorded side by side in good standing in major dictionaries, it would be outrageous to claim that one pronunciation is wrong. In this situation, the right pronunciation becomes a matter of personal choice. For whenever there are hairs to be split, people will forever split them (along with their infinitives whenever it sounds better that way). Modern authorities are about evenly divided: for example, Lass & Lass (1976) and the *NBC Handbook* (1984) prefer ki-LAHM-i-tur, while *Everyday Reader's* (1985) and Burchfield (1996) prefer **KIL**-uh-MEE-tur.

So what should one do? If you are accustomed to saying ki-LAHM-i-tur, you have plenty of good company; indeed, your pronunciation shows signs of winning out. *M-W 9* (1985) and *10* (1993) claim that "in North American speech *kilometer* is most often pronounced with primary stress on the second syllable," and "this pronunciation is also frequently heard in British speech."† However, if you are a **KIL**-uh-MEE-tur sayer, you can rest easy in the knowledge that it is the pronunciation supported by anal-

---

* Curiously enough, members of the scientific community may be the only American speakers who use *kilometer* on anything approaching a regular basis. The drive to adopt metric values in common contexts, begun in earnest in the 1970s, has faltered in the U.S. The kilometer is standard in Canada and Mexico, and kph (kilometers per hour) are now a feature on the speedometers of most automobiles sold in the U.S., but most Americans still don't know a kilometer from a parking meter.

† Don't be misled by this statement into assuming that ki-LAHM-i-tur either prevails or is generally accepted in British speech. *OED 2* (1989) and Jones (1991) prefer **KIL**-uh-MEE-tur, and the *Oxford Guide* (1983) labels the second-syllable accent as "especially to be avoided."

ogy as well as long-standing usage. And if you are unsure and would like a recommendation — well, you can follow me. I'd walk a mile before I said ki-LAHM-i-tur. It does roll nicely off the tongue, I admit, but **KIL-uh-MEE-tur** seems "more right" to me. See **centimeter**.

kimono ki-MOH-noh.

I had never — repeat, never — heard anyone pronounce this word ki-MOH-nuh, with the *uh* sound of *sofa* in the last syllable (this sound is called a *schwa*, pronounced SHWAH), until one day recently I was looking over my six-year-old daughter's shoulder as she was playing with the *American Heritage Children's Dictionary*, Multimedia Edition (1995), on CD-ROM. She was investigating various words that begin with *k*, and when she clicked on a picture of a woman wearing a kimono a recorded voice uttered the word, pronouncing it ki-MOH-nuh (rhyming with *Ramona*).

Before I could register my surprise, my precocious daughter cried, "Dad, she mispronounced it! It's not *kimo*-NUH, it's *kimo*-NOH, with an *o* at the end. Right?"

"That's what I thought, sweetheart," I said. "But let me take a look," I added, ever the circumspect orthoepist.

The first source I checked, of course, was *American Heritage 3* (1992), to see if this ki-MOH-nuh might have been an oversight at the studio production level. (Having done a considerable amount of voice-work and narration myself, some of it for CD-ROMs, I know that despite one's own and the production team's best efforts, mistakes sometimes slip by.) But no, ki-MOH-nuh was in fact the first pronunciation listed there. It was also the first pronunciation in *RHWC* (1997) and *WNW 3* (1997), which, to my chagrin, slapped the label *also* on my long *o* pronunciation, meaning in the opinion of the editors it was considerably less common. Of the four leading current American dictionaries, only *M-W 10* (1993) gave priority to ki-MOH-noh. Perplexed, I checked three recent authorities and was flabbergasted to find that all of them — Lass & Lass (1976), the *NBC Handbook* (1984), and Barnhart (1988) — preferred ki-MOH-nuh.

I was stunned. What was going on here? Was this some sort of lexicographic conspiracy, or was there simply something wrong with my ears? How could a pronunciation I had never heard in my entire life, and that my daughter instinctively sensed was eccentric, have all that authority behind it? I wanted answers, and I wanted them fast. A few minutes later, after a flurry of page-flipping, I emerged from the fine print convinced that my long *o* pronunciation was indeed the better one and that some of our lexicographers must be sleeping on the job.

Kimono was first recorded in English in 1886. Funk & Wagnalls *Standard* (1897), the *Century* (1914), *Webster's Collegiate* (1917), and Phyfe (1926) sanction only -noh (like *no*) for the last syllable. The trouble starts with

Webster 2 (1934), which gives ki-MOH-noh and then adds "popularly" ki-MOH-nuh. Opdycke (1939) also prefers -noh and calls the schwa "colloquial," but Kenyon & Knott (1949) and *American College* (1952) list it first and *Webster 3* (1961) — a dictionary whose treatment of pronunciation never ceases to amaze me — calls the long *o* in the last syllable "infrequent."

My friend and fellow language maven Richard Lederer — author of *Crazy English, Anguished English, The Word Circus,* and many other delightful books — who also prefers ki-MOH-noh, assures me that he has frequently heard ki-MOH-nuh. (Where are these people?) Lederer suggests that the pronunciation with a final schwa may be based on analogy with words like *potato, tomato,* and *tobacco,* which are often pronounced puh-TAY-tuh, tuh-MAY-tuh, tuh-BAK-uh. In my opinion these are less-than-cultivated pronunciations, and any association between them and the schwa at the end of *kimono* is all the more reason to avoid it. Although I have no reason to doubt Lederer's theory, I can't help noticing that there are a great many more trisyllabic words ending in a single *o* with the accent on the middle syllable that in educated speech are always pronounced with a clear and unmistakable long final *o: fiasco, volcano, commando, torpedo, tornado, flamingo, embargo, casino, lumbago, farrago,* and tons of words from music: *piano, allegro, concerto, crescendo, staccato, legato,* and so on. Why did these words keep their long *o* while *kimono,* not exactly an everyday sort of word like *potato,* was singled out for a lowly schwa? Unfortunately I can't answer that question, but I can tell you one thing: if *kimono* is analogous with anything it should logically be another Japanese loanword, *mikado,* which is never pronounced mi-KAH-duh, always mi-KAH-doh.

"The ordinary rendering [of *kimono*] (rhyming with *Jonah*)," writes Alfred H. Holt (1937), "follows neither the Japanese sound nor the English spelling. The Japanese accent the *kim,* concluding with 'oh no.' A correct anglicization is to accent the *mo,* but round out the final *o* too."

The schwa may once have been ordinary and the long *o* may once have been infrequent, but at the close of the millennium there is no question the reverse is true. When the mammoth *OED 2* came out in 1989, it recognized only one pronunciation for *kimono* — ki-MOH-noh. In giving priority to ki-MOH-noh, *M-W 10* (1993) is the only current American dictionary that gets it right. The rest of them should stop kowtowing to the uncultivated ki-MOH-nuh and get with it.

kindergarten KIN-dur-GAHRT'n or **KIN**-dur-GARD'n.
The *d* should have its full sound, and the *t* is lightened but still audible. Don't say *kinner-garden.* See **fundamental, gentle, mental, rental, ventilate.**

kismet KIZ-met or KIS-met.

Until the 1930s, sources preferred KIS-met; since then the weight of authority has shifted to KIZ-met, although dictionaries continue to list KIS-met in good standing. Also acceptable are the variants KIZ-met and KIS-met, in which the *e* is lightened so that it sounds like *e* in *item*.

knoll NOHL (rhymes with *bowl*).

Knopf (Alfred Abraham) KNAHPF. Pronounce the *k*.

Koran ko-RAHN (recommended) or ko-RAN.

Do not say KOR-an or KOH-ran, with the stress on the first syllable. Stress the second syllable, which may sound like *Ron* or *ran*.

kudos KOO-dahs (-dahs rhyming with *-hos* in *hostage*).

The variants KOO-dohs, KYOO-dohs (-dohs like *dose*) and KOO-dohz, KYOO-dohz are used by many educated speakers and are now often listed in dictionaries, but many authorities and cultivated speakers — including me — take exception to them, especially the variants ending in a *z* sound. "Even people who are careful to treat the word syntactically as a singular often pronounce it as if it were a plural," says *American Heritage 3* (1992). "Etymology would require that the final consonant be pronounced as a voiceless (s) rather than as a voiced (z)."

Here's what Bergen Evans (1959) has to say about *kudos:* "If you want to be very highfalutin (and in using such a word you might as well be), you will pronounce it *kyoo'doss*. However, if you prefer your Greek with a homely, folksy flavor, you are within your rights if you pronounce it *koo'doss*. It's downright vulgar, though, to say *koo'dose*."

Although the pronunciation preferred by the most authorities, past and present, is KYOO-dahs, I agree with Evans that KYOO- sounds a tad too precious. Therefore I recommend KOO-dahs on the grounds that it is unpretentious, it is faithful to the original Greek, it has been acceptable for at least sixty years — Opdycke (1939) conferred his blessing on it — and nearly all current sources list it. Finally, and perhaps most important, it is the one variant that is least likely to attract unfavorable attention.

A few words on usage: some current dictionaries include lengthy notes justifying the singular back formation *kudo* and the use of *kudos* as a plural. Those who would be lulled by these arguments into accepting *a kudo* and *these kudo(e)s are* should know that many authorities vehemently object to these forms. Evans (1959) said it, Bernstein (1965) said it, Shaw (1972) said it, Hook (1990) said it, Burchfield (1996) said it, and Morris & Morris's *Harper Dictionary of Contemporary Usage* (1985), which I quote, said it: "There is no such thing as a 'kudo.' The word is *kudos* and it is singular." Evans puts it nicely: "Sometimes one sees a false singular, *kudo*. . . . From this it is simply best to avert the gaze."

Ku Klux Klan KOO-kluhks-**KLAN**.

Don't put an *l* in *Ku* and say KLOO. There is no *clue* in *Ku Klux Klan*. Or, to put that another way, the Klan is clueless.

Kuwait kuu-WAYT (kuu- as in *could* and *cookie*) or koo-WAYT (koo- as in *coop* and *food*).

The accent is on the second syllable (which sounds like *wait*), never the first. The variant kuu-WYT (-WYT rhyming with *bite*), which still appears in a few current sources, is old-fashioned and rarely heard.

L

laboratory **LAB**-ruh-TOR-ee or **LAB**-uh-ruh-TOR-ee.

The British stress the second syllable, luh-BOR-uh-tree.

Don't say **LAB**-ur-TOR-ee (like *labbertory*) or **LAB**-uh-TOR-ee (like *labbatory*). These are beastly mispronunciations.

Some older speakers may insist that only the five-syllable **LAB**-uh-ruh-TOR-ee is correct, and that the four-syllable **LAB**-ruh-TOR-ee — the result of syncope (SING-kuh-pee), the loss or omission of sounds or letters from the middle of a word — is careless. This is a misconception. The four-syllable pronunciation is listed first in Kenyon & Knott (1949), *American College* (1952), and *Random House II* (1987), and is preferred by Lass & Lass (1976), the *NBC Handbook* (1984), and *WNW Guide* (1984). For more on syncope, see **chocolate, temperature, vegetable**.

labyrinthine LAB-uh-**RIN**-thin.

Rhyme this word with *dabber in thin,* says Opdycke (1939). For the final syllable, *-thine,* older authorities all prefer and current dictionaries all give priority to -thin (or -th<u>i</u>n). Eschew the variants -theen (rhymes with *seen*), now often listed second, and -thyn (rhymes with *wine*), which is British. The alternative spelling *labyrinthian* is pronounced LAB-uh-**RIN**-thee-in. To avoid confusion, use the preferred forms, which are far more common in good writing and speech. See **Minotaur**.

lackadaisical LAK-uh-**DAY**-z<u>i</u>-kuul. Don't say LAKS-uh-**DAY**-z<u>i</u>-kuul.

The odd and beastly mispronunciation *lax*-adaisical is heard from careless speakers not accustomed to listening to what they are saying. *Lackadaisical*

---

a = at / <u>a</u> = final / ah = spa / ahr = car / air = fair / ay = hay / aw = saw
ch = chip / e = let / <u>e</u> = item / ee = see / eer = deer / i = sit / <u>i</u> = April
ng = sing / <u>o</u> = carrot / oh = go / oo = soon / or = for / oor = poor
ow = cow / oy = toy / sh = she / th = thin / <u>th</u> = this / <u>u</u> = focus / uh = up
ur = turn / uu = pull, took / y, eye = by, I / zh = measure / (see full key, p. xiv)

connotes laxness, but it begins with *lack* and should be pronounced as it is spelled. The word comes from the archaic interjection *lackaday* (used to express sorrow, regret, or dismay), which in turn comes from *alackaday.* Dictionaries do not recognize the *lax-* mispronunciation.

laissez-faire LES-ay-**FAIR** (rhymes with *guess way there*).

Laissez-faire came into English from French about 1825. The *Century* (1889–1914), *Webster's Collegiate* (1917), *Webster 2* (1934), and Kenyon & Knott (1949) pronounce it LES-ay-**FAIR**. Funk & Wagnalls *Standard* (1897), Phyfe (1926), and Vizetelly (1929) give LAY-say-**FAIR**. After *Webster 3* (1961) listed a host of dubious and infrequent variants, one would expect subsequent dictionaries to accommodate some of them. Not so. Three of the four leading current American dictionaries countenance only LES-ay-**FAIR**, and Lass & Lass (1976), the *NBC Handbook* (1984), *Everyday Reader's* (1985), and Barnhart (1988) prefer it.

lambaste lam-BAYST (rhymes with *waste*), not lam-BAST (rhymes with *fast*).

I once mistakenly pronounced this word lam-BAST, until one day someone properly lam-BAY-stid me for it and I now know the correct pronunciation. Lam-BAYST is the first pronunciation in *M-W 10* (1993), *RHWC* (1997), and *WNW 3* (1997), the only pronunciation in the *Century* (1889–1914), *Webster 2* (1934), *American College* (1952), *OED 2* (1989), and *American Heritage 3* (1992), and the preference of Lass & Lass (1976), the *NBC Handbook* (1984), and Barnhart (1988).

lamentable Traditionally, LAM-in-tuh-buul. Now usually luh-MEN-tuh-buul.

Lamentable entered English in the 15th century. In the late 16th century, Spenser and Shakespeare placed the accent on the first syllable, and for the next three hundred years this was the only acceptable pronunciation in cultivated speech. In the first half of the 20th century the variant luh-MEN-tuh-buul (accented on analogy with *lament*) caught on and began to spread, though it went unrecognized by dictionaries and was severely criticized by various authorities. *Webster 3* (1961) was the first to recognize luh-MEN-tuh-buul, which it labeled with an obelus [÷] to indicate that many speakers took "strong exception" to it. This esoteric mark did nothing to deter the unwary from saying luh-MEN-tuh-buul, and its meaning probably eluded most readers.

Today, luh-MEN-tuh-buul is so widespread that the traditional pronunciation now seems old-fashioned to many speakers — William Safire is one prominent example. Although the day may not be far off when the traditional LAM-in-tuh-buul goes on life support, at the close of the millennium there are still a good many cultivated speakers — Supreme Court Justice Antonin Scalia is one prominent example — who are conscientiously keeping it alive. Lass & Lass (1976), the *NBC Handbook* (1984), *Everyday Reader's* (1985), and Burchfield (1996) prefer it, and two of the four major current American dictionaries — *WNW 3* (1997) and *M-W 10* (1993) — list it first, the latter (like its predecessor, *Webster 3*) labeling luh-MEN-tuh-buul with an obelus [÷] to indicate that some of us, at least, still find it unacceptable.

lapsus linguae (English) LAP-s<u>u</u>s LING-gwee; (Latin) LAHP-suus LING-gwy. Careful speakers take pains to avoid a *lapsus linguae*, slip of the tongue.

Caution: use either the English or the Latin pronunciation, as you prefer, but take care not to mix them up. Avoid the hybrid forms LAP-s<u>u</u>s LING-gwy and LAHP-suus LING-gwee.

largess Traditionally, LAHR-jis or LAHR-jes. Now usually lahr-JES, which I accept with reluctance, or lahr-ZHES, which I reject as affected and beastly.

Largess dates back to the 13th century and is related to the word *large* — which at one time meant generosity, bounty — as *riches* (formerly spelled *richesse*) is related to *rich;* hence, the traditional pronunciation with the accent on the first syllable. "If the word had remained in common use," writes H. W. Fowler (1926), who recommends the spelling *largess* and the pronunciation LAHR-jis, "it would doubtless have come to be spelt, as it often formerly was, *larges.*"

For several centuries the spellings *larges, largess,* and *largesse* were all in use. By 1800 *larges* had begun to disappear. From then until now, *largess* has been the preferred spelling and *largesse* the runner-up, but for several decades *largesse* has been staging a strong comeback, and one current dictionary, *M-W 10* (1993), now lists it first.

The predominance of the two double *s* spellings in the 20th century undoubtedly has influenced the change in this word's pronunciation. A reader encountering *largess* for the first time might easily assume the *-ess* is stressed, as in *caress, success, impress, express,* and *undress.* To the speaker unfamiliar with the word's long history in English, the spelling *largesse,* with its final *e,* looks French, and would therefore seem to be pronounced with stress on *-esse* like *finesse, politesse,* and *noblesse.*

Until the mid-20th century dictionaries recognized only LAR-jis and LAR-jes, but since the 1960s — when *Webster 3* (1961) and *RH College* (1968) listed lahr-JES first — most speakers have accented the word on the second syllable and the traditional pronunciation, though still listed in current dictionaries, is infrequently heard. Regardless of where you choose to put the accent, the *g* should be pronounced as in *large,* as was the custom for centuries. To say lahr-ZHES, giving it a French *zh* sound as in *mirage,* is an illogical, pretentious, pseudo-French de-anglicization and an ignorant affront to the nearly eight hundred years of service this word has given the English language. Because of its popularity, two of the four major current American dictionaries now list lahr-ZHES first, but the other two do not even recognize it. For more on de-anglicization, see **cadre, junta**.

larvae (plural of *larva*) LAHR-vee. Don't say LAHR-vy.

See **alumnae, antennae, formulae, minutiae, papilla(e), vertebrae**.

larynx LAR-ingks (LAR- as in *Larry*, -ingks rhyming with *rinks*).

Careless speakers transpose the *y* and *n* in this word and say LAHR-niks, as if the spelling were *larnyx*. *Webster 3* (1961) labels this substandard; in this book (and to most educated speakers, I think) it's beastly. Other dictionaries do not recognize LAHR-niks, further proof of its unacceptability.

The plural of *larynx* is *larynges* (luh-RIN-jeez) or *larynxes* (LAR-inks-iz). The adjective is *laryngeal* (luh-RIN-jee-ul). The branch of medicine dealing with the larynx is *laryngology* (LAR-in-**GAHL**-uh-jee), and a specialist in that branch is called a *laryngologist* (LAR-in-**GAHL**-uh-jist).

Las Vegas LAHS VAY-gus.

No one mispronounces *Vegas* — except actor Bronson Pinchot in the silly TV sitcom *Perfect Strangers,* who said VAY-gahs (with the *ah* sound of *bomb*) because he played a schlemiel with a fake foreign accent. The trouble here occurs with *Las,* which a growing number of people are pronouncing like the word *loss.* This is fitting, in one sense, considering what happens to most folks who go to Vegas, but it's a mispronunciation nonetheless, no doubt reinforced by this gambling city's popular nickname, *Lost Wages.* In Spanish and in English, *los* and *las* have different pronunciations. The *Los* in *Los Angeles* is pronounced like *loss,* but the *Las* in *Las Vegas* is properly pronounced LAHS, with the open *ah* sound of *pot* and *father.*

lath (wood strips) LATH (rhymes with *bath*); plural, LATHZ (TH as in *rather*).

lathe (woodworking tool) LAYTH (rhymes with *bathe*, TH as in *rather*).

learned (adjective) LUR-nid; (participle) LURND.

A wise or scholarly person is *learned* (LUR-nid). When you are taught a lesson, presumably it is *learned* (LURND). See **aged**.

legacy LEG-uh-see, not LEE-guh-see.

There is no *league* in *legacy.* The *leg-* in this word is pronounced like your *leg*. Dictionaries do not recognize the beastly mispronunciation LEE-guh-see.

leisure LEE-zhur. Also, LEZH-ur. Don't say LAY-zhur.

The battle between the LEE-zhur sayers and the LEZH-ur sayers is one of the oldest in the language. Curiously, among the orthoepists, the feud has been settled (fairly amicably) for some time. Here is a compendium of historical commentary on LEE- vs. LEZH-.

John Walker (1791): "*Leisure* is sometimes pronounced as rhyming with *pleasure;* but, in my opinion, very improperly; for if it be allowed that custom is equally divided, we ought, in this case, to pronounce the diphthong long, as more expressive of the idea annexed to it."

Joseph Emerson Worcester (1860), who prefers LEE-zhur, notes that most authorities from Walker's day to his, including Noah Webster (1828), also prefer LEE-. However, he quotes Benjamin Humphrey Smart (1836), who says that between LEE-zhur and LEZH-ur "there is little, in point of good usage, to choose."

Alfred Ayres (1894) declares, presumably with a loud harrumph, that LEE-zhur "is the only way of pronouncing this word that nowadays is admissible in this country. In England, however, [LEZH-ur] is common, although sanctioned by only one modern orthoepist."

Vizetelly (1929) says LEE-zhur "indicates American usage and former British usage," and LEZH-ur "represents modern English usage." H. W. Fowler (1926) and *Webster 2* (1934) corroborate this, both noting that LEE-zhur is rare in British speech. And Kenyon & Knott, in their *Pronouncing Dictionary of American English* (1949), label LEZH-ur "less frequent."

Since then American dictionaries have given priority to LEE-zhur but continued to list LEZH-ur in deference to our English cousins and to the minority of Americans who prefer this pronunciation. The current state of affairs is perhaps best expressed by the *Oxford Guide* (1983), a British source, which remarks rather derisively that in British speech *leisure* rhymes with *pleasure,* but in American speech with *seizure.* Apparently, the British know that free time is serious business on this side of the Atlantic, no matter what you call it. (Just don't call it LAY-zhur, please! That's beastly.) See **lever, measure, pleasure.**

length LENGKTH. Do not say LENTH or LAYNTH. See **strength.**

lethargy LETH-ur-jee. Do not say luh-THAR-jee.

The noun *lethargy* is accented on the first syllable, the adjective *lethargic* on the second.

lever LEV-ur (rhymes with *clever*) or LEE-vur (rhymes with *cleaver*).

According to Morris & Morris (1985), "British pronunciation of this word has always used the long 'e.' . . . American pronunciation has long favored the short 'e' and today all American dictionaries indicate that [LEV-ur] is more widely used than [LEE-vur]. However, though [LEE-vur] may sound affected, it is still acceptable."

This assessment is generally accurate, but a bit too cut-and-dried. LEV-ur and LEE-vur have coexisted in educated American speech for at least two hundred years. Vizetelly (1929) explains that LEV-ur "indicates American usage, first noted by [Noah] Webster (1828)," and LEE-vur "indicates

British usage" since at least the mid-1700s (when the word was often spelled *leaver*). The leading American authorities in the hundred-odd years after Webster were divided. Worcester (1860), *Webster's New International* (1909), and *Webster 2* (1934) gave priority to LEE-vur; Funk & Wagnalls *Standard* (1897) and the *Century* (1889–1914) gave priority to LEV-ur. Not until 1940–1960 did LEV-ur emerge as the dominant American pronunciation. The British continue to favor LEE-vur.

Today both pronunciations are still equally acceptable. Authorities agree, however, that LEV-ur is more common everywhere but in the South, where, as Kenyon & Knott (1949) observe, LEE-vur is preferred by many cultivated speakers.

liaison LEE-uh-ZAHN, lee-AY-zahn, **LEE**-ay-ZAHN.

Of the many and sometimes strange ways of saying this word, the three listed above are the ones countenanced by the most current authorities. Evidence indicates that the first two pronunciations are, for the time being, the dominant ones in American speech. **LEE**-uh-ZAHN is the preference of Lass & Lass (1976) and listed first in *WNW Guide* (1984), Barnhart (1988), and *M-W 10* (1993). Lee-AY-zahn is listed first in *WNW 3* (1997) and second in *WNW Guide*, Barnhart, *American Heritage 3* (1992), and *M-W 10*. **LEE**-ay-ZAHN is my preference, and listed first in *American Heritage 3*. According to Burchfield (1996), the British favor lee-AY-z̲u̲n, which is listed first in *RHWC* (1997), and lee-AY-zahn.

Burchfield also notes that "William Safire made fun of the pronunciation of the word by President Reagan and others as [LAY-uh-zahn]." It's true: LAY- for the first syllable is a ridiculous and beastly mispronunciation, and I am grateful that *M-W 10* labels the LAY- variant with an obelus [÷] to indicate that many speakers find it objectionable. Also to be avoided is the bizarre -ZOHN (like *zone*) for the final syllable, which only *WNW 3* recognizes. Some authorities still list the Frenchified LEE-ay-ZAW(N), but this pronunciation is now passé and should be jettisoned in favor of one of the anglicized variants sanctioned above. See **foyer, lingerie, penchant**.

library LY-brer-ee.

Don't say LY-ber-ee, as if the word were spelled *liberry*. There is no *berry* in *library*.

The mispronunciation LY-ber-ee, according to *M-W 9* (1985) and *10* (1993), is heard "from educated speakers, including college presidents and professors, as well as with somewhat greater frequency from less educated speakers." That is the kind of insidious factoid that makes one view what little usage advice today's dictionaries dispense with a skeptical and cynical eye. If a few college presidents and professors say LY-ber-ee, does that somehow make it less beastly? Are these anomalous academics paragons of elocution? Should we now emulate them and their bedfellows in beastliness, the "less educated speakers"?

I have been involved in public library advocacy in San Diego since 1988 and have served on that city's Board of Library Commissioners since 1993. Consequently, I have spent countless hours discussing library issues, campaigning for libraries, attending city council meetings, appearing on radio talk shows, and listening to the testimony of hundreds of people from all walks of life, and in all that time and all that talk I could count on my ten fingers the number of people — educated and not-so-well educated — I have heard who said LY-ber-ee. The fact is, most children in literate homes are admonished at an early age not to say LY-ber-ee, in the same way they are admonished not to say *puhsketty* for *spaghetti*, *cinnamon* for *synonym*, or *pacific* for *specific*. Let's be honest here: in anyone older than twelve, LY-ber-ee is certain evidence of sloppy speech habits and inadequate education.

I don't doubt that Merriam-Webster's files, as they assert, contain LY-ber-ee citations from educated speakers. But when an educated person says LY-ber-ee the plain truth is that he or she loses credibility in others' eyes (or ears, as it were). Some well-educated people do speak poorly, but they are generally exceptions, and most of their mistakes involve difficult rather than common words. If your college professor, or your child's professor, said LY-ber-ee — or *perfessor*, for that matter — wouldn't you raise a concerned eyebrow? The note in *Random House II* (1987) and *RHWC* (1997) seems closer to the truth: "[LY-ber-ee] is more likely to be heard from less educated or very young speakers and is often criticized."

The variant LY-bruh-ree, though chiefly British, is also standard in American speech. Properly, *library* should have three syllables, but a two-syllable variant, LY-bree, occurs in educated speech and is listed in good standing in some current dictionaries. See **arctic, February, nuclear.**

liege LEEJ. Do not say LEEZH.

The *g* in *liege* should have the sound of *g* in *page*. The variant LEEZH, with a Frenchified *g*, is an affectation. It appears in *Webster 3* (1961), labeled *sometimes*, and as an unlabeled alternative in *Random House II* (1987) and its most recent abridgment, *RHWC* (1997). Other dictionaries do not sanction it, however, and no pronunciation maven with a reputation to lose would either. See **siege.**

lien LEEN (rhymes with *seen*).

"The British puzzle over this more than we do," says Holt (1937). "By analogy with *mien*, we customarily pronounce it 'leen,' though Webster [1934] joins OED [1928] in approval of 'lee'en.'" Since the 1940s American authorities have favored the monosyllabic LEEN, and the two-syllable pronunciation, although still often listed, is now rare. The usual pronunciation in England remains LEE-in, says *OED 2* (1989).

lieutenant (American always) loo-TEN-int; (British) lef-TEN-int.

See the discussion of Noah Webster under **aunt**.

lilac LY-l<u>a</u>k or LY-lak. Don't say LY-lahk.

There is no *lock* in *lilac,* or at least there shouldn't be. It's an affectation. From John Walker (1791), Noah Webster (1828), and Walt Whitman — "When Lilacs Last in the Dooryard Bloom'd" (1866) — to the *Century* (1914), *Webster 2* (1934), and *American College* (1952), there were two acceptable pronunciations of this word in cultivated speech: LY-l<u>a</u>k, with a "mute" or "obscure" *a* whose sound falls somewhere between the *i* of *lick* and the *u* of *luck,* and LY-lak, second syllable like *lack.* The *lock* variant sprang up sometime toward the end of the 19th century and, despite the disapproval of Ayres (1894), Phyfe (1926), Holt (1937), Opdycke (1939), and other orthoepists, it hung on like a hardy weed until it finally achieved recognition in *Webster 3* (1961), which listed it third. With that nourishment, it grew more quickly. *RH College* (1968) and *AHNC* (1969) list it second, and *M-W 10* (1993) is the first dictionary to give it priority. The other three major current American dictionaries, however, list LY-l<u>a</u>k first. Lass & Lass (1976) prefer -lak, the *NBC Handbook* (1984) and I prefer -l<u>a</u>k, and Barnhart (1998) sanctions LY-l<u>a</u>k and LY-lak. Take your pick.

lingerie Properly, but rarely, lan-zh<u>e</u>-REE or LAN-zh<u>e</u>-ree (first syllable as in *land*). Also acceptable, but less frequent, lahn-zh<u>e</u>-REE or LAHN-zh<u>e</u>-ree. Popularly, and erroneously, lahn-zh<u>e</u>-RAY, LAHN-zh<u>e</u>-ray, lahn-j<u>e</u>-RAY, or LAHN-j<u>e</u>-ray.

Lingerie, which came into English from French in the 19th century, has been so mangled by English speakers that it is now almost impossible to pronounce it correctly and be understood. Words taken into English from other languages that occur frequently in speech soon become anglicized in pronunciation. This is natural and appropriate. With *lingerie,* however, the process of anglicization has backfired and resulted in an inept and ludicrous imitation of the original French. The pronunciations popular today bear no resemblance to the French, nor do they sound English. It would be kind but inaccurate to call them anglicizations. They are best described as "manglicizations."

The French is la(n)zh-REE, and until about 1940 it was the only pronunciation countenanced in cultivated speech. *Webster 2* (1934) prefers la(n)zh-REE but notes that the word is popularly pronounced LAHN-zh<u>e</u>-ree. Kenyon & Knott (1949) prefer LAN-zh<u>e</u>-ree; *American College* (1952), however, puts lahn-zh<u>e</u>-RAY first and LAN-zh<u>e</u>-ree second. Finally, *Webster 3* (1961) covers all the bases by placing lahn-j<u>e</u>-RAY at the head of a long series of variants followed by the admonition that vowels other than short *a* (as in *land*) in the first syllable and long *e* (as in *reed*) in the last syllable are regarded by many as substandard. So who said a dictionary was the place to go for a little straightforward advice?

In the 1959 film *Anatomy of a Murder,* in which a certain pair of panties figures prominently as evidence in a trial, Jimmy Stewart and George C. Scott both say lahn-zhe-ree, their stress varying from the first to third syllables. This variant, recorded in *Webster 2* as the "popular" pronunciation, appears in most current dictionaries and Morris & Morris (1985) and Barnhart (1988) prefer it (with stress on the last syllable). Though it is a hybrid, it is preferable to the variants ending in -RAY because it at least properly anglicizes the final vowels -*ie* to conform with *reverie, coterie, bourgeoisie, jalousie,* and other analogous loanwords from French.

My preferred pronunciations, lan-zhe-REE and LAN-zhe-ree, are the most faithful to the original vowel sounds of the French. They are still listed in several current dictionaries and favored by Lass & Lass (1976), who prefer lan-zhe-REE, and the *NBC Handbook* (1984), which prefers LAN-zhe-ree. Unfortunately, these pronunciations are now incomprehensible to most Americans. I offer them here, not with any false hope that they will catch on, only to bring to light a bit of bungled pretentiousness that somehow became the norm.

The funny thing about all this confusion is that *lingerie,* when you think about it, is a pretty silly word — a euphemism we have adopted to make something intimate and titillating sound innocuous at social gatherings and over department store loudspeakers. In *Anatomy of a Murder,* the judge asks counselors Stewart and Scott if there is an Anglo-Saxon word they can use in place of *lingerie* to make the testimony clearer and more specific. When Stewart slyly suggests *panties,* the jury snickers, but the judge, realizing that panties are precisely what they are talking about, prudently lectures the jurors to keep their prurient connotations out of his courtroom. Since blank or puzzled faces usually meet my attempts to pronounce *lingerie* properly, and since I cannot bring myself to "manglicize" the word, these days, whenever I am about to utter it I say "women's underwear" instead — a plain English phrase that gets the point across just fine. See **Parisian.**

Linnaean li-NEE-in, not li-NAY-in.

Carolus Linnaeus (KAR-uh-lus li-NEE-us), 1707–1778, was a Swedish botanist who developed the binomial system of scientific nomenclature (genus, species, and all that). In his name, and in the adjective *Linnaean,* the stress falls on the second syllable, in which the ligature *ae* is properly pronounced like the long *e* in *need.* The alternative spelling *Linnean* is pronounced the same way.

liqueur li-KUR.

This is the traditional American pronunciation, the preference of modern authorities, and the first pronunciation listed in all four major current American dictionaries. The variant li-KYUR (-KYUR rhyming with *sir*) is originally (and still) British, and the variant li-KYOOR (-KYOOR rhyming with *poor*), now often heard, is an affected overpronunciation that dictionaries do not recognize. See **amateur, connoisseur, de rigueur, entrepreneur, restaurateur, voyeur.**

lissome LIS-um (rhymes with *miss 'em*).

lithe LY<u>TH</u> (<u>TH</u> as in *then*), not LYTH (TH as in *path*).
Lithe should rhyme with *writhe.* See **blithe, loath.**

litigious li-TIJ-us (rhymes with *religious*).
Litigious is often mispronounced li-TEE-jus or li-TIJ-ee-us. There is no *tea* in *litigious* and the word should have three, not four, syllables. Occasionally I have even heard (arrgh!) LIT-uh-gus, evidence that the mis-speaker discovered the word in print but never checked the pronunciation in a dictionary or heard it pronounced correctly.

litotes LY-tuh-teez (LY- like *lie*), not ly-TOH-teez.
The weight of authority, past and present, heavily favors LY-tuh-teez. Among those preferring it are Worcester (1860), Phyfe (1926), Fowler (1926), Kenyon & Knott (1949), *WNW 2* (1984), the *NBC Handbook* (1984), Barnhart (1988), *OED 1* (1928) and *2* (1989), and Jones (1991). It is the first pronunciation listed in *Webster 2* (1934), *American College* (1952), *Random House II* (1987), and numerous other sources including all four major current American dictionaries.

An alternative pronunciation, LIT-uh-teez (LIT- as in *little*), preferred by Funk & Wagnalls *Standard* (1897) and the *Century* (1914) and listed second in *Webster 2,* has coexisted with LY-tuh-teez in good standing for over a hundred years. No modern authority prefers it, however. A third variant, ly-TOH-teez, which shifts the accent to the second syllable, first appeared in *Webster 3* (1961) and is listed third in current American dictionaries. Burchfield (1996), a New Zealander who edited *OED 2,* says that in his teaching he and his colleagues always pronounced *litotes* "with a short initial /-ɪ-/ and with the main stress on the second syllable": li-TOH-teez. With all due respect for this formidable scholar, his preferred variant, which does not appear in any of my other sources, strikes me as an academic eccentricity. For further comment on *litotes,* see **apotheosis.**

-lived See **long-lived, short-lived.**

loath LOH<u>TH</u> (rhymes with *both*). Do not say LOH<u>TH</u> (<u>TH</u> as in *bathe*).
Many experienced speakers — the TV journalist and documentarian Bill Moyers, for example — fail to make the proper distinction in pronunciation between the verb to *loathe,* to detest, and the adjective *loath,* unwilling. They say *loathe* (rhymes with *clothe*) when they mean *loath* (rhymes with *both*).

This regrettably common beastly mispronunciation sometimes is reflected in print. Here is *Elle* magazine as quoted in an ad for Cristina García's novel *The Agüero Sisters* that appeared in *The New York Times Book Review:* "A rich, velvety world one is loathe to leave." Make that *loath,* reluctant, as in "I am loath to read *Elle* magazine because I loathe it." "Today," writes Michiko Kakutani in *The New York Times Magazine*, "we are loathe to condemn anyone or anything for fear of being labeled ourselves as judgmental or politically incorrect."* That sentence, you may imagine, filled me with fear and loathing. But I'm not afraid of labels, nor loath to condemn, and I hereby vociferously denounce, as both grammatically and phonologically incorrect, the use of the verb *loathe* when the adjective *loath* is meant.

The verb to *loathe*, because it has an *e* at the end, is pronounced with the "voiced" *th* of *bathe, clothe, lathe, seethe, tithe,* and *breathe*. The adjective *loath* has no final *e* and so should be pronounced with a "voiceless" *th* like *both, quoth, cloth, broth,* and *growth*. (The alternative spelling *loth,* common in the 19th century but now old-fashioned, better illustrates the proper pronunciation.) "When **th** is final," explains *Webster 2* (1934), "it is usually voiceless [with a few exceptions, such as *smooth* and the verb to *bequeath*]; when final and voiced, it is usually spelled -**the**."

I don't think the verb to *loathe* is ever mispronounced or misspelled, but the adjective *loath* is so often mispronounced like the verb *loathe* that the voiced *th* pronunciation of *loathe* for *loath* is recognized by all four current American dictionaries, and several of the Merriam-Webster dictionaries — *Webster 3* (1961) and *M-W 8* (1975), *9* (1985), and *10* (1993) — take the abominable liberty of listing the misspelling *loathe* for *loath* as an acceptable variant. It never ceases to amaze me how our lexicographers are never *loath* to embrace the latest solecism, affectation, or fad. Is there no such thing as a mistake? It's enough to make a language lover loony!

The distinction in pronunciation and spelling between *loath* and *loathe* is both traditional and useful, and it would be a shame to forfeit it out of sheer ignorance and carelessness. Dictionaries may now countenance the mispronunciation — and in Merriam-Webster's case, the misspelling — of *loathe* for *loath,* but good speakers, writers, editors, teachers, and scholars of the language most emphatically do not. *The New York Times Manual of Style and Usage* (1976) prescribes "**loath** (unwilling), **loathe** (to hate)." "Note the spellings," admonishes J. N. Hook, a professor of English emeritus and former director of the National Council of Teachers of English, in *The Appropriate Word* (1990). In *loath,* he says, "the *th* is pronounced as in *thin,*" in *loathe,* "the *th* as in *this.*" Shaw (1972), Lass & Lass (1976), the *NBC Handbook* (1984), *WNW Guide* (1984), and Barnhart (1988) all uphold the distinction in pronunciation and spelling, and R. W. Burchfield (1996), editor of the monumental second edition of the *OED* (1989), asserts that

---

* December 7, 1997, p. 38.

loath "is to be carefully distinguished from the verb *loathe*... which, apart from its different spelling, has a fully voiced *th*."

For anyone having trouble keeping the words apart, Shaw suggests this sentence as a mnemonic device: "A kind person, Jack was *loath* to say that he *loathed* the foreman." See **bequeath, blithe,** and, for more on mispronunciations affecting spelling, **entrepreneur** and **minuscule.**

loathe See **loath.**

loathsome LOH<u>TH</u>-s<u>u</u>m, not LOHTH-s<u>u</u>m.

Loathsome should be pronounced like the verb to *loathe* (LOH<u>TH</u>) plus *some,* but spelled without the final *e* of *loathe.* Not surprisingly, the misspelling *loathesome,* with a spurious medial *e,* which better reflects the proper pronunciation, is as common as the mispronunciation LOHTH-s<u>u</u>m, which better reflects the proper spelling *loathsome.* See **loath.**

longevity lahn-JEV-<u>i</u>-tee or lawn-JEV-<u>i</u>-tee.

Remember: there is no *long* in *longevity.* Do not say lahng- or lawng-JEV-<u>i</u>-tee, or lahng- or lawng-GEV-<u>i</u>-tee. The first syllable, *lon-,* may be pronounced to rhyme with *on* or *lawn.* The *g* is soft, as in *gem* and *gel.*

long-lived LAWNG-LYVD, not LAWNG-LIVD.

The *i* in *long-lived* is properly long, as in *alive.*

WNW Guide (1984) says the pronunciation LIVD for *-lived* "stems from the notion that the form (as in *long-lived*) comes from the verb *live,* but it is formed from the noun *life* plus the suffix *-ed.*" Hence, the pronunciation LYVD (rhymes with *arrived*), which is listed first in *American Heritage 3* (1992), *WNW 3* (1997), and *RHWC* (1997) and preferred by Lass & Lass (1976), the *NBC Handbook* (1984), and Morris & Morris (1985), who echo *WNW Guide* with this advice:

> Two of the most common mispronunciations heard on the air and in the speech of average and otherwise literate Americans are *long-lived* and *short-lived* pronounced with the short "i" of the verb "live." Both words should be pronounced with a long "i," as heard in the noun "life." Why? Simply because the adjectives are formed from the noun "life," not from the verb "live."

Want a mnemonic device to help you get it right? Think of the *-lived* part as meaning *of life.* Thus, *long-lived* means long-of-life, and *short-lived* means short-of-life.

The popular but erroneous LAWNG-LIVD (with the short *i* of the verb to *live*) has been disparaged in pronunciation guides for most of the 20th century. According to *Webster 2* (1934), it is a British import. This is corroborated by the *Oxford Guide* (1983), a British authority, which says "originally rhyming with *arrived,* but now usually like past tense *lived.*" Two other British authorities, Jones (1991) and Burchfield (1996), also give the short *i* as the usual British pronunciation. Thus it may be asserted that the true-blue American pronounces *long-lived* and *short-lived* to rhyme with *revived*, while the Benedict Arnold turncoat uses the short *i* of *give*.

Louisville (Kentucky) Locally, LOO-uh-vul. Generally, LOO-ee-vil.

luxury LUHK-shuh-ree (LUHK- like *luck*) or LUHG-zhuh-ree (LUHG- like *lug*).

Despite the persistent criticism of some, the LUHG- pronunciation is perfectly acceptable. I have used it all my life, which of course makes it permissible automatically. But some of you may need more persuasive evidence, so here you are:

The LUHG- in *luxury* definitely dates back to the 19th century and possibly to the time of the venerated English elocutionist John Walker (1791). Walker made quite a fuss about the sound of the *x* in *luxury* and *luxurious,* arguing that because the accent fell before the *x* in *luxury* and after the *x* in *luxurious,* "the words ought to be pronounced *luckshury* and *lugzurious.*" For many in the 19th century, Walker's *Critical Pronouncing Dictionary* was second in authority only to the Bible, and most subsequent orthoepists echoed this pronouncement.

Vizetelly (1929), however, noted that the *Imperial Dictionary* (1882) prefers LUHG-zyoo-ree, and Phyfe (1926) remarked that LUHG-zuur-ee has "the sanction of eminent authorities." After *OED 1* (1928) countenanced LUHG-zhuu-ree, the respectability of LUHG- was assured. Kenyon & Knott (1949) recognized LUHG-zhuh-ree, calling it "much less frequent," but by the 1960s it was in all the dictionaries, as it is today. *American Heritage 3* (1992) lists it first, and the *NBC Handbook* (1984) prefers it.

As various authorities point out, LUHG-zhuh-ree is the result of analogy with *luxurious,* for which the traditional pronunciation is luhg-ZHUUR-ee-us. Likewise, the alternative pronunciation luhk-ZHUUR-ee-us for *luxurious* — preferred by Morris & Morris (1985) and used by many educated speakers — has come about from analogy with the traditional LUHK-shuh-ree pronunciation of *luxury.*

lysine LY-seen.

Lately I have heard several speakers mispronounce the name of this amino acid. One reporter on National Public Radio said ly-ZEEN, doubly distorting the word by giving the *s* the sound of *z* and shifting the accent to the second syllable. There is no authority for this eccentric variant. Some sources — including *Webster 2* (1934), *Mosby's Medical* (1990), *American Heritage 3* (1992), and *RHWC* (1997) — sanction the alternative pronunciation LY-sin, which I have never heard. (Have you?) The careful speaker would be wise to stick with LY-seen, which is the first pronunciation in the sources just cited and the only pronunciation in *Webster 3* (1961), *Taber's Medical* (1970), *Stedman's Medical* (1972), *OED 2* (1989), *M-W 10* (1993), and *WNW 3* (1997).

M

macerate MAS-ur-ayt (MAS- rhyming with *pass*).

Recently I heard a thirty-something Canadian doctor (a graduate of McGill in Montreal) pronounce the adjective *macerated* as **MAY**-sur-**AY**-ted, an eccentricity for which there is no authority.

machination MAK-i-**NAY**-shin. Do not say MASH-i-**NAY**-shin.

Properly, there is no *mash* in *machination*. The *ch* should be pronounced like *k*, as in *Machiavelli*, not as in *machine*.

This word entered English in the 15th century. From the time that dictionaries began indicating pronunciation in the 18th century until the 20th century, authorities countenanced only one pronunciation: MAK-i-**NAY**-shin. The MASH- variant arose sometime in the mid–20th century, based on false analogy with *machine,* a word that Walker (1791) notes is exceptional for preserving the French -sheen for -*chine. Webster 3* (1961) was the first to recognize MASH-i-**NAY**-shin, but the variant appeared preceded by that dictionary's infamous Obelus of Opprobrium, an esoteric mark [÷] used to indicate a controversial pronunciation, one that occurs in educated speech but that many find unacceptable. (The reader of this book, who presumably wishes to speak well and avoid pronunciations that other good speakers find objectionable, may safely assume that any pronunciation in a Merriam-Webster dictionary that is labeled with an obelus [÷] is best avoided.) The lure of the false analogy with *machine* was irresistible for many, however, and the MASH- variant has since proliferated. It now appears after the traditional pronunciation in three of the four

---

a = at / a̲ = final / ah = spa / ahr = car / air = fair / ay = hay / aw = saw
ch = chip / e = let / e̲ = item / ee = see / eer = deer / i = sit / i̲ = April
ng = sing / o̲ = carrot / oh = go / oo = soon / or = for / oor = poor
ow = cow / oy = toy / sh = she / th = thin / t̲h̲ = this / u̲ = focus / uh = up
ur = turn / uu = pull, took / y, eye = by, I / zh = measure / (see full key, p. xiv)

---

major current American dictionaries. However, *WNW 3* (1997) sanctions only MAK-i-**NAY**-shin, which is preferred by Lass & Lass (1976), *WNW Guide* (1984), the *NBC Handbook* (1984), *Everyday Reader's* (1985), and Burchfield (1996). Careful speakers should make an extra effort to hold the line on this word.

Magdalen (college at Oxford); **Magdalene** (college at Cambridge)
   MAWD-lin (like *maudlin*). See **Cholmondeley**.

magi MAY-jy (rhymes with *say bye*).
   Occasionally one hears the pronunciation MAJ-eye (MAJ- rhyming with *badge*), which — with the sole exception of *Webster 3* (1961), which labels it infrequent — dictionaries do not recognize and no authority I know of sanctions. *Magi* is the plural of *magus* (MAY-gus).

maintenance MAYN-tuh-nints, not MAYNT-nints.
   Pronounce the word in three syllables, not two. Also, be sure to place the stress on *main-*. The variant mayn-TAYN-ints is beastly. There is no *maintain* in *maintenance*.

malaise ma-LAYZ or muh-LAYZ.
   The Frenchified variant ma-LEZ is sometimes listed but not recommended. The *a* in the first syllable may be short as in *mat* or obscure as in *machine* or *malign* (muh-LYN). The stress is on the second syllable, *-laise*, not the first. I once heard a prominent epidemiologist say MAL-ayz, a pronunciation for which there is no authority.

maleficent muh-LEF-uh-sint.
   In Disney's animated film *Sleeping Beauty* (1958) one hears the name of the evil witch *Maleficent* mispronounced muh-LIF-uh-sint. The careful speaker is advised not to repeat this cartoonish mistake. There is no *-lif-* in *maleficent*. It's *-lef-*, as in *left* — connoting *sinister*, which means literally "on the left" or "lefthanded." See **beneficent**.

malpractice mal-PRAK-tis. Do not say MAL-prak-tis.
   Malpractice, with the accent on the second syllable, is the failure of a professional person to render competent services. MAL-prak-tis, with the accent on the first syllable, is the failure of any person to render the pronunciation of this word properly. Authorities do not countenance first-syllable stress. Those guilty of misplacing the accent are hereby advised to secure stress-related mal-PRAK-tis in-SHUUR-ints immediately.

Maori MOW-ree.
   Some authorities also countenance MAH-oh-ree (which, said rapidly, becomes MOW-ree). Only one source, *WNW 3* (1997), recognizes may-OR-ee, labeling it infrequent. It is best avoided.

maraschino MAR-uh-**SKEE**-noh, not MAR-uh-**SHEE**-noh.
   Maraschino is a loanword from Italian. In Italian, the consonant blend *sch* is pronounced like *sk*, as in the musical term *scherzo* (SKAIRT-soh), and

this sound is properly retained in the pronunciation of *maraschino*. "The common pronunciation MAR uh **SHEE** noh," says *WNW Guide* (1984), "apparently arose from a misreading of Italian *sch* as the German cluster pronounced *sh*." The -**SHEE**- was first recognized by *Webster 3* (1961). No authority I know of prefers it, and current dictionaries all list MAR-uh-**SKEE**-noh first.

margarine MAR-juh-rin.

While browsing in my dictionaries one day I was astonished to discover that *margarine* has not always been pronounced the way I have always heard it: MAR-juh-rin. My older sources countenance three variants: MAR-guh-rin, with a hard *g* (as in *gum*); MAR-guh-reen, with a hard *g* and -een (rhymes with *bean*) for the last syllable; and MAR-juh-reen.

Authorities from Evans (1959) to Burchfield (1996) agree unequivocally that the *g* is now soft, like *j*, but some current dictionaries still list the variant MAR-juh-reen. I say no way. The hard *g* (as in *go*) and -reen for the final syllable are as antique and whimsical as the 150 varieties of apple peelers patented in the 19th century. Today it's MAR-juh-rin, period. If you don't like it, eat butter.

marital MAR-i-tul. In Britain, formerly also, but now rarely, muh-RY-tul.

Márquez, Gabriel García MAHR-kez, GAH-bree-**EL** gahr-SEE-uh.

Most people have no trouble pronouncing *Gabriel* with the Spanish open *a* (-ah as in *spa*) and stress on the final syllable. *García* also presents no problem; it is a familiar name and the accented *í* directs our stress. But many speakers misplace the stress in this Nobel Prize–winning novelist's last name. Note the accent over the *a* in *Márquez* and take care to observe it: MAHR-kez.

marquis MAHR-kwis. Now usually mahr-KEE.

Marquis denotes a nobleman below a duke and above an earl or count. The alternative spelling *marquess* is the official one in England, where it is officially pronounced MAHR-kwis. American usage prefers *marquis*, the French spelling, and American authorities favor the traditional anglicized pronunciation MAHR-kwis; Lass & Lass (1976) and the *NBC Handbook* (1984) prefer it, and Barnhart (1988) and all four leading current American dictionaries list it first. Current dictionaries, however, also countenance the Frenchified mahr-KEE, which the evidence of my ears tells me is far and away the dominant pronunciation in the U.S.

Nevertheless, to distinguish *marquis* from the word *marquee* (mahr-KEE), which refers to the rooflike projection over the entrance to a movie theater on which titles or names are displayed, I recommend MAHR-kwis. Thus, if you get into an argument about pronunciation and it escalates into a fight, at least you can agree to battle it out according to the Marquis of Queensberry (or Marquess of Queensberry) rules for boxing, and pronounce it MAHR-kwis regardless of how you choose to spell it. (These rules, by the way, were developed in 1867 and supervised by the eighth Marquis/Marquess of Queensberry, Sir John Sholto Douglas; they stipulated the use of gloves instead of bare knuckles, the division of a match into rounds, and the ten-second count for knockdowns.) Simply put your names on a *marquee* (mahr-KEE), put up your dukes (an odd idiom, considering who made the rules), and may the best MAHR-kwis win.

Now, here's where it gets confusing: the plural of *marquis* is *marquises,* the plural of *marquess* is *marquesses,* and both are pronounced MAHR-kwi-siz; however, *marquis* is also listed as a plural of *marquis,* and for this alternative spelling the pronunciations given are mahr-KEEZ and mahr-KEE (French). A woman holding the rank of *marquis* is called a *marquise* (mahr-KEEZ), and several women of this rank are *marquises* (mahr-KEEZ-iz or mahr-KEEZ).

Is there any rhyme or reason in this aristocratic mess? Not really. That's why we have democracy — and its offspring, bureaucracy, which everyone understands. But if Robin Leach ever comes knocking to invite you to fulfill your champagne wishes and caviar dreams, you can try this: call the man a MAHR-kwis *(marquis);* call the woman a mahr-KEEZ *(marquise);* call the men MAHR-kwi-siz *(marquises);* and call the women mahr-KEEZ-iz *(marquises).* That should get you by all right, unless these aristocrats speak French. Then you're on your own. (And don't ask me about the plural of *mongoose.*)

masonry MAYS'n-ree.

Masonry has three syllables. The four-syllable MAYS'n-er-ee is beastly.

mature muh-TUUR, muh-TOOR, muh-TYUUR, muh-TYOOR, or, now very often, muh-CHUUR or muh-CHOOR.

"The pronunciation is [muh-TYOOR]," says Opdycke (1939), "not [muh-TOOR] or [muh-CHOOR]." The phonetic scenery has changed since that pronouncement was made. The traditional pronunciation, still used by many cultivated speakers, is muh-TYOOR, with a long *u* or YOO sound, as in *cute* and *cure;* in many current sources this has been modified to muh-TYUUR (YUUR as in *Europe*). The pronunciations muh-TUUR (TUU as in *took*) and muh-TOOR (TOOR like *tour*) have been countenanced by authorities since the 1940s and listed first in most dictionaries since the 1960s. Perhaps the most commonly heard pronunciation today is muh-CHUUR (or muh-CHOOR), with the *ch* sound of *choose* replacing the *t,* as in *nature* and *picture.*

As Opdycke indicates, this pronunciation was heard in the first half of the 20th century but was considered unacceptable; it is still sometimes criticized, but unjustly in my opinion. It is entirely reasonable, and likely inevitable, for speakers to associate *mature* with the numerous other words ending in *-ture* that are pronounced -chuur: e.g., *feature, creature, furniture, manufacture, temperature, architecture, signature, literature,* and so on. That *mature* hasn't long since followed in this word family's footsteps probably is due only to its anomalous second-syllable stress.

I must confess that I am inconsistent with this word. Although I usually say either muh-TYOOR or muh-TYUUR, there is no denying that muh-CHUUR is calling me like a siren to abandon these traditional pronunciations, which are now on the wane. All four major current American dictionaries sanction muh-CHUUR, the *NBC Handbook* (1984) prefers it, and if it is not already the dominant pronunciation in American speech, there is no doubt it will be in the 21st century.

mausoleum MAW-suh-**LEE**-um (MAW- rhyming with *paw*).
There is no *mouse* in *mausoleum*. Dictionaries do not recognize the beastly mispronunciation MOW-suh-**LEE**-um (MOW- rhyming with *how*). Traditionally, the *s* in *mausoleum* is hard, as in *sassy,* but current dictionaries also countenance a soft *s,* as in *rose:* MAW-zuh-**LEE**-um.

mauve MOHV (rhymes with *stove*), not MAWV.
The variant MAWV (AW for *au* as in *Maude* and *gauze*) was first recorded in *Webster 3* (1961) as "appreciably less frequent." Today it is substantially more frequent, and two of the four major current American dictionaries now list it, with one putting it first. The other two dictionaries, however, along with *OED 2* (1989), countenance only MOHV, the traditional pronunciation, which is preferred by Lass & Lass (1976), the *NBC Handbook* (1984), Barnhart (1988), and Jones (1991).

mayonnaise **MAY**-uh-NAYZ or MAY-uh-**NAYZ**. Don't say MAY-nayz.
You may stress *mayonnaise* either on the first or last syllable, but take care to give the word three syllables. Don't drop the middle syllable and say MAY-nayz (or MAN-ayz, as my wife is wont to do, which of course drives me to distraction). Dictionaries do not recognize this two-syllable variant.

mayoral **MAY**-ur-ul. Do not say may-OR-ul.
In the 1980s the trendy variant may-OR-ul, which erroneously shifts the accent to the second syllable, came screaming like a banshee out of Pandora's Box of Extremely Beastly Mispronunciations and now seems to have the majority of educated American speakers by the throat. Younger speakers (those under the age of forty), following the bad example of many older boomers, are especially prone to use it. It is also rampant among newsreaders and news "analysts" on radio and TV, who deserve to have their mouths washed out with soap for disseminating this egregious affront to the language.

The truth is, may-OR-ul and its lowbrow pal, EE-lek-**TOR**-ul (for *electoral*), are nothing but vogue pronunciations, which — to borrow a phrase here from the venerable H. W. Fowler — are taken up merely for "the joy of showing that one has acquired them." I also suspect, especially in the case of the newsreaders, that they have been adopted because they are easier to say and sound more orotund than the proper pronunciations, MAY-ur-ul and ee-LEK-tur-ul.

Pronouncing something in a new or unusual way is not a sign of ready intelligence. It is a sign of ignorance, carelessness, pseudosophistication, or sycophancy — take your beastly pick. The pathetic faddishness of may-OR-ul is manifest in the historical evidence. Funk & Wagnalls *Standard* (1897), the *Century* (1914), *Webster 2* (1934), *Webster 3* (1961), and *Random House II* (1987) countenance only first-syllable stress for *mayoral*. By about 1980, second-syllable stress had burst on the scene. *WNW Guide* (1984), with its ear to the ground, noted that "may **AWR** ul, which is heard increasingly, is not yet considered standard." *WNW 3* (1988), getting the stress confused, said "often" **MAY**-OR-ul. And as the vogue peaked in the 1990s, *M-W 10* (1993) and *WNW 3* (1997) recognized may-OR-ul as a "standard" alternative. However, three other major current dictionaries — *OED 2* (1989), *American Heritage 3* (1992), and *RHWC* (1997) — do not find anything "standard" about it and countenance only MAY-ur-ul.

My fellow careful speakers, I implore you not to fall prey to this beastly mania for may-OR-ul. Come this phonetic election day, please vote no on second-syllable stress and pronounce *mayor* and *mayoral* with the accent on the first syllable, where it rightfully belongs. See **electoral, pastoral, pectoral**.

measure MEZH-ur. Do not say MAY-zhur.

Pronounce the *mea-* in *measure* like *me-* in *met* or *mesh*. See **leisure, pleasure**.

Medici (the) **MED-i-CHEE**.

One of your pronunciation maven's many diligent spies recently caught Sister Wendy, public television's winsome, wimpled art critic, pronouncing the name of this famed Italian family with the accent on the second syllable: me-DEE-chee. Sorry, sister, that's beastly. There is no authority for second-syllable stress. If the muse compels you to mimic the Italian, say **MED**-ee-CHEE or **MAY**-dee-CHEE, but you still must keep the primary accent on the *first* syllable.

medieval MEE-dee-**EE**-vul or MED-ee-**EE**-vul.

Medieval should be pronounced in four syllables. Some current dictionaries list the three-syllable variants mee-DEE-vul, med-EE-vul, and mid-EE-vul, which do not articulate the *i* in the second syllable. These relatively recent and unfortunately rather common corruptions are best avoided — especially mid-EE-vul, which manages also to mispronounce the first syllable. You may begin the word either with MEE- or MED-. The former, which is my preference, is the traditional American pronunciation; the latter is originally British.

memento muh-MEN-toh. Do not say moh-MEN-toh.

There is no *moment* in *memento*.

Memento is now so often misspelled *momento*, no doubt because of the prevalence and persistence of the beastly mispronunciation moh-MEN-toh, that three current dictionaries record *momento* as a variant spelling of the word. *M-W 10* (1993), quite irresponsibly I think, calls it simply a "*var of* MEMENTO," as if it were perfectly acceptable for you to use *momento* instead of *memento* if you feel so inclined. (I pity the poor high school or college student who, after consulting *M-W 10*, uses *momento* in a term paper.) *WNW 3* (1997) handles the situation more appropriately by noting that *memento* is an "*erroneous sp. of* MEMENTO." *RHWC* (1997) offers this helpful (but too cautiously worded) usage note: "MEMENTO is sometimes spelled MOMENTO. Though this spelling occurs frequently in edited writing, it is usually considered an error." And *American Heritage 3* (1992) handles the situation best, in my opinion, by not recognizing the erroneous spelling at all.

To its credit, *M-W 10* does at least label the mispronunciation moh-MEN-toh with its Obelus of Opprobrium, the symbol ÷, to indicate that it "is considered by some to be unacceptable." (I would argue by *many*.) *M-W 10* could have gone one better, however, by imitating the other three current American dictionaries noted above, which ignore the ignorant and odious moh-MEN-toh and countenance only muh-MEN-toh. What this adds up to, dear careful speaker, is that both the pronunciation moh-MEN-toh and the nonword *momento* are, in the lingo of the linguists and lexicographers, nonstandard, which in this book means beastly.

Memento, a remembrance, keepsake, comes from a Latin word meaning remember. If you remember that *memento* begins with the *mem-* of *memory* and *remember*, you should have no trouble pronouncing and spelling it properly.

The Latin phrase *memento mori* is pronounced muh-MEN-toh MOR-ee, as in classical Latin, or sometimes MOR-eye, in anglicized Latin.

For more on mispronunciation influencing spelling, see **entrepreneur, minuscule**.

memorabilia MEM-uh-ruh-**BIL**-ee-uh or MEM-uh-ruh-**BIL**-yuh.

American Heritage 3 (1992) and *RHWC* (1997) do not recognize the popular mispronunciation MEM-uh-ruh-**BEEL**-yuh (-**BEEL**- rhyming with *peel*), which is pseudo-Latin. The accented syllable in *memorabilia* (-bil-) is properly pronounced like *bill*. See **filial, familial, -philia**.

menstruation MEN-stroo-**AY**-shin, not men-STRAY-shin.

Terry Gross, host of *Fresh Air* on National Public Radio, told me she once was badgered mercilessly by a listener who claimed that the proper way to say this word is MIN-i-**STRAY**-shin. Dictionaries do not recognize this pronunciation, which is apparently a confusion of the words *menstrua-*

tion and *ministration*. However, a quick survey of the four major current American dictionaries reveals that men-STRAY-sh*in*, with three syllables instead of four, appears as an alternative in *M-W 10* (1993) and *RHWC* (1997) and is listed first in *WNW 3* (1997). If the listener was in fact saying men-STRAY-sh*in* (or min-STRAY-sh*in*) and Ms. Gross misheard it, does that mean the listener is right and Ms. Gross is wrong?

Capital *N*, long *o*. The proper pronunciations for *menstrual, menstruate,* and *menstruation* are MEN-stroo-*ul*, MEN-stroo-ayt, and MEN-stroo-AY-sh*in*, with -*stru*- clearly pronounced -stroo- (like *strew*). You should not slur over the -*stru*- and say MEN-str*ul*, MEN-strayt, and men-STRAY-sh*in*, cutting a syllable from each word. These clipped pronunciations did not appear in a dictionary until *Webster 3* (1961), where they were labeled unacceptable to many. Though the three dictionaries cited above recognize the clipped variants, modern authorities — including Lass & Lass (1976), the *NBC Handbook* (1984), *Everyday Reader's* (1985), and Jones (1991) — and nearly all other recent dictionaries — including Funk & Wagnalls *Standard* (1980), *OED 2* (1989), and *American Heritage 3* (1992) — countenance only the fully articulated -stroo- pronunciations. Why? Because that's the way most educated speakers pronounce these words, and because the slurred pronunciations are still unacceptable to many.

As for pronouncing *men*- like *min*-, it's beastly. (In case you're wondering, the *men*- in these words has nothing to do with men, but comes from the Latin *mensis,* month; the Latin plural *menses* [MEN-seez] is used in English as the formal, physiological term for menstruation.) Many women are administrators, but they do not *ministrate* (or *minstrate*), nor do they have *minstrel* cycles during which, as this pronunciation suggests, they leave their jobs and go around playing music. Let the minstrels be mincing, leave the ministrations to the ministers, and pronounce *menstrual, menstruate,* and *menstruation* as they are divided: men-stru-al, men-stru-ate, and men-stru-a-tion.

mental MENT'l.
In *mental* and *dental,* be sure to pronounce the *t* clearly. Do not say *mennal* and *dennal.* Also take care to pronounce the *t* in words incorporating *mental* (*fundamental, instrumental, sentimental, incremental, temperamental*) and *dental* (*accidental, incidental, occidental*). See **gentle, kindergarten, rental, ventilate**.

mentor MEN-tur (recommended) or MEN-tor.
Mentor, spelled with a capital *M,* refers to the friend and adviser of Odysseus in Greek mythology. Spelled with a lowercase *m,* it means any wise and trusted counselor.

Three of the four major current American dictionaries give priority to MEN-tor, and it could be argued that this is more proper for the name

(MEN-tor is the classical Greek pronunciation); however, this would necessitate making an awkward distinction between a Greek pronunciation for the name and an anglicized pronunciation for the English word that has developed from it. No speaker I know makes this distinction, but many use the Greek MEN-tor for both senses of the word. This can hardly be called wrong, for the pronunciation MEN-tor for both senses is recorded as far back as Worcester (1860), but it seems more sensible to accept the fully English MEN-tur, which is consistent with other English words ending in -or (*sculptor, factor, pastor, doctor, motor*) and which is preferred by most older authorities and by the *NBC Handbook* (1984). See **juror, predator, vendor.**

mercantile MUR-kun-TEEL or **MUR**-kun-TYL or, traditionally but infrequently, **MUR**-kun-TIL.

The pronunciation of the last syllable as -TEEL dates back to the mid-1800s but did not gain acceptance until the mid-1900s. Worcester (1860), who prefers **MUR**-kun-TIL, says, "This word is often incorrectly pronounced in this country [mur-KAN-til] and [**MUR**-kun-TEEL]; but these modes have no countenance from the orthoepists." Holt (1937) says, "Choose between 'till' (American) and 'tile' (British) — but no 'teel.'" And Opdycke (1939) says, "Don't make the last syllable rime with *steal*." In 1949 Kenyon & Knott recognized **MUR**-kun-TEEL as a less frequent but acceptable alternative, and in 1961 *Webster 3* gave it priority. Lass & Lass (1976) and the *NBC Handbook* (1984) prefer it, and three of the four major current American dictionaries list it first.

So what about -TYL and -TIL? Until the ascendancy of -TEEL it was a British vs. American thing. Today -TIL (my obstinate preference), favored only by Barnhart (1988), is obsolescent, and -TYL, long the British preference, has become the backup American pronunciation, preferred by *WNW Guide* (1984) and listed first in *WNW 3* (1997). For more on the American vs. British pronunciation of -*ile*, see **textile.**

merchandise (noun and verb) MUR-chin-DYZ, not **MUR**-chin-DYS.

Note the *z* sound in the last syllable, -*dise*, which should rhyme with *size*. Don't pronounce it like the word *dice*. The suffix -*ise*, which takes its spelling from French, is equivalent to the suffix -*ize*, which comes from Greek. In *advertise, compromise, enterprise, improvise, exercise, supervise,* and *merchandise,* -*ise* is properly pronounced like -*ize*.

meteorologist MEE-tee-ur-**AHL**-uh-jist.

Six syllables, please: *meteor* (MEE-tee-ur) + -*ologist* (-**AHL**-uh-jist). Don't slur the word, drop a syllable, and pronounce it as if it were a combination of *meter* + -*ologist*.

Morris & Morris (1985) note that one of the readers of their column "reported that the newscaster on a network 'flagship' station in New York

City introduced the weatherman as the staff mee-ter-OL-uh-jist and the meteorologist proceeded to top the earlier mispronunciation by predicting VAIR-uh-b'l (for 'variable') cloudiness. Such obvious mispronunciations can find no defenders" (p. 493).

miasma my-AZ-muh (like *my asthma*).

The pronunciation mee-AZ-muh is also acceptable; Funk & Wagnalls *Standard* (1897) gave it priority and authorities since have listed it as an alternative. The weight of authority, however, strongly favors my-AZ-muh. It is the first pronunciation in all four major current American dictionaries and the preference of Lass & Lass (1976), the *NBC Handbook* (1984), and Barnhart (1988). The plural is *miasmas* (my-AZ-muhz) or *miasmata* (my-AZ-muh-tuh).

Michelangelo MY-kul-AN-juh-loh.

How should we pronounce the *Michel-* in *Michelangelo?* Like *Michael*, or to rhyme with *nickel?*

Phyfe (1926), Opdycke (1939), *Webster 2* (1934), the *Columbia Encyclopedia* (1963), and the *NBC Handbook* (1984) prefer MY-kul-AN-juh-loh, as though the name were spelled *Michael Angelo* (which formerly it often was). The *Michael* pronunciation is also listed first in Kenyon & Knott (1949), *American College* (1952), *WNW Guide* (1984), *Random House II* (1987), and all four major current American dictionaries. *Webster 3* (1961) lists an adjective, *Michelangelesque,* for which it gives one pronunciation: MY-kul-AN-juh-LESK. Only McConkey (1986) prefers the pronunciation rhyming with *nickel.*

In the 1989 documentary *Michelangelo: A Self-Portrait,* directed by the Oscar-winning filmmaker Robert Snyder, the narrator twice says MIK-ul-AHN-yuh-loh and once MIK-ul-AHN-juh-loh. Both are apparently attempts at the Italian pronunciation, and both are inaccurate. The latter, with its slurred vowels and broad *a,* is bad Italian and affected English. The former renders the name as if it were spelled *Michelagnolo;* hence, the rolled *gn* sound of -AHN-yuh- as in *lasagna.* The Italian pronunciation, as transcribed by Kenyon & Knott and the *Columbia Encyclopedia,* is MEE-kay-LAHN-jay-loh. Funk & Wagnalls *Standard* (1897) and *Random House II* (1987) transcribe it as MEE-kel-AHN-je-loh. See **cognoscenti, Modigliani, seraglio**.

midwifery Traditionally, MID-wyf-ree or MID-wyf-ur-ee. Now usually mid-WIF-uh-ree or mid-WIF-ree. Sometimes mid-WYF-ree or mid-WYF-uh-ree.

Vizetelly (1929), who prefers MID-wyf-ree, notes that from 1775 to 1860, authorities both in England and America preferred the pronunciation MID-wif-ree. The English elocutionist John Walker (1791), for example, in prescribing the pronunciation MID-wif-ree, says, "Though the *i* is long in

Midwife, it is always short in its derivative *Midwifery*." Worcester (1860), who sides with Walker, cites eleven other authorities who also favor MID-wif-ree and only one who prefers MID-wyf-ree. Who was the one? That grumpy granddaddy of the American language, Noah Webster.

Webster, a son of the American Revolution, expended a great deal of energy trying to distinguish the English of America from the English of England in vocabulary, spelling, and pronunciation. His most famous work, you'll recall, is titled *An American Dictionary of the English Language* (1828). I wouldn't be at all surprised if he invented the pronunciation MID-wyf-ree himself and put it in his dictionary in the hope that Americans would abandon their sinful Anglophilic ways and adopt the long *i*, which, as authorities liked to say in those days, was "more agreeable to analogy."

If that indeed was Webster's stratagem, it worked — for quite a long while, at least. MID-wyf-ree or MID-wyf-uh-ree, with the long *i*, are preferred or listed first by Ayres (1894), Funk & Wagnalls *Standard* (1897), the *Century* (1889–1914), *Webster's Collegiate* (1917), Phyfe (1926), *Webster 2* (1934), Opdycke (1939), Kenyon & Knott (1949), the *Winston Dictionary* (1951), *American College* (1952), *Webster 3* (1961), *RH College* (1968), *AHNC* (1969), *M-W 7* (1972), *M-W 8* (1975), *WNW 2* (1984), and the *NBC Handbook* (1984). At that point Webster's spell wore off, authoritative preference for the long *i* dried up, and the Anglophilic pronunciation with short *i* returned in full force. It returned, however, in a slightly altered form, for while the Americans were dallying with Webster's MID-wyf-ree (-uh-ree), the restless Brits had taken Walker's MID-wif-ree and moved the accent forward: mid-WIF-ree or mid-WIF-uh-ree.

In contemporary British speech, says Burchfield (1996), *midwifery* is "now mostly pronounced as four syllables, [mid-WIF-uh-ree], but it is only relatively recently that the second syllable has settled down as [-WIF-]. . . . In AmE, usage is divided but [-WYF-] is commonly used for the second syllable." Not so commonly anymore, for all four major current American dictionaries list mid-WIF-uh-ree or mid-WIF-ree first.

The British may have lost the American Revolution, but it appears they have won the Battle of Midwifery. Noah Webster must be ranting in his grave.

milieu meel-YUU or mil-YUU.

Milieu's cluster of vowels makes it a particularly daunting word for English speakers to pronounce. Odd variations I have heard, some of which appear in recent dictionaries, include meel-YOO, MEEL-yoo, mil-YOO, MIL-yoo, mayl-YOO, and MAY-loo. All of these should be avoided, particularly the last, which is unutterably beastly.

Milieu comes from French and retains much of its foreign flavor in its pronunciation. The first syllable is pronounced meel-, like *meal,* or mil-, like the first syllable of *million.* The second syllable, which receives the accent, is pronounced like the *Eu-* in *Europe.* The plural may be spelled *milieus* or *milieux,* and may be pronounced like the singular or with a *z* sound at the end. I recommend the final *z* to distinguish the plural from the singular.

mineralogy   Properly, MIN-ur-**AL**-uh-jee, not MIN-ur-**AHL**-uh-jee.

"Be sure to pronounce the third syllable of this word *al* so that it will rhyme with *pal* and not with *doll,*" writes Gilmartin (1936).

For well over a century this word has been mispronounced as if it were spelled *minerology,* with *-ology* instead of *-alogy* at the end. Ayres (1894), Phyfe (1926), Holt (1937), and Opdycke (1939) frown upon the *-ology* mispronunciation, but as the popularity of the fallacious *-ology* analogy grew, lexicographers eventually recorded it as an acceptable alternative. (Kenyon & Knott (1949) and *American College* (1952) were the first to do so.) Today the beastly critter is listed first in three of the four leading American dictionaries — although it should be noted that the fourth, *WNW 3* (1997), sanctions only the traditional MIN-ur-**AL**-uh-jee. And at least two modern authorities, *WNW Guide* (1984) and *Everyday Reader's* (1985), have fallen into the miner-*ology* trap.

I can be lenient about some mispronunciations, especially when they predominate so thoroughly that the correct pronunciation sounds hopelessly old-fashioned or eccentric. But there are a number of words for which I cannot, in good conscience, make an exception, and this is one. There is absolutely no reasonable basis for tacking *-ology* on the end of a word created from *mineral* and *-logy,* the combining form meaning science or theory of (from Greek *logos,* word).

I urge you to be hard as a rock about the way you say *mineralogy* — and don't misspell it *-ology* either, please. Disregard those sources that countenance the *-ology* mispronunciation, and take your cue from Lass & Lass (1976), the *NBC Handbook* (1984), *OED 2* (1989), and *WNW 3* (1997), which prefer MIN-ur-**AL**-uh-jee. See **genealogy**.

Minotaur   MIN-uh-TOR.

Don't say **MIN**-uh-TOW-ur. There is no *tower* in *Minotaur.* Rhyme *Minotaur* with *win a war.*

minuscule   Properly, mi-NUHS-kyool. Now almost always **MIN**-uh-SKYOOL.

Don't say **MIN**-yuh-SKYOOL, as I once heard an astronomer eccentrically pronounce it on NPR's *Talk of the Nation.*

Minuscule comes from the Latin *minusculus* (mi-NUUS-kuu-luus), somewhat small. As an adjective it may mean very small, or written in small or lowercase letters; in this latter sense it is the opposite of *majuscule* (muh-JUHS-kyool), written in capital letters. As a noun it may mean a small letter or refer to a small, cursive style of ancient and medieval writing.

The pronunciation **MIN**-uh-SKYOOL is almost universally heard today, but dictionaries of the first half of the 20th century did not recognize it. Authorities of the 1920s and 1930s make no mention of it, so it must have caught on between 1940 and 1960, perhaps influenced by the pronunciation of its French counterpart, *minuscule,* in which the first syllable sounds like *me* and the primary accent falls on *-cule. Webster 3* (1961), the first of my sources to recognize it, lists it first, an indication of its popularity by then. Nearly all dictionaries since have followed suit — *WNW 2* (1984) and *WNW 3* (1988, 1997) are notable exceptions — and most authorities, including the *NBC Handbook* (1984), *Everyday Reader's* (1985), and Barnhart (1988), now prefer **MIN**-uh-SKYOOL. Burchfield (1996), who also favors **MIN**-uh-SKYOOL, says "until about the mid-20c. almost always [mi̯-NUHS-kyool]."

With the ascendancy of **MIN**-uh-SKYOOL came the inevitable misspelling of the word as *miniscule.* This misspelling is based on the assumption, reinforced by the popular pronunciation, that a word meaning "very small" must begin with the combining form *mini-,* small. Of course the assumption is false and illogical, because the function of *mini-* is to inform us that whatever follows is small or short — as in *minibus, minicomputer, mini-crisis, miniskirt* — and there is no *-scule* for *mini-* to minify.

Nevertheless, since the 1960s the misspelling *miniscule* has flourished, and today all four major American dictionaries list it, although their treatment of it differs considerably and is worth noting. The apathetic *M-W 10* (1993) calls it simply a *"var of* MINUSCULE." *WNW 3* (1997) — the only current dictionary that gives priority to the traditional mi̯-NUHS-kyool — shows some backbone by labeling it an *"erroneous sp. of* MINUSCULE," the implicit message being that "We can't ignore the frequency of this mistake in 'edited' writing, but why can't you folks out there get it right?" The more circumspect *RHWC* (1997) lists the variant and includes a usage note explaining that "MINUSCULE, from Latin *minus* meaning 'less,' has frequently come to be spelled MINISCULE, probably under the influence of the prefix *mini-* in the sense 'of a small size.' Though this spelling occurs frequently in edited writing, it is usually considered an error." Finally, *American Heritage 3* (1992), apparently "under the influence," as it were, does the utmost — both intentionally and unwittingly — to encourage the spelling confusion. First, like *M-W 10* it lists *miniscule,* calling it a variant of *minuscule.* Then it goes one better than *M-W 10* by presenting the erroneous variant as a legitimate alternative spelling in the entry for *minuscule.* Then it goes beyond the pale and actually uses the misspelling in definition 2: "Of, relating to, or written in miniscule [*sic*]."

Was this mistake a Freudian *lapsus calami* (LAP-s<u>u</u>s KAL-uh-my), slip of the pen? Do the lexicographers at American Heritage subconsciously favor *miniscule?* Could what appears to be an innocuous typo in fact be an instance of subliminal advertising, a devious attempt to encourage us to use the "alternative" spelling?

Careful speakers and careful spellers, I exhort you to stand fast. Don't let the apathetic editors at Merriam-Webster, or the circumspect editors at Random House, or the squiffy-eyed editors at American Heritage bamboozle you into believing that it's acceptable, or at worst a venial offense, to put a *mini-* in *minuscule*. However you choose to pronounce this one small word, it is no small matter how you choose to spell it. *Minuscule* is the only acceptable spelling, and only a dimbulb would intentionally write *miniscule*. Of course, if you pronounce it in the traditional manner, with the stress on the second syllable, it is almost impossible to misspell.

Incidentally, when I finished writing this discussion I thought it would be interesting to run my computer's spell checker — now listed in *RHWC* (1997) — through the entry and see what caught its electronic eye. And what do you think it did? It burped on *lapsus calami* and *squiffy* (a British colloquialism for "drunk") and a few other insignificant things, but it didn't bat a binary eyelash at a single misspelled *miniscule*. How about that? I guess that means my computer is a dimbulb, or perhaps there really is a conspiracy to overthrow King Minuscule after all.

For more on how mispronunciation influences spelling, see **Brobdingnagian, chaise longue, conservatism, daiquiri, doctoral, entrepreneur, loath, memento,** and **unequivocally**. For more on recessive stress — the shift of the accent toward the beginning of a word — see **acclimate, acumen, inculcate, infiltrate, obfuscate, precedence, promulgate, sonorous, vagaries,** and, for an overview of the subject, **confiscate**.

minutiae m<u>i</u>-N(Y)OO-shee-ee.

The *-ti-* is pronounced like *she*, as it properly also is in *negotiate, consortium,* and *propitiate*. The terminal *-ae* is properly pronounced like double *e* in *need*. *Minutiae* is plural; the singular is *minutia,* pronounced m<u>i</u>-N(Y)OO-shee-uh. See **alumnae, antennae, larvae, papilla(e), vertebrae.**

mirror MIR-ur or MEER-ur.

Mirror has two syllables. Avoid the pronunciation of the slovenly speaker who says MEER, like the word *mere,* and the illiterate speaker who says MUR. See **error.**

misanthrope MIS-<u>a</u>n-THROHP.

Pronounce the *mis-* like *miss,* not with a *z* sound as in the title *Ms.* (MIZ). The final syllable, *-thrope,* rhymes with *slope*. The corresponding noun *misanthropy* is pronounced mis-AN-thruh-pee, with the accent on the second syllable.

mischievous MIS-ch<u>i</u>-v<u>u</u>s. Three syllables, stress on the *first*.

Mischievous is subject to two beastly mispronunciations: mis-CHEE-vu̱s and, more often, mis-CHEE-vee-u̱s. Both place the accent on the wrong syllable; the latter adds an erroneous syllable to the word. *OED 2* (1989) says, "The stressing on the second syllable was common in literature till about 1700; it is now dialectal, vulgar, and jocular." *M-W 10* (1993) dubs the second-syllable accent "nonstandard" but notes that "our pronunciation files contain modern attestations" of mis-CHEE-vee-u̱s "ranging from dialect speakers to Herbert Hoover." That's not much of a range, in my humble opinion. If Hoover is your model of cultivated speech, I feel for you. I'll stick with the majority of educated Americans who say MIS-chi̱-vu̱s, thank you. See **heinous, grievous, intravenous**.

Missouri mi̱-ZUUR-ee (preferred by a clear majority of Missourians and nearly all "foreigners"); mi̱-ZUUR-uh (preferred by a significant but dwindling minority of Missourians and by many speakers in Kansas and across the South).

In the April 1976 issue of *The Midwest Motorist* (published in St. Louis) a stately debate erupted over the pronunciation of *Missouri*. The antagonists were Martin Quigley, the contributing editor of the magazine, and the late Bill Vaughan, syndicated newspaper columnist and former associate editor of *The Kansas City Star*. At issue was the proper sound of the final *i:* Should it be pronounced -uh, like the *a* in *sofa*, or -ee, like the *y* in *lonely?* Each argued passionately for his preference, Vaughan for -uh and Quigley for -ee. Then the magazine, which claims to be "the only Missouri publication that goes into homes in every county of the state," invited its readers to fill out a ballot stating their preference, "to settle this question once and for all." The results of the survey directly contradicted the conclusion drawn forty-three years earlier by the eminent linguist Allen Walker Read.*

In "The Pronunciation of the Word 'Missouri,'" a scrupulously documented article that appeared in the December 1933 issue of *American Speech*, Read asserts that the -uh ending "has, in defiance of spelling, shown remarkable vitality. An actual counting of heads in Missouri would show, I believe, that it has the decided majority."

Read's view, I think, is the popular opinion of many non-Missourians today. But hold your horses, folks — this is the Show Me State. When the results were reported in the June 1976 issue, 60 percent of Missourians chose -ee. (The overall count — including the far smaller number of "nearby" voters from Kansas, Illinois, and Arkansas — was 59 percent to 41

---

* Chief among Read's many contributions to the study of language is his uncovering of the complex origin of *O.K.* (or *okay*). Any current dictionary will note perfunctorily that the initials stand for *oll korrect*, a facetious alteration of *all correct*, but for curious readers who want to know more, the complete skinny can be found in an article on Read called "At Play in the Language" in the September 4, 1989, issue of *The New Yorker.*

percent, because Kansas residents favored -uh by 74 percent.) Those who'd lived in Missouri for zero to twenty years preferred -ee by a wide margin of 78 percent, while residents of more than twenty years preferred -ee by 57 percent. "Nearly 90 percent of those under 21 and 62 percent of those in the 21 to 45 age bracket preferred 'EE,'" the magazine reported.

That is strong evidence for the predominance of -ee, but for all you doubters who know from reading your newspapers that one study does not an empirical truth make, here's the coup de grace: in 1989 *The Midwest Motorist* repeated its survey, and nearly 4,000 readers responded (almost twice as many as in the first poll). This time the result was 66 percent in favor of -ee. Here's how the magazine broke down the returns:

> Geographically the preference for EE is statewide except in the northwest corner, with pockets of UH in Central and Western counties. Kansas Citians, who were 58 percent for UH 12 years ago are now 54 percent for EE. . . .
>
> Age is a factor in the EE preference. Respondents under 21 prefer EE by about 89 percent today, just as they did 12 years ago, but those in the 21 to 45 age bracket, comprising 30 percent of the total vote, prefer EE today by 79 to 21, compared with 62 percent to 38 percent 12 years ago. Those over 45, comprising 66 percent of the total, haven't switched much — a 59 percent EE preference now and 56 percent 12 years ago. . . .
>
> A majority of Illinois and Arkansas voters still prefer EE, while a big majority of Kansas voters (nearly 75 percent) are — and were — on the UH side.

After the 1976 survey the magazine noted that "these preferences are strongly held and not likely to be changed by debate or 'proof' of any kind." And even after the 1989 landslide it concluded that "one thing is certain — the numbers do not change the intensity of the convictions held by both factions." That is true. Once one has chosen sides on the issue, there is no debate. The chance of persuading a mi-ZUUR-uh sayer to become a mi-ZUUR-ee sayer, or vice versa, is as remote as the chance of discovering life on Jupiter. But all this acrimony and divisiveness raises the question: how did this civil war in pronunciation get started, anyway?

There is convincing evidence to show that the controversy probably is rooted in the age-old bitterness between North and South. Among the many letters from survey voters printed in *The Midwest Motorist* are two that suggest this interpretation.

Howard Lollar writes, "My parents, both born in the 1890s, pronounced it Missour-a also, as did their parents, born in Missouri around Civil War days. So undoubtedly my great-grandparents pronounced it the same way. This would take us back to [1830–1840] when some of my great-grandparents moved to Missouri from Kentucky and Tennessee. Do you suppose that Missour-uh could have been the southern pronunciation of the state while the Yankee pronunciation was the more harsher [*sic*] sounding Missour-ee?"

John H. Windsor, Jr., writes that "Missouri's first settlers were predominantly from Virginia and Kentucky and brought with them the softer, more open pronunciations of the South; hence *Missour-a*. Subsequently, the migration source for Missouri moved to the North and from Europe with *Missour-ee* the result. Oil and water don't mix!"

Allen Walker Read (in the article cited above) corroborates the North vs. South theory. There was a "consensus of observation," he writes, "that the 'a' ending was most prevalent among those people whose speech background lay in Virginia, Kentucky, and the South. As a Saint Louisan said [in 1897], 'I call it Missoura. That is the Southern pronunciation and if we are an integral part of the South, it should be so called.'"

In a two-fisted debate like this, where pride and territory are at stake, what the dictionaries say is practically worthless. Orthoepic asseveration is also suspect — *WNW Guide* (1984), for example, incorrectly states that "the usual pronunciation in Missouri is mi ZOOR uh." Sometimes questions of pronunciation transcend any concept of "correctness" and become a matter of identity, of self-esteem. What counts most in these situations is one's experience and the unshakable certainty arising from it that says, "I'll be doggoned if I'll pronounce it any other way!"*

However, without intending to belittle the intense conviction of those who prefer -uh, I will take the liberty of throwing in a foreigner's two cents. My experience confirms the results of the survey. For what it's worth, nearly all the Missourians I have come in contact with — from St. Louis (where I have been a guest on many radio shows on KMOX) to Kansas City to Cape Girardeau to Columbia — have preferred the -ee ending. Bill Vaughan, in his dignified essay in defense of -uh, may celebrate "the gentle tolerance with which we who know how to pronounce Missouri regard those who don't," but his complacent confidence in the propriety of his pronunciation isn't likely to win many converts. What sticks in my mind is

---

* On the other hand, sometimes one must lay such deep-seated prejudices aside and strike a conciliatory note. For example, in *Watching My Language* (1997) William Safire relates this anecdote: "A sandpapered-fingertip sensitivity to pronunciation was shown by the [Bush-Clinton] debate's moderator, Jim Lehrer of PBS. In his introduction, he said the program originated in St. Louis, 'Miz-oor-uh.' In his conclusion, he said good-bye from 'Miz-oor-ee.'

Caught out in this straddle, [Lehrer] confesses: 'I did it deliberately. I went to the University of Miz-oor-uh. "Miz-oor-uh! Tigers!" That was a signal to my friends that I knew that's the way it's pronounced there.

"'But everybody else says "Miz-oor-ee,"' says the national broadcaster, 'so I closed on that'" (pp. 34–35).

the image of the elderly, gregarious Missourians I met at a baseball game in San Diego who, upon learning that I wrote about pronunciation, suddenly turned pink with passion and implored me to defend the righteousness of -ee in this book. Well, then, here you are: I prefer mi-ZUUR-ee, and I am gratified to know that most Missourians now do too.

A historical postscript: until about 1930, many authorities favored mi-SOOR-i and mi-SOOR-ee, with *s* as in *miss* instead of like *z*. Beginning in the late 19th century, attempts were made in the schools and universities to teach one or the other as the proper pronunciation. This caused an uprising among many Missourians at all levels of society, who considered the hissing-*s* pronunciations an imposition of foreigners, particularly Easterners, and particularly Bostonians.* Vehement denunciation from academics, journalists, politicians, and other public figures (often vented on the editorial pages of the state's newspapers), combined with the constitutional stubbornness of average Missourians (who have always preferred a *z* sound for the double *s*, despite their differences over the final *i*), eventually put the kibosh (KY-bahsh, see the entry) on mi-SOOR-i and mi-SOOR-ee, and they have since disappeared from the dictionaries.

In conclusion, all I can say is that there is not likely to be a new Missouri Compromise. The lines are plainly drawn, and though one side appears to be winning, it is still a battle to the death (well, almost). At this point perhaps the best advice I can give is to heed the admonition of Elbert Hubbard: "Be from Missouri, of course; but for God's sake forget it occasionally." See **St. Louis.**

mobile (adjective) MOH-bul (rhymes with *noble*); (art object) MOH-beel. For the adjective, British and Canadian speakers prefer MOH-byl (-byl like *bile*). For Mobile, Alabama, the pronunciation is moh-BEEL (or sometimes MOH-beel depending on syntax). For more on American vs. British pronunciation of words ending in *-ile,* see **textile.**

---

* Read [op. cit.] quotes numerous editorial pronouncements of the day, including a judge who, "in denouncing Easterners, spoke of 'the nasal-twanged manufacturer of wooden nutmegs who demands that we shall sound a discordant "s" rather than a mellifluous "z,"'" and a congressman who wrote, "I resent the assumption of eastern authors of our school books that they know more about the pronunciation of our own name than we ourselves do." One of the most outspoken critics of the hissing-*s* pronunciation was Walter Williams, editor of the Columbia, Missouri, *Herald* and later president of the University of Missouri, who called it "a fad, a monstrosity tasting of codfish and baked beans."

Apparently the regional quandary of the Missourian is a sticky one indeed. As William Least Heat Moon writes in *Blue Highways* (1982), "A Missourian gets used to Southerners thinking him a Yankee, a Northerner considering him a cracker, a Westerner sneering at his effete Easternness, and the Easterner taking him for a cowhand." This may account for the doggedness with which Missourians cling to their preferences and the fervor they sometimes display in defending them.

modem MOH-d<u>u</u>m (first syllable rhymes with *go*, second syllable as in *kingdom*).

I thought everybody, and I mean *everybody*, pronounced this word MOH-d<u>u</u>m until one day I came across a letter from John Strother of Princeton, New Jersey, to William Safire, language maven of *The New York Times*, which appears in Safire's *Watching My Language* (1997). "The way I and my acquaintances pronounce *modem*," writes Strother, "is specifically 'MO-dem,' with a secondary accent on the second syllable, not 'MOWED-'m,' with a throwaway second syllable using a schwa vowel sound."

That made my baud rate skip and stopped me in my digital tracks. Was this guy actually in favor of saying MOH-dem, with the second syllable like *dem-* in *democrat?*

Figuring Mr. Strother and his acquaintances were either quacksalvers or visiting Venusians, I swaggered over to my ponderous pile of wordbooks to reaffirm my presumption that MOH-d<u>u</u>m was the only pronunciation in the universe. Ten seconds later I uttered a *eureka shriek* — that sharp, guttural exclamation you emit upon finding precisely what you didn't want to find. Strother and company's unearthly MOH-dem not only was listed in all four major American dictionaries of the 1990s, it was the *only* pronunciation in two of them — *American Heritage 3* (1992) and *M-W 10* (1993). What in telecommunication tarnation was going on here? I had to dig deeper and find out.

Modem entered English in the 1950s — the first citation in *OED 2* (1989) is from 1958 — but the word didn't get into the dictionaries until the boom in personal computers in the 1980s. After surveying all my sources from that decade, here is what I found: *modem* appears in *WNW 2* (1984), the *NBC Handbook* (1984), *WNW Guide* (1984), *M-W 9* (1985), *AHSC* (1985), Barnhart (1988), and *OED 2* (1989), all of which give only one pronunciation. Can you guess which one? Yup, MOH-dem. Only two dictionaries — *WNW 3* (1988) and the unabridged *Random House II* (1987) — recognize MOH-d<u>u</u>m; the former labels it less common, but the latter lists it first.

Stunned by what seemed to me a glaring discrepancy between what these sources had recorded and what people actually said, I decided to consult several members of the digerati — which *RHWC* (1997) defines as "people skilled with or knowledgeable about computers" — to determine if I, rather than the editors of all these estimable references, was the one who suffered from a superfluity of cerumen.

First I called Robert J. Hawkins, editor of *ComputerLink,* a weekly supplement to *The San Diego Union-Tribune,* and asked him to pronounce *m-o-d-e-m* for me. "MOH-d<u>u</u>m," he said, twice. Have you ever heard MOH-dem? I asked. He pondered for a moment. "No, actually I haven't," he said, "and hearing you say it sounds so strange." What if you heard someone else say it that way? "I would think it was a regional dialect of some sort." I told him MOH-dem was the only pronunciation in two of our four current dictionaries and in nearly all sources since 1980. "I'm shocked," he said.

I reached Linda Stern, contributing editor of *Home Office Computing* magazine, in (where else?) her home office in Takoma Park, Maryland. MOH-dum, she said, was her pronunciation and that of all her colleagues and friends. Have you ever heard MOH-dem? I asked. "Not that I can recall," she said. "It hasn't stuck in my mind." Would it sound strange if you heard someone say it? "Yes."

Next I connected with Katrina Heron, editor in chief of *Wired*, just as her May 1998 issue was hitting the newsstands with the magazine's latest neologism on the cover: *modemnity*. This high-wired editor, I was impressed to discover, was not too high and mighty to answer her own phone. Her pronunciation of *m-o-d-e-m*? "MOH-dum." Had she ever heard MOH-dem? "*Nunca*," she replied without hesitation, using the Spanish for *never*. What would be her response if she heard someone say MOH-dem? "I believe in pronunciatory* democracy," Heron said. "I wouldn't think anything except that they said it a different way."

Next I hooked up with Constance Hale, the author of *Wired Style: Principles of English Usage in the Digital Age* (1996), a woman who knows her bits from what bytes in the land of compuspeak. "I have absolutely never heard it pronounced any other way than MOH-dum," she told me. When I asked what she thought about the dominance of MOH-dem in the dictionaries, Hale said she wasn't surprised. "I've found often that mainstream reference books on language do poorly when it comes to the language of technology. Go look at the computer page in the 14th edition of *The Chicago Manual of Style*. You are given zero guidance for all the new words." What would be her response if she happened to hear someone say MOH-dem? "I'd correct them," declared our regnant digistylist. "I'd use the word in my next sentence."

According to another cyberlinguist, Gareth Branwyn, a contributing editor of *Wired* magazine and the author of *Jargon Watch: A Pocket Dictionary for the Jitterati* (1997), "MOH-dum is universal." Had he ever heard MOH-dem? I asked. "Yes, I sure have," he said confidently, but then had trouble remembering who had pronounced it that way. "It's probably happened on more than one occasion. I think it was somebody unfamiliar with computers, somebody who had not spent a bunch of time among

---

* Yes, it's a real word, although you won't find it in your average college dictionary. It appears in Worcester (1860), the *Century* (1914), *Webster 2* (1934), *Webster 3* (1961), *Random House II* (1987), and *OED 2* (1989).

computer people, and that was just their guess at how you would pronounce it." What's interesting about the pronunciation of *modem*, Branwyn pointed out, is that it didn't wind up being MAH-dem or MAH-dum because the word is an abbreviation for *modulator-demodulator*. I asked him how long he thought the now universal MOH-dum had been around. "I remember MOH-dum all the way back to the time of acoustical modems, which were the first modems," he said. "I probably saw my first one in 1980–81, when personal computers started to make their way into people's homes. I clearly remember that the first people using these devices called them MOH-dumz."

At this point, satisfied that MOH-dum was indeed the prevailing pronunciation and that our dictionaries had some catching up to do, I decided it was time to call John Strother, the man whose letter to William Safire got me into this geekophonetic mess, and sound him out on his preference for MOH-dem.

I reached Strother at home in New Jersey, and when I explained the purpose of my call, he amiably agreed to discuss himself and his pronunciation. He said he was "just a curmudgeon, retired" who had been "in the space business" as an electrical, optical, and systems engineer. How did he come to say MOH-dem rather than MOH-dum? I asked. He began by noting that he first became familiar with modems in their infancy, long before the word was a part of everyone's vocabulary. "I'm an engineer, not in telecommunications as such," he said, "but I worked with people who were, and they were the people who invented it [the modem], so I thought [MOH-dem] was something that was authoritative in its own right. Authoritative literally: The authors pronounced it that way."

I asked Strother what he thought of the fact that *modem* took three decades to get into a dictionary. "I'm not really surprised," he said, "because the terminology was dormant, or a private lingo among a small group of people, until modems became an inseparable part of the personal computer — until they became a commodity. Until that time the term was only used among electrical engineers, people who were designing and repairing telephone equipment." So how did he think we got from the esoteric MOH-dem to the exoteric MOH-dum? "For economy of communication among themselves, the producers and users of later modems quit articulating both syllables," he surmised, quite reasonably in my opinion.

What can we conclude from this inquiry into the second syllable of *modem?* Three things. First, that MOH-dem indeed has every right to be in the dictionary. Second — given the testimony quoted above and the overwhelming dominance of MOH-dum since the early 1980s — that MOH-dem has no right to be the only pronunciation in a current dictionary, or even the one listed first. And third, that in the midst of the verbal revolution of the Digital Age, in which the cult of neophilia reigns supreme, it's nice to know there are still a few techno-curmudgeons like John Strother around to help keep a window open to the past.

Modena (Italy) MOHD'n-uh or MAWD'n-uh.

modernity muh-DUR-ni-tee.

There is no *dare* in *modernity*. The pompous momes* who say muh-DAIR-ni-tee (or moh-DAIR-ni-tee) apparently think that the word is formed from *moderne* + *-ity*. Problem is, *moderne* is French and does not appear in English dictionaries.

It is also permissible to pronounce the first syllable mah- (chiefly British) or moh-. I recommend muh- because the vowel is unstressed and weak and therefore most naturally pronounced as a schwa.

Modigliani moh-DEE-lee-**AH**-nee or MOH-deel-**YAH**-nee.

I have heard many good speakers, including novelist John Updike, mispronounce this name moh-DIG-lee-**AH**-nee. No matter how much you *dig* this artist's work, don't pronounce the *g*. Authorities countenance only the silent *g* pronunciation moh-DEE-lee-**AH**-nee or the more authentically Italian pronunciation MOH-deel-**YAH**-nee, in which *gl* sounds like *l* and *y* rolled together. See **cognoscenti, seraglio**.

Monday see **-day**.

months MUHNTHS. Don't say MUHNTS.

Be sure to stick your tongue between your teeth and pronounce the *th* blend. See **depths**.

mores MOR-ayz or MOR-eez. Avoid MOH-rays or MOR-rays.

Mores, which entered English about 1900 as the gift of the budding discipline of sociology, comes directly from the Latin *mores,* the plural of *mos,* custom, manner. At first it was pronounced MOH-reez (rhyming with *go seize*), in anglicized Latin; this is the only pronunciation in *Webster 2* (1934) and *OED 2* (1989), and the first in *WNW 3* (1997). By the 1940s many speakers had understandably softened that sonorous first syllable to sound like *more,* and Kenyon & Knott (1949) recognized MOR-eez. In 1961, *Webster 3* gave priority to another variant, MOR-ayz (rhymes with *door haze*), a partly re-Latinized — or what I would call de-anglicized — pronunciation (the Latin is MOH-rays, rhyming with *slow race*), which has since been dominant. Burchfield (1996) and I still favor MOR-eez, but three of the four major current American dictionaries give priority to MOR-ayz, and Lass & Lass (1976), the *NBC Handbook* (1984), *Everyday Reader's* (1985), Barnhart (1988), and Jones (1991) prefer it.

The Latin MOH-rays (or MOR-ays), with an *s* rather than *z* sound at the end, is not listed in most dictionaries but is sometimes heard from dis-

---

* Rhymes with *homes*. This rare word means a stupid, boring person, a buffoon, or a captious critic.

gruntled pedants who take exception to MOR-ayz, the prevailing pronunciation, and MOR-eez, which is usually listed second.

Moscow MAHS-kow (-kow like *cow*). Often among the broadcast media, and in Britain, MAHS-koh.

"There is no 'cow' in Moscow," writes Bart Benne in *Waspleg and Other Mnemonics* (1988). "It is a long 'o.'" If you believe what you hear on radio and TV these days, it would appear that Mr. Benne's dictum is correct. Since the 1980s I have noticed that the broadcast media have made a striking shift from saying *Moscow* with the *cow* to saying it with a long *o* as in *go*. Listen carefully and you will hear what I mean — you will be hard put to find a *cow* on the networks today.

Among the many broadcasters I have heard say MAHS-koh are Ted Koppel, Peter Jennings, Forrest Sawyer, Brit Hume, and Jim Laurie of ABC; Dan Rather, Mike Wallace, and Bill McLaughlin of CBS (Lesley Stahl, however, says -kow); Judy Woodruff and Robert MacNeil (formerly) of PBS; and Bob Edwards, host of NPR's *Morning Edition.* All the NPR newsreaders now say MAHS-koh (not all of them did before) and the BBC correspondents reporting on NPR use the long *o* as well. Finally, while on a trip across Canada in 1989 I asked a producer for the CBC in Vancouver if that network had a preference. She said that individual broadcasters had been pronouncing it differently but recently "the word had come down" that everyone should now say -koh.

When I interviewed Bob Edwards in 1989 for San Diego's public broadcasting magazine, I asked him why he preferred the long *o.* "I've always said it that way," he replied. "It was reinforced early, and then again later in graduate school by my journalism professor, Edward Bliss." Edwards also said he recalled MAHS-koh's being the preferred pronunciation in NPR's standard reference on place names, *The Columbia Lippincott Gazetteer of the World* (1952, 1962).

That authority actually lists both pronunciations, with *cow* first (transcribed MAH-skow). It then goes on to give the pronunciations for seven U.S. localities named *Moscow,* as follows: for Moscow, Latah County, Idaho, MAHS-koh (for more on this city, the largest Moscow in the country, see the end of this entry); for Moscow, Stevens County, southwest Kansas, MAHS-koh; for Moscow, Somerset County, west central Maine, MAHS-kow; for Moscow, Clermont County, southwest Ohio, MAHS-kow; for Moscow, Lackawanna County, northeast Pennsylvania, MAHS-kow; for Moscow, Fayette County, southwest Tennessee, MAHS-kow or -koh; and for Moscow Mills in Lincoln County, Missouri, on the Cuivre (like *quiver*) River, both -kow and -koh. All in all there are at least thirteen Moscows in the U.S., including ones in Arkansas, Indiana, Iowa, and Vermont. A flyer issued by the chamber of commerce in Moscow, Idaho, notes that "there are twelve other communities that share our name with us."

On the basis of the *Columbia Lippincott Gazetteer* alone it is reasonable to doubt the propriety of the "no cow in Moscow" mnemonic, and it is also reasonable to call into question the media's current preference for a *cow*-less pronunciation. But before I tell you what the rest of my sources say, let me discuss briefly the history of the name and relate the opinions of three eminent professors on how it should be pronounced.

The Russian name for *Moscow* is *Moskva,* pronounced muhsk-VAH or mahsk-VAH.* *Moscow* therefore is an exonym, a useful term that has appeared in various monographs on language (including William Safire's column in *The New York Times*) but that to my knowledge has yet to be recorded in a dictionary. In *Crazy English* (1989), wordsmith Richard Lederer defines *exonym* as "a place name that foreigners use instead of the name that natives use: *Cologne* for Köln, *Florence* for Firenze, *Morocco* for Maroc." Some other examples of exonyms are *Rome* for Roma, *Germany* for Deutschland (DOYCH-lahnt), and *Sweden* for Sverige (SVER-yuh).

The first academic expert I contacted for a ruling was Vytas Dukas, emeritus chair of the Russian and East European Studies Department at San Diego State University and a Lithuanian whose mother, he said, was from Moscow. "*Moskva* means muddy waters in Finnish," he explained. "The tribes that lived there were Finnish before Slavic tribes came in." The English spelling, he said, is based on the Germanic *Moskau,* because "the Germans are the ones who 'discovered' Russia and wrote the books." Since the Germanic pronunciation is MAWS-kow (with *cow*), "English linguistically requires -kow," he asserted. "Spell it *Moscow* and pronounce it *cow*." When I asked him what he thought of the pronunciation MAHS-koh, with long *o*, he said, "It's affectation."

Next I wrote to a man William Safire once dubbed "the nearest we have to a Mr. Pronunciation in America,"† Karl V. Teeter, emeritus professor of linguistics at Harvard. His reply was simple and blunt: "I am not aware of any pronunciation of Moscow other than that you spell MAHS-kow."

Finally I called Richard Pipes, professor of Russian history at Harvard and former director of the university's Russian Research Center. Professor Pipes, who was born and raised in Poland and came to the U.S. in 1940, is a polyglot who speaks Russian "almost like a native," he said. "In academic circles I always call it MAHS-kow," he told me, adding that his colleagues all use the *cow* pronunciation as well. "If anybody called it MAHS-koh my ears would perk up. I would find it a little bit affected to say MAHS-koh."

When I mentioned that the long *o* pronunciation was rampant on TV and radio, and that it had been listed in dictionaries for a long time,

---

* *Webster's Collegiate* (1917) and *Webster 2* (1934) prefer this native pronunciation for the Russian capital and MAHS-koh for the city in Idaho.

† See p. 399 of Safire's *I Stand Corrected* (1984).

Professor Pipes also seemed surprised. Then he asked me to hold the line for a minute. When he returned he had a copy of a 1591 work by the Elizabethan poet and diplomat Giles Fletcher entitled *Of the Russe Commonwealth*. (Pipes edited the 1966 facsimile edition.) This was "the first full-scale, systematic description of the country" in English, Pipes explained, and just as he suspected, throughout the book Fletcher had often used the spelling *Mosko*. The professor suggested that this spelling (and perhaps other variants used before *Moscow* was established) might be the source of the pronunciation MAHS-koh (long *o*). Then could -koh originally have been British? I asked. Pipes wasn't sure. "I spent almost two years in England," he said, "and I always said MAHS-kow and nobody corrected me and I wasn't aware that anybody pronounced it differently."

Most likely the British refrained from correcting the good professor out of politeness, for there is conclusive evidence that MAHS-koh is in fact the British pronunciation. William Perry's *Royal Standard English Dictionary* (1775) — the earliest dictionary to include proper names — and Daniel Jones's *English Pronouncing Dictionary* (14th edition, 1991) — a leading authority on British pronunciation since its initial publication in 1917 — give only MAHS-koh, while *OED 2* (1989) sanctions MAHS-koh and labels MAHS-kow American. According to Ralph H. Emerson, an authority on English spelling and pronunciation who was kind enough to do some research on *Moscow* and share his opinions with me, MAHS-kow "is *only* an American pronunciation, and of fairly recent vintage at that. The sole historical pronunciation was [MAHS-koh], and that remains the sole pronunciation in England. This has given it enough prestige to be preferred by upscale American broadcasters."* (We will hear more from Mr. Emerson regarding the origin and development of the *cow* pronunciation in a moment.)

The British are not the only ones with a penchant for the long *o*. A significant number of Russians also prefer MAHS-koh when speaking English. During a radio talk show in Denver on which I was the guest, a caller remarked that he had just returned from a trip to Moscow. On a bus tour of the city, he said, the Russian guide had pronounced it MAHS-koh. One of my readers in rural Tennessee told me that she frequently picks up Radio Moscow on shortwave, and that all the announcers use -koh. And on ABC's *Nightline* and on NPR I have heard a number of Russians pronounce *Moscow* with a long *o*.

It is conceivable, of course, that all these Russians, like most Europeans, learned British English in school rather than American English, and that the announcers on Radio Moscow are simply imitating the BBC or following the trend in the American media toward -koh in an effort to sound

---

* Personal correspondence of July 2, 1997.

more "natural" to their Anglophone listeners. It is also possible, however, that the three wise professors are on the losing side of an academic coin toss, and that the long *o* is on the verge of achieving a popularity it has not enjoyed since Giles Fletcher used the spelling *Mosko*.

On the other hand, the evidence of my ears tells me that most Americans — of all ages and stripes — put a *cow* in *Moscow*. I have said MAHS-kow all my life, and it wasn't until the 1980s that I heard anyone pronounce it with a long *o*, and then it was only from "upscale American broadcasters." Only later did I hear it occasionally from John and Jane Doe. In recent years I have informally queried scores of people from various parts of the U.S., and nearly all of them said they are more comfortable with the *cow* pronunciation, that they have used it all their lives. The few who prefer -koh usually admitted to having switched their allegiance. Bob Edwards is the only person who told me he has always said MAHS-koh. All of this leads me to surmise that, despite the prevalence of -koh on the airwaves, if we counted heads in America today the results would show an overwhelming preference for *cow*.

Perhaps that is why most American sources published since the 1940s give priority to MAHS-kow. Here is a breakdown:

MAHS-koh (long *o*) *only:*

Worcester (1860)
Webster (1864, 1868)
Funk & Wagnalls *Standard* (1897)
Phyfe (1926)
Vizetelly (1929) — "not [MAHS-kow]"
Opdycke (1939) — "should rime with *Ma's toe,* not *Ma's brow*"
Witherspoon (1943)
Greet (1948)*

MAHS-koh *first:*

Funk & Wagnalls *New Practical Standard* (1962)
Scribner-Bantam (1979)
RH College (1968)
Random House II (1987)
RHWC (1991, 1997)
WNW 3 (1988, 1997)
M-W 10 (1993)

---

* Greet, who was a professor of English at Columbia University and speech consultant to CBS, notes in *World Words* (1948) that MAHS-koh "is the pronunciation usually recorded in dictionaries, and radio speakers should therefore adopt it as probably the most convenient. However, a spelling pronunciation, [MAHS-kow], is very common in the United States and deserves dictionary recognition."

MAHS-kow (with *cow*) *only:*

Century (1897 ed.)
New Century (1927–42)
Macmillan World Gazetteer and Geographical Dictionary (1961)
NBC Handbook (1984)

MAHS-kow *first:*

Webster's Geographical Dictionary (1949 and 1997)
Kenyon & Knott (1949)
American College (1952)
New Century Cyclopedia of Names (1954)
Webster 3 (1961)
Columbia Lippincott Gazetteer (1952, 1962)
Columbia Encyclopedia (1963)
AHNC (1969) and *AHSC* (1985)
Funk & Wagnalls *Standard* (1980)
WNW 2 (1984)
M-W 9 (1985)
American Heritage 3 (1992)

As you can see from this list, MAHS-koh was once preferred by many authorities — when it was more fashionable, perhaps, for educated Americans to model their pronunciation after the British. There is no doubt, however, that there is ample authority for MAHS-kow, and perhaps better authority if you choose to agree with Professors Dukas, Teeter, and Pipes, which I do. In this case I side with the professors and the plain folk. In their book and in mine, there is a *cow* in *Moscow*.

That should settle things as far as contemporary American and British preferences are concerned. But, as Ralph H. Emerson points out, two questions remain: "Why did it used to be 'kō' and where did 'kow' come from?" Here is Emerson's explanation:*

> According to the *Century* [1897 ed.], *Moscow* is derived immediately from French *Moscou,* and I can fill in that since English rarely allows final *u* in spelling, the *u* changed to *w*.

> I would guess that the spellings *Moskow* and *Mosko* (Giles Fletcher's preference) competed for a while, with *Moskow* eventually winning out (probably encouraged by the German *Moskau*) and eventually becoming further anglicized to *Moscow*.

---

* Taken from his letter of July 2, 1997.

Emerson continues:

The pronunciation of unstressed final -*ow* in English is always ō, as in *borrow, narrow, hollow,* etc., and both *Moscow* and the anglicized *Cracow* (formerly KRAY-koh) derived their original final ō by analogy with these words. In other words, by conservation shift.

"Conservation shift," says Emerson, is an instance of "conserving the familiar by preferring to pronounce an unfamiliar word according to the analogy of some more familiar word that looks or sounds similar, as I suppose 'air' for *err* is a conservation shift from *error* and *errant.*"

So where did 'kow' come from? I suspect again from conservation shifts. No other two-syllable English words end in -*cow* — only the monosyllables *scow* and *cow* itself do. So, in a case of competing analogies, the conservation shift from *cow* and *scow* won out over that from *borrow,* etc. . . .

Why here and not in England? We were further away, and had less reason to talk about the place and keep up the traditional pronunciation. . . . Moscow was comparatively obscure until it leapt into prominence with the Revolution, and in the midst of the Red Scare that followed, the fears the name evoked must have made the ugly sound "ow" seem a more appropriate way to end the word than the neutral ō, and this finally tipped the scales in favor of the "kow" pronunciation for good in this country. . . . Maybe the contempt or amusement that Americans felt for the "backwards" Russians helped favor a new pronunciation. . . .

In any case, I'm sure the decisive reason for the switch was the spelling. If it had been spelled simply *Mosco* in the first place the change in pronunciation would never have happened. Whatever else it may be, [MAHS-kow] is certainly a spelling pronunciation, though as I said above it results from competing analogies — the old pronunciation came from the analogy that unstressed final -*ow* is pronounced ō, the new pronunciation from the analogy that final -*cow* should be pronounced "kow," regardless of stress.

Some final words (as promised earlier) on Moscow, Idaho. In 1989 I spoke with Mary Reed, director of the Latah (LAY-tah) County Historical Society, who informed me that the only acceptable pronunciation of her city is MAHS-koh, with the long *o*. The proper pronunciation is reinforced in the school system, from the primary grades up. "You're quickly corrected if you say MAHS-kow," she told me. "It's how you tell outsiders, people who are not Idahoans, who are newcomers." Then Ms. Reed said something fascinating about how the long *o* pronunciation came to be preferred for the city: "One of the intentions was to make a difference between it and the Soviet capital."

moths MAW<u>TH</u>Z (<u>TH</u> as in *then* or *bathe*).

In the singular *moth*, the *th* is voiceless, as in *path* and *bath*. In the plural *moths,* and in the plurals *paths* and *baths,* the *th* is voiced, as in *bathe* and *lathe,* and the final *s* has the sound of *z.*

motif moh-TEEF (rhymes with *no grief*).

This is the only recognized pronunciation. Don't say MOH-tif.

museum myoo-ZEE-um, not MYOO-zee-um.

Stress the second syllable, never the first.

myopic my-AHP-ik. Do not say my-OH-pik.

The host of a sports-talk radio show whom I recently heard say my-OH-pik didn't realize that *myopic* and *myopia* properly have different pronunciations. *Myopia* has a long *o,* as in *opal:* my-OH-pee-uh. *Myopic* has a short *o,* as in *optic:* my-AHP-ik.

"But hey," Mr. Sports-Talk objects, "my my-OH-pik pronunciation's in the dictionary, pal. You can't tell me it's wrong."

"I'm glad to know you can read a dictionary, and that you use one," I shoot back, "but the fact that your my-OH-pik appears in current dictionaries means only that enough other people like you have made the mistake of mispronouncing the word that way so that dictionary editors feel compelled to record it as a prevalent variant. Perhaps you might change your mind if you knew something about the word *myopic* and the history of its pronunciation."

"Such as?" asks Mr. Sports-Talk skeptically.

"To begin with, *OED 2* (1989), which gives only my-AHP-ik, shows that *myopic* entered English in 1800, about fifty years after *myopia.* From then until about thirty years ago — when *AHNC* (1969) and *M-W 7* (1972) recognized your pronunciation — authorities sanctioned only my way of saying the word: my-AHP-ik. Two hundred years of acceptance in educated speech is a bit more impressive than thirty, wouldn't you agree?"

Mr. Sports-Talk doesn't respond.

"On top of that," I go on, "there is the matter of analogy. For your pronunciation, my-OH-pik, which retains the long *o* of its parent word, *myopia* (my-OH-pee-uh), there is none. But for my pronunciation, my-AHP-ik, in which the *o* changes from long (as in *go*) to short (as in *hot*), there is plenty of good analogy — for example, *telescope* and *telescopic, philanthropy* and *philanthropic, misanthrope* and *misanthropic, isotope* and *isotopic.* So, based on that evidence I can in fact tell you that even though your pronunciation is listed in dictionaries, it is wrong. Besides, this is my book, not your show, and I call the shots here. *Comprende?*"

I wait for Mr. Sports-Talk to tell me he once was blind but now he sees, but all I hear are the sounds of silence. He's hung up on me.

N

Nabokov, Vladimir nuh-BAW-k<u>o</u>f (or -BOH-), vluh-DEE-m<u>u</u>r.

"It is indeed a tricky name," Nabokov remarks in *Strong Opinions* (1973), a collection of interviews and occasional prose. "As to pronunciation," says the famously meticulous writer,

> Frenchmen of course say Nabo*koff*, with the accent on the last syllable. Englishmen say *Nab*okov, accent on the first, and Italians say Nabokov, accent in the middle, as Russians also do. Na-*bo*-kov. A heavy open "o" as in "Knickerbocker". My New England ear is not offended by the long elegant middle "o" of Nabokov as delivered in American academies. The awful "Na-bah-kov" is a despicable gutterism. Well, you can make your choice now. Incidentally, the first name is pronounced Vladeemer—rhyming with "redeemer"—not Vladimir rhyming with Faddimere (a place in England, I think).

In light of Nabokov's pronounced distaste for "Na-bah-kov," I would surmise that his preferred "heavy open 'o'" is not the *o* of *Knickerbocker*, which is light as in *hot, sock,* and *bottom,* but rather the rounder *o* of *soft, dog,* and *bought;* and so I have given nuh-BAW-k<u>o</u>f and also nuh-BOH-k<u>o</u>f, with the "long elegant middle 'o.'" Well, you can make your choice now.

naiveté NAH-eev-**TAY**.

In American English, the standard spelling is *naiveté* (with an accent) and the variant *naïveté* (with an accent and a dieresis) is now less common.

---

a = at / <u>a</u> = final / ah = spa / ahr = car / air = fair / ay = hay / aw = saw
ch = chip / e = let / <u>e</u> = item / ee = see / eer = deer / i = sit / <u>i</u> = April
ng = sing / <u>o</u> = carrot / oh = go / oo = soon / or = for / oor = poor
ow = cow / oy = toy / sh = she / th = thin / <u>th</u> = this / <u>u</u> = focus / uh = up
ur = turn / uu = pull, took / y, eye = by, I / zh = measure / (see full key, p. xiv)

The variant *naivety,* pronounced nah-EEV-tee, is rare; evidence indicates it is chiefly British.

With *naive* and *naiveté* many speakers blend the *a* and *i* into a long *i* sound, which results in ny-EEV and NY-eev-**TAY.** These are so close to the proper pronunciations, nah-EEV and NAH-eev-**TAY,** as to be nearly indistinguishable from them. However, they appear in only one of my sources — *Webster 3* (1961), which is assiduous to a fault about recording variants. I suggest that if you can hear the distinction between nah- and ny- in the first syllable of *naive* and *naiveté,* you should cultivate the preferred pronunciations nah-EEV and NAH-eev-**TAY.**

Some current sources countenance nah-EEV-uh-tay, and I have also frequently heard ny-EEV-uh-tee. These four-syllable variants are illogical and erroneous. *Naiveté* combines *naive* and *té,* and standard word division calls for three syllables: na-ive-té. Don't add a spurious fourth syllable. It is acceptable to stress the middle syllable (nah-EEV-tay), but the weight of authority favors the primary accent on the final syllable (NAH-eev-**TAY**), which should rhyme with *day,* never with *tea.*

nascent NAS-int (*a* as in *fascinate*) or NAY-sint (NAY- rhyming with *say*). The first pronunciation above, with short *a,* is recommended.

NAY-sint, with a long *a,* was originally a mispronunciation that stubbornly refused to go away. Worcester (1860), Funk & Wagnalls *Standard* (1897), and the *Century* (1889–1914) countenance only NAS-int, and Ayres (1894), Phyfe (1926), and Vizetelly (1929) all proscribe NAY-sint, the last remarking, "frequently, but erroneously, [NAY-sint], perhaps by confusion with *natal.*" In 1934, however, *Webster 2* granted NAY-sint respectability as an alternative pronunciation, and since then American dictionaries have listed it in good standing and numerous authorities — including Lass & Lass (1976), the *NBC Handbook* (1984), *Everyday Reader's* (1985), and Barnhart (1988) — prefer it.

That said, I must still register my objection to NAY-sint. I fail to comprehend how a word that authorities agree is divided *nas · cent* could logically be pronounced as if it were divided *na · scent.* There is no *scent* in *nascent;* the word comes from the Latin *nasci,* to be born, divided *nas · ci* and pronounced NAHS-kee. Given the hard-won acceptability of NAY-sint in educated speech, I won't presume to tell you it's wrong, but I will tell you, emphatically, that NAS-int is the more sensible and cultivated pronunciation. In this rare instance I side with the Brits: NAS-int is the only pronunciation in *OED 2* (1989), and the preference of the *Oxford Guide* (1983) and Jones (1991). It is also worth noting that all four major current American dictionaries — *American Heritage 3* (1992), *M-W 10* (1993), *WNW 3* (1997), and *RHWC* (1997) — list NAS-int first.

nausea NAW-zee-uh or NAW-shuh; **nauseate** NAW-zee-AYT; **nauseous** NAW-shus.

The nightmarish thought of attempting to navigate a safe course through all the variant pronunciations for these words that have been heard in educated speech and recorded in 20th-century dictionaries is enough to make a pronunciation maven sick to his stomach. (Current sources list from three to five variants for each word.) Suffice it to say that the pronunciations recommended above are in widespread cultivated use, listed in current dictionaries, and preferred by various authorities. For *nauseous,* evidence indicates that NAW-shus now prevails in American speech; for the others it's a toss-up. That's as far as I can guide you through this swamp of sound. You're on your own now. Hope you feel better soon.

Nazi NAHT-see (like *not see*).

NAT-see (rhymes with *bat see*) is also sanctioned but much less common. In the 1946 film *The Stranger,* in which Orson Welles plays a Nazi war criminal hunted down by Edward G. Robinson, only Loretta Young says NAT-see, and it sticks out like a sore tongue. I do not recommend it. Also avoid the beastly NAH-zee and NAZ-ee.

For the doctrine or practices of the Nazis, *Nazism* is the preferred spelling, and the three-syllable NAHT-siz'm is the preferred pronunciation.

negotiate ne-GOH-shee-ayt. Do not say ne-GOH-see-ayt.

The corresponding noun *negotiation* is properly pronounced ne-GOH-shee-**AY**-shin, not ne-GOH-see-**AY**-shin.

In *There Is No Zoo in Zoology* (1988) I called *negoseeate* "the Great Beastly Mispronunciation of the 1980s," for it was in that decade that millions of speakers suddenly replaced the traditional *shee* sound in this word with the oh-so-precious *see*. I have since found evidence that the *see* for *shee* substitution in this word, though it did not become rampant until the early 1980s, is in fact much older than that, dating back to at least the early 1930s.

In *How to Speak English Effectively* (1933), a compilation of lectures "delivered to the members of the Announcing Staff of the Columbia Broadcasting System," Frank H. Vizetelly, general editor of Funk & Wagnalls *New Standard Dictionary* (1913), remarks that "such words as *appreciate, appreciation, associate, association, negotiate, negotiation,* have been repeatedly mispronounced before the microphone during the past six months. The *cia* or *tia* in these words is correctly pronounced *she,* not *see.*" The *see* sound has long since gained acceptance in *associate, association,* but not so in the other words; to most educated American speakers, I would wager, a *see* sound in *negotiate, negotiation* seems prissy, and in *appreciate, appreciation* it's ridiculous.

As Vizetelly suggests, much of the fault lies with our broadcasters, who all too often are in the vanguard of the vogue. Broadcasters may be professional speakers, but few have had any formal preparation for the job and most are no more knowledgeable about pronunciation than the next person. Long gone are the days when the networks relied on speech consultants like Vizetelly and W. Cabell Greet and local stations subjected announcers to pronunciation exams. Unlike the BBC in England, whose announcers have long been widely regarded as models of careful speech, American broadcasters today are too often exemplars of vulgarity, carelessness, and affectation. If you wouldn't take John or Jane Doe's word on how to pronounce something, why take theirs? The next time you hear an unfamiliar pronunciation on the air, don't take it for granted that it's right. Go to a dictionary (or two) and find out.

Authorities ignored whatever currency the prissy *see* sound in *negotiate* and *negotiation* may have had until *Webster 3* (1961), a controversial tome that has been roundly criticized for its permissiveness. In its treatment of pronunciation, certainly, *Webster 3* is a paragon of painstaking descriptivism, its guiding principle apparently being to record every variant ever uttered by anyone with more than an eighth-grade education. Merriam-Webster's next three *Collegiate* dictionaries — *M-W 7* (1972), *8* (1975), and *9* (1985), all based on *Webster 3* — along with *Random House II* (1987) list *see* as an alternative for *negotiation* but do not countenance it for *negotiate*. A survey of the four major American dictionaries of the 1990s, I am happy to report, reveals an unusual reluctance to grant unqualified approbation — which keeps alive my hope that perhaps this voguish, foppish substitution has seen its heyday and will eventually disappear.

Although *RHWC* (1997) sanctions the *see* sound for *negotiation,* it still lists only *shee* for *negotiate*. *WNW 3* (1997) qualifies the *see* variants with the label *often,* which (along with the labels *also* and *sometimes*) is a coded way dictionaries have of implying that the variant so labeled has limited acceptance among educated speakers and may be trendy, obsolescent, eccentric, or of questionable propriety.* *M-W 10* (1993), duly recognizing that many find the *see* sound not only questionable but reprehensible, confers its inscrutable symbol of infamy, the obelus [÷], upon the *see* sound, meaning, as the front matter explains, that it "occurs in educated speech but . . . is considered by some to be unacceptable." *American Heritage 3* (1992), in an admirable display of backbone, refuses to acknowledge the *see* variants at all.

A final word: though it may be true that nego-*see*-ate and nego-*see*-ation are more often heard in England (the BBC announcers I hear on NPR use *see* frequently), lest you jump to the conclusion that the British have foisted this snooty *see* sound upon unsuspecting Americans I hasten to point out that both Jones (1991) and Burchfield (1996) prefer *shee* (the lat-

---

* For more on the subtleties of pronunciation labels, see the footnote under *divisive* on p. 122.

ter emphatically), and *shee* is the only pronunciation in *OED 2* (1989). Just because the United States is a democracy doesn't mean its citizens are immune to affectation. If anything, the *see* for *shee* substitution is an international disgrace. See **Beijing, consortium, controversial, oceanic, Social Security,** and **species.**

neither NEE-<u>th</u>ur. See **either.**

neologism nee-AHL-uh-jiz'm.

The beastly mispronunciation NEE-uh-**LOH**-jiz'm, for which there is no authority, is often heard from educated speakers who have learned the meaning of this word but who have not bothered to learn how to pronounce it properly. The variant NEE-uh-**LAWG**-iz'm, which is even beastlier, is thankfully less often heard.

neologist nee-AHL-uh-jist; **neology** nee-AHL-uh-jee. See previous entry.

new Preferably, NYOO. Now usually NOO.

Traditionally, *new* is pronounced with a *y* sound between the *n* and *o* (NYOO), and many cultivated speakers today preserve this sound not only in *new* but also in words incorporating it: *newspaper, newsletter, newlywed, newfangled, newt,* and so on. See **dew.**

Newfoundland (Canadian province and dog) N(Y)OO-f<u>u</u>n(d)-l<u>u</u>nd.

When *Newfoundland* is used as an attributive, notes W. Cabell Greet in *World Words* (1948), "the second syllable is stressed and is pronounced 'found.'" As shown above by (d), you may articulate or swallow the *d,* as you please.

New Orleans (Louisiana) N(Y)OO OR-l<u>i</u>nz or N(Y)OO OR-lee-<u>i</u>nz.

The variant NOO or-LEENZ is often heard,* but it is not the usual pronunciation either in the city or in the South, where *New Orleans* is usually compressed to NAW-l<u>i</u>nz and *Louisiana* to LOOZ-ee-**AN**-uh. This compression is natural for Southerners, but I don't recommend imitating it if you are not from the South, for it will probably sound affected, even mocking or condescending — like suddenly adopting British enunciation in the presence of a Brit, or a Brooklyn accent in the presence of a Brooklynite. The non-Southern speaker is best off saying N(Y)OO OR-l<u>i</u>nz (or OR-lee-<u>i</u>nz), loo-EE-zee-**AN**-uh. These pronunciations are countenanced by all current authorities, they have the greatest currency nationally, and they are generally unobjectionable to Southerners.

newspaper N(Y)OOZ-pay-pur.

---

* Linguist Charles-James N. Bailey, an expert on Southern-states phonetics, has told me that he suspects NOO or-LEENZ has its roots in the speech and songs of African-American jazz musicians. He's probably right. The New Orleans radio and TV broadcaster Mel Leavitt, in his *Short History of New Orleans* (1982), writes that "the pronunciation that raises local hackles is New Or-LEENS, as sung in 'Way Down Yonder (in New Orleans)' — composed here!" (As quoted in William Safire's *What's the Good Word?* New York: Times Books, 1982, p. 244.)

There is no *noose* in *newspaper.* Do not say NOOS-pay-pur. The *s* should have the sound of *z*. See **dew, new**.

Nicaragua NIK-uh-**RAH**-gwuh.

Native speakers of English should not affect a Spanish pronunciation. The British, who say things funny, add a syllable and stuff a *rag* in it: NIK-uh-**RAG**-yoo-uh.

The new breed of politically correct broadcast journalists, many of whom inhabit the airwaves of public radio and TV, insist on an overprecise imitation of the original Spanish: NEE-kah-**RAH**-gwah, with vowels agape and a self-consciously trilled *r*. What ever happened to good old NIK-uh-**RAH**-gwuh, which gives a polite nod to Spanish but doesn't make you sound as if you're suddenly (and inexplicably) switching languages in the middle of a sentence?

Saturday Night Live once spoofed this strange new hyperarticulate tendency to de-anglicize Spanish proper nouns that have been adopted into English. In the skit, the members of an all-Anglo TV news team go out of their way to impress a newly hired Latino reporter, played by guest host Jimmy Smits, with their ethnic sensitivity by using "authentic" Spanish pronunciations for names and words with established anglicized pronunciations. Finally, an exasperated Smits tells them all to stop putting on the dog and speak naturally. The point here is that it's silly to give a personal or place name a foreign pronunciation when there's a long-standing, widely accepted anglicization.

nicety NY-si-tee. Three syllables, not two.

niche NICH.

"French no longer," says Holt (1937). "Rhyme it with *ditch.*"

OED 2 (1989) traces *niche* back to 1611. Since at least the mid-18th century the anglicized NICH has been preferred in cultivated speech. Walker (1791) preferred NICH, and it is the only pronunciation countenanced by Worcester (1860), Funk & Wagnalls *Standard* (1897), the *Century* (1914), *OED 1* (1928), *Webster 2* (1934), *American College* (1952), and *RHWC* (1997). Orthoepists who prefer NICH include Ayres (1894), Phyfe (1926), Vizetelly (1929), Opdycke (1939), Kenyon & Knott (1949), Lass & Lass (1976), *WNW Guide* (1984), and the *NBC Handbook* (1984). Need I say more?

Yes. This word's long history has yielded two alternative pronunciations, NEESH and NISH. The latter is eccentric, the former is pseudo-French, and both are best avoided. NISH, which arose sometime in the 19th century, was stigmatized by Ayres and Opdycke and ignored by other authorities. *Webster 3* (1961) lists it, labeling it infrequent, but it does not appear in any current dictionaries. *WNW 3* (1997) calls NEESH British (*OED 2* does list it after NICH), but I have heard many very un-British speakers use it

— for example, Ed Koch, the former New York City mayor turned TV judge.* *American Heritage 3* (1992) sanctions NEESH as an alternative, but careful speakers would be wise to heed *M-W 10* (1993), which gives priority to NICH and labels NEESH with an obelus [÷], indicating that it "is considered by some to be objectionable." I would argue that those "some" are in fact many, and those many are the cultivated speakers who defend their traditional NICH.

nihilism NY-i-LIZ-um (NY- rhyming with *high*).

NY-i-LIZ-um is the first pronunciation listed in all four major current American dictionaries and *OED 2* (1989), and it is preferred by Lass & Lass (1976), the *NBC Handbook* (1984), *Everyday Reader's* (1985), and Burchfield (1996). The variant **NEE**-i-LIZ-um, first recorded by dictionaries in the 1960s, is listed as alternative; only Barnhart (1988) prefers it. Apparently it is modeled after the classical pronunciation of the Latin root word of *nihilism* — *nihil*, nothing, correctly pronounced NI-hil (both *i*'s are short in Latin) but often misrendered NEE-hil. Classical Latin pronunciations (especially *incorrect* ones) for established, anglicized English words are at best eccentricities and at worst asininities. For **NI**-hil-IZ-um there would be some remote authority, but **NEE**-i-LIZ-um has only its dubious current popularity to recommend it.

The *nihil* in *nihilism* and *annihilate* should be pronounced with the initial *i* long, as in *nice*, and the *h* silent. Formerly it was proper to pronounce the *h* in both words, but since the 1930s it has almost entirely disappeared from cultivated speech in the U.S. and Britain. Today *nihilism* with the *h* sounded still appears in some dictionaries, but the *h* sound in *annihilate* has not been recorded for about forty years.

Nin, Anaïs NEEN or NIN, AH-nah-**EES**.

"How should novelist Anaïs Nin's first name be pronounced?" asks McConkey (1986). "A respected American encyclopedia says *uh-nigh-is*. Her long-time friend, Lawrence Durrell [DUR-ul, rhymes with *squirrel*] (certainly knowledgeable, but not an American), renders it *an-i-eece*. And the author herself gave instructions to pronounce it *anna-ees*. The reader, mindful that it is a question of acceptability rather than correctness, can decide."

Frankly, that sort of advice is no advice at all — McConkey is planting his feet firmly in midair. In matters of pronunciation it is always a question of acceptability *and* correctness, and of discerning the uneasy relationship between them. It is impossible to consider the acceptability of a given pronunciation without the issue of correctness lurking in the background, and vice versa, and it is at the very least disingenuous to imply that one is a

---

* In an interview on TV's *Hard Copy*, November 21, 1997.

legitimate concern while the other is not. Acceptability and correctness are joined at the hip.

That said, in the matter of how to pronounce a person's name, the best rule to follow is to say it as that person wishes it to be said, in the manner he or she finds both acceptable and correct. With foreign names, the prudent speaker will strike a balance between the authentic and the intelligible, between what is correct to the foreign ear and acceptable to the native.

With *Anaïs Nin,* one must weigh what many find acceptable against what the author has told us is correct. The many seem to have settled on NIN (rhymes with *sin*) for her last name and uh-NY-is (rhymes with *a bias*) for her first. Although NIN is not quite what the author stipulated (answers in a moment), it does no injustice to her last name and is close enough to what she preferred so as to be unobjectionable. On the other hand, uh-NY-is is an idiotic pronunciation that to make any sense would require a spelling of *Anaïis, Aniïs, Anayis,* or some such thing. It is clearly just a bad guess that got passed around an uninformed and unsuspecting public. The careful speaker has an obligation to be more discriminating, to base judgment upon verifiable evidence wherever possible — and here is the evidence.

In the December 1996 issue of *English Language Notes,* Ralph H. Emerson (1996), an authority on the proper pronunciation of literary names, offers this report on the author's own preferences: "For her Spanish last name she used the Spanish pronunciation NEEN, like *clean.* Her French first name she pronounced ah-nah-EECE, last syllable as in *fleece.* You can more or less hear the sound of the name embedded in *Donna East.*" Emerson's source for this information was about as close to unimpeachable as you can get. "I verified all this with her husband, Rupert Pole," he told me.*

Now here's my two cents: for *Nin,* if NEEN seems too precious or just doesn't sit well with you, there's no harm in saying NIN. But follow the author's instructions exactly for *Anaïs* and show this entry to anyone who's foolish enough to give you a hard time about it. See **bolivar.**

nomenclature (American) **NOH**-men-KLAY-chur; (British) noh-MEN-kluh-chur.

nonage (American) NAHN-ij; (British) NOH-nij.

nonchalant NAHN-shuh-**LAHNT** or **NAHN**-shuh-LAHNT.

The usual British pronunciation, which was listed first in American dic-

---

* Emerson also noted in a letter to me (July 2, 1997) that "readers can hear her saying her first name aloud in the documentary *Anaïs Nin Observed,* sometimes called *Anaïs Observed,* which is available on videotape."

tionaries until the 1960s, is NAHN-shuh-lunt. It is now rare in American speech.

noon NOON (rhymes with *soon*).

The hypercorrect speaker inserts a spurious *y* and says NYOON.

Norwich (American) NOR-wich (like *nor witch*); (British) NAHR-ij (rhymes with *porridge*).

not at all NAHT-at-AWL, as spelled.

The would-be sophisticates who say NAH-tuh-TAWL give me heartburn: *not a tall* what? In an American speaker, *nah tuh tall* for *not at all* is a preposterous pretense that only the most egregious Anglophile would affect. This absurd pronunciation is excusable in old Hollywood movies, in which fake upper-crust accents were *de rigueur* (q.v.), but not in real life.

nuclear N(Y)OO-klee-ur. For Pete's sake, don't say NOO-kyuh-lur.

In his introduction to the fourth edition of the *NBC Handbook of Pronunciation* (1984), veteran broadcaster and language commentator Edwin Newman remarks that when the nuclear age began in August 1945, so did the *nucular* age as well.

Ever since *nuclear* entered the national vocabulary (a hundred years after entering English in the 1840s) it has been mispronounced by millions of educated and otherwise careful speakers, including scientists, lawyers, professors, and presidents of the United States. According to Newman, Dwight D. Eisenhower "could not get it right"; Jimmy Carter, who had been an officer aboard nuclear-powered submarines, pronounced it NOO-kee-ur; and Walter Mondale, in his 1984 bid for the presidency, repeatedly said NOO-kyuh-lur. "The word, correctly pronounced," writes Newman, "somehow is too much for a fair part of the population, and education and experience seem to have nothing to do with it." In *The Diabolical Dictionary of Modern English*, R. W. Jackson dryly echoes that sentiment by defining *nuclear* simply as "nucyaler."

Newman's and Jackson's cynicism reminds me of a debate I once heard between William F. Buckley, Jr., and the philosopher Mortimer Adler on whether everyone is inherently "educable," or whether some people, by nature or by circumstance, are "ineducable." Of course, Adler, as a teacher, was of the former opinion, and Buckley, who earns his living trying to make his ideological opponents look hopelessly dull and impervious to illumination, was of the latter.

I choose to believe that anyone in possession of physiologically normal organs of speech and at least half a brain is capable of pronouncing *nuclear* correctly. As R. W. Burchfield (1996) points out, "the spectacular blunder of pronouncing [*nuclear*] as if it were spelled *nuc-u-lar*" is the result of a tempting misassociation with the many words ending in -*ular* (*circular, particular, cellular, secular, molecular, jocular, avuncular*, etc.). This error is one of the ear and eye more than the tongue, and it has persisted not because it is too difficult for some to say N(Y)OO-klee-ur but because they do not heed the spelling and hear the difference between the proper and improper pronunciations — which brings us to the matter of correction.

Those who do hear the mispronunciation and who say the word right (still a substantial majority of us, I think) are understandably reluctant to correct those who do not. Can you imagine, as Edwin Newman puts it, "how other and lesser members of the Carter administration found it tactful to pronounce [*nuclear*] during Cabinet meetings," when President Carter and Vice President Mondale were mangling the word, albeit unwittingly, at every turn?* In Shaw's *Pygmalion*, the arrogant dialectician Henry Higgins "experiments" without the slightest compunction on his social inferior, the "guttersnipe" Liza Doolittle, teaching her to speak Received Standard English so he can win a bet. But who else feels comfortable correcting the pronunciation of anyone but a child without being asked to do so? It is a tricky matter even to correct family members and friends, and so with a neighbor, acquaintance, or coworker, most of us will not — and should not — presume to offer an unsolicited opinion. (Writing a book on the subject is different, for a book lays open its opinions only to those who freely choose to read it, and who are equally free to accept or reject the advice it contains without compromising their dignity.)

On the other hand, we should and do reserve the right, in matters of language, to speak as we see fit, to decide for ourselves what is acceptable and unacceptable, and to pass tacit judgment on our peers. When I began writing this book nearly every person with whom I discussed its contents asked (and in some cases implored) me to decry NOO-kyuh-lur, which made me wonder whether it might be the Most Disdained and Detestable Beastly Mispronunciation in the language. People who care at all about how words are pronounced (with the exception of linguists and lexicographers) seem to reserve their most vehement antipathy for NOO-kyuh-lur, and it comes as no surprise to me that a whopping 99 percent of the usage panel of Morris & Morris's *Harper Dictionary of Contemporary Usage* (1985) condemned it. In usage notes devoted to a lame defense of the mispronunciation, *M-W 10* (1993) and *RHWC* (1997) both admit that

* In *I Must Say* (1988), Newman writes, "Those who make it nucular must hear themselves saying it and must hear others who don't. How do they account for the difference? Do they think the others are wrong, and are they too polite to correct them? Evidently they never look up the word in a dictionary. Maybe the word 'muscular' leads them astray, or 'circular' or 'molecular.' Only a fiend would distribute a circular written by a molecular biologist and recommending a muscular nuclear policy. It is embarrassing to hear Russians and other foreigners snapping off the word as it should be when so many Americans cannot manage it" (p. 274).

NOO-kyuh-lur is "disapproved of by many," yet by just how many it is impossible to determine. On behalf of the indeterminate many who pronounce the word correctly, then, I appeal to the inadvertent many who do not: listen, and be errant no longer.

Molecular comes from *molecule*, and *particular* comes from *particle*, but there is no *nucule* to support *nucular*. *Nuclear* comes from *nucleus* — N(Y)OO-klee-<u>us</u> — which is almost never mispronounced. If you can say *nucleus* and you can say *nuke* (the informal verb meaning to attack with nuclear weapons or, humorously, to microwave), then the proper pronunciation of *nuclear* is but a suffix away.

For more on correcting others' pronunciation, see **gondola**. Also see **arctic, cupola, diminution, February, irrelevant, jewelry, Realtor**.

nucleic noo-KLEE-ik, not noo-KLAY-ik.

Properly, there is no *clay* in *nucleic*. The beastly mispronunciation noo-KLAY-ik — which has become so popular in recent years that it is now sanctioned as an alternative by all four major current American dictionaries and *OED 2* (1989) — is a pure piece of pseudo-Latin poop. The word, formed from the *nucle-* of *nucleus* plus *-ic*, entered English in 1892 in the phrase *nucleic acid*. *Webster's Collegiate* (1917), *Webster 2* (1934), and *American College* (1952) sanction only noo-KLEE-ik, and then suddenly *Webster 3* (1961) recognizes noo-KLAY-ik as an acceptable alternative. Scientists and other smart people pronounce *nucleolus* noo-KLEE-uh-l<u>us</u>, never noo-KLAY-uh-l<u>us</u>, so why say noo-KLAY-ik? It defies all logic and the evidence of etymology and analogy. One can only conclude that it's an affectation. The careful speaker is advised to follow the *NBC Handbook* (1984), *WNW Guide* (1984), and *Everyday Reader's* (1985), which sensibly prefer noo-KLEE-ik.

nuptial NUHP-sh<u>ul</u>. Pronounce in *two* syllables, not three.

NUHP- rhymes with *cup;* -sh<u>ul</u> as in *spatial* and *partial*.

NUHP-sh<u>ul</u> is the only pronunciation in *OED 2* (1989) and the first given in all four major current American dictionaries. The only acceptable alternative is NUHP-ch<u>ul</u>, which authorities have sanctioned since the 1940s.

Nuptial has two syllables. Do not say NUHP-shoo-<u>ul</u> or NUHP-choo-<u>ul</u>. No authority with a reputation to lose countenances these beastly three-syllable mispronunciations, and they appear only in *M-W 10* (1993), which labels them with an obelus [÷] to alert the careful speaker that they are controversial and objectionable variants.

O

obeisance oh-BAY-s<u>i</u>nts or oh-BEE-s<u>i</u>nts.

Pronounce the last syllable, *-sance,* like *since,* not *sins.* The accent falls on the second syllable, which you may pronounce either like *bay* or *bee.* Both pronunciations given above have been in cultivated use in America and England since the 1700s. However, if you are not already accustomed to using one or the other, it may be helpful to bear in mind that the preponderance of authority in the 19th and 20th centuries favors oh-BAY-s<u>i</u>nts. Of seven current authorities polled, only the *NBC Handbook* (1984) prefers oh-BEE-s<u>i</u>nts.

obelisk AHB-uh-lisk, not OH-buh-lisk.

AHB-uh-lisk is the only pronunciation in *OED 2* (1989), *American Heritage 3* (1992), and *RHWC* (1997). No authority I am aware of prefers OH-buh-lisk. It is useful to remember that the word is divided *ob • e • lisk.*

obelus AHB-uh-l<u>u</u>s.

The *obelus* is more commonly known as the division symbol: ÷. Since the 1960s the dictionaries of Merriam-Webster have used the obelus to indicate a controversial or objectionable pronunciation. *Webster 3* (1961), which first employed the obelus, says it "precedes variants which occur in educated speech but to the acceptability of which many take strong exception. . . ." The most recent Merriam-Webster dictionaries, *M-W 9* (1985) and *10* (1993), modify that awkward language, explaining that the obelus "is placed before a pronunciation variant that occurs in educated speech but that is considered by some to be unacceptable."

---

a = at / <u>a</u> = final / ah = spa / ahr = car / air = fair / ay = hay / aw = saw
ch = chip / e = let / <u>e</u> = item / ee = see / eer = deer / i = sit / <u>i</u> = April
ng = sing / <u>o</u> = carrot / oh = go / oo = soon / or = for / oor = poor
ow = cow / oy = toy / sh = she / th = thin / <u>th</u> = this / <u>u</u> = focus / uh = up
ur = turn / uu = pull, took / y, eye = by, I / zh = measure / (see full key, p. xiv)

Did you notice how *Webster 3*'s "many" who "take strong exception" to a given variant have become, in *M-W 9* and *10*, the "some" who find it "unacceptable"? That calculated diminution in passion as well as number speaks volumes about the hidden agenda of the modern dictionary, which is to offend as few as possible by embracing — and apologizing for — as much as possible. In my years of close work with dictionaries I have rarely come across a variant labeled with an obelus that I did not find objectionable and that had not already been censured by numerous language mavens and laypeople alike. The lesson here is this: the careful speaker who consults a Merriam-Webster dictionary would be wise to cast a cold eye upon any pronunciation preceded by an obelus.

obfuscate ahb-FUHS-kayt or AHB-fuh-skayt.

The pronunciation with first-syllable stress is without doubt now the dominant pronunciation in the U.S., but it is worth noting that the historical evidence indicates it was an early-20th-century import from Britain. Worcester (1860), Funk & Wagnalls *Standard* (1897), and the *Century* (1914) give only ahb-FUHS-kayt, and Phyfe (1926) and Vizetelly (1929) disapprove of AHB-fuh-skayt. *Webster 2* (1934), however, sanctioned second-syllable stress as an alternative, and since then it has gradually displaced the traditional accent on the first syllable. In the 20th century, recessive stress — where the accent moves toward the beginning of the word — has affected numerous words, and a fair number of recessive-stress pronunciations now common in American speech have been British imports. See **inculcate, infiltrate, precedence, promulgate,** and **sonorous.** For a general discussion of recessive and progressive stress, see **confiscate.**

oblique uh-BLEEK.

The pronunciation uh-BLYK (-BLYK rhyming with *like*), which enjoyed its heyday in the 19th century, is still heard in military usage.

Though some dictionaries now give priority to oh-BLEEK (oh- rhyming with *go*), it is an overpronunciation. Because the first syllable is unstressed, the quantity of the *o* is neither short (as in *opt*) nor long (as in *pope*) but lightened to sound like the initial *o* in *oppose, oblige,* and the verb to *object.* See **occasion, occult, occur, official, opinion,** in which the first syllable should be pronounced uh-, not oh-.

obscurantism uhb-SKYUR-in-tiz'm or ahb-SKYUR-in-tiz'm.

As in *obscure,* the stress in *obscurantism* properly falls on the second syllable. That has been the accepted pronunciation of the word since it entered the language in the 1830s. In 1961, *Webster 3* recognized a variant with penultimate primary stress, AHB-skyu-RAN-tiz'm, which is now sanctioned as an alternative by most current dictionaries. It is not recommended for two simple reasons: it's ugly and it's ugly. It may also be British in origin, for Jones (1991), who reflects the pronunciations "current among speakers of the middle generations" in England, prefers the penultimately stressed variant and lists the traditional pronunciation as a "somewhat less common" alternative.

obscure uhb-SKYUUR.

The *ob-* in *obscure* is properly pronounced like *ab-* in *about.* Lately there has been a tendency among educated speakers to overpronounce this unstressed *ob-* and say ahb-SKYUUR (ahb- rhyming with *slob*). This overly audible *ob-* is fastidious to a fault and unnecessary. Although *American Heritage 3* (1992) and *M-W 10* (1993) now list the ahb- variant first, *WNW 3* (1997) gives priority to the established uhb-, and *Webster 2* (1934), *American College* (1952), *WNW Guide* (1984), and *RHWC* (1997) countenance only uhb-.

obsequies AHB-si-KWEEZ (rhymes with *bob the knees*).

obsequious uhb-SEE-kwee-us.

occasion uh-KAY-zhun.

There is no *shun* in *occasion.* The last syllable, *-sion,* properly has the *zh* sound of *vision,* not the *sh* sound of *tension.* The first syllable is a schwa, as in *ago* and *allow.* Do not say oh-KAY-zhun with a long *o* as in *go.* That is an overpronunciation. See **oblique, occult, occur, official, opinion**.

occult uh-KUHLT.

Properly, the *o* is a schwa (SHWAH) and should sound like *uh,* as in *ago* and *occlude.* Always stress the second syllable. See **oblique, occasion, occur, official, opinion**.

occur uh-KUR (like *a cur*).

Do not say oh-KUR. Current sources do not recognize this long *o* (oh-), which is an overpronunciation. Pronounce the *o* like *a* in *accord* and *allow.* See **oblique, occasion, occult, official, opinion**.

oceanic OH-shee-AN-ik.

There is no *sea* in *oceanic.* It's a *she.*

Some speakers have been seduced into thinking that a pure *s* (as in *sister*) is preferable to the traditional *sh* sound in such words as *controversial, negotiate, species,* and *oceanic.* They say *controver-see-al, nego-see-ate, spee-seez,* and *o-see-anic* instead of *controver-shul, nego-shee-ate, spee-sheez,* and *o-shee-anic.* Are these innovations more precise, or are they merely precious? Should we now say pruh-SHYS for *precise* and PRES-ee-us for *precious?*

The substitution of a pure *s* in words that have traditionally had the *sh* sound is now rampant. SPEE-seez is threatening to make SPEE-sheez an endangered species, KAHN-truh-**VER**-see-ul has become the darling of millions of baby boomers (especially white-collar ones), and since the 1980s ne-GOH-see-ayt has become so popular on radio and TV that it is hard to find a broadcaster who says it the traditional way. However, OH-see-**AN**-ik — which I have heard on NPR — has not yet disgraced the dictionaries.* Let's keep it that way, or pretty soon we'll all be swimming in the OH-see-i̱n.

Oceania is pronounced OH-shee-**AN**-ee-uh. See **Beijing, consortium, controversial, negotiate, Social Security,** and **species.**

Odysseus oh-DIS-yoos (recommended) or oh-DIS-ee-u̱s. See **Theseus.**

Oedipus ED-i̱-pu̱s (ED- as in *bed*).

EE-di̱-pus (EE- as in *need*) is the usual British pronunciation, says *Webster 2* (1934), and this is confirmed by Jones (1991), a current British authority.

offense see **defense.**

official uh-FISH-u̱l. Don't say oh-FISH-u̱l.

Some speakers think it sounds more uh-FISH-u̱l to say oh-FISH-u̱l, with the initial *o* long, as in *no*. This is an overpronunciation. Modern phoneticians call the initial vowel sound in this word a *schwa* (SHWAH). Lexicographers of the 19th and early 20th century called it "obscure." All that means is that the first syllable of *official,* because it is not stressed, is pronounced like the *a* in *ago,* not like the *o* in *open*. See **oblique, occasion, occult, occur, opinion.**

often AWF-i̱n or AHF-i̱n. Do not pronounce the *t*.

Before I give you my two cents on the *t* in *often,* let's take a look at what various authorities have said about it since the late 18th century.

John Walker (1791), whose *Critical Pronouncing Dictionary* was one of the most respected and popular references both in England and America well into the 19th century, declared that "in *often* and *soften* the *t* is silent."

"The sounding of the *t*," proclaims the legendary H. W. Fowler in *Modern English Usage* (1926), "which as the OED says is 'not recognized by the dictionaries', is practised by two oddly consorted classes — the academic speakers who affect a more precise enunciation than their neighbours . . . & the uneasy half-literates who like to prove that they can spell. . . ."

"The *t* in *glisten* is silent, even as it is in *castle* and *often,*" says Frank H. Vizetelly (1929), editor of Funk & Wagnalls *New Standard* (1913), "yet one occasionally hears pedants and provincials pronounce them [GLIS-ten] and [AWF-ten]. No pronouncing dictionary with a reputation to lose ever sounds the *t* in these words."

"You don't want a *t* in here any more than in *soften,*" advises Alfred H. Holt (1937).

Webster 2 (1934), which sanctions only AWF-i̱n, notes that "the pronunciation [AWF-ti̱n], until recently generally considered as more or less

---

* It appears only in Jones (1991), a British authority, who records it as a "somewhat less common" variant in educated British speech.

illiterate, is not uncommon among the educated in some sections, and is often used in singing."

According to *Random House II* (1987),

OFTEN was pronounced with a *t-* sound until the 17th century, when a pronunciation without the (t) came to predominate in the speech of the educated, in both North America and Great Britain, and the earlier pronunciation fell into disfavor. Common use of a spelling pronunciation has since restored the (t) for many speakers, and today [AWF-in] and [AWF-tin] . . . exist side by side. Although it is still sometimes criticized, OFTEN with a (t) is now so widely heard from educated speakers that it has become fully standard once again.

"Nowadays," says R. W. Burchfield (1996), editor of *OED 2* (1989), "many standard speakers use both [AWF-in] and [AWF-tin], but the former pronunciation is the more common of the two."

What is going on here? After two hundred years of censure, has the *t* in *often* scratched and clawed its way back into acceptability? I would caution those who might be consoled by the comments of *Random House II* and Burchfield to heed the admonitions of the past and avoid pronouncing the *t*. Current dictionaries, including *Random House II,* do not give priority to AWF-tin, and it is much less common in educated speech and far more often disapproved of by cultivated speakers — particularly teachers of English, drama, and speech — than *Random House II* makes it appear. In 1932 the English lexicographer Henry Cecil Wyld called AWF-tin "vulgar" and "sham-refined," and today the bad odor of class-conscious affectation still clings to it as persistently as ever. As if that were not enough, analogy is entirely unsupportive: no one pronounces the *t* in *soften, listen, fasten, moisten, hasten, chasten, christen,* and *Christmas* — so, once and for all, let's do away with the eccentric AWF-tin.

ogle OH-gul (*o* as in *open, -gle* as in *bugle*).
The variants AH-gul (rhymes with *boggle*) and AW-gul are best avoided. Authorities of the first half of the 20th century did not recognize them. AH-gul first appeared in *Webster 3* (1961) labeled *sometimes,* meaning it was infrequent; AW-gul appears only in the American Heritage line of dictionaries — *AHNC* (1969), *AHSC* (1985), and *American Heritage 3* (1992) — as an alternative to the established OH-gul. *M-W 10* (1993) and *WNW 3* (1997) also label AH-gul uncommon, and Lass & Lass (1976), Funk & Wagnalls *Standard* (1980), the *NBC Handbook* (1984), *WNW Guide* (1984), Barnhart (1988), *OED 2* (1989), and *RHWC* (1997) all sanction only OH-gul.

olfactory ahl-FAK-tur-ee, not ohl-FAK-tur-ee.
This word has nothing to do with an old factory. It comes from the Latin *olfacere,* to smell, and in English the *ol-* is properly pronounced ahl-, as in

olive, ology, and *oligarchy* (see the next entry). Lass & Lass (1976) are the only authorities I am aware of who prefer the variant ohl-FAK-tur-ee (long *o* as in *hole*), which first appeared in *Webster 3* (1961). *Taber's Medical* (1970) and *Mosby's Medical* (1990) countenance only ahl- for the first syllable, ahl-FAK-tur-ee is the preference of the *NBC Handbook* (1984), *WNW Guide* (1984), *Everyday Reader's* (1985), Barnhart (1988), and *OED 2* (1989), and all four major current American dictionaries list ahl-FAK-tur-ee first.

oligarchy AHL-i-GAHR-kee, not OH-li-GAHR-kee.

Oligarchy means "government by the few," and very few members of the current oligarchy of lexicographers and language mavens countenance the pronunciation OH-li-GAHR-kee, with the long *o* of *no*, which first appeared in *M-W 8* (1975). *OED 2* (1989), *RHWC* (1997), and *WNW 3* (1997) list only AHL-i-GAHR-kee, with the *ol-* pronounced as in *olive, ology,* and *olfactory* (see the previous entry).

oncology ahng-KAHL-uh-jee. Now also ahn-KAHL-uh-jee.

Oncology has four syllables. Avoid the recent and proliferating beastly mispronunciation AHN-uh-**KAHL**-uh-jee (like *onacology*), which adds a spurious fifth syllable.

Of the two pronunciations sanctioned above, the traditional (and recommended) one is ahng-KAHL-uh-jee, with the *n* in *on-* pronounced as an *ng* consonant blend (as in *gong*). Because the *n* precedes a hard *c* (pronounced like *k*), it is more natural to pronounce it as an *ng* blend (*ong-cology*) than to separate the *n* from the *c* (*on-cology*). The same blending can be heard in *ankle* (ANG-kul), *bronchitis* (brahng-KY-tis), *synchronize* (SING-kruh-nyz), *banquet* (BANG-kwit), and *conquest* (KAHNG-kwest).*
Recently a "more precise" pronunciation of *oncology* has developed in which *on-* is separated from the *c* and distinctly pronounced: ahn-KAHL-uh-jee. This is the only pronunciation in *AHSC* (1985) and the first in *American Heritage 3* (1992), *M-W 10* (1993), and *WNW 3* (1997). The *ng*-blended ahng- pronunciation, however, is the preference of *Taber's Medical* (1970) and *Mosby's Medical* (1990), and the only one sanctioned by the *Century* (1914), *Webster 2* (1934), *American College* (1952), *WNW Guide* (1984), Barnhart (1988), and *RHWC* (1997).

onerous AHN-ur-us, not OHN-ur-us.

Properly, there is no *owner* in *onerous*. It should be pronounced like *honor us*.

Though *onerous,* burdensome, and *onus,* a burden, are related etymo-

---

* Linguists call this *assimilation,* the tendency of neighboring sounds to become similar or identical for "ease of articulation," as *WNW Guide* (1984) puts it. Thus, *inliterate* evolved into *illiterate, horseshoe* is pronounced *horshoe, cupboard* is pronounced *cubberd, Grandpa* becomes *grampa,* and so on.

logically, they have different pronunciations. The *o* of *onus,* which is divided *o · nus,* is long as in *bone.* The *o* of *onerous,* which is divided *on · er · ous,* has the short sound of *on.*

Onerous was first recorded in English in 1400. The variant OHN-ur-<u>us</u>, with the first syllable pronounced like *own,* was first recorded in *Webster 3* (1961). Lass & Lass (1976) is the only authority that prefers it. Walker (1791), Worcester (1860), Funk & Wagnalls *Standard* (1897), the *Century* (1914), *Webster 2* (1934), *American College* (1952), the *NBC Handbook* (1984), *WNW Guide* (1984), *Everyday Reader's* (1985), and Barnhart (1988) all sanction only AHN-ur-<u>us</u>, and all four major current American dictionaries list it first.

onomatopoeia AHN-uh-MAT-uh-**PEE**-uh.

This challenging word is often mispronounced AHN-uh-MAHN-uh-**PEE**-uh. There is no *mono* in *onomatopoeia.* It's a *mat.* The adjective is either *onomatopoeic* (AHN-uh-MAT-uh-**PEE**-ik) or *onomatopoetic* (AHN-uh-MAT-uh-poh-**ET**-ik).

ophthalmologist AHF-thuul-**MAHL**-uh-jist. See next entry.

ophthalmology AHF-thuul-**MAHL**-uh-jee.

For the second syllable, many authorities sanction -thal- (rhymes with *pal*). Because the syllable is unstressed I see no reason to extend the quantity of the vowel, and so I recommend -thuul- (rhymes with *pull*) as more fluent and natural.

Now, let's begin this discussion with an experiment. Read the following aloud:

> I call it the Cardiff Theory: to get off therapy, swallow a rough thermometer and cough thoroughly. It's a tough thing to do.

Did you get through that nonsense without slurring or stumbling? I'll bet you did. That means you are living proof that it is possible to pronounce the *ph* and *th* sounds in *diphthong, diphtheria, ophthalmology,* and *ophthalmologist* properly — enunciating and smoothly blending their adjacent *f* and *th* sounds rather than turning the *f* into *p.*

The trouble with -*phth*- began way back in the 18th century. In his vastly influential *Critical Pronouncing Dictionary* (1791), the English elocutionist John Walker* prescribed dip- for the first syllable of *diphthong* and ahp- for the first syllable of *ophthalmic* — which, being an 18th-century gent, Walker spelled *ophthalmick.* (*Ophthalmologist* didn't come along until 1834; *ophthalmology* appeared in 1842.) "Two aspirations in succession seem disagreeable to the English ear, and therefore one of them is generally sunk," Walker wrote in defense of his preference. "It is no wonder we hear

---

* For more on Walker's popularity, see the footnote under **educate.**

the first *h* dropped in *ophthalmy* and *ophthalmick,* which is the pronunciation I have adopted as agreeable to analogy." I can't help wondering if
Walker also would have countenanced dropping the first *l* in *ophthalmologist* and *ophthalmology,* which many do today, because it is hard to enunciate before *m* in an unstressed syllable — certainly harder, in my opinion,
than enunciating the "voiceless" *ph-th* sound. But more on that missing *l*
in a moment.

Worcester (1860), who sanctions ahp- and ahf- (in that order) for words
beginning with *oph-*, shows that the authorities who preceded him were
sharply divided. Along with Walker, Perry (1775), Jones (1798), Jameson
(1827), and Smart (1840) also favored ahp-, while ahf- was the preference of
Sheridan (1780), Enfield (1807), Knowles (1835), Reid (1844), Craig (1849),
and Wright (1855). Webster's *Academic Dictionary* of 1867 (based on the
unabridged 1864 Webster) gives ahf- and ahp-, reversing Worcester's order,
and from that point on ahp- began falling out of favor.

For over half a century, from the 1880s to the 1950s, ahp- seems to have
disappeared (or gone dormant). The dictionaries of that period do not
recognize it and the orthoepists make no mention of it — except for Phyfe
(1926), who attributes it to Worcester. The only authority that cites another
pronunciation is Opdycke (1939), who proscribes the peculiar and obviously short-lived ahf-THAL-mahl-jee.

The ahp- variant got its wake-up call in *Webster 3* (1961), which labeled
both it and -thuh- for the second syllable unacceptable to many — which I
suppose makes the popular AHP-thuh-**MAHL**-uh-jist/-jee a doubly objectionable pronunciation. Other dictionaries of the 1960s and 1970s were
quick to recognize ahp- and -thuh-, but without any warning labels. *WNW
Guide* (1984) notes that "thuh is also heard as the second syllable," and Lass
& Lass (1976), I was surprised to discover, prefer AHF-thuh-**MAHL**-uh-
jist. Two current dictionaries, however — *American Heritage 3* (1992) and
WNW 3 (1997) — do not recognize the dropped first *l.*

So is there a current consensus regarding *ophthalmologist* and *ophthalmology?* Yes indeed. Although AHP-thuh-**MAHL**-uh-jee (like *opthamol-
ogy*) probably now prevails in popular usage, careful speakers and the
weight of authority still clearly favor pronouncing the first syllable ahf-
and making the *l* in the second syllable audible. Three of the four major
current American dictionaries list AHF-thuul- first, with the fourth giving
priority to AHF-thal-. *Everyday Reader's* (1985) prefers AHF-thuul-; the
NBC Handbook (1984) and *OED 2* (1989) prefer AHF-thal-. Not surprisingly, my three medical dictionaries — *Taber's* (1970), *Stedman's* (1972),
and *Mosby's* (1990) — give only AHF-thal-**MAHL**-uh-jee/-jist. No modern authority I am aware of prefers ahp- for *oph-*, and only *WNW Guide*
sanctions it as an alternative. With all due respect for the great John

Walker, apparently "two aspirations in succession" are not so disagreeable to the (cultivated) English ear after all. See **diphtheria, diphthong.**

opine oh-PYN (rhymes with *so fine*).

This is the only recognized pronunciation.

opinion uh-PIN-yin. Don't say oh-PIN-yin.

It is an overpronunciation to make the initial *o* long, as in *open*. Because it is unstressed it is properly a schwa, like *a* in *appear, ago,* and *away.* (You don't say "long ay-GOH and far ay-WAY," do you?).

The overpronounced oh-PIN-yin is quite common today, especially (as might be expected) in more formal situations where the speaker is making an extra effort to be clear and precise. But in this instance the effort is wasted and unnecessary, for the only thing achieved by the meticulous enunciation of a long *o* at the beginning of *opinion* is an unnatural, stilted effect. In his article on pronunciation in the front matter of *American College* (1952), W. Cabell Greet — a professor of English at Columbia who for many years was a speech consultant to CBS — writes that "we must realize that unstressed and therefore reduced vowels are a respectable and essential element in the English language. No broadcaster is so tedious, annoying, and difficult to understand as he who 'overpronounces,' stressing syllables and preserving vowel sounds that are neglected in idiomatic and correct English speech."

I have my uh-PIN-yin, and I am willing to listen to your uh-PIN-yin, but if you are one of those folks who always oh-verpronounce their oh-*pinions,* then forget it. I'm not interested. See **oblique, occasion, occult, occur, official,** and also **a, the.**

orangutan uh-**RANG**-uh-TAN.

Also, for the first syllable, aw- or, less often, oh-.

Properly, there is no *tang* in *orangutan,* but a variant spelling with a *g* at the end, *orangoutang,* has been hanging around ever since the word entered the language in the 1690s, which explains why the next time you pay a visit to the monkey house at your local zoo you are sure to hear Joe and Jane Average and their unexceptional kids say uh-**RANG**-uh-TANG. Current dictionaries all sanction this pronunciation (some only for the -*tang* alternative spelling), but modern authorities prefer *tan* for the last syllable, and *OED 2* (1989) says the word is "more correctly" spelled and pronounced without the final *g.*

orator OR-uh-tur. Regionally (and also British), AHR-uh-tur.

There is no *ray* in *orator.* Don't say **OR**-RAY-tur, or worse, or-RAY-tur, shifting the stress to the second syllable. The former is a beastly overpronunciation, the latter a beastly and affected overpronunciation. (In case you're wondering, it's not British.) Dictionaries do not recognize these oratorical abominations. The noun *oratory* is pronounced **OR**-uh-TOR-ee in the U.S. and AHR-uh-tree in Britain.

orchestral or-KES-tr<u>u</u>l.

Stress the second syllable. Don't say OR-k<u>e</u>s-tr<u>u</u>l.

Oregon OR-uh-g<u>u</u>n.

I had to relearn the pronunciation of this state when I moved to California and met some native Oregonians (OR-uh-**GOH**-nee-<u>i</u>nz). As a native Easterner I had always said AH-ruh-gahn, but as those in other parts of the U.S. know, Easterners have their own peculiar ways of saying things. The indigenous pronunciation is OR-uh-g<u>u</u>n, and that is the way most other American speakers say it as well.

My philosophy about place names is, "When in Rome. . . ." Easterners who, like me, are accustomed to saying AH-rinj for *orange* (instead of OR-inj), HAHR-uh-b<u>u</u>l for *horrible* (instead of HOR-uh-b<u>u</u>l), and FLAHR-uh-duh for *Florida* (instead of FLOR-uh-duh, first syllable like *floor*) can probably get away with saying AH-ruh-gun instead of OR-uh-gun. Just don't pronounce the last syllable -gahn (rhymes with *John*). That's a dead giveaway that you're an out-of-stater. One final warning: don't pronounce *Oregon* so that it sounds like *organ.* That's sloppy. Always give the word three syllables.

organization OR-guh-n<u>i</u>-**ZAY**-sh<u>i</u>n, not OR-guh-ny-**ZAY**-sh<u>i</u>n.

The *i* in the third syllable should be short as in *nip,* not long as in *nice.* In other words, pronouncing the suffix *-ization* like *eyes-ation* is overnice, overmeticulous, and, whether you realize it or not, Anglophilic. Of the four major current American dictionaries, only one — *WNW 3* (1997) — recognizes the -ny- pronunciation. See **civilization.**

orthoepist OR-thoh-uh-pist or or-THOH-uh-pist; **orthoepy** OR-thoh-
uh-pee, or-THOH-<u>i</u>-pee, or **OR**-thoh-**EP**-ee.

Orthoepy is the art and study of correct pronunciation, and an *orthoepist* is an authority on proper pronunciation. Both words hail from the Greek *orthos,* right, and *epos,* a word. The funny thing is — and wouldn't you just know it — the doggone orthoepists can't seem to agree how to pronounce them. The main point of disagreement is whether the stress should fall on the first or second syllable. (I prefer the accent on *or-,* but I bear no ill will toward the many who stress *-tho-.*) Then there is the ridiculously pedantic question, among those who prefer first-syllable stress, of whether the penultimate syllable should be pronounced -uh-, -e- (as in *step*), or -ee- (as in *keep*), which is chiefly British. About the only thing the orthoepists can agree on is that these two words must have four syllables. And that, my friend, is the estimable (that's ES-t<u>i</u>-muh-b<u>u</u>l) and exact science of orthoepy (select your pronunciation with care). The pronunciations countenanced above are the ones most often listed in current dictionaries. Most modern authorities prefer second-syllable stress.

otiose OH-shee-ohs.

Pronounce the first syllable to rhyme with *go,* the second like *she,* and the third to rhyme with *dose*. Chief among the variants countenanced in modern dictionaries is OH-tee-ohs, with the second syllable pronounced like *tee* instead of *she*. *OED 2* (1989) and Jones (1991) indicate that this is the usual British pronunciation; be apprised that in an American speaker it is an affectation. English speakers of all persuasions should avoid the beastly variants OH-shee-u̱s (sloppy), OH-see-ohs (precious), and OH-shu̱s (aargh!).

P

Pachelbel (Johann) PAHK'l-bel or, with a German guttural *ch*, PA<u>KH</u>'l-bel. The *Pach-* should sound like *pock*, not *pack*. Be sure to pronounce the first *l.*

paean PEE-<u>i</u>n. Do not say PAY-<u>i</u>n.

This word — which means a song, hymn, or fervent expression of praise or joy — is often mispronounced PAY-<u>i</u>n by the quasi-cultured. There is no *pay* in *paean.* PEE-<u>i</u>n is the only recognized pronunciation.

paella pah-AY-yuh, or, if you must, pah-EL-uh.

Paella was first recorded in English in 1892. Like the flavor of this Iberian dish, which can vary considerably depending on the quality of the ingredients and the skill of the chef, the word's pronunciation is unstable. Dictionaries recognize several variants: the anglicized pah-EL-uh (or pah-YEL-uh) and pah-AY-luh (or pah-AYL-yuh), and the more Spanish pah-AY-yuh. Pronounce the *l*'s if you want to, but where I come from (California), and for many gastronomically cultivated speakers elsewhere, there is only one way to say it: pah-AY-yuh.

palliative PAL-ee-uh-tiv; **palliate** PAL-ee-ayt. Pronounce PAL- like the word *pal.*

I have heard the first syllable pronounced PAHL- (rhymes with *doll*) by a news anchor on NPR. There is no authority for this eccentricity.

panegyric PAN-uh-**JIR**-ik, not PAN-uh-**JY**-rik.

The word means formal or elaborate praise, a eulogy in speech or writing. It should rhyme with *lyric* and *satyric,* not with *high stick* or *Bye, Rick.*

---

a = at / <u>a</u> = final / ah = spa / ahr = car / air = fair / ay = hay / aw = saw
ch = chip / e = let / <u>e</u> = item / ee = see / eer = deer / i = sit / <u>i</u> = April
ng = sing / <u>o</u> = carrot / oh = go / oo = soon / or = for / oor = poor
ow = cow / oy = toy / sh = she / th = thin / <u>th</u> = this / <u>u</u> = focus / uh = up
ur = turn / uu = pull, took / y, eye = by, I / zh = measure / (see full key, p. xiv)

(Some speakers lengthen the short *i* sound of the *y* in *panegyric, lyric,* and *satyric* so that the syllables come out sounding like *jeer, leer,* and *tier,* respectively. This is okay.)

Although you will see the -**JY**-rik variant listed second in current dictionaries, be apprised that (a) it is probably based on false analogy with *gyrate;* (b) it is relatively recent, countenanced first by *Webster 3* (1961); and (c) no reputable authority recommends it. PAN-uh-**JIR**-ik is the only pronunciation in Worcester (1884), the *Century* (1914), *Webster 2* (1934), and *American College* (1952), and Ayres (1894), Phyfe (1926), Vizetelly (1929), Opdycke (1939), Kenyon & Knott (1949), Lass & Lass (1976), the *NBC Handbook* (1984), and Burchfield (1996) all prefer it.

The adjective *panegyrical* is pronounced PAN-uh-**JIR**-i-kul; the verb *panegyrize* is pronounced PAN-i-ji-ryz; the noun *panegyrist* is pronounced PAN-uh-**JIR**-ist (the older PAN-i-ji-rist is sometimes heard).

papal PAY-pul. Don't say PAP-ul.

The first syllable in *papal* should sound like *pay,* and that's no bull.

papier-mâché PAY-pur muh-SHAY.

Papier-mâché, literally "chewed paper," came into English from French about 1750. Until the early 20th century authorities marked it as a foreign word and gave either the French pronunciation, pap-YAY muh-SHAY, or the partly anglicized (and peculiar) PAP-yay MAH-shay, with the stress on the first syllable of each word. *Webster 2* (1934) recognized the more anglicized PAY-pur muh-SHAY and listed it first as the prevailing pronunciation. Since then all sources have preferred the anglicized PAY-pur muh-SHAY, and some current ones no longer list the French pronunciation.

Although technically the French pronunciation is still permissible, it is now so rarely heard that using it may mark a person as one of the following: (a) an older speaker who has clung to his or her obsolescent ways; (b) a speaker out of touch with accepted changes in pronunciation; (c) a speaker who has studied French and cannot resist a display of pedantry; (d) a visiting Martian. In general, the more common the word and the longer it has been part of English, the more likely it will have or soon acquire an anglicized pronunciation. If, in your estimation, the anglicized form is widespread, and if it is countenanced by dictionaries, then usually it is prudent to use it. See **foyer, penchant**.

papilla puh-PIL-uh; **papillae** (plural) puh-PIL-ee (rhymes with *so silly*).

A *papilla* is any small, nipplelike projection, or, more specifically, one of the bumps on your tongue containing a taste bud.

For the plural, *papillae,* the mispronunciation puh-PIL-eye is frequently heard, and one dictionary now recognizes it as an alternative. If you were speaking classical Latin, puh-PIL-eye would be correct; we are not speaking Latin, however, and I see no reason to re-Latinize a word that has been well established in English for three hundred years. Another error, common even among dental professionals and biologists (who ought to know better), is pronouncing the plural *papillae* puh-PIL-uh, like the singular *papilla*. On TV recently I heard an expert on the sense of taste make this mistake! As the crusty but venerable H. W. Fowler says in *Modern English Usage* (1926), "Our learned persons and possessors of special information should not . . . presume to improve the accepted vocabulary. . . ." For more on the pronunciation of plurals formed with *-ae,* see **alumnae, antennae, larvae, minutiae, vertebrae**.

paradigm Traditionally, PAR-uh-dim (-dim like *dim*). Now usually PAR-uh-dym (-dym like *dime*).

This is one of the many strange-looking English words that make the language such a beastly one to spell and pronounce properly. In *paradigm,* the odd placement of a *g* before an *m* poses a problem — is it sounded, and if so, how? The answer is the *g* is left over from the Latin and ancient Greek forms of the word, and, like those languages, is dead, unspoken. In the noun *paradigm* the *g* is silent, but in the adjective *paradigmatic* the *g* is pronounced: PAR-uh-dig-**MAT**-ik.

Then there is the matter of the *i* in *-digm.* Is it short or long? PAR-uh-dim is the traditional pronunciation both in England and America; it was preferred by Walker (1791), Worcester (1860), Funk & Wagnalls *Standard* (1897), and the *Century* (1914). Sometime before 1900 the variant PAR-uh-dym gained currency and was sanctioned as an alternative by *Webster's Collegiate* (1917), Phyfe (1928), Vizetelly (1929), and *OED 1* (1928), and preferred by Fowler (1926). *Webster 2* (1934) preferred -dim and labels -dym "especially British," but subsequent sources listed -dym without comment, and current dictionaries — with the exception of *OED 2* (1989) — list PAR-uh-dym first. *Everyday Reader's* (1985) favors -dim, but other recent authorities — including Lass & Lass (1976), the *NBC Handbook* (1984), Barnhart (1988), Jones (1991), and Burchfield (1996) — prefer -dym, and *WNW Guide* (1984) says "fewer and fewer people are saying PAR uh dim." For what it's worth, I am one of them.

paraplegic PAR-uh-**PLEE**-jik. Do not say PAR-uh-puh-**LEE**-jik.

Paraplegic has four syllables. Do not add a fifth. The five-syllable mispronunciation may account for the frequent misspelling *parapalegic.* The alternative pronunciation PAR-uh-**PLEJ**-ik, despite its appearance in some current sources, is now rare.

parental puh-REN-tul. Do not say PAR-en-tul.

In *parent* (both the noun and the relatively new verb) the accent is on the first syllable, but in *parental* it shifts to the second. Dictionaries do not recognize first-syllable stress for *parental,* and *WNW Guide* (1984) calls it "not standard" — in other words, beastly.

Parisian Properly, puh-RIZH-in. Now usually puh-REE-zhin.

The older variant puh-RIZ-ee-in is still usual in Britain but now obsolete in the U.S.

We don't say pa-REE for *Paris,* so why do many say puh-REE-zhin for *Parisian?* Frierson (1988) points out that both *Paris* and *Parisian* have long been anglicized to PAR-is and puh-RIZH-in, therefore puh-REE-zhin, a half-baked imitation of the French *parisien,* "doesn't exist," he says. It does exist, of course, because millions say puh-REE-zhin and many sources now recognize it. However, that does not nullify the fact that it is pseudo-French.

Americans love to embellish certain words with French sounds, often creating hybrid pronunciations or a mangled version of the French original. For instance, why do many speakers pronounce the *en-* in *envelope* like *on?* How did we manage to come up with lahn-zhe-RAY for *lingerie* when the French is la(n)zh-REE? The *l*'s in *guillotine* have been pronounced (GIL-uh-teen) almost since the word came into English in the 1790s, but in the last few decades a de-anglicized pronunciation, with the *l*'s elided (GEE-yuh-teen), has become widespread. And *ambience* has been an English word for over a hundred years and nearly all current sources list the anglicized pronunciation AM-bee-ints first, yet hordes of people prefer the French spelling *ambiance* and pronounce the word AHM-bee-ahnts or ahm-bee-AHNTS.

Americans favor so many Frenchified — or perhaps I should say French-fried — pronunciations that one could reasonably argue that "pseudo-French" is an American dialect. The dramatic rise during the 20th century in the number of people who have earned college degrees may have contributed to our peculiar predilection for French sounds, for many of these educated speakers have studied French just enough to forget everything about the language except how to misapply it to established English words. A subtler but more compelling reason for the "pseudo-French phenomenon" may be our association of the French language and culture with romance and sophistication, which makes French sounds (often factitious ones), and Continental vowels in general, strangely alluring. Whatever the reason, one thing is clear: wherever a pseudo-French pronunciation exists for a word, there are always many speakers who use it, it is usually recognized by dictionaries, and the expostulations of hidebound orthoepists like Frierson and me are not likely to persuade many to abandon a partiality so comfortably entrenched. Authorities before 1960 did not recognize puh-REE-zhin and the three major current American dictionaries that list the word give priority to puh-RIZH-in. However, most speakers, it seems, now favor the pseudo-French puh-REE-zhin, the *NBC Handbook* (1984) prefers it, and in the early 21st century the balance of authority will probably shift in their favor. *C'est la vie.* See **ambience, Elysian, enclave, envelope, guillotine, lingerie, papier-mâché.**

parley PAHR-lee; **parlay** PAHR-lay.

Don't confuse the pronunciation of *parley* (rhymes with *barley* and *Charlie*), the conference, with *parlay* (rhymes with *parkway*), the bet.

paroxysm PAR-u̱k-SIZ'm, not puh-RAHK-siz'm. Stress the first syllable, not the second.

As justification for their beastliness, mispronouncers of *paroxysm* (who perhaps mistakenly associate it with *peroxide*) may point to *M-W 9* (1985) and *10* (1993), where the variant puh-RAHK-siz'm appears preceded by the label "also," meaning it is "appreciably less common." What these mispronouncers fail to apprehend is that second-syllable stress is appreciably *absent* from all other sources, past and present, including *Webster 3* (1961), the unabridged predecessor of *M-W 9* and *10*.

I urge you not to follow the perverse and often pompous few who are now altering the pronunciation of this four-hundred-year-old word. There is no authority for second-syllable stress; even Merriam-Webster's own pronunciation editor, Brian M. Sietsema, Ph.D., eschews it. "I used to pronounce flaccid as FLASS-id and paroxysm as puh-ROX-i-zim," he confessed to a reporter from *The New York Times.** "And now? It's FLAK-sid and PAIR-ux-i-zim." (The reporter's transliteration of the first syllable as PAIR- is a bit off: the dictionaries, including Sietsema's, mark it PAR- with the short *a* of *act* and *ash*.) See **flaccid**.

pastoral PAS-tur-u̱l. Do not say pa-STOR-u̱l. (The variant PAHS-tur-u̱l is British.)

There is no *store* in *pastoral*. Authorities do not countenance the increasingly heard and extremely beastly mispronunciation pa-STOR-u̱l, with second-syllable stress. Please help preserve the proper pronunciation of this word: the stress should be on the *first* syllable, as in *pastor*. See **electoral, mayoral, pectoral**.

patent (obvious) PAYT'nt; (other general senses) PAT'nt.

pathos PAY-thahs (-thahs rhyming with *pos* in *posse*) or PAY-thaws (rhymes with *play toss*).

The first pronunciation has the greater authority and is recommended.

In *pathos, bathos,* and *ethos,* the first vowel should have its long sound (PAY-, BAY-, EE-) and *-os* is preferably pronounced -ahs, with a short *o* as in *hot* and *jostle*.

PAY-thahs is preferred by Lass & Lass (1976), the *NBC Handbook* (1984), *Everyday Reader's* (1985), and Barnhart (1988), it is the only pronunciation in *Oxford American* (1980), Funk & Wagnalls *Standard* (1980), and *OED 2* (1989), and it listed first by all four major current American dictionaries. These same four also recognize the alternative PAY-thaws; only two list the

---

* July 22, 1993, p. C8.

variant PAY-thohs (with a long *o* as in *dose*), which is not recommended. See **cosmos, ethos.**

patina PAT-i-nuh or PAT'n-uh. Do not say puh-TEE-nuh.

The stress should be on the *first* syllable, not the second.

The variant puh-TEE-nuh, with the accent on the second syllable, is a vogue pronunciation apparently based on false analogy with *patine,* an alternative spelling of *patina* often pronounced puh-TEEN. It probably was encouraged by association with such words as *farina, sestina,* and *ballerina,* and it may also be an ignorant attempt to imitate Italian or Latin. Whatever the reason, the second-syllable accent is erroneous. *Patina* comes through Italian, where the accent falls on the first syllable, from Latin, where the accent also fell on the first syllable. Properly, *patina* follows the pattern of *retina, stamina,* and *lamina,* also trisyllabic words from Latin with antepenultimate stress.

Patina was first recorded in English in 1748. *Webster 3* (1961) was the first dictionary to recognize puh-TEE-nuh, and for the next twenty years the variant appeared only in *Webster 3*'s offspring, the Collegiate dictionaries of Merriam-Webster. In the 1980s we enter the heyday of this vogue pronunciation, with *WNW 2* (1984), *AHSC* (1985), and *Random House II* (1987) sanctioning puh-TEE-nuh as an alternative, *M-W 9* (1985) listing it first, and the *NBC Handbook* (1984) selecting it (for some unfathomable reason) as its preferred pronunciation. The weight of recent authority, however, still favors the traditional PAT-i-nuh. *American Heritage 3* (1992), *RHWC* (1997), and *WNW 3* (1997) list it first, and Lass & Lass (1976), *Everyday Reader's* (1985), Barnhart (1988), and *OED 2* (1989) prefer it.

Want my opinion? Second-syllable stress in *patina* is bogus, trendy, and (to borrow a good putdown from H. W. Fowler) sham-refined. Stress the first syllable.

patriarch (American and British) PAY-tree-ahrk.

patriot PAY-tree-it.

According to Burchfield (1996), the British say PA-tree-it (PA- as in *pat*) or PAY-tree-it (PAY- like *pay*), "with the first perhaps slightly more common." In the U.S. PAY-tree-it rules the roost. Current American dictionaries also recognize the variant PAY-tree-aht (-aht rhyming with *dot*). I have never heard anyone use that pronunciation, which strikes me as ridiculously exagerrated and pretentious, like saying chari-*aht* for *chariot* or idi-*aht* for *idiot*. Americans and Brits may differ on how to pronounce the first syllable of *patriot,* but we are happy to agree that the last syllable has an obscure *o,* as in *riot* and *carrot.*

patronize (American) PAY-truh-nyz; (British) PA-truh-nyz.

The vast majority of Americans say *pay,* with a long *a,* for the first syllable of *patronage* and *patronize.* The short *a* sound, as in *pat,* is the British preference, and coming from an American speaker it sounds Anglophilic and stilted.

pecan pi-KAHN (-KAHN ryming with *John*) or pi-KAN (-KAN like *can*).
These are the pronunciations most often listed, and sometimes the only ones listed. Older authorities often preferred pi-KAN, but in American speech today there is no doubt that pi-KAHN is the dominant pronunciation, and the four leading American dictionaries all list it first. Other recognized variants, in descending order of frequency listed, include PEE-kan, which the evidence of my ears tells me is chiefly Eastern and which Lass & Lass (1976) prefer, and PEE-kahn, which my ears tell me is chiefly Southern. Don't say (ugh) PEEK-in.

pectoral PEK-tur-ul. Do not say pek-TOR-ul. Stress the *pec-*, not the *-tor-*.
In recent years the semiliterate have taken to saying pek-TOR-ul, with the accent on the second syllable instead of the first. There is no authority whatsoever for this faddish and thoroughly beastly mispronunciation. See **electoral, mayoral, pastoral**.

pedagogy PED-uh-GOH-jee or **PED**-uh-GAH-jee.
The final *-gy* is pronounced *-jee*, as in *gee whiz*.

The noun *pedagogue* is pronounced **PED**-uh-GAHG (rhymes with *fed a hog*). The adjective *pedagogic* is pronounced PED-uh-**GAH**-jik (rhymes with *head of logic*).

pejorative pi-JOR-uh-tiv or pi-JAHR-uh-tiv.
Stress the second syllable, *-jor-*, which may rhyme with *door* or sound like *jar.*

The pronunciations **PEE**-jur-AY-tiv and **PEJ**-ur-AY-tiv, preferred by older sources, are now rare in American speech, and in British speech the formerly preferred PEE-juh-ruh-tiv has also given way to pi-JAHR-uh-tiv.

penalize PEE-nuh-lyz, not PEN-uh-lyz.
The first syllable of the verb to *penalize,* which entered English in the 1860s, is pronounced PEE- (like *pea*) because the word is formed from the adjective *penal* (PEE-nul) plus the suffix *-ize.* Although the alternative PEN-uh-lyz, which is based on false analogy with *penalty* (PEN-ul-tee), has been recorded in dictionaries since the 1940s, the weight of authority clearly favors PEE-nuh-lyz. It is the first pronunciation given by the four leading current American dictionaries, it is the only pronunciation in *OED 2* (1989), and it is preferred by Lass & Lass (1976), the *NBC Handbook* (1984), and Jones (1991).

penchant PEN-chint.
The anglicized PEN-chint has been the dominant pronunciation in American speech since the 1940s and current American authorities all prefer it. The French pronunciation, paw(n)-SHAW(N), still appears in three of the

four leading current dictionaries, but two of them, *M-W 10* (1993) and *RHWC* (1997), note that it is especially British. (A French pronunciation that's especially British? I find that exquisitely ironic.) In American speech today, the French/British pronunciation sounds odd or affected — at least to anyone too young to make mandatory withdrawals from an IRA.

For example, my mother (born 1920), with the venerable *Webster 2* (1934) in her living room to guide and defend her, still clings to the French pronunciation of *penchant*, bless her soul. Though her pronunciation, to my forty-year-old ear, seems as quaint as running boards, place prefixes for phone numbers, and movie stars who chain-smoke Chesterfields, I indulge her in her preference. After all, she was brought up by a well-educated New England mother who was a stickler for good French, and that was the way she was taught to say the word.

On the other hand, one has to consider the effect (or perhaps affect) of continuing to use a foreign pronunciation when most people have adopted the anglicization — and particularly when the foreign pronunciation is a French one that's especially British. (That's double trouble!) When does one dare say paw(n)-SHAW(N)? Among those one's own age, who might also pronounce it that way? Among tolerant family members? Among Francophones and Brits? Is it worth it to stick with a foreign pronunciation when it's bound to raise eyebrows or induce puzzled stares?

The answers to these questions are ultimately personal. Depending on your age, your upbringing, and where you live, your preferred pronunciation of *penchant* (and, for that matter, many of the words in this book) may not be the popular or current one, and that's all right. The main thing is to be consistent; stick to your guns, as they say. Don't use paw(n)-SHAW(N) when hobnobbing with highbrows and PEN-chint when hanging out with hoi polloi. As long as your pronunciation is recognized by current dictionaries (preferably by more than one), you have every right to continue using it. The worst you have to fear is that some people will think you are hopelessly behind the times — which, in the long view, is not always such a bad thing to be. See **centimeter, crème de menthe, deluxe, double entendre, foyer, papier-mâché, Parisian.**

penitentiary PEN-i-TEN-shuh-ree, not PEN-i-TEN-shee-er-ee.
This word should have five syllables, never six. Pronounce the suffix *-iary* in two syllables (-uh-ree), not three. Three syllables are appropriate for *-iary* in (q.v.) **beneficiary, judiciary, plenipotentiary,** and **subsidiary.**

pentathlon pen-TATH-lahn or pen-TATH-lun. See **decathlon.**

penult PEE-nuhlt (like *peanut* with an *l: peanult*). Also, pi-NUHLT.
The *penult* is the next-to-last syllable of a word. "The weight of authority favors first-syllable accent," says Opdycke (1939), "but second-syllable accent is likewise correct." Historically, American authorities generally prefer PEE-nuhlt, while British ones prefer pi-NUHLT. See **antepenult.**

penultimate pi-NUHL-ti-mit. See **penult**.

percolator PUR-kuh-LAY-tur (like *perk a later*).

There is no *you* in *percolator*. Pronouncing this word as if it were spelled *perculator* is 100 percent beastly.

perfume (noun) PUR-fyoom; (verb) pur-FYOOM.

Always stress the second syllable of the verb: "The scent of flowers pur-FYOOMD the garden." Some speakers like to stress the second syllable of the noun, and Morris & Morris (1985) find this acceptable, but it sounds chichi to my ear: "My, your pur-FYOOM is LUH-vuh-lee, DAH-ling." Lass & Lass (1976), *WNW Guide* (1984), the *NBC Handbook* (1984), Barnhart (1988), and Jones (1991) prefer PUR-fyoom for the noun and pur-FYOOM for the verb. This conforms to the rule for stressing two-syllable words that function both as nouns and verbs, explained under **decrease**.

permit (noun) PUR-mit; (verb) pur-MIT.

Don't say pur-MIT for both noun and verb. The noun a *permit* is properly accented on the first syllable and the verb to *permit* is accented on the second. See **decrease**.

persevere PUR-suh-**VEER** (just like *per* + *severe*).

Always stress the last syllable, and don't stick an *r* sound in the middle and say the word as if it were spelled *per-ser-vere* (a mistake I made for many years in my wayward youth). PUR-sur-**VEER** is wrong, and pur-SEV-ur — based on the old spelling *persever*, used by Shakespeare and obsolete by the mid-17th century — is straight out of a time warp.

persona pur-SOH-nuh.

From the 1950s to the 1980s the variant pur-SAHN-uh (-SAHN- as in *sonic*) had limited currency, but at millennium's end it has quietly disappeared without, thank goodness, having made a splash in the dictionaries. All four major current American dictionaries and *OED 2* (1989) countenance only pur-SOH-nuh.

The plural of *persona* is either *personae* (pur-SOH-nee) or *personas* (pur-SOH-nuhz). The Latin phrase *persona non grata,* meaning "unacceptable, unwelcome," is best pronounced pur-SOH-nuh NAHN GRAH-tuh.

Petrarch PEE-trahrk, not PE-trahrk; **Petrarchan** pi-TRAHR-kin.

Petruchio (*Taming of the Shrew*) pi-TROO-kee-oh (or -chee-oh), not pi-TROO-shee-oh.

phenomenon fi-NAHM-uh-nahn.

Pronounce the final -*non* in *phenomenon* like the *non-* in *nonsense*. The variant fi-NAHM-uh-nun, in which -*non* sounds like *none,* is originally (and still chiefly) British.

philatelist fi-LAT'l-ist (-LAT'l- rhyming with *tattle* and *battle*).

Don't say fi-LAYT'l-ist (-LAYT like *late*) or fi-LAHT'l-ist (-LAHT like *lot*). These are beastly mispronunciations.

Some time ago I called the U.S. Postal Service and heard a recording, of course. I gathered up my blanket and pillow, put some water for coffee, and prepared to wait for "the next available operator" to return from vacation. Just then, over the somnolent sound of Muzak, a taped voice asked, "Are you a fį-LAYT'l-ist?"

Oh my gosh! I thought. What if I am? Will I grow hair on my palms? Is my picture going to be in those Most Wanted lists in all the post offices? I could see the headlines: "Fį-LAYT'l-ist found guilty of language molestation." And I saw the judge handing down my sentence: twenty years of licking millions of Christmas Seals.

Then it came to me. The voice wasn't trying to accuse me of doing something dirty. I simply had been the victim of yet another beastly mispronunciation. The fancy word for stamp collecting is *philately* (pronounced fį-LAT'l-ee, with a short *a* as in *bat*), the adjective is *philatelic* (FIL-uh-**TEL**-ik), and a person who collects stamps is a *philatelist* (fį-LAT'l-ist). (*Timbromaniac* was the word originally proposed for a stamp collector, but it quickly got licked by *philatelist*.)

When my fears subsided, I began to wonder how the Postal Service could allow its spokesperson to mispronounce this word. Surely there were philatelists calling up who would be flabbergasted by the mistake. Surely they would see the error of their ways.

A few months later I had reason to call again, and, lo and behold, the recorded voice's pronunciation had changed. This time the question was, "Are you a fį-LAHT'l-list?" Sometimes you wonder how they ever manage to get the mail sorted and delivered.

But I shouldn't be too tough on these people. They work hard under a great deal of stress. Why should I fault them for allowing some talking head to say (on a tape that no one pays attention to) fį-LAYT'l-ist and fį-LAHT'l-ist instead of fį-LAT'l-ist? Does it matter that fį-LAT'l-ist is the only pronunciation you will find in any current dictionary when, for example, no less a personage than David Letterman says fį-LAHT'l-ist? After all, Letterman is funny; dictionaries are dull.

As all you philatelists and English teachers and careful speakers know, it does make a difference, no matter how many David Lettermans mispronounce the word and no matter how many people try to hand you that line about how the essence of language is change, which is usually just a pompous excuse to cover up an insecurity or a mistake. If trend is our god, and change our only creed, now that a Postal Service voice-over and Letterman — who, with a name like that, should know better — say fį-LAHT'l-ist, does that mean it's time to tinker with the pronunciations of *deltiologist* (DEL-tee-**AHL**-uh-jist), a postcard collector, and *numismatist* (noo- or nyoo-MIZ-muh-tist), a coin collector?

When Douglas Martin of *The New York Times* asked the etymologist David Shulman (who is credited with finding the earliest citation of the nickname "the Big Apple" for New York City) what difference "all this verbal pickiness" makes, Shulman responded, "Why, the same difference as being literate or illiterate, accurate or inaccurate, telling the truth or spreading yarns." Shulman the *etymologist*, a scrutinizer of words, would not take kindly, I'm sure, to being called an *entomologist*, a scrutinizer of bugs. Saying it right *does* make a difference, and often a "meaningful" one.

The only acceptable pronunciation of *philatelist* is fi-LAT'l-ist. That is the only pronunciation sanctioned by 20th-century authorities and the only one you will find in every 20th-century dictionary but one — *Webster 3* (1961), which gives fi-LAT'l-ist followed by fi-LAYT'l-ist labeled as less common.

-phile Always like *file*, never like *feel*. For more on *-ile*, see **textile**.

-philia FIL-ee-uh (also FIL-yuh); **-philiac** -FIL-ee-ak.

Properly, there is no *feel* in *-philia* and *-philiac*. It should be *filly*, with a short *i* as in *fit*. These combining forms, which come from the Greek *philos*, loving, are frequently mispronounced in such words as *hemophiliac* and *necrophilia*. When *phil(o)-* appears as a prefix, no one pronounces it with this pseudoclassical *feel*. You don't say FEEL-*osophy* for *philosophy* (love of learning), FEEL-*anthropy* for *philanthropy* (love of humankind), or FEEL-*adelphia* for *Philadelphia* (city of brotherly love). So why say HEE-muh-FEEL-ee-uh for *hemophilia*? See **memorabilia**.

philippic fi-LIP-ik. Stress the second syllable.

phlegmatic fleg-MAT-ik (rhymes with *egg static*).

This is the only recognized pronunciation. Anything else is beastly. The most common mistake is pronouncing the *g* like *j*.

Phnom Penh puh-NAWM PEN.

Greet's *World Words* (1948), the *Columbia Encyclopedia* (1963), and the *NBC Handbook* (1984) prefer the anglicized pronunciation without the initial *p*: NAHM PEN. But *Webster's Geographical* (1949) and *WNW 3* (1997) give only puh-NAWM PEN, which Greet acknowledges reflects the local pronunciation, and this is the first pronunciation in *American Heritage 3* (1992) and *Webster's Geographical 3* (1997).

Phoenician fi-NISH-in (rhymes with *remission*).

This is the traditional and proper way to say it, but dictionaries now sanction fi-NEE-shin, a pseudoclassical pronunciation that is probably more frequently heard. Whatever you do, don't (as someone once told me he had been taught to) pronounce the first syllable foh-.

phraseology FRAY-zee-**AHL**-uh-jee (five syllables).

One of the most common mistakes I hear educated speakers make is pronouncing *phraseology* in four syllables instead of five. (What do you bet the same folks who make this beastly booboo also mispronounce *verbiage* in two syllables instead of three?)

There is no *phrase* in *phraseology.* In other words, don't pronounce it like *phrase* + *ology:* frayz-AHL-uh-jee. The word is divided *phra • se • ol • o • gy* and is properly pronounced in five syllables, with *phra • se* rhyming with *crazy:* FRAY-zee-**AHL**-uh-jee.

The frequency of the four-syllable mispronunciation in educated speech has led the round-heeled lexicographers at Merriam-Webster to list it (after the correct pronunciation) in their modern dictionaries, beginning with the unabridged *Webster 3* (1961) and continuing in four subsequent abridgments through *M-W 10* (1993). It is significant, however, and the careful speaker should take careful note, that the three other major current American dictionaries — *American Heritage 3* (1992), *RHWC* (1997), and *WNW 3* (1997), along with the British *OED 2* (1989) — countenance only the five-syllable FRAY-zee-**AHL**-uh-jee, and no authority with a reputation to lose prefers the four-syllable pronunciation. See **verbiage**.

pianist pee-AN-ist (or PYAN-ist). PEE-uh-nist is chiefly British.

It has been my experience — as the son of two professional musicians, both of whom pronounce this word pee-AN-ist — that those who say PEE-uh-nist seem quite sure that those who say pee-AN-ist are wrong, whereas those who say pee-AN-ist tend to wonder whether those who say PEE-uh-nist are putting on the dog.

According to *The Barnhart Dictionary of Etymology* (1988), *piano,* the instrument, dates from 1803, and *pianist* came along in 1839, "borrowed from French *pianiste,* from Italian *pianista,* formed from *piano* piano + *ista* -ist." Worcester (1860), Webster's *Academic Edition* (1868), and Ayres (1894) give pee-AH-nist (rhymes with *be honest*), with the so-called Italian or broad *a,* but this pronunciation disappeared shortly after 1900. Funk & Wagnalls *Standard* (1897) gives pee-AN-ist, the *Century* (1914) and Phyfe (1926) sanction both pee-AN-ist and PEE-uh-nist, and *OED 1* (1928) prefers PEE-uh-nist. Vizetelly (1929), who also countenances both pee-AN-ist and PEE-uh-nist, says that the latter "is common in England," and Holt (1937) says, "The first syllable accent is more English than American." This and other evidence indicates that PEE-uh-nist is British in origin, and since the early 20th century it has been the dominant British pronunciation. The four major current American dictionaries all list PEE-uh-nist, but three give priority to pee-AN-ist, which is the preference of the *NBC Handbook* (1984).

What this boils down to is that if you say PEE-uh-nist you are not being "more correct," only a bit different and RAH-thur more British. On the other hand, if you say pee-AN-ist, you won't need a tuxedo to play along with anyone. See **flutist, viola**.

picture PIK-chur.

Don't say PITCH-ur (like *pitcher*). This is a common and venial error in children that, if not corrected, can become a persistent beastly mispronunciation in adults. At the other end of the misguided spectrum is the over-elegant and undereducated mispronunciation PIK-tyoor, which is used by those who sit on PAH-tee-oh FUR-ni-tyoor, gazing out at their PAS-tyoor and enjoying NAY-tyoor. If I were sheriff, I'd have these folks CAP-tyoord and put in *gaol*.

Pierre (capital of South Dakota) PEER.

Pietà pyay-TAH or PEE-ay-**TAH**, not pee-AY-tah.

The word comes directly from the Italian *pietà*, pity, mercy, piety, and the grave accent is there for a reason.

piquant PEE-ki̱nt.

PEE-ki̱nt has been established in cultivated speech for over a hundred years and is favored by most current authorities. It is the first pronunciation listed in *American Heritage 3* (1992), *M-W 10* (1993), and *RHWC* (1997), and the only pronunciation in *OED 2* (1989) and *WNW 3* (1997). An acceptable alternative is PEE-kahnt (-kahnt rhyming with *want*), which usually appears second in current sources. A third variant, pee-KAHNT, is unattractive because it shifts the traditional accent to the second syllable. Other recent variants include PEE-kant, pee-KANT, PEE-kwu̱nt, PEE-kwahnt, and the increasingly common but erroneous PIK-wu̱nt. All of these are best avoided. Say PEE-ki̱nt, which is neither pretentious nor difficult to pronounce.

plantain PLAN-ti̱n, not PLAN-tayn.

Current dictionaries do not recognize the spelling pronunciation PLAN-tayn (-tayn rhyming with *cane*). The *-tain* in *plantain* is properly pronounced like the *-tain* in *captain*, and the word should sound like *plan* + *tin*.

pleasure PLEZH-ur (*ple-* as in *pledge* and *plenty*).

There is no *play* in *pleasure*. Don't say PLAY-zhur. See **leisure, measure**.

plenipotentiary PLEN-i̱-puh-**TEN**-shee-er-ee.

Take care to pronounce this powerful mouthful of a word in seven syllables. Don't chop off the second-to-last syllable and say PLEN-i̱-puh-**TEN**-shur-ee. See **beneficiary, judiciary, penitentiary, subsidiary**.

plethora PLETH-uh-ruh. Stress the *first* syllable, which rhymes with *breath*. The ignorant and the unwary commonly mispronounce this word ple̱-THOR-uh, erroneously placing the accent on the second syllable. Authorities from the 18th century to the present have preferred PLETH-uh-ruh, and current dictionaries do not recognize ple̱-THOR-uh. The adjective *plethoric*, however, is best pronounced with the accent on the second syllable, ple̱-THOR-ik, but PLETH-uh-rik is also acceptable.

poem POH-u̱m, not POYM or POHM (rhymes with *home*).

The monosyllabic nonword POYM — which I have heard, most prominently, from a college professor who discusses contemporary poets and poetry on NPR — is an affront to the language. "The word pronounced POME," says Shaw (1972), "refers to a fleshy fruit, such as an apple or pear." In *The King's English* (1998), the late British novelist Kingsley Amis complains that "PWETry and POYtry [for *poetry*] are devilish noises. Make three syllables of it." And make two audible syllables out of *poem*, please, to rhyme with *show 'em*.

pogrom po-GRAHM (po- as in *polite*).

There is considerable difference of opinion on the proper pronunciation of this Russian loanword. The noun *pogrom* was first recorded in English in 1882. The earliest sources in which I found it listed — *Webster's Collegiate* (1917), *OED 1* (1928), and *Webster 2* (1934) — give one pronunciation: po-GRAHM. The *OED* includes this 1906 quotation from the *Westminster Gazette:* "The Russian word 'pogrom' (pronounced with stress on the final syllable) is generally translated 'desolation, devastation.'"

As is often the case with loanwords, recessive stress (the movement of the accent toward the beginning of a word) soon went to work on *pogrom*, and by the 1940s two variants with first-syllable stress had appeared. Kenyon & Knott (1949) sanctioned POH-grum and PAH-grum, followed by poh-GRAHM; *American College* (1952) gave priority to POH-grum, followed by poh-GRAHM. *Webster 3* (1961) juggled that order, listing puh-GRAHM first followed by POH-grahm, POH-grum, and "sometimes" PAH-grum.

Since then second-syllable stress has continued to hold its own, and today the evidence of my ears tells me that first-syllable stress — perhaps because it invites confusion with *program* (and its mispronunciation, PROH-grum) — has leveled off and may be on the wane. Only *M-W 10* (1993) gives priority to POH-grum, which is preferred by the *NBC Handbook* (1984) and Barnhart (1988). *American Heritage 3* (1992) lists puh-GRAHM first, *WNW 3* (1997) lists poh-GRAHM first, and *RHWC* (1997) countenances only puh-GRUHM — the preference of Lass & Lass (1976) and *Everyday Reader's* (1985) — and puh-GRAHM (or poh- for the first syllable of both). PAH-grum survives in Britain, where *OED 2* (1989) lists it as an alternative to poh-GRAHM and Burchfield (1996) and Jones (1991) prefer it.

poignant POYN-yint. The *g* is silent.

A number of people have told me that this word gives them trouble. If that's true for you, try remembering these two things: that *poign-* rhymes with *coin;* and that the *gn* has the same rolled *n*-to-*y* sound as in *lasagna* (luh-ZAHN-yuh).

poinsettia poyn-SET-ee-uh (four syllables).

There is no *point* in *poinsettia*. The mispronunciation poynt-SET-ee-uh is especially beastly, and poynt-SET-uh is beyond the pale.

This hardy, colorful plant is named after the American diplomat J. R. Poinsett (1779–1851), who brought it from Mexico to the U.S. in 1828. No doubt certain words ending in -*etta*, such as *operetta* and *vendetta*, as well as names like *Henrietta* and *Rosetta*, have encouraged the common three-syllable mispronunciation poyn-SET-uh. But *poinsettia*, from what I can tell, appears to be the only word in the language that ends in -*ettia*, and properly, that lonesome little penultimate *i* should be pronounced. "Why omit the last *i?*" asks Holt (1937). "'Setta' is common, but wrong. Who says 'gar-dee′na' or 'mag-no′-la'?"

Current American dictionaries have succumbed to the frequency of the error and listed poyn-SET-uh as a secondary pronunciation, but no authority I have consulted prefers the three-syllable variant and careful speakers frown upon it — a fact that is acknowledged by *M-W 10* (1993), which labels both poyn-SET-uh and poynt- (like *point*) for the first syllable with an obelus [÷], meaning they are "considered by some to be unacceptable." If you aren't already a member of that "some," you are best off becoming one pronto.

pointillism POYN-ti̱-LIZ'm. Also, **PWAN**-ti̱-LIZ'm.

Is there a *point* in *pointillism*, or should it be *pwant*? And how should we handle the double *l* — like a regular *l* or a semi-audible *y*? For broad-brush answers and a few fine points, read on.

There are three recognized (i.e., dictionary-sanctioned) ways of saying this word: the fully anglicized **POYN**-ti̱-LIZ'm, which I recommend; the half-anglicized **PWAN**-ti̱-LIZ'm, the traditional and most often recorded pronunciation, which is also acceptable; and the de-anglicized, or re-Frenchified, **PWAN**-tee-IZ'm, which I will argue is affected and unacceptable. But first, a brief history lesson.

OED 2 (1989) traces *pointillist* to 1891 and *pointillism* to 1901. *Webster's Collegiate* (1917, 1923) is the earliest of my sources to record *pointillism*, with the half-anglicized pronunciation **PWAN**-ti̱-LIZ'm, and this is the only pronunciation in *OED 1* (1928), *Webster 2* (1934), the *Winston Dictionary* (1951), *American College* (1952), and *M-W 6* (1956). *Webster 3* (1961) is the first of my sources to record the de-anglicized (re-Frenchified) **PWAN**-tee-IZ'm, which it lists first, followed by the established **PWAN**-ti̱-LIZ'm. *RH College* (1968) is the first of my sources to record the fully anglicized **POYN**-ti̱-LIZ'm, listing it third after the half-anglicized and de-anglicized variants.

This chronology raises an interesting question: why did these two new ways of saying the word — one more French, the other more English than the established pronunciation — emerge at about the same time? My theory is that the spread of **PWAN**-tee-IZ'm is linked to the growing popularity and tremendous increase in the value of impressionist and postimpressionist paintings. As we all know, the art world is no stranger to snobbery.

Since the 1960s the pseudosophisticated **PWAN**-tee-IZ'm has gradually displaced the original **PWAN**-ti-LIZ'm undoubtedly because of its snob appeal — because it sounds "more French" and therefore somehow more intellectual or refined. Meanwhile, however, as an appreciation of *pointillism* spread from the art world's cognoscenti to hoi polloi, its pronunciation quite naturally evolved in the opposite direction and became more plebeian and hence more English.

I reject the re-Frenchified **PWAN**-tee-IZ'm because it is the product and the property of those who wish to call attention to their more elevated position on the ladder of culture. I accept, without rancor, the half-anglicized **PWAN**-ti-LIZ'm because it has been standard since the word entered the language and because several current authorities — including *Everyday Reader's* (1985) and *WNW 3* (1997) — still prefer it. Nevertheless, I think its color is fading fast. I endorse **POYN**-ti-LIZ'm because after a hundred years full anglicization is not only sensible but in most cases inevitable as well. English has a salutary habit of abandoning French sounds whenever they become overnice, old-fashioned, unintelligible, or *pwant*less. In my book, there *is* a *point* in *pointillism*. This word has hitched its palette, and our palate, to English, and despite all the prissy forces of re-Frenchification I predict there will be no going back. The future clearly belongs to **POYN**-ti-LIZ'm. The *NBC Handbook* (1984) and Jones (1991) agree.

pomace PUHM-is, not PAHM-is.

Properly, there is no *palm* in *pomace*. PUHM-is is the only pronunciation in *OED 2* (1989) and *WNW 3* (1997), and the preference of *WNW Guide* (1984) and *Everyday Reader's* (1985).

pommel (noun) PAHM-ul (recommended) or PUHM-ul; **pummel** (verb) PUHM-ul.

I am in agreement with Alfred H. Holt, who in *You Don't Say!* (1937) writes that

> a frequent distinction in spelling is between the noun (part of a saddle), spelled [*pommel*], and the verb (what a saddle does to a beginner — though that is not the origin of the word), spelled *pummel*. Both are now supposed to be pronounced "pummel," but I favor an eventual distinction in pronunciation as well.

The *pommel horse* used in gymnastics, however, is usually PUHM-ul.

Popocatépetl (famed volcano in central Mexico) POH-poh-kah-**TEP**-et'l. There's some authoritative disagreement on this one. W. Cabell Greet's *World Words* (1948), the *NBC Handbook* (1984), *American Heritage 3* (1992), and *Webster's Geographical* (1997) say POH-puh-**KAT**-uh-PET'l, with the primary stress on -*cat*-. *M-W 8* (1975) and *9* (1985) say POH-puh-

KAT-uh-**PET**'l, with the primary stress on *-pet-*. And *Random House II* (1987) says PAW-paw-kah-**TE**-PET'l, a variant listed in several other current sources as an alternative and the pronunciation closest to the Mexican Spanish POH-poh-kah-**TEP**-et'l. This is the pronunciation we ought to use, it seems to me, since it is the native one and no more exotic or difficult to pronounce than any of the anglicized variants. Of course, if you're in Mexico, all you have to do is use the colloquial *Popo* (POH-poh) and they'll know what you're talking about.

porcupine POR-kyuh-pyn.

The pronunciation POR-kee-pyn (like *porky* + *pine*) is not recognized by dictionaries. In children it can be endearing, but not in adults. Pronounce the *-cu-* in *porcupine* like the *-cu-* in *occupy*.

Porsche PORSH.

In my experience, how you pronounce this word/name depends largely on whether you own the automobile in question. *Porsche* does not appear in any of my references, so I must rely solely on the evidence of my ears, which tells me that those who own a Porsche (or wish they did) tend to prefer the disyllabic POR-shuh, while those who don't (and could not care less) tend to prefer the monosyllabic PORSH. Because the great majority of us don't own (or aspire to own) a Porsche, I recommend the monosyllabic pronunciation as less ostentatious.

Portuguese POR-chuh-GEEZ.

There are no *geese* in *Portuguese*. Rhyme the final syllable with *bees* and *knees*. See **Japanese**.

possess puh-ZES. Do not say poh-ZES.

There is no *pose* in *possess*. A long *o* (poh-) in the first syllable is an over-pronunciation. See **official**.

posthumous PAHS-chuu-mus or, chiefly British, PAHS-tyuu-mus.

Stress the *pos-*, which should sound like *pos-* in *posse*.

It is natural to look at this word, see *post-* and *-humous*, and assume that the pronunciation should be pohst-HYOO-mus (or sometimes pahst-HYOO-mus). What is astonishing is how many well-educated people then blithely go about using this conjectural pronunciation, never bothering to check a dictionary and apparently oblivious of the many careful speakers who pronounce the word correctly.

I have heard businesspeople, lawyers, professors, engineers, writers, editors, and even doctors say pohst-HYOO-mus. Despite what you hear from these folks (and some of them may get huffy and defend the mispronunciation), there is no authority for stressing the second syllable, unless one happens to be referring to the character *Posthumus Leonatus* (pahst-HYOO-mus LEE-oh-**NAY**-tus) in Shakespeare's *Cymbeline*.

The modern dictionaries of Merriam-Webster — from the unabridged

Webster 3 (1961) through its most recent abridgment, *M-W 10* (1993) —
are the only dictionaries that recognize the mispronunciation. (*M-W 10*
labels it less frequent.) No other authority I know of — from Walker (1791)
to *RHWC* (1997) — countenances it. Merriam-Webster's irresponsible bit
of lexicography in this instance is a snub to the many cultivated speakers
who pronounce the word properly and a great disservice to those who
don't, for they will be encouraged to find their mistake ratified by Merriam-Webster but fail to grasp that most educated speakers consider the
second-syllable accent unacceptable, as evidenced by its conspicuous absence from other dictionaries and lack of any other authoritative approval.
The careful speaker is advised to heed the words of *WNW Guide* (1984),
which says, "Some people manage a tongue-twisting spelling pronunciation **PAHS** thyoo mus. That and another spelling pronunciation, pohst
HYOO mus, are not standard." (In this book, "not standard" = *beastly*.)

potpourri POH-puu-**REE**.

precedence PRES-i-dents. Formerly, but now rarely, pri-SEE-dents.

First-syllable stress in *precedence* is an early-20th-century British innovation that was endorsed by H. W. Fowler, who declared in *Modern English
Usage* (1926) that the *OED*'s preference for second-syllable stress was "a
very disputable account of present usage" and recommended first-syllable
stress "for all alike" on the assumption that it would prevail — which it
has, on both sides of the Atlantic. Although Lass & Lass (1976) and the
NBC Handbook (1984) prefer second-syllable stress, and Morris & Morris
(1985) recommend that "the pronunciation of PRESS-ih-denss might be
reserved for *precedents* and the pronunciation preh-SEE-denss given to
precedence," for at least forty years the matter has been settled beyond
debate. The British import, PRES-i-dents, is far and away the dominant
pronunciation in American speech, and although current American dictionaries still list pri-SEE-dents, it is heard only once in a blue moon.

predator PRED-uh-tur. Do not say PRED-uh-tor.

The terminal *-or* is pronounced like *-er* (UR). See **juror, mentor, vendor**.

predecessor PRED-uh-SES-ur.

The British say **PREE**-duh-SES-ur. Note that the terminal *-or* should
rhyme with *sir*, not *soar*.

preferable PREF-ur-uh-buul.

Stress the first syllable. Do not say pruh-FUR-uh-buul.

Despite the fact that two current American dictionaries recognize pruh-
FUR-uh-buul (labeling it less frequent), and despite what you may have
heard from the Great Communicator, Ronald Reagan, and other prominent educated speakers, the words *preferable* and *prefer* should have different accents. *Prefer* is accented on the second syllable; *preferable* is properly
accented on the first syllable, like *preference*. For Shaw (1972), Lass & Lass

(1976), the *Oxford Guide* (1983), the *NBC Handbook* (1984), *WNW Guide* (1984), Morris & Morris (1985), *American Heritage 3* (1992), Burchfield (1996), and *WNW 3* (1997), PREF-ur-uh-buul is preferable.

prelate PREL-it (rhymes with *smell it*).

prelude PREL-yood. Don't say PRAY-lood or PREL-ood.

PREL-yood has been the customary pronunciation in cultivated speech since the influential English elocutionist John Walker indicated it as such in his *Critical Pronouncing Dictionary* of 1791. The American lexicographer Joseph Emerson Worcester (1860), who also favors PREL-yood, shows that it was also the preference of William Perry (1775), Thomas Sheridan (1780), Benjamin Humphrey Smart (1836), and several other prominent English orthoepists of the early 19th century. Only Noah Webster (1806, 1828), that crotchety godfather of the American language, struck out on his own and opted for PREE-lood,* which has survived to this day (albeit barely) in educated American speech. In deference to Grandpa Webster, perhaps, the Merriam-Webster dictionaries of the 19th and early 20th centuries listed both PREE-lood and PREL-yood, and other dictionaries of the period — including Funk & Wagnalls *Standard* (1897) and the *Century* (1889–1914) — followed suit. *Webster 2* (1934), however, gave priority once again to PREL-yood, and since then the weight of authority has remained solidly on its side. Morris & Morris (1985) and Barnhart (1988) give priority to PREL-yood and sanction PREE-lood as an alternative, and Lass & Lass (1976), the *NBC Handbook* (1984), and Burchfield (1996) prefer PREL-yood.

The mid-20th century witnessed the rise of a vogue pronunciation, PRAY-lood, which has since caught on to the point where all four major current American dictionaries now recognize it. (All four, however, give priority to the traditional pronunciation, PREL-yood.) *Webster 3* (1961) was the first to record PRAY-lood (and also the preposterously stuffy and artificial PRAYL-yood), noting that it was more commonly heard for the word's "musical senses." I know plenty of musicians who would vehemently dispute that, but that's beside the point, which is this: PRAY-lood is an affectation, a pathetic descent into pseudo-French masquerading as an ascent to refinement and culture. It is what I call a de-anglicization, an

---

* This was undoubtedly a pedanticism on his part, based on the word's origin: Latin *prae-*, before (pronounced PREE in Noah's day), the source of the English prefix *pre-*, and *ludere*, to play. It may also have been prompted by his ardent desire to drive a chauvinistic wedge between the English of England and the English of America. "As an independent nation," Webster wrote in his *Dissertations on the English Language* (1789), "our honor requires us to have a system of our own, in language as well as government. Great Britain, whose children we are, and whose language we speak, should no longer be *our* standard: for the taste of her writers is already corrupted, and her language on the decline."

ostentatious attempt to return to what the offending speakers imagine is the original, or foreign, pronunciation of the word. Suddenly to say PRAY-lood after over 200 happy years of saying PREL-yood (and also PREE-lood) is like one day deciding that BLAWNSH is a superior way to pronounce *blanch*, or that ROH-mawn-**TEEK** sounds classier than roh-MAN-tik. I say let's leave this pretentious PRAY-lood where it probably began — with that peculiar clan of pseudosophisticated radio and TV voice-overs who hawk cheap wine, luxury cars, and low-calorie TV dinners. (For more on de-anglicization, see **cadre, junta, largess,** and **lingerie.**)

Careful speakers are also advised to avoid one other beastly mispronunciation. "Many rhyme [*prelude*] with '*swell* food,' without bothering to insert 'you,'" says Holt (1937). "But this annoys purists excessively." And why shouldn't it? PREL-ood, without that *y* (or long *u*) sound, is ugly as sin. If you can pronounce *volume* (VAHL-yoom), then you have no excuse for not pronouncing *prelude* properly — especially if you think it's more erudite to insert a *y* before the *u* in *erudite*. See **erudite.**

premier pri-MEER; (British) PREM-yur (swallow the *r*).

premiere pri-MEER (recommended) or pri-MYAIR; (British) PREM-ee-er (swallow the *r*).

premises PREM-i-siz, not PREM-i-seez.

There is no *seize* at the end of *premises*. Say *premise* + *is*. See **basis, crisis, process.**

premonition PREE-muh-**NISH**-in, not PREM-uh-**NISH**-in.

Premonition entered English from Latin in the 15th century. Authorities from Walker (1791) to Funk & Wagnalls *Standard* (1897) to *American College* (1952) countenance only one pronunciation: PREE-muh-**NISH**-in, first syllable rhyming with *see*. The variant PREM-uh-**NISH**-in, first syllable rhyming with *stem*, was first recognized by *Webster 3* (1961). Jones (1991) lists it as the prevailing pronunciation in educated British speech today; *OED 2* (1989), however, gives priority to PREE-. Current American authorities are divided. Lass & Lass (1976), *WNW Guide* (1984), and *WNW 3* (1997) favor PREM-; the *NBC Handbook* (1984) and Barnhart (1988) favor PREE-; and *American Heritage* (1992), *M-W 10* (1993), and *RHWC* (1997) list PREE- first.

preparatory pri-**PAR**-uh-TOR-ee, not **PREP**-uh-ruh-TOR-ee or **PREP**-ruh-TOR-ee.

Preparatory has five syllables, and the accent properly should fall on the second (*-par-*), which is pronounced as in *parent*. The five- and four-syllable variants that shift the accent to the first syllable, *prep-*, have been recognized by dictionaries since the 1960s. It is possible that they arose based on analogy with *laboratory*, but I suspect a more insidious influence was at work. I think they are pseudo-British, affected vogue pronunciations that were initially popular among the affluent Eastern prep school set and that, through fawning imitation, later spread to the rest of us lesser mortals. Current American dictionaries all recognize the five-syllable **PREP**-uh-ruh-TOR-ee (though only one lists the four-syllable **PREP**-ruh-TOR-ee), but all give priority to the traditional pri-**PAR**-uh-TOR-ee, which Lass & Lass (1976) and the *NBC Handbook* (1984) prefer. In case you were wondering, *OED 2* (1989) and Jones (1991) indicate that the British also stress the second syllable, but slur the fourth: pri-PAR-uh-tur-ee.

prerogative pruh-RAHG-uh-tiv.

No matter how rapidly you say this word, you must take care not to transpose the *r* and *e* of *pre-* and say pur-. There is no *purr* in *prerogative* (which is why you sometimes hear the jocular overpronunciation pree-RAHG-uh-tiv). It's okay to say pur- when you're being *per*-snickety, but you may find yourself in a *pruh*-dicament if you say pur- when exercising your pruh-RAHG-uh-tiv. See **repercussion**.

presage (noun) PRES-ij (rhymes with *message*); (verb) pri-SAYJ (second syllable like *sage*). See **decrease.**

prescience PREE-shints or PREE-shee-ints; PRESH-ints or PRESH-ee-ints. All these pronunciations are acceptable. The *sc* is pronounced like *sh,* the word may have two or three syllables, and the first syllable may have a long *e,* as in *preen,* or a short *e,* as in *pressure.* My preference is two syllables, long *e:* PREE-shints.

Holt (1937) says the word "was formerly pronounced like *pre* plus *science,* and still 'pree' is preferred to 'presh'; but the *science* has collapsed into 'shence.'" Kenyon & Knott (1949), Lass & Lass (1976), the *NBC Handbook* (1984), and Barnhart (1988) prefer "presh." Vizetelly (1929), Opdycke (1939), *WNW Guide* (1984), and *Everyday Reader's* (1985) prefer "pree."

In British English, says Burchfield (1996), the "customary pronunciations" of *prescience* and *prescient* are now PRES-ee-ints and PRES-ee-int. See **prescient.**

prescient PREE-shint or PREE-shee-int; PRESH-int or PRESH-ee-int. See **prescience, sentient, transient.**

presentation PREZ-in-**TAY**-shin (recommended) or PREE-zen-**TAY**-shin. The recommended pronunciation is the traditional one and one of my (many) passionate preferences. Walker (1791), Worcester (1860), Funk & Wagnalls *Standard* (1897), the *Century* (1914), *Webster's Collegiate* (1917), Phyfe (1926), and Vizetelly (1929) give only PREZ-, and Ayres (1894) and Opdycke (1939) caution against saying PREE-. However, since *Webster 2* (1934) listed PREE- as an alternative in good standing, it has become nearly as common as PREZ- in educated American speech. Current authorities are divided. Lass & Lass (1976) prefer PREE-, which *WNW Guide* (1984) and *M-W 10* (1993) list first; the *NBC Handbook* (1984) prefers PREZ-, which *American Heritage 3* (1992), *WNW 3* (1997), and *RHWC* (1997) list first.

Under the circumstances, I suppose I must accept PREE- as respectable; however, there is no law that says I have to like it. The PREE- in *presentation* has always struck me as a stilted overnicety used by those who ostentatiously attempt to be more precise than their peers and who are somehow convinced, without anything to back it up, that *presentation* is formed from the verb to *present*, which of course is pronounced PREE-zent in *presentation*. These same fastidious people no doubt would become flustered should you inquire why you have to make a fancy PREE-*sentation* just to give them a *present* at the *present* time. They may come around to your point of view *presently*, but if they get peribleptic (PER-i-**BLEP**-tik, wild-eyed and delirious), just tell them you have to go in the interest of *self*-PREE-*servation*.

I would wager that many speakers who say PREZ- (still the majority of us, I believe) feel the same way I do. Maybe the PREZ-sayers no longer can accuse the PREE-sayers of being wrong, but what we think is another matter.

presentiment pri-ZEN-ti-ment, not pri-SEN-ti-ment.
This may surprise you, but there is no *sentiment* in *presentiment*. The *s* has the sound of *z*, as in *present, presently,* and *presentable*. Dictionaries do not recognize the erroneous variant with *s* as in *presto*.

president PREZ-uh-dint (or -dent).
Don't drop the middle syllable (-*i*-) from *president* and say PREZ-dint. That is sloppy. Also, even in your most rapid speech, don't ever, ever slur over both the *i* and the *d* and pronounce *president* PREZ'nt, like *present*. I was astonished to discover that *M-W 9* (1985) and *10* (1993) actually list this slovenly variant, implying that it is acceptable in cultivated speech. It is not! It's beastly, and no other dictionary countenances it. Finally, don't say PRES-uh-dint, with an *s* as in *press*. I have heard numerous newscasters make this mistake, and it irks me that they do not realize they are confusing the pronunciations of *president* (*z* for *s*) and *precedent* (*s* for *c*). The *s* in *president* should have the sound of *z*, and a peek into any dictionary will prove it.

Presley (Elvis) PRES-lee (first syllable like *press*).
Ed Sullivan, Steve Allen, and Milton Berle, on their respective TV shows, all introduced the King as Elvis PREZ-lee, with the *s* pronounced as in *present*. Two current dictionaries list PREZ-lee as an alternative and it is the *only* pronunciation in *WNW 3* (1988, 1997).* Is the *z*-influenced pronunciation more correct than plain *s*?

---

* *WNW 3*'s failure to recognize PRES-lee is remarkable evidence that dictionary editors, who

When I began investigating this question the evidence of my ears told me that PRES-lee prevailed among non-Southerners (myself included), and so I suspected that PREZ-lee might be the Southern pronunciation, and perhaps Elvis's own preference. A telephone call to the Elvis Presley birthplace in Tupelo (TOO-puh-loh), Mississippi, quickly dispelled this erroneous notion.

"I've never heard anything but PRES-lee in the South," said the woman who answered the phone. She then handed the receiver to the director, who declined to give her name but asserted that "the correct pronunciation is PRES-lee, like *go to press*. There's no *z* in it. In the South, where he was born, that's the way you say it."

Okay, I thought, but what about the King himself? For an answer I called Graceland (GRAYS-lund, with *-land* as in *island*), Elvis's opulent home in Memphis, Tennessee. I was referred to Todd Morgan, Graceland's long-time director of creative resources. "Elvis pronounced his last name PRES-lee," he told me, "and that's what we go with."

Never one to take such assertions entirely on faith, I trudged down to my local video store and picked up a couple of Elvis documentaries, and in *This Is Elvis* (1981) I struck gold — or platinum, as the case may be. In a comedy skit with Milton Berle, Berle mistakes Elvis for an importunate fan, and the King has to set him straight. "I'm Elvis PRES-lee," he says. So there. If that doesn't im*press* you, nothing will.

prestigious pre-STIJ-u̲s, not pre-STEE-ju̲s.

We don't say -TEE- for the second syllable of *litigious,* or -DEE- for the second syllable of *prodigious,* or -LEE- for the second syllable of *religious.* Why, then, do so many people say -STEE- for the second syllable of *prestigious?* It's a simple case of misapplied analogy. *Litigious, prodigious,* and *religious* have no accompanying nouns *litige, prodige,* and *relige,* but *prestigious* has *prestige,* and the pronunciation of the noun has unduly influenced the adjective. *Prestige* is preferably pronounced pre-STEEZH, although the less common pre-STEEJ is also acceptable. For *prestigious,* three of the four major current American dictionaries, *OED 2* (1989), and *WNW Guide* (1984) give priority to pre-STIJ-u̲s, which is the preference of Lass & Lass (1976), Barnhart (1988), and Jones (1991).

A word on former pronunciations: for *prestige,* the variant PRES-tij is obsolete. For *prestigious,* the four-syllable pre-STIJ-ee-u̲s, the only pronunciation in *Webster 2* (1934), is on its way out. Only one current dictionary lists it. See **capricious**.

presumptuous pri-ZUMP-choo-u̲s.

---

pride themselves on their "truly scientific (i.e. quantitative) approach" to language and claim to record those pronunciations "widely used by good speakers," can sometimes be strangely deaf to usage. (The quoted phrases are from *WNW 3*'s front matter.)

The word has four syllables, not three. Don't say pri-ZUMP-shus (a hoary and tenacious vulgarism that Walker decried in 1791).

primer (introductory textbook) PRIM-ur; (paint) PRY-mur.

pristine PRIS-teen (recommended) or pri-STEEN. British also PRIS-tyn.

"Forget *Christine* and her second syllable accent — nobody seems to approve of her as a rhyme for this," writes Alfred H. Holt in *You Don't Say!* (1937). "[PRIS-tin] is preferred by most to a long *i* in the last syllable. But Webster [2] has rushed boldly into an endorsement of a rhyme with *Sistine;* i.e., 'priss'-teen.'"

Holt issued this report on the eve of a major shift in the pronunciation of *pristine.* Webster's bold endorsement of PRIS-teen marked the beginning of its dominance in American speech and the beginning of the end for the older PRIS-tin, which disappeared by the mid-20th century. (I was born in 1957 and I have never in my life heard anyone say PRIS-tin. Only one current dictionary still records it.) Holt was quite wrong, of course, about the variant pri-STEEN, rhyming with *Christine.* By the 1970s it had gained respectability — Lass & Lass (1976) prefer it — and all four major American dictionaries of the 1990s list it after PRIS-teen, which is the preference of the *NBC Handbook* (1984), *WNW Guide* (1984), *Everyday Reader's* (1985), Barnhart (1988), Jones (1991), and Burchfield (1996).

privilege PRIV-uh-lij.

Careful speakers pronounce the word in three syllables, not two.

proboscis proh-BAH-sis (or pruh- in rapid speech).

The legendary comedian W. C. Fields used to say pruh-BAHS-kis, with a *k* sound for the *c.* Perhaps the mispronunciation was a subtle part of his comic style, perhaps not. At any rate, anyone who knows anything about trunks and noses knows that there is no *kiss* in *proboscis.* The -*sc*- should be pronounced as in *scene* and *science.*

Because of the prevalence of the *kiss* mispronunciation, three of the four major current American dictionaries now list it as an alternative, but *OED 2* (1989) and *American Heritage 3* (1992) sanction only proh-BAH-sis, and Lass & Lass (1976), the *NBC Handbook* (1984), *WNW Guide* (1984), *Everyday Reader's* (1985), and Barnhart (1988) prefer it. Burchfield (1996) says "the medial *c* is silent."

process (American) PRAH-ses; (British) PROH-ses.

processes PRAH-ses-iz. Do not say PRAH-ses-eez.

The final -*es* is pronounced as in *kisses* and *excuses,* and there are no excuses for the beastly mispronunciation PRAH-ses-eez. It is an affected, ostentatious, faddish, pseudo-Latin overpronunciation. The plural of *face* is not FAY-seez, the plural of *base* is not BAY-seez, the plural of *abuse* is not uh-BYOO-seez, and you are abusing the language if you put a spurious *seize* at the end of *processes.* See **bases, premises**.

[318]

processor PRAH-ses-ur. Do not say PRAH-ses-or.

The final -*or* should rhyme with *sir,* not with *for.* See **juror.**

prodigy PRAH-di-jee.

Be careful not to switch the *d* and *g* sounds and say PRAH-juh-dee.

produce (noun) PROH-doos or PRAH-doos.

You may wonder why a defender of the YOO/long *u* sound (see **dew**) would not recommend -dyoos for the second syllable here, and this is my answer: because the second syllable receives neither primary nor secondary stress. In an unstressed syllable, YOO/long *u,* to my ear, usually sounds precious and overprecise rather than fluent and euphonious. It's a personal call. If you prefer PRAH-dyoos (the modern British pronunciation) or PROH-dyoos, fine. Just bear in mind that both are rarely heard today in American speech.

Now let's look at the question of short *o,* PRAH-, for the first syllable versus long *o,* PROH-. Walker (1791), who prefers PRAH-, notes that the noun *produce* was "very often, but improperly, pronounced like the verb, with the accent on the second syllable. Some speakers, who attempt to be wonderfully accurate, preserve the accent on the first syllable, but pronounce the *o* long and open" — in other words, PROH-. Walker concluded that "this is contrary to analogy."

Nearly all authorities of the 19th century and early 20th century shared Walker's disdain for PROH-. *Webster 2* (1934) pronounced PROH- all but dead ("*formerly also* prō′ dūs," it said), but apparently it was still alive and growing because Holt (1937) and Opdycke (1939) both proscribed it. By the 1940s PROH- had gained enough respectability for Kenyon & Knott (1949) and *American College* (1952) to sanction it as an alternative. Current American sources all give priority to PRAH-, with the short *o,* but the evidence of my ears tells me that the dominant pronunciation in the U.S. today is PROH-. My advice? Go with the pronunciation you are accustomed to hearing or are more comfortable with. For me, that's PROH-doos.

productivity PROH-duk-**TIV**-i-tee (recommended) or PRAHD-.

This word, formed from *productive* + -*ity,* was first recorded in 1809 in the writing of Samuel Taylor Coleridge — that's KOHL-rij, in two syllables, not three (see the entry). Worcester (1860) and Funk & Wagnalls *Standard* (1897) give PRAHD-uk-**TIV**-i-tee with a short *o* in the first syllable. The *Century* (1914), *Webster's Collegiate* (1917), *OED 1* (1928), *Webster 2* (1934), and *American College* (1952) give only PROH-duk-**TIV**-i-tee with a long *o.* Three of the four major current American dictionaries give priority to PROH- with the long *o,* and this is the only pronunciation in the fourth, *RHWC* (1997).

program PROH-gram. Do not say PROH-grum.

In a letter to *New York Times* language maven William Safire, John Strother of Princeton, New Jersey, calls the slurred PROH-grum "a voguish pronunciation among public-radio announcers and other people who wish to sound erudite, or at least British. . . ."* Yes, PROH-grum is voguish, yes, it's pretentious, and yes, it's regrettably rampant on public radio, but no, it's not an Anglophilic affectation. It's simply an illogical bit of beastliness that made its way into the dictionaries over the objections of numerous authorities.

"Do not slur over the *a* in the second syllable," counsels Gilmartin (1936). "You do not say *telegr'm* — do not say *progr'm*. The *gram* should be clearly pronounced." Ayres (1894), Phyfe (1926), Vizetelly (1929), Holt (1937), Witherspoon (1943), the *NBC Handbook* (1984), *WNW Guide* (1984), *Everyday Reader's* (1985), and Morris & Morris (1985) agree: the second syllable should be pronounced -gram, not grum. One need only compare the sound of -*gram* in *diagram, anagram, telegram, milligram, monogram,* and *cryptogram* to see that their verdict is sound. English words ending in -*gram* rhyme with *ham* and *cram*, not *some* and *dumb*. (Only in the name *Seagram* does -*gram* have an obscure *a*.)

project (noun) PRAH-jekt; (verb) pruh-JEKT.
Pronounce the *t*. "Projeck" is a Major Beastly Mispronunciation.

promulgate Traditionally, pro-MUHL-gayt. Now usually **PRAHM-ul-GAYT.**
Recessive stress — a shift in accent toward the beginning of a word — has taken *promulgate* by storm. The pronunciation **PRAHM-ul-GAYT**, with the primary stress on *prom-*, is a British innovation, first recorded in *OED 1* (1928). (The *OED* also recognized **PROH-mul-GAYT**, which flopped in England and America.) *Webster 2* (1934), Opdycke (1939), Kenyon & Knott (1949), and *American College* (1952) all preferred pro-MUHL-gayt and labeled first-syllable stress British, but that probably only added to its cachet. Since *Webster 3* (1961) gave priority to **PRAHM-ul-GAYT** it has steadily pushed pro-MUHL-gayt to the brink of extinction. At present I know of only two speakers who say pro-MUHL-gayt — William F. Buckley, Jr., and me — and I wouldn't be surprised if our reason for sticking with the traditional pronunciation is the same: an idiosyncratic and obstinate brand of patriotism. Barnhart (1988) also prefers second-syllable stress, but all other current authorities have surrendered to the British and all four major current American dictionaries list **PRAHM-ul-GAYT** first. See **inculcate, infiltrate, obfuscate, precedence, sonorous.** For a discussion of recessive and progressive (forward-moving) stress, see **confiscate.**

pronounciation Don't say it.
There is no *pronoun* in *pronunciation*. It's a *nun*. There is also no verb to

---

* See *Watching My Language* (1997), p. 228.

[320]

pronounciate. It's *pronounce.* Both of these are regrettably common and beastly errors, even among educated speakers. Be sure to distinguish *pronounce* and *pronunciation* in speech and spelling. See **pronunciation**.

pronunciation pruh-NUHN-see-**AY**-shin.

Many who regard themselves as careful speakers boast of their good pruh-NOWN-see-**AY**-shin, saying this word as if it were spelled — which it sometimes mistakenly is, after the mispronunciation. Remember, there is no *pronoun* in *pronunciation.* (See the next entry.)

This subtle and beastly error has been around for a long time. John Walker (1791), for example, wrote that "there are few words more frequently mispronounced than [*pronunciation*]. A mere English scholar, who considers the verb to *pronounce* as the root of it, cannot easily conceive why the *o* is thrown out of the second syllable, and therefore, to correct the mistake, sounds the word as if written *Pronounciation.*"

Incidentally, Walker argued vigorously that the *c* in *pronunciation* should have the sound of *sh;* he marked the word proh-NUHN-shee-**AY**-shuhn. Authorities of the 19th century were divided: Worcester (1860), for example, sided with Walker, but Smart (1836) claimed that "most speakers say *pro-nun-si-a'shun.*" By the beginning of the 20th century cultivated usage and authority had settled on *s* for *c,* and the *sh* pronunciation soon became obsolete.

protein PROH-teen, not PROH-tee-in.

Protein now should be pronounced as the overwhelming majority of speakers pronounce it — in two syllables. The earlier pronunciation with three syllables, PROH-tee-in, is obsolescent, and, because it is old-fashioned, it also sounds overpronounced.

I realize that some older speakers will take exception to my ruling and cling to their three-syllable PROH-tee-in, which of course they have every right to do. But I can offer more than just the winds of change to defend my case. PROH-tee-in (almost identical to PROH-tee-in) is the pronunciation for the adjective *protean,* literally "like Proteus" (PROH-tee-us), the Greek god who could assume different shapes and forms. Pronouncing *protein* in two syllables and *protean* in three reinforces a useful aural distinction between the words.

protest (noun) PROH-test; (verb) pruh-TEST.

In days of yore, the noun *protest* was stressed on the second syllable, but from about the time of Worcester (1860) to the present, it has been stressed on the first syllable. For the verb *protest* and its participles *protesting, protested,* cultivated speakers place the accent on the *-test-,* not on the *pro-,* following the rule for disyllabic nouns and verbs explained under **decrease**.

provenance PRAH-vuh-nints.

psalm SAHM. The *l* is silent. See **calm**.

psychiatry sy-KY-uh-tree; **psychiatrist** sy-KY-uh-trist.

Although mentally ill people are commonly called "sick," nobody puts a *sick* in the first syllable of *psychosis* and *psychotic*. The *psy-* is always a *sigh*. Likewise with *psychology*. So why do so many speakers today slip a *sick* into the same unstressed *psy-* of *psychiatry* and *psychiatrist*, pronouncing them *sick-EYE-a-tree* and *sick-EYE-a-trist*? As is often the case, the answer lies buried in the yellowing pages of the dictionaries.

Psychiatry, says *OED 2* (1989), was first recorded in the 1846 edition of Worcester's dictionary. I have the 1860 edition, a peek into which elicited what I have come to call a *eureka shriek* — a sharp cry uttered upon finding the very thing one hoped not to find. Worcester marks the *y* as "slight or obscure," meaning it has an indefinite quality somewhere between the *i* of *sister* and the *u* of *summer,* in this case closer to *sister*. Hence, *sick-EYE-a-tree,* which when said rapidly sometimes sounds almost like *suck-EYE-a-tree*. (For the much older word *psychology* — c. 1650s — Worcester prefers *sigh* in the first syllable, as do all sources since.) *Psychiatrist,* says *OED 2,* first appeared in the 1890 edition of the *Century,* which gives only *sigh-* for it and its fifty-something father *psychiatry*. From then on it's *sigh-* all the way — not exactly from your first couchant cry to your last dying day, but from Funk & Wagnalls *Standard* (1897) to *Webster 2* (1934) to *American College* (1952), supported by Phyfe (1926), Vizetelly (1929), Opdycke (1939), and Kenyon & Knott (1949).

All this orthoepic harmony over *sigh-,* without a peep uttered either in acknowledgment or disapproval of *sick-,* would seem to indicate that *sick-* was but a distant memory buried in Worcester's 19th-century brain. Not so. *Sick-* was only latent, and when it resurfaced in *Webster 3* (1961) it appeared to have already turned the tables on *sigh-,* for that dictionary gave *sick-* top billing and labeled *sigh-* "appreciably less frequent." It's been that way ever since. Only one of the four major current American dictionaries, *WNW 3* (1997), gives priority to *sigh-,* and only one modern American authority, Lass & Lass (1976), prefers it. In Britain, however, *sigh-* remains the preferred pronunciation.

I suspect that what's at work here is that old bugbear dissimilation — the term linguists use for the tendency of one of two similar neighboring sounds in a word to become different from the other. For example, dissimilation is how we got GUHV-uh-nur for *governor,* which is fine, and **FEB**-yoo-ER-ee for *February,* which is not fine. (Just because it's a "linguistic process" doesn't mean I have to like everything it does.) Not surprisingly, dissimilation exerts a mighty force, and when it gets a good grip on a word it rarely lets go. Unlike the British, American speakers are major suckers for dissimilation because it allows us to get from point A to point B with as little conscious effort as possible. But the purpose of speech is not simply to make oneself heard. An infant or a pet can accomplish that without benefit of words. To speak, in my opinion, is to attempt to express oneself well, an act that requires a certain amount of thought and labor. Don't get me wrong here. I'm not opposed to natural fluency in speech, an end that dissimilation often serves admirably. What I dislike is mere expediency, the slovenly couch-potato approach to pronunciation, for which dissimilation all too often is just a joystick or a jumbo bag of chips.

Worcester couldn't have marked the first *y* in *psychiatry* obscure because of dissimilation; the word was still wet behind the ears and barely finding its voice. Instead he seems to have based his *sick-EYE-a-tree* pronunciation on the New Latin *psychiatria,* an early, evanescent synonym of *psychiatry* that he pronounces si-KY-uh-**TRY**-uh. Having the benefit of longer familiarity with the word, authorities later sensibly settled on *sigh-* on analogy with *psychology.* Related words with second-syllable stress — e.g., *psychosis* (1847), *psychopathy* (1847), *psychometry* (1854), *psychography* (1883), and *psychotic* (1890) — followed suit, and everything was hunky-dory for a while.

So why are *psychiatry* and *psychiatrist* the only members of the entire family of *psych-* words that have fallen prey to dissimilation? Because, with their adjacent rhyming sy- and -ky- sounds, they were the only ones vulnerable to it. Speakers found it more expedient to let their *sigh-* become *sick-,* and the neurosis swiftly became the norm. You don't have to be a psychiatrist to diagnose that as the couch-potato syndrome.

For a comment on the former practice of sounding the *p* in *psychiatry* and other words beginning with *ps-,* see the footnote under **facet**.

puerile (American) PYOOR-ul; (British) PYOOR-ryl. See **textile**.

puerperal pyoo-UR-pur-ul.

puissant PYOO-i-sint or pyoo-IS-int or PWIS-int.

All three variants are sanctioned by modern authority. My preference, PYOO-i-sint, appears to have a bit of an edge; *Webster 2* (1934), *Random House II* (1987), *OED 2* (1989), and *WNW 3* (1997) give it priority, and it is preferred by the *NBC Handbook* (1984), *Everyday Reader's* (1985), and Barnhart (1988). But of course I'm biased. I don't have anything personal against pyoo-IS-int, a pronunciation often required in old poetry, but I must admit that PWIS-int is just too *pwissy* for my taste.

pulpit PUUL-pit, not PUHL-pit.

The *pul-* in *pulpit* should sound like the verb to *pull.* The variant PUHL-pit, in which *pul-* rhymes with *dull,* was not listed in dictionaries before the 1960s. Current dictionaries all give priority to the traditional PUUL-pit, and no modern authority I am aware of prefers the variant pronunciation.

pummel PUHM-ul. See **pommel**.

pumpkin PUHMP-kin (just like *pump* + *kin*).

Pronounce the medial *p* and avoid saying PUHNG-kin (like *punkin*), unless you're joking or using it as a term of endearment for a child.

Q

quagmire KWAG-myr (recommended) or KWAHG-myr.

KWAG- rhymes with *bag*, KWAHG- rhymes with *bog*; second syllable like *mire*.

In American speech KWAG- has long been the dominant pronunciation, and some older authorities — Ayres (1894) and Phyfe (1926), for example — objected to KWAHG-. In 1934, however, *Webster 2* sanctioned KWAHG-, and since then it has been listed in good standing. Burchfield (1996), referring chiefly to British speech, calls both pronunciations "equally acceptable."

qualm KWAHM. The *l* is properly silent. See **calm**.

quandary KWAHN-duh-ree or KWAH-dree.

The chiefly British variant kwahn-DAIR-ee, with second-syllable stress, is an archaism. By as long ago as the 1940s it was rarely heard in America. Burchfield (1996) says *quandary* "has firmly joined the group of words in which -*ary* is unstressed (*aviary, boundary, burglary*, etc.)."

quasi KWAY-zy or KWAY-sy.

The *a* should be long, as in *quake;* the *i* should be long, as in *sigh;* and the *s* may be either soft, as in *rose*, or hard, as in *case*. Older sources generally prefer KWAY-sy, with the hard *s;* most current ones prefer KWAY-zy, with a soft *s*. (Both follow the rule for the English pronunciation of Latin discussed under **data**.) The popular variants KWAH-zee (which is relatively recent) and KWAH-see (the classical Latin pronunciation) are recognized by current dictionaries but not recommended. Why say it in classical Latin or pseudo-Latin when you can say it in English? The same goes for

---

a = at / a̱ = final / ah = spa / ahr = car / air = fair / ay = hay / aw = saw
ch = chip / e = let / e̱ = item / ee = see / eer = deer / i = sit / i̱ = April
ng = sing / o̱ = carrot / oh = go / oo = soon / or = for / oor = poor
ow = cow / oy = toy / sh = she / th = thin / t̲h̲ = this / u̱ = focus / uh = up
ur = turn / uu = pull, took / y, eye = by, I / zh = measure / (see full key, p. xiv)

the Latin-English hybrid KWAH-zy — an eccentric variant I once heard from a book reviewer on NPR — for which there is no authority.

The *quasi-* in *Quasimodo* (the ecclesiastical term for the first Sunday after Easter as well as the name of Victor Hugo's hunchbacked character) is an exception. Because *Quasimodo* is formed from the first words of the Latin Introit, *Quasi modo geniti infantes* ("As newborn babes . . ." 1 Pet. 2:2), it is pronounced either like the classical Latin, KWAH-si-**MOH**-doh, or — more often in American speech — like the Italian, KWAH-zee-**MOH**-doh.

quay KEE (like *key*).

Two influential early English authorities, William Perry (1775) and Thomas Sheridan (1780), preferred KAY, and two important literary figures, Jonathan Swift and Alfred, Lord Tennyson, rhymed the word with *day* and *today*, respectively. However, the highly esteemed English elocutionist John Walker (1791) and the venerated American lexicographer Noah Webster (1828) both preferred KEE, and nearly all authorities since then on both sides of the Atlantic have agreed. Today, KEE is listed first in three of the four major current American dictionaries and it is the only pronunciation in the fourth — *WNW 3* (1997). The spelling pronunciation KWAY, which appears only in *M-W 10* (1993), is best avoided.

Quebec (English) kwi-BEK; (French) kay-BEK.

The host of the TV game show *Jeopardy!*, Alex Trebec — a French Canadian, I believe — says kay-BEK. One could do much worse than emulate Mr. Trebec's pronunciation in general, and I'm certainly not about to lecture a French Canadian on how to pronounce *Quebec* (they've got language police up there, you know). American speakers, however, should bear in mind that the predominant pronunciation in the U.S. and among other English speakers outside of Quebec is kwi-BEK, and that Americans are generally skeptical, and sometimes derisive, of any native speaker of English who displays a fondness for French pronunciations.

querulous KWER-uh-lus or KWER-yuh-lus. Do not say KWEER-uh-lus.

Past and present authority is fairly evenly divided between the two pronunciations sanctioned above. For what it's worth, I favor the first to be consistent in my manner of pronouncing the medial *u* in *querulous, garrulous, erudite,* and *virulent* (which see).

Properly, there is no *queer* in *querulous,* but in recent years the word has so often been mispronounced KWEER-uh-lus that *M-W 9* (1985) and *10* (1993) list the variant. Be careful to avoid this beastly vogue pronunciation. Also, don't say KWAHR-uh-lus or KWOR-ul-lus (like *quarrel + us*); this especially beastly mispronunciation is a resurrection of the obsolete word *quarrelous,* which was once used to mean either quarrelsome or querulous.

query KWEER-ee (like *queer* + *y*).

Query is increasingly mispronounced KWAIR-ee. This vogue variant was first recorded in *Webster 3* (1961). In 1984, *WNW Guide* gave KWEER-ee as its preference and added "now occasionally" KWAIR-ee. Transcribed as /kwer'ē/, it now can be found in three of the four major current American dictionaries. *American Heritage 3* (1992) and *OED 2* (1989), however, give only the traditional KWEER-ee, which is the preference of all authorities I have consulted from Walker (1791) to the present.

quiescent kwy-ES-int, not kwee-ES-int.

A silent battle is raging over how to pronounce the first syllable of this word. Should *qui-* be said kwy-, as in *quiet*, or kwee-, rhyming with *we?*

Before the 1960s, all was quiet on the *quiescent* front. Dictionaries and orthoepists sanctioned one pronunciation, kwy-ES-int, and peace and kwy-it reigned. But then came *Webster 3* (1961), which listed kwee-ES-int as an alternative, and *RH College* (1968), which listed *only* kwee-ES-int, and suddenly we had pronunciation mitosis. The language "grew" as more and more speakers came across *quiescent*, looked it up, and found that kwee- was now a "standard" — or in the case of Random House, the *only* standard — pronunciation, then began saying it that way and influencing others in turn. And apparently no one knew or cared that kwee-ES-int was in fact pseudo-Latin, for in the so-called classical method of pronouncing Latin, *qui-* is kwee-. Never mind that Latin is a dead language, that *quiescent* has been an English word for nearly four hundred years, or that previous dictionaries listed only the anglicized pronunciation.

At any rate, kwee-ES-int is now so popular that *RHWC* (1997) and *American Heritage 3* (1992) list it first, and *Oxford American* (1980) and *Everyday Reader's* (1985) prefer it. However, Lass & Lass (1976), the *NBC Handbook* (1984), *WNW Guide* (1984), Barnhart (1988), and Jones (1991) prefer the traditional kwy-ES-int, which is listed first in *OED 2* (1989), *M-W 10* (1993), and *WNW 3* (1997).

The battle is on. Choose your weapon: English or Latin. And remember, in the speech dodge there is no peace with honor, and no honor either, I suppose, in speaking your piece.

quietus kwy-EE-tus.

Because the word *quiet* is so prominent in *quietus*, many speakers mistakenly pronounce it with the accent on the first syllable: KWY-it-us. This mispronunciation has persisted since the early part of the 20th century but has yet to find its way into a dictionary. The pseudo-Latin variant kwy-AYT-us appears as an alternative in *M-W 10* (1993); other dictionaries do not recognize it, either, and it is best avoided.

Quietus is properly stressed on the second syllable, which has a long *e* as in *eat*. You can hear it in the iambic rhythm of these lines from the famous soliloquy in Shakespeare's *Hamlet:*

For who would bear the whips and scorns of time . . .
When he himself might his quietus make,
With a bare bodkin?

quixotic kwik-SAHT-ik.

This is the only acceptable pronunciation. Occasionally one hears, from some unfortunate soul, kee-HOH-tik, presumably based on analogy with the common American pronunciation of *Don Quixote*.

In Spanish, *Quixote* is pronounced kee-HOH-te (-te as in *test*). English speakers attempting to approximate this often say kee-HOH-tay (-tay rhyming with *day*). Authorities sanction two English pronunciations: kee-HOH-tee and KWIK-sit (rhymes with *fix it*). In the U.S., kee-HOH-tee is the dominant pronunciation and the quasi-Spanish kee-HOH-tay, though not usually listed, is often heard. KWIK-sit — the only pronunciation in *OED 2* (1989) and Jones (1991) — is British. I have never heard an American say KWIK-sit, yet all four major current American dictionaries list it and the *NBC Handbook* (1984) prefers it. That is indeed perplexing. Any American who says KWIK-sit should stop tilting at windmills and get with the program.

quoin KOYN.

Quoin — a corner of a building or, more often, a cornerstone — should be pronounced like the word *coin*, of which it is a variation. The alternative KWOYN, however, has been around since the mid-1700s, although few authorities since then have favored it. It was sanctioned by Phyfe (1926) and *Webster 2* (1934), and since then most sources have countenanced both, with KOYN listed first. Care for a ruling from architects? Under *quoins* in the glossary to their *AIA Guide to New York City,* third edition (1988), Willensky and White advise us to "say 'coins.'"

R

rabid RAB-id. Do not say RAY-bid.

Rabid and *rabies* have different pronunciations. *Rabid* properly has a short *a*, as in *rabbit*. *Rabies* has a long *a*, as in *ray*.

The beastly mispronunciation RAY-bid, with the long *a* of *ray*, is quite recent; *M-W 7* (1972) is the first of my sources to record it. Two current dictionaries list RAY-bid — *M-W 10* (1993) and *WNW 3* (1997) — but both label it infrequent, and the two other leading current American dictionaries, *American Heritage 3* (1992) and *RHWC* (1997), sanction only the proper pronunciation, RAB-id.

Be careful: this recent RAY-bid is now running wild. Don't let it bite *you*. If it does, you will surely start foaming at the mouth and uttering all sorts of other beastly monstrosities.

Raleigh (Sir Walter) RAW-lee, not RAH-lee or RAL-ee.

RAW-lee is the first pronunciation in *American Heritage 3* (1992), *M-W 10* (1993), and *RHWC* (1997), the only pronunciation in *WNW 3* (1997), and the preference of the *NBC Handbook* (1984), Emerson (1996), and Jones (1991), a British authority, who notes that "the family of the late Sir Walter Raleigh pronounced [RAW-lee]."

Rand, Ayn *Rand* rhymes with *sand*; *Ayn* rhymes with *wine* and *dine*.

Ayn is *not* pronounced like *Anne*. You don't believe me? McConkey (1986), *Random House II* (1987), and *M-W 10* (1993) all say it rhymes with *fine*. Go argue with them.

---

a = at / a̱ = final / ah = spa / ahr = car / air = fair / ay = hay / aw = saw
ch = chip / e = let / e̱ = item / ee = see / eer = deer / i = sit / i̱ = April
ng = sing / o̱ = carrot / oh = go / oo = soon / or = for / oor = poor
ow = cow / oy = toy / sh = she / th = thin / ṯẖ = this / u̱ = focus / uh = up
ur = turn / uu = pull, took / y, eye = by, I / zh = measure / (see full key, p. xiv)

rapport ra-POR or ruh-POR. See **en rapport**.

rapprochement RA-prohsh-**MAH(N)** or RA-prawsh-**MAH(N)**.

This word, which entered English in 1809, still retains most of its French flavor. Pronounce *rap-* like English *rap* (one current dictionary gives RAHP-, which is not recommended). Pronounce *-roche-* to rhyme with *gauche* (GOHSH) or with the *o* like *awe*. Place the primary stress on the final syllable and, if you can do it, nasalize the *n* in the French manner, -**MAH(N)**; if this sound is difficult for you, -**MAH**. The *t* is silent, always.

M-W 10 (1993) lists and *WNW Guide* (1984) gives priority to the half-anglicized ra-PROSH-mah(n), with second-syllable stress. It is not recognized by other authorities and is best avoided. The fully anglicized ruh-PROHCH-ment (like *reproach* + *-ment*), which I have heard occasionally, is not countenanced by dictionaries or orthoepists. See **denouement**.

ratatouille RAH-tuh-**TOO**-ee or RAT-uh-**TOO**-ee.

This word was first recorded in English in 1877. It was confined to the cookbooks for decades and did not appear in a dictionary until *Webster 3* (1961), which gives the tough-to-transcribe, still-French-behind-the-ears pronunciation / rätätüy /, with no stress indicated; as best I can render it, this is rah-tah-tooy with the -tooy like -too-ee compressed into one syllable. Some later sources render this RAH-tah-**TWEE** — *WNW 3* (1997) gives only this pronunciation — or sometimes RA-ta-**TWEE**, with the flat *a* of *at*, which *M-W 10* (1993) lists first. I cannot recommend these three-syllable variants, however, partly because they are rarely heard and chiefly because that twangy -**TWEE** in the final syllable makes you sound like a visiting Martian, which is probably why it's so rarely heard. The two pronunciations sanctioned above are the most common in American speech today and the ones most commonly recorded in current American dictionaries. If you prefer a subtle foreign flavor in your ratatouille, start off with *rot*. If you find that unappetizing, put a *rat* in it.

rather RA**TH**-ur (rhymes with *gather*). Don't say RAH-**th**ur (rhymes with *father*).

There has been, of late, a marked increase in the number of educated American speakers who perhaps think they will sound *rather* more educated if they say RAH-**th**ur — with an aristocratic open or broad *a*, as in *spa* — instead of saying RA**TH**-ur with a good old American flat *a* as in *rat*.

In their *Pronouncing Dictionary of American English* (1949), Kenyon & Knott state that the British form is RAH-**th**ur, which is also often heard in Canada, but "the most regular form, historically," is RA**TH**-ur. In the U.S. as a whole, they say, RA**TH**-ur "overwhelmingly prevails," with RAH-**th**ur "being only sporadic." They also note that even in New England — where a broad or intermediate *a* is traditional in such words as *ask, fast, dance,* and the perennially ridiculed *park* and *car* — a flat *a* in *rather* is more common among cultivated speakers.

In *The Treasure of Our Tongue* (1964), Lincoln Barnett gives an interesting account of the historical divergence between the British broad and the American flat *a:*

> One of the most striking instances of phonetic deviation — indeed a badge of nationality in the English-speaking world — is the contrasting treatment of the letter *a* in such sentences as: *The calf came down the path to take a bath.* Where most Americans, confronted with these words, use the flat *a* of *cat,* most Englishmen (save in the North) employ the [broad] *a* of *father,* and the sentence emerges from his lips as: *The cahff came down the pahth to take a bahth.* Such a pronunciation was unknown in Elizabethan times, at least not in polite court circles where *calf, path,* and *bath* were pronounced as they are in American English today. As late as 1791 an English pronouncing dictionary [John Walker's] classified the broad *a* as vulgar and the flat *a* as "characteristic of the elegant and learned world." Precisely why the broad *a* began to gain a foothold is not known, but its origins were, ironically, Cockney. Not until the second quarter of the nineteenth century did it become a hallmark of the cultivated Old School accent in British society. It is in American speech, therefore, that the older "elegant" pronunciation has been preserved, while the adoption of a once-vulgar form occurred in the linguistic homeland [pp. 175–76].*

Lest there be any doubt left in your mind over which pronunciation is appropriate in American speech today, consider this brutal bit of obloquy: the *Reader's Digest* guide *Write Better, Speak Better* (1972) classifies RAH-thur as affected and ostentatious, and places it in a list of "conspicuous, less popular, hence ineffective" pronunciations that includes VAHZ for *vase* (preferred: VAYS, rhymes with *space;* also VAYZ, rhymes with *days*); uh-GAYN for *again* (preferred: uh-GEN); and AHNT for *aunt* (preferred: ANT). See **aunt, vase.**

rathskeller RAHT-skel-ur.

Avoid the half-anglicized RAT-skel-ur and the spelling pronunciation RATH-skel-ur.

ratiocination RASH-ee-AHS-i-**NAY**-shin.

ration RASH-in (recommended) or RAY-shin.

Both pronunciations are acceptable and have been heard in cultivated speech since the word entered English in the mid–19th century. *OED 1* (1904 ed.) gave priority to RAY-shin, but by the 1930s RASH-in was the prevailing pronunciation in England. American dictionaries gave priority

---

* For more on American vs. British preferences regarding the broad, flat, short, and long *a* sounds, see pp. 334–39 of H. L. Mencken's *The American Language* (1937).

to RAY-shin until the 1940s, but since then RASH-in has been listed first (as it is in the four leading current American dictionaries).

raucous RAW-kus. Don't say ROW-kus.

There is no *row* (rhymes with *how*) in *raucous*. Current dictionaries and modern authorities countenance only RAW-kus, first syllable like *raw*.

Realtor REE-ul-tur. Do not say REE-luh-tur.

A great many educated speakers have difficulty with this word. I have heard it mispronounced by radio and TV newspeople, by businesspeople, professionals, and people in high places, and by Realtors themselves. The problem comes from inadvertently switching the *l* and the *a*, making *rela-* out of *real-*, which results in the beastly mispronunciation REE-luh-tur. It can be resolved by carefully saying the word *real* and following it with -tur. See **athlete, February, irrelevant, jewelry, nuclear.**

realty REE-ul-tee. Don't say REE-luh-tee. See **Realtor.**

recess (break or intermission) REE-ses; (alcove or niche) ri-SES or REE-ses; (verb) ri-SES.

The following historical commentary should suffice to illustrate the stressful changes that have occurred with this word.

Worcester (1860) says, "Although all the orthoepists [from 1775 to his time] accent this word on the second syllable, yet we often hear it pronounced with the accent on the first."

Ayres (1894) says, "I leave this word unmarked for two reasons: Because I do not wish to mark it [REE-ses], in opposition to all the authorities; and because I doubt whether [ri-SES], when the word is used in its literal sense, is the prevailing pronunciation. That it is not the pronunciation that will finally prevail I am confident."

Larsen and Walker (1930) say, "No doubt many Americans who speak of a [REE-ses] in 'school work' would speak of a [ri-SES] in a 'school wall'."

Holt (1937) says, "The second syllable accent in *recess* (noun) has long had the preference, but the first is gaining."

Lass & Lass (1976) prefer second-syllable stress, period. *WNW Guide* (1984), the *NBC Handbook* (1984), and Barnhart (1988) prefer REE-ses for all senses of the noun and ri-SES for the verb.

The plural noun *recesses* is preferably pronounced ri-SES-iz, but now acceptably pronounced REE-ses-iz. The participial adjective *recessed* is always stressed on the second syllable. See **decrease,** and also **recourse, redress, repeat,** and **research.**

recluse REK-loos or ri-KLOOS.

All four major current American dictionaries give these two pronunciations, in this order. Only one, *M-W 10* (1993), recognizes a third, RE-klooz. This, and its counterpart ri-KLOOZ, are beastly mispronunciations. The *-luse* in *recluse* should sound like *loose*, never *lose*. Modern American authorities generally favor REK-loos, while British authorities favor ri-KLOOS.

recognize REK-ug-nyz.

Be sure to pronounce the *g*. Careful speakers do not say REK-uh-nyz.

recourse Traditionally, ri-KORS. Now usually REE-kors.

I strongly prefer second-syllable accent in this word and I cannot help cringing a bit whenever I hear the ungainly REE-kors, which in the mouths of many speakers sounds like a donkey trying to say *wreak horse*. Nevertheless, I'll readily admit that I am at odds with almost all current American authorities and that my pronunciation is fast going the way of the dodo in American speech. It survives in good health in Britain, however, so maybe it's time to retire to the Cotswolds. See **decrease,** and also **recess, redress, repeat,** and **research**.

redolent RED'l-int. Stress the *red.*

This is the only acceptable pronunciation. There is no authority for ri-DOH-lint, or any other beastly variant you may hear. The corresponding noun, *redolence,* is also stressed on *red:* RED'l-ints.

redress (noun) REE-dres; (verb) ri-DRES.

First-syllable stress for the verb is beastly.

In the past, both the noun and verb were stressed on the second syllable, as in these lines from Dryden —

> Fair majesty, the refuge and redress
> Of those whom fate pursues and wants oppress.

— but in the 20th century this word has gradually been conforming with the general tendency, which I call Phyfe's rule, for disyllabic words that function both as nouns and verbs to have their accent on the first syllable as nouns and on the second as verbs. For consistency's sake, I say let's give *redress* a good shove in that direction. For a full discussion of Phyfe's rule, see **decrease**. See also **recess, recourse, repeat,** and **research**.

refuge REF-yooj. Do not say REF-yoozh.

Do not be misled by *M-W 10* (1993), which gives REF-yooj followed by *also* REF-yoozh (the *also* meaning "appreciably less common"). REF-yoozh is a beastly (and vogue) mispronunciation. The *g* in *refuge* is properly pronounced as in *huge,* not as in *mirage.* That, undoubtedly, is why the three other major current American dictionaries — *American Heritage 3* (1992), *RHWC* (1997), and *WNW 3* (1997) — give only one pronunciation: REF-yooj. See **refugee, regime, rouge, siege**.

refugee REF-yoo-JEE or REF-yoo-jee.

This word is now frequently mispronounced REF-yoo-**ZHEE** or **REF**-yoo-ZHEE, with a *zh* sound for the *g* (as in *collage, mirage*) instead of the traditional soft *g* (as in *page, gem*). Dictionaries do not recognize the *zh* sound for *g* in *refugee.* Properly, the *g* has the sound of *j.* Three of the four major current American dictionaries give the two pronunciations countenanced above, in that order, and the fourth, *American Heritage 3* (1992), lists only the first. I think many good speakers use both pronunciations, quite acceptably, depending on the rhythm and stress demands of the context: e.g., "Thousands of REF-yoo-**JEEZ** were crossing the border every day"; "We visited the **REF**-yoo-JEE center." See **refuge, regime, rouge, siege**.

refund (noun) REE-fuhnd; (verb) ri-FUHND.

The careful speaker does not say REE-fuhnd for the verb. See **decrease**.

regime ri-ZHEEM or ray-ZHEEM.

Be careful not to say ri-JEEM or ray-JEEM. Unlike *refuge,* which has been fully anglicized so that the *g* has a *j* sound, the *g* in *regime* retains its French *zh* sound, as in *collage* and *mirage.* Do not be misled by *M-W 10* (1993), which gives the *zh* pronunciations sanctioned above followed by *also* ri-JEEM (the *also* meaning "appreciably less common"). Ri-JEEM is a beastly (and vogue) mispronunciation, which undoubtedly is why the three other major current American dictionaries — *American Heritage 3* (1992), *RHWC* (1997), and *WNW 3* (1997) — do not recognize it and countenance only ri-ZHEEM and ray-ZHEEM. See **refuge, rouge, siege**.

remnant(s) REM-nints (two syllables).

I once heard a vice president of a prominent San Diego bank pronounce this word with a vowel sound between the *m* and *n,* as though it were spelled *reminants* or *remanants.* Take care to give *remnants* two syllables, never three.

remonstrate ri-MAHN-strayt, not REM-un-strayt. Stress the second syllable.

The accent in *remonstrate* follows *demonstrative* (di-MAHN-struh-tiv), not *demonstrate.*

remuneration ri-MYOO-nuh-**RAY**-shin.

The second syllable should sound like -*mu*- (-MYOO-) in *community.*

Take care to distinguish the words *remuneration* and *renumeration* in pronunciation and spelling. *Renumeration,* pronounced ri-N(Y)OO-muh-**RAY**-shin, is a little used word meaning renumbering, recalculation, that probably gets most of its play being misused for the far more common *remuneration.* The confusion of these two words occurs frequently not only in speech but also in print, as this passage from a *New York Times* story printed in the *Sacramento Bee* attests:

> The government . . . said it would pay her room and board for teaching English to Foreign Ministry officials. The government offer never came through, she said. Vietnam finally gave her a visa, but no *renumeration* [my italics].

The trick here is to remember that there is no *renew* in *remuneration.* The word begins with *rem-,* as in *remit.* When you get a bill, you are asked to *remit* because the company wants *remuneration,* payment.

[333]

rental REN-tul.

Do not — on pain of eviction — say REN-ul. Pronounce the *t*.

In a TV commercial for a San Diego rental company a woman and a man each had to say *rental* a half-dozen times within thirty seconds. The woman said *rental*, but the man kept saying *rennel*. Was he listening to her when they made the recording? Can't he hear the difference? Is there a director in the house? Some folks complain about all the *g*-dropping going on in such words as *going (goin')*, *doing (doin')*, and *nothing (nothin')*. Muhself, I'm bothered by all the *t*-droppin' goin' on in words like *rental*, *dental*, and *gentle*. Either way, all this droppin' jus' adds up to guano. See **gentle, kindergarten, mental, ventilate**.

reparable REP-ur-uh-buul, not ruh-PAIR-uh-buul.

There is no *repair* in *reparable*. Stress the *rep-*. See **admirable, comparable, formidable, irreparable**.

repartee REP-ur-**TEE** or REP-ahr-**TEE**.

The last syllable, *-tee*, is often mispronounced -tay (rhymes with *day*).

Repartee came into English in the mid–17th century from the French *repartie*, a retort. At first it was often spelled like the French, or sometimes *reparty*, but the modern spelling, which had appeared by 1712, predominated by 1800.

From the beginning the English pronunciation, as indicated by John Walker (1791), has retained the French accent on the final syllable and the French long *e* sound (as in *bee*) of *-ie*. This was the only pronunciation recognized by dictionaries until the 1960s, when REP-ur-**TAY** gained currency. The -tay variant is wrong because it is pseudo-French. It is based on false analogy with the current English pronunciations of such French words as *negligee* (NEG-li-**ZHAY**), *soiree* (swah-RAY), *née* (NAY) — and perhaps *touché*, which is so often used to acknowledge a trenchant remark — instead of on the original French source of *repartee*, in which the final syllable, *-tie*, is pronounced like *tea*. (No doubt we settled on the spelling *repartee* to better indicate that long *e* sound. Oh well. Another example of pseudosophisticated re-Frenchification, or what one pronunciation guru has called "bargain-basement French.")

REP-ur-**TAY** is so common today that all four leading current American dictionaries recognize it, although they all give priority to the proper pronunciation, REP-ur-**TEE**. Lass & Lass (1976) and the *NBC Handbook* (1984) favor -tay, which I find highly peculiar, but *Oxford American* (1980), *Everyday Reader's* (1985), Barnhart (1988), and *OED 2* (1989) prefer -tee. For more on pseudo-French pronunciations, see **envelope, lingerie**.

repast ri-PAST. Stress the second syllable.

The variant ri-PAHST, with the broad *a* of *spa*— which appears after ri-PAST in two current American dictionaries — is British. The variant

REE-past, with first-syllable stress — recognized only by *M-W 10* (1993) — is beastly.

repeat (verb, noun, and adjective) r<u>i</u>-PEET.

The careful speaker always stresses the word *repeat,* in all parts of speech, on the *second* syllable, never on the first. When you ask someone to say something again, you say, "Would you please *rePEAT* that?" (never *repeat that again,* which is redundant). When speaking of a TV or radio show that comes on the air again, you say it is a rebroadcast, a rerun, or a *rePEAT,* not a *REpeat.* And when using the word in its newest sense, as an adjective, you say that it's a *rePEAT* performance, not a *REpeat* performance, and that someone is a *rePEAT* offender, not a *REpeat* offender.

First-syllable stress for the noun *repeat* dates back at least to the 1930s, when Opdycke (1939) sternly objected to it. His disapproval is shared by many cultivated speakers today, apparently, for only one of the four leading current American dictionaries recognizes REE-peet as an alternative pronunciation, while the other three sanction only r<u>i</u>-PEET.

Larsen & Walker (1930) point out that most disyllabic words beginning with *re-* have their stress on the second syllable, "whether used as verbs, nouns, or adjectives" — for example, *refrain, relate, release, remove, reply, repeal, report, request, respect, result, retreat, return, revenge, revolt,* and *reward.* The word *repeat* belongs squarely in this category and is a longstanding exception to the rule for disyllabic nouns and verbs discussed under **decrease.** See also **recess, recourse, redress,** and **research,** which traditionally have their accent on the second syllable but which in varying degrees have been bucking the trend.

repercussion REE-pur-**KUHSH**-<u>i</u>n, not REP-ur-**KUHSH**-<u>i</u>n.

Older sources — including *Webster 2* (1934), Opdycke (1939), Kenyon & Knott (1949), and *American College* (1952) — recognize only REE-pur-**KUHSH**-<u>i</u>n (REE- rhyming with *me*). Among current authorities, Lass & Lass (1976) favor REP- for the first syllable, but Funk & Wagnalls *Standard* (1980), the *NBC Handbook* (1984), *Everyday Reader's* (1985), and *OED 2* (1989) prefer REE-, and all four major current American dictionaries give priority to this pronunciation.

Take care to avoid the beastly mispronunciation REP-ruh-**KUHSH**-<u>i</u>n, in which the medial *-er-* gets turned around and the word comes out sounding as if it's spelled *rep-re-cussion.* See **prerogative.**

reportage r<u>i</u>-POR-tij (recommended) or REP-ur-**TAHZH**.

The *NBC Handbook* (1984) and two British authorities, *Oxford Guide* (1983) and Jones (1991), prefer the Frenchified REP-ur-**TAHZH**, but *OED 2* (1989) and three of the four leading current American dictionaries list the anglicized r<u>i</u>-POR-tij first. *Reportage* has been English for more than a hundred years, time enough in my opinion for the word to fall in line with analagous words (*encourage, advantage, percentage, appendage, assemblage, envisage*) in which -*age* rhymes with *ridge*.

reportorial REP-ur-**TOR**-ee-ul (recommended). Also, REE-pur-**TOR**-ee-ul. This word was first recorded in print in 1858. The *Century* (1889–1914) and *New Century* (1927) prefer REE- for the first syllable, but Funk & Wagnalls *Standard* (1897), *New Standard* (1913), and *OED 1* (1928) prefer REP-, and authorities since *Webster 2* (1934), which lists REP- first, have overwhelmingly favored REP-. Three major current American dictionaries list REP-first, it is the only pronunciation in *OED 2* (1989) and *WNW 3* (1997), and the *NBC Handbook* (1984), the chief authority for many in the news business, prefers REP-.

reprise (music) ri-PREEZ; (law) ri-PRYZ.

research (noun and verb) Traditionally, ri-SURCH. Now often REE-surch for the noun. Careful speakers avoid REE-surch for the verb.

In *Modern American Usage* (1966), Wilson Follett writes, "The word *research,* both noun and verb, is generally accented on the second syllable by those who are most familiar with the thing it denotes."

Follett's point is a bit heavy-handed. It's true that most 20th-century authorities favor second-syllable accent; however, there is also authority for first-syllable accent, at least for the noun. I much prefer second-syllable stress in both cases, but I have no trouble accepting first-syllable accent for the noun and second-syllable accent for the verb. This conforms to the long-standing custom of stressing disyllabic noun-verbs on the first syllable for the noun and the second syllable for the verb, as in *conflict, digest, incense, progress, rebel, subject, survey,* and so on. Most speakers, however, do not make such a distinction with *research,* either consciously or unconsciously. Nowadays, those who say REE-surch tend to do so for *both* noun and verb. To my ear this is ungainly, and it becomes even more clumsy when the speaker stresses the first syllable in the corresponding words *researcher* and *researchable.*

Since the *search* is the important part of *research,* it makes *sound* sense to stress the second syllable. Unless you can be consistent about making a distinction between REE-surch, noun, and ri-SURCH, verb, make it easy on yourself and your listeners and always stress the *search.* That is the preference of older authorities, and of Shaw (1972), Lass & Lass (1976), and the *NBC Handbook* (1984).

It is worth noting, as a postscript to this discussion, that on the popular educational TV show for children on PBS, *The Magic Schoolbus,* Ms. Frizzle and her science-savvy pupils pronounce the noun *research* with the accent on the second syllable: ri-SURCH. Wilson Follett would be pleased.

See **recess, recourse, redress,** and **repeat,** which traditionally have their accent on the second syllable but which in varying degrees have been bucking the trend.

respiratory RES-pur-uh-TOR-ee. Primary stress on the first syllable.

If you are an American, don't say ruh-**SPY**-ruh-TOR-ee (as I have heard TV news anchor Dan Rather pronounce it). That's an affectation of the British pronunciation, which is more clipped: ruh-SPY-ruh-tur-ee.

respite RES-pit. Do not say ruh-SPYT.

In American speech, the accent in *respite* should be on the first syllable, and the second syllable should be pronounced like *pit*. The British, according to Burchfield (1996), are about evenly divided between RES-pit and RES-pyt.

The mispronunciation ruh-SPYT, which misplaces the accent and changes the short *i* to a long *i*, appears as an "appreciably less common" alternative in only one of the four major current American dictionaries, *M-W 10* (1993), and no authority prefers it. It has been heard for most of the 20th century, however — Phyfe (1926) and Opdycke (1939) frown on it — and so deserves membership in the infamous Antiquarian Beastly Mispronunciation Club, whose disreputable members include AWF-tin for *often*, HEE-nus for *heinous*, HYT-th and HITH for *height*, and mis-CHEE-vus or mis-CHEE-vee-us for *mischievous*. (See the entries for these words.)

restaurateur RES-tur-uh-**TUR**.

There is no *restaurant* in *restaurateur*. Don't insert a spurious *n* before the second *t* and say RES-tuh-rawn-**TUR**. Also, the final, stressed syllable (-*teur*) should rhyme with *sir*, not *poor*. See **amateur, connoisseur, de rigueur, entrepreneur, liqueur**.

ribald RIB-uld. Do not say RY-bald.

There is no *rye* in *ribald*. It's a *rib*. Properly, the word should rhyme with *dribbled* and *scribbled*, as in this limerick I have composed for the occasion:

> William Shakespeare, whenever he scribbled,
> Used a quill that incessantly dribbled;
>   When his pen leaked a lot,
>   It made Willy quite hot,
> And he wrote something suitably *ribald*.

Unfortunately, the spelling pronunciation *rye bald* is now so common that three of the four major current American dictionaries list it. Please hold the line on this one.

ridiculous ri-DIK-yuh-lus.

The beastly mispronunciations ri-DIK-lus and ri-DIK'l-us — when not intentionally jocular, as in the film *The Wizard of Oz* — are illiterate and inexcusable.

rococo ruh-KOH-koh (or roh-).

This word was first recorded in English in 1836. Worcester (1860) and Ayres (1894) do not list it. Funk & Wagnalls *Standard* (1897), the *Century* (1914), and Phyfe (1926) give only second-syllable stress, but *Webster 2* (1934) lists an alternative pronunciation, ROH-kuh-**KOH**, with primary stress on the last syllable. American dictionaries have since continued to list this variant but they continue to give priority to ruh-KOH-koh (or roh-). This is the preference of Lass & Lass (1976), the *NBC Handbook* (1984), *WNW Guide* (1984), *Everyday Reader's* (1985), and Barnhart (1988), and the only pronunciation in *OED 2* (1989).

rodeo ROH-dee-oh. For certain proper nouns, roh-DAY-oh.

Rodeo entered English from Spanish about 1830. At first it was pronounced with the accent on the second syllable, following the Spanish: roh-DAY-oh. The second-syllable accent persisted for more than a hundred years, although there was some dispute over how to pronounce the *e*. The *Century* (1914) and Vizetelly (1929) give roh-DAY-oh, with the latter disapproving of roh-DEE-oh. Opdycke (1939), on the other hand, prefers roh-DEE-oh, adding that ROH-dee-oh "is threateningly in the air, and the dictionaries will probably succumb pretty soon." He was already behind the times. *Webster 2* (1934) already had given ROH-dee-oh priority over roh-DAY-oh (with no sign of roh-DEE-oh), Kenyon & Knott (1949) and *American College* (1952) followed suit, and since then first-syllable stress has prevailed.

Though it is still listed by current dictionaries, roh-DAY-oh is now a quaint exception rather than a thriving alternative pronunciation. *WNW 3* (1997) labels it infrequent and says it is used especially for a roundup of cattle, a sense labeled "now rare." In everyday speech, ROH-dee-oh predominates, and roh-DAY-oh persists chiefly in the traditional pronunciation of a handful of proper nouns, such as *Rodeo Drive* in Los Angeles and the 1942 ballet *Rodeo* composed by Aaron Copland and choreographed by Agnes de Mille.

Roosevelt (Theodore, Franklin D., and Eleanor) ROH-zuh-velt, not
    ROOZ-uh-velt.

Roosevelt may also acceptably have two syllables, ROHZ-velt, but the *Roos-* should always sound like *rose,* not rhyme with *snooze.*

Older authorities do not recognize the erroneous ROOZ-uh-velt and current ones do not favor it. *Random House II* (1987) calls it a spelling pronunciation and *WNW 3* (1997) says it is used "by some." The *Columbia Encyclopedia* (1963) and the *NBC Handbook* (1984) countenance only ROH-zuh-velt, which *M-W 10* (1993) notes is the Roosevelts' usual pronunciation.

rouge ROOZH (ZH as in *mirage, collage*), not ROOJ.

Only the modern dictionaries of Merriam-Webster — *Webster 3* (1961) through *M-W 10* (1993) — recognize the variant ROOJ, which they label "especially Southern." That may be so, but in the name of the capital of Louisiana, Baton Rouge, the *rouge* "gets its French value locally," says H. L. Mencken in *The American Language* (1937); "the *Baton* becomes *bat'n,* with the *bat* rhyming with *cat,* and the *o* reduced to a neutral vowel." See **refuge, regime, siege.**

route ROOT or ROWT.

ROOT has been preferred or listed first in dictionaries since the mid–19th century. ROWT, however, has as long a history as ROOT, and was preferred by many of the earliest authorities. In the first half of the 20th century ROWT was often labeled colloquial, provincial, or military; it is now well established in various engineering, transportation, delivery, and sales contexts.

I prefer ROOT for all senses of the word *route,* but it is difficult to fashion an argument for it that goes further than saying that is how I was taught to pronounce it, that is how most educated speakers around me said it, and that is the pronunciation that feels right and cultivated to me. In my vocabulary, *route* will always be ROOT and *rout* ROWT, but many speakers nowadays prefer to pronounce both words ROWT. Since it cannot be stated unequivocally that one pronunciation of *route* is right and the other wrong, I present the following historical evidence, which you can use to make up your mind, bolster your case, or live and let live, as you prefer.

In his *Critical Pronouncing Dictionary* of 1791, the English elocutionist John Walker prefers ROOT but notes that the word "is often pronounced so as to rhyme with *doubt* by respectable speakers." In a later edition, Walker changed his course. "Upon a more accurate observation of the best usage," he wrote, "I must give the preference to [ROWT] . . . notwithstanding its coincidence in sound with another word of a different meaning; the fewer French sounds of this diphthong we have in our language the better."

Worcester (1860), who prefers ROOT, says, "Most of the orthoepists more recent than Walker give the preference to the pronunciation [ROOT]." Ayres (1894) says that "there is abundant authority for pronouncing this word *rowt;* but this pronunciation is now very generally considered inelegant." Vizetelly (1929) says the "best modern usage pronounces the word as if written *root,*" and Opdycke (1939) assigns ROWT to "colloquial and provincial usage."

Funk & Wagnalls *Standard* (1897) countenances only ROOT, but the *Century* (1889–1914) sanctions ROWT as an alternative. *Webster 2* (1934) says that ROOT "is now the generally accepted pronunciation, but in certain special cases *rout* (*ou* in *out*) prevails, as in military use, among railroad men, and, colloquially, of a delivery route."

Since then ROWT has gained a good deal of ground, but ROOT still appears to hold the lead among educated speakers, and all four major current American dictionaries list it first.

Morris & Morris (1985) observe that "people like Army engineers, bus and plane dispatchers, and others professionally engaged in planning routes tend to pronounce *route* so it rhymes with 'out.' Pronouncing it as if it were spelled 'root' is, however, equally acceptable."

In *Watching My Language* (1997), William Safire writes, "[President George] Bush frowned on 'the tax-and-spend route, which he pronounced 'ROWT.' That is not incorrect. . . . Most of us, however, have come to use 'ROOT' to mean 'way, itinerary, journey, map,' spelled *route,* and pronounced the same as the root of a plant. We use 'ROWT' to pronounce the word spelled *rout,* meaning 'resounding defeat; disorderly flight from battle; electoral debacle'" [p. 34]. It is perhaps worth noting that if Safire received any letters objecting to this assessment when it first appeared in his column in *The New York Times Magazine,* he does not reprint them in his book.

rubric ROO-brik.

Rubric has two syllables. Don't add a third and say ROO-buh-rik.

ruse ROOZ (rhymes with *shoes* and *lose*). Do not say ROOS (rhymes with *moose*).

Ruse, a trick, deception, came into English from French in 1625, and for the next three hundred years cultivated speakers pronounced it with the French *z* for the *s:* ROOZ. Then all of a sudden, in the first half of the 20th century, a variant with pure *s* as in *loose* sprang up and quickly became a vogue pronunciation. Opdycke (1939) objected to it, and *Webster 2* (1934), Kenyon & Knott (1949), and *American College* (1952) all ignored it. By 1960, however, it was apparently common enough to make its dictionary debut in *Webster 3* (1961), where — lo and behold — it was listed *first.*

That was quite a ruse that *ruse* pulled, but it didn't fool everyone and most current authorities are not amused. Although *American Heritage 3* (1992) and *M-W 10* (1993) — *Webster 3*'s latest offspring — give priority to ROOS and Barnhart (1988) prefers it, careful speakers should take note that ROOZ is the only pronunciation countenanced by Funk & Wagnalls *Standard* (1980), *OED 2* (1989), *WNW 3* (1997), and *RHWC* (1997), and it is the preference of Lass & Lass (1976), the *NBC Handbook* (1984), and *WNW Guide* (1984).

S

sacerdotal SAS-ur-**DOH**-tul, not SAK-ur-**DOH**-tul.

Sacerdotal properly should rhyme with *pass her total*, not *pack her total*.

This word comes from the Latin word for priest and ultimately from the Latin *sacer,* sacred. In classical Latin, *c* is pronounced like *k,* and for this reason, apparently, certain enterprising neoclassicists have taken to pronouncing the *c* in *sacerdotal* like *k. Webster 3* (1961) is the first of my sources to recognize this pronunciation, and its gradual spread has led three of the four major current American dictionaries to list it as an alternative (one labels it occasional).

Whence, and wherefore, this disposition to adopt Latin ways? English has taken thousands of words from Latin and anglicized them both in spelling and pronunciation. Would these *sack-erdotal* sayers now have us separate those Latinate words that pertain to the Latin-saturated clerical tradition and re-Latinize them? I fear that any strategy based on that sort of reasoning would only create speakers like Salvatore the hunchbacked monk in Umberto Eco's novel *The Name of the Rose,* "who looks like an animal and speaks the language of Babel." (See **Babel.**)

Sacerdotal has been an English word since 1400, and when it is used — whether in or out of church — it is used in English, not Latin. In a Latin sentence it would be a foreign word. Thus, one must conclude that the *k* for *c* substitution is either an affectation or an eccentric and misguided bit of pedantry for which there is no authority. Current American dictionaries give priority to the traditional SAS-ur-**DOH**-tul, which is the only

a = at / a̱ = final / ah = spa / ahr = car / air = fair / ay = hay / aw = saw
ch = chip / e = let / e̱ = item / ee = see / eer = deer / i = sit / i̱ = April
ng = sing / o̱ = carrot / oh = go / oo = soon / or = for / oor = poor
ow = cow / oy = toy / sh = she / th = thin / tẖ = this / u̱ = focus / uh = up
ur = turn / uu = pull, took / y, eye = by, I / zh = measure / (see full key, p. xiv)

pronunciation in *RHWC* (1997) and *OED 2* (1989), and the preference of Lass & Lass (1976), the *NBC Handbook* (1984), *WNW Guide* (1984), *Everyday Reader's* (1985), Barnhart (1988), and Jones (1991).

sacral SAY-kr<u>u</u>l, not SAK-r<u>u</u>l.

Put a *say* in your *sacral,* not a *sack.*

This word has two meanings: pertaining to religious rites or observances, and pertaining to the sacrum (SAY-kr<u>u</u>m), a bone in the lower spine. The bone sense dates from the mid-1700s, the religious sense from 1882. At first, one pronunciation served for both meanings; *Webster's Collegiate* (1917), *OED 1* (1928), *Webster 2* (1934), Kenyon & Knott (1949), and *American College* (1952) list only SAY-kr<u>u</u>l. In recent years, however, certain speakers apparently decided that we needed another pronunciation to go along with the distinction in usage, and so the alternative SAK-r<u>u</u>l sprang up and gained currency among language mavens fond of splitting hairs, especially on a bald man's head. (William F. Buckley, Jr., for example, says SAK-r<u>u</u>l for the religious sense; I do not know how he pronounces the word in its anatomical sense.)

The problem is that the distinction is not consistent. Some speakers use SAY- for holy and SAK- for the bone, some do it the other way around, and some have dismissed the long *a* altogether and use SAK-r<u>u</u>l for both meanings. When this sort of thing happens it is clear that the attempt to clarify has misfired, and it is best to go back to square one.

That seems to be the opinion of most current authorities. Although the *NBC Handbook* (1984) and *M-W 10* (1993) favor SAY- for the religious sense and SAK- for the bone sense, *American Heritage 3* (1992) and *WNW 3* (1997) list only SAY-kr<u>u</u>l for both senses and *OED 2* (1989) and *RHWC* (1997) give priority to SAY-.

There is much to support a preference for the long *a*. In its religious sense *sacral* is related to *sacred,* which is always pronounced SAY-krid. In its physiological sense *sacral* is related to *sacrum,* for which the traditional pronunciation is SAY-kr<u>u</u>m. Wouldn't it simplify things nicely to use long *a* all around — for *sacred, sacrum,* and *sacral?*

To those who would object to this argument on the ground that one pronunciation for a word with two meanings invites confusion, I say this: the word *set* has one pronunciation and 119 definitions in *Random House II* (1987). Have you ever had trouble using it? *Sacral's* two senses are so specific and so different that the chance of confusing them is remote, if not impossible. I doubt that if a doctor tells us we have a *sacral* inflammation we will think our faith has swelled, nor are we likely to imagine that a cleric's reference to *sacral* obligations implies we should put our backs into being good. Why make things troublesome when the solution is clear? SAY-kr<u>u</u>l for both senses makes best sense to me.

sacrilegious SAK-ri-**LIJ**-us. Formerly, but now rarely, SAK-ri-**LEE**-jus.

Yes, Virginia, there is a *religious* in *sacrilegious* — but only in pronunciation, not spelling.

SAK-ri-**LIJ**-us, like *sack* + *religious,* was once a beastly mispronunciation, but it has long been used by educated speakers and now unquestionably prevails in cultivated speech.

Need I say more? Yes — a word of explanation for those of you who might still take exception to SAK-ri-**LIJ**-us, and some consolation for anyone who has been unjustly censured for saying it that way.

Ayres (1894), *Webster's New International* (1909), and Phyfe (1926) disapproved of SAK-ri-**LIJ**-us, but Vizetelly (1929) noted that "the word is now more frequently heard [SAK-ri-**LIJ**-us]." No doubt because of that fact, *Webster 2* (1934) sanctioned SAK-ri-**LIJ**-us as an alternative, Gilmartin (1936) and Opdycke (1939) gave it their blessing — Holt (1937), however, frowned on it — and by the 1940s SAK-ri-**LIJ**-us was so prevalent that Kenyon & Knott (1949) and *American College* (1952) gave it priority, the former remarking that for British and American speakers alike, SAK-ri-**LIJ**-us was probably based on analogy with *sacrilege* (SAK-ri-lij) and the unrelated *religious.*

Modern authorities are still divided, although the scale is tipping in favor of the *religious* pronunciation. Shaw (1972), Lass & Lass (1976), and the *NBC Handbook* (1984) stick by the older SAK-ri-**LEE**-jus, while *WNW Guide* (1984), *Everyday Reader's* (1985), and Burchfield (1996) favor SAK-ri-**LIJ**-us, with *WNW Guide* noting that "the earlier standard [SAK-ri-**LEE**-jus] is much less frequently heard." In corroboration of that assessment, all four major current American dictionaries and *OED 2* (1989) give priority to the *religious* pronunciation — although one dictionary, *M-W 10* (1993), labels it unacceptable to some.

That, I hope, will settle the issue. Let there be no more bad blood between the orthodox pronouncers who say SAK-ri-**LEE**-jus and the recusant pronouncers who say SAK-ri-**LIJ**-us. Dogma has changed, and the offense has now become law. However, a final word of caution to both parties: do be careful to *spell* the word properly. Even eagle-eyed copyeditors sometimes overlook the misspelling *sacreligious*. See **schism**. Also, for more on pronunciation affecting spelling, see **entrepreneur, minuscule**.

St. Louis (Missouri) SAYNT LOO-is (like *Lewis*), not LOO-ee.

Speaker, beware! Many current sources list the alternative pronunciation SAYNT LOO-ee for this city, which is wrong — at least as far as the locals are concerned, and when it comes to place names, local preference is what counts most.

In *World Words* (1948), W. Cabell Greet, a professor of English at Columbia University and speech consultant to CBS, says that LOO-ee for

Louis "is seldom heard locally," and in *The American Language* (1937), H. L. Mencken notes that *"St. Louis,* to the people of the city, is *St. Lewis."* Martin Quigley, contributing editor of *The Midwest Motorist* and a long-time St. Louis resident, vehemently agrees. Quigley is an authority on the pronunciation of various Midwestern place names, and in an article on the subject he declares, "Not a single one of us who calls St. Louis our home lives in a place called St. Looey!" Putting the case more mildly, *WNW Guide* (1984) calls SAYNT LOO-ee "old-fashioned." Kenyon & Knott (1949), the *Columbia Encyclopedia* (1963), the *NBC Handbook* (1984), and *Webster's Geographical* (1997) also sanction only LOO-is.

I asked Mr. Quigley if LOO-ee was permissible for the old song "The St. Louis Blues." The answer: "No way." However, for the famous lyric celebrating the World's Fair of 1904, "Meet me in St. Louis, Louis / Meet me at the fair," Quigley makes an exception. "That is the only acceptable use of LOO-ee," he said. But he adds that for the movie *Meet Me in St. Louis* starring Judy Garland, the pronunciation is still SAYNT LOO-is. See **Missouri**.

salmon SAM-<u>u</u>n.

L silent, *a* as in *ham.* Anything else is beastly — er, fishy. See **salmonella**.

salmonella SAL-muh-**NEL**-uh.

There is no *salmon* in *salmonella.* Pronounce all the *l*'s.

My conscience compels me to confess that I was well into adulthood before I realized that *salmon* and *salmonella* have different pronunciations. I had always pronounced *salmon* properly, with a silent *l* (SAM-<u>u</u>n), but I made the mistake of carrying this silent *l* over into *salmonella.*

Opdycke (1939) states that there is no authority for pronouncing the *l* in *salmon,* and he's right. No authority — from Walker (1791) to Worcester (1860) to *Webster 2* (1934) to *WNW 3* (1997) — countenances an *l*-full pronunciation. The opposite is true for *salmonella,* the genus of bacteria that takes its name from the name of American pathologist Daniel Elmer Salmon — pronounced SAL-m<u>u</u>n like the biblical name and not SAM-<u>u</u>n like the lowly fish. Despite what you may hear on radio and TV from certain educated, but misguided, speakers, all authorities agree that all the *l*'s are pronounced in *salmonella:* SAL-muh-**NEL**-uh. That's the way it's always been and the way it still is, and if you don't like it, find me an authority that says otherwise.

salutary SAL-yuh-TER-ee (or -TAIR-ee).

Do not say **SAL**-yuh-TOR-ee, a beastly mispronunciation reflected in the beastly misspelling *salutory,* which appears occasionally in edited writing — even in the august pages of *The New York Times.** There is no *tory* in *salutary.* It's *salu-terry.*

---

* "That, he believes, is not a salutory [*sic*] legacy." Sunday, March 22, 1998, p. 41.

salve (noun, medicinal ointment, and verb, to apply it) SAV or SAHV.

The variant SAHLV (like *solve*) was common in the 18th and 19th centuries; Walker (1791) preferred it and Worcester (1860) listed it after SAHV. Today it is probably obsolete and only one current dictionary records it. The variant SALV — according to the *Oxford Guide* (1983), Jones (1991), and Burchfield (1996) — is British. A different verb to *salve,* a back formation from *salvage* meaning to salvage, is pronounced SALV.

sandwich SAND-wich.

This word should be pronounced exactly as it is spelled. Do not drop the *d* and say SAN-wich, even in rapid speech, for this seemingly innocuous mispronunciation is construed by many as a sign of a careless speaker.

sanguine SANG-gwin (-gwin rhyming with *win*).

This is the only acceptable, recognized pronunciation. Avoid the beastly mispronunciations SANG-gwyn (-gwyn rhyming with *wine*) and SANG-gween (-gween rhyming with *queen*).

sans SANZ (rhymes with *fans*).

saran (plastic wrap, formerly a trademark) suh-RAN, not SAR-an.

All four major current American dictionaries and *OED 2* (1989) give only suh-RAN.

Saturday see -**day**.

savant suh-VAHNT.

This is the only acceptable pronunciation in American speech. Some dictionaries still list the French pronunciation, sah-VAH(N), and also SAV-unt, which is British. In the U.S. the latter is unintelligible and the former survives only as an affectation.

savvy SAV-ee.

Savvy has the flat *a* of *hat.* I once heard a college professor say SAH-vee, with the broad *a* of *father.* There is no authority for this pronunciation.

scallop SKAH-lup or SKAL-up.

Both pronunciations have been used by cultivated speakers since at least the mid–18th century. Walker (1791), who prefers SKAH-lup, acknowledges that "this word is irregular, for it ought to have the *a* in the first syllable like that in *tallow;* but the deep sound of *a* is too firmly fixed by custom to afford any expectation of a change." All four current American dictionaries give both pronunciations, with SKAH-lup first, but the evidence of my ears tells me that, except in New England and along the eastern seaboard, SKAL-up, my own pronunciation and the preference of the *NBC Handbook* (1984), is probably now more common in the U.S. SKAH-lup remains the British preference. Take your pick.

scenario suh-NAIR-ee-oh, suh-NAR-ee-oh, suh-NAH-ree-oh.

All three pronunciations are recognized by current dictionaries. In the first, the second syllable rhymes with *hair;* in the second, the *a* is flat as in *gnat;* in the third, the *a* is broad as in *spa.*

The first two pronunciations given above are the most common in educated American speech. Suh-NAIR-ee-oh is usually listed first in dictionaries and has the greatest currency; it is my own preference. Suh-NAR-ee-oh is chiefly a regional variation of suh-NAIR-ee-oh common among those speakers who tend to use a flat *a* before *r*, as in the pronunciation of the verb to *vary* as VAR-ee rather than VAIR-ee. Suh-NAH-ree-oh is listed in three of the four major current American dictionaries; my British sources indicate that it is the preferred pronunciation in England. Although suh-NAH-ree-oh is now common in educated American speech, it is worth noting that when I discussed the pronunciation of *scenario* with various colleagues and friends, a number of them remarked that they thought suh-NAH-ree-oh sounded either old-fashioned or affected — which in my experience is usually what a British pronunciation sounds like to an American who doesn't know it's British. The old-fashioned pronunciation of this word is shi-NAH-ree-oh, which reflects the original Italian pronunciation. Dictionaries no longer record this variant, which would sound affected indeed if anyone were to use it today.

schedule SKEJ-uul or SKEJ-ool.

In British and, to a lesser extent, Canadian English, SHED-yool and SHEJ-ool are the prevailing pronunciations. To the American ear these sound unnatural and stilted, as the American SKEJ-uul and SKEJ-ool likely do to the British ear. For more on *schedule*, see Bill Bryson's comments on Noah Webster quoted in **aunt**.

schism Traditionally and properly, SIZ'm. Now usually SKIZ'm.

Most words beginning with *sch-* are pronounced either SK-, as in *school* and *scheme*, or (generally only in words and names of German, Yiddish, or Hebrew origin), SH-, as in *schwa, schnauzer, Schmidt,* and *schmaltz. Schism*, however, because of its history, is a special exception.

Schism entered English in the late 14th century from the Greek and Latin *schisma*, through the Old French *cisme* or *scisme* and the Middle English *scisme*. Of the numerous spellings that arose in its first two hundred years in the language, *scisme* was the most common, and it was not until the 17th century that writers began reinserting the *h* from the original Latin and Greek. In 1644 Milton used *scism;* twenty-four years later Izaak Walton spelled it *schism.* The burgeoning crop of English dictionaries in the 18th century served to establish *schism* as the standard spelling, but the pronunciation SIZ'm, based on earlier spellings without the *h,* had already been established for centuries. Thus English gained yet another incongruity between a word's form and its sound — but that, my friend, is what gives the language its character (and, unfortunately, what makes it so difficult to pronounce).

Perry (1775), Sheridan (1780), Walker (1791), Webster (1828), Smart

(1836), Worcester (1860), and other authorities of the 18th and 19th centuries endorsed this schism between the word's spelling and its pronunciation, but Walker, unlike the others, was unhappy about it, and in his famous *Critical Pronouncing Dictionary* he issued this complaint:

> The common pronunciation of this word [as SIZ'm] is contrary to every rule for pronouncing words from the learned languages, and ought to be altered. *Ch* in English words, coming from Greek words with χ, ought always to be pronounced like *k;* and I believe the word in question is almost the only exception throughout the language. However strange, therefore, *skizm* may sound, it is the only true and analogical pronunciation; and we might as well pronounce *scheme, seme,* as *schism, sizm,* there being exactly the same reason for both.

It is a testament to Walker's profound influence and the popularity of his dictionary that SKIZ'm, based on analogy with the original Latin and Greek, eventually became the norm in the 20th century. Usually, when it comes to fine points of language, the general public is deaf to the pleas of pundits and pedants. This is one of the rare instances in which a novel pronunciation recommended by an authority was adopted by hoi polloi. (For more on Walker's influence, see the footnote under **education**.)

Sometime in the early 1900s SKIZ'm began to catch on among educated speakers, who, unfamiliar with the word's history, no doubt made the natural (but at the time erroneous) association with other English words beginning with *sch-*. Dictionaries and authorities from Funk & Wagnalls *Standard* (1897) to *American College* (1952) countenanced only SIZ'm. "Don't say *shism* or *skism,*" counseled Opdycke (1939). Despite this disapproval, SKIZ'm relentlessly continued to spread and made its dictionary debut in *Webster 3* (1961). It was hardly an auspicious appearance, however, for it was labeled with Merriam-Webster's Obelus of Opprobrium, the symbol ÷, meaning it was unacceptable to many. Since then it has been happily adopted by many, and all four major current American dictionaries and *OED 2* (1989) now list it — after the traditional SIZ'm, however.

I was born in 1957 and until the early 1980s I had no idea that SIZ'm existed in a dictionary or in educated speech. I had always heard and said SKIZ'm, so I never thought to look it up and make sure it was correct. If you are accustomed to saying SKIZ'm, and you are not a member of the clergy, I imagine you will be as shocked as I was to discover that SIZ'm is the first or only pronunciation in *every* dictionary and pronunciation guide I have consulted, which includes over a dozen published since 1980, several of which do not recognize SKIZ'm.

As a SKIZ'm sayer, there are two ways you can respond to this information. You can defenestrate your dictionary and dismiss the entire profession of lexicography as a bow-tied bunch of ivory-tower eggheads with too much wax in their ears, or you can sit back for a moment and consider why the weight of authority is still so steadfastly behind SIZ'm. You can ponder the singular history of the word, how ancient, hoary, and venerable the traditional pronunciation is compared with SKIZ'm, the impertinent offspring of 18th-century pedantry and 20th-century ignorance; and you can ruminate on the fact that the clergy, who undoubtedly are most knowledgeable about schisms, are generally conscientious about pronouncing (and denouncing) them properly. (The dictionaries of Merriam-Webster from *Webster 3* on duly note that SIZ'm is the usual pronunciation among the clergy.) I don't think you'll have to mull things over too long before you come around, and — take my word for it — after you've said it a few times, SIZ'm won't seem odd to your ear at all, especially when you know you have every authority (including Walker, who sanctioned SIZ'm in spite of his protest) and every dictionary ever printed to back you up. If that doesn't give you confidence in SIZ'm, nothing will.

The peculiar variant SHIZ'm, noted and frowned upon by Opdycke in 1939, appears in *M-W 9* (1985) and *10* (1993) labeled "appreciably less common." No other authority that I know of, British or American, recognizes this pronunciation, and careful speakers would be wise to avoid it. I certainly have never heard anyone say SHIZ'm, and if I did I would probably laugh out loud.

schizophrenia SKIT-suh-**FREE**-nee-uh, not SKIT-suh-**FREN**-ee-uh.
The variant SKIT-suh-**FREN**-ee-uh, now countenanced by some authorities, is an illogical mispronunciation, as I will demonstrate in a moment. The variant SKIT-suh-**FRAY**-nee-uh, which I have occasionally heard and which appears only in *WNW 3* (1988, 1997), is beastly and should be avoided by anyone who wishes to be thought of as a careful speaker.

Schizophrenia is divided *schiz • o • phre • ni • a.* Because the third syllable, *-phre-*, is stressed and ends in a vowel, the vowel (e) is properly long, making the syllable sound like *free.* The mispronunciation SKIT-suh-**FREN**-ee-uh, third syllable like *friend* minus the final *d,* is based on false analogy with *schizophrenic,* pronounced SKIT-suh-**FREN**-ik and divided *schiz • o • phren • ic.* To justify the short *e* of -**FREN**- for the third syllable, *schizophrenia* would have to be divided *schiz • o • phren • i • a.* Moreover, the handful of other words ending in *-enia* all are pronounced with long *e* as in *seen: gardenia, Armenia, neurasthenia, Taenia* (a genus of worms), and *catamenia* (an obscure term for menses).

The -**FREN**- variant first appeared in *Webster 3* (1961) preceded by the word *sometimes,* meaning it was infrequently heard. Today it is listed after the proper pronunciation in three of the four major current American dictionaries. The fourth, *M-W 10* (1993), which is usually the most permis-

sive of the bunch, sanctions only SKIT-suh-**FREE**-nee-uh, which is pre-
ferred by Lass & Lass (1976), *Oxford American* (1980), Funk & Wagnalls
Standard (1980), the *NBC Handbook* (1984), *Everyday Reader's* (1985),
Barnhart (1988), *OED 2* (1989), and Jones (1991).

A historical postscript to this discussion: *schizophrenia* was first recorded in English in 1912. Until the 1960s the preferred pronunciation was
SKIZ-uh-**FREE**-nee-uh, with the *z* pronounced like *z* in *whiz* and *jazz*
instead of like *ts* in *skits*. This is the only pronunciation in *Webster 2* (1934)
and *American College* (1952), and from a purely linguistic standpoint it is
the correct pronunciation of the word. Look in any American dictionary at
words beginning with the combining form *schiz(o)-* and you will see that
for all the words *not* having to do with schizophrenia the first or only
pronunciation given begins with SKIZ-, not SKITS-: e.g., *schizocarp, schiz-
ogenesis, schizogamy, schizopod, schizolite, schizospore, schizomycosis,* and
schizotrichia, a medical term for the splitting of a hair. The SKIZ- at the
beginning of these (albeit obscure) words follows the Greek — although
SKIDZ- (like *skids*), listed second in *OED 2* for the first syllable of *schizophrenia,* is more faithful to the original Greek pronunciation of *z*. As far as
I can tell, *schizophrenia, schizophrenic,* and *schizoid* are the only wholly
English words (as opposed to loanwords) in which *z* is pronounced like *ts*.

So how did *schizophrenia* and its friends come to have the SKITS-
pronunciation? To begin with, these words swiftly traveled from the jargon
of psychology into the general vocabulary, making them fair game for
mispronunciation; the other *schiz-* words remained chiefly the property of
scientists. Then there is the sophisticated allure of Continental pronunciation to be reckoned with, namely, the Italian *z*, usually pronounced like
English *ts* (e.g., *scherzo, forza, grazie*), and especially — when you think of
Freud, Jung, et al. — the German *z*, which is also pronounced like *ts*. *OED
2* says that the SKITS- pronunciation is "probably influenced by the German pronunciation" of *schiz-*, which is SHITS-. I don't think I need to
explain why we adopted the *-its-* but decided to pass on the *sh-* part.
scimitar SIM-i̠-tur, not SIM-i̠-tahr.

There is no *tar* in *scimitar,* which should rhyme with *perimeter*. The -tahr
variant, which first appeared in *Webster 3* (1961) labeled "appreciably less
common," is a spurious attempt to give this word an exotic flavor. Problem
is, *scimitar* has been English since the 16th century and has been pronounced SIM-i̠-tur at least since Walker (1791). Contemporary authorities
all prefer -tur, *OED 2* (1989) sanctions only this pronunciation, and all four
major current American dictionaries list it first. See **bursar**.
scion SY-u̠n (rhymes with *lion*). This is the only acceptable pronunciation.
secretary **SEK**-ri̠-TER-ee. Don't say **SEK**-uh-TER-ee.
Be sure to pronounce the *r* in the second syllable. Dropping it has long

been regarded as beastly. Unfortunately, the many educated speakers who are careless with this word have induced *M-W 9* (1985) and *10* (1993) to recognize **SEK**-uh-TER-ee. Don't let this cameo appearance mislead you into thinking that this sloppy pronunciation is now acceptable. All authorities and all other current American dictionaries countenance only **SEK**-ṛi-TER-ee, with an audible *r*. The British pronunciation is **SEK**-ṛi-tree.

secreted sị-KREE-tid, not SEE-kṛi-tid.

When *secreted* means discharged through secretion, no educated speaker mispronounces it. However, when it means hidden, concealed, there has been a tendency of late to shift the accent to the first syllable, and this sometimes also occurs with the infinitive *secrete* in this sense.

There once was a verb to *secret*, meaning to conceal. It became obsolete by the mid–18th century, and since then *secrete* has been the standard spelling. Had the verb *secret* survived, perhaps the pronunciations SEE-krit and SEE-kri-tid (for *secreted*) would be the norm today. It did not, however, and *OED 2* (1989) and three of the four major current American dictionaries countenance only second-syllable stress for *secrete* and *secreted*. Only *M-W 10* (1993) recognizes SEE-krit and SEE-kṛi-tid as alternatives.

The adjective *secretive* is now pronounced SEE-kṛi-tiv, with the accent on the first syllable, when it means disposed to keep secrets. However, when it means pertaining to secretion, it is pronounced sị-KREE-tiv.

semi- SEM-ee (rhymes with *Emmy*), not SEM-eye.

Only a nitwit would say *sem-eye-colon* and *sem-eye-circle*, so why the big attraction to SEM-eye in so many other *semi-* words? "Don't follow those who affectedly make the *i* long," counsels Opdycke (1939). Avoid the appearance of semiliterate affectation. For all words beginning with the combining form *semi-*, say SEM-ee. However, for the word *semi*, meaning a tractor-trailer, SEM-eye is acceptable. See **anti-**.

seminal SEM-ị-nụl (*sem-* rhymes with *hem*).

Occasionally you come across an educated speaker who for some reason is not aware that there is no *seem* in *seminal*. Most recently for me, that person was none other than William Safire of *The New York Times*. "The word *seminal*," Safire wrote (on April 6, 1997), "is slipped in here to assert its correct pronunciation, SEE-men-ul, contrary to what you hear from bowdlerizing academics on the air."

Your alert pronunciation maven shot back with this letter:

Those bowdlerizing academics may be impotent in other ways, but they're shooting straight with this word. Despite what the sperm banker would assert, there is no SEE-men in *seminal*, nor in artificial *insemination*, *dis-*

seminate, seminary, and *seminar,* all of which sprang from the same seed (Latin *semen*) as *seminal,* which is correctly pronounced not with a long but with a short *e:* SEM-uh-nul.

It's an open-and-shut, *seem*-less case: I consulted a passel of orthoepists — from Walker (1791) to Kenyon & Knott (1949) to the *NBC Handbook* (1984) — and a pile of dictionaries — from Worcester (1860) to *Webster 2* (1934) to *OED 2* (1989). Though I was much aroused and perspired by my labors between those many pages, no hide, nor hair, nor errant DNA could I find of SEE-men-ul. If in fact your pronunciation has a pedigree, chances are it's seedy at best.

A couple of months later (in his column of June 22, 1997) Safire recanted, noting that "pronunciation fans have objected to my recent diktat about *seminal*" and quoting my admonishment. "No doubt I'm in a minority," Safire admitted. *"Merriam-Webster's Third* [New] *International* gives my way as a less-common alternative, and only old British pronunciation guides say SEE-mun-ul. 'The SEE was a deviation,' Edmund Weiner, the deputy chief editor of the *OED,* informs me, 'used by people who wanted to emphasize the connection (hardly more than etymological now) with *semen.*' With that point made, I will now adopt SEM-un-ul. . . ."

senile SEE-nyl (like *see Nile*). Do not say SEN-yl.
Senile is accented on the first syllable, which rhymes with *glee,* and the second syllable should rhyme with *file.*

Formerly the word was sometimes pronounced with a short *i,* SEE-nil, second syllable rhyming with *pill.* In the 20th century this variant has gradually faded from the dictionaries and since the 1960s a new one has risen in its place: SEN-yl (SEN- as in *send,* -yl like *aisle*). The evidence indicates it is a homegrown American variant. It may have been a pedanticism based on the source of the word, the Latin *senilis,* pronounced se-NEE-lis, which comes in turn from *senex,* old, pronounced SEN-eks. Of course this "etymological pronunciation" ignores the more pertinent fact that the English word is divided se • *nile,* which calls for a long *e* in the stressed first syllable.

At any rate, the eccentric SEN-yl first appeared in *Webster 3* (1961) labeled "appreciably less frequent"; today all four major American dictionaries list it as an alternative, with two labeling it less common. *OED 2* (1989) and Jones (1991), both British authorities, give only the traditional SEE-nyl, which, despite its venerable age — it was the preference of John Walker (1791) and other orthoepists of his day — shows no signs of infirmity or dotage. For a discussion of American vs. British pronunciation of *-ile,* see **textile.**

sentence SEN-tints.

Don't drop the *t* and pronounce the word as if it were spelled *sennence.* See **fundamental, gentle, inter-, kindergarten, mental, rental.**

sentient SEN-sh<u>i</u>nt (recommended) or SEN-shee-<u>i</u>nt.

For the noun *sentience,* I recommend the pronunciation SEN-sh<u>i</u>nts. The three-syllable SEN-shee-<u>i</u>nts is also acceptable.

Recently, from a car salesman on TV, I heard the peculiar pronunciation SEN-tee-<u>i</u>nt. Never one to assume that something peculiar, preposterous, or beastly would *not* be in a dictionary, I quickly checked the four major current American ones to see if there was any sign of this eccentric SEN-tee-<u>i</u>nt. With the first three — *American Heritage 3* (1992), *RHWC* (1997), and *WNW 3* (1997) — I came up dry, much to my relief. I was not so lucky with the fourth, *M-W 10* (1993), which elicited the dreaded *eureka shriek* — a sharp cry uttered upon finding the very thing one hoped not to find. Several more minutes of frantic digging through other dictionaries and guides revealed that SEN-tee-<u>i</u>nt first appeared in *M-W 8* (1975) and was carried over into *M-W 9* (1985) and *10.* Only these three fraternal Merriam-Webster dictionaries recognize it.

In this book the presence of a variant in one publisher's dictionaries does not an authoritative consensus make. Anyone who says SEN-tee-<u>i</u>nt and anyone who is wondering about its propriety would be wise to give greater heed to the conspicuous absence of this unorthodox spelling pronunciation from all my other references. Compare **consortium, prescience, transient**.

sepulcher SEP-<u>u</u>l-kur.

Don't transpose the *u* and *l* and say SEP-luh-kur, as if the word were spelled *seplucher.* Linguists, who can't bring themselves to call anything a mispronunciation, call this transposition of sounds metathesis (muh-TATH-uh-sis). Common examples of mispronunciation due to metathesis are REE-luh-tur for *Realtor* (REE-<u>u</u>l-tur); JOO-luh-ree for *jewelry* (JOO-wuul-ree); and NOO-kyuh-lur (like *nucular*) for *nuclear* (NYOO- or NOO-klee-ur).

Another, less frequent mispronunciation of *sepulcher* is suh-PUHL-kur, which puts the accent, as the saying goes, "on the wrong *syl-LAH-ble.*" The beastliest mispronunciations of *sepulcher* are (ugh) SEF-<u>u</u>l-kur and (aarrrgh) SEF-luh-kur. Both major boo-boos manage to insinuate an *h* between the *p* and *u (seph-ul-cher),* and the latter, by metathesis, transposes the *u* and *l* as well *(seph-lu-cher).*

To pronounce *sepulcher* correctly you need remember only two things: stress the first syllable, SEP-, which rhymes with *step,* and pronounce *-ul* like *-le* in *ripple* or *supple.* In the adjective *sepulchral* the accent shifts to the second syllable: suh-PUHL-kr<u>u</u>l.

sequel SEE-kw<u>u</u>l (rhymes with *equal*).

Have you noticed how some speakers pronounce the second syllable of *sequel* like the word *quell?* For a while I relegated this pronunciation to a small back room in the storehouse of language with a door labeled "Pronunciations Preferred by the Absurdly Fastidious." But when one day I heard Mark Russell, public television's songwriter-satirist, say SEE-kwel with a meticulous *-el* (not in song but in regular speech), I knew something insidious was up and I would have to speak out and attempt to quell the SEE-kwel insurrection.

The best thing I can say about SEE-kwel is that it's old-fashioned — or perhaps antiquated would be the better word. It is the pronunciation of Walker (1791) — who also marks *equal* as rhyming with *See, pal* — of Funk & Wagnalls *Standard* (1897), and of the *Century* (1889–1914). And that's where the SEE-kwel story ends. Worcester (1860), *Webster's Collegiate* (1917), *OED 1* (1928), and *Webster 2* (1934) countenance only SEE-kwul, and Opdycke (1939) says it should rhyme with *equal.* SEE-kwul is the only pronunciation in Kenyon & Knott (1949), *American College* (1952), *Webster 3* (1961), *Random House II* (1987), *OED 2* (1989), *American Heritage 3* (1992), and *RHWC* (1997). Only two current sources, *WNW 3* (1997) and *M-W 10* (1993), recognize SEE-kwel, the latter labeling it "appreciably less common." No authority I am aware of prefers it.

Those speakers today who have revived the superannuated SEE-kwel apparently are motivated by the belief that they must all-ways prohnounce ev-e-ry syll-a-ble pree-cise-ly or they will not be understood, or respected, or noticed — who knows? But everyday speaking, and even everyday broadcasting, is not like announcing at a baseball stadium. If you start sounding like the hyperarticulate voice on a public-address system, your friends either will rise to salute the flag or think there's an emergency and run screaming from the building. Okay, I'm exaggerating. They'll just think you're a geeked-out android with a freaky speech chip.

There are thousands of English words in which the vowel in an unstressed syllable is lightened or obscure — *obscure* (uhb-SKYUUR, not ahb-SKYUUR) is one of them — and natural (and proper) speech requires that you go with the flow and obscure it. No one says *l* at the end of *shovel, sentinel,* or *doggerel,* or puts a *well* in *towel, bowel,* and *vowel.* Why put a *quell* in *sequel?* It's more natural, and correct, to rhyme *sequel* with *equal* — and that goes for its recent (early 1970s) companion word *prequel,* too.

seraglio si-RAL-yoh or si-RAHL-yoh.

Don't pronounce the *g.* The *a* may be short as in *pal* or open as in *arm* and *spa.*

Seraglio comes from Italian, and in that language *gl* nearly always has the sound of final *l* and initial *y* in *will you* (pronounced quickly). When such a word enters English directly, it keeps this gliding sound. Thus, *intaglio*, incised carving, is in-TAL-yoh; *imbroglio*, a complicated situation or misunderstanding, is im-BROHL-yoh; and *seraglio* is si̱-RAL-yoh. Don't pronounce it the way a friend of mine told me his professor in graduate school did, with the hard *g* of *rag;* si̱-RAG-lee-oh and si̱-RAHG-lee-oh are seriously beastly. See **cognoscenti, Modigliani.**

serpentine SUR-pi̱n-teen or SUR-pi̱n-tyn.

The last syllable, -*tine,* may rhyme with *dean* or *dine.*

Many American authorities of the early 20th century considered SUR-pi̱n-teen incorrect and preferred -tin (rhymes with *din*) for the last syllable, often giving -tyn, the British pronunciation, as an alternative. By the 1930s, -tin was on its way out and -teen had wound its wily way to the top. *Webster 2* (1934) put -teen first, -tyn second, and most American dictionaries since have followed suit. Lass & Lass (1976) prefer -tyn, but the *NBC Handbook* (1984) and *WNW Guide* (1984) go with -teen. Take your pick.

servile SUR-vi̱l (American); SUR-vyl (British).

The American pronunciation of *servile* originally had a short *i* as in *villa* or *pill,* but, as Kenyon & Knott (1949) indicate, since at least the 1940s most Americans have pronounced *servile* with the obscure or "silent" *i* of *evil, fossil,* and *hostile.* The pronunciation with a long *i,* SUR-vyl, which sounds like *Sir Vile* (stress on *Sir*), is a British innovation that caught on in England in the second half of the 19th century and was dominant there by 1900. *Webster's Collegiate* (1917), the *New Century* (1927), and *Webster 2* (1934) label SUR-vyl "chiefly British," while the British *Shorter OED* (1933) conversely labels SUR-vil (short *i*) American. *Webster 3* (1961) and subsequent American dictionaries have listed SUR-vyl as an alternative to SUR-vi̱l without comment, but to my ear, a *vile* in *servile* still sounds peculiar coming from an American speaker. For more on American vs. British pronunciation of -*ile,* see **textile.**

shallot SHAL-i̱t or shuh-LAHT.

Until the mid-20th century, shuh-LAHT, with the accent on the second syllable, was the only acceptable pronunciation of this word. In the 1960s and early 1970s, however, recessive stress — a shifting of the accent toward the beginning of a word — set to work on *shallot* and sprouted an alternative pronunciation, SHAL-i̱t, which has spread like onion grass. SHAL-i̱t made its debut in *M-W 8* (1975) labeled "appreciably less common." *WNW Guide* (1984) noted that "in recent years [SHAL-i̱t] has become common." *AHSC* (1985) listed it as an alternative without comment, the unabridged *Random House II* (1987) put it first, and it is the only pronunciation sanctioned by Barnhart (1988).

If you've been browsing through this book for a while you probably are well aware that I am not a big fan of newly minted pronunciations. Unlike the editors of most current dictionaries, I do not rush to embrace every phonetic aberration that comes down the pike. I am by nature skeptical of innovations in speech and inclined to defend established pronunciations. That noted, however, I must now say this: as a liberal purist, I believe in evaluating things on a case-by-case basis, and sometimes there are cases that present compelling reasons to chuck the old in favor of the new. It would be a grave mistake to assume that just because a pronunciation is new it must be objectionable. It all depends on who's doing the changing and whether there's any justification for it.

I would argue that the recessive-stress SHAL-it is one of the exceptional cases. This variant is not the result of ignorance or affectation but rather of the natural and inevitable pressure of anglicization, which for *foyer* led us to discard fwah-YAY and FOY-ay and arrive at FOY-ur, and for *insouciant* led us from a(n)-soo-SYAH(N) to in-SOO-see-int. By shifting its accent to the first syllable, *shallot* (from obsolete French *eschallotte*) — perhaps influenced by its food cousins *scallion* (from Norman French *scaloun* and Old French *eschaloigne*) and *carrot* (from French *carotte*), and words such as *ballot* (from Italian *balotta*), *pilot* (from French *pilote*), and *harlot* (from Old French *herlot*), along with *spigot, zealot, abbot, pivot,* etc. — is simply becoming more English. In my book that's a good thing, and so I welcome this new pronunciation with open arms. SHAL-it is on the way in, shuh-LAHT is on the way out. The dictionaries don't yet reflect that, but eventually they will.

sherbet SHUR-bit (rhymes with *blurb it* and near rhymes with *serve it*).

Sherbet does not rhyme with *Herbert*. The reduplicated SHUR-burt is a bad habit of childhood — like *liberry* for *library* and *pacific* for *specific* — that some poor souls never manage to shake. The variant spelling *sherbert*, which you will find in current dictionaries, is also erroneous, says *WNW 3* (1997). I wholeheartedly agree.

short-lived SHORT-LYVD, not SHORT-LIVD.

The *i* is properly long as in *alive*, not short as in *give*. Why? See **long-lived**.

siege SEEJ. Do not say SEEZH.

Siege and *besiege* should be pronounced with the *g* of *rage* and *cage*, not with the *g* of *mirage* and *rouge*.

Siege came into the language in the early 13th century, and for at least as long as dictionaries have recorded pronunciation (about 250 years) the only acceptable pronunciation has been SEEJ. The beastly mispronunciation SEEZH, with the *zh* sound of *seizure*, appears to have come on the scene about 1975–1980. I first heard it in the early 1980s from some of the announcers on National Public Radio's news programs. I have heard it since from numerous television newscasters and, of course, various educated speakers who ought to know better than to re-Frenchify an eight-hundred-year-old English word. I can't say whether broadcasters are responsible for SEEZH, but they certainly have helped elevate it to the level of a vogue pronunciation. SEEZH now appears in *M-W 9* (1985) and *10* (1993), which label it "appreciably less common," but other sources do not recognize it. Let's keep it that way, please. See **liege, refuge, refugee.**

similar SIM-i-lur.

Be careful not to insert a *y* sound in the second syllable of *similar* and say SIM-yuh-lur, as if the word were spelled *simular*. This is a major-league beastly mispronunciation. See **jubilant.**

simony SY-muh-nee or SIM-uh-nee.

Both pronunciations have been heard in cultivated speech since the 18th century. SIM-uh-nee prevailed from the time of John Walker (1791) until the 1930s; of the ten early authorities surveyed by Worcester (1860), only one — William Kenrick (1773) — preferred SY-muh-nee. Kenyon & Knott (1949) and *American College* (1952) were the first to give priority to SY-muh-nee, which has since been dominant. All four major current American dictionaries list SY-muh-nee first, and it is the preference of Lass & Lass (1976), *Everyday Reader's* (1985), and Burchfield (1996), who notes that this pronunciation conforms with the name of the biblical sorcerer Simon Magus, "who seems to have been the first to attempt this malpractice (Acts 8:18)." The *NBC Handbook* (1984) and I buck the trend and stick by SIM-uh-nee. Take your pick.

simpatico sim-PAHT-i-koh.

The British, who love the broad *a* except when it comes to Spanish and Italian names and loanwords, prefer to put a flat *pat* in their *simpatico*. Americans, with the exception of some idiosyncratic New Englanders, prefer a broad *pot*. I see no compelling reason to flatten the *a* and several compelling reasons not to mimic the British pronunciation.

simultaneity SY-mul-tuh-**NEE**-i-tee.

Properly, there is no *nay* in *simultaneity*. It's a *knee*. The last three syllables, -*neity*, should rhyme with *see a flea*, not *say a flea*. SY-mul-tuh-**NEE**-i-tee is the first pronunciation in *American Heritage* (1992) and *M-W 10* (1993), the only pronunciation in *RHWC* (1997) and *WNW 3* (1997), and the preference of the *NBC Handbook* (1984). See **deity, homogeneity, spontaneity.**

sinecure SY-nuh-KYOOR (recommended) or **SIN**-uh-KYOOR.

The last syllable, -*cure*, is also acceptably pronounced -kyuur.

SY-nuh-KYOOR is the traditional pronunciation, the only one countenanced by authorities from Walker (1791) and Worcester (1860) to the *Century* (1914) and *OED 1* (1928). The pronunciation **SIN**-uh-KYOOR, no doubt influenced by the classical Latin pronunciation of the word's source, *sine cura*, without a care, was disapproved of by Ayres (1894), Phyfe (1926),

Vizetelly (1929), and Holt (1937), who says, "We *sigh* for a *sinecure*. Don't *sin* for one, though some folks do." However, *New Century* (1931 edition), the *Shorter OED* (1933), and *Webster 2* (1934) all listed **SIN-** as an acceptable alternative, and Opdycke (1939) and Witherspoon (1943) gave it the nod. Although **SIN-** has now achieved respectability, **SY-** still enjoys the weight of authority. **SY-** is the first pronunciation listed in all four major current American dictionaries, *OED 2* (1989), *WNW Guide* (1984) and Barnhart (1988) give it priority, and it is the preference of Lass & Lass (1976), the *NBC Handbook* (1984), and Jones (1991).

Sisyphean SIS-uh-**FEE**-in.

One occasionally hears the pronunciation si-SIF-ee-in, for which there is no authority.

slough For the noun meaning cast-off skin, as of a snake, and the verb meaning to shed or discard, SLUHF (rhymes with *tough*); for a marsh or swamp, either SLOO (rhymes with *true*) or SLOW (rhymes with *cow*); for despair or degradation, and the Slough of Despond in Bunyan's *Pilgrim's Progress*, SLOW (rhymes with *cow*).

Social Security SOH-shul si-KYUUR-i-tee.

Take care not to say SOH-sul (or worse, SOH-suh) si-KYUUR-i-tee, as President Bill Clinton usually does. This is slovenly. Even in rapid-fire speech the *ci* in *social* should have a clear *sh* sound, as in *special, racial,* and *crucial.* See **Beijing, consortium, controversial, negotiate, oceanic, species.**

soigné swahn-YAY.

soiree swah-RAY.

solar SOH-lur. Do not say SOH-lahr.

Solar properly rhymes with *molar* and *polar,* not with *go far.* See **bursar.**

Solzhenitsyn (Alexander) SOHL-zhuh-**NEET**-sin.

sonogram SAHN-uh-GRAM (first syllable rhymes with *Ron* and *John*).

Sonogram was first recorded in print in 1956. It did not appear in a dictionary until the unabridged *Random House II* (1987), which lists **SAHN**-uh-GRAM, in which the first syllable rhymes with *don* and *con,* followed by **SOHN**-uh-GRAM, in which the first syllable rhymes with *phone* and *bone.* Although **SOHN**-uh-GRAM appears as an alternative in three of the four major current American dictionaries, **SAHN**-uh-GRAM is by far the dominant pronunciation. **SOHN**-uh-GRAM, the only pronunciation countenanced by *OED 2* (1989) and Jones (1991), prevails in Britain.

In 1986, a year before *sonogram* appeared in a dictionary, I queried Merriam-Webster's Language Research Service about its pronunciation. Assistant Editor (now Senior Editor) Stephen J. Perrault responded that "our evidence indicates" that the first syllable could be pronounced either to rhyme with *lawn* or with *loan,* and that the former pronunciation was the more common one. I found that curious, for the evidence of my own ears indicated that **SAHN-** as in *sonic,* not **SAWN-** rhyming with *lawn* (which sounds New Englandy), was the common pronunciation. Even curiouser, when *sonogram* eventually appeared in a Merriam-Webster dictionary — in *M-W 10* (1993) — there was only one pronunciation for the word: **SAHN**-uh-GRAM. For once, I had no objections.

sonorous Traditionally, suh-NOR-<u>u</u>s. Now usually SAHN-ur-<u>u</u>s.

The pronunciation SAHN-ur-<u>u</u>s, which prevails in American speech today, is a British import — and a fairly old one at that. It apparently caught on in the late 19th century, for Ayres (1894) disapproved of it and *Webster's New International* (1909) noted "now often, especially in British usage, [SAHN-ur-<u>u</u>s]." *Webster 2* (1934) also labeled first-syllable stress British. Holt (1937) and Opdycke (1939) frowned upon it, the latter writing, "Don't say *son' o ris* or *son' rus* even tho persons whose use of English you respect may tempt you to do so." The playwright G. B. Shaw didn't like first-syllable stress either. In a 1934 letter to the *Times* of London, Shaw wrote, "An announcer who pronounced decadent and sonorous as dekkadent and sonnerus would provoke Providence to strike him dumb."

Providence remained indifferent, however, and by the 1960s SAHN-ur-<u>u</u>s was listed in all American dictionaries as a non-British alternative. No doubt the recessive stress (shift in accent toward the beginning of a word) in *sonorous* was encouraged by the numerous trisyllabic words ending in -*rous* that have their accent on the first syllable: *vigorous, rigorous, glamorous, humorous, decorous* (formerly stressed on the second syllable), *amorous, dangerous, ludicrous, boisterous, chivalrous, murderous,* and so on. Although the evidence of my ears tells me that SAHN-ur-<u>u</u>s is now the dominant pronunciation, all four major current American dictionaries and even *OED 2* (1989) still give priority to suh-NOR-<u>u</u>s, and *Everyday Reader's* (1985) and Barnhart (1988) prefer it. Lass & Lass (1976), the *NBC Handbook* (1984), and Jones (1991), a British authority, prefer SAHN-ur-<u>u</u>s. For a discussion of recessive and progressive stress, see **confiscate.**

soothsayer **SOOTH**-SAY-ur (first syllable rhymes with *tooth*).

There is no *soothe* in *soothsayer,* so don't say *soothe-sayer* with *th* as in *bathe* and *then.* The *sooth* in *forsooth* (for-SOOTH) and *soothsayer* means truth, and in both words it rhymes with *truth.*

sophomore SAHF-mor or SAHF-uh-mor.

Two beastly mispronunciations to avoid: do not insert a *t* and say SAHFT-mor, and may the gods of good speech have mercy upon you if you say SOWF-mor or SOWTH-mor (SOWTH- like *south*). Also, avoid saying SAWF- as in *soft* for *soph-,* in which the *o* properly is short as in *pot* and *shop.*

Sophomore is acceptably pronounced either in two or three syllables. It is no longer true that only the three-syllable pronunciation is correct. The disyllabic SAHF-mor — the result of syncope (SING-kuh-pee) the loss of sounds or letters from the middle of a word — is the more common pronunciation today among educated speakers. Like many other victims of syncope — for example, GROHS-ree for *grocery,* CHAWK-lit for *chocolate,* AHP-ruh for *opera,* and VEJ-tuh-buul for *vegetable* — SAHF-mor does not compromise the clarity and harmony of one's speech. Except perhaps to the most hard-line traditionalist, it is unobjectionable. *WNW Guide* (1984) prefers SAHF-mor, Barnhart (1988) and *M-W 10* (1993) list it first, and *American Heritage 3* (1992) and *RHWC* (1997) sanction it as an alternative. Among current dictionaries, *WNW 3* (1988, 1997) is alone in countenancing only the three-syllable SAHF-uh-mor, which Lass & Lass (1976) and the *NBC Handbook* (1984) prefer. For more on syncope, see **temperature.**

sovereignty SAHV-ur-in-tee or SAHV-rin-tee.

There is no *-ity* at the end of *sovereignty.* Watch out for the beastly mispronunciations SAHV-uh-**REN**-i-tee and sahv-REN-i-tee, which add a syllable to the word.

species SPEE-sheez, not SPEE-seez.

The origin of the spurious SPEE-seez — with a horrible hissing *s* for the *c* — begins not in the slime of billions of years past but just a paleontologic wink of an eye ago in *Webster 3* (1961), where it appeared labeled "appreciably less frequent." Whether it was endogenous (born in America) or exogenous (imported from Great Britain, Canada, Australia, or outer space) is not certain. What is certain is that SPEE-seez proved to be a very hardy little beast, for by the 1970s it had invaded several other dictionaries and by 1980 it had reached maturity as a major-league vogue pronunciation.

Yes, what was once but a lowly *SPEE-seez infrequentus* has in just a few brief decades become the formidable *SPEE-seez reiteratus.* These days it seems that every other speaker — whether biologist, member of the bar, bartender, or bezonian* — is saying SPEE-seez. Yet, despite this variant's astounding popularity, not one authority prefers it, several — including *Everyday Reader's* (1985), Barnhart (1988), and *OED 2* (1989) — do not recognize it, and no current American dictionary lists it first. Burchfield (1996) calls it prissy. Of all my sources, only one — *Mosby's Medical* (1990) — gives priority to SPEE-seez, which makes me wonder if this preposterous pomposity may have been foisted upon us by American physicians and scientists.

The overwhelming authoritative disdain for SPEE-seez makes my heart

---

* *bezonian* (bi-ZOH-nee-in), a beggar or scoundrel.

glad, for to me it is pretentious and painfully overrefined. No one would be caught dead saying PRES-ee-us for *precious* or SPES-ee-ul for *special*, lest he or she be accused of being SOH-see-uh-lee (socially) am-BIS-ee-us (ambitious) and intellectually SOO-pur-FIS-ee-ul (superficial). In a word, SPEE-seez is specious (SPEE-shus) and should go the way of all faddish and fallacious pronunciations — into extinction.

spherical SFER-i-kul, not SFEER-i-kul.

Properly there is no *sphere* in *spherical*. SFER-i-kul, rhyming with *clerical, hysterical, numerical,* and *chimerical,* was the only recognized pronunciation from John Walker (1791) to *Webster 3* (1961), which lists the illogical SFEER-i-kul first. *Sphere* is monosyllabic, which makes the *e* long. *Spheroid* is divided *sphe • roid,* and because the *e* ends the accented syllable, it is long. The first syllable of *spherical,* however, ends after the *r, spher • i • cal,* and so the *e* is short as in *fetch* and *ferry.* Although *American Heritage 3* (1992) and *M-W 10* (1993) give priority to the upstart SFEER-i-kul — no doubt because it is now the more common pronunciation — *WNW Guide* (1984), *WNW 3* (1997), and *RHWC* (1997) list the traditional SFER-i-kul first, Lass & Lass (1976) and the *NBC Handbook* (1984) prefer it, and it is the only pronunciation in *OED 2* (1989). See **atmospheric, hemispheric.**

Spokane (Washington) spoh-KAN, not spoh-KAYN.

There is no *cane* in *Spokane.* It's a *can.*

spontaneity SPAHN-tuh-**NEE**-i-tee, not SPAHN-tuh-**NAY**-i-tee.

Pronounce the third, accented syllable with a long *e,* as in *knee,* not with a long *a,* as in *nay.* See **deity, homogeneity, simultaneity.**

status Traditionally, STAY-tus. Now usually STAT-us in America and STAY-tus in Britain. See **data.**

steroid STER-oyd (recommended) or STEER-oyd.

Some speakers pronounce *steroid* with the long *e* of *steer,* STEER-oyd, or sometimes with a half-long *e,* STIR-oyd. Others pronounce it STER-oyd, with the short *e* of *step* and *sterile.* Some put a *stair* in it: STAIR-oyd. Are all these variants acceptable?

The short answer is no. Variant number three, STAIR-oyd, is incorrect. Dictionaries do not recognize it and neither should you. Variants one and two, on the other hand, are both prevalent in educated speech and both enjoy authoritative sanction. Does one have more merit than the other? The following information should help you decide.

Steroid made its print debut in 1936. It made its dictionary debut in *American College* (1952, originally published 1947), which offers one pronunciation: STER-oyd. Its next appearance was in *M-W 6* (1956), which also gives only STER-oyd. *Webster 3* (1961) — the dictionary that never met a variant it didn't like — lists STER-oyd and introduces STI-royd, with an ambiguous short-long *e. AHNC* (1969) and Funk & Wagnalls *New*

Practical Standard (1962) countenance only STER-oyd, but *RH College* (1968) gives STER-oyd followed by STEER-oyd, and in the 1970s the tide begins to shift in favor of long *e*. Lass & Lass (1976) prefer STEER-oyd, *WNW Guide* (1984) gives it priority, and the *NBC Handbook* (1984) prefers STI-royd. *OED 2* (1989) and the four major American dictionaries of the 1990s all list STEER-oyd first, with *M-W 10* (1993) labeling STER-oyd (inaccurately in my opinion) "appreciably less common."

One could easily be tempted to assume, based on this current consensus, that STEER-oyd is the more meritorious pronunciation. It is not. Its thirty-something-year record of respectability prevents me from calling it wrong, but I can call it untrue to the word's roots. *Steroid* comes from *sterol* (STER-awl or STER-ohl), which was plucked from *cholesterol* (see the entry for this word). It is formed from the Greek *ster(eós)*, solid, and the suffix *-oid*, like, resembling. Given this derivation, *steroid* is properly divided between its etymological elements, *ster · oid*, which can suggest only the short *e* of *sterile*. The two current dictionaries that mistakenly divide it *ste · roid* — *M-W 10* (1993) and *RHWC* (1997) — defy linguistic logic and betray their partiality for the aberrant pronunciation STEER-oyd, which they list first.

The earliest sources in which *steroid* appeared were not the last to favor STER-oyd. *Taber's Medical* (1970), *Stedman's Medical* (1972), *Oxford American* (1980), Funk & Wagnalls *Standard* (1980), *Everyday Reader's* (1985), and Barnhart (1988) also prefer this pronunciation, which the (albeit unscientific) evidence of my ears tells me is still more common in everyday educated speech. STEER-oyd, my ears say, is often heard from sportscasters, which may account for its growth in popularity since 1970.

stigmata STIG-muh-tuh (recommended) or stig-MAH-tuh.
A third variant, stig-MAT-uh, appears in several current dictionaries but is not recommended.

Stigmata is the Latinate plural of *stigma* (STIG-muh). The anglicized plural is *stigmas* (STIG-muz). In its most specific sense, *stigmata* refers to marks resembling the wounds on the crucified body of Jesus Christ that are believed to have been supernaturally impressed on the bodies of certain persons, such as St. Francis of Assisi.

STIG-muh-tuh, with the stress on the first syllable, follows the Latin and Greek accentuation and is the traditional English pronunciation. It is the only one countenanced by Worcester (1860), the *Century* (1889–1914), Funk & Wagnalls *Standard* (1897), *Webster's Collegiate* (1917), *OED 1* (1928), *Webster 2* (1934), Kenyon & Knott (1949), and *American College* (1952). Opdycke (1939) stigmatized stig-MAH-tuh by saying, "Don't accent the second syllable." This suggests that second-syllable accent has been heard since the 1920s.

Webster 3 (1961), the first to recognize stig-MAH-tuh, listed it first, indicating equal or greater currency than STIG-muh-tuh in the opinion of the editors. Several subsequent authorities — most notably Lass & Lass (1976) and the *NBC Handbook* (1984) — prefer stig-MAH-tuh, and today the word is perhaps more likely to be stressed on the second syllable.

Those are the facts. Now here is a ruling. Despite its popularity and authoritative sanction, there is no escaping that stig-MAH-tuh (with its ostentatiously broad *a*) is a pseudoclassical pronunciation, and anyone with any sensitivity to such things — *OED 2* (1989) and Burchfield (1996), for example — sensibly prefers first-syllable stress. If you are just learning the word or are trying to decide which pronunciation to use, remember this: stig-MAH-tuh is now respectable, but there was never any stigma on STIG-muh-tuh, which has greater authority and a long track record of acceptability.

The verb is *stigmatize* (STIG-muh-tyz); the adjective is *stigmatic* (stig-MAT-ik).

strength STRENGKTH. Do not say STRENTH or STRAYNTH. See **length**.
subsidiary suhb-**SID**-ee-ER-ee (five syllables).

British and Canadian speakers say suhb-SID-ee-ur-ee, with no secondary accent on the penultimate syllable.

Subsidiary has become a victim of two beastly mispronunciations: the four-syllable suhb-SID-ur-ree, as though the word were spelled *subsidary;* and the five-syllable suhb-**SID**-uh-RAIR-ee, which has a spurious *r* sound in the penultimate syllable, as if the word were spelled *subsidirary.* Watch out for these slip-ups, and see **beneficiary, judiciary, penitentiary, plenipotentiary**.

substantive SUHB-stin-tiv, not suhb-STAN-tiv.

Substantial is stressed on the second syllable, but *substance, substitute,* and *substantive* are stressed on the first syllable. Three of the four major current American dictionaries give only SUHB-stin-tiv, and the fourth — *M-W 10* (1993) — labels suhb-STAN-tiv "appreciably less common."

succeed suk-SEED (like *suck seed* or *sick seed* said quickly).

The slovenly speaker pronounces *succeed* like *secede* (suh-SEED). The careful speaker preserves the *k-s* sound of the *cc*. See **success**.

success suk-SES. Pronounce the *cc* like *k-s*.

Occasionally one hears a semiliterate speaker pronounce *succeed* and *success* as if they were spelled *sussess.* There is only one word for this: *beastly.* See **accessory, flaccid, succinct**.

succinct suhk-SINGKT.

This word is increasingly mispronounced suh-SINGKT, as if it were spelled *sussinct.* No authority with a reputation to lose countenances this beastly mispronunciation. The *cc* should be pronounced like *k-s:* suhk-

SINGKT. This is the only pronunciation in *OED 2* (1989) and three of the four major current American dictionaries: *American Heritage 3* (1992), *WNW 3* (1997), and *RHWC* (1997). Only the modern dictionaries of Merriam-Webster recognize the slovenly suh-SINGKT, beginning with *Webster 3* (1961), which labeled it objectionable to many. See **accessory, flaccid, success.**

suggest sug-JEST or suh-JEST.

In *suggest* and *suggestion,* the first *g* may be sounded (sug-JEST, sug-JES-chin) or silent (suh-JEST, suh-JES-chin), as you prefer. The audible first *g* is here recommended, but if you are accustomed to silent first *g* there is no compelling reason to change.

In *Modern American Usage* (1966), Wilson Follett criticizes those who say sug-JEST (audible *g*) for using an "overnice" pronunciation. Not only is this charge unfair, it is also historically inaccurate; in fact, many American speakers would make just the opposite claim — that suh-JEST (silent first *g*) is the chichi pronunciation. For example, in *We Who Speak English* (1938), Charles Allen Lloyd observes that

> the new [*Webster 2* (1934)] is the only dictionary that gives the preference to "sugjest." The *Oxford* and *Standard* give only "sujest," a fact which is still incredible to me and will be to most of us who say "sugjest," and feel that it is as slovenly to omit the "g" in this word as the one in "length." But it must be admitted that English pronunciation does not always go by reason, though I think it is undoubtedly true that the editors of *Webster* are right in feeling that "sugjest" prevails in this country. May it long continue to do so!

In his celebrated and influential *Critical Pronouncing Dictionary* (1791), John Walker gives suhg-JEST followed by this comment:

> Though the first *g* in *Exaggerate* is, by a carelessness of pronunciation, assimilated to the last, this is not always the case in the present word. For though we sometimes hear it sounded as if written *sudjest,* the most correct speakers generally preserve the first and last *g* in their distinct and separate sounds.

In a later edition (as quoted in Worcester), Walker added this:

> Mr. Sheridan [1780], Mr. Scott [1797], and Mr. Nares [1784] pronounce the *g* in both syllables soft, as if written *sud-jest.* Dr. Kenrick [1773], Mr. Perry [1775], and Barclay [1774] make the first *g* hard, as I have done; for, as the accent is not on these consonants, there is not the same apology for pronouncing the first soft as there is in *exaggerate.*

The audible first *g* was also the preference of Noah Webster (1828), Worcester (1860), Ayres (1894), Funk & Wagnalls *Standard* (1897), *Webster's*

Collegiate (1917), Phyfe (1926), Vizetelly (1929), Gilmartin (1936), Holt (1937), Opdycke (1939), and Witherspoon (1943). Kenyon & Knott (1949) labeled suh-JEST less frequent, but more recent evidence shows that it is alive and well in America. (It has been the dominant pronunciation in Britain since the early 20th century.) Lass & Lass (1976), the *NBC Handbook* (1984), and *WNW Guide* (1984) prefer su̱g-JEST, but the *Guide* notes that the "British suh JEST is becoming common in the U.S." That is true. Although all four major current American dictionaries give priority to su̱g-JEST, you don't have to be Henry Higgins to tell that suh-JEST is probably now just as frequently heard in America as su̱g-JEST.

Which leads me to my point: both pronunciations have been around since the 1700s, and both are acceptable today. One is more American, the other more British, but at this stage of the game it would be foolish to say that one or the other is wrong or "overnice." Though I, along with many American speakers, prefer the more American su̱g-JEST, in this case I cannot see the need, as Follett did, to adjure anyone to select one pronunciation and castigate the other. Why draw battle lines when the lines are in the process of being erased? Clearly, both pronunciations are hale and hearty and likely to coexist for a long time to come. May I suggest (your call) that we let them do so in peace?

suit, suite The former is SOOT (rhymes with *boot*), the latter SWEET (like *sweet*).

I am frequently asked if it's acceptable to pronounce *suite* like *suit* when using the word to mean a set of rooms *(a penthouse suite)* or a set of matched furniture *(a bedroom suite)*. Often those asking the question cite as the source of their confusion and distress a radio or TV commercial for some flimflamming furniture dealer in which *suite* was pronounced *suit*. There is no denying this crossover is common, and most dictionaries now recognize it without comment. Authorities from Phyfe (1926) to Burchfield (1996), however, vociferously condemn it. Here are three representative opinions:

Opdycke (1939): "**suite** — a number of connected rooms or a group of persons; a set of articles having a certain relationship — is pronounced *sweet*, and no two ways about it."

Shaw (1972): "In standard usage, only *suite* can be applied to 'matched furniture pieces,' but in this usage *suite* is often pronounced (incorrectly) like *suit*. Why not avoid difficulty and say '*set* of furniture'?"

Morris & Morris (1985): "The correct pronunciation of *suite* is SWEET. However, in the furniture trade the pronunciation SOOT (the same as for 'suit') is very commonly heard, especially in shops specializing in what the trade privately calls *borax* [shoddy and gaudy] and *schlock* [inferior, cheaply made] merchandise. The fact that the pronunciation SOOT is widely heard does not make it acceptable in literate speech."

summarily Traditionally, SUHM-ur-uh-lee. Now suh-MAIR-uh-lee.

Until the 1950s *summarily* was properly stressed on the first syllable, like many adverbs formed from three-syllable adjectives that have their accent on the first syllable: *similar, similarly; succulent, succulently; sumptuous, sumptuously; seminal, seminally; summary,* SUMmarily. But in the first half of the 20th century, an "emphatic" pronunciation with the accent on the second syllable — recorded by *Webster 2* (1934), Kenyon & Knott (1949), and *American College* (1952) — gradually began supplanting the traditional pronunciation, and in 1961 *Webster 3* gave second-syllable stress priority and labeled first-syllable stress "appreciably less frequent." Since then SUHM-ur-uh-lee has almost disappeared from American speech; although Lass & Lass (1976) prefer it, all four major current American dictionaries give only suh-MAIR-uh-lee. First-syllable stress survives in Britain, however; SUHM-ur-uh-lee is the only pronunciation in *OED 2* (1989) and Jones (1991).

Sunday see **-day**.

superfluity SOO-pur-**FLOO**-i-tee (primary stress on *-flu-*).

This is the only recognized pronunciation. See **superfluous**.

superfluous soo-PUR-floo-us (also suu- for the first syllable).

The beastly mispronunciation SOO-pur-**FLOO**-us is regrettably common among educated speakers, yet (remarkably) no dictionary records it, not even as an objectionable or erroneous variant. Even more beastly is soo-PUR-fuh-lus, which transposes the *l* and *u* and makes the word sound as if it were spelled *superfulous.* I have never heard this mispronunciation myself, but I note it here because it appears in the doggedly descriptive *Webster 3* (1961), labeled with an obelus — the symbol ÷, pronounced AHB-uh-lus — to show that many speakers take "strong exception" to it.

supine (adjective) soo-PYN (rhymes with *you mine*).

Stress the *-pine*, not the *su-*.

In his column "On Language" (June 22, 1997) in *The New York Times Magazine*, William Safire writes, "I pronounce *supine* soo-PINE; most younger people, and most modern American dictionaries, prefer SOO-pine."

I don't know which "modern American dictionaries" Safire consulted, but if he had checked the four major current ones — *American Heritage 3* (1992), *M-W 10* (1993), *RHWC* (1997), and *WNW 3* (1997) — he would have discovered that only the last gives priority to SOO-pyn. And if he had checked *OED 2* (1989) he would have seen that the pressure to move the accent to the first syllable seems to be coming not from younger speakers but from British ones, for the *OED* gives SOO-pyn and says "formerly" soo-PYN. Burchfield (1996) also says the British pronunciation is now SOO-pyn, although Jones (1991) still prefers soo-PYN.

American authorities of the first half of the 20th century were unanimous in preferring second-syllable stress for the adjective *supine;* since the 1970s there has been some disagreement but most favor soo-PYN. Lass & Lass (1976) and *Everyday Reader's* (1985) go with SOO-pyn; the *Quintessential Dictionary* (1978), *WNW Guide* (1984), the *NBC Handbook* (1984), and Barnhart (1988) go with soo-PYN.

supposed suh-POHZD, not suh-POH-zid.

When *supposed* is used as the past tense or past participle of *suppose*—"We suh-POHZD they were there"—it is always pronounced in two syllables. However, when the word is used as an adjective, it is often pronounced in three rather than two syllables: "a suh-POH-zid infraction"; "her suh-POH-zid friend." In this adjectival sense, the word means imagined, believed, received as true. We do not say imagin-*ed,* believ-*ed,* or receiv-*ed.* Why say suppos-*ed?* Doubtless the temptation to pronounce *supposed* in three syllables comes from the adverb *supposedly* (see next entry) and by analogy with the three-syllable mispronunciation of **alleged.**

supposedly suh-POH-zid-lee.

Mispronounced *supposably* by the careless. Say it in four syllables, and don't forget *Ed.* See **unequivocally.**

surprise sur-PRYZ or — often, and now acceptably — suh-PRYZ.

Is it true, as some say, that the pronunciation suh-PRYZ, with the *r* in *sursilent,* is incorrect? Only if you choose to flout the evidence of your ears and bullheadedly insist on it. Though orthoepists from Ayres (1894) to Shaw (1972) have mandated sur-PRYZ and disapproved of the omission of the first *r,* at the same time there has been a gradual acceptance of what apparently has been true all along: that suh-PRYZ is probably more common than sur-PRYZ and most educated speakers consider it acceptable.

In their respected *Pronouncing Dictionary of American English* (1949), Kenyon and Knott give priority to suh-PRYZ, noting that it is a product of "a phonetic tendency" called *dissimilation.* This occurs, they explain,

> in English words in which an *r* sound in one syllable is lost if there is another *r* sound in the word. Thus in those regions where *r* is usually sounded in all positions the commonest colloquial pronunciation of *surprise* is [suh-PRYZ]. Here the presence of the second *r* has led to the loss of the first. . . .
>
> Another example of *r* loss is [GUH-vuh-nur], the prevailing pronunciation of *governor* in the North. That this is due to the other *r* sound and not to slovenly pronunciation is shown by the fact that the same speakers who say [GUH-vuh-nur] do not omit the *r* sound in *governess, govern, governing, governance, government,* which have no second *r.* . . .
>
> The pronunciations [suh-PRYZ] and [GUH-vuh-nur] are "correct" forms, not because they are phonetically normal, but solely because they are in wide use by cultivated speakers. [p. xlvi]

If you want to stay on the safe side, say *sir* when you say sur-PRYZ; but if you're more comfortable with one *r* in your suh-PRYZ, or if you're like me and use both pronunciations without noticing or caring or attracting attention, you can use this entry to defend your case. For the record, three of the four major current American dictionaries countenance suh-PRYZ as an alternative, and it is the only pronunciation in the British *OED 2* (1989) and Jones (1991).

swathe (to wrap, bind) Traditionally, SWAY<u>TH</u>. Now often SWAH<u>TH</u>.
I find it nothing short of remarkable that — viewed from the perspective of the dictionaries — a pronunciation that has prevailed in cultivated speech for more than 150 years can be replaced, seemingly overnight, by a newly minted variant that no authority has recognized, rejected, or even remarked upon.

SWAY<u>TH</u>, rhyming with *scathe* and *bathe,* was the only acceptable pronunciation of the verb to *swathe* from the 18th-century British English of John Walker (1791) to the 20th-century American English of *American College* (1952). Then *Webster 3* (1961), in an astonishing bit of lexicographic legerdemain, gave priority to the heretofore unknown and unbaptized SWAH<u>TH</u> and labeled the traditional SWAY<u>TH</u> "infrequent." In an another remarkable turn of events, authorities since have swiftly embraced the young SWAH<u>TH</u> and cast a cold eye upon the old SWAY<u>TH</u> to the extent that a poll of recent sources makes it appear that the upstart pronunciation is the one with the pedigree: Lass & Lass (1976), the *NBC Handbook* (1984), and *Everyday Reader's* (1985) prefer SWAH<u>TH</u>, and all four major current American dictionaries list it first. Only *WNW Guide* (1984) and the British *OED 2* (1989) and Jones (1991) hold out for SWAY<u>TH</u>.

The noun *swath* (SWAHTH or SWAWTH, *th* as in *path*) and the verb to *swaddle* both have the broad *a* of *swat* and *spa,* and undoubtedly this modern SWAH<u>TH</u> has gained many followers by analogy with these words. But the proper analogy is not one of similarity but of difference between the noun and verb in the treatment of the vowel, as in *breath* and *breathe, cloth* and *clothe, bath* and *bathe.* I doubt that point will sway many to drop their spurious SWAH<u>TH</u> in favor of my SWAY<u>TH</u>, but at least I've had my say in defense of this endangered pronunciation.

And that about wraps it up for *swathe,* except for one important thing: however you choose to pronounce the *a,* do not, under any circumstances, pronounce the *th* with a dental hiss as in *breath* and *death.* It must be voiced, as in *seethe, breathe,* and *rather.* Many speakers are prone to this mistake with the form *swathed.*

sycophant SIK-uh-f<u>u</u>nt.
The *-phant* in *sycophant* should sound just like the *-phant* in *elephant.*

SIK-uh-fant, with -fant as in *phantom,* is now often heard. It is a spelling pronunciation — that is, a guess-pronunciation based on how a word is spelled rather than on established usage and lexical authority. Because *sycophant* is far less common in speech than *elephant,* and because most people probably learn it from reading and do not check a dictionary to see how it is pronounced, the spelling pronunciation has thrived. (I was tempted to write *thriven,* but that venerable form is swiftly doing the opposite of what it denotes.) The interesting thing about this spelling pronunciation, however, is that it is not recent. It is *old.* SIK-uh-fant is the only pronunciation in Walker (1791), Worcester (1860), and Phyfe (1926), and the alternative in Vizetelly (1929). However, the *Century* (1889–1914), Funk & Wagnalls *Standard* (1897), *Webster's Collegiate* (1917), *Webster 2* (1934), Kenyon & Knott (1949), and *American College* (1952) all countenance only the rhyme with *elephant.*

SIK-uh-fant reappeared in *Webster 3* (1961), where it was labeled "infrequent." Since then its revival in American speech may have been abetted by the British, for Jones (1991) shows that -fant prevails in England. No modern American authority countenances -fant, however, and no current American dictionary lists it first.

Careful speakers, take note: some current dictionaries recognize the variant SY-kuh-funt, first syllable like *sigh.* I can only speculate that this eccentric pronunciation, which Opdycke (1939) frowned upon, is perhaps a pedanticism based on the bizarre notion that because the first vowel in the Greek *sukophantēs* was long, the quantity of the English *y* used to represent it must be long as well. However it came about, all I can say about SY- for the first syllable of *sycophant* is that it has no pedigree and no authority. In a word, it's weird.

The *a* is also obscure in the noun *sycophancy* (SIK-uh-fun-see), but in the adjective *sycophantic* it is short as in *fan:* SIK-uh-**FAN**-tik (-**FAN**-tik rhyming with *frantic*).

synecdoche si-NEK-duh-kee. Stress the second syllable.

The rhetorical term *synecdoche* rhymes roughly with *select a key* or *Schenectady.*

William Safire relates a humorous story of an interview he had with Jerry Brown, the former governor of California, during which Brown used *synecdoche* correctly but mispronounced it (as Safire transcribes it) SY-neck-doash.* Notables who know big words but neglect to look up their pronunciation also commonly mispronounce *synecdoche* as **SIN**-ek-DOHSH. See **Beijing, consortium, controversial, negotiate, oceanic,** and **Social Security.**

---

* See *On Language* (1980), pp. 301–3.

syringe suh-RINJ.

"In my view second-syllable stressing is now dominant," says Burchfield (1996), referring to British speech. It has been dominant in American speech probably since the 1950s. Opdycke (1939) advised not to stress the second syllable but acknowledged that "the man in the street is doing so a great deal and his accent will ultimately prevail." *American College* (1952) was the first to recognize suh-RINJ as an alternative; recent authorities prefer it and all four major current American dictionaries list it first.

syrup SIR-up or SUR-up.

John Walker (1791) and Noah Webster (1828), among other early authorities, preferred the pronunciation SUH-rup (first syllable as in *supper*). In the 20th century, this was modified to SUR-up (first syllable like *sir*). Though older authorities preferred SIR-up, *Webster 2* (1934) noted that *syrup* "is nearly always pronounced [SUR-up] by makers of maple syrup" and Holt (1937) reluctantly acknowledged that the first syllable was "headed in the same direction" as *stir, stirrup,* and *squirrel.* Today SUR-up (my preference) is perfectly acceptable, and "both pronunciations seem to be heard with equal frequency," says *WNW Guide* (1984).

T

Taurus TOR-u̲s (TOR- as in *torn*).

I have heard certain well-educated folk mispronounce this word TOW-ru̲s (TOW- as in *tower*). This is an example of how a little learning can be a misleading thing. TOW-ru̲s reflects the Latin pronunciation, in which the diphthong *au* is pronounced OW. In English, however, this *au* diphthong has the sound of AW, which becomes OR when *au* precedes *r*, as in *aural* and *auricle*. Seeing as *taurus* has been an English word since 1400, it is foolish and bullheaded not to pronounce it TOR-u̲s.

Tchaikovsky (Peter Ilich) chy-KAWF-skee. Regionally, often chy-KAHF-skee.

Probably because of the variant spelling *Tchaikowsky* (or *Tschaikowsky*) — preferred by Phyfe (1926) and Vizetelly (1929) but now almost obsolete — the mispronunciation chy-KOW-skee is sometimes heard. Regardless of the spelling, chy-KAWF-skee has always been the only acceptable pronunciation, and since the 1930s the dominant spelling has been *Tchaikovsky*.

technical TEK-ni̲-kuul.

Take care to pronounce the *tech-*. Careless speakers say TET-ni̲-kuul.

technique tek-NEEK. Always stress the *second* syllable, never the first.

temperamental TEM-pruh-**MEN**-tu̲l or TEM-pur-uh-**MEN**-tu̲l. See **temperature**.

temperature Properly, TEM-pur-uh-chur. Now often TEM-pruh-chur (acceptable) or TEM-pur-chur (beastly) or TEM-puh-chur (very beastly). For every weather forecaster who says TEM-puh-chur there are probably

---

a = at / a̲ = final / ah = spa / ahr = car / air = fair / ay = hay / aw = saw
ch = chip / e = let / e̲ = item / ee = see / eer = deer / i = sit / i̲ = April
ng = sing / o̲ = carrot / oh = go / oo = soon / or = for / oor = poor
ow = cow / oy = toy / sh = she / th = thin / th = this / u̲ = focus / uh = up
ur = turn / uu = pull, took / y, eye = by, I / zh = measure / (see full key, p. xiv)

thousands of listeners who cringe to hear the word pronounced in three syllables, and thousands more who groan to hear it uttered with no *r*. But there are also just as many who notice but don't feel compelled to cringe (they have accepted the variant) and probably even more who don't notice at all because they say it that way, too. Does that mean it's now okay to say TEM-puh-chur? Let's take a look.

Temperature has become a victim of syncope (SING-kuh-pee), the loss or omission of sounds or letters from the middle of a word. This natural and often ineluctable process affects numerous English words. For example, long before any of us were born syncope had whittled *Worcester* and *Gloucester* down to WUUS-tur and GLAHS-tur; long before many of us were born it had pruned *interesting, vegetable, several, diaper,* and *vacuum* to IN-tris-ting, VEJ-tuh-buul, SEV-rul, DY-pur, and VAK-yoom; and mostly since the mid–20th century it has been hewing the middle vowel sounds from *family, grocery, chocolate,* and *conference,* leaving FAM-lee, GROHS-ree, CHAWK-lit (or CHAHK-lit), and KAHN-frints. So it is with *temperature.* Most modern authorities sanction the syncopated three-syllable variants TEM-pruh-chur and TEM-pur-chur (with the *r* sound intact), and William Safire, language guru of *The New York Times* (who has described himself as "a roundheels on pronunciation"), goes so far as to countenance the *r*-less TEM-puh-chur.

That's good news for the say-it-as-you-please crowd, who will turn on the TV tonight and smile benignly as the local meteorologist — who calls himself a *meter*-ologist — rattles off statistics on the variable conditions — which he calls VAIR-uh-bul conditions — around the country.* However, for you, the careful, discriminating speaker, allow me to offer the following advice.

Like *nucular* for *nuclear* and *liberry* for *library,* TEM-puh-chur is one of many shibboleths identifying the careless, slovenly, or indifferent speaker. To quote William Safire (this time out of context and in disservice to his permissive cause), if you say TEM-puh-chur "you'll have a lot of company, but many of us who will refrain from correcting you won't respect you in the morning."

The traditional pronunciation TEM-pur-uh-chur, with four syllables, still has the weight of authority. Lass & Lass (1976) and the *NBC Handbook* (1984) prefer it, and three of the four major current American dictionaries give it priority. The runner-up is TEM-pruh-chur, favored by *WNW Guide* (1984) and Jones (1991) and usually listed second in dictionaries. Given the natural tendency toward syncope throughout the language, I find TEM-pruh-chur unobjectionable, for the clipped syllable incorporates the *r* in

---

* I have borrowed these examples from Morris & Morris (1985), p. 493. "Such obvious mispronunciations," they write, "can find no defenders."

a manner analogous to similar syncopated pronunciations: TEM-pruh-**MEN**-tul for *temperamental,* **LAB**-ruh-TOR-ee for *laboratory,* AHP-ruh for *opera,* and so on.

The third variant, TEM-pur-chur (which if spelled out would be *temperture*), is objectionable because of its similarity to many pronunciations widely considered careless. Like *temper-mental* for *temperamental, labbertory* for *laboratory, figger* for *figure, reckanize* for *recognize, inneresting* for *interesting,* and *akkerit* for *accurate,* TEM-pur-chur falls into that vast category of slovenly pronunciations for which you may be criticized, and so should be scrupulously avoided.

At the bottom of the list is TEM-puh-chur, perhaps now the most common variant in general American speech but also the worst, for two reasons: dictionaries are reluctant to recognize it, and no orthoepist I know of countenances it; and, Safire notwithstanding, a great number of careful speakers — even those who are tolerant and flexible about many controversial pronunciations — still look upon the dropping of the medial *r* in *temperature* as inexcusably sloppy. See **accurate, figure, interesting, laboratory, library, nuclear, recognize.** For more on syncope, see **chocolate.**

Templar TEM-plur.

I have heard the literary and media critic John Leonard say TEM-plahr, the second syllable rhyming with *car.* This is an overpronunciation, like saying SEK-yoo-LAHR for *secular* (SEK-yuh-lur). In *Templar* and *exemplar* (eg-ZEM-plur), the unstressed *-plar* is lightened to -plur. See **bursar.**

tepid TEP-id.

There is no *tea* in *tepid.* Don't say TEE-pid. The *e* is short, as in *step.*

tercel TUR-sul.

A *tercel* is a male hawk, especially a peregrine falcon. The name of the popular economy car made by Toyota, pronounced tur-SEL (stress on *sell,* of course), comes from this bird. I am not suggesting that we change the pronunciation of the car, only that we retain the proper pronunciation for the bird. See **prelude.**

Terpsichore turp-SIK-uh-ree.

Terpsichore is the Muse of dance and song. The adjective *terpsichorean* (TURP-si-kuh-**REE**-in) means pertaining to dancing, and the noun *terpsichorean* (same pronunciation) is a twenty-dollar synonym for a dancer.

The other Muses of Greek mythology are Calliope (kuh-LY-uh-pee), eloquence and epic or heroic poetry;* Clio (KLY-oh), history; Erato (ER-

---

* This pronunciation is also used for *calliope,* the keyboard instrument whose steam-whistle sound we associate with the circus; however, dictionaries also recognize KAL-ee-ohp, which I am told many circus veterans prefer. See **calliope.**

uh-toh), lyric and love poetry; Euterpe (yoo-TUR-pee), music (and pa-
troness of flutists); Melpomene (mel-PAHM-i-nee), tragedy; Polymnia
(puh-LIM-nee-uh) or, more often, Polyhymnia (PAHL-i-**HIM**-nee-uh),
sacred poetry and song, rhetoric, and mime (the ancient poets say she
invented the lyre); Thalia (thuh-LY-uh), comedy and pastoral poetry; and
Urania (yuu-RAY-nee-uh), astronomy. All are daughters of Zeus (ZOOS
or ZYOOS) and Mnemosyne (ni-MAHS-i-nee).

tête-à-tête TAYT-uh-TAYT (recommended) or TET-ah-TET ("more
French").

Both pronunciations are acceptable, but several authorities — Lass & Lass
(1976), the *NBC Handbook* (1984), *Everyday Reader's* (1985), Barnhart
(1988), and the British Jones (1991), who gives -ah- for the unstressed (à)
— sanction only TAYT-uh-TAYT.

textile TEKS-til or TEKS-tyl.

Americans today pronounce most words ending in -*ile* with an obscure or
"silent" *i*, as in *evil, pupil,* and *fossil.* British speakers generally do the
opposite, pronouncing them with a long *i*, as in *file* and *mile.*

This distinction, I was surprised to learn, is relatively recent. "The division seems not to have become clear-cut until about 1900," says R. W.
Burchfield (1996). Before that, throughout the 18th and 19th centuries,
both British and American speakers pronounced -*ile* either with a short *i*
(as in *pill*) or an obscure/silent *i* (as in *fossil*). For example, the English
elocutionist John Walker, whose *Critical Pronouncing Dictionary* (1791) had
a profound influence on both sides of the Atlantic well into the 19th
century, favored the short *i* in nearly all -*ile* words, including *juvenile,
mercantile,* and *puerile,* citing only *reconcile, chamomile,* and *infantile* as
long *i* exceptions.

In the 20th century Americans have been less consistent in their customary preference than the British have been in their newfound preference, and the long *i* has been making some inroads in American speech.
Here is what the evidence of my ears tells me is going on with long *i* vs.
obscure/silent *i* in American speech at the close of the millennium.

Words of two syllables or more that cut both ways include *reptile* (long *i*
seems to be winning out); *juvenile, servile,* and *puerile* (more still favor
obscure/silent *i*); *projectile* and *prehensile* (long *i* is gaining); *nubile* (long *i*
is now in vogue and threatening to supplant obscure/silent *i*); and *erectile*
(often long *i*, probably because of its quasi-scientific sound). *Textile* is also
among this variable group and seems to be joining the list of converts to
the long *i*. Although American dictionaries of the first half of the 20th
century gave priority to the short or obscure/silent *i* and Lass & Lass (1976)
and the *NBC Handbook* (1984) prefer TEKS-til, all four major current
American dictionaries list the long *i* first and *WNW Guide* (1984) prefers it.

In case you're wondering, I favor the obscure/silent *i* for *textile* and *reptile*, I adamantly prefer it for *juvenile, servile, puerile, prehensile,* and *nubile,* but I'm ambivalent on *projectile* and *erectile.* (Were you expecting bland consistency? Sorry, I'm only human.)

Words of two syllables or more for which most Americans prefer obscure/silent *i* include *hostile, missile, (in)fertile, fragile, futile, agile, imbecile* — which the British have strangely decided to rhyme with *what a deal* — *(im)mobile, docile* (British DOH-syl), *ductile, facile, febrile, fictile, gracile, insectile, motile, sextile, sterile, tactile, tensile, versatile, volatile,* and *virile.*

Words of two syllables or more in which most Americans prefer the long *i* include *senile* (SEE-nyl, see entry), *domicile* (see entry), *penile, gentile,* and *chamomile* (now often -eel for the last syllable — see entry). The statistics terms *decile* and *quartile* are also usually pronounced with long *i.*

Words of two syllables or more that are always pronounced with long *i* in American English include *exile, crocodile, infantile, percentile, profile, reconcile, (turn)stile.* The combining form -*phile,* as in *Anglophile, bibliophile,* is also now always pronounced with a long *i,* like *file.* (Pronouncing -*phile* like *feel* is beastly.)

At present there are only five common exceptions to the long *i* vs. obscure/silent *i* division: *automobile; facsimile* (which doesn't really count because it is based on *simile*); *campanile* (KAM-puh-**NEE**-lee, after the Italian); *mobile* (see entry), which in the sense of "art object" is pronounced MOH-beel; and *mercantile,* in which -*ile* traditionally has a short or obscure/silent *i* but which now is usually pronounced like *eel* or *aisle* (see the entry for a full discussion).

the THUH before a word beginning with a voiced (pronounced) consonant sound: *the woman, the man, the one;* THEE, often variable to THI, before a word beginning with a vowel sound: *the actor, the idea, the only;* THEE when emphatic: THEE *best,* THEE *worst.*

One day, as I came off the set of an early-morning TV show in San Diego, where, between interminable commercials, I had been trying to make the subject of commonly mispronounced words sound thrilling, a camera operator rushed up to me and asked breathlessly, "Which is right, THUH or THEE?"

"Both," I answered. (You have to keep your responses short on TV.)

"Then is there some sort of rule about when we should say THUH and when THEE?"

"Yes. Say THUH before words beginning with a consonant: you are THUH camera operator for THUH show. Say THEE before words beginning with a vowel sound: THEE operator wins THEE around-the-world tour."

"Hey, tell that to my boss!"

"Occasionally it's okay to use THEE for emphasis. For example, recently I heard Michael Medved of PBS's *Sneak Previews Goes Video* say, 'Nosferatu is *thee* greatest vampire movie of all time.'"

"That makes sense. But if the rule is so simple, how come I hear everyone breaking it, especially on TV?"

"Rules are usually simple, but usage is not. And wherever there are rules they will be broken, of course."

"Then what should we do? Should we even bother?"

This was not a question suited to a pithy answer. It was time to wax eloquent.

"We certainly should," I said, putting on my most authoritative voice. "Unlike some rules, this one was not made to enforce something unnatural; it was deduced empirically from our normal patterns of speech. Try forcing yourself to say THEE all the time and you'll see it feels awkward. Listen to people who habitually use THEE where THUH belongs and you'll hear that it sounds self-conscious and often affected. Here's what you should do. Observe the rule as best you can, wherever it feels natural, but if you slip or decide to make an exception once in a while, no harm done. As long as you don't make a habit of saying THEE, you'll be fine."

Indeed, it's the habit that hurts, and we — as a society, en masse — have the habit *bad*. (Did you say THUH habit, or THEE?) I have heard highly educated speakers, such as John Updike, and highly regarded speakers, such as Alistair Cooke, say THEE before words beginning with a consonant. I have also heard many prominent politicians and most network newscasters use THEE unnecessarily (or obnoxiously), as I'm sure you have too.*

So where *did* all these unnecessary THEEs come from, anyway? I suspect that our popular culture bears as much responsibility as our public speakers for creating the confusion, and surely the disinformation program starts early. Take, for example, Kermit THEE Frog and the Sesame Street gang, who love to overpronounce *the* as they prance through their ABCs and other antics. Or how about the way James Taylor sings, "Shower THEE people you love with love; show them THEE way that you feel"? I don't mean to pick on Kermit or Taylor — I have great affection for what they do — but the point is that wherever you turn these days you can find THEE everywhere it shouldn't be. THEE for THUH is so widespread that

---

* I once came across an especially bad case during a radio interview. The talk show host, who mentioned that he had thirty years in the business, must have said THEE nine times out of every ten, regardless of what word followed in his sentence. What's more, he seemed to be using THEE almost belligerently, to establish vocal superiority over me and his audience.

you have to wonder whether we should just forget T<u>HEE</u> rule and give up on T<u>HEE</u> whole thing.

That last sentence shows, I think, how artificial and even ridiculous T<u>HEE</u> can sound when used indiscriminately or automatically. The problem does not stem from inattention to detail; it is an overnicety that has gotten out of hand. Most of us, when speaking naturally, get T<u>HUH</u> distinction between T<u>HEE</u> and T<u>HUH</u> right without even thinking about it. It's when we start dwelling on it and imposing a misguided standard of correctness on ourselves that we begin to make a fetish out of saying T<u>HEE</u>. Then our speech becomes stilted and stagy, because we are trying always to say things T<u>HEE</u> "right" way instead of T<u>HUH</u> natural way. So just relax and say T<u>HUH</u> before all words beginning with a consonant, and T<u>HEE</u> only before words beginning with a vowel sound, or for emphasis. That, in my opinion, is T<u>HEE</u> best way to go. See **a**.

theater THEE-uh-tur.

Properly, this word has three syllables, but when pronounced quickly in the flow of conversation it often comes out in two, THEER-tur. That is unobjectionable compared with the beastly mispronunciation thee-AY-tur, which *Random House II* (1987) calls "characteristic chiefly of uneducated speech" and *WNW Guide* (1984) affirms is "generally disapproved."

Theseus THEE-syoos or THEE-see-<u>u</u>s.

The two-syllable THEE-syoos is the preference of Worcester (1860), *Webster 2* (1934), and the *Columbia Encyclopedia* (1963). The three-syllable THEE-see-<u>u</u>s is the preference of the *NBC Handbook* (1984) and *WNW 3* (1997).

Worcester says "the termination *eus* in most Greek proper names" is "to be pronounced in one syllable," arguing that because the *eu* is a diphthong in Greek it should have a gliding sound in English rather than being treated as distinct vowels sounded in separate syllables. Common usage, however, has shown a marked tendency to treat the *eu* separately in most cases, e.g., *Orpheus, Morpheus, Prometheus,* perhaps influenced by Latin names and words ending in *-eus* and *-ius,* e.g., *nucleus, gluteus, caduceus, malleus, Aquarius, Sagittarius, Sirius, radius,* etc. But the diphthong has persevered in *Theseus, Perseus* (PUR-syoos), *Odysseus* (oh-DIS-yoos), and *Zeus* (which is never pronounced *Ze-us,* in two syllables), and many cultivated speakers today, including me, pronounce *-eus* as *-yoos* in *Theseus, Perseus,* and *Odysseus* and as *-ee-<u>u</u>s* in *Orpheus, Morpheus,* and *Prometheus,* without losing a moment's sleep over the inconsistency.

thesis (singular) THEE-sis; **theses** (plural) THEE-seez.

No literate speaker would be caught dead saying *my books is* or *my pets is,* but certain speakers who think their "higher education" requires them to speak a "higher" form of English will say *my* THEE-seez *is on. . . . .* Be careful to distinguish the singular *thesis* from the plural *theses* in pronunciation and spelling. The same distinction applies to the singular *hypothesis* (hy-PAHTH-uh-sis) and plural *hypotheses* (hy-PAHTH-uh-seez). See **basis, crisis, diagnosis.**

Thoreau (Henry David) THOR-oh. Popularly, but incorrectly, thuh-ROH.
Most Americans pronounce this name thuh-ROH, with the accent on the second syllable. All four major current American dictionaries, however, also record THOR-oh, with first-syllable stress, and *WNW 3* (1997) gives priority to this pronunciation.

According to Ralph H. Emerson (1996), an authority on the pronunciation of literary names, *Thoreau* should rhyme with *four oh,* stress on *four.* "There is no doubt that he himself said it this way," Emerson asserts. "The first dictionary to deal with modern biographical pronunciations at length," the 1864 Webster edited by Noah Porter, "gives THOR-oh," and "this is also the only pronunciation given by dictionaries until the 1920s, when the modern guess-pronunciation [thuh-ROH] (almost like *throw*) began to appear."* The evidence shows that Concord residents have long stressed the first syllable, says Emerson, "and this being settled, the arguments focus on the sound of the first *o* . . . is it as in *thorough* or as in *Thor?*"

In the Spring 1990 issue of *The Thoreau Society Bulletin,* James Dawson relates that "when Bronson Alcott met Thoreau for the first time in 1839, he spelled the name phonetically in his journal as Thorough. However, when Hawthorne met Thoreau in 1842, he seems to have heard the name differently. He wrote, 'Sept. 1st Thursday. Mr. Thorow dined with us yesterday.' . . . How did Henry Thoreau pronounce Thoreau? Perhaps we get a clue in *Cape Cod* [1865] when he playfully compares himself with a viking: 'But whether Thor-finn saw the mirage or not, Thor-eau, one of the same family, did.'"

Thursday see **-day.**

Tijuana (Baja California, Mexico) tee-HWAH-nuh, with the Spanish aspirated *j,* but tee-WAH-nuh is also acceptable.
Tijuana should have three syllables, not four. The old-fashioned pronunciation, TEE-uh-**WAH**-nuh, though still common among Americans, is erroneous.

You'll have to take my word for it on this one, because many current authorities have got it all wrong. In the 1860s a tiny community known as rancho de Tía Juana formed just south of what is now the international

---

* I have taken the liberty here of combining remarks Emerson published in the journal *English Language Notes* (cited in "Authorities Consulted") with remarks he made in his letter to me of July 2, 1997.

border between San Diego and Tijuana. After a flood in 1891, the people moved to a safer area nearby and adopted the name Tijuana for their town. In 1925, Mexican President Plutarco Elías Calles tried to change the name to Zaragoza, but it didn't stick and the name Tijuana was officially reinstated in 1929.

Today, the people of Tijuana, and the savvier citizens of its U.S. neighbor, San Diego (where I live), know that there is no *tia* in *Tijuana*. But many Americans are unaware of the correct pronunciation and may even misspell it *Tiajuana* or *Tia Juana* to conform to their four-syllable mispronunciation. American popular culture has certainly done its share to reinforce the error. To cite only two of many examples: in the idiotic movie *Losin' It* (1982), starring Shelley Long and Tom Cruise, all the Anglo characters mispronounce *Tijuana*, and in the theme song to Eddie Murphy's movie *Coming to America* (1988), *Tijuana* is pronounced TEE-uh-**WAH**-nuh in the lyric "I've seen Ghana and Tijuana."

Dwight MacDonald wrote that "simple illiteracy is no basis for linguistic evolution." Unfortunately, in the case of *Tijuana*, a survey of current sources shows that most are concerned not with historical fact, local preference, and linguistic propriety but with the tendency of Americans to ignore them. All of the four major current American dictionaries give the proper spelling but three list the four-syllable variant first. Only *WNW 3* (1997) gets it right, listing tee-WAH-nuh and tee-HWAH-nuh with no sign of the beastly TEE-uh-**WAH**-nuh. The *NBC Handbook* (1984), sadly misguided in this instance, prefers TEE-uh-**WAH**-nuh, but *Webster's Geographical* (1997) gives priority to tee-HWAH-nuh, which is the only pronunciation countenanced by *Webster 2* (1934), Greet (1948), and the *Columbia Encyclopedia* (1963).

timbre (English) TIM-bur; (more French) TAM-bur.

Timbre, which by derivation means "bell," entered English in the mid–19th century. Both pronunciations given above are heard today in cultivated speech. Authorities of the first half of the 20th century preferred TIM-bur; those in the second half have shifted in favor of TAM-bur. Burchfield (1996), recommending TAM-bur, says the word is "still not fully anglicized in pronunciation" — overlooking the fact that Funk & Wagnalls *Standard* (1897), the *Century* (1914), *Webster 2* (1934), and *American College* (1952) all give priority to TIM-bur, which is also my preference. Take your pick, and we'll see for whom the bell tolls.

tomato tuh-MAY-toh. Regionally (chiefly New England) and in Britain, tuh-MAH-toh. Canadian also tuh-MAT-oh.

I have a wonderful cartoon above my desk that captures everything I could say in ten books on pronunciation. It shows two scowling men standing back-to-back at daybreak. Each is holding a basket of tomatoes, one marked *tomato*, the other marked *to-mah-to*. In a moment, one presumes, they will engage in a duel to a saucy death.

My mother, having grown up outside of Boston, has always said tuh-MAH-toh, even after fifty-odd years of living in New York City, where just about everyone says tuh-MAY-toh, and after forty-odd years of living with my father, who grew up in Indiana and also says tuh-MAY-toh. Miraculously, they have managed to get along, though duels over language, and language duels (at twenty paces), have been known to break out.

The majority of Americans say tuh-MAY-toh — which, despite my mother's formidable influence, is my pronunciation — but it is clear that the tuh-MAH-toh sayers are not going to give in (they'll just die out, I suppose), and there is no reason why they should. Not only is it what they grew up with and are accustomed to saying, it is also a matter of pride for many of them. So if you are a New Englander who says tuh-MAH-toh, or perhaps a Southerner who prefers tuh-MAH-toh, or if you are a Brit trying to fathom the (from your perspective) nasal-twanged U.S. of A., by all means do your thing. Just don't criticize the rest of us for saying tuh-MAY-toh. If you lay off, we'll lay off. Besides, there are lot more of us than there are of you.

A warning for all speakers: do not slur the last syllable into an -uh or -ur sound. In his book *On Language* (1980), William Safire prints a letter from Liz Smith of *The New York Daily News*:

> In regard to "You say potato, I say potahto" there is a joke that when this unusual song was sung in English theater auditions, nobody got it because the singers invariably sang it: "You say potahto and I say potahto, You say tomahto and I say tomahto. . . ." But when I was at the University of Texas, we had our own linguistic joke that went like this: "You say potato and I say pertayter, You say tomato and I say termayter!"

tortuous TOR-choo-<u>us</u>; **torturous** TOR-chur-<u>us</u>.
There is no *torture* in *tortuous*.

The words *tortuous* and *torturous* are frequently confused. *Torturous* means involving torture, extremely painful. It is spelled *tortur* + *ous* and pronounced like *torture* + *us*. *Tortuous* means crooked — either literally, in the sense of winding, twisted, or figuratively, in the sense of tricky, devious. It is spelled *tortu* + *ous* and pronounced like *torch* + *oo* + *us*. If you are careful to distinguish these words in usage, you should have no trouble with their pronunciation.

tousled TOW-zuuld.
TOW- rhymes with *how*, -zuuld rhymes with *pulled*. Make sure the *s* sounds like *z*. Don't say TOW-suuld or TUH-suuld (like *tussled*).

transfer (verb) tran(t)s-FUR; (noun) TRAN(T)S-fur.

Sometimes the *s* in *trans-* has a mild *z* sound. This is acceptable.

Everyone accents the noun *transfer* on the first syllable, which is correct, but many speakers today also accent the verb to *transfer* on the first syllable when it is properly the second that should receive the stress.

When a disyllabic word serves as both a noun and a verb, it is the general rule (or, if that word reminds you of schoolmarms wielding rulers, custom) that the noun is accented on the first syllable and the verb on the second. Thus *transfer, transport,* and *transplant* are accented on the first syllable as nouns, but as verbs they should be accented on the second: to *trans-*FUR, to *trans-*PORT, to *trans-*PLANT.

Furthermore, most of the disyllabic verbs beginning with the prefix *trans-* that do not also function as nouns are also properly accented on the second syllable. This is generally observed with *transpire, transgress,* and *transmute,* but with *transpose, transact, transcend, transmit, transcribe,* and especially *translate,* many speakers today misplace the accent, putting it on the first syllable when it should be on the second. For more on disyllabic noun-verb accent, see **decrease**.

transient Traditionally and properly, TRAN-shint.

Transience is properly pronounced TRAN-shints.

If you prefer to speak like a Brit, then say TRAN-zee-int or TRAN-see-int. These pronunciations were first recorded by *OED 1* (1928) and other British authorities of the 1920s and 1930s. They did not appear in an American dictionary until *Webster 3* (1961), where they were labeled infrequent. Today — largely thanks to your friends and mine, those bumbling broadcasters — these British imports are threatening to revenge the Boston Tea Party and kick poor old TRAN-shint out the door and into the street.

My fellow Americans, do not be misled by the unwitting Anglophile in your midst or the talking head on your TV. Heed the word of your country's authorities. TRAN-shint is the preference of Lass & Lass (1976), the *NBC Handbook* (1984), *WNW Guide* (1984), *Everyday Reader's* (1985), and Barnhart (1988), and the first pronunciation in all four major current American dictionaries: *American Heritage 3* (1992), *M-W 10* (1993), *WNW 3* (1997), and *RHWC* (1997). See **prescient, sentient**.

trauma Traditionally and properly, TRAW-muh. Now often TROW-muh.

I hope that those who take this book to heart, especially those in the professions of medicine (nowadays known as the health-care industry) and psychology, will join me in holding the line for the traditional TRAW-muh. From the time the word entered English about 1700 to the 1940s, the only acceptable pronunciation was TRAW-muh. Since Kenyon & Knott (1949) recognized TROW-muh, however, it has become widespread and now appears to be the dominant pronunciation in American speech.

Taber's Medical (1970) and *Stedman's Medical* (1972) give only TRAW-muh, but *Mosby's Medical* (1990), reflecting the ascendancy of TROW-muh, lists it first. Three of the four major current American dictionaries also give TROW-muh priority, and it is the preference of Lass & Lass (1976), the *NBC Handbook* (1984), and *Everyday Reader's* (1985). The British still favor TRAW-muh, but Barnhart (1988) is the only American authority I can find who prefers it.

So why am I bucking the tide and sticking my neck out for TRAW-muh? Because it's the correct pronunciation, doggone it, and TROW-muh is wrong. The vowels *au* are pronounced OW in classical Latin and in German (and in a few loanwords from German), but in English they are pronounced AW. Open any dictionary and check the words beginning with *au*- and you'll see what I mean. Not counting *auf Wiedersehen* and a handful of other foreignisms, I think the only one (and there are a least a couple of hundred) that isn't pronounced AW is *aunt*. And think of all the words incorporating *au* somewhere in their midst. A computer search elsewhere in this book quickly yielded over a dozen, all pronounced AW (*because, taught, faucet, Chaucer, Paul, pause, nautical,* etc.). Tell me, can you think of any English word — again not counting German loanwords like *schnauzer* and *sauerkraut* and foreign place names like *Aulie Ata* (a city in Kazakhstan) — in which *au* has the sound of OW (as in *cow*)? It's just not a natural English thing, and there is no sensible reason for making *trauma* an exception.

I'm guessing that the big shift over to TROW-muh may have been the fault of the chief proprietors of the word — physicians and nurses, but particularly their teachers. Pedagogues are infamous for pedanticism, and it's quite possible that the esteemed professors in our medical schools, knowing that in the original Latin and Greek *trauma* is pronounced TROW-mah, arbitrarily decided that TROW- was "more correct." Another likely possibility is that once *trauma* entered the jargon of psychiatry about 1890, American speakers gradually were influenced by the many European — especially German, Austrian, and Swiss — psychoanalysts who no doubt pronounced it TROW-muh, with a rumbly German *r*. Who knows? All I can say is it's illogical, it's weird, it's wrong, and it's unfortunately here to stay.

Pronounce the adjective *traumatic* truh-MAT-ik or traw-MAT-ik. See **glaucoma.**

traverse Traditionally, TRAV-urs. Now usually truh-VURS.

"This represents one of the few cases — exceptions to the general rule," writes Gilmartin (1936), "in which a verb of two syllables must be accented on the first syllable." Historically, he is right. Vizetelly (1929) shows that all the major authorities from the 18th century to his day — including Dr.

Johnson (1755), John Walker (1791), and Noah Webster (1828) — preferred first-syllable accent for the verb to *traverse*. *Webster 2* (1934) also preferred it and *American College* (1952) listed it first, but since then American usage has firmly settled on second-syllable stress. *Everyday Reader's* (1985) is the only modern authority in my library that sticks with the traditional TRAV-urs. Apparently it is still the usual pronunciation in British speech, for *OED 2* (1989) and Jones (1991) give it priority.

In 1755, Samuel Johnson noted in his famous dictionary that *traverse* "was anciently accented upon the second syllable." What queer atavism is this, that truh-VURS should reemerge after several hundred years? Though down on its luck in the late 20th century, TRAV-urs has not disappeared from cultivated speech in America. If truh-VURS can be resurrected, then surely TRAV-urs — the *modern* pronunciation — can recover from its wounds and rise again. See **decrease, transfer**.

trespass (noun and verb) TRES-pus (-pus like -*pass* in *compass* or -*pice* in *hospice*). *Trespasses* is pronounced TRES-puh-siz (TRES- as in *trestle*, -puh-siz as in *compasses*).

"I should be greatly interested in your thoughts about the pronunciation of the words *trespass* and *trespasses*, both of which appear in the Lord's Prayer," writes Ehney A. Camp, Jr., of Birmingham, Alabama. "Because these words are repeated millions of times each day throughout our country, I think the correct pronunciation is extremely important.

"In the Lord's Prayer, where the word *trespasses* appears as a noun," Mr. Camp continues, "I find that some emphasize the first syllable and some emphasize the second syllable. The same problem arises with the verb *trespass*. It seems to me that most Catholic and Episcopalian ministers emphasize the first syllable whereas the ministers in my own Methodist denomination seem to be divided."

That *trespass* and *trespasses* are repeated millions of times each day is the very reason different pronunciations exist. However, orthoepists and cultivated speakers have always preferred the stress on the first syllable, and until quite recently TRES-pus and TRES-puh-siz were the only pronunciations recorded in dictionaries. Modern authorities still prefer these pronunciations, but current dictionaries now also list an alternative, TRES-pas (-pas like *pass*), and several note that this pronunciation is especially common for the verb. TRES-pas is a spelling pronunciation; we see *pass* in the word so we think it must be pronounced that way. Strictly speaking, this is an overpronunciation, but its popularity in recent years has made it acceptable.

I can accept TRES-pas as long as the accent remains on the first syllable. In other words, I can forgive those who TRES-pas against me (rather than TRES-pus), but if they tres-PAS against me I'm not sure I can turn the other cheek. Likewise with *trespasses*. If my neighbor in the pew says

TRES-pas-iz (rhymes with *press passes*), I'm not going to deliver a sermon on proper pronunciation. However, if I hear someone either from the laity or the clergy say tres-PAS-iz, I will be strongly tempted to exhort the offender to go straight to the first syllable and sin no longer.

In short, there is no authority for second-syllable stress in these words.* In the Lord's Prayer you may say "forgive us our TRES-puh-siz as we forgive those who TRES-pus against us," which is traditional and preferred, or "forgive us our TRES-pas-iz as we forgive those who TRES-pas against us," which is now acceptable. However, it is beastly mispronunciation — and in this book a cardinal sin — to say "forgive us our tres-PAS-iz as we forgive those who tres-PAS against us." See **baptize, blasphemous**.

tribunal try-BYOO-nul.

Pronounce *tri-* like *try*, and stress the second syllable, never the first.

The noun *tribune* is properly accented on the first syllable, TRIB-yoon, but when it occurs in the names of newspapers one often hears second-syllable stress.

triumvirate try-UHM-vur-it.

I once heard a three-piece-suited speaker — a smooth-talking "director of resource development" — mispronounce this word TRY-um-**VY**-rit. This type of ghastly illiteracy results from one or more of three common problems: learning a word from reading but neglecting to check the pronunciation in a dictionary; saying it the way the boss says it (hey, the dictionary doesn't pay my salary, right?); and never learning the lesson that no matter how much your clothes cost, you're going to look pretty poor if you pull a big word out of your bag and mispronounce it, especially if you're talking to someone whose pockets you are hoping to pick for your nonprofit needs. As Shakespeare wrote, "Mend your speech a little, lest it mar your fortunes."

Tuesday see **-day**.

tumult T(Y)OO-mult or T(Y)OO-muhlt.

The first *u* may be obscure, as in *column* and *singular*, or short, as in *insult*.

Tumult is a word I habitually mispronounced when I was young. All through school I said TUHM-ult (TUHM- as in *tumble*) because TUH was the sound I thought I heard in the first syllable of *tumultuous*, which is actually a too- softened by lack of stress into tuu- or tuh-. Not until I began working as an editor after college did I bother to check the pronunciation in a dictionary, where to my surprise I found that the *u* in the first syllable should be pronounced like the *u* in *tumor*. I don't care much for surprises

---

* A caveat to those who use *American Heritage 3* (1992): don't be misled by the accent after the element -păs, used to indicate the alternative pronunciation TRES-pas. Look closely and you'll see it's smaller than the accent after trĕs. That's because it's a *secondary* stress mark. The primary stress still falls on the first syllable.

like that, so now I make it a habit to confirm my pronunciation of even the most familiar words. It's a good habit to develop if you like to be right.

turgid TUR-jid.

The *g* in *turgid* is soft, which means it has the sound of *j*, as in *rage* and *gym*. Do not say TUR-gid with a hard *g*, as in *bargain* and *gaggle*.

turquoise TUR-koyz or TUR-kwoyz.

Both pronunciations are acceptable. TUR-koyz, my own pronunciation, is preferred by many older authorities. TUR-kwoyz is preferred by most current ones.

tyrannical ti-RAN-i-kul, not ty-RAN-i-kul.

The *y* in *tyrant* has the sound of long *i:* TY-rint. However, the *y* is like short or obscure *i* in *tyranny* (TIR-uh-nee), *tyrannous* (TIR-uh-nus), and *tyrannical* (ti-RAN-i-kul).

U

ukase yoo-KAYS (like *you case*, stress on *case*).

Historically, a *ukase* is an edict from the czar of Russia, having the power of law. Today it is used generally to mean any authoritative order or proclamation.

The word entered English about 1730, coming from Russian through French. Worcester (1860), Funk & Wagnalls *Standard* (1897), the *Century* (1914), Phyfe (1926), H. W. Fowler (1926), and *OED 1* (1928) all give only one pronunciation: yoo-KAYS.

In 1934 *Webster 2* listed an alternative, YOO-kays, with the accent shifted to the first syllable. This became the first pronunciation in Kenyon & Knott (1949) and *American College* (1952), both of which gave as their second pronunciation yet a third variant: yoo-KAYZ (-KAYZ rhyming with *daze*). Put some recessive stress on that and you get a fourth variant now commonly listed in dictionaries: YOO-kayz.

With four possible pronunciations, it appears the time has come for a ukase on *ukase*. As the self-styled Czar of the Spoken Word, I issue this decree: do not pronounce the *s* as *z*. YOO-kayz and yoo-KAYZ, being the newest of the variants (and apparently British), are hereby banned. Since YOO-kays is closest to the original anglicized pronunciation and has been sanctioned since the 1930s, I will not send those who embrace it on a one-way trip to Siberia. However, they are strongly encouraged (by force of the Imperial Guard of the Spoken Word, if necessary) to see the eminent wisdom in saying it the traditional way: yoo-KAYS.

That's my dictum. Here is how other modern authorities weigh in: Lass

---

a = at / a̲ = final / ah = spa / ahr = car / air = fair / ay = hay / aw = saw
ch = chip / e = let / e̲ = item / ee = see / eer = deer / i = sit / i̲ = April
ng = sing / o̲ = carrot / oh = go / oo = soon / or = for / oor = poor
ow = cow / oy = toy / sh = she / th = thin / t̲h̲ = this / u̲ = focus / uh = up
ur = turn / uu = pull, took / y, eye = by, I / zh = measure / (see full key, p. xiv)

& Lass (1976), the *NBC Handbook* (1984), and Barnhart (1988) prefer yoo-KAYS. *WNW Guide* (1984) and *Everyday Reader's* (1985) prefer YOO-kays. The British authorities Jones (1991) and Burchfield (1996) prefer yoo-KAYZ.

ultimatum UHL-ti̱-**MAY**-tu̱m, not UHL-ti̱-**MAH**-tu̱m.

Ultimatum, which entered English about 1730, comes directly from Latin. Until the 1960s dictionaries recognized only UHL-ti̱-**MAY**-tu̱m, with the penultimate syllable pronounced with a long *a*, as in *may*. Since then most dictionaries have also sanctioned UHL-ti̱-**MAH**-tu̱m, with the penultimate syllable pronounced with a broad *a*, like *ma-* in *mama*. This variant with the broad *a* is a de-anglicized pronunciation, an illogical and unnecessary regression from the established English way of saying the word to a classical Latin affectation. It is a trendy, pseudosophisticated pronunciation that the careful speaker should scrupulously avoid. For more on the English pronunciation of words from Latin, see **data**. For more on de-anglicization, see **cadre, junta**.

unequivocally UHN-i-**KWIV**-uh-kuh-lee (six syllables).

The clipped, or syncopated, form UHN-i-**KWIV**-uh-klee (five syllables) is also acceptable. Because the *e* (second syllable) is unstressed, it usually has the sound of short or lightened *i*, as in *picky* or *divide;* some sources, however, mark the *e* long, as in *equal.*

Watch out for the Major Beastly Mispronunciation UHN-i-**KWIV**-uh-kuh-blee, in which a spurious *b* creeps into the last syllable, making the word sound as if it were spelled *unequivocably. Unequivocally* ends in *vocally,* not *vocably,* and there is no such word as *unequivocably* — at least not a legitimate one, at any rate. Unfortunately, over the years so many people have mistakenly said *unequivocably* instead of *unequivocally* that a spurious alternative spelling has cropped up based on the mispronunciation.

Two brief examples should serve to illustrate the regrettable infiltration of *unequivocably* into educated discourse. Several years ago I was a guest on a popular radio talk show in Maryland where the host, a veteran of thirty years in the business who prided himself on his impeccable (and, I might add, imperious) speech, said *unequivocably.* And in *Imperial Masquerade* (1990), a collection of essays by Lewis H. Lapham, editor of *Harper's Magazine,* I found this: "Not the greatest recording artist of all time, not the greatest rock singer or break dancer of all time, but, simply and *unequivocably,* the greatest artist" (p. 78, my emphasis).

OED 2 (1989) contains citations of the "irregular" forms *unequivocable* and *unequivocably* dating back to 1917, and since the 1970s the dictionaries of Merriam-Webster have recorded *unequivocably,* with the pronunciation UHN-i-**KWIV**-uh-kuh-blee, followed by the label *nonstand* — which I'm sure sends shivers down every dictionary-user's spine. The other leading American dictionaries do not recognize this impropriety, however, and R. W. Burchfield, in his *New Fowler's MEU* (1996), is unequivocal: "The standard corresponding adverb is *unequivocally*, not *unequivocably*." See **minuscule**.

Uranus YUUR-uh-n<u>u</u>s, not yuu-RAY-n<u>u</u>s.

The accent is properly on the *first* syllable, which has the sound of *Eur-* in *Europe*.

The once beastly, now sanctioned pronunciation yuu-RAY-n<u>u</u>s (also yuh-), which shifts the accent to the second syllable, took root sometime in the early 20th century and gained recognition in a few references by mid-century. It is now probably the dominant pronunciation, certainly in the U.S.

Nevertheless, it's hard for me to imagine how anyone can feel comfortable saying it this way, and it's even harder to imagine how the first person who used this pronunciation managed to do so with a straight face. To put it bluntly, yuu-RAY-n<u>u</u>s sounds like "your anus." That is reason enough to avoid it — unless, of course, you intend to be crudely humorous, as Johnny Carson once did when he gave sidekick Ed McMahon this minilesson in scatological astronomy: "Across from *Uranus*," he said, accenting the second syllable, "is Constellation H."

I should point out that the pronunciation YUUR-uh-n<u>u</u>s did not come about because polite speakers in the more prudish past felt a need for a phonic euphemism. The name of the planet *Uranus* comes from the Late Latin *Uranus*, which in turn comes from the Greek *Ouranos*, the heaven, first ruler of the universe and father of the Titans. In Greek the accent fell on the last syllable, but in Latin the *u* was long and the *a* was short, so the stress shifted to the first syllable; hence, the English YUUR-uh-n<u>u</u>s. Until the middle of this century, nearly two hundred years after the planet's discovery in 1781, the only recognized pronunciation placed the accent on the first syllable. Thus there is no precedent (other than a popular misconception, perhaps based on a false notion of how the Latin was pronounced) for stressing the second syllable.

In his *New Fowler's MEU* (1996), R. W. Burchfield has this to say about the matter:

> One hears this word stressed on the first syllable from time to time . . . but more often, in my subjective judgment, on the second. . . . I am bound to report, however, that most of the standard desk dictionaries in Britain and America give priority to first-syllable stressing.

The only other recent authorities I found who list *Uranus*, the *NBC Handbook* (1984) and Jones (1991), both prefer YUUR-uh-n<u>u</u>s.

usage YOOS-ij.

Believe it or not, it used to be YOOZ-ij. *Webster 2* (1934) says, "Though the preponderance of lexical authority is for [YOOZ-ij], investigation shows that [YOOS-ij] strongly prevails in America."

usual YOO-zhoo-<u>ul</u>.

This word has three syllables. Don't say YOO-zh<u>ul</u>, which Burchfield (1996) calls "slipshod."

usurp yoo-SURP. Formerly, and now chiefly British, yoo-ZURP.

The traditional pronunciation, preferred by American and British authorities from Walker (1791) to *Webster 2* (1934), is yoo-ZURP. In the 1940s yoo-SURP gained recognition in the dictionaries and soon became the dominant pronunciation in the U.S. The British still favor yoo-ZURP, but most modern American authorities — including Lass & Lass (1976), *WNW Guide* (1984), the *NBC Handbook* (1984), *Everyday Reader's* (1985), and Barnhart (1988) — prefer yoo-SURP. In preferring the traditional yoo-ZURP, I am anomalous — but not Anglophilic.

usurpation YOO-sur-**PAY**-sh<u>in</u>.

usury YOO-zhuh-ree.

The *s* in *usury* should have the *zh* sound of *s* in *vision* and *measure*. Don't say YOO-zuh-ree or YOO-suh-ree. Dictionaries do not recognize these beastly mispronunciations.

uvula YOOV-yuh-luh.

V

vaccinate VAK-s<u>i</u>-NAYT. Don't say **VAS-<u>i</u>-NAYT.**

The *cc* has the sound of *x* or *k-s.* See **accept, accessory, flaccid, succinct.**

vacuum VAK-yoom.

With the advent of the vacuum cleaner in the early 20th century the three-syllable VAK-yoo-<u>um</u> swiftly became endangered. Apparently it survives in Britain — *OED 2* (1989) and Jones (1991) prefer it — but in American speech it is as rare as a spotted owl. Nevertheless, current American dictionaries all list it and will probably continue doing so for several generations after the poor creature is extinct.

vagaries Traditionally, vuh-GAIR-eez. Now usually VAY-guh-reez.

Vagaries is the plural of *vagary* — a wild fancy, eccentric action, or unpredictable event — which entered English in the late 16th century, formed apparently from the Latin *vagari* (wuh-GAH-ree), to wander. Like the Latin, *vagary* and *vagaries* were accented on the second syllable, as in these 17th-century lines from Milton: "They changed their minds / Flew off, and into strange *vagaries* fell / As they would dance."

Walker (1791) and 19th-century authorities preferred vuh-GAY-ree, with a long *a* in the second syllable, following the rule for the English pronunciation of words taken from Latin, in which vowels ending accented syllables have their long English sounds. (See **data** for more on this rule.) Eventually, as speakers began to blend the long *a* of *gay* into the adjacent *r*, *vagary* came to be pronounced vuh-GAIR-ee — which "rhymes satisfactorily with *canary*," says Holt (1937) — and the shift was reflected in diction-

---

a = at / <u>a</u> = final / ah = spa / ahr = car / air = fair / ay = hay / aw = saw
ch = chip / e = let / <u>e</u> = item / ee = see / eer = deer / i = sit / <u>i</u> = April
ng = sing / <u>o</u> = carrot / oh = go / oo = soon / or = for / oor = poor
ow = cow / oy = toy / sh = she / th = thin / <u>th</u> = this / <u>u</u> = focus / uh = up
ur = turn / uu = pull, took / y, eye = by, I / zh = measure / (see full key, p. xiv)

---

aries of the first half of the 20th century, including *OED 1* (1928), *Webster 2* (1934), and *American College* (1952).

Between about 1900 and 1930, however, the pronunciation VAY-guh-ree, with the accent on the first syllable (presumably based on analogy with *vague*), began to gain currency in educated British speech. It appeared as an alternative in Daniel Jones's *English Pronouncing Dictionary* (1924) — which records the colloquial pronunciation of those who have been "educated at the great public boarding schools" — and in the *Shorter OED* (1933). It soon traveled from England's upper crust to America's Angloma-niacs, who snapped up this latest Etonian gewgaw and, through the infa-mous trickle-down effect, bestowed it on the masses. VAY-guh-ree did not appear in American dictionaries until the 1960s, but by then it had become so prevalent in American speech that *Webster 3* (1961) listed it first, and *AHNC* (1969) followed suit.

Authorities since are divided. Lass & Lass (1976), *WNW Guide* (1984), and *Everyday Reader's* (1985) stick by the traditional vuh-GAIR-eez, while the *NBC Handbook* (1984), Barnhart (1988), and Burchfield (1996) prefer VAY-guh-reez. William Safire, in his *New York Times* column "On Lan-guage," has argued that most people now say VAY-guh-reez (the evidence of my ears says he's right), and he has adjured the dictionaries to "get with it." Whether you prefer to be with it or, like me, are ever skeptical of the imported pronunciation and defer to tradition over trend — that will determine which way the dictionaries go, for there are few vuh-GAIR-eez or VAY-guh-reez in lexicography. Just don't say VAG-uh-ree (VAG- as in *vagabond*), which is an out-and-out beastly mispronunciation. For a dis-cussion of recessive and progressive stress, see **confiscate**.

vaginal (American) VAJ-i-nul; (British) vuh-JY-nul.

valance VAL-ints (rhymes with *balance*).

valence VAY-lints (VAY- as in *vapor*).

valet Traditionally, VAL-it, but in the U.S. now usually va-LAY or VAL-ay.

"The overwhelming majority of Americans say 'vaLAY,' which they think is the French pronunciation, but which finds, somewhat strangely, no sup-port in any dictionary," writes Charles Allen Lloyd in *We Who Speak English* (1938).

> Our lexicographers apparently argue that people who have no dealings with valets are not entitled to be consulted about the pronunciation of the word. Those who have them — mostly Englishmen — say "VALett," sounding the "t" in good English fashion, and this is the pronuncia-tion favored by the dictionaries, though it was almost unknown to the great mass of the American people before the advent of the talking pic-tures. . . .
>
> But the difficulty of pleasing everybody in the matter of pronunciation is

shown by my experience with this word in a hotel in New York. Wishing to have some pressing done, in accordance with printed instructions on the wall I took down the telephone receiver and said to the operator:

"Give me the VALett's office, please."

"Do you mean the va-LAY?" came the reply, and feeling properly rebuked, I was forced to admit that I did. [p. 149]

Alfred H. Holt, a contemporary of Lloyd's, offers a different opinion in *You Don't Say!* (1937): "Since 1755, it has been considered a little unpatriotic, if not downright vulgar, to do this the French way. Rhyme it with *mallet*."

So what should we do? Rhyme *valet* with *mallet,* or with *chalet* and *sashay?*

In America, where most gentlemen prefer to dress themselves and do their own errands, there is little use for this word. It survives, however, as the term for an anthropomorphic rack for holding clothing and other personal effects, and in the odd custom of "valet parking," which seems to have been invented to provide a socially acceptable outlet for the destructive impulses of young male drivers. For "valet parking," the pronunciation VAL-ay is now so entrenched that it would be pedantic and pointless to take exception to it. The rack, on the other hand, since it is designed to substitute for the servant, ought to have the traditional pronunciation, VAL-it. (If the thing could talk, it probably would respectfully request that you say it that way.)

Kenyon & Knott (1949) call va-LAY and VAL-ay "pseudo-French," and *Webster 2* (1934), noting that the word has been anglicized since the 17th century, says "the best usage still prefers [VAL-it]." Like *claret* and *jacket,* also old disyllabic borrowings from French that end in -*et,* the word *valet* — "a corruption of the old French *varlet* [also *vaslet* or *valet*], a knight's page or attendant," says Opdycke (1939) — is traditionally pronounced VAL-it, but I doubt anyone will disagree that the pseudo-French variants predominate in American speech today. Lass & Lass (1976) and the *NBC Handbook* (1984) favor the traditional VAL-it, but Barnhart (1988) prefers va-LAY and Burchfield (1996) prefers VAL-ay. Current dictionaries countenance all three pronunciations. For more on pseudo-French pronunciations, see **envelope**.

valetudinarian VAL-i-T(Y)OO-di-**NAIR**-ee-in.

This twenty-dollar word may denote either an invalid or a hypochondriac.

Van Gogh (Vincent) van-GOH (like *van go*).

There are three dictionary-sanctioned ways to pronounce the last name of this great Dutch painter: in Dutch; in half-English, half-Dutch; or in English. In other words, that means an English speaker may choose a pronunciation that is (a) foreign and extremely awkward; (b) awkward and affected; or (c) natural and comfortable. Gosh, which do you think I recommend? Before I give it away, let's discuss each variant in turn.

The Dutch pronunciation is entirely appropriate when speaking Dutch, of course. However, those who insist on using the Dutch pronunciation in English conversation had better be prepared for their interlocutors to look at them as though they were about to spit on the floor. In Dutch, both the *G* and *gh* of *Gogh* are voiceless velar fricatives, that is, gutturalized like *ch* in German *ach:* (roughly) vahn-<u>KH</u>AW<u>KH</u>. For the English speaker, this double guttural is a double whammy; not only is it unnatural to pronounce, it is also alarming to hear. With all due respect for the Dutch, the unfortunate truth is the Dutch pronunciation sounds like an attempt to clear phlegm from the throat with the mouth open. Even those English speakers who take the greatest pains to reproduce the authentic pronunciation of foreign names are bound to have second thoughts about saying it the Dutch way. When the choice is between authenticity and intelligibility, most speakers quite sensibly opt for the latter.

In the half-Dutch, half-English pronunciation, the initial *G* is hard, as in *go,* and the *gh* is guttural: GAW<u>KH</u> or GAH<u>KH</u>. Though this hybrid falls less harshly upon all-English ears, it presents another problem: trying to be in two places at once without being anywhere at all. If you try to say *Van Gogh* in two languages at once you won't be saying it properly in either one, and then where will you be? Dutch speakers will know you are faking it and English speakers will think you're a snoot. Thus, to use the half-anglicized vahn- or van-GAW<u>KH</u> only draws attention to the fact that you are capable of creating a voiceless velar fricative (hooray for you!) and that your pronunciation is different from most everyone else's.

And so that brings us to door number three, behind which lies the anglicized, natural, and entirely acceptable van-GOH. No matter what you may have heard from your art history professor in college, your local art critic, or the culture snobs who condescend to lecture you at cocktail parties, the anglicized pronunciation is *not* wrong. If these fussy fools ever start getting guttural with you over Van Gogh, clear your throat and give them this: *American College* (1952), the *Columbia Encyclopedia* (1963), and all four major current American dictionaries list van-GOH first, and the *NBC Handbook* (1984) and McConkey (1986) prefer it.

vapid VAP-id.

This is the preference of Lass & Lass (1976), the *NBC Handbook* (1984), *Everyday Reader's* (1985), and Jones (1991), and the only pronunciation in *OED 2* (1989), *RHWC* (1997), and *WNW 3* (1997).

varicose VAR-<u>i</u>-kohs (or VAIR- for the first syllable).

The *-cose* in *varicose* should rhyme with *dose,* not *doze.*

variegated VAIR-ee-uh-GAY-tid (five syllables).

vase VAYS (rhymes with *case* and *lace*) or VAYZ (rhymes with *haze*).
VAYS has been the prevailing American pronunciation since the days of
Noah Webster, though VAYZ is just as venerable and is used by many
cultivated speakers today. Both pronunciations were once widely heard in
cultivated speech in England. In his *Critical Pronouncing Dictionary,* John
Walker (1791) prefers VAYZ but remarks that

> Mr. [Thomas] Sheridan [1780] has pronounced this word so as to rhyme
> with *base, case,* &c. I have uniformly heard it pronounced with the *s* like *z,*
> and sometimes, by people of refinement, with the *a* like *aw;* but this, being
> too refined for the general ear, is now but seldom heard.

OED 2 (1989) notes that Jonathan Swift (1731) rhymed *vase* with *face,* and
Lord Byron (1822) and Ralph Waldo Emerson (1847) rhymed it with *grace.*
The pronunciations VAHZ and VAWZ, noted by Walker above, are
British. The former is the prevailing pronunciation, but the latter "has still
some currency in England," says *OED 2.* In an American speaker, say
Morris & Morris (1985), VAHZ "is a mark of affectation." I agree.

In *You Don't Say!* Alfred H. Holt (1937) offers this amusing bit of verse:

> Some greet with lusty "Rah"s
> A reference to a *vase.*
> Another bares his claws
> At folks who don't say *vase.*
> But many use the phrase,
> "Please put these in a *vase,*"
> While still a stronger case
> We now can make for *vase.*

vaudeville VAWD-vil. Less often, VOHD-vil or VAW-duh-vil.
Until the mid–20th century, American authorities preferred VOHD-vil.
Since the 1960s, however, VAWD-vil — preferred by Lass & Lass (1976) and
the *NBC Handbook* (1984) — has thoroughly eclipsed VOHD-vil, which is
now probably on the verge of obsolescence. Also acceptable, but much less
common, is the three-syllable variant VAW-duh-vil, which appeared as an
alternative in *Webster 2* (1934) and *American College* (1952) and was listed
first by Kenyon & Knott (1949). Another three-syllable variant, VOHD-uh-
vil, is especially British, says *Webster 2,* but two current British authorities,
Jones (1991) and Burchfield (1996), prefer VAWD-uh-vil.

vector VEK-tur (rhymes with *Hector*). Don't say VEK-tor. See **juror,
vendor**.

vegan VEE-gin.
This word was coined in 1944 to designate a vegetarian who shuns all
animal products. *OED 2* (1989), which prefers VEE-gin, says VEJ-in is the

American pronunciation, but current evidence on this side of the Atlantic contradicts that assessment. The earliest American source in which I found the word is *M-W 7* (1972), which gives VEJ-in and the short-lived VEJ-an. VEE-gin first appears as an alternative pronunciation in *M-W 9* (1985). A survey of current sources shows that it is now the dominant American pronunciation: VEE-gin is listed first in *American Heritage 3* (1992), *M-W 10* (1993), and *RHWC* (1997), and it is the only pronunciation in *WNW 3* (1997).

vegetable VEJ-tuh-buul.

One day you may encounter a member of the Language Police who will insist that the proper pronunciation of *vegetable* is VEJ-i-tuh-buul, with four painfully distinct syllables. I include this entry for your protection should this ever happen to you.

Opdycke (1939) frowned upon the three-syllable VEJ-tuh-buul, but Kenyon & Knott (1949) and *American College* (1952) listed it first, and since then it has thoroughly dominated the four-syllable pronunciation, which is now rarely heard in American speech. Four syllables are appropriate when reading old poetry aloud, as in this 17th-century couplet from Andrew Marvell's "To His Coy Mistress": "My *veg-e-ta-ble* love should grow / Vaster than empires and more slow." In all other situations, however, the pedantic VEJ-i-tuh-buul sticks out like an armoire in a studio apartment. "To everything there is a season," sayeth the prophet, "a time to plant, and a time to pluck up that which is planted." Current sources still dutifully record the four-syllable variety of vegetable, but it is now less common than VEJ-tuh-buul in British speech, as Jones (1991) indicates, and in American speech it is practically extinct.

The technical term for the loss of this syllable in pronunciation is *syncope* (SING-kuh-pee), which is discussed under **temperature**.

vehement VEE-uh-mint.

Stress the first syllable, never the second, and don't pronounce the *h*. The same goes for the adverb *vehemently:* first-syllable stress, silent *h*. Second-syllable stress is, in dictionary lingo, "nonstandard," which in this book means beastly. See **vehicle**.

vehicle VEE-i-kuul.

The *h* is properly silent. Stress the first syllable, never the second.

Ah, how fashions change — and sometimes for the better. Formerly in the U.S., *vehicle* and *vehement* were pronounced with an audible *h* in cultivated speech. Worcester (1860) and Funk & Wagnalls *Standard* (1897), for example, preferred the audible *h* (with the accent on the *first* syllable in both words), but early in the 20th century enthusiasm for it began to wane. *OED 1* (1928) and *Webster 2* (1934) both favored a silent *h* pronunciation for *vehement* and *vehicle* and listed the audible *h* as alternative. Since then the audible *h* has steadily disappeared from educated speech and fallen into much disfavor among authorities. "The 'h' should be silent and the accent on the first, not the second, syllable," say Morris & Morris (1985) of *vehicle.* Of *vehicle* and *vehement,* Burchfield (1996) says, "In Standard English now, the *h* is never pronounced."

velodrome VEE-luh-drohm.

vendor VEN-dur, not VEN-dor or (in legalese) ven-DOR.

Lawyers and judges habitually overpronounce certain common words, perhaps because they were taught to do so in law school but more likely because it keeps the layperson appropriately in awe of the solemnity and grandiloquence of the legal profession and the law. Whatever the case, I hereby declare that VEN-dorz and ven-DORZ, along with dee-FEN-dants and JOOR-orz — which the average citizen calls VEN-durz, di-FEN-dints, and JOOR-urz — constitute a menace to society. Therefore, they should stay in the courtroom and not be released on their own recognizance, until such time as they can be tried, pronounced properly, and banished from the realm. See **juror, mentor, predator**.

venerable VEN-ur-uh-buul.

The word has four syllables. Don't say VEN-ruh-buul.

venereal vuh-NEER-ee-ul. Don't say vuh-NAIR-ee-ul.

There is no *nary* in *venereal.* It's ve-*near*-eal.

TV's Geraldo Rivera says vuh-NAIR-ee-ul, and, as we all know, when someone with a microphone mispronounces something, it can quickly lead to an epidemic of imitation. The Pronunciation-General's Warning is here provided for your protection: dictionaries do not recognize this *air*-y pronunciation, nor is it sanctioned by any authorities I am aware of.

ventilate VEN-ti-layt.

Be sure to pronounce the *t.* Don't say *vennilate.* See **gentle, kindergarten, mental, rental**.

verbatim vur-BAY-tum.

verbiage VUR-bee-ij. Do not say VUR-bij.

The two-syllable VUR-bij is a thoroughly beastly mispronunciation that unfortunately has become so common that two current dictionaries recognize it. *Marriage* and *carriage* have two syllables, but, traditionally and properly, *foliage* (FOH-lee-ij) and *verbiage* (VUR-bee-ij) have three. For the full story, see **foliage**.

Verdi (Giuseppe) VAIR-dee.

"VUR dee is also heard," says *WNW Guide* (1984), "but is not applauded by those who play or listen to Verdi's music."

verdigris VUR-di-GREES (-GREES like *grease*).

All four major current American dictionaries list **VUR**-di-GREES first, and Lass & Lass (1976), the *NBC Handbook* (1984), and Barnhart (1988) prefer it. **VUR**-di̱-GRIS (-GRIS as in *gristle*), favored by *OED 2* (1989) and Jones (1991), is the British preference. Burchfield (1996) prefers a third variant, **VUR**-di̱-GREE, which is on its way out.

versatile VUR-suh-ti̱l, not VUR-suh-tyl.

In American speech, the last syllable, *-tile*, is pronounced with an obscure *i*, as in *hostile, futile, missile*, and *fertile*. In British speech, the *-tile* in these words has a long *i*, as in *mile* and *file*. For more on American vs. British pronunciation of *-ile*, see **textile**.

vertebrae VUR-tuh-BREE, not **VUR**-tuh-BRAY.

The final syllable properly should rhyme with *see*, not *say*.

Vertebra (VUR-tuh-bruh), the singular, and *vertebrae* (**VUR**-tuh-BREE), the Latinate plural (the anglicized *vertebras* is also acceptable), are both often mispronounced **VUR**-tuh-BRAY, an illegitimate pronunciation that is neither English nor Latin. If this **VUR**-tuh-BRAY, with a donkey honk at the end, is correct, then why don't we say uh-LUM-nay for *alumnae* — properly uh-LUM-nee; *alumni* ends in -ny — and AL-jay for *algae*? Why, for that matter, don't we say **VUR**-tuh-BRY, pronouncing *-ae* like long *i*, as in classical Latin? I'll tell you why: because of the simple, straightforward, sensible, and consistent rule that words borrowed from Latin that form their plurals in *-ae* properly have a long *e* sound at the end. (For more on this rule, and words governed by it, see **algae, alumnae, antennae, formulae, larvae, minutiae, papilla(e)**).

For the singular *vertebra*, **VUR**-tuh-BRAY is simply a flagrant, ludicrous, beastly blunder. For the plural *vertebrae*, however, **VUR**-tuh-BRAY is an old mistake, and, like most long-standing violations of good usage, this one has its distinguished defenders. In *The American Language* (1937), H. L. Mencken claims that for *vertebrae* the pronunciation "*vertebray* is commoner than *vertebree*,"* and cites its appearance seven years earlier as a variant in Larsen & Walker (1930).

Despite the august advocacy of Mencken and this putative prevalence, Kenyon & Knott (1949), *American College* (1952), and other authorities of the time ignored **VUR**-tuh-BRAY, and it did not get into a dictionary until 1961, when *Webster 3* labeled it with an obelus [÷], meaning that many took "strong exception" to it. Regrettably, since then resistance to **VUR**-tuh-BRAY has faded in the U.S., and current American dictionaries sanction it without comment. The British continue to hold the line, however: Jones (1991) and Burchfield (1996) prefer the traditional **VUR**-tuh-BREE, which is the only pronunciation in *OED 2* (1989).

via VY-uh (recommended) or VEE-uh.

---

* *Commoner* is an interesting choice of word here, when you consider its other senses — "one of the common people" and "more vulgar, less refined."

Twentieth-century authority heavily favors VY-uh (VY- rhyming with *buy*), but VEE-uh (VEE- rhyming with *be*), first recognized by *Webster 3* (1961), is probably now the dominant pronunciation in the U.S.

viand VY-und.

vibrato vi-BRAH-toh. Do not say vy-BRAH-toh.

The *i* in *vibrato* is short as in *vivid* and *vision*, not long as in *vibration*.

vice versa VY-suh-VUR-suh or VY-see VUR-suh. Don't say VYS VUR-suh.

This is not the same *vice* as in *vice squad*. That *vice*, which rhymes with *ice* and *nice*, comes from the Latin *vitium*, a fault, defect, and means depravity, immoral behavior. The *vice* in *vice versa* is the ablative of the Latin *vicis*, change, turn, alternation, and is used in English as a preposition meaning in place of, instead of. This *vice* is properly pronounced in two syllables, not one.

The traditional pronunciation of *vice versa*, favored by older authorities, is VY-see VUR-suh, with both vowels in *vice* long (rhyming with *high* and *sea*). When the phrase is said quickly, though, the second, unstressed syllable of *vice* is often lightened or obscured to VY-suh (or VY-si). This pronunciation is perfectly acceptable; it is used today by many good speakers and it is preferred by many authorities from *Webster 2* (1934) and Opdycke (1939) to Lass & Lass (1976), *WNW Guide* (1984), the *NBC Handbook* (1984), Burchfield (1996), and your humble pronunciation maven.

The monosyllabic VYS (rhymes with *rice*) — which first appeared in *Webster 3* (1961), listed last — is common today, but other than that it has nothing to recommend it and no authority I am aware of prefers it. If you've been accustomed to using the vicious VYS, and if the venerable VY-see sounds overpronounced or a bit precious to your ear, then how about going with the versatile, and entirely acceptable, VY-suh? It's an attractive compromise.

vicissitudes vi-SIS-i-T(Y)OODZ.

The *vicissitudes* of speech are such that this word is sometimes mispronounced vik-SIS-i-toodz, as if it were spelled *viccisitudes*, with a double *c* pronounced like *k-s*, as in *accident*. But there is no double *c* or *k-s* sound in *vicissitudes*. The *c* is soft, as in *vicinity*. See **accept, flaccid, vaccinate**.

victuals VIT'lz (rhymes with *whittles*).

You can take your cue on this word from Jed Clampitt and the other Beverly Hillbillies: VIT'lz is the correct and only acceptable pronunciation.

Victuals dates back to 1300. The *c* is left over from the Latin root, *victualis*, pertaining to food. It was dropped in the Middle English *vitaille*, provisions, and reinstated in the 16th and 17th centuries. The spelling pronunciation VIK-choo-ulz, which is sometimes heard in educated speech, is not countenanced by authorities or dictionaries.

vigilante VIJ-i-LAN-tee (-LAN- as in *land*).

The de-anglicized variant VIJ-i-**LAHN**-tee is sometimes heard. Only one current dictionary, *WNW 3* (1997), recognizes it.

viola (stringed instrument) vee-OH-luh.

For plants of the genus *Viola,* such as the violet and the pansy, both VY-uh-luh and vy-OH-luh are acceptable. For the character *Viola* in Shakespeare's *Twelfth Night,* the proper pronunciation is VY-uh-luh, "as the meter invariably requires," says Opdycke (1939). The first or last name *Viola* is generally vy-OH-luh or vee-OH-luh, depending on personal preference. For the stringed instrument, past and present authority overwhelmingly favors vee-OH-luh.

WNW Guide (1984), which prefers vee-OH-luh, says that the word is occasionally pronounced vy-OH-uh, "but no viola player says it [that way]." I was curious to know how this statement would stand up against the experience of some professional musicians, so I called the two I know best — my parents. Had they ever heard musicians, or anyone else, say vy-OH-luh? They both said yes. "I've heard it many, many times," said my mother, "even from people who I thought would know better — even from violists [she said vee-OH-lists] and people who play chamber music." What do you think of it? I asked them. "There's no question of preference here: vy-OH-luh is wrong," said my mother. "It's from Lower Slobbovia," my father quipped. "The Lower Slobbovia Philharmonic."

After that verdict you can imagine how hard things could get for me if I tried to go easy on the vy-OH-luh sayers. No, my destiny is clear — to defend the integrity of music and the honor of the family. But seriously, folks, I don't care for vy-OH-luh either; frankly, I'd never heard it and was surprised to find it listed. This is how I would revise the statement in *WNW Guide:* "vy-OH-luh, which was formerly sanctioned as an alternative, is still sometimes heard, even among musicians; however, today no *self-respecting* viola player — or *any* educated speaker who has even a cursory knowledge of the proper pronunciation of musical terms — says it that way." To my ear, vy-OH-luh for *viola* is like py-AN-uh for *piano.* It's cacophonous (kuh-KAHF-uh-nus), not euphonious (yoo-FOH-nee-us). It strikes a sour note and grates on the ear. See **flutist, pianist.**

virago vi-RAY-goh (recommended) or vi-RAH-goh.

Originally, a *virago* was "a woman of extraordinary stature, strength, and courage . . . a female warrior," says the *Century* (1914). Not surprisingly, it wasn't long before that sense degenerated into "a bold, impudent, turbulent woman," which the *Century* notes is "now the usual meaning." The word comes from the Latin *vir,* man, and by derivation means "resembling a man."

Authorities from Walker (1791) to Kenyon & Knott (1949) favored -RAY-for the second, stressed syllable but differed on how best to sound the first:

vee-, vy-, or (no, not vum-) vi-. By the early 20th century, vee- had gone the way of the dodo and vy- was passing out of use. In modern cultivated speech the short *i* sound (as in *sit*) of the winner, *vi-*, is generally softened to vi̠- (i̠ as in *April* or *sanity*) because the *i* occurs in an unstressed syllable.

The variant vi̠-RAH-goh, with a broad *a* as in *spa*, appears to have originated in Britain in the early 20th century and arrived in the U.S. by mid-century. *OED 1* (1928) gives only vi-RAY-goh, but *Webster 2* (1934) shows that the *Shorter OED* (1933) and Daniel Jones (1924 ed.) both sanction vi-RAH-goh as an alternative. *Webster 3* (1961) is the first of my American sources to recognize vi̠-RAH-goh, listing it first. Current American authorities are about evenly divided between -RAY- and -RAH- for the second syllable, but current British authorities clearly prefer -RAH-. Because I am predisposed to favor traditional American pronunciations over British imports, I recommend vi̠-RAY-goh.

Webster 3 (1961) and *American Heritage 3* (1992) record a third variant: VEER-uh-goh, an offspring of recessive stress that is heard infrequently. Let's keep it that way.

virulent VIR-uh-li̠nt or VIR-yuh-li̠nt.

Some cultivated speakers put a *y* sound before the *u* in *virulent*, others don't. (I don't.) The pronunciation with *y* probably is more common today, but both pronunciations have been heard in educated speech for a very long time. Walker (1791) and British authorities of the 19th century preferred -yoo- or -yuh- for the second syllable; Worcester (1860) and American dictionaries and orthoepists of the late 19th and early 20th centuries favored -uu- or -uh- and sometimes frowned on -yuh-. In 1934, however, *Webster 2* listed -yuh- first, and since then both pronunciations have been acceptable. See **erudite, garrulous, querulous.**

visa VEE-zuh, not VEE-suh. The *s* is properly soft, as in *rose.*

In recent years, more and more people have been pronouncing this word VEE-suh (with *s* as in *sun*), no doubt in part because of the numerous TV commercials for the popular credit card, in which the voice-overs habitually mispronounce it VEE-suh. *Webster 3* (1961) was the first to recognize the variant, marking it "appreciably less common." Today it is unfortunately quite common, although two of the four major current American dictionaries — *American Heritage 3* (1992) and *RHWC* (1997) — do not sanction it, and *OED 2* (1989) also lists only VEE-zuh.

Visa came into English from French around 1830. In French, a single *s* between vowels is soft — pronounced like English *z* in *maze* or *s* in *rose* (e.g., *maison*) — and this has been the established way of pronouncing the *s* in *visa* since the word entered English. VEE-suh, with a hard *s* as in *vista*, is appropriate in Spanish, but not in English. Be sure to put some pizzazz in your *visa*. Say VEE-zuh. See **vis-à-vis.**

visage VIZ-ij.

Some extremely misguided speakers affect the pronunciation vi-ZAHZH, which rhymes with *massage*. There is no authority whatsoever for this preposterous and pretentious bit of pseudo-French. *Visage,* which dates back to the 14th century, has only one acceptable pronunciation: VIZ-ij, which sounds like *vizzidge.*

vis-à-vis VEEZ-uh-VEE.

Don't say VEES-uh-VEE. The first *s* is soft, as in *rose.* The final *s* is silent. See **visa.**

viscount VY-kownt. The *i* is long, the *s* is silent. Don't say VIS-kownt.

Pronunciation mavens aren't perfect, in case you hadn't noticed. Consider this advice from one of my illustrious predecessors, Alfred H. Holt (1937), regarding *viscount:*

> It is likely that more Americans pronounce this as it is spelled than give it the silly long *i* and silent *s* of tradition. If our peerage-minded friends want to preserve that pronunciation, let them spell the word "vicount" and get closer to the French.

When Holt wrote those words he clearly had no idea that he was alone and way out on a limb, sawing vigorously on the wrong side of it. Regardless of how many Americans have mistakenly employed "the silly long *i* and silent *s* of tradition," the spelling pronunciation VIS-kownt has never been acceptable in educated speech. Current sources, along with the older ones, all sanction only one pronunciation — the one with long *i* and silent *s.*

And now it's time for your humble pronunciation maven to 'fess up. When I think how I learned the proper pronunciation of *viscount,* I have to laugh. Like many an average American, I suppose, I too had always thought it was pronounced VIS-kownt. Of course, like many an average American, I again suppose, I had never actually heard the word, only seen it in print, and quite naturally — but stupidly, for I should have checked a dictionary — I assigned it a spelling pronunciation.

One night I was flipping through the TV channels when the nasal, stentorian voice of Robin Leach narrating *Lifestyles of the Rich and Famous* stopped me dead in my tracks. He was babbling away about some "fabulously wealthy" viscount, which he pronounced VY-kownt. You've got to be kidding, I thought. Was this just another tawdry bit of pseudosophistication he was trying to foist on the American public? A quick trip to the dictionary, then to another and another, proved that it was time for me, Mr. Beastly Mispronunciation, to eat crow.

The *vis-* of *viscount* means, by derivation, a deputy or subordinate, and is related to the *vice* in *vice chancellor, vice president, vice regent,* and so on (from the Latin *vice*, in the place of another). From the Latin root we inherit the long *i*, and when the word passed from the Old French *viscomte* into Middle English, the *s* remained silent.

So, Mr. Leach, I owe you one: if I ever become a fabulously wealthy VY-kownt, I'll be sure to invite you up to my castle for caviar and champagne. See **marquis**.

volatile VAHL-uh-tul (VAHL- as in *volume*).

In American speech the *i* in the final syllable of *volatile* is properly obscure or "silent," as in *pupil* and *fossil*. In British speech it is long, as in *mile*. For a discussion of American vs. British pronunciation of *-ile*, see **textile**.

vouchsafe vowch-SAYF. Do not say vow-SAYF.

Pronounce as spelled: *vouch* rhyming with *couch*, accent on *safe*.

vox populi VAHKS PAHP-yuh-ly (rhymes with *fox hop July*).

voyeur voy-UR.

Voyeur entered English about 1900, and after a full century I say it's time to let go of the Frenchified vwah- for the first syllable and go with the anglicizing flow. Although the British stubbornly continue to say vwah-YUR with a bow in the direction of France, most American speakers today sensibly prefer voy-UR. See **foyer**.

vulnerable VUHL-nur-uh-buul.

Sloppy speakers drop the initial *l* and say *vunnerable*. Even sloppier speakers drop the *l* and a syllable and say *vun-rable*. Take care to preserve the *l* and all four syllables.

W

waft WAHFT or WAFT.

"Rhyme this with *craft, draft, graft, raft,*" says Holt (1937), "with a flat *a* instead of a ritzy 'ah.'" Current authorities disagree. Lass & Lass (1976), *WNW Guide* (1984), the *NBC Handbook* (1984), Barnhart (1988), and Jones (1991) prefer the "ritzy 'ah,'" as I do (I'm entitled to a little ritziness once in a while), and all four major current American dictionaries — *American Heritage 3* (1992), *M-W 10* (1993), *WNW 3* (1997), and *RHWC* (1997) — list WAHFT first.

wainscot WAYN-sk<u>u</u>t (recommended) or WAYN-skaht.

The British sometimes pronounce the first syllable WEN-.

In the pronunciation recommended, the first syllable sounds like *Wayne* and the second has an obscure *o* somewhere between the *scut-* in *scuttle* and the *-scuit* in *biscuit.* Three of the four major current American dictionaries and *WNW Guide* (1984) list WAYN-sk<u>u</u>t first, and the *NBC Handbook* (1976) prefers it. Lass & Lass (1976) prefer WAYN-skaht (-skaht like *Scot*), which is usually listed second. Barnhart (1988) prefers WAYN-skoht (like *Wayne's coat*), but *WNW 3* (1997) does not recognize it and Opdycke (1939) says there is no authority for rhyming the second syllable with *coat.*

waistcoat WES-k<u>u</u>t or WAYS(T)-koht.

In his *Critical Pronouncing Dictionary* (1791), the English elocutionist John Walker gives WES-k<u>u</u>t but says, "This word has fallen into the general contraction observable in similar compounds, but, in my opinion, not so irrecoverably as others have done. It would scarcely seem pedantic if both

---

a = at / <u>a</u> = final / ah = spa / ahr = car / air = fair / ay = hay / aw = saw
ch = chip / e = let / <u>e</u> = item / ee = see / eer = deer / i = sit / <u>i</u> = April
ng = sing / <u>o</u> = carrot / oh = go / oo = soon / or = for / oor = poor
ow = cow / oy = toy / sh = she / th = thin / <u>th</u> = this / <u>u</u> = focus / uh = up
ur = turn / uu = pull, took / y, eye = by, I / zh = measure / (see full key, p. xiv)

parts of the word were pronounced with equal distinctness." Perhaps taking their cue from Walker, many speakers of the 19th century began to do just that.

In *Modern English Usage,* the crusty H. W. Fowler recommended WES-kut, but *OED 1* (1928) labeled it "colloquial or vulgar." *Webster 2* (1934), which gives priority to WAYS(T)-koht, says that WES-kut "is the phonetically regular traditional pronunciation" and WAYS(T)-koht "is a recent spelling pronunciation . . . now widely used." The *Century* (1914) and Phyfe (1926) also call WES-kut colloquial, and Opdycke (1939) pronounces it "provincial" and "corrupted." Holt (1937), however, comes to its defense, remarking that "though the British are usually scornful of spelling-pronunciation, in this case they indorse 'waist-coat' and condemn as vulgar the 'weskit' which American students of English literature have tried so hard to learn."

Today the controversy has settled down and become largely a matter of American vs. British preference. Fowler lost his battle on his home turf, and — as the *Oxford Guide* (1983), Jones (1991), and Burchfield (1996) attest — in Britain WES-kut is rare and old-fashioned and WAYS(T)-koht is the preferred pronunciation. Although many educated American speakers say WAYS(T)-koht, authority on this side of the pond favors the traditional (and unjustly maligned) WES-kut. Lass & Lass (1976), *WNW Guide* (1984), and the *NBC Handbook* (1984) prefer it, and three of the four major current American dictionaries list it first.

wash WAHSH or WAWSH. Do not say WAHRSH or WAWRSH.

Some speakers allow the sound of *r* to insinuate itself between the *a* and *s* of *wash,* pronouncing the word as if it were spelled *warsh.* M-W 9 (1985) and 10 (1993) label WAHRSH and WAWRSH "chiefly Midland" and "appreciably less common"; *Webster 3* (1961) labels them "chiefly substandard." In the cautious and often inscrutable lingo of linguists, what this chiefly means is that these *r*-colored pronunciations of *wash* are in circumscribed use by an indeterminate portion of the U.S. population, perhaps mostly in the Midwest; they do not reflect the general practice of the nation (Noah Webster's influential standard of propriety); and they are disapproved of and considered uncultivated by many. No doubt that is why other dictionaries politely avert their gaze from these beastly mispronunciations. The careful speaker is advised to do the same.

Washington WAHSH-ing-tun (or WAWSH-).

Don't let an *r* creep into the first syllable: *Warsh*-ington is beastly. Also, don't drop the *g* and say WAHSH-in-tun (careless), or clip a syllable and say WAHSH-tun (slovenly). See **wash**.

wassail WAHS'l (rhymes with *fossil* and *jostle*).

Some speakers put a *sail* in *wassail* and say WAH-sayl or wah-SAYL, and these variants can be heard in certain old Christmas songs. Others pronounce the first syllable with a flat *a* as in *wag:* WAS'l or WAS-ayl — so say the dictionaries, anyway, though I have never heard these variants. All these pronunciations, along with WAHS'l, are represented in 20th-century dictionaries. However, the preponderance of authority from Walker (1791) to Worcester (1860) to *Webster 2* (1934) to the *NBC Handbook* (1984) favors WAHS'l, and all four major current American dictionaries list this pronunciation first.

Wassailing — as in *Here we go a-wassailing* — is pronounced WAHS'l-ing, rhyming with the nonce word *fossiling,* and *wassailer* is pronounced WAHS'l-ur, rhyming with *jostle 'er.*

wastrel WAY-strul. Do not say WAH-strul (rhymes with *nostril*).

Occasionally one hears this word pronounced with a broad *a,* as in *spa* and *father.* This is not just beastly. It is asinine. *Wastrel* comes from *waste,* which would stink to high heaven if you put a broad *a* in it. Like other derivatives of *waste* (*wasteful, wastage, wasteland, wastebasket,* etc.), *wastrel* is properly pronounced with a long *a,* as in *way.* Unfortunately, the modern dictionaries of Merriam-Webster — from *Webster 3* (1961) through *M-W 10* (1993), with the curious exception of *M-W 7* (1972) — list this preposterous pronunciation, labeling it "appreciably less common." No other dictionary or authority I know of will touch the ugsome WAH-strul with a ten-foot pole. Let's hope it stays that way.

Wednesday see **-day**.

werewolf WEER-wuulf or WUR-wuulf or WAIR-wuulf.

All three of these pronunciations are recorded in current dictionaries and acceptable in cultivated speech. Think of them as forming the question "We were where?" The *We* variant, WEER-wuulf (WEER- as in *weary*), is my preference; Lass & Lass (1976) also prefer it and *WNW Guide* (1984) lists it first. The *were* variant, WUR-wuulf, is less frequently heard today. The *where* (or *wear*) variant, WAIR-wuulf, first recorded in *Webster 3* (1961), is most commonly heard in popular contexts and probably is now also the dominant pronunciation in educated American speech.

wh- In most words, preferably HW-, but often W- in American speech.

In the 20th century the traditional *hw-* sound in such words as *whale, whimper,* and *whistle* has been steadily disappearing from American speech, and Morris & Morris (1985) are not happy about it. "American people, from the lowest to the highest," they write, "tend to leave the 'h' sound out of words beginning with 'wh' and 'White House' becomes 'Wite House.' The slurring of such words is deplorable."

Deplorable? I don't feel that strongly. The words that come to my mind are regrettable, understandable, venial. I know some will vehemently disagree with me on this, but I just can't condemn everyone who says *wite* instead of *white* to the Underworld of Uncultivated Speakers.

With most words beginning with *wh-*, cultivated speakers ought to make an effort to put in a little *hw-*. But if you don't, I won't think any less of you for it. As what I hope may be a happy medium between the high dudgeon of Morris & Morris and the mass of Americans who are wholly deaf to *hw-*, I humbly offer the following guidelines regarding words beginning with *wh-*:

Elster's Rule of Wh-
(Otherwise known as "Whistlin' in the Wind")

No HW- sound:
who, whose, whole, wharf, whore
Sometimes HW-, sometimes not:
why, what, where, when, while, wheat, wheel (and compounds),
whoop(ee)
HW- is preferable:
whack, whale, overwhelm and underwhelm, whence,
whether (to distinguish it from *weather*), *whey, which* (to distinguish
it from *witch*), *whiff, whimper, whimsical, whine, whinny, whip,*
whirl(wind), whisk, whisker, whiskey, whisper, whist, whistle,
white (and compounds), *whither, whittle, whiz*
HW- is requisite:
wheedle, wheeze, whet (to distinguish it from *wet*), *Whig, whim,*
whilom (HWY-l<u>um</u>), *whilst, whir, whit, whorl* (HWORL).

Willamette (Oregon river) wi-LAM-it.

Opdycke (1939) says that "few proper nouns are more frequently misspelt and mispronounced than this name of the river in Oregon." Apparently that is still the case, for Bob Edwards, host of NPR's *Morning Edition*, once told me that many Oregon listeners have written NPR to insist on the proper pronunciation. *Willamette* has its accent on the second syllable, which rhymes with *ham*. Do not say **WIL**-uh-MET (beastly), WIL-uh-**MET** (beastlier), or, like the name *William*, WIL-y<u>um</u>-et (beastliest).

wintry WIN-tree, not WIN-tur-ee.

Wintry, the proper spelling, is pronounced in two syllables, not three. The variant spelling *wintery* and its three-syllable pronunciation are best avoided.

wisteria wi-STEER-ee-uh.

Wisteria was named in honor of Caspar Wistar, an American anatomist (1761–1818), and is sometimes spelled *wistaria* with the *a* of *Wistar* instead of the *e*. *Webster 2* (1934) prefers *Wistaria*, with a capital *W*, calling it the correct form for the genus and the only spelling approved by the International Code of Botanical Nomenclature. This opinion, however, is not shared by most other dictionaries, past and present, which give priority to *wisteria* and list *wistaria* as an alternative in good standing. Apparently the confusion is the fault of a Harvard naturalist, Thomas Nuttall (1786–1859). In publishing the name of this genus Nuttall intended to print *Wistaria* but accidentally printed *Wisteria* instead, and the typographical error has since become the norm.

This creates a quandary for the pronouncer of the word. Is wi-STEER-ee-uh correct when the word is spelled *wistaria?* Some dictionaries say yes. Is wi-STAIR-ee-uh permissible for the more common spelling *wisteria?* Some dictionaries allow it. Does that mean that you can say and spell it however you want to? Well, yes and no.

Consistency is always the best solution to this sort of problem. Usage has long shown a preference for the spelling *wisteria,* with an *e,* and the pronunciation wi-STEER-ee-uh, and I recommend spelling and pronouncing the word this way. Considering how entrenched this spelling and pronunciation are, to insist on the spelling *wistaria,* with an *a,* and the pronunciation wi-STAIR-ee-uh seems a pointless pedanticism. See **hysteria, schizophrenia**.

with WI<u>TH</u> (*th* as in *this* and *there*), not WITH (rhymes with *pith* and *myth*).

This is an avowed pet peeve of mine, and by no means do all authorities agree with me on this punctilio, though many do. I believe firmly that in cultivated speech, *with* and words beginning with it — *withal* (with-AWL), *withdraw, wither, withhold, within, without, withstand* — should be pronounced with the "voiced" *th* of *bathe, lather,* and *rather,* and not with the "voiceless" *th* of *path* and *bath.* One advantage of following this rule is stronger, clearer speech. The voiced *th* is resonant; the voiceless *th* is lispy and weak.

wizened WIZ'nd (WIZ- as in *wizard*).

Wizened rhymes with *risen* + *d*.

The participial adjective *wizened* was created in the early 1500s from one of the oldest words in English, the verb to *wizen* (WIZ'n, rhymes with *risen*), to dry up, wither, which dates back to the 9th century. In the late 18th century, *wizen* also became an adjective and for the next hundred-odd years was used interchangeably with *wizened.* To further confuse things, in the 19th century the words were often spelled *weazen* and *weazened; OED 2* (1989) cites examples of these forms from Irving, Godwin, Dickens, Thackeray, and W. S. Gilbert. From these obsolete variant spellings came the pronunciations WEEZ'n and WEEZ'nd, which still appear in some current dictionaries.

The pronunciation WYZ'nd (WYZ- like *wise*), which is not recognized by dictionaries, is what I would call a "conjectural pronunciation," one based on a guess. It is sometimes heard today from educated speakers who are familiar with the word from reading but who have arrived at their pronunciation on no better authority than their own conjecture.

Wollstonecraft (middle name of Mary Shelley) WUUL-stun-kraft.

Woll- like *wool, -stone-* like *-ston* in *Boston* and *Houston,* and *craft* just like *craft.* "As if describing the industry of a town named for the wool it produces," comments Ralph H. Emerson (1996), an expert on the pronunciation of literary names.

wont WAWNT (rhymes with *gaunt*) or WAHNT (like *want*) or WUHNT (rhymes with *hunt*).

The first two are the most common pronunciations in American speech; the third is my preference and the traditional pronunciation, which all four major current American dictionaries still list although it is much less often heard today. All four dictionaries also list a fourth variant, WOHNT (like *won't*), which is British.

"The traditional pronunciation [WUHNT]," says R. W. Burchfield (1996), editor of *OED 2* (1989), "useful in differentiating this word from *won't* (= will not), has been preserved in AmE (as one of at least three standard pronunciations), but not in BrE, in which the standard pronunciation is [WOHNT]."

Worcester WUUS-tur (or, for *r*-droppers, WUUS-tuh).

Kenyon & Knott (1949) note that the first *r* in *Worcester* was lost by the 16th century. See **temperature.**

Worcestershire WUUS-tur-sheer or WUUS-tuh-sheer.

worsted (yarn) WUUS-tid; (past tense of *worst,* verb) WUR-stid.

Though WUR-stid is often heard and listed, WUUS-tid is the traditional pronunciation for the yarn or the adjective meaning made of this type of yarn. If you ever have occasion to use the past tense of the somewhat old-fashioned verb to *worst,* to defeat, say WUR-stid, with the *r.*

Wuthering (Heights) WUH<u>TH</u>-ur-ing (rhymes with *mothering*).

This is the only pronunciation in *Webster 2* (1934), Kenyon & Knott (1949), *American College* (1952), *Random House II* (1987), and Jones's *English Pronouncing Dictionary* (1991), a British authority. However . . .

In a March 19, 1989, letter to the editor in *The New York Times Magazine,* Adeline Naiman of Lincoln, Massachusetts, writes,

> A. Scott Berg should not declare so assuredly that Mr. [Samuel] Goldwyn was wrong to pronounce "wuthering" as "withering." Years ago, several professors of English at Harvard taught me to pronounce the title of Emily Brontë's novel as Mr. Goldwyn did. My father, a Yorkshireman, always called it "woothering" (as in wood), which sounds more like withering than like wuthering. Perhaps an itinerant British scholar passed through Hollywood and, for once, Mr. Goldwyn's ear served him well.

See **Brontë.**

XYZ

Xanthippe, Xantippe zan-TIP-ee.

Xanthippe was the wife of Socrates, and she is almost as well known for henpecking and browbeating the ugly old gadfly as he is for dismembering his disciples with hairsplitting rhetoric. Since the late 17th century we have been using *Xanthippe,* with a capital *X,* to mean an ill-tempered, shrewish woman — a termagant (TUR-muh-gint), virago (vi-RAY-goh, see the entry).

Since at least the 19th century the spelling pronunciation zan-THIP-ee has competed with zan-TIP-ee. Two of the four major current American dictionaries, *American Heritage 3* (1992) and *M-W 10* (1993), give priority to zan-THIP-ee, while the other two, *WNW 3* (1997) and *RHWC* (1997), countenance only zan-TIP-ee. *American College* (1952), the *Columbia Encyclopedia* (1963), the *NBC Handbook* (1984), *Everyday Reader's* (1985), and *OED 2* (1989) prefer zan-TIP-ee, while only Jones (1991), a British authority, favors zan-THIP-ee. Regardless of which spelling you choose to use — the *OED* says it is properly *Xanthippe,* which most sources prefer — the pronunciation zan-TIP-ee is recommended as having the weight of authority.

Xavier ZAY-vee-ur (recommended), ZAV-ee-ur, ZAY-vyur, ZAV-yur.

The Spanish pronunciation is hah-VYAIR.

xenophobia ZEN-uh-**FOH**-bee-uh, not ZEE-nuh-**FOH**-bee-uh.

Xenophobia, fear and hatred of foreigners or of anything strange or foreign, first appeared in print in 1919. Its antonym, *xenomania* (ZEN-uh-

---

a = at / a̱ = final / ah = spa / ahr = car / air = fair / ay = hay / aw = saw
ch = chip / e = let / e̱ = item / ee = see / eer = deer / i = sit / i̱ = April
ng = sing / o̱ = carrot / oh = go / oo = soon / or = for / oor = poor
ow = cow / oy = toy / sh = she / th = thin / t̲h̲ = this / u̱ = focus / uh = up
ur = turn / uu = pull, took / y, eye = by, I / zh = measure / (see full key, p. xiv)

MAY-nee-uh), an inordinate attachment to foreign things, was coined about 1879 but is rarely used today. *OED 1* (1928) recorded *xenophobia* as a nonce word and *Webster 2* (1934) deemed it unworthy of its own entry, but both were kind enough to give its proper pronunciation: ZEN-uh-**FOH**-bee-uh, first syllable rhyming with *men*.

Until quite recently there was no confusion about this word. People pronounced the first syllable ZEN- and dictionaries continued to record only that pronunciation. Then one day, as the story goes, someone unfamiliar with the conventions of the language — probably a foreign spy — malevolently and methodically began to mispronounce the first syllable ZEE-. Soon all the xenomaniacs — in particular those members of the literati who delight in finding new outlets for their xenophilia (ZEN-uh-**FIL**-ee-uh), love of foreigners and foreign cultures — began copying this evil example, and the beastly mispronunciation ZEE-nun-**FOH**-bee-uh slipped into the dictionaries. For those who like to keep a dossier on such events, the point of infiltration was *M-W 8* (1975).

No authority I am aware of favors this alien and erroneous ZEE-. All four major current American dictionaries and *WNW Guide* (1984) give ZEN- priority, and Lass & Lass (1976), the *Quintessential Dictionary* (1978), the *NBC Handbook* (1984), *Everyday Reader's* (1985), Barnhart (1988), *OED 2* (1989), and Jones (1991) prefer it.

xiphoid ZIF-oyd (recommended). Also ZY-foyd.

Anyone who has taken a class in CPR (cardiopulmonary resuscitation) has probably heard the word *xiphoid* or, more likely, the phrase *xiphoid process*. The xiphoid process is the lowermost, cartilaginous (KAHR-t̲i-**LAJ**-i̲-nu̲s) segment of the sternum (breastbone); it is also called the *xiphisternum*, always pronounced ZIF-i̲-**STUR**-nu̲m. *Xiphoid* literally means sword-shaped, and the xiphoid process is so named because of its resemblance to the broad, pointed tip of a sword.

One of the preliminary steps in CPR is locating the xiphoid process with the fingers and measuring from there up the sternum to the proper place to apply pressure over the heart. Years ago, when I was training to be an emergency medical technician in New York State, the instructor demonstrating this procedure pronounced the word ZY-foyd (ZY- rhyming with *high*). Naturally I adopted that pronunciation, assuming it was correct. The instructor always knows what he or she is pronouncing, right?

If you have ever been a victim of a Miss Thistlebottom, a Sister Elizabeth, or a General Jean Martinet — the eponymous source of the word *martinet*, a strict disciplinarian — then you are probably suffering from a disorder I call the Teacher Infallibility Fallacy. Think of it: how many times in your life have you adopted a pronunciation used by a professor, boss, or mentor only to discover — sometimes years later, and usually in embarrassing circumstances — that it is at best eccentric, or at worst, flat-out wrong? It is unfortunate but all too common that we allow those in authority to ram a pronunciation down our throats, even when we feel it is stilted, old-fashioned, or trendy. (See **facet** for more on the inculcation of eccentric pronunciations.)

It was my own fault, of course, that I never bothered to look up *xiphoid* in a dictionary and instead accepted my instructor's pronunciation as infallible. But now I have a chance to redeem myself and get a load off my chest, so to speak. ZY-foyd has been around for a long while — it's not a beastly mispronunciation — but so has ZIF-oyd (ZIF- rhyming with *whiff*), and the preponderance of authority favors ZIF-. How did I come to that heart-stopping conclusion? I put it to a vote.

All those in favor, say ZY-: the *Century* (1914), *Stedman's Medical* (1972), and the *NBC Handbook* (1984) prefer ZY-, and *M-W 7* (1972) through *10* (1993) give it priority. Worcester (1860), *Webster's Collegiate* (1917), and Phyfe (1926) record it as alternative.

All those opposed, say ZIF-: ZIF-oyd is the only pronunciation recognized by *OED 1* (1928) and *2* (1989), *Webster 2* (1934), *American College* (1952), *Webster 3* (1961), *Taber's Medical* (1970), *Everyday Reader's* (1985), *Random House II* (1987), *Mosby's Medical* (1990), *American Heritage 3* (1992), *WNW 3* (1997), and *RHWC* (1997).

The ZIFs have it, wouldn't you say?

yarmulke YAHR-m<u>u</u>l-kuh.

I grew up in New York City hearing Jews and gentiles alike pronounce this word YAH-muh-kuh, without an *r* and without an *l*, as if it were spelled *yamaka*. This is pure laziness and an affront to the word's linguistic and sacral tradition. "The caplet perched on the top of the head by observing Jewish males," says Leo Rosten in *The Joys of Yinglish* (1989), is "pronounced YAHR-*m'l-keh*, to rhyme with 'bar culpa.'" YAHR-m<u>u</u>l-kuh is the preference of Lass & Lass (1976), the *NBC Handbook* (1984), *Everyday Reader's* (1985), and Barnhart (1988), and the first pronunciation in *WNW Guide* (1984) and three of the four major current American dictionaries. Only *M-W 10* (1993) gives priority to the uncultivated YAH-muh-kuh.

ye (article, meaning "the") TH<u>UH</u> or TH<u>EE</u>.

Ye, meaning "the," is very often confused in pronunciation with *ye*, the archaic form of *you*, which is pronounced YEE. This is because most people are unaware that the *y* in the *ye* that means "the" is not a real *y*. It's the modern transcription of the Anglo-Saxon *th* character thorn, which resembles *y*. Thus, *ye*, meaning "the," should be pronounced just like *the*: TH<u>UH</u> before a word beginning with a consonant, TH<u>EE</u> before a word beginning with a vowel. YEE, I'm afraid, is just a beastly old spelling pronunciation.

So, dear reader, when next thou goest to *Ye* Olde Laundromat or *Ye* Olde Taco Shoppe, or lodge at *Ye* Compleat Motor Inne, say *ye* word right and show thy friends how clever thou art.

yesterday see -**day**.

yolk YOHK (like *yoke*).

The spelling pronunciation YOHLK, with an audible *l*, was Noah Webster's preference in his dictionary of 1828 and the preference of several earlier English authorities. This was undoubtedly due to the variant spelling *yelk,* pronounced YELK, which Dr. Johnson (1755), Walker (1791), and Smart (1836) favored. Since Worcester (1860), however, the spelling *yolk* and the pronunciation YOHK have prevailed, while *yelk* has disappeared and YOHLK has fallen into disfavor. According to *M-W 10* (1993), YOHLK survives in the South among some cultivated speakers.

Yom Kippur For *Yom,* YAHM, YOHM, YAWM, and YUHM are all accept-
    able. For *Kippur,* the Yiddish is KIP-ur (rhymes with *slipper*), the He-
    brew is ki-POOR or kee-POOR.

The way you pronounce this Jewish High Holy Day depends on who you are, what your heritage is, what you heard when you were growing up, and whether you studied Hebrew. Among older Jews, especially those who speak or have some knowledge of Yiddish, *Yom Kippur* is commonly stressed on the *Kip-*. Among Jews who speak or have studied Hebrew, or who have traveled or lived in Israel, it is commonly stressed on the final syllable, *-pur,* which sounds like *poor.*

In his glorious *Joys of Yinglish* (1989), Leo Rosten gives this explanation: "In Yiddish, pronounced *yum*-KIP-*per,* to rhyme with 'hum dipper.' . . . But in Hebrew, the pronunciation is YOM-*kip*-POOR, to rhyme with 'Tom Mature.' The latter pronunciation, adopted by virtually all radio and tele-vision newscasters, discombobulated Jews everywhere — who did not know there was a Hebrew pronunciation."

The discombobulation caused by the promulgation of the Hebrew pro-nunciation raises an interesting question: is there an unresolved socio-linguistic tension among Jews between Yiddish and Hebrew? Although the Hebrew pronunciation is now often heard from Jews and gentiles alike, some speakers feel uneasy using it. For example, Arthur Salm, books editor of *The San Diego Union-Tribune,* told me he used to say YAHM KIP-ur before he lived in Israel and learned Hebrew. He now pre-fers YOHM kee-POOR but believes "it sounds affected to the American ear." Consequently, Salm says, he doesn't feel comfortable saying the name at all.

One other point worth noting: the four major current American dic-tionaries countenance YAHM, YOHM, and an intermediate YAWM for *Yom,* but none recognize Rosten's Yiddish YUHM (like *yum*). According to the evidence of my ears, which grew up in New York City, Rosten is right on target. I would wager that *yum* is at least as common as the other variants, especially in areas with a high concentration of Jews of European descent, and the dictionaries ought to include it.

zealous ZEL-u̱s. Do not say ZEE-lu̱s.

A *zealous* person is full of *zeal* (rhymes with *real*), but there is no *zeal* in *zealous.* Careful speakers frown upon the beastly spelling pronunciation ZEE-lu̱s, and dictionaries do not recognize it. The corresponding noun *zealot* is pronounced ZEL-i̱t.

zodiacal zoh-DY-uh-kuul.

The accent is on the second syllable, which rhymes with *dry.* The beastly mispronunciation **ZOH**-dee-AK-u̱l is neither in the dictionaries nor in the stars.

zoological ZOH-uh-**LAHJ**-i̱-ku̱l. See **zoology.**

zoologist zoh-**AHL**-uh-JIST. See **zoology.**

zoology zoh-AHL-uh-jee, not zoo-AHL-uh-jee.

There is no *zoo* in *zoology.* The first syllable, *zo-,* rhymes with *go,* not with *do.*

The mispronunciation zoo-AHL-uh-jee, with the first syllable pronounced like *zoo,* has been around for over a century. Funk & Wagnalls *Standard* (1897), in its supplement on "Faulty Diction," notes that *zoology* and *zoological* "and other words with the same first element are in many instances oddly pronounced [zoo-] . . . a mistake that begot *Zoo* as the abbreviation in England for the Zoological Gardens." In the 20th century the *zoo*-ology mispronunciation has been heard from many otherwise cultivated speakers — the actress Katharine Hepburn, for example, in the 1938 film *Bringing Up Baby.* Despite its longevity and its frequency in educated speech, modern authorities have consistently frowned upon it and dictionaries — from Nathan Bailey (1726) to *Random House II* (1987) — stubbornly refused to countenance it.

Zoo-AHL-uh-jee made a cameo appearance in *Webster 3* (1961), but even the 20th century's most permissive dictionary found it wanting in respectability and deserving of its Obelus of Opprobrium — the symbol ÷, used to indicate "variants which occur in educated speech but to the acceptability of which many take strong exception." (Talk about tortured syntax!) Subsequent Merriam-Webster dictionaries — *M-W 7* (1972) through *10* (1993) — do not record zoo-AHL-uh-jee, instead cleverly listing the alternative pronunciation zuh-WAHL-uh-jee, in which the ambiguous zuh-, with its obscure vowel, could suggest either an underarticulated zoh- or zoo-. In 1984, *WNW Guide* noted that zoo-AHL-uh-jee "is heard, but is not considered standard." Four years later, however, it appeared in *WNW 3* (1988, 1997) preceded by the label *often,* and the next year it popped up in *OED 2* (1989), which says *popularly* zoo-. (Although the lexicographers doubtless would deny any judgmental intent behind these labels, the careful speaker would be wise to interpret *often* and *popularly* as indicating that the pronunciation in question is prevalent but not reputable.)

Zoology formerly was often printed with a dieresis (dy-ER-uh-sis) — two small dots — above the second *o* to show that it is pronounced as a separate syllable. Likewise, until the 1950s *cooperate* and *preeminent* were printed either *coöperate, preëminent* or *co-operate, pre-eminent* to indicate that *oo* and *ee* are pronounced separately. Now all three words appear without these pronunciation aids, and though no one would dream of saying koo-AHP-ur-ayt and PREE-muh-ni̲nt, millions blithely say zoo-AHL-uh-jee. This pronunciation is ridiculous, for it requires three *o*'s (*zoo-ology*) and makes the word sound as if it means the study of zoos. ZOO-luh-jee has more basis in reason, but no one has had the sense to mispronounce it that way. Perhaps we should return to printing the word with a dieresis or a hyphen between the *o*'s. I will support any measure, however draconian, that will help speakers separate the *zo-* from its *-ology*.

zounds ZOWNDZ (rhymes with *sounds* and *hounds*).

Zounds, which was first recorded in print in 1600, is an archaic exclamation of wonder or anger, "a euphemistic abbreviation," says *OED 2* (1989), of the oath *by God's wounds.* The word appears occasionally in the plays of Shakespeare, Marlowe, and other English dramatists of the 17th and 18th centuries, and in productions of such works that I have seen the actors usually mispronounce it ZOONDZ or ZWOONDZ.

I suspect this is the result of an assumption on the part of certain speech and dialect coaches, or directors, that because *zounds* incorporates the word *wounds* it should be pronounced with an OO as in *soon* rather than an OW as in *out,* the usual sound of the diphthong *ou.* This assumption is false.

The noun *wound,* an injury, and the verb to *wound,* to hurt, were originally pronounced WOWND, like the past tense of the verb to *wind.* According to Vizetelly (1929), Chaucer (d. 1400), Marlowe (d. 1593), Shakespeare (d. 1616), and Pope (d. 1744) rhymed *wound* with *found, hound, bound,* and *ground.* By the close of the 18th century, WOOND (rhyming with *marooned*) had come to prevail in cultivated speech, leading the celebrated English orthoepist John Walker, in his *Critical Pronouncing Dictionary* (1791), to remark that "*wound* is sometimes pronounced so as to rhyme with *found;* but this is directly contrary to the best usage." However, in a later edition quoted in Worcester (1860), Walker defended the older WOWND, which he called "the established sound of the word" and "still so among the great bulk of speakers, who learn this sound at school and are obliged to unlearn it again when they come into the conversation of the polite world." WOOND, wrote Walker, is "a capricious novelty" that "ought to be entirely banished." Although Benjamin Humphrey Smart (1836), another influential English orthoepist, called WOWND "the old-fashioned pronunciation," for another hundred years — through *Webster 2* (1934) — dictionaries continued to list WOWND as an acceptable alternative.

Zounds, therefore, being an old-fashioned word, should properly follow the old-fashioned pronunciation of *wounds* and rhyme with *hounds.* That is the simplest explanation. But as is often the case, things are somewhat more complicated than that. Like many old words, the spelling of this oath was unstable; *OED 2* shows that although *zounds* has been used since the early 1600s (when it appeared in the earliest editions of Marlowe and Shakespeare), a dozen other variants have had their moments on the stage as well. Among these are *zownes, dzowns,* and *zownds,* which indicate the rhyme with *sounds,* and *zoones* and *zoons,* which suggest the pronunciation ZOONDZ. Although I do not doubt that ZOONDZ had some currency in the 17th and 18th centuries, there is little doubt concerning its questionable propriety then and no doubt as to its impropriety since. "Zoons is only us'd by the disbanded Officers and Bullies: but Zauns is the Beaux pronunciation," wrote the Irish playwright George Farquhar in *Love and a Bottle* (1699). My oldest source to record *zounds* is Worcester (1860), who gives ZOWNDS, and this is the only pronunciation countenanced by all subsequent major dictionaries, including Funk & Wagnalls *Standard* (1897), the *Century* (1914), *Webster 2* (1934), *Webster 3* (1961), *Random House II* (1987), *American Heritage 3* (1992), and both editions of the *OED.* Of all my sources, only three — *M-W 8* (1975), *9* (1985), and *10* (1993) — recognize the mispronunciations now popular on the stage, ZOONDZ and ZWOONDZ, along with a third variant, ZWOWNDZ, which should also be avoided.

A historical nicety is at stake here, which actors, directors, speech coaches, and dramaturges in particular should take care to preserve. Let the record show that there is no reliable authority for any pronunciation other than ZOWNDZ. The word should not follow the OO sound of the modern pronunciation of *wound.* It must have the OW sound of the old-fashioned pronunciation. See **dramaturge.**

zydeco ZY-duh-KOH (rhymes with *try to go*).
Random House II (1987) dates the word from 1955–1960, noting that it comes from the Louisiana French *les haricots* in "the dance-tune title *Les haricots sont pas salés.*" I once heard a radio disk jockey, of all people, mispronounce the word zy-DEK-oh. Was he thinking of art deco? The stress is on *zy-.*

[414]

Some Terms Often Used in This Book

Except where otherwise indicated, boldfaced cross-references in this list refer to other entries in the list.

alternative (pronunciation) (1) Any pronunciation not listed first in a dictionary or guide, or (2) a pronunciation other than the traditional or established one. *Alternative* implies that a pronunciation is less prevalent or favored by fewer authorities; it does not necessarily imply that it is unacceptable or objectionable. The term is broadly synonymous with *variant*, but *variant* often has a disparaging connotation that *alternative* usually does not. See **established, list first, traditional, variant**.

anglicize, anglicization To *anglicize* is to make English, conform to English modes and usages. *Anglicization* is the act or process of making something English.

authority, weight of authority "An accepted source of expert information or advice," says *American Heritage 3* (1992). *Authority* is also often used to mean the approval of pronunciation experts and recognition in dictionaries: *There is no authority for this pronunciation.*

Throughout this book I have tried to distinguish *authorities* from *dictionaries*. *Authorities* are individual experts who express their opinion on what pronunciations are acceptable or unacceptable at a given time. *Dictionaries* (modern ones, at least) are collectively produced records of acceptable pronunciations at a given time. The phrase *weight of authority* may refer to a majority of authorities consulted, or, more often, to a majority of authorities and dictionaries consulted.

beastly mispronunciation In this book *beastly* means flagrantly wrong, wholly unacceptable, odious, repugnant. A *beastly mispronunciation* is a pronunciation that flouts established usage, one abhorrent to the ear. I should emphasize that beastliness is by no means restricted to coarse or uneducated speakers.

In fact, most of the pronunciations labeled *beastly* here occur in educated speech — which does not imply careful speech, just the speech of people with an education. Beastly mispronunciations may be the result of laziness, carelessness, pretentiousness, or affectation. See **educated speakers, speech**.

careful speakers, speech Same as **cultivated speakers, speech**.

colloquial Conversational, of everyday speech. Colloquial pronunciation is not necessarily incorrect or uncultivated. Each case must be considered individually.

countenance To approve, authorize (or tolerate) as acceptable.

cultivated speakers, speech One meaning of the verb to *cultivate* is to devote special attention to with the aim of improving. In this book the adjective *cultivated* means refined by study and training, marked by skill and taste. Cultivated pronunciation occurs at all levels of society, in every region, just as uncultivated speech is heard from rich and poor, educated and uneducated alike in all areas. In short, *cultivated speakers* are those who have arrived at their pronunciation not simply by imitation and conjecture but by careful consideration and practice. *Cultivated speech* refers to the consensus of such conscientious speakers, and to how that consensus is represented in our dictionaries and pronunciation guides. See **educated speakers, speech**.

current Used of dictionaries to mean in general circulation in the 1990s. Used of authorities it means "since about 1975–80." The phrase *the four major current American dictionaries* refers specifically to *American Heritage 3* (1992), *M-W 10* (1993), *RHWC* (1997), and *WNW 3* (1997). (See "Authorities Consulted" for more information on these sources.)

dominant (pronunciation) Prevailing; used by most speakers; heard more than any other pronunciation.

educated speakers, speech An *educated speaker* is anyone who possesses the credentials of an education — from a high school diploma to a Ph.D. — and who can read, write, and speak English passably. *Educated speech* is the speech of this vast group, within which there is substantial variation and incongruity. Although educated speech comprises cultivated speech, the two are not synonymous. And while educated speech is for the most part acceptable, educated speakers run the gamut from cultivated to beastly. For just as knowledge does not guarantee wisdom, so an education does not necessarily result in careful speech. Some of the sloppiest and some of the most affected speakers I have ever heard had doctoral degrees. In short, good pronunciation is not something you are born with or that accompanies a sheepskin. It is acquired. See **cultivated speakers, speech**.

established Settled by usage, rooted in tradition, accepted by many authorities. See **traditional**.

four major (or leading) current American dictionaries see **current**.

give priority to same as **list first**.

list first When I say a certain pronunciation is *listed first*, that means it appears before any other pronunciation in that dictionary or guide. When I say a dictionary or guide *gives priority to* a certain pronunciation, it means the same thing — that it appears first. I would like to say that no more is implied by these two phrases, but . . .

Many, if not most, users of dictionaries assume — quite naturally — that the first pronunciation listed is "preferred." Consult the explanatory notes of any current dictionary, however, and you get a different story. All variants listed for a given word occur in educated speech, these notes assert, and all are acceptable regardless of the order in which they appear. One pronunciation must necessarily precede another, and the order is of no significance.

The problem with this disclaimer of preference becomes clear when one consults several dictionaries and compares the order in which they list pronunciations for a given word. It is striking how often most or all of them list the same one first. For example, for *clitoris,* all four major current American dictionaries (see **current** for a definition of this phrase) list KLIT-ur-is first rather than kli-TOR-is; for *schism,* all four list SIZ'm first rather than SKIZ'm; and for *gymnast,* three of the four list JIM-nast first, not JIM-nist, and the fourth gives only JIM-nast. When one works closely with many dictionaries, as I do, one cannot help noticing such congruities. Given their frequency, it is hard to believe they are merely coincidence. Such agreement must signify something, right?

The dictionary editors insist that the order in which they list pronunciations means nothing, yet it would doubtless be a blow to their professional pride if one were to suggest that they arranged them haphazardly, perhaps by drawing straws or flipping coins. While the makers of our dictionaries want us to believe they are indifferent, which they generally are, we want to believe they are making informed choices for us, which they generally are. They won't admit they are discriminating, and we can't believe they're as disinterested as they claim. It's a knotty problem.

My way out of it, or around it, is simply to do what the dictionaries profess to do — record the facts and let the reader decide. When a number of dictionaries all list a certain pronunciation first, that is noteworthy, and when some list one pronunciation first and some another, that is also revealing. Throughout this book I provide evidence of such unanimity or division and offer my opinion on its significance. You, of course, are free to draw your own conclusions. See **educated speech, prefer.**

modern When used of the English language, *modern* means since A.D. 1500. In this book *modern* means of the 20th century — modern times. It is distinguished from *current,* which here refers to that which is in print, in use, in vogue, or pertinent at the present time.

orthoepist An authority on pronunciation. For more on this word, see the entry in the Guide.

prefer Because the concept of "preferred pronunciation" is anathema to many linguists and lexicographers and repudiated in the explanatory notes of recent dictionaries, which assert that the most common pronunciations are listed with no significance attached to their order, I have refrained from stating or implying what older dictionaries acknowledge and what most people today still assume — that the first pronunciation listed in a dictionary is the "preferred pronunciation." Instead, in a spirit of fairness and for the sake of clarity, in this book I have used the terms *prefer, preferred,* and *preference* only when a dictionary or pronunciation guide gives one pronunciation for a word. When you read that a source *prefers* a certain pronunciation, it means that is the only pronunciation listed by that source. Compare **list first.**

recent *Recent* may suggest, depending on context, anything from the 1960s to the present.

recognize A *recognized pronunciation* is simply one that appears in a dictionary. To *recognize* a pronunciation is similar to *listing* it, but the two differ in one important way. To *list* generally implies that a pronunciation is acceptable, whereas *recognize* is entirely neutral; a recognized pronunciation may be controversial or objectionable. If an entry says a certain pronunciation is *not* recognized, you may assume, unless the text says otherwise, that it is beastly.

regional (pronunciation) A *regional pronunciation* is one that is prevalent in a particular area of the U.S., such as New England, the Midwest, or the South. I have tried to note any regional pronunciation that is in good standing in the dictionaries or that is fundamentally the same as the dominant pronunciation but for a slight variation in the sound of a vowel or consonant. Compare **dominant (pronunciation).**

sanction Same as **countenance.**

spelling pronunciation A pronunciation based on how a word is spelled that differs from the established pronunciation. Spelling pronunciations often occur when the word is unfamiliar and its pronunciation is either guessed at or mimicked. In their *Pronouncing Dictionary of American English* (1949), Kenyon & Knott write that "such pronunciations originate, as the *Oxford Dictionary* puts it, by taking a 'shot' at the word from the spelling. Every such pronunciation is at first an error (departs from established usage); but innumerable pronunciations of this origin have come to be so general that they are now in unquestioned good standing."

traditional *Traditional* refers to a pronunciation that has a long track record in dictionaries and the approval of many authorities. A *traditional pronunciation* is one that has a history of acceptability in cultivated speech but that is usually in some stage of being challenged or supplanted by an alternative pronunciation.

variant (pronunciation) A *variant pronunciation,* like an *alternative pronunciation,* is any pronunciation not listed first in a dictionary or guide. Broadly speaking, the terms are synonymous, but they differ considerably in connotation. *Alternative* is generally descriptive and dispassionate, suggesting simply that a pronunciation has less currency or less authority, whereas *variant* usually is unfavorable or disparaging, implying that the pronunciation is objectionable or of questionable standing. See **alternative, list first.**

Authorities Consulted

In writing this book, I have relied upon the pronunciations and opinions noted in the following authorities. For ease of reference they are listed in alphabetical order and each source is preceded by the abbreviation for it used in the text.

AHNC (**1969**) *The American Heritage Dictionary.* New college ed. Boston: Houghton Mifflin Company, 1969.

AHSC (**1985**) *The American Heritage Dictionary.* 2nd college ed. Boston: Houghton Mifflin Company, 1985. First published in 1982.

American College (**1952**) Clarence L. Barnhart, ed. *The American College Dictionary.* New York: Random House, 1952 (first published 1947). *The American College Encyclopedic Dictionary,* 2 vols. Chicago: Spencer Press, 1953.

American Heritage 3 (**1992**) *The American Heritage Dictionary of the English Language.* 3rd ed. Boston: Houghton Mifflin Company, 1992.

Ayres (1894) Ayres, Alfred. *The Orthoëpist: A Pronouncing Manual.* New York: D. Appleton and Company, 1894.

Barnhart (1988) Robert K. Barnhart and Sol Steinmetz, ed. *The Barnhart Dictionary of Etymology.* Bronx, New York: H. W. Wilson Company, 1988.

Burchfield (1996) R. W. Burchfield, ed. *The New Fowler's Modern English Usage.* 3rd ed. Oxford: Clarendon Press, 1996.

Century (**1914**) **or** (**1889–1914**) William Dwight Whitney and Benjamin E Smith, ed. *The Century Dictionary: An Encyclopedic Lexicon of the English Language.* Rev. & enlarged edition. 10 vols. New York: The Century Company, 1914. Compiled and published from 1889–1914.

Columbia Encyclopedia (**1963**) William Bridgwater and Seymour Kurtz, ed. *The Columbia Encyclopedia.* 3rd ed. New York & London: Columbia University Press, 1963.

Emerson (1996) or Ralph H. Emerson Emerson, Ralph H. "The Unpronounceables: Difficult Literary Names 1500–1940." *English Language Notes* 34.2 (December 1996): 63–74.

Evans (1959) or Bergen Evans Evans, Bergen. *Comfortable Words.* New York: Random House, 1959.

***Everyday Reader's* (1985)** Laurence Urdang, ed. *The New York Times Everyday Reader's Dictionary of Misunderstood, Misused, and Mispronounced Words.* Rev. ed. New York: New American Library, 1985.

Follett (1966) Follett, Wilson (ed. by Jacques Barzun et al.). *Modern American Usage.* New York: Hill & Wang, 1966.

Fowler (1926) or H. W. Fowler Fowler, H. W. *A Dictionary of Modern English Usage.* Oxford: Clarendon Press, 1961.

Frierson (1988) Frierson, David E. *Orthoëpy: The Correct Pronunciation of Words.* Mt. Pleasant, S.C.: The Spoken Word, 1988. Audiotape produced with the assistance of WSCI-FM and the South Carolina Educational Radio Network.

Funk & Wagnalls (sources listed in chronological order)

Funk, Isaac K., ed. *A Standard Dictionary of the English Language.* New York: Funk & Wagnalls Company, 1897.

Frank H. Vizetelly, ed. *Funk & Wagnalls New Standard Dictionary of the English Language.* New York: Funk & Wagnalls Company, 1913.

Funk & Wagnalls New Practical Standard Dictionary. New York: Funk & Wagnalls Company, 1962.

Funk & Wagnalls Standard Dictionary. New York: Lippincott & Crowell, 1980.

Gilmartin (1936) Gilmartin, John G. *Everyday Errors in Pronunciation.* New York: Walter J. Black, Inc., 1936.

Greet (1948) or W. Cabell Greet Greet, W. Cabell. *World Words: Recommended Pronunciations.* 2nd ed. New York: Columbia University Press, 1948.

Holt (1937) or Alfred H. Holt Holt, Alfred H. *You Don't Say! A Guide to Pronunciation.* New York: Thomas Y. Crowell Company, 1937.

Jones (1991) Jones, Daniel. *English Pronouncing Dictionary,* 14th ed. Edited by A. C. Gimson with revisions and supplement by Susan Ramsaran. Cambridge, England: Cambridge University Press, 1991. The fourteenth edition was originally published in 1977, and the revisions and supplement in 1988. The first edition of this respected British authority was published in 1917. *Webster 2* (1934) relied on the 1924 edition.

Kenyon & Knott (1949) Kenyon, John Samuel, and Thomas Albert Knott. *A Pronouncing Dictionary of American English.* Springfield, Mass.: G. & C. Merriam Company, 1949 (first published in 1944).

Larsen & Walker (1930) Larsen, Thorleif, and Francis C. Walker. *Pronunciation: A Practical Guide to American Standards.* London: Oxford University Press, 1930.

Lass & Lass (1976) Lass, Abraham, and Betty Lass. *Dictionary of Pronunciation.* New York: Quadrangle/The New York Times Book Co., 1976.

Lloyd (1938) Lloyd, Charles Allen. *We Who Speak English, and Our Ignorance of Our Mother Tongue.* New York: Thomas Y. Crowell Company, 1938.

McConkey (1986) McConkey, Wilfred J. *Klee as in Clay.* Boston: Hamilton Press, 1986.

Morris & Morris (1985) Morris, William, and Mary Morris. *Harper Dictionary of Contemporary Usage.* 2nd ed. New York: Harper & Row, 1985.

***Mosby's Medical* (1990)** *Mosby's Medical, Nursing, and Allied Health Dictionary.* 3rd ed. St. Louis, Mo.: C. V. Mosby Company, 1990.

***M-W 6* (1956)** *Webster's New Collegiate Dictionary.* 6th ed. Springfield, Mass.: G & C. Merriam Co., 1956. Based on *Webster 2* (1934) and first published in 1949.

***M-W 7* (1972)** *Webster's New Collegiate Dictionary.* 7th ed. Springfield, Mass.: G & C. Merriam Co., 1972. Based on *Webster 3* (1961) and first published in 1963.

***M-W 8* (1975)** *Webster's New Collegiate Dictionary.* 8th ed. Springfield, Mass.: G & C. Merriam Co., 1972. Based on *Webster 3* (1961) and first published in 1973.

***M-W 9* (1985)** *Webster's Ninth New Collegiate Dictionary.* Springfield, Mass.: Merriam-Webster Inc., 1985. Based on *Webster 3* (1961) and first published in 1983.

***M-W 10* (1993)** *Merriam-Webster's Collegiate Dictionary.* 10th ed. Springfield, Mass.: Merriam-Webster, Inc., 1993. Based on *Webster 3* (1961).

***NBC Handbook* (1984)** Ehrlich, Eugene, and Raymond Hand, Jr. *NBC Handbook of Pronunciation.* 4th ed. New York: Harper & Row, 1984.

***New Century* (1927)** H. G. Emery and K. G. Brewster, ed. *The New Century Dictionary.* New York: D. Appleton-Century Company, 1942. First published in 1927.

***OED 1* (1928)** Sir James A. H. Murray, ed. *The Oxford English Dictionary.* Compact ed. 2 vols. Oxford: Oxford University Press, 1971. Compiled from 1891 to 1928, with supplement published in 1933.

***OED 2* (1989)** R. W. Burchfield, ed. *The Oxford English Dictionary.* 2nd ed. Oxford: Clarendon Press (Oxford University Press), 1989. Compact edition published in 1991.

Opdycke (1939) Opdycke, John B. *Don't Say It: A Cyclopedia of English Use and Abuse.* New York and London: Funk & Wagnalls Company, 1939.

***Oxford American* (1980)** *The Oxford American Dictionary.* New York: Avon Books and Oxford University Press, 1980.

***Oxford Guide* (1983)** Weiner, E. S. C., ed. *The Oxford Guide to English Usage.* Oxford: Clarendon Press, 1983.

Phyfe (1926) or W. H. P. Phyfe Phyfe, W. H. P. *18,000 Words Often Mispronounced.* New ed. with supplement of 2,000 words. Compiled by Frederick A. Sweet and Maude D. Williams. New York & Chicago: A. L. Burt Company, 1926. Previous editions published in 1889, 1894, 1903, 1908, and 1914.

***Quintessential Dictionary* (1978)** Hunsberger, I. Moyer. *The Quintessential Dictionary.* New York: Hart Publishing Company, Inc., 1978.

Random House II (1987)   *The Random House Dictionary of the English Language.* 2nd ed. — unabridged. New York: Random House, 1987.

RH College (1968)   *The Random House Dictionary of the English Language.* College ed. New York: Random House, 1968.

RHWC (1997) **and** (1991)   *Random House Webster's College Dictionary.* New York: Random House, 1997 and 1991.

Scribner-Bantam (1979)   *The Scribner-Bantam English Dictionary.* New York: Bantam Books, 1979.

Shaw (1972)   Shaw, Harry. *Say It Right!* New York: Barnes & Noble Books, 1972.

Stedman's Medical (1972)   *Stedman's Medical Dictionary.* 22nd ed. Baltimore: The Williams & Wilkins Company, 1972.

Taber's Medical (1970)   Taber, Clarence Wilbur. *Taber's Cyclopedic Medical Dictionary.* 11th ed. Philadelphia: F. A. Davis Company, 1970.

Vizetelly (1929) **and** (1933)

Vizetelly, Frank H. *A Desk-Book of Twenty-Five Thousand Words Frequently Mispronounced.* 4th ed. New York: Grosset & Dunlap, 1929.

————. *How to Speak English Effectively.* New York: Funk & Wagnalls Company, 1933.

Walker (1791) **or John Walker**   Walker, John. *A Critical Pronouncing Dictionary and Expositor of the English Language.* Facsimile of the original 1791 edition. Menston, England: The Scolar Press Limited, 1968.

Webster 2 (1934)   *Webster's New International Dictionary.* 2nd ed. Springfield, Mass.: G. & C. Merriam Company, 1941. First published in 1934. Contains the invaluable supplement "Synopsis of Words Differently Pronounced by Different Orthoepists," which covers about 1,100 words "whose present pronunciation is a matter of doubt or controversy" and gives the opinions of eight other sources: *Century* (1911 ed.); *New Century* (1931 ed.); *OED* (1928); *Shorter OED* (1933); Jones's *English Pronouncing Dictionary* (1924 ed.); H. C. Wyld's *Universal Dictionary* (1932); Funk & Wagnalls *New Standard* (1931 ed.); and Passy and Hempl's *International French-English and English-French Dictionary* (1904).

Webster 3 (1961)   *Webster's Third New International Dictionary.* Springfield, Mass.: G. & C. Merriam Company, 1961.

Webster's Collegiate (1917) **and** (1923)   *Webster's Collegiate Dictionary.* 3rd ed. Springfield, Mass.: G. & C. Merriam Company, 1917 and 1923 printings. First published in 1916.

Webster's Geographical (1997) **and** (1949)

Merriam-Webster's Geographical Dictionary. 3rd ed. Springfield, Mass.: Merriam-Webster, Inc., 1997.

Webster's Geographical Dictionary. Springfield, Mass.: G. & C. Merriam Company, 1949.

Winston Dictionary (1951)   *The Winston Dictionary.* Advanced ed. Philadelphia: The John C. Winston Company, 1951.

Witherspoon (1943) Witherspoon, Alexander M. *Common Errors in English and How to Avoid Them*. Totowa, N.J.: Littlefield, Adams & Co., 1983. Originally published by Copeland & Lamm, Inc., New York: 1943.

***WNW* 2 (1984)** *Webster's New World Dictionary*. 2nd college ed. New York: Simon & Schuster, 1984.

***WNW* 3 (1997) and (1988)** *Webster's New World Dictionary*. 3rd college ed. New York: Simon & Schuster, 1997 and 1988.

***WNW Guide* (1984)** Chisholm, William S., Jr. *Webster's New World Guide to Pronunciation*. New York: Simon & Schuster, 1984.

Worcester (1860) Worcester, Joseph Emerson. *A Dictionary of the English Language*. Philadelphia: J. B. Lippincott & Company, 1884. Rev. ed. of Worcester's dictionary of 1860.

Other Sources Cited or Consulted

American Heritage Children's Dictionary. Multimedia ed. Boston and London: Houghton Mifflin Interactive and Dorling Kindersley, 1995.

Amis, Kingsley. *The King's English: A Guide to Modern Usage.* New York: St. Martin's Press, 1998.

Baker, Josephine Turck. *Ten Thousand Words: How to Pronounce Them.* Evanston–Chicago, Ill.: The Correct English Publishing Company, 1905.

Barnett, Lincoln. *The Treasure of Our Tongue.* New York: Alfred A. Knopf, 1964.

Barnhart, Clarence L., Sol Steinmetz, and Robert K. Barnhart. *The Second Barnhart Dictionary of New English.* New York: Barnhart/Harper & Row, 1980.

Benne, Bart. *Waspleg and Other Mnemonics.* Dallas: Taylor Publishing Company, 1988.

Bernstein, Theodore M. *The Careful Writer.* New York: Atheneum, 1983. Originally published in 1965.

Bryson, Bill. *The Mother Tongue: English and How It Got That Way.* New York: William Morrow and Company, Inc., 1990.

Burchfield, Robert. *The English Language.* Oxford, New York: Oxford University Press, 1986.

Collocott, T. C., and J. O. Thorne. *The Macmillan World Gazetteer and Geographical Dictionary.* Rev. ed. New York: Macmillan, 1961.

Dawson, James. "A Pronouncing Guide to the Name Thoreau." Concord, Mass: *The Thoreau Society Bulletin,* no. 191 (1990), 1.

Dickson, Paul. *Labels for Locals.* Springfield, Mass.: Merriam-Webster, Inc., 1997.

Ehrlich, Eugene. *Amo, Amas, Amat, and More.* New York: Harper & Row, 1985.

Elster, Charles Harrington. *There Is No Zoo in Zoology, and Other Beastly Mispronunciations.* New York: Collier Macmillan, 1988.

———. *Is There a Cow in Moscow? More Beastly Mispronunciations and Sound Advice.* New York: Collier Macmillan, 1990.

Emerson, Ralph H. "English Spelling and Its Relation to Sound." *American Speech* 72.3 (1997): 260–88.

Espy, Willard R. *Say It My Way.* New York: Doubleday, 1980.

Fowler, H. W., and F. G. Fowler. *The King's English.* 3rd ed. Oxford: Oxford University Press, 1931.

Hanks, Patrick, and Flavia Hodges. *A Dictionary of Surnames.* Oxford: Oxford University Press, 1988.

Hendrickson, Robert. *The Dictionary of Eponyms: Names That Became Words.* New York: Dorset Press, 1972.

Hook, J. N. *The Appropriate Word.* New York: Addison-Wesley, 1990.

Jackson, R. W. *The Diabolical Dictionary of Modern English.* New York: Dell, 1986.

Jennings, Charles B., Nancy King, and Marjorie Stevenson, ed. *Weigh the Word.* New York: Harper & Brothers, 1957.

Johnson, Samuel. *A Dictionary of the English Language.* Facsimile of the original 1755 edition. London: Times Books, 1979.

Jordan, Lewis, ed. *The New York Times Manual of Style and Usage.* New York: Times Books, 1976.

Landau, Sidney I. *Dictionaries: The Art and Craft of Lexicography.* New York: Charles Scribner's Sons, 1984.

Lederer, Richard. *Crazy English.* New York: Pocket Books, 1989.

McNamee, Lawrence F., and Kent Biffle. *A Few Words.* Dallas: Taylor Publishing Company, 1988.

Mencken, H. L. *The American Language.* 4th ed. New York: Alfred A. Knopf, 1937.

Moon, William Least Heat. *Blue Highways.* Boston/Toronto: Atlantic–Little, Brown and Company, 1982.

Nabokov, Vladimir. *Strong Opinions.* New York: McGraw-Hill Book Company, 1973.

The New Century Cyclopedia of Names. New York: Appleton-Century-Crofts, Inc., 1954.

Newman, Edwin. *I Must Say.* New York: Warner Books, 1988.

O'Connor, Johnson. *English Vocabulary Builder.* 3 vols. Boston: Human Engineering Laboratory, 1948, 1951, 1974.

Pinckert, Robert C. *Pinckert's Practical Grammar.* Cincinnati, Ohio: Writer's Digest Books, 1986.

Pointon, G. E. *BBC Pronouncing Dictionary of Family Names.* 2nd ed. Oxford: Oxford University Press, 1983.

Reader's Digest. *Write Better, Speak Better.* Pleasantville, N.Y.: Reader's Digest, 1972.

Ricks, Christopher, and Leonard Michaels, ed. *The State of the Language.* Berkeley and Los Angeles: University of California Press, 1990.

———. *The State of the Language.* Berkeley and Los Angeles: University of California Press, 1980.

Rosten, Leo. *The Joys of Yinglish.* New York: Plume, 1989.

Safire, William. *Watching My Language: Adventures in the Word Trade.* New York: Random House, 1997.

———. *In Love with Norma Loquendi.* New York: Random House, 1994.

————. *Quoth the Maven*. New York: Random House, 1993.

————. *Coming to Terms*. New York: Doubleday, 1991.

————. *Take My Word for It*. New York: Times Books, 1986.

————. *I Stand Corrected*. New York: Avon Books, 1984.

————. *What's the Good Word?* New York: Times Books, 1982.

————. *On Language*. New York: Avon Books, 1980.

Seltzer, Leon, ed. *The Columbia Lippincott Gazetteer of the World*. New York: Columbia University Press, 1952, 1962.

Simpson, D. P., ed. *Cassell's Latin Dictionary*. London: Cassell & Company, and New York: Macmillan, 1968.

Tedeschi, Alberto, and Carlo Rossi Fantonetti. *Mondadori's Pocket Italian-English Dictionary*. New York: Pocket Books, 1959.

Walker, John. *The Rhyming Dictionary of the English Language*. Rev. enlarged ed. Edited by Lawrence H. Dawson. London: George Routledge and Sons, and New York: E. P. Dutton and Co., n.d. Originally published in 1775.

Webster, Noah. *Dissertations on the English Language*. Facsimile of the original 1789 edition. Menston, England: The Scolar Press Limited, 1967.

Webster's II New Riverside Dictionary. New York: Berkley Books, 1984.

Webster's New Twentieth Century Dictionary. 2nd ed. unabridged. New York: Simon & Schuster, 1983.

Wentworth, Harold, and Stuart Berg Flexner. *Dictionary of American Slang*, 2nd supplemented edition. New York: Thomas Y. Crowell, 1975.

Willensky, Elliot, and Norval White. *AIA Guide to New York City*. 3rd edition. San Diego: Harcourt Brace Jovanovich, 1988.

Wood, Clement, ed. *The Complete Rhyming Dictionary and Poet's Craft Book*. Garden City, N.Y.: Garden City Books, 1936.